Lecture Notes in Computer Science

Lecture Notes in Artificial Intelligence 16021
Founding Editor

Jörg Siekmann

Series Editors

Randy Goebel, *University of Alberta, Edmonton, Canada*
Wolfgang Wahlster, *DFKI, Berlin, Germany*
Zhi-Hua Zhou, *Nanjing University, Nanjing, China*

The series Lecture Notes in Artificial Intelligence (LNAI) was established in 1988 as a topical subseries of LNCS devoted to artificial intelligence.

The series publishes state-of-the-art research results at a high level. As with the LNCS mother series, the mission of the series is to serve the international R & D community by providing an invaluable service, mainly focused on the publication of conference and workshop proceedings and postproceedings.

Inês Dutra · Mykola Pechenizkiy · Paulo Cortez ·
Sepideh Pashami · Alípio M. Jorge ·
Carlos Soares · Pedro H. Abreu · João Gama
Editors

Machine Learning and Knowledge Discovery in Databases

Applied Data Science Track

European Conference, ECML PKDD 2025
Porto, Portugal, September 15–19, 2025
Proceedings, Part IX

Editors
Inês Dutra
University of Porto
Porto, Portugal

Paulo Cortez
University of Minho
Guimarães, Portugal

Alípio M. Jorge
University of Porto
Porto, Portugal

Pedro H. Abreu
University of Coimbra
Coimbra, Portugal

Mykola Pechenizkiy
Eindhoven University of Technology
Eindhoven, The Netherlands

Sepideh Pashami
Halmstad University
Halmstad, Sweden

Carlos Soares
University of Porto
Porto, Portugal

João Gama
University of Porto
Porto, Portugal

ISSN 0302-9743 ISSN 1611-3349 (electronic)
Lecture Notes in Artificial Intelligence
ISBN 978-3-032-06117-1 ISBN 978-3-032-06118-8 (eBook)
https://doi.org/10.1007/978-3-032-06118-8

LNCS Sublibrary: SL7 – Artificial Intelligence

© The Editor(s) (if applicable) and The Author(s), under exclusive license
to Springer Nature Switzerland AG 2026
Chapter "CNN-Transformer with Absolute Positional Encoding Optimized for Low-Dimensional Inputs: Applied to Estimate Sliding Drop Width" is licensed under the terms of the Creative Commons Attribution 4.0 International License (http://creativecommons.org/licenses/by/4.0/). For further details see license information in the chapter.

This work is subject to copyright. All rights are solely and exclusively licensed by the Publisher, whether the whole or part of the material is concerned, specifically the rights of translation, reprinting, reuse of illustrations, recitation, broadcasting, reproduction on microfilms or in any other physical way, and transmission or information storage and retrieval, electronic adaptation, computer software, or by similar or dissimilar methodology now known or hereafter developed.
The use of general descriptive names, registered names, trademarks, service marks, etc. in this publication does not imply, even in the absence of a specific statement, that such names are exempt from the relevant protective laws and regulations and therefore free for general use.
The publisher, the authors and the editors are safe to assume that the advice and information in this book are believed to be true and accurate at the date of publication. Neither the publisher nor the authors or the editors give a warranty, expressed or implied, with respect to the material contained herein or for any errors or omissions that may have been made. The publisher remains neutral with regard to jurisdictional claims in published maps and institutional affiliations.

This Springer imprint is published by the registered company Springer Nature Switzerland AG
The registered company address is: Gewerbestrasse 11, 6330 Cham, Switzerland

If disposing of this product, please recycle the paper.

Preface

The 2025 edition of the European Conference on Machine Learning and Principles and Practice of Knowledge Discovery in Databases (ECML PKDD 2025) was held in the vibrant city of Porto, Portugal on September 15–19, 2025. This marks a significant return of the conference to Porto, following successful editions in 2005 and 2015, underscoring the city's enduring appeal as a hub for scientific exchange.

The annual ECML PKDD conference stands as a premier worldwide platform dedicated to showcasing the latest advancements and fostering insightful discussions in the fields of machine learning and knowledge discovery in databases. Held jointly since 2001, ECML PKDD has firmly established its reputation as the leading European conference in these disciplines. It provides researchers and practitioners with an unparalleled opportunity to exchange knowledge, share innovative ideas, and explore the latest technical advancements. Furthermore, the conference deeply values the synergy between foundational theoretical advances and groundbreaking practical data science applications, actively encouraging contributions that demonstrate how Machine Learning and Data Mining are being effectively employed to address complex real-world challenges.

A Hub for Responsible AI and Cutting-Edge Research

As the technological landscape continues to evolve and societal needs shift, the conference remains committed to adapting to and reflecting these dynamic changes. This year's event saw a robust engagement from the global research community with a substantial increase in the number of submissions.

The three main conference days were organised into five distinct tracks:

- The Research Track received an impressive number of 924 submissions, with 226 papers ultimately accepted, reflecting a highly competitive acceptance rate of 24.5%.
- The Applied Data Science Track received a total of 299 submissions, accepting 74 papers, resulting in an acceptance rate of 24.7%.
- The Journal Track continued to bridge the gap between conference and journal publications, accepting 43 papers (27 for the Machine Learning journal and 16 for the Data Mining and Knowledge Discovery journal) out of 297 submissions.
- The Nectar Track, focusing on recent scientific advances at the frontier of machine learning and data mining, received 30 submissions.
- The Demo Track showcased practical applications and prototypes, accepting 15 papers from a total of 30 submissions.

These proceedings cover the papers accepted in the Research and Applied Data Science tracks.

The high quality and diversity of the accepted papers across all tracks underscore the continued vitality and intellectual breadth of the machine learning and data mining communities. We extend our sincere gratitude to all authors for their valuable contributions, to the program committee members and reviewers for their diligent efforts in ensuring the rigorous double-blind review process, and to the organising committee for their tireless work in making ECML PKDD 2025 a resounding success. We believe these proceedings will serve as a valuable resource, inspiring future research and innovation in these rapidly advancing fields.

This year's conference featured seven insightful keynote talks that focused on crucial and emerging areas within Responsible AI, including trustworthy AI, interpretability, and explainability. The keynotes also explored fundamental theoretical issues, covering causality, neural-symbolic systems, large language models (LLMs), and AI for science. We were honoured to host leading experts who shared their valuable perspectives:

- Cynthia Rudin (Duke University) presented on "Many Good Models Lead to ...";
- Elias Bareinboim (Columbia University) discussed "Towards Causal Artificial Intelligence";
- Francisco Herrera (University of Granada) addressed "Not Just a Trend: Institutionalizing XAI for Responsible and Compliant AI Systems";
- Mirella Lapata (University of Edinburgh) explored "Compositional Intelligence: Coordinating Multiple LLMs for Complex Tasks";
- Nuria Oliver (ELLIS Alicante Foundation, Spain) spoke on "Towards a Fairer World: Uncovering and Addressing Human and Algorithmic Biases";
- Pedro Domingos (University of Washington) shared insights on "A Simple Unification of Neural and Symbolic AI"; and
- Sašo Džeroski (Jožef Stefan Institute, Slovenia) presented on "Artificial Intelligence for Science".

Fostering Diversity and Inclusion

Our Diversity and Inclusion initiative proudly awarded 10 scholarship grants of €500 to early-career researchers. These grants enabled individuals from developing countries and communities underrepresented in science and technology to attend the conference, present their work, and become integral members of the ECML PKDD community.

Acknowledging Our Contributors and Supporters

We extend our sincere gratitude to everyone who contributed to making ECML PKDD 2025 such a success. Our heartfelt thanks go to the authors, workshop and tutorial organisers, and all participants for their valuable scientific contributions.

An outstanding conference program would not be possible without the immense dedication and substantial time investment from our area chairs, program committee, and organising committee. The smooth execution of the event was also largely due to the hard work of our many volunteers and session chairs. A special acknowledgement goes to the local organisers for meticulously handling every detail, making the conference a truly memorable experience.

Finally, we are incredibly grateful for the generous financial support from our wonderful sponsors. We also appreciate Springer's ongoing support and Microsoft's provision of their CMT software for conference management, as well as their continued assistance. Our sincere thanks also go to the ECML PKDD Steering Committee for their invaluable advice and guidance over the past two years.

September 2025

João Gama
Pedro H. Abreu
Alípio M. Jorge
Carlos Soares
Rita P. Ribeiro
Pedro Larrañaga
Nathalie Japkowicz
Bernhard Pfahringer
Inês Dutra
Mykola Pechenizkiy
Sepideh Pashami
Paulo Cortez

Organization

Honorary Chair

Pavel Brazdil — University of Porto, Portugal

General Chairs

João Gama — University of Porto, Portugal
Pedro H. Abreu — University of Coimbra, Portugal
Alípio M. Jorge — University of Porto, Portugal
Carlos Soares — University of Porto, Portugal

Research Track Program Chairs

Bernhard Pfahringer — University of Waikato, New Zealand
Nathalie Japkowicz — American University, USA
Pedro Larrañaga — Technical University of Madrid, Spain
Rita P. Ribeiro — University of Porto, Portugal

Applied Data Science Track Program Chairs

Inês Dutra — University of Porto, Portugal
Mykola Pechenisky — TU Eindhoven, The Netherlands
Paulo Cortez — University of Minho, Portugal
Sepideh Pashami — Halmstad University, Sweden

Journal Track Chairs

Ana Carolina Lorena — Instituto Tecnológico de Aeronáutica, Brazil
Arlindo Oliveira — Instituto Superior Técnico, Portugal
Concha Bielza — Technical University of Madrid, Spain
Longbing Cao — Macquarie University, Australia
Tiago Almeida — Federal University of São Carlos, Brazil

Nectar Track Chairs

Ricard Gavaldà Amalfi Analytics, Spain
Riccardo Guidotti University of Pisa, Italy

Demo Track Chairs

Arian Pasquali Faktion, Belgium
Nuno Moniz University of Notre Dame, USA

Local Chairs

Bruno Veloso University of Porto, Portugal
Rita Nogueira INESC TEC, Portugal
Shazia Tabassum INESC TEC, Portugal

Workshop Chairs

Irena Koprinska University of Sydney, Australia
João Mendes Moreira University of Porto, Portugal
Paula Branco University of Ottawa, Canada

Tutorial Chairs

Alicia Troncoso Universidad Pablo de Olavide, Spain
Nikolaj Tatti University of Helsinki, Finland

PhD Forum Chairs

Raquel Sebastião Polytechnic Institute of Viseu, Portugal
Yun Sing Koh University of Auckland, New Zealand

Awards Committee Chairs

André Carvalho	University of São Paulo, Brazil
Amparo Alonso-Betanzos	University of A Coruña, Spain
Katharina Morik	TU Dortmund, Germany
Vítor Santos Costa	University of Porto, Portugal

Proceedings Chairs

João Vinagre	European Commission (JRC), Spain
Miriam Santos	University of Porto, Portugal
Shazia Tabassum	INESC TEC, Portugal

Diversity and Inclusion Chairs

Inês Sousa	Fraunhofer, Portugal
Zahraa Abdallah	University of Bristol, UK

Discovery Challenge Chairs

Carlos Ferreira	Polytechnic Institute of Porto, Portugal
Peter van der Putten	Leiden University, The Netherlands
Rui Camacho	University of Porto, Portugal

Panel Chairs

Pedro H. Abreu	University of Coimbra, Portugal
Paula Brito	University of Porto, Portugal

Publicity Chair

Carlos Ferreira	Polytechnic Institute of Porto, Portugal

Sponsorship Chairs

Mariam Berry BNP Paribas, France
Nuno Moutinho University of Porto, Portugal
Rui Teles Accenture, Portugal

Social Media Chairs

Luis Roque ZAAI.ai, Portugal
Ricardo Pereira University of Coimbra, Portugal
Dalila Teixeira Creative Matter, USA

Web Chair

Thiago Andrade University of Porto, Portugal

Senior Program Committee – Research Track

Adam Jatowt University of Innsbruck, Austria
Andrea Passerini University of Trento, Italy
Anthony Bagnall University of Southampton, UK
Arno Knobbe Leiden University, Netherlands
Arno Siebes Universiteit Utrecht, Netherlands
Arto Klami University of Helsinki, Finland
Bernhard Pfahringer University of Waikato, New Zealand
Bettina Berendt TU Berlin, Germany
Celine Robardet INSA Lyon, France
Celine Vens KU Leuven, Belgium
Cesar Ferri Universitat Politècnica Valencia, Spain
Charalampos Tsourakakis Boston University, USA
Chedy Raissi Inria, France
Chen Gong Nanjing University of Science and Technology, China
Danai Koutra University of Michigan, USA
Dimitrios Gunopulos University of Athens, Greece
Donato Malerba Università degli Studi di Bari Aldo Moro, Italy
Dragi Kocev Jožef Stefan Institute, Slovenia
Dunja Mladenic Jožef Stefan Institute, Slovenia
Eirini Ntoutsi Universität der Bundeswehr München, Germany

Emmanuel Müller	TU Dortmund, Germany
Ernestina Menasalvas	Universidad Politécnica de Madrid, Spain
Esther Galbrun	University of Eastern Finland, Finland
Evaggelia Pitoura	University of Ioannina, Greece
Evangelos Papalexakis	University of California, Riverside, USA
Fabio A. Stella	University of Milano-Bicocca, Italy
Fabrizio Costa	Exeter University, UK
Fragkiskos Malliaros	CentraleSupélec, France
Georg Krempl	Utrecht University, Netherlands
Georgiana Ifrim	University College Dublin, Ireland
Gustavo Batista	University of New South Wales, Australia
Heikki Mannila	Aalto University, Finland
Hendrik Blockeel	KU Leuven, Belgium
Henrik Bostrom	KTH Royal Institute of Technology, Sweden
Henry Gouk	University of Edinburgh, UK
Ioannis Katakis	University of Nicosia, Cyprus
Jan N. Van Rijn	LIACS, Leiden University, Netherlands
Jefrey Lijffijt	Ghent University, Belgium
Jerzy Stefanowski	Poznań University of Technology, Poland
Jesse Davis	KU Leuven, Belgium
Jesse Read	Ecole Polytechnique, France
Jessica Lin	George Mason University, USA
Jesus Cerquides	IIIA-CSIC, Spain
Jilles Vreeken	CISPA Helmholtz Center for Information Security, Germany
João Gama	INESC TEC - LIAAD, Portugal
Jörg Wicker	University of Auckland, New Zealand
José Hernández-Orallo	Universitat Politècnica de Valencia, Spain
Junming Shao	University of Electronic Science and Technology of China, China
Kai Puolamaki	University of Helsinki, Finland
Manfred Jaeger	Aalborg University, Denmark
Marius Kloft	TU Kaiserslautern, Germany
Marius Lindauer	Leibniz University Hannover, Germany
Mark Last	Ben-Gurion University of the Negev, Israel
Matthias Renz	University of Kiel, Germany
Matthias Schubert	Ludwig-Maximilians-Universität München, Germany
Michele Lombardi	University of Bologna, Italy
Michèle Sebag	LISN CNRS, France
Nathalie Japkowicz	American University, USA
Paolo Frasconi	Università degli Studi di Firenze, Italy

Parisa Kordjamshidi — Michigan State University, USA
Pasquale Minervini — University of Edinburgh, UK
Pauli Miettinen — University of Eastern Finland, Finland
Pedro Larrañaga — Technical University of Madrid, Spain
Peer Kroger — Christian-Albrechts-Universität Kiel, Germany
Peter Flach — University of Bristol, UK
Ricardo B. Prudencio — Universidade Federal de Pernambuco, Brazil
Rita P. Ribeiro — University of Porto and INESC TEC, Portugal
Salvatore Ruggieri — University of Pisa, Italy
Sebastijan Dumancic — TU Delft, Netherlands
Sibylle Hess — TU Eindhoven, Netherlands
Sicco Verwer — Delft University of Technology, Netherlands
Siegfried Nijssen — Université catholique de Louvain, Belgium
Sophie Fellenz — RPTU Kaiserslautern-Landau, Germany
Stefano Ferilli — University of Bari, Italy
Stratis Ioannidis — Northeastern University, USA
Szymon Jaroszewicz — Polish Academy of Sciences, Poland
Tijl De Bie — Ghent University, Belgium
Ulf Brefeld — Leuphana University of Lüneburg, Germany
Varvara Vetrova — University of Canterbury, New Zealand
Wannes Meert — KU Leuven, Belgium
Wei Ye — Tongji University, China
Wenbin Zhang — Florida International University, USA
Willem Waegeman — Universiteit Gent, Belgium
Wouter Duivesteijn — Technische Universiteit Eindhoven, Netherlands
Xiao Luo — University of California, Los Angeles, USA
Yun Sing Koh — University of Auckland, New Zealand
Zied Bouraoui — CRIL CNRS and Université d'Artois, France

Senior Program Committee – Applied Data Science Track

Albrecht Zimmermann — Université de Caen Normandie, France
Andreas Hotho — University of Würzburg, Germany
Anirban Dasgupta — IIT Gandhinagar, India
Anna Monreale — University of Pisa, Italy
Annalisa Appice — University of Bari Aldo Moro, Italy
Bruno Cremilleux — Université de Caen Normandie, France
Carlotta Domeniconi — George Mason University, USA
Dejing Dou — BCG, USA
Fabio Pinelli — IMT Lucca, Italy
Fuzhen Zhuang — Beihang University, China

Gabor Melli	PredictionWorks, USA
Giuseppe Manco	ICAR-CNR, Italy
Glenn Fung	Independent Researcher, USA
Grzegorz Nalepa	Jagiellonian University, Poland
Hui Xiong	Hong Kong University of Science and Technology (Guangzhou), China
Inês Dutra	University of Porto, Portugal
Ioanna Miliou	Stockholm University, Sweden
Ira Assent	Aarhus University, Denmark
Jiayu Zhou	Michigan State University, USA
Jiliang Tang	Michigan State University, USA
Jingrui He	University of Illinois at Urbana-Champaign, USA
João Gama	INESC TEC - LIAAD, Portugal
Jose A. Gamez	Universidad de Castilla-La Mancha, Spain
Ke Liang	National University of Defense Technology, China
Kurt Driessens	Maastricht University, Netherlands
Lars Kotthoff	University of Wyoming, USA
Liang Sun	Alibaba Group, China
Martin Atzmueller	Osnabrück University and DFKI, Germany
Michael R. Berthold	KNIME, Germany
Michelangelo Ceci	University of Bari, Italy
Min-Ling Zhang	Southeast University, China
Mykola Pechenizkiy	TU Eindhoven, Netherlands
Myra Spiliopoulou	Otto-von-Guericke-Universität Magdeburg, Germany
Niklas Lavesson	Blekinge Institute of Technology, Sweden
Nikolaj Tatti	Helsinki University, Finland
Panagiotis Papapetrou	Stockholm University, Sweden
Paolo Frasconi	Università degli Studi di Firenze, Italy
Paulo Cortez	University of Minho, Portugal
Peggy Cellier	INSA Rennes, IRISA, France
Rayid Ghani	Carnegie Mellon University, USA
Sahar Asadi	King (Microsoft), UK
Sandeep Tata	Google, USA
Sepideh Pashami	Halmstad University, Sweden
Slawomir Nowaczyk	Halmstad University, Sweden
Sriparna Saha	IIT Patna, India
Thomas Liebig	TU Dortmund, Germany
Thomas Seidl	LMU Munich, Germany
Tom Diethe	AstraZeneca, UK
Tony Lindgren	Stockholm University, Sweden

Vincent S. Tseng   National Yang Ming Chiao Tung University, Taiwan
Vítor Santos Costa   Universidade do Porto, Portugal
Xingquan Zhu   Florida Atlantic University, USA
Yi Chang   Jilin University, China
Yinglong Xia   Meta, USA
Yongxin Tong   Beihang University, China
Yun Sing Koh   University of Auckland, New Zealand
Zhaochun Ren   Shandong University, China
Zheng Wang   Alibaba DAMO Academy, China
Zhiwei (Tony) Qin   Lyft, USA

Program Committee – Research Track

Christoph Bergmeir   Monash University, Australia
A. K. M. Mahbubur Rahman   Independent University, Bangladesh
Abdulhakim Qahtan   Utrecht University, Netherlands
Abhishek A.   Fujitsu Research, India
Acar Tamersoy   Microsoft, USA
Ad Feelders   Universiteit Utrecht, Netherlands
Adam Goodge   I2R, A*STAR, Singapore
Adele Jia   China Agricultural University, China
Adem Kikaj   KU Leuven, Belgium
Aditya Mohan   Leibniz Universität Hannover, Germany
Ajay A. Mahimkar   AT&T, USA
Akka Zemmari   Université de Bordeaux, France
Akshay Sethi   MasterCard, USA
Alborz Geramifard   Meta, USA
Alessandro Antonucci   IDSIA, Switzerland
Alessandro Melchiorre   Johannes Kepler University Linz, Austria
Alexander Dockhorn   Leibniz University Hannover, Germany
Alexander Schiendorfer   Technische Hochschule Ingolstadt, Germany
Alexander Schulz   CITEC, Bielefeld University, Germany
Alexandre Termier   Université de Rennes 1, France
Alexandre Verine   Ecole Normale Supérieure - PSL, France
Alexandru C. Mara   Ghent University, Belgium
Ali Ayadi   University of Strasbourg, France
Ali Ismail-Fawaz   IRIMAS, Université de Haute-Alsace, France
Alicja Wieczorkowska   Polish-Japanese Academy of Information Technology, Poland
Alipio M. G. Jorge   INESC TEC/University of Porto, Portugal

Alireza Gharahighehi	KU Leuven, Belgium
Alistair Shilton	Deakin University, Australia
Alneu A. Lopes	University of São Paulo, Brazil
Alper Demir	Izmir University of Economics, Turkey
Alvaro Figueira	CRACS and Universidade do Porto, Portugal
Amal Saadallah	TU Dortmund, Germany
Aman Chadha	Stanford University and Amazon, USA
Amer Krivosija	TU Dortmund, Germany
Amir H. Payberah	KTH Royal Institute of Technology, Sweden
Ammar Shaker	NEC Laboratories Europe, Europe
Ana Rita Nogueira	INESC TEC, Portugal
Anand Paul	Louisiana State University HSC, USA
Anastasios Gounaris	Aristotle University of Thessaloniki, Greece
Andre V. Carreiro	Fraunhofer Portugal AICOS, Portugal
André C. P. L. F. de Carvalho	University of São Paulo, Brazil
Andrea Cossu	University of Pisa, Italy
Andrea Mastropietro	University of Bonn, Germany
Andrea Pugnana	University of Trento, Italy
Andrea Tagarelli	DIMES - UNICAL, Italy
Andreas Bender	LMU Munich, Germany
Andreas Nürnberger	Otto-von-Guericke-Universität Magdeburg, Germany
Andreas Schwung	Fachhochschule Südwestfalen, Germany
Andrei Paleyes	University of Cambridge, UK
Andrzej Skowron	University of Warsaw, Poland
Andy Song	RMIT University, Australia
Angelica Liguori	ICAR-CNR, Italy
Anirban Dasgupta	IIT Gandhinagar, India
Anke Meyer-Baese	Florida State University, USA
Anna Beer	University of Vienna, Austria
Anna Krause	Universität Wurzburg and Chair X Data Science, Germany
Anna Monreale	University of Pisa, Italy
Annelot W. Bosman	Universiteit Leiden, Netherlands
Antoine Caradot	Hubert Curien Laboratory, France
Antonio Bahamonde	University of Oviedo, Spain
Antonio Mastropietro	Università di Pisa, Italy
Antonio Pellicani	Università degli Studi di Bari, Aldo Moro, Italy
Antonis Matakos	Aalto University, Finland
Antti Laaksonen	University of Helsinki, Finland
Aomar Osmani	LIPN-UMR CNRS, France
Aonghus Lawlor	University College Dublin, Ireland

Aparna S. Varde	Montclair State University, USA
Apostolos N. Papadopoulos	Aristotle University of Thessaloniki, Greece
Aritra Konar	KU Leuven, Belgium
Arjun Roy	Freie Universität Berlin, Germany
Arthur Charpentier	UQAM, Canada
Arunas Lipnickas	Kaunas University of Technology, Lithuania
Atsuhiro Takasu	National Institute of Informatics, Japan
Aurora Esteban	University of Cordoba, Spain
Baosheng Zhang	Tsinghua University, China
Barbara Toniella Corradini	University of Florence and University of Siena, Italy
Bardh Prenkaj	Technical University of Munich, Germany
Barry O'Sullivan	University College Cork, Ireland
Beilun Wang	Southeast University, China
Benjamin Halstead	University of Auckland, New Zealand
Benjamin Paassen	Bielefeld University, Germany
Benjamin Quost	Université de Technologie de Compiègne, France
Benoit Frenay	University of Namur, Belgium
Bernardo Moreno Sanchez	University of Helsinki, Finland
Bernhard Pfahringer	University of Waikato, New Zealand
Bertrand Cuissart	University of Caen, France
Bin Liu	Chongqing University of Posts and Telecommunications, China
Bin Shi	Xi'an Jiaotong University, China
Bin Wu	Zhengzhou University, China
Bin Zhou	National University of Defense Technology, China
Bitao Peng	Guangdong University of Foreign Studies, China
Bo Kang	Ghent University, Belgium
Bogdan Cautis	Université Paris-Saclay, France
Bojan Evkoski	Central European University, Hungary
Boshen Shi	Institute of Computing Technology, Chinese Academy of Sciences, China
Boualem Benatallah	Dublin City University, Ireland
Brandon Gower-Winter	Utrecht University, Netherlands
Bunil K. Balabantaray	NIT Meghalaya, India
Carlos Ferreira	INESC TEC, Portugal
Carlos Monserrat-Aranda	Universitat Politècnica de Valencia, Spain
Carson K. Leung	University of Manitoba, Canada
Catarina Silva	University of Coimbra, Portugal
Cecile Capponi	Aix-Marseille University, France
Celine Rouveirol	LIPN Université de Sorbonne Paris Nord, France

Cesar H. G. Andrade	Porto University, Portugal
Chandrajit Bajaj	University of Texas, Austin, USA
Chang Rajani	University of Helsinki, Finland
Charlotte Laclau	Polytechnique Institute, Télécom Paris, France
Charlotte Pelletier	Université de Bretagne du Sud, France
Chen Wang	DATA61, CSIRO, Australia
Cheng Cheng	Carnegie Mellon University, USA
Cheng Xie	Yunnan University, China
Chenglin Wang	East China Normal University, China
Chenwang Wu	University of Science and Technology of China, China
Chiara Pugliese	IIT Institute of National Research Council, Italy
Chien-Liang Liu	National Chiao Tung University, Taiwan
Chihiro Maru	Chuo University, Japan
Chongsheng Zhang	Henan University, China
Christian Beecks	FernUniversität in Hagen, Germany
Christian M. M. Frey	University of Technology Nuremberg, Germany
Christian Hakert	TU Dortmund, Germany
Christine Largeron	LabHC Lyon University, France
Christophe Rigotti	INSA Lyon, France
Christophe Rodrigues	DVRC Pôle universitaire Léonard de Vinci, France
Christos Anagnostopoulos	University of Glasgow, UK
Christos Diou Harokopio	University of Athens, Greece
Chuan Qin	Chinese Academy of Sciences, China
Chunchun Chen	Tongji University, China
Chunyao Song	Nankai University, China
Claire Nedellec	INRAE, MaIAGE, France
Claudio Borile	CENTAI Institute, Italy
Claudio Gallicchio	University of Pisa, Italy
Claudius Zelenka	Kiel University, Germany
Colin Bellinger	NRC and Dalhousie University, Canada
Collin Leiber	Aalto University, Finland
Cong Qi	New Jersey Institute of Technology, USA
Congfeng Cao	University of Amsterdam, Netherlands
Corrado Loglisci	Università degli Studi di Bari, Aldo Moro, Italy
Cuicui Luo	University of Chinese Academy of Sciences, China
Cuneyt G. Akcora	University of Central Florida, USA
Cynthia C. S. Liem	Delft University of Technology, Netherlands
Dalius Matuzevicius	Vilnius Gediminas Technical University, Lithuania

Dan Li	Sun Yat-sen University, China
Danai Koutra	University of Michigan, USA
Dang Nguyen	Deakin University, Australia
Daniel Neider	TU Dortmund, Germany
Daniel Schlor	Universität Würzburg, Germany
Danil Provodin	TU Eindhoven, Netherlands
Danyang Xiao	Sun Yat-sen University, China
Dario Garcia-Gasulla	Barcelona Supercomputing Center (BSC), Spain
Dario Garigliotti	University of Bergen, Norway
Darius Plonis	Vilnius Gediminas Technical University, Lithuania
Dariusz Brzezinski	Poznań University of Technology, Poland
David Gomez	Universidad Politecnica de Madrid, Spain
David Holzmüller	University of Stuttgart, Germany
David Q. Sun	Apple, USA
Davide Evangelista	University of Bologna, Italy
Debo Cheng	University of South Australia, Australia
Deepayan Chakrabarti	University of Texas at Austin, USA
Deng-Bao Wang	Southeast University, China
Denilson Barbosa	University of Alberta, Canada
Denis Huseljic	University of Kassel, Germany
Denis Lukovnikov	Ruhr-Universität Bochum, Germany
Destercke Sebastien	UTC, France
Di Jin	TikTok, USA
Di Wu	Chongqing Institute of Green and Intelligent Technology, Chinese Academy of Sciences, China
Diana Benavides Prado	University of Auckland, New Zealand
Dianhui Wang	Independent Researcher, Australia
Diego Carrera	STMicroelectronics, Switzerland
Diletta Chiaro	Università degli Studi di Napoli Federico II, Italy
Dimitri Staufer	TU Berlin, Germany
Dimitrios Katsaros	University of Thessaly, Greece
Dimitrios Rafailidis	University of Thessaly, France
Dino Ienco	INRAE, France
Dmitry Kobak	University of Tübingen, Germany
Domenico Redavid	University of Bari, Italy
Dominik M. Endres	Philipps-Universität Marburg, Germany
Dominique Gay	Université de La Réunion, France
Dong Li	Baylor University, USA
Duarte Folgado	Fraunhofer Portugal AICOS, Portugal
Duo Xu	Georgia Institute of Technology, USA

Edoardo Serra	Boise State University, USA
Edouard Fouche	Karlsruhe Institute of Technology (KIT), Germany
Eduardo F. Montesuma	Université Paris-Saclay, France
Edward Apeh	Bournemouth University, UK
Edwin Simpson	University of Bristol, UK
Ehsan Aminian	INESC TEC, Portugal
Ekaterina Antonenko	Mines Paris - PSL, France
Eliana Pastor	Politecnico di Torino, Italy
Emanuela Marasco	George Mason University, USA
Emilio Dorigatti	LMU Munich, Germany
Emilio Parrado-Hernandez	Universidad Carlos III de Madrid, Spain
Emmanouil Krasanakis	CERTH, Greece
Emmanouil Panagiotou	Freie Universität Berlin, Germany
Emre Gursoy	Koc University, Turkey
Engelbert Mephu Nguifo	Université Clermont Auvergne, CNRS, LIMOS, France
Eran Treister	Ben-Gurion University of the Negev, Israel
Erasmo Purificato	Otto-von-Guericke Universität Magdeburg, Germany
Erik Novak	Jožef Stefan Institute, Slovenia
Erwan Le Merrer	Inria, France
Esra Akbas	Georgia State University, USA
Esther-Lydia Silva-Ramirez	Universidad de Cadiz, Spain
Evaldas Vaičiukynas	Kaunas University of Technology, Lithuania
Evangelos Kanoulas	University of Amsterdam, Netherlands
Evelin Amorim	INESC TEC, Portugal
Fabian C. Spaeh	Boston University, USA
Fabio Fassetti	Università della Calabria, Italy
Fabio Fumarola	Prometeia, Italy
Fabio Mercorio	University of Milan-Bicocca, Italy
Fabio Vandin	University of Padova, Italy
Fandel Lin	University of Southern California, USA
Federica Granese	Inria, Université Côte d'Azur, France
Federico Baldo	University of Bologna, Italy
Federico Sabbatini	National Institute for Nuclear Physics (INFN), Italy
Feifan Zhang	China Agricultural University, China
Felipe Kenji Nakano	KU Leuven, Belgium
Fernando Martinez-Plumed	Universitat Politècnica de Valencia, Spain
Filipe Rodrigues	Technical University of Denmark (DTU), Denmark

Flavio Giobergia	Politecnico di Torino, Italy
Florent Masseglia	Inria, France
Florian Beck	JKU Linz, Austria
Florian Lemmerich	University of Passau, Germany
Francesca Naretto	University of Pisa, Italy
Francesco Piccialli	University of Naples Federico II, Italy
Francesco Renna	Universidade do Porto, Portugal
Francisco Pereira	DTU, Denmark
Franco Raimondi	Gran Sasso Science Institute, Italy
Frederic Koriche	Université d'Artois, CRIL CNRS, France
Frederic Pennerath	CentraleSupélec - LORIA, France
Furong Peng	Shanxi University, China
Gabriel Marques Tavares	LMU Munich, Germany
Gabriele Sartor	University of Turin, Italy
Gabriele Venturato	KU Leuven, Belgium
Gaetan De Waele	Ghent University, Belgium
Gaia Saveri	University of Trieste, Italy
Gang Li	Deakin University, Australia
Gaoyuan Du	Amazon, USA
Gavin Smith	University of Nottingham, UK
Geming Xia	National University of Defense Technology, China
Geng Zhao	Heidelberg University, Germany
Gennaro Vessio	University of Bari Aldo Moro, Italy
Geoffrey I. Webb	Monash, Australia
Georgia Baltsou	Centre for Research & Technology, Greece
Geraldin Nanfack	Concordia University, Canada
Germain Forestier	University of Haute Alsace, France
Gerrit Grossmann	DFKI, Germany
Gerrit J. J. van den Burg	Alan Turing Institute, UK
Gherardo Varando	Universitat de Valencia, Spain
Giacomo Medda	University of Cagliari, Italy
Gilberto Bernardes	INESC TEC and University of Porto, Portugal
Giorgio Venturin	University of Padova, Italy
Giovanna Castellano	University of Bari Aldo Moro, Italy
Giovanni Ponti	ENEA, Italy
Giovanni Stilo	Università degli Studi dell'Aquila, Italy
Gisele Pappa	UFMG, Brazil
Giuseppe Manco	ICAR-CNR, IT, Italy
Gizem Gezici	Scuola Normale Superiore, Italy
Gjergji Kasneci	TU Munich, Germany
Goreti Marreiros	ISEP/GECAD, Portugal

Graziella De Martino	University of Bari, Aldo Moro, Italy
Grazina Korvel	Vilnius University, Lithuania
Grigorios Tsoumakas	Aristotle University of Thessaloniki, Greece
Guangyin Jin	National University of Defense Technology, China
Guangzhong Sun	University of Science and Technology of China, China
Guanjin Wang	Murdoch University, Australia
Guilherme Weigert	Cassales University of Waikato, New Zealand
Guillaume Derval	UC Louvain - ICTEAM, Belgium
Guorui Quan	University of Manchester, UK
Guoxi Zhang	Beijing Institute of General Artificial Intelligence, China
Gustau Camps-Valls	Universitat de Valencia, Spain
Gustav Sir	Czech Technical University, Czech Republic
Gustavo Batista	University of New South Wales, Australia
Hachem Kadri	Aix-Marseille University, France
Hadi Asghari	Humboldt Institute for Internet and Society, Germany
Haifeng Sun	University of Science and Technology of China, China
Haihui Fan	Institute of Information Engineering, Chinese Academy of Sciences, China
Haizhou Du	Shanghai University of Electric Power, China
Hajer Salem	AUDENSIEL, France
Hakim Hacid	TII, United Arab Emirates
Hamid Bouchachia	Bournemouth University, UK
Han Wang	Xidian University, China
Hang Yu	Shanghai University, China
Hanna Sumita	Institute of Science Tokyo, Japan
Hao Niu	KDDI Research, Japan
Hao Xue	University of New South Wales, Australia
Hao Yan	Carleton University, Canada
Haowen Zhang	Zhejiang Sci-Tech University, China
Harsh Borse	IIT Kharagpur, India
Heitor M. Gomes	Victoria University of Wellington, New Zealand
Helder Oliveira	FCUP and INESC TEC, Portugal
Helge Langseth	Norwegian University of Science and Technology, Norway
Hendrik Blockeel	KU Leuven, Belgium
Henrique O. Marques	University of Southern Denmark, Denmark
Henryk Maciejewski	Wroclaw University of Science and Technology, Poland

Hideaki Ishibashi	Kyushu Institute of Technology, Japan
Hilde J. P. Weerts	Eindhoven University of Technology, Netherlands
Holger Froening	University of Heidelberg, Germany
Holger Karl	HPI, Germany
Hongbo Bo	University of Bristol, UK
Hongyang Chen	Zhejiang Lab, China
Hua Chu	Xidian University, China
Huaiyu Wan	Beijing Jiaotong University, China
Huaming Chen	University of Sydney, Australia
Huandong Wang	Tsinghua University, China
Huanlai Xing	Southwest Jiaotong University, China
Hui Ji	University of Pittsburgh, USA
Hui (Wendy) Wang	Stevens Institute of Technology, USA
Huiping Chen	University of Birmingham, UK
Humberto Bustince	Universidad Publica de Navarra, Spain
Huong Ha	RMIT University, Australia
Idir Benouaret	Epita Research Laboratory, France
Ines Sousa	Fraunhofer AICOS, Portugal
Ingo Thon	Siemens AG, Germany
Inigo Jauregi Unanue	University of Technology Sydney, Australia
Ioannis Sarridis	Centre for Research & Technology, Greece
Issam Falih	Université Clermont Auvergne, CNRS, LIMOS, France
Ivan Vankov	iris.ai, Norway
Ivor Cribben	University of Alberta, Canada
Jaemin Yoo	KAIST, South Korea
Jakir Hossain	University at Buffalo, USA
Jakub Klikowski	Wroclaw University of Science and Technology, Poland
Jalaj Bhandari	Columbia University, USA
Jaleed Khan	University of Oxford, UK
James Goulding	University of Nottingham, UK
Jan Kalina	Czech Academy of Sciences, Czech Republic
Jan P. Mielniczuk	Polish Academy of Sciences, Poland
Jan Ramon	Inria, France
Jan Verwaeren	Ghent University, Belgium
Jannis Brugger	TU Darmstadt, Germany
Jean-Marc Andreoli	Naverlabs Europe, Netherlands
Jedrzej Potoniec	Poznań University of Technology, Poland
Jeronimo Arenas-Garcia	Universidad Carlos III de Madrid, Spain
Jhony H. Giraldo	Télécom Paris, Institut Polytechnique de Paris, France

Jia Cai	Guangdong University of Finance and Economics, China
Jiahui Jin	Southeast University, China
Jiang Zhong	Independent Researcher, China
Jianwu Wang	University of Maryland, Baltimore County, USA
Jiawei Chen	Tianjin University, China
Jiaxin Ding	Shanghai Jiao Tong University, China
Jidong Yuan	Beijing Jiaotong University, China
Jie Song	Zhejiang University, China
Jie Wu	Fudan University, China
Jie Yang	University of Wollongong, China
Jimeng Shi	Florida International University, USA
Jin Chen	Hong Kong University of Science and Technology, China
Jin Liang	South China Normal University, China
Jing Ren	NUDT, China
Jing Wang	Amazon, USA
Jinghui Zhong	South China University of Technology, China
Jingtao Ding	Tsinghua University, China
Jinli Zhang	Beijing University of Technology, China
Jiri Sima	Czech Academy of Sciences, Czech Republic
João Gama	University of Porto, Portugal
Joao Mendes-Moreira	University of Porto, Portugal
Joao Vinagre	European Commission (JRC), Spain
Joaquim Silva	NOVA LINCS, Universidade Nova de Lisboa, Portugal
Jochen De Weerdt	KU Leuven, Belgium
Joe Mellor	University of Edinburgh, UK
Johanne Cohen	LISN-CNRS, France
Johannes Jakubik	IBM Research, USA
John W. Sheppard	Montana State University, USA
Jonata Tyska Carvalho	Federal University of Santa Catarina, Brazil
Jordi Guitart	Barcelona Supercomputing Center (BSC), Spain
Joris Mattheijssens	Ghent University, Belgium
Jose M. Costa Pereira	University of Porto, Portugal
Jose Oramas	University of Antwerp, sqIRL/IDLab, imec, Belgium
Jose Tomas Palma	University of Murcia, Spain
Joydeep Chandra	Indian Institute of Technology, Patna, India
Juan A. Botia	University of Murcia, Spain
Juan Rodriguez	Universidad de Burgos, Spain
Jukka Heikkonen	University of Turku, Finland

Julien Delaunay	Inria, France
Julien Ferry	Polytechnique Montreal, Canada
Julien Perez	EPITA, France
Jun Zhuang	Boise State University, USA
Jun Yu Hou	Nanjing University, China
Junbo Zhang	JD Intelligent Cities Research, USA
Junze Liu	University of California, Irvine, USA
Jurgita Kapočiūtė-Dzikienė	Tilde SIA, University of Latvia and Tilde IT, Vytautas Magnus University, Lithuania
Justina Mandravickaitė	Vytautas Magnus University, Lithuania
Kamil Adamczewski	Max Planck Institute for Intelligent Systems, Germany
Kamil Michal Ksiazek	Jagiellonian University, Poland
Karim Radouane	Université Sorbonne Paris Nord, France
Kary Framing	Umeå University, Sweden
Katerina Taskova	University of Auckland, New Zealand
Katharina Dost	Jožef Stefan Institute, Slovenia
Kaushik Roy	University of South Carolina, USA
Kejia Chen	Nanjing University of Posts and Telecommunications, China
Ken Kobayashi	Tokyo Institute of Technology, Japan
Khaled Mohammed Saifuddin	Northeastern University, USA
Khalid Benabdeslem	Université de Lyon 1, France
Kim Thang Nguyen	LIG, University Grenoble-Alpes, France
Kira Maag	Heinrich-Heine-Universität Düsseldorf, Germany
Koji Maruhashi	Fujitsu Research, Japan
Koyel Mukherjee	Adobe Research, USA
Kristen M. Scott	KU Leuven, Belgium
Krzysztof Ruda	Polish Academy of Sciences, Poland
Krzysztof Slot	Lodz University of Technology, Poland
Kuldeep Singh	Cerence, Germany
Kushankur Ghosh	University of Alberta, Canada
Lamine Diop	EPITA, France
Latifa Oukhellou	IFSTTAR, France
Laurence Park	Western Sydney University, Australia
Laurens Devos	KU Leuven, Belgium
Len Feremans	Universiteit Antwerpen, Belgium
Lena Wiese	Goethe University Frankfurt, Germany
Lenaig Cornanguer	CISPA Helmholtz Center for Information Security, Germany
Lennert De Smet	KU Leuven, Belgium
Lev Reyzin	University of Illinois at Chicago, USA

Li Wang	National University of Defense Technology, China
Liang Du	Shanxi University, China
Lianyong Qi	China University of Petroleum (East China), China
Lijie Hu	King Abdullah University of Science and Technology, Saudi Arabia
Lijing Zhu	Bowling Green State University, USA
Lingling Zhang	Capital Normal University, China
Lingyue Fu	Shanghai Jiao Tong University, China
Linh Le Pham Van	Deakin University, Australia
Livio Bioglio	University of Turin, Italy
Lixing Yu	Yunnan University, China
Liyan Song	Harbin Institute of Technology, China
Longlong Sun	Chang'an University, China
Luca Corbucci	University of Pisa, Italy
Luca Ferragina	University of Calabria, Italy
Luca Romeo	University of Macerata, Italy
Lucas Pereira	LARSyS, Tecnico Lisboa, Portugal
Luciano Caroprese	ICAR-CNR, Italy
Ludovico Boratto	University of Cagliari, Italy
Luis Rei	Jožef Stefan Institute, Slovenia
Mahardhika Pratama	University of South Australia, Australia
Maiju Karjalainen	University of Eastern Finland, Finland
Makoto Onizuka	Osaka University, Japan
Manali Sharma	Samsung, South Korea
Maneet Singh	MasterCard, India
Manuel M. Garcia-Piqueras	Universidad de Castilla La Mancha, Spain
Manuele Bicego	University of Verona, Italy
Mao A. Cheng	University of California, Berkeley, USA
Marc Plantevit	EPITA, France
Marc Tommasi	Lille University, France
Marcel Wever	Leibniz University Hannover, Germany
Marcilio de Souto	LIFO/Université d'Orleans, France
Marco Lippi	University of Florence, Italy
Marco Loog	Radboud University, Netherlands
Marco Mellia	Politecnico di Torino, Italy
Marco Podda	University of Pisa, Italy
Marco Polignano	Università di Bari, Italy
Marco Viviani	Università degli Studi di Milano Bicocca, Italy
Maria Vasconcelos	Fraunhofer Portugal AICOS, Portugal
Maria Sofia Bucarelli	Sapienza University of Rome, Italy

Mariana Oliveira	Universidade do Porto, Portugal
Mariana Vargas Vieyra	MostlyAI, Austria
Marielle Malfante	CEA, France
Marina Litvak	Shamoon College of Engineering, Israel
Mario Antunes	Universidade de Aveiro, Portugal
Mario Andres Munoz	University of Melbourne, Australia
Marius Koppel	Johannes Gutenberg University Mainz, Germany
Mark Junjie Li	Shenzhen University, China
Marko Robnik-Sikonja	University of Ljubljana, Slovenia
Marta Soare	Université d'Orleans, France
Martin Holena	Czech Academy of Sciences, Czech Republic
Martin Pilat	Charles University, Czech Republic
Martino Ciaperoni	Aalto University, Finland
Marwan Hassani	TU Eindhoven, Netherlands
Masahiro Suzuki	University of Tokyo, Japan
Massimo Guarascio	ICAR-CNR, Italy
Matej Mihelcic	University of Zagreb, Croatia
Mathias Verbeke	KU Leuven, Belgium
Mathieu Lefort	Université de Lyon, France
Matteo Francobaldi	University of Bologna, Italy
Matteo Riondato	Amherst College, USA
Matteo Salis	University of Turin, Italy
Matthew B. Middlehurst	University of Southampton, UK
Matthia Sabatelli	University of Groningen, Netherlands
Mattia Cerrato	JGU Mainz, Germany
Mattia Setzu	University of Pisa, Italy
Mattis Hartwig	German Research Center for Artificial Intelligence, Germany
Matyas Bohacek	Stanford University, USA
Maximilian T. Fischer	University of Konstanz, Germany
Maximilian Münch	University of Applied Sciences, Würzburg-Schweinfurt, Germany
Maximilian Stubbemann	University of Hildesheim, Germany
Maximilian Thiessen	TU Wien, Austria
Maximilian von Zastrow	Southern Denmark University, Denmark
Megha Khosla	TU Delft, Netherlands
Meiyun Zuo	Renmin University of China, China
Meng Liu	National University of Defense Technology, China
Mengying Zhu	Zhejiang University, China
Michael Granitzer	University of Passau, Germany
Michael B. Ito	University of Michigan, USA

Michael G. Madden	National University of Ireland, Galway, Ireland
Michal Wozniak	Wroclaw University of Science and Technology, Poland
Michele Fontana	Università di Pisa, Italy
Michiel Stock	Ghent University, Belgium
Miguel Rocha	University of Minho, Portugal
Miguel Silva	INESC TEC, Portugal
Mike Holenderski	Eindhoven University of Technology, Netherlands
Milos Savic	University of Novi Sad, Serbia
Mina Rezaei	LMU Munich, Germany
Minh P. Nguyen	University of Texas, Austin, USA
Minyoung Choe	Korea Advanced Institute of Science and Technology, South Korea
Minyu Chen	Shanghai Jiaotong University, China
Miquel Perello-Nieto	University of Bristol, UK
Mira Kristin Jurgens	Ghent University, Belgium
Miriam Santos	University of Porto, Portugal
Mirko Bunse	TU Dortmund, Germany
Mirko Polato	University of Turin, Italy
Mitra Baratchi	LIACS, University of Leiden, Netherlands
Mohammed Elbamby	Telefonica Scientific Research, Spain
Moises Rocha dos Santos	University of Porto, Portugal
Monowar Bhuyan	Umeå University, Sweden
Morteza Rakhshaninejad	Ghent University, Belgium
Mounim A. El Yacoubi	Télécom SudParis, France
Muhammad Rajabinasab	University of Southern Denmark, Denmark
Muhao Guo	Arizona State University, USA
Mustapha Lebbah	Paris Saclay University-Versailles, France
Nabeel Hussain Syed	Rheinland-Pfälzische Technische Universität, Kaiserslautern-Landau, Germany
Nandyala Hemachandra	Indian Institute of Technology Bombay, India
Nannan Wu	Tianjin University, China
Nanqing Dong	Shanghai Artificial Intelligence Laboratory, China
Naresh Manwani	International Institute of Information Technology, Hyderabad, India
Natan Tourne	Ghent University, Belgium
Nate Veldt	Texas A&M, USA
Nathalie Japkowicz	American University, USA
Natthawut Kertkeidkachorn	Japan Advanced Institute of Science and Technology (JAIST), Japan
Ngoc-Son Vu	ENSEA, France
Nhat-Tan Bui	University of Arkansas, USA

Nian Li	Tsinghua University, China
Nick Lim	University of Waikato, New Zealand
Nico Piatkowski	Fraunhofer IAIS, Germany
Nicolas Roque dos Santos	University of São Paulo, Brazil
Niklas A. Strauss	LMU Munich, Germany
Nikolaj Tatti	Helsinki University, Finland
Nikolaos Nikolaou	University College London, UK
Nikolaos Stylianou	Information Technologies Institute, Greece
Nikos Kanakaris	University of Southern California, USA
Ning Xu	Southeast University, China
Nripsuta Saxena	University of Southern California, USA
Nuwan Gunasekara	Halmstad University, Sweden
Olga Kurasova	Vilnius University, Lithuania
Olga Slizovskaia	AstraZeneca, UK
Olivier Teste	IRIT, University of Toulouse, France
Oswald C.	NIT Trichy, India
Oswaldo Solarte-Pabon	Universidad del Valle, Colombia
Ozge Alacam	University of Bielefeld, Germany
P. S. Sastry	Indian Institute of Science, India
Pablo Olmos	Universidad Carlos III de Madrid, Spain
Panagiotis Karras	University of Copenhagen, Denmark
Panagiotis Symeonidis	University of the Aegean, Greece
Pance Panov	Jožef Stefan Institute, Slovenia
Paolo Bonetti	Politecnico di Milano, Italy
Paolo Merialdo	Università degli Studi Roma Tre, Italy
Paolo Mignone	University of Bari Aldo Moro, Italy
Pascal Welke	TU Wien, Austria
Patrick Y. Wu	American University, USA
Paul Caillon	LAMSADE Université Paris Dauphine - PSL, France
Paul Davidsson	Malmo University, Sweden
Paul Prasse	University of Potsdam, Germany
Paulo J. Azevedo	Universidade do Minho, Portugal
Pawel Teisseyre	Warsaw University of Technology, Poland
Pawel Zyblewski	Wroclaw University of Science and Technology, Poland
Pedro G. Ferreira	University of Porto, Portugal
Pedro Larrañaga	Technical University of Madrid, Spain
Pedro Ribeiro	University of Porto, Portugal
Pedro H. Abreu	CISUC, Portugal
Peijie Sun	Tsinghua University, China
Peng Wu	Shanghai Jiao Tong University, China

Pengpeng Qiao	Institute of Science Tokyo, Japan
Peter Karsmakers	KU Leuven, Belgium
Peter Schneider-Kamp	SDU, Denmark
Peter van der Putten	Leiden University, Netherlands
Petia Georgieva	University of Aveiro, Portugal
Philipp Vaeth	Technical University of Applied Sciences Würzburg-Schweinfurt and Universität Bielefeld, Germany
Philippe Preux	Inria, France
Phung Lai	SUNY-Albany, USA
Pierre Geurts	Montefiore Institute, University of Liège, Belgium
Pierre Monnin	Université Côte d'Azur, Inria, CNRS, I3S, France
Pierre Schaus	UC Louvain, Belgium
Pierre Wolinski	Paris Dauphine University - PSL, France
Pieter Robberechts	KU Leuven, Belgium
Pietro Sabatino	ICAR-CNR, Italy
Pingchuan Ma	HKUST, China
Piotr Habas	Amazon, USA
Piotr Lipinski	University of Wroclaw, Poland
Piotr Porwik	University of Silesia, Katowice, Poland
Prithwish Chakraborty	IBM Corporation, USA
Lucie Flek	Marburg University, Germany
Przemyslaw Biecek	Warsaw University of Technology, Poland
Qiang Sheng	Institute of Computing Technology, Chinese Academy of Sciences, China
Qiang Zhou	Nanjing University of Aeronautics and Astronautics, China
Rafet Sifa	Fraunhofer IAIS, Germany
Raha Moraffah	Arizona State University, USA
Raivydas Simanas	Vilnius University, Lithuania
Rajeev Rastogi	Amazon, USA
Ranya Almohsen	Baylor College of Medicine, USA
Raphael Romero	Ghent University, Belgium
Raquel Sebastiao	ESTGV-IPV & IEETA-UA, Portugal
Ravi Kolla	Sony Research India, India
Raza Ul Mustafa	Loyola University, USA
Remy Cazabet	Université de Lyon 1, France
Renhe Jiang	University of Tokyo, Japan
Reza Akbarinia	Inria, France
Ricardo P. M. Cruz	University of Porto (FEUP), Portugal
Ricardo B. Prudencio	Universidade Federal de Pernambuco, Brazil
Ricardo Rios	Federal University of Bahia, Brazil

Ricardo Santos	Fraunhofer Portugal AICOS, Portugal
Riccardo Guidotti	University of Pisa, Italy
Robertas Damasevicius	Vytautas Magnus University, Lithuania
Roberto Corizzo	American University, USA
Roberto Interdonato	CIRAD, France
Rocio Chongtay	University of Southern Denmark, Denmark
Rohit Babbar	University of Bath, UK and Aalto University, Finland
Romain Tavenard	Université de Rennes, LETG/IRISA, France
Rosana Veroneze	LBiC, Italy
Ruggero G. Pensa	University of Turin, Italy
Rui Meng	BNU-HKBU United International College, USA
Rui Yu	University of Louisville, USA
Ruixuan Liu	Emory University, USA
Runqun Xiong	Southeast University, China
Runxue Bao	University of Pittsburgh, USA
Ruochun Jin	National University of Defense Technology, China
Ruta Juozaitiene	Vytautas Magnus University, Lithuania
Rytis Maskeliunas	Polsl, Poland
Salvatore Ruggieri	University of Pisa, Italy
Sam Verboven	Vrije Universiteit Brussel, Belgium
Sangkyun Lee	Korea University, South Korea
Sara Abdali	University of California, Riverside, USA
Sarah Masud	LCS2, IIIT-D, India
Sarwan Ali	Georgia State University, USA
Satoru Koda	Fujitsu Limited, Japan
Sebastian Buschjager	Lamarr Institute for ML and AI, Germany
Sebastian Jimenez	Ghent University, Belgium
Sebastian Meznar	Jožef Stefan Institute, Ljubljana, Slovenia
Sebastian Ventura Soto	University of Cordoba, Spain
Sebastien Razakarivony	Safran, France
Selpi Selpi	Chalmers University of Technology, Sweden
Sergio Greco	University of Calabria, Italy
Sergio Jesus	Feedzai, Portugal
Sha Lu	University of South Australia, Australia
Shalini Priya	Indian Institute of Technology Patna, India
Shanqing Guo	Shandong University, China
Shaofu Yang	Southeast University, China
Shazia Tabassum	INESCTEC, Portugal
Shengxiang Gao	Kunming University of Science and Technology, China

Shichao Pei	University of Massachusetts, Boston, USA
Shin Matsushima	University of Tokyo, Japan
Shin-ichi Maeda	Preferred Networks, Japan
Shiwen Ni	Chinese Academy of Sciences, China
Shiyou Qian	Shanghai Jiao Tong University, China
Shu Zhao	Anhui University, China
Shuai Li	University of Cambridge, UK and University of Tokyo, Japan, Tsinghua University, China
Shuang Cheng	Institute of Computing Technology, Chinese Academy of Sciences, China
Shubhranshu Shekhar	Brandeis University, USA
Shurui Cao	Carnegie Mellon University, USA
Shuteng Niu	Mayo Clinic, USA
Siamak Ghodsi	Leibniz University of Hannover, Germany
Sihai Zhang	University of Science and Technology of China, China
Silvia Chiusano	Politecnico di Torino, Italy
Silviu Maniu	Université de Grenoble Alpes, France
Simon Gottschalk	L3S Research Center, Leibniz Universität Hannover, Germany
Simona Nistico	University of Calabria, Italy
Simone Angarano	Politecnico di Torino, Italy
Sinong Zhao	Nankai University, China
Siwei Wang	Intelligent Game and Decision Lab, China
Sofoklis Kitharidis	LIACS, Netherlands
Songlin Du	University of Melbourne, Australia
Songlin Du	Southeast University, China
Soumyajit Chatterjee	Nokia Bell Labs, USA
Sourav Dutta	Huawei Research Centre, China
Stefan Duffner	University of Lyon, France
Stefan Heindorf	Paderborn University, Germany
Stefan Kesselheim	Forschungszentrum Jülich, Germany
Stefano Bortoli	Huawei Research Center, China
Stefanos Vrochidis	Information Technologies Institute, CERTH, Greece
Steffen Thoma	FZI Research Center for Information Technology, Germany
Stephan Doerfel	Kiel University of Applied Sciences, Germany
Steven D. Prestwich	University College Cork, Ireland
Suman Banerjee	IIT Jammu, India
Sunil Aryal	Deakin University, Australia
Surabhi Adhikari	Columbia University, USA

Susan McKeever	TU Dublin, Ireland
Swati Swati	Universität der Bundeswehr München, Germany
Szymon Wojciechowski	Wroclaw University of Science and Technology, Poland
Talip Ucar	AstraZeneca, UK
Taro Tezuka	University of Tsukuba, Japan
Tatiana Passali	Aristotle University of Thessaloniki, Greece
Tatiane Nogueira Rios	UFBA, Brazil
Telmo M. Silva Filho	University of Bristol, UK
Teng Lin	Hong Kong University of Technology (Guangzhou), China
Teng Zhang	Huazhong University of Science and Technology, China
Thach Le Nguyen	Insight Centre, Ireland
Thang Duy Dang	Fujitsu Limited, Japan
Thanh-Son Nguyen	A*STAR, Singapore
Theresa Eimer	Leibniz University Hannover, Germany
Thiago Andrade	INESC TEC & University of Porto, Portugal
Thomas Bonald	Telecom Paris, France
Thomas Guyet	Inria, Centre de Lyon, France
Thomas Lampert	University of Strasbourg, France
Thomas L. Lee	University of Edinburgh, UK
Thomas Mortier	Ghent University, Belgium
Tianyi Chen	Boston University, USA
Tie Luo	University of Kentucky, USA
Tiehang Duan	Mayo Clinic, USA
Tijl De Bie	Ghent University, Belgium
Timilehin B. Aderinola	University College Dublin, Ireland
Timo Bertram	Johannes-Kepler Universität, Germany
Timo Ropinski	Ulm University, Germany
Tobias A. Hille	University of Kassel, Germany
Tom Hanika	University of Hildesheim, Germany
Tomas Kliegr	University of Economics, Prague, Czech Republic
Tomasz Michalak	University of Warsaw and Ideas NCBiR, Poland
Tomasz Walkowiak	Wroclaw University of Science and Technology, Poland
Tommaso Zoppi	University of Florence, Italy
Tong Li	Hong Kong University of Technology, China
Tong Mo	Peking University, China
Tongya Zheng	Hangzhou City University, China
Tonio Weidler	Maastricht University, Netherlands
Tony Lindgren	Stockholm University, Sweden

Tsunenori Mine	Kyushu University, Japan
Tuan Le	New Mexico State University, USA
Tuwe Lofstrom	Jönköping University, Sweden
Ulf Johansson	Jönköping University, Sweden
Vadim Ermolayev	Ukrainian Catholic University, Ukraine
Vahan Martirosyan	CentraleSupélec, Belgium
Vana Kalogeraki	Athens University of Economics and Business, Greece
Vanessa Gomez-Verdejo	Universidad Carlos III de Madrid, Spain
Vasileios Iosifidis	SCHUFA Holding, Germany
Vasilis Gkolemis	ATHENA RC, Greece
Victor Charpenay	Mines Saint-Etienne, France
Vincent Derkinderen	KU Leuven, Belgium
Vincent Lemaire	Orange Research, France
Vincenzo Pasquadibisceglie	University of Bari, Aldo Moro, Italy
Virginijus Marcinkevicius	Vilnius University, Lithuania
Vitor Cerqueira	University of Porto, Portugal
Vivek Kumar	Universität der Bundeswehr München, Germany
Vivek Srikumar	University of Utah, USA
Wagner Meira Jr.	UFMG, Brazil
Wei Wu	Ben Gurion University of the Negev, Israel
Weichen Li	RPTU Kaiserslautern-Landau, Germany
Weifeng Xu	Independent Researcher, China
Weike Pan	Shenzhen University, China
Weiwei Jiang	Beijing University of Posts and Telecommunications, China
Weiwei Sun	Carnegie Mellon University, USA
Weiwei Yuan	Nanjing University of Aeronautics and Astronautics, China
Weixiong Rao	Tongji University, China
Wen-Bo Xie	Southwest Petroleum University, China
Wenhao Li	Tongji University, China
Wenhao Zheng	Shopee, Singapore
Wenjie Feng	National University of Singapore, Singapore
Wenjie Xi	George Mason University, USA
Wenshui Luo	Nanjing University of Science and Technology, China
Wentao Yu	Nanjing University of Science and Technology, China
Wenzhe Yi	Wuhan University, China
Wenzhong Li	Nanjing University, China
Wojciech Rejchel	Nicolaus Copernicus University, Torun, Poland

Xi Jiang	Southern University of Science and Technology, China
Xiang Li	East China Normal University, China
Xiang Lian	Kent State University, USA
Xiao Ma	Beijing University of Posts and Telecommunications, China
Xiao Zhang	Shandong University, China
Xiaobing Zhou	Yunnan University, China
Xiaofeng Cao	University of Technology Sydney, Australia
Xiaofeng Gao	Shanghai Jiaotong University, China
Xiaojun Chen	Institute of Information Engineering, Chinese Academy of Sciences, China
Xiao-Jun Zeng	University of Manchester, UK
Xiaoming Zhang	Beihang University, China
Xiaoting Zhao	Etsy, USA
Xiaowei Mao	Beijing Jiaotong University, China
Xiaoyu Shi	Chinese Academy of Sciences, China
Xin Du	University of Edinburgh, UK
Xin Qin	California State University, Long Beach, USA
Xing Tang	Tencent, China
Xing Xing	Tongji University, China
Xinning Zhu	Beijing University of Posts and Telecommunications, China
Xinpeng Lv	National University of Defense Technology, China
Xintao Wu	University of Arkansas, USA
Xinyang Zhang	University of Illinois at Urbana-Champaign, USA
Xinyu Guan	Xi'an Jiaotong University, China
Xixun Lin	Chinese Academy of Sciences, China
Xiyue Zhang	University of Bristol, UK
Xuan-Hong Dang	IBM T.J. Watson Research Center, USA
Xue Li	University of Queensland, Australia
Xue Yan	Institute of Automation, Chinese Academy of Sciences, China
Xuefeng Chen	Chongqing University, China
Xuemin Wang	Guilin University of Electronic Technology, China
Yachuan Zhang	East China University of Science and Technology, China
Yan Zhang	Peking University, China
Yang Li	University of North Carolina at Chapel Hill, USA
Yang Shu	East China Normal University, China
Yang Wei	Nanjing University of Science and Technology, China

Yanhao Wang	East China Normal University, China
Yanmin Zhu	Shanghai Jiao Tong University, China
Yansong Y. L. Li	University of Ottawa, Canada
Yao-Xiang Ding	Nanjing University, China
Yaqi Xie	Carnegie Mellon University, USA
Yasutoshi Ida	NTT, Japan
Yaying Zhang	Tongji University, China
Ye Zhu	Deakin University, Australia
Yeon-Chang Lee	Ulsan National Institute of Science and Technology, South Korea
Yexiang Xue	Purdue University, USA
Yi Wang	Xinjiang Technical Institute of Physics and Chemistry, Chinese Academy of Sciences, China
Yifeng Gao	University of Texas, Rio Grande Valley, USA
Yilun Jin	Hong Kong University of Science and Technology, China
Yin Zhang	University of Electronic Science and Technology of China, China
Ying Chen	RMIT University, Australia
Yinsheng Li	Fudan University, China
Yong Li	Huawei European Research Center, China
Yongyu Wang	JD Logistics, China
Youhei Akimoto	University of Tsukuba/RIKEN AIP, Japan
You-Wei Luo	Sun Yat-sen University and Jiaying University, China
Yuchen Li	Baidu, China
Yuchen Yang	Harbin Institute of Technology, China
Yudi Zhang	Eindhoven University of Technology, Netherlands
Yuhao Li	University of Melbourne, Australia
Yuheng Jia	Southeast University, China
Yujia Zheng	CMU, USA
Yulong Pei	TU Eindhoven, Netherlands
Yuncheng Jiang	South China Normal University, China
Yuntao Shou	Xi'an Jiaotong University, China
Yunyun Wang	Nanjing University of Posts and Telecommunications, China
Yutong Ye	East China Normal University, China
Yuzhou Chen	University of California, Riverside, USA
Zahraa Abdallah	University of Bristol, UK
Zaineb Chelly Dagdia	UVSQ, Paris-Saclay, France
Zehua Cheng	University of Oxford, UK
Zeyu Chen	University of Auckland, New Zealand

Zhaocheng Ge	Huazhong University of Science and Technology, China
Zhe Yang	Soochow University, China
Zhen Liu	Guangdong University of Foreign Studies, China
Zheng Chen	Osaka University, Japan
Zhenghao Liu	Northeastern University, China
Zhenyu Yang	Macquarie University, Australia
Zhi Li	Tsinghua University, China
Zhichao Han	ETHZ, Switzerland
Zhihui Wang	Fudan University, China
Zhilong Shan	South China Normal University, China
Zhipeng Yin	Florida International University, USA
Zhipeng Zou	Nanjing University of Science and Technology, China
Zhiwen Xiao	Southwest Jiaotong University, China
Zhiwen Zhang	LocationMind, Japan
Zhixin Li	Guangxi Normal University, China
Zhiyong Cheng	Shandong Academy of Sciences, China
Zhong Chen	Southern Illinois University, USA
Zhong Li	Leiden University, Netherlands
Zhong Zhang	Tsinghua University, China
Zhongjing Yu	Peking University, China
Zhuang Liu	Dongbei University of Finance and Economics, China
Zhuo Cao	Forschungszentrum Jülich, Germany
Zhuoming Xie	Guangdong University of Technology, China
Zhuoqun Li	Louisiana State University, USA
Zicheng Zhao	Nanjing University of Science and Technology, China
Zichong Wang	Florida International University, USA
Zifeng Ding	University of Cambridge, UK
Ziheng Chen	Walmart, USA
Zijie J. Wang	Georgia Tech, USA
Zirui Zhuang	Beijing University of Posts and Telecommunications, China
Zixing Song	Chinese University of Hong Kong, China
Ziyu Wang	University of Tokyo, Japan
Ziyue Li	University of Cologne, Germany
Zongxia Xie	Tianjin University, China
Zongyue Li	LMU Munich, Germany
Zuojin Tang	Zhejiang University, China

List of Editors

Inês Dutra	University of Porto, Portugal
Mykola Pechenisky	TU Eindhoven, The Netherlands
Paulo Cortez	University of Minho, Portugal
Sepideh Pashami	Halmstad University, Sweden
Alípio M. Jorge	University of Porto, Portugal
Carlos Soares	University of Porto, Portugal
João Gama	University of Porto, Portugal
Pedro H. Abreu	University of Coimbra, Portugal

Program Committee – Applied Data Science Track

Nasrullah Sheikh	IBM Research, USA
Aakarsh Malhotra	MasterCard, USA
Aakash Goel	Amazon, USA
Abdoulaye Sakho	Artefact, France
Abhijeet Pendyala	Ruhr-Universität Bochum, Germany
Abu Shad Ahammed	University of Siegen, Germany
Adi Lin	Didi, China
Aditya Gautam	Meta, USA
Ahmed K. Mohamed	Meta, USA
Akihiro Yoshida	Kyushu University, Japan
Akshay Sethi	MasterCard, USA
Alejandro Kuratomi	Stockholm University, Sweden
Alessandro Gambetti	Nova School of Business and Economics, Portugal
Alessandro Leite	INSA Rouen, Inria, France
Alessio Russo	Politecnico di Milano, Italy
Alex Beeson	University of Warwick, UK
Alexander Galozy	Halmstad University, Sweden
Alexander Karlsson	University of Skovde, Sweden
Alexander Kovalenko	Czech Technical University in Prague, Czech Republic
Alexey Zaytsev	Skoltech, Russia
Alina Bazarova	Forschungszentrum Jülich, Germany
Alix Lheritier	Amadeus SAS, France
Allan Tucker	Brunel University London, UK
Alvaro Figueira	CRACS and Universidade do Porto, Portugal
Aman Gulati	Amazon, USA
Amira Soliman	Halmstad University, Sweden

Ana Gjorgjevikj	Jožef Stefan Institute, Slovenia
Anders Holst	RISE SICS, Sweden
André C. P. L. F. de Carvalho	University of São Paulo, Brazil
Andrea Seveso	University of Milan-Bicocca, Italy
Andreas Bender	LMU Munich, Germany
Andreas Henelius	Independent Researcher, Finland
Andreas Holzinger	University of Natural Resources and Life Sciences, Vienna, Austria
Andrei Shelopugin	Independent Researcher, Brazil
Angelo Impedovo	Niuma, Italy
Aniket Chakrabarti	Amazon, USA
Animesh Prasad	Roku, USA
Anisio Lacerda	UFMG, Brazil
Anli Ji	Georgia State University, USA
Antoine Doucet	La Rochelle Université, France
Anton Borg	Blekinge Institute of Technology, Sweden
Antonio Bevilacqua	Meetecho, Italy
Antonis Klironomos	University of Mannheim, Germany
Aron Henriksson	Stockholm University, Sweden
Artur Chudzik	Polish-Japanese Academy of Information Technology, Poland
Arun Venkitaraman	EPFL, Switzerland
Arunabha Choudhury	ASML, Netherlands
Asem Omari	Higher Colleges of Technology, UAE
Ashman Mehra	Birla Institute of Technology and Science, India
Ashwani Rao	Amazon, USA
Asier Rodriguez	BBVA, Spain
Asma Atamna	Ruhr-Universität Bochum, Germany
Atiye Sadat Hashemi	Halmstad University, Sweden
Atul Anand Gopalakrishnan	SUNY Buffalo, USA
Avani Wildani	Emory University, USA
Aviv Rovshitz	Ben-Gurion University of the Negev, Israel
Axel Brando	Barcelona Supercomputing Center (BSC) and Universitat de Barcelona (UB), Spain
Azadeh Alavi	RMIT University, Australia
Beihong Jin	Institute of Software, China
Benoit Frenay	University of Namur, Belgium
Berkay Aydin	Georgia State University, USA
Bijaya Adhikari	University of Iowa, USA
Bin Li	Alibaba Group, China
Bo Pang	University of Auckland, New Zealand
Bogdan Ruszczak	Opole University of Technology, Poland

Bohao Qu	Agency for Science, China
Bruno Veloso	INESC TEC, FEP-UP, Portugal
Buyue Qian	Xi'an Jiaotong University, China
Camille Kurtz	Université Paris Cité, France
Cangbai Li	Guangdong University of Technology, China
Carlo Metta	ISTI CNR, Italy
Carlos N. Silla	Pontifical Catholic University of Paraná (PUCPR), Brazil
Cecile Bothorel	IMT Atlantique, France
Cesar Ferri	Universitat Politècnica Valencia, Spain
Chang Li	Apple, USA
Chang-Dong Wang	Sun Yat-sen University, China
Chaofan Li	Karlsruhe Institute of Technology, Germany
Chaoyuan Zuo	Nankai University, China
Chen Gao	Tsinghua University, China
Chen Li	Computer Network Information Center, China
Chen Zhao	Baylor University, USA
Chen-Wei Chang	Virginia Tech, USA
Chenxi Xue	Nanjing Normal University, China
Chongke Bi	Tianjin University, China
Christian M. Adriano	Hasso-Plattner Institute, Germany
Christophe Rodrigues	DVRC Pôle universitaire Léonard de Vinci, France
Chuan Li	Sorbonne University, LIPADE, France
Chunhui Zhang	Dartmouth College, USA
Cristina Soguero Ruiz	Rey Juan Carlos University, Spain
Daheng Wang	Amazon, USA
Daifeng Li	Sun Yat-sen University, China
Damien Fay	HPE Labs, Ireland
Dania Herzalla	Technology Innovation Institute, UAE
Daniel Lemire	University of Quebec (TELUQ), Canada
Daniel Trejo Banos	SDSC, USA
Daochen Zha	Rice University, USA
Dawei Cheng	Tongji University, China
Dayne Freitag	SRI International, USA
Di Yao	Institute of Computing Technology, China
Dimitris Nick Dimitriadis	Aristotle University of Thessaloniki, Greece
Diogo F. Soares	Universidade de Lisboa, Portugal
Dirk Pflueger	University of Stuttgart, Germany
Doheon Han	University of Notre Dame, USA
Dongxiang Zhang	Zhejiang University, China
Dongxiao Yu	Shandong University, China

Dugang Liu	Guangdong Laboratory of Artificial Intelligence and Digital Economy (Shenzen), China
Ece Calikus	Uppsala University, Sweden
Edwyn Brient	Thales LAS/Mines Paris PSL, France
Efstathios Stamatatos	University of the Aegean, Greece
Elaine Faria	UFU, Brazil
Elio Masciari	University of Naples, Italy
Emilie Devijver	Université Grenoble Alpes, Inria, CNRS, Grenoble INP, LIG, France
Emmanuelle Claeys	IRIT, France
Enayat Rajabi	Halmstad University, Sweden
Enda Barrett	University of Galway, Ireland
Enyan Dai	Hong Kong University of Science and Technology (Guangzhou), China
Eric Peukert	ScaDS.AI, Germany
Eric Sanjuan	Avignon University, France
Erik Frisk	Linköping University, Sweden
Eui-Hong (Sam) Han	The Washington Post, USA
Eunil Park	Sungkyunkwan University, South Korea
Fabio Carrara	CNR-ISTI, Italy
Fabiola Pereira	Federal University of Uberlandia, Brazil
Fan Yang	Rice University, USA
Fangzhao Wu	MSRA, China
Fangzhou Shi	Didi Chuxing, China
Fathima Nuzla Ismail	State University of New York, USA
Flavio Bertini	University of Parma, Italy
Francesco Dente	EURECOM, France
Francesco Guerra	University of Modena e Reggio Emilia, Italy
Francesco Scala	CNR-ICAR, Italy
Francesco Spinnato	University of Pisa, Italy
Francesco Paolo Nerini	Sapienza University of Rome, Italy
Francisco P. Romero	UCLM, Spain
Franco Maria Nardini	ISTI-CNR, Italy
Francois Schwarzentruber	ENS Lyon, France
Fudong Lin	University of Delaware, USA
Gabriel Augusto Pinheiro	UNIFESP, Brazil
Gan Sun	South China University of Technology, China
Gargi Srivastava	Rajiv Gandhi Institute of Petroleum Technology Jais, India
Giacomo Boracchi	Politecnico di Milano, Italy
Giuseppe Garofalo	DistriNet, KU Leuven, Belgium
Giuseppina Andresini	University of Bari Aldo Moro, Italy

Goran Falkman	University of Skovde, Sweden
Grzegorz Nalepa	Jagiellonian University, Poland
Guanggang Geng	Jinan University, China
Guojun Liang	Halmstad University, Sweden
Haifang Li	Baidu, China
Haina Tang	University of Chinese Academy of Sciences, China
Hancheng Ge	Amazon, USA
Hao Li	National University of Defense Technology, China
Haohui Chen	CSIRO, Australia
Haomin Yu	Aalborg University, Denmark
Haoyi Xiong	Baidu, China
Hiba Najjar	DFKI, Germany
Hillol Kargupta	Agnik, USA
Hong Zhou	Meta, USA
Hongbin Pei	Xi'an Jiao Tong University, China
Hou-Wan Long	Chinese University of Hong Kong, China
Hua Wei	Arizona State University, USA
Huaiyuan Yao	Xi'an Jiaotong University, China
Huan Song	Amazon, USA
Hubert Baniecki	University of Warsaw, Poland
Hyunsung Kim	KAIST, Fitogether, South Korea
Ibtihal El Mimouni	Inria, France
Ildar Baimuratov	L3S Research Center, Germany
Ilir Jusufi	Blekinge Institute of Technology, Sweden
Inaam Ashraf	Bielefeld University, Germany
Ines Sousa	Fraunhofer AICOS, Portugal
Iris Heerlien	Saxion, Netherlands
Isak Samsten	Stockholm University, Sweden
Ishan Verma	TCS Research, India
Ismail Hakki Toroslu	METU, Turkey
Ivan Carrera	EPN, Ecuador
Jaakko Hollmen	Stockholm University, Sweden
Jairo Cugliari	Laboratoire ERIC, France
Jakub Nalepa	Silesian University of Technology, Poland
Jelica Vasiljević	Hoffmann-La Roche, Switzerland
Jens Lundstrom	Halmstad University, Sweden
Jesse Davis	KU Leuven, Belgium
Jiahui Bai	Meta, USA
Jiajun Gu	Carnegie Mellon University, USA
Jiali Pan	Department of Information Management, USA

Jian Yu	Auckland University of Technology, New Zealand
Jiangbin Zheng	Westlake University, China
Jianhua Yin	Shandong University, China
Jingbo Zhou	Baidu, China
Jingjing Liu	MD Anderson Cancer Center, USA
Jingwen Shi	Michigan State University, USA
Jingxuan Wei	University of Chinese Academy of Sciences, China
Jinyoung Han	Sungkyunkwan University, South Korea
Jiue-An Yang	City of Hope Beckman Research Institute, USA
Joao R. Campos	University of Coimbra, Portugal
Jochen De Weerdt	KU Leuven, Belgium
Joe Tekli	Lebanese American University, Lebanon
Joel Ky	University of Lorraine, CNRS, Inria, France
John McCall	Robert Gordon University, UK
John Mitros	University College Dublin, Ireland
Jonas Fischer	Ruhr-Universität Bochum, Germany
Jonas Nordqvist	Linnaeus University, Sweden
Joydeep Chandra	Indian Institute of Technology Patna, India
Julian Martin Rodemann	LMU Munich, Germany
Jun Shen	University of Wollongong, Australia
Junichi Tatemura	Google, USA
Junxuan Li	Microsoft, USA
Jyun-Yu Jiang	Amazon Science, USA
Kai Wang	Shanghai Jiao Tong University, China
Kaiping Zheng	National University of Singapore, Singapore
Kaiwen Dong	University of Notre Dame, USA
Katarzyna Bozek	University of Cologne, Germany
Katerina Schindlerova	UniVie, Austria
Katharina Dost	Jožef Stefan Institute, Slovenia
Katsiaryna Mirylenka	Zalando SE, Germany
Keith Burghardt	ISI, Germany
Klaus Brinker	Hamm-Lippstadt University of Applied Sciences, Germany
Koki Kawabata	Osaka University, Japan
Korbinian Randl	Stockholm University, Sweden
Krzysztof Krawiec	Poznań University of Technology, Poland
Krzysztof Kutt	Jagiellonian University, Poland
Kwan Hui Lim	Singapore University of Technology and Design, Singapore
Lamija Lemes	University of Zenica, Bosnia & Herzegovina
Le Nguyen	University of Oulu, Finland

Lei Li	Hong Kong University of Science and Technology (Guangzhou), China
Lei Liu	York University, Canada
Li Liu	Chongqing University, China
Li Zhang	University College London, UK
Liang Tang	Google, USA
Liang Tong	NEC Labs America, USA
Liang Wang	Alibaba Group, China
Lina Yao	University of New South Wales, Australia
Lingxiao Li	Michigan State University, USA
Lingyang Chu	McMaster University, Canada
Lixin Zou	Wuhan University, China
Lluis Garcia-Pueyo	Meta, USA
Lou Salaun	Nokia Bell Labs, USA
Luca Corbucci	University of Pisa, Italy
Luca Pappalardo	ISTI, Italy
Luca Romeo	University of Macerata, Italy
Luis Ferreira	Olympus Medical Products Portugal, Portugal
Luis Miguel Matos	ALGORITMI Centre, Portugal
Lukas Grasmann	TU Wien, Austria
Lukas Pensel	Johannes Gutenberg University Mainz, Germany
Maciej Grzenda	Warsaw University of Technology, Poland
Maciej Piernik	Poznań University of Technology, Poland
Madiraju Srilakshmi	Dream Sports, India
Mads C. Hansen	A.P. Moller-Maersk, Denmark
Mahardhika Pratama	University of South Australia, Australia
Mahmoud Rahat	Halmstad University, Sweden
Man Tianxing	Jilin University, China
Manish Gupta	Microsoft, USA
Manos Papagelis	York University, Canada
Manuel Lopes	Instituto Tecnico Superior, Portugal
Manuel Portela	Universitat Pompeu Fabra, Spain
Marc Tommasi	Lille University, France
Marco Fisichella	Leibniz Universität, Hannover, Germany
Maria Riveiro	Jonkoping University, Sweden
Maria Ulan	RISE Research Institutes of Sweden, Sweden
Marian Scuturici	LIRIS, France
Marianne Clausel	IECL, France
Mario Doller	University of Applied Sciences, Kufstein, Austria
Marius Schwammle	DLR/BT, Germany
Markus Gotz	Karlsruhe Institute of Technology (KIT), Germany

Markus Leyser	Technische Universität Dresden, Germany
Martin Boldt	Blekinge Institute of Technology, Sweden
Martin Mladenov	Google, USA
Martin Vita	Institute of Physics, Czech Academy of Sciences, Czech Republic
Matthias Demant	Fraunhofer ISE, Germany
Matthias Galipaud	SDSC, Switzerland
Matthias Petri	Amazon, USA
Matthieu Latapy	CNRS, France
Maurice Van Keulen	University of Twente, Netherlands
Maxime Cordy	University of Luxembourg, Luxembourg
Maxwell J. Jacobson	Purdue University, USA
Md Nahid Hasan	Miami University, USA
Md Zia Ullah	Edinburgh Napier University, UK
Mehtab Alam Syed	CIRAD, France
Melanie Neubauer	University of Leoben, Austria
Meng Chen	Shandong University, China
Mengxuan Zhang	Australian National University, Australia
Miao Fan	NavInfo, China
Michael Bain	University of New South Wales, Australia
Michele Bernardini	Uni eCampus.It, Italy
Michiel Dhont	EluciDATA Lab of Sirris, Belgium
Mickael Coustaty	L3i Laboratory, France
Miguel Couceiro	LORIA, France
Mihaela Mitici	Utrecht University, Netherlands
Min Lee	Singapore Management University, Singapore
Min Hun Lee	Singapore Management University, Singapore
Mina Rezaei	LMU Munich, Germany
Ming Ma	Inner Mongolia University, China
Minghao Chen	Tencent, China
Mirco Nanni	CNR-ISTI Pisa, Italy
Mirjam Wattenhofer	Google, USA
Mirko Marras	University of Cagliari, Italy
Mitra Heidari	University of Melbourne, Australia
Modesto Castrillon-Santana	Universidad de Las Palmas de Gran Canaria, Spain
Mohammadmehdi Saberioon	German Research Centre for Geosciences, Germany
Mohammed Amer	Fujitsu Research of Europe, Germany
Mohammed Ghaith Altarabichi	Halmstad University, Sweden
Mojgan Kouhounestani	University of Melbourne, Australia
Moonki Hong	Sogang University, South Korea

Munira Syed	Procter & Gamble, USA
Nan Li	Microsoft, USA
Narendhar Gugulothu	TCS Research, India
Nedra Mellouli	LIASD, Portugal
Ngoc Son Le	University of Hildesheim, Germany
Niklas Lavesson	Blekinge Institute of Technology, Sweden
Niraj Kumar	Fujitsu, Japan
Nitish Kumar	MasterCard, USA
Nuno Cruz Garcia	FCUL, Portugal
Nuno R. P. S. Guimaraes	INESC TEC, University of Porto, Portugal
Nuwan Gunasekara	Halmstad University, Sweden
Pablo Picazo-Sanchez	Halmstad University, Sweden
Pablo Torrijos Arenas	Universidad de Castilla-La Mancha, Spain
Pablo Jose Del Moral Pastor	Ekkono.ai, Finland
Pan He	Auburn University, USA
Panagiotis Kanellopoulos	University of Essex, UK
Panagiotis Papadakos	FORTH-ICS, Greece
Pandey Shourya Prasad	International Institute of Information Technology, Bangalore, India
Panpan Xu	Amazon AWS, USA
Paola Velardi	Sapienza University of Rome, Italy
Paolo Cintia	Kode, Italy
Pascal Plettenberg	Intelligent Embedded Systems, Italy
Paul Boniol	Inria, France
Pavel Blinov	Sber AI Lab, Russia
Pawel Parczyk	Wroclaw University of Science and Technology, Poland
Pedro M. Ferreira	University of Lisbon, Portugal
Pedro Seber	MIT, USA
Peng Qiao	NUDT, China
Pengyuan Wang	University of Georgia, USA
Petr Olegovich Sokerin	Skoltech, Russia
Philipp Bach	University of Hamburg, Germany
Philipp Froehlich	TU Darmstadt, Germany
Philipp Schmidt	Amazon Research, USA
Philipp Zech	University of Innsbruck, Austria
Pinar Karagoz	Middle East Technical University (METU), Turkey
Ping Luo	Chinese Academy of Sciences, China
Po Yang	University of Sheffield, UK
Pop Petrica	Technical University of Cluj-Napoca, Romania
Prathap Manohar Joshi R	Zoho Corporation, India

Praveen Borra	Florida Atlantic University, USA
Praveen Paruchuri	IIIT Hyderabad, India
Qian Li	Curtin University, Australia
Qihang Yao	Georgia Institute of Technology, USA
Qiwei Han	Nova School of Business and Economics, Portugal
Quentin Duchemin	Université Gustave Eiffel, France
Radu Tudor Ionescu	University of Bucharest, Romania
Rafal Kucharski	Jagiellonian University, Poland
Rafet Sifa	Fraunhofer IAIS & University of Bonn, Germany
Ramasamy Savitha	I2R A*STAR, Singapore
Ran Yu	DSIS Research Group, Singapore
Ranga Raju Vatsavai	North Carolina State University, USA
Raphael Couturier	University of Bourgogne Franche-Comte (UBFC), France
Renato M. Assuncao	ESRI, USA
Renaud Lambiotte	University of Oxford, UK
Reuben Kshitiz Borrison	ABB, Switzerland
Reza Shirvany	Zalando SE, Germany
Ricardo R. Pereira	Feedzai, Portugal
Riccardo Rosati	Università Politecnica delle Marche, Ancona, Italy
Richard Allmendinger	University of Manchester, UK
Richard Nordsieck	XITASO GmbH IT and Software Solutions, Germany
Richi Nayak	Queensland University of Technology, Australia
Roberto Trasarti	CNR, Italy
Rogerio Luis de C. Costa	Polytechnic of Leiria, Portugal
Romain Ilbert	Huawei Paris Research Center, France
Roy Ka-Wei Lee	Singapore University of Technology and Design, Singapore
Ruilin Wang	University of Aberdeen, UK
Sabrina Gaito	Università degli Studi di Milano, Italy
Sai Karthikeya Vemuri	Computer Vision Group Jena, Italy
Saisubramaniam Gopalakrishnan	Quantiphi, USA
Sajjad Shumaly	Max-Planck-Institut for Polymer Research, Germany
Salvatore Rinzivillo	KDD Lab, ISTI, CNR, Italy
Samaneh Shafee	LASIGE, Portugal
Sandra Wissing	Fachhochschule Münster, Germany
Sarwan Ali	Georgia State University, USA
Sebastian Becker	Fraunhofer ISST, Germany

Sebastian Honel	Linnaeus University, Sweden
Selin Colakhasanoglu	Saxion University of Applied Sciences, Netherlands
Senzhang Wang	Central South University, China
Sepideh Nahali	York University, Canada
Shahrooz Abghari	Blekinge Institute of Technology, Sweden
Shahroz Tariq	CSIRO, Australia
Shang Yanlei	BUPT, China
Shen Liang	Paris Cité University, France
Shengheng Liu	Southeast University, China
Shereen Elsayed	University of Hildesheim, Germany
Shi-ting Wen	NingboTech University, China
Shiv Krishna Jaiswal	Walmart Global Tech, USA
Shoujin Wang	Macquarie University, Australia
Shuai Li	University of Cambridge, UK and University of Tokyo, UK
Shuchu Han	Capital One Financial Group, Japan
Simon F. Weinberger	EssilorLuxottica, France
Siyuan Chen	Guangzhou University, China
Snehanshu Saha	BITS Pilani Goa Campus, India
Souhaib Ben Taieb	University of Mons, Abu Dhabi
Sriparna Saha	IIT Patna, India
Stefan Rueping	Fraunhofer IAIS, Germany
Stephane Chretien	Université Lyon 2, France
Sunil Aryal	Deakin University, Australia
Susana Ladra	University of A Coruña, Spain
Szymon Bobek	Jagiellonian University, Poland
Szymon Jaroszewicz	Institute of Computer Science, Poland
Szymon Wilk	Poznań University of Technology, Poland
Tanel Tammet	Tallinn University of Technology, Estonia
Thanh Thi Nguyen	Monash University, Australia
Thiago Zangato	Université Sorbonne Paris Nord, France
Theodora Tsikrika	Information Technologies Institute, Greece
Thibault Girardin	Université Jean Monnet, France
Thomas Czernichow	Darwinlabs, Portugal
Thorsteinn Rognvaldsson	Halmstad University, Sweden
Tiago Mendes-Neves	FEUP/INESC TEC, Portugal
Tianshu Yu	Chinese University of Hong Kong (Shenzhen), China
Ting Su	Imperial College London, UK
Tingrui Qiao	University of Auckland, New Zealand
Tobias Glasmachers	Ruhr-Universität Bochum, Germany

Tomas Olsson — RISE SICS, Sweden
Tome Eftimov — Jožef Stefan Institute, Slovenia
Topon Paul — Toshiba Corporation, Japan
Tsuyoshi Okita — Kyushu Institute of Technology, Japan
Unmesh Padalkar — Dream Sports, India
Vahid Shahrivari Joghan — Utrecht University, Netherlands
Valerio Bonsignori — Unipisa, Italy
Vanessa Borst — University of Würzburg, Germany
Venkata Sai Prakash Mukkamala — Quantiphi Analytics, USA
Veselka Boeva — Blekinge Institute of Technology, Sweden
Viacheslav Komisarenko — University of Tartu, Estonia
Vikas Gupta — HPCL, India
Vinayak Gupta — University of Washington, Seattle, USA
Vincent Auriau — Artefact Research Center, France
Vincenzo Pasquadibisceglie — University of Bari, Aldo Moro, Italy
Vincenzo Scotti — KASTEL, Germany
Vinothkumar Kolluru — Stevens Institute of Technology, USA
Vladimir Mic — Aarhus University, Denmark
Wang-Zhou Dai — Nanjing University, China
Wee Siong Ng — Institute for Infocomm Research, Singapore
Wei Cheng — NEC Laboratories America, USA
Wei Li — Harbin Engineering University, China
Wei Wang — Tsinghua University, China
Wei-Peng Chen — Fujitsu Research of America, USA
Wentao Wang — Michigan State University, USA
Wentao Wu — Microsoft Research, USA
Wray Buntine — VinUniversity, Vietnam
Xianchao Wu — Nvidia, USA
Xiang Lian — Kent State University, USA
Xianli Zhang — Xi'an Jiaotong University, China
Xiaobo Jin — Xi'an Jiaotong-Liverpool University, China
Xiaofei Zhou — University of Chinese Academy of Sciences, China
Xiaofeng Gao — Shanghai Jiaotong University, China
Xiaolin Han — Northwestern Polytechnical University, China
Xin Huang — Hong Kong Baptist University, China
Xin Liu — East China Normal University, China
Xing Tang — Tencent, China
Xiuqiang He — Tencent, China
Xiuyuan Hu — Tsinghua University, China
Xueping Peng — University of Technology Sydney, Australia
Yanchang Zhao — CSIRO, Australia

Yang Guo	Xidian University Hangzhou Institute of Technology, China
Yang Song	Apple, USA
Yijun Zhao	Fordham University, USA
Yinghui Wu	Case Western Reserve University, USA
Yingzhen Lin	Harbin Institute of Technology (Shenzhen), China
Yintao Yu	University of Illinois at Urbana-Champaign, USA
Yixiang Fang	Chinese University of Hong Kong, China
Yixuan Cao	Institute of Computing Technology, China
Yizheng Huang	York University, Canada
Yongchao Liu	Ant Group, China
Yu Huang	Indiana University, USA
Yu Wang	University of Oregon, USA
Yuantao Fan	Halmstad University, Sweden
Yucheng Zhou	University of Macau, China
Yue Shi	Meta, USA
Yueyuan Zheng	Beihang University, China
Yunchuan Shi	University of Sydney, Australia
Yunjun Gao	Zhejiang University, China
Yuting Ding	Southeast University, China
Yuzhuo Li	University of Auckland, New Zealand
Zahra Kharazian	Stockholm University, Sweden
Zahra Taghiyarrenani	Halmstad University, Sweden
Zahraa Abdallah	University of Bristol, UK
Zeyi Wen	Hong Kong University of Science and Technology (Guangzhou), China
Zeyu Zhu	National University of Defense Technology, China
Zhanyu Liu	Shanghai Jiao Tong University, China
Zhaogeng Liu	Jilin University, China
Zhaohui Liang	National Library of Medicine, USA
Zhen Zhang	Shandong University, China
Zhendong Chu	Squirrel Ai Learning, China
Zheng Zhang	University of California, USA
Zhengze Li	University of Göttingen, Germany
Zhibin Gu	Hebei Normal University, China
Zhuang Liu	Dongbei University of Finance and Economics, China
Ziyu Guan	Xidian University, China
Zoltan Miklos	Université de Rennes, France
Zunlei Feng	Zhejiang University, China

Program Committee – Demo Track

Andrzej Wójtowicz	Adam Mickiewicz University, Poznań, Poland
Anna Sokol	University of Notre Dame, USA
Arian Pasquali	Faktion AI, Belgium
Bruno Veloso	INESC TEC - FEP-UP, Portugal
Chongsheng Zhang	Henan University, China
Christos Doulkeridis	University of Piraeus, Greece
Danqing Zhang	PathOnAI.org, USA
Fátima Rodrigues	INESC TEC, Portugal
Grigorii Khvatskii	University of Notre Dame, USA
Joe Germino	University of Notre Dame, USA
Jungwon Seo	University of Stavanger, Norway
Ke Li	University of Exeter, England
Manfred Jaeger	Aalborg University, Denmark
Marcin Luckner	Warsaw University of Technology, Poland
Mehwish Alam	Institut Polytechnique de Paris, France
Nuno Moniz	University of Notre Dame, USA
Tânia Carvalho	FCUP, Portugal
Vitor Cerqueira	FEUP, Portugal
Wei-Wei Du	National Yang Ming Chiao Tung University, Taiwan

Additional Reviewers

Andrea D'Angelo
Patrick Altmeyer
Guiseppina Adresini
Vedangi Bengali
Michele Bernardini
Zhi Cao
Louis Carpentier
Alessio Cascione
Lilia Chebbah
Meng Ding
Roberto Esposito
Alina Fastowski
Roger Ferrod
Michele Fontana
Chang Gong
Michal Grzejdziak-Zdziarski
Paul Hahn

Antonia Hain
Md Athikul Islam
Michael Ito
Philipp Jahn
Rahul Kumar
Bishal Lakha
Yuwen Liu
Jerry Lonlac
Shijie Luo
Francesca Naretto
Navid Nobani
Diego Coello de Portugal
Joana Santos
Francesco Scala
Richard Serrano
Nuno Silva
Francesco Spinnato

Pedro C. Vieira
Xiao Wang
Yunyun Wang
Qi Wen
Jianye Xie

Huaiyuan Yao
Yutong Ye
Obaidullah Zaland
Efstratios Zaradoukas
Nan Zhang

Sponsors

Diamond

Platinum

liv   Organization

Gold

Silver

Bronze

Other Sponsors

Partners

Keynotes

Many Good Models Leads to ...

Cynthia Rudin

Duke University, USA

Abstract. As it turns out, many good models leads to amazing things! The Rashomon Effect, coined by Leo Breiman, describes the phenomenon that there exist many equally good predictive models for the same dataset.

This phenomenon happens for many real datasets, and when it does it sparks both magic and consternation, but mostly magic. In light of the Rashomon Effect, my collaborators and I propose to reshape the way we think about machine learning, particularly for tabular data problems in the nondeterministic (noisy) setting. I'll address how the Rashomon Effect impacts (1) the existence of simple-yet-accurate models, (2) flexibility to address user preferences, such as fairness and monotonicity, without losing performance, (3) uncertainty in predictions, fairness, and explanations, (4) reliable variable importance, (5) algorithm choice, specifically, providing advanced knowledge of which algorithms might be suitable for a given problem, and (6) public policy. I'll also discuss a theory of when the Rashomon Effect occurs and why: interestingly, noise in data leads to a large Rashomon Effect. My goal is to illustrate how the Rashomon Effect can have a massive impact on the use of machine learning for complex problems in society.

Towards Causal Artificial Intelligence

Elias Bareinboim

Columbia University, USA

Abstract. While a significant portion of AI scientists and engineers believe we are on the verge of achieving highly general forms of AI, I offer a critical appraisal of this view through a causal lens. In particular, building on foundational developments in the field, I will present my perspective on the relationship between intelligence and causality – and the central role of the latter in building intelligent systems and advancing credible data science.

I frame this discussion in terms of five core capabilities that we should expect from an intelligent AI system: performing causal reasoning and articulating explanations; making precise, surgical, and sample-efficient decisions; generalizing across changing conditions and environments; generating and simulating in a causally consistent manner; and learning causal structures and variables.

In this talk, I will elaborate on this perspective and share current progress toward building causally intelligent AI systems. A more detailed discussion of this thesis is provided in my forthcoming textbook, a draft of which is available here: https://causalai-book.net/.

Not Just a Trend: Institutionalizing XAI for Responsible and Compliant AI Systems

Francisco Herrera

Granada University, Spain

Abstract. As artificial intelligence (AI) systems increasingly mediate decisions in high-stakes domains – from healthcare and finance to public policy – the demand for explainable AI (XAI) has grown rapidly. Yet many current XAI approaches remain disconnected from the practical needs of stakeholders and the requirements of emerging regulatory frameworks. This talk argues that XAI must not be treated as a passing trend or optional technical add-on, but as a foundational principle in the design and deployment of AI systems. We critically examine the state of the field, exposing the gap between model-centric explainability and stakeholder-centric accountability. In response, we propose a framework that aligns explainability with legal, ethical, and social responsibilities, emphasizing co-design with affected users, sensitivity to institutional contexts, and governance over opacity. Our goal is to advance XAI from superficial compliance toward deeply integrated transparency that fosters trust, accountability, and responsible innovation.

Compositional Intelligence: Coordinating Multiple LLMs for Complex Tasks

Mirella Lapata

University of Edinburgh, UK

Abstract. Recent years have witnessed the rise of increasingly larger and more sophisticated language models (LMs) capable of performing every task imaginable, sometimes at (super)human level. In this talk, I will argue that in many realistic scenarios, solely relying on a single general-purpose LLM is suboptimal. A single LLM is likely to underrepresent real-world data distributions, heterogeneous skills, and task-specific requirements. Instead, I will discuss multi-LLM collaboration as an alternative to monolithic generative modeling. By orchestrating multiple LLMs, each with distinct roles, perspectives, or competencies, we can achieve more effective problem-solving while being more inclusive and explainable. I will illustrate this approach through two case studies: narrative story generation and visual question answering, showing how a society of agents can collectively tackle complex tasks while pursuing complementary subgoals. Additionally, I will explore how these agent societies leverage reasoning to improve performance.

Towards a Fairer World: Uncovering and Addressing Human and Algorithmic Biases

Nuria Oliver

ELLIS Alicante Foundation, Spain

Abstract. In my talk, I will first briefly present ELLIS Alicante1, the only ELLIS unit that has been created from scratch as a non-profit research foundation devoted to responsible AI for Social Good. Next, I will provide an overview of AI with a focus on the ethical implications and limitations of today's AI systems, including algorithmic discrimination and bias. On this topic, I will present a few examples of our work on uncovering and mitigating both human and algorithmic biases with AI.

On the human front, I will present the body of work that we have carried out in the context of AI-based beauty filters that are so popular on social media. On the algorithmic front, I will explain the main approaches to address algorithmic discrimination and I will present three novel methods to achieve fairer decisions.

Tensor Logic: A Simple Unification of Neural and Symbolic AI

Pedro Domingos

University of Washington, USA

Abstract. Deep learning has achieved remarkable successes in language generation and other tasks, but is extremely opaque and notoriously unreliable. Both of these problems can be overcome by combining it with the sound reasoning and transparent knowledge representation capabilities of symbolic AI. Tensor logic accomplishes this by unifying tensor algebra and logic programming, the formal languages underlying respectively deep learning and symbolic AI. Tensor logic is based on the observation that predicates are compactly represented Boolean tensors, and can be straightforwardly extended to compactly represent numeric ones. The two key constructs in tensor logic are tensor join and project, numeric operations that generalize database join and project. A tensor logic program is a set of tensor equations, each expressing a tensor as a series of tensor joins, a tensor project, and a univariate nonlinearity applied elementwise. Tensor logic programs can succinctly encode most deep architectures and symbolic AI systems, and many new combinations.

In this talk I will describe the foundations and main features of tensor logic, and present efficient inference and learning algorithms for it. A system based on tensor logic achieves state-of-the-art results on a suite of language and reasoning tasks. How tensor logic will fare on trillion-token corpora and associated tasks remains an open question.

Artificial Intelligence for Science

Sašo Džeroski

Jožef Stefan Institute, Slovenia

Abstract. Artificial intelligence is already transforming science, with its future impact expected to be even greater. Realizing this potential requires addressing key scientific challenges, such as ensuring explainability (of models and their predictions), learning effectively from limited data, and integrating data with prior domain knowledge. It also requires the provision of support for open and reproducible science through formalizing and sharing scientific knowledge.

I will present an overview of my research on the development of AI methods suitable for use in science. These include methods for explainable machine learning – including multi-target prediction and relational learning – that deliver accurate yet interpretable models suitable for complex scientific domains. These methods have been applied in environmental science, life science and materials science. Learning from limited data is critical in science. I will discuss two complementary approaches: semi-supervised learning, which leverages unlabeled data directly, together with labeled data, and foundation models, which use representations learned from vast unlabeled data to support downstream tasks with minimal supervision, i.e., limited amounts of labeled data. Both paradigms expand AI's reach into data-scarce scientific problems.

I will then present our work on automated scientific modeling, where we learn interpretable models of dynamical systems – such as process-based models and differential equations – from time series data and domain knowledge. Finally, I will highlight the role of ontologies and semantic technologies in experimental computer science, including machine learning and optimization. In these areas, we have developed ontologies for the representation and annotation of both data and other artefacts produced by science, such as algorithms, models, and results of experiments.

Contents – Part IX

Engineering and Technology

CNN-Transformer with Absolute Positional Encoding Optimized
for Low-Dimensional Inputs: Applied to Estimate Sliding Drop Width 3
  Sajjad Shumaly, Fahimeh Darvish, Mahsa Salehi,
  Navid Mohammadi Foumani, Oleksandra Kukharenko,
  Hans-Jürgen Butt, Ulrich Schwanecke, and Rüdiger Berger

Personalized Contest Recommendation in Fantasy Sports 22
  Madiraju Srilakshmi, Kartavya Kothari, and Kamlesh Marathe

Talk is Cheap, Energy is Not: Towards a Green, Context-Aware Metrics
Framework for Automatic Speech Recognition 36
  Maria Ulan, Erik Johannes Husom, and Jeriek Van den Abeele

Sequential Rule Analysis of ICU Patient Vital Signals and Alarms 55
  Michela Venturini, Len Feremans, Wouter De Corte, and Celine Vens

Continuous Learning of Ordinal User Preferences on Wearable Devices 71
  Simón Weinberger, Jairo Cugliari, and Aurélie Le Cain

Iterative Corpus Refinement for Materials Property Prediction Based
on Scientific Texts 89
  Lei Zhang and Markus Stricker

CARIS: Cache Affinity-Aware Reinforced Intelligent Strategy 104
  Yu Zuo and Yanlei Shang

Finance, Economy, Management or Marketing

Better Capturing Interactions Between Products in Retail: Revisited
Negative Sampling for Basket Choice Modeling 125
  Jules Désir, Vincent Auriau, Martin Možina, and Emmanuel Malherbe

Transaction Categorization with Relational Deep Learning in QuickBooks 143
  Kaiwen Dong, Padmaja Jonnalagedda, Xiang Gao, Ayan Acharya,
  Maria Kissa, Mauricio Flores, Nitesh V. Chawla, and Kamalika Das

Attribute-Aware Sequential Recommendation Model for Used Car
Auctions 161
   *Shereen Elsayed, Ngoc Son Le, Ahmed Rashed, Lukas Hestermeyer,
   Radoslaw Wlodarczyk, Maximilian Stubbemann,
   and Lars Schmidt-Thieme*

Attribute and Context-Aware Multi-Behavior Model for Unique-Item
Recommendation 178
   Shereen Elsayed, Ngoc Son Le, Ahmed Rashed, and Lars Schmidt-Thieme

On the Performance of LLMs for Real Estate Appraisal 195
   *Margot Geerts, Manon Reusens, Bart Baesens, Seppe vanden Broucke,
   and Jochen De Weerdt*

InterDiff: Synthesizing Financial Time Series with Inter-Stock
Correlations via Classifier-Free Guided Diffusion 212
   *Hou-Wan Long, Zhoufei Tang, Jianhui Zhang, Zhuoyang Zhan, Tao Lu,
   and Xiaoquan Michael Zhang*

Evaluating Transfer Learning Methods on Real-World Data Streams:
A Case Study in Financial Fraud Detection 230
   *Ricardo Ribeiro Pereira, Jacopo Bono, Hugo Ferreira, Pedro Ribeiro,
   Carlos Soares, and Pedro Bizarro*

Harnessing Mixed Features for Imbalance Data Oversampling: Application
to Bank Customers Scoring 247
   *Abdoulaye Sakho, Emmanuel Malherbe, Carl-Erik Gauthier,
   and Erwan Scornet*

Proactive Detection of Model Degradation in Financial Fraud Prediction
with Delayed Labels 265
   *Akshay Sethi, Priyanshi Gupta, Sparsh Kansotia, Kamal Kant,
   and Nitish Srivasatava*

Health, Biology, Bioinformatics or Chemistry

WoundAmbit: Bridging State-of-the-Art Semantic Segmentation
and Real-World Wound Care 285
   *Vanessa Borst, Timo Dittus, Tassilo Dege, Astrid Schmieder,
   and Samuel Kounev*

Offline Reinforcement Learning for Community-Acquired Pneumonia
Management: A Feasibility Study 304
   Alex Beeson, Keith Couper, and Giovanni Montana

TempEHR: A Temporal Dependency-Based Approach for Synthesizing
Electronic Health Records 321
  *Emmanuella Budu, Amira Soliman, Farzaneh Etminani,
  and Thorsteinn Rögnvaldsson*

Federated Learning Towards the Unknown: A Deep Dive Into Diabetic
Retinopathy Prediction from Real-World EHR Structured Data on Unseen
Diabetic Centers 338
  *Alessandro Cacciatore, Mariachiara Di Cosmo, Emanuele Frontoni,
  and Michele Bernardini*

HAGAPS: Hierarchical Attentive Graph Neural Networks for Predicting
Alternative Polyadenylation Site Quantification 356
  Eleni Giovanoudi and Dimitrios Rafailidis

Do Protein Transformers Have Biological Intelligence? 373
  *Fudong Lin, Wanrou Du, Jinchan Liu, Tarikul Milon, Shelby Meche,
  Wu Xu, Xiaoqi Qin, and Xu Yuan*

SigBERT: Combining Narrative Medical Reports and Rough Path
Signature Theory for Survival Prediction in Oncology 391
  *Paul Minchella, Loic Verlingue, Stéphane Chrétien, Rémi Vaucher,
  and Guillaume Metzler*

TIDS: A Thermal Imaging Dataset for Subclinical Mastitis in Dairy Sheep 408
  *Georgios Botsoglou, Marios Lysitsas, Dimitris Dimitriadis,
  Constantina Tsokana, George Valiakos, and Grigorios Tsoumakas*

Mitigating Data Scarcity in Polymer Property Prediction via Multi-task
Auxiliary Learning 426
  *Gabriel A. Pinheiro, Marcos G. Quiles, Juarez L. F. Da Silva,
  and Xiaoli Z. Fern*

Enhancing Detection of *Leishmania* spp. Amastigotes in Canine Lymph
Node Smear Images: Evaluating the Effectiveness of Synthetic Data
in Augmenting Existing Datasets 443
  *Dimitrios Tsikos, Irene Chatzipanagiotidou, Dimitris Dimitriadis,
  Constantina N Tsokana, George Valiakos, Labrini V Athanasiou,
  and Grigorios Tsoumakas*

ActiveVisium: Leveraging Active Learning to Enhance Manual Pathologist
Annotation in 10x Visium Spatial Transcriptomics Experiments 459
  *Jelica Vasiljević, Ines Berenguer Veiga, Kerstin Hahn, Petra Schwalie,
  and Alberto Valdeolivas*

TEMPOBIGEN: A Curated Generative Model for Healthcare Mobility Logs
with Visit Duration 476
   Hieu Vu, Alberto M. Segre, and Bijaya Adhikari

Industry (4.0, 5.0, Manufacturing, ...)

Near-Infrared Spectroscopy and Image Classification of Refuse Derived
Fuels to Increase Cement Production Quality 495
   Jonas Fischer, Luca Fehler, Kevin Treiber, and Viktor Scherer

From Lab to Factory: Pitfalls and Guidelines for Self-/Unsupervised
Defect Detection on Low-Quality Industrial Images 511
   Sebastian Hönel and Jonas Nordqvist

Author Index 529

Engineering and Technology

CNN-Transformer with Absolute Positional Encoding Optimized for Low-Dimensional Inputs: Applied to Estimate Sliding Drop Width

Sajjad Shumaly[1]([✉]), Fahimeh Darvish[1], Mahsa Salehi[2], Navid Mohammadi Foumani[2], Oleksandra Kukharenko[1], Hans-Jürgen Butt[1], Ulrich Schwanecke[3], and Rüdiger Berger[1]

[1] Max Planck Institute for Polymer Research (MPI-P), Mainz, Germany
shumalys@mpip-mainz.mpg.de
[2] Department of Data Science and Artificial Intelligence, Monash University, Melbourne, VIC, Australia
[3] Department of Computer Science and Media, RheinMain University of Applied Sciences, Wiesbaden, Germany

Abstract. High-speed video recordings are crucial for investigating drop dynamics and their interactions with surfaces. Measuring the width of sliding drops, a key parameter linked to frictional forces, requires additional equipment like cameras or mirrors, complicating experimental setups and limiting observable areas. This study introduces a novel method that simplifies the measurement process by employing artificial neural networks to estimate millimeter-scale drop width directly from side-view video data. Our approach processes raw video footage to dynamically identify features most indicative of drop width. By treating drop behavior as an extrinsic time-series problem, our model effectively captures temporal dependencies in video sequences. We propose a VGG8-inspired architecture optimized for small and low information density video datasets. This architecture is combined with our novel position invariant video processing methodology that efficiently removes non-essential regions, reducing computation time by 84%. We further integrate ConvTran, a state-of-the-art time-series classification model, with an enhanced Absolute Position Encoding, improving the encoding's dot-product and lowering drop width estimation errors. Our novel neural network architecture achieved a root mean square error of 48 µm (1.7% relative error), where each pixel corresponds to approximately 44 µm. Code and data are open-sourced at: https://github.com/shumaly/position_invariant_cnn_transformer.

Supplementary Information The online version contains supplementary material available at https://doi.org/10.1007/978-3-032-06118-8_1.

Keywords: position invariant video processing · low-dimensional absolute positional encoding · extrinsic time series · spatiotemporal CNNTransformer

1 Introduction

Video analysis of sliding drops enables quantitative studies of sliding forces and liquid-solid interfacial properties [1,2]. Sliding forces depend on drop width [3,4]. A recent investigation by Li et al. focused on drops sliding down an inclined surface, presenting an empirical equation of the friction force F_f versus drop velocity U [3]:

$$F_f = F_0 + \beta w U \eta \tag{1}$$

Here, β is a dimensionless friction coefficient, w is the width of the drop while sliding, η is the viscosity of the liquid, and F_0 is the friction force extrapolated to velocity $U = 0$. The friction force of drops that just start sliding is described by the Furmidge equation [5–8]:

$$F = k\gamma w(\cos\theta_r - \cos\theta_a) \tag{2}$$

where γ is the liquid-air surface tension, θ_a is the advancing contact angle, θ_r is the receding contact angle, and k is a geometry factor [4,9]. The Furmidge equation also appears of frictional forces at low velocities [10]. The dynamic contact angles vary with velocity and can be easily measured from a side view.

Friction force is essential for detecting surface inhomogeneities, assessing interfacial stability, monitoring viscoelastic energy dissipation [43], and also is critical in anti-icing [41] and surface coating quality [42]. However, determining the drop width during a standard sliding drop experiment remains a challenging task. Adding cameras for bottom- or top-view measurements is not feasible since these views show the drop's central width, not the drop's contact line width. The drop's contact line width is narrower on surfaces with contact angles $> 90°$. Front-view imaging of drops is feasible by installing two mirrors or a second, time-synchronized high-speed camera [10,11]. However, it is limited to a sliding length of only ≈ 1.5 cm, as the drop moves toward the mirror and cannot stay within the camera's focus range for an extended period. To address these limitations, Shumaly et al. recently proposed a deep learning-based multivariate time-series analysis approach that leverages side-view measurements to estimate the front-view drop width, eliminating the need to add additional cameras or devices and without limiting sliding length [12].

Practical Significance. Previous research has relied on predefined measures extracted from side-view videos—such as contact angles, drop length, height, and the velocity of the drop's center—to estimate drop width. While these features are deemed important by existing literature, they may not capture all the nuanced interactions that occur, especially when drops encounter surface defects. When a drop moves over a surface with a single defect, its center velocity decreases upon encountering a defect and increases after surpassing it (Fig. 1, black line). Meanwhile, the advancing and receding velocities exhibit distinct behaviors as they interact with surface defects in different ways (Fig. 1, red and blue lines). Monitoring only the center velocity fails to account for these differences, limiting estimation accuracy. The advancing and receding contact lines engage with the defect differently, revealing nuanced behaviors that are not captured when considering only the center velocity.

The gap in knowledge lies in the absence of a comprehensive method that can autonomously extract and prioritize relevant features from raw video data to describe the physics of sliding drops. Current models do not leverage the full potential of video data to identify subtle but important features that could enhance measurement precision, especially in challenging scenarios involving surface defects. Moreover, if we can automatically extract features, it will open up new opportunities to explore which segments of the drop contour line are crucial. For instance, we could investigate whether a combination of pixels in the drop's receding section or even the reflections within the drop itself might provide essential information on drop width (Fig. 1, green drop curves). Furthermore, this method enhances estimation accuracy and increase robustness against environmental variations, including optical distortions such as minor defocusing and focus irregularities, motion blur, lighting fluctuations, as well as dust within the lenses and scattered lights that cause noise in video frames.

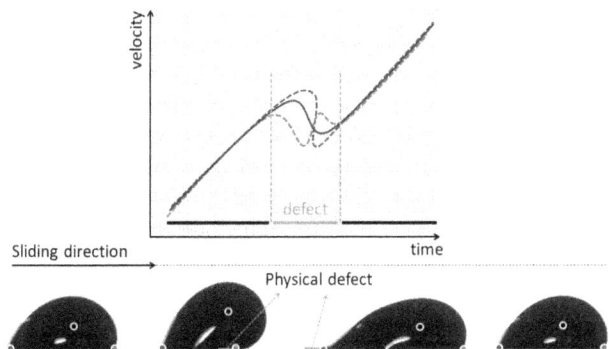

Fig. 1. Velocity profiles of a sliding drop over a surface defect. The diagram depicts the velocities at the drop's center (black), advancing edge (red), and receding edge (blue). Colors in the plot match the colored points on the schematic. As the drop interacts with the defect, the center velocity decreases, while the advancing and receding edges respond differently, revealing nuanced behaviors beyond center velocity analysis. Green curves indicate potential areas of interest for a more detailed investigation of drop dynamics. (Color figure online)

1.1 Main Contributions

In this study, we introduced a novel deep learning approach for accurately estimating the width of sliding drops directly from side-view video data. Key outcomes and advancements of our work include:

- **Position Invariant Video Processing:** Our proposed position invariant video processing method mitigates overfitting due to positional bias while significantly reducing computational load by approximately 84%. It is applicable to scientific problems involving the motion of small objects of interest, especially when data availability is limited.
- **Low-Dimensional Absolute Position Encoding:** Our proposed ldAPE effectively addresses the anisotropic limitations commonly encountered in conventional positional encoding methods for low-dimensional time-series data. Empirically, it outperforms both tAPE and Sin-APE on 32-dimensional data, with theoretical advantages extending up to 128 dimensions.
- **Optimized CNN-Transformer Architecture:** We developed a custom VGG8-inspired CNN architecture specifically designed for video datasets characterized by low information density. Coupled with the ConvTran time-series transformer, our model efficiently captures intricate spatiotemporal interactions. We achieved an RMSE of 48.4 µm, corresponding to a low error rate of just 1.7%. This demonstrates a considerable improvement over previous state-of-the-art models, especially in challenging scenarios involving surface defects.
- **Robustness and Interpretability:** Based on Grad-CAM visualizations, we confirmed that our model robustly identifies critical drop features, including subtle edges and reflections. This capability not only improves estimation accuracy but also enhances interpretability, offering insights into the underlying physics of drop-surface interactions.
- **Open Source Contribution:** To support future research and foster collaboration within the scientific community, we release our comprehensive sliding drop video dataset and the source code. This contribution enhances reproducibility, supports model inference, and promotes advancements in ML-based experimental fluid dynamics research.

2 Related Work

2.1 Machine Learning and Surface Science

The integration of machine learning into surface science enhances drop dynamics and contact angle analysis, improving complexity handling. Yancheshme et al. applied a random forest model to predict the behavior of impacting drops on hydrophobic and superhydrophobic surfaces [13]. Their goal was to determine the optimal conditions for inducing bouncing behavior during drop impact. They analyzed a broad set of predefined measures, including the drops' physical properties, kinematic characteristics, and surface attributes. Similarly, Zhang et al. developed a method to optimize the contact angle on rice leaf surfaces by comparing artificial neural networks (ANN) and response surface methodology (RSM) [14]. They focused on factors such as temperature, humidity, and pesticide concentration to determine the best conditions for minimizing the contact angle. ANN outperformed RSM in contact angle prediction, with pesticide concentration as the key factor. Kokalis et al. proposed a method to classify composite insulators into hydrophobicity classes using convolutional neural networks (CNNs) [15]. They used a spray method to collect images and train CNNs for insulator classification, removing human subjectivity. In the same way, Roy et al. introduced a method for detecting the hydrophobicity grade of polymeric insulators using Bi-directional Long Short-Term Memory (Bi-LSTM) classifier [16]. Rabbani et al. employed two deep learning models with fully connected dense layers to predict contact angles in tomography images of porous materials [17]. Kabir et al. used ResNet-50 to estimate contact angles, overcoming fitting limitations on hydrophilic surfaces [18]. A recent deep learning study in surface science developed a method (4S-SROF), enabling systematic analysis of sliding drops, even when occupying a small image region [19]. Shumaly et al. introduced a method based on regressions and Recurrent Neural Networks (RNNs) to estimate sliding drop width using predefined side-view features [12]. Their Long Short-Term Memory (LSTM) model demonstrated the best performance, estimating sliding drop width with a low error of 2.4% (67.6 μ m RMSE), eliminating the need for cumbersome equipment while maintaining an unrestricted view of sliding drops. We now introduce more advanced end-to-end deep learning models capable of extracting features without relying on predefined physics-based measurements, enhancing accuracy to estimate sliding drop width.

2.2 Time Series Extrinsic Regression

Time series extrinsic regression (TSER) is a regression task aimed at understanding the relationship between a time series and continuous scalar variables. Although numerous papers are published annually on time series classification [20,21] and time series forecasting [22–24], time series extrinsic regression has received limited attention [25]. In this study, we address a TSER problem, reconstructing a time series (front-view) from a set of time series (side-view). Our approach employs a machine learning framework, formulating the task as a regression problem where the input consists of consecutive drop images and the output is a scalar value. Regression involves predicting a continuous numeric value based on a set of input features [26]. However, our goal is to estimate values that may extend the input time series or be indirect to it, without being restricted to future values.

Similar studies on regression involve estimating heart rate based on data gathered from accelerometers [27,28]. Random Convolutional Kernel Transform (ROCKET) has demonstrated state-of-the-art results in various time series tasks by leveraging a set of random convolutional kernels to extract informative features efficiently [29]. InceptionTime, a deep learning-based approach inspired by the Inception architecture, enhances feature extraction, making it effective for capturing both short- and long-term temporal dependencies [30]. Similarly, Transformer for Time Series (TST) has been proposed as an attention-based model that excels in capturing intricate relationships within time series data by leveraging self-attention mechanisms [31]. ConvTran, a convolutional transformer model, has recently gained recognition. By combining convolutional feature extraction with transformer-based sequence modeling, ConvTran achieves superior performance in handling both local and global dependencies, making it particularly well-suited for tasks like TSER [32].

3 Materials and Methods

3.1 Data Collection

The sliding drop setup consists of a high-speed camera with a telecentric lens to record drop motion under uniform backlighting. Two parallel mirrors capture the front view by reflecting the backlight. The entire optical system is mounted on a rotatable breadboard to maintain alignment. Distilled water drops (32 µl) are deposited onto a tilted plane using a peristaltic pump connected to a grounded syringe needle. The technical details and a schematic of the setup and sample preparation are presented in Supplementary Information (SI) Sections S.1, and S.2. Installing the mirrors restricted the focus of the front-view camera to the last ≈1.5 cm of the slide path. Data was collected only within this region. Therefore, defects were fabricated on the last centimeter of the samples. The dataset was filtered to include videos with 20–250 frames for consistency. The dataset consists of 235 videos with a resolution of 1280×1024 pixels, containing a total of 11,944 frames. The number of frames per video varies depending on the drop velocity.

3.2 Data Augmentation

We applied data augmentation to mimic real-world imaging variations and enhance robustness. The techniques included brightness adjustment, Gaussian blur filtering, and artifact generation. Brightness adjustment varied image intensity by ±15% to account for ambient fluctuations. Gaussian blur was applied with randomly selected kernel sizes (1×1, 3×3, 5×5) to simulate defocusing and motion blur. Image artifacts were introduced as irregular stains and radiance spots to mimic lens smudges and reflections. Irregular stains were generated using sinusoidal perturbations on random circular shapes, followed by transformations such as stretching, rotation, and scaling. Radiance spots were simulated using Canny edge detection to localize drop edges, followed by circular gradient overlays. More details and pseudo-codes are provided in SI Section S.3.

3.3 Position Invariant Video Processing Methodology

Captured high-speed video frames of sliding drops have a resolution of 1280×1024 pixels. In our dataset, the largest drops reach 216×99 pixels. An initial approach involved cropping frames to 1280×99 pixels, preserving the drop's horizontal path while removing unnecessary upper and lower portions (Fig. 2a). However, this approach introduced several challenges.

Firstly, the drop occupies only a small fraction of the cropped frame, leaving extensive empty space. Secondly, the model may overfit by associating drops with their absolute positions in the image rather than focusing on their shape and velocity, which are the relevant features. For instance, surface defects are always located in the last centimeter of the sliding path due to video capture constraints [12]. This carries the risk that the model becomes too closely adapted to the droplet's dynamic behavior at a specific location, thereby limiting its ability to generalize to defects appearing at other positions.

To address these challenges, we introduced a 3D sliding window centered on the drop, which we call the sliding spatiotemporal window (SSW). We set the window size to 216×99 pixels, matching the maximum observed drop dimensions (Fig. 2b). This window follows the drop's movement, keeping it centered in the frame and reducing irrelevant background. The impact of input tensor size on memory usage and computation time was obtained using a dummy input. It assesses the general computational footprint of the model's forward pass. The total memory usage M and total time T were computed as follows:

$$M = \sum_{i=1}^{n} S_i, \quad T = \sum_{i=1}^{n} t_i, \tag{3}$$

Here, S_i and t_i represent the memory usage (in bytes) and time (in milliseconds) of the i-th operation, respectively. Two experiments were conducted with different input tensor sizes: (216 × 99) notated as "SSW", and (1280 × 99) notated as "original". The percentage reduction in memory usage and computation time was computed as

$$\Delta M\% = \left(1 - \frac{M_{\text{ssw}}}{M_{\text{original}}}\right) \times 100\% = \left(1 - \frac{1796.8 \text{ MB}}{10153.8 \text{ MB}}\right) \times 100\% \approx 82.3\%, \tag{4}$$

$$\Delta T\% = \left(1 - \frac{T_{\text{ssw}}}{T_{\text{original}}}\right) \times 100\% = \left(1 - \frac{239.5 \text{ ms}}{1518.1 \text{ ms}}\right) \times 100\% \approx 84.2\%. \tag{5}$$

These results indicate that reducing the input tensor size led to an approximately 82% decrease in memory usage and an 84% decrease in computation time, while the number of model parameters remained unchanged.

Capturing temporal dynamics is essential for accurate drop width estimation. To track the drop's movement over time, we set the sequence length to 20 frames, meaning each model input consists of 20 consecutive frames with the drop centered within the SSW. Studies show that 20-frame sequences effectively capture key drop dynamics without overloading the model [12]. In general, frames 1 to 9 correspond to the past relative to the target frame (frame 10), whose width we aim to estimate, while frames 11 to 20 represent its future.

However, centering drop images inadvertently removes the drop's relative positional information within the sequence, which carries valuable temporal cues about its motion. To retain motion cues, we tracked the drop's center relative to its start. However, directly including the drop's center position could lead the model to overfit to absolute drop locations. To avoid this, we incorporated the first derivative of the drop's position with respect to time, which corresponds to its velocity. We approximated the velocity using a first-order finite difference. Specifically, we calculated it as $v_t = (x_t - x_{t-1})/\Delta t$, where x_t is the horizontal position of the drop in frame t, and Δt is the time interval between frames. The resulting velocity time series was added as an input to the model. This helped us retain temporal motion cues while removing the risk of overfitting to absolute drop positions. Incorporating the velocity time series serves two key purposes. First, velocity is crucial for understanding drop dynamics, as it reflects frictional forces, surface interactions, and acceleration. Most importantly, with a fixed frame rate, velocity encodes positional changes and establishes a temporal link between frames.

Our approach ensures that the model focuses on the drop's shape and motion rather than its position. Additionally, it extracts only the drop region (216 × 99) from the original frame (1280 × 99), achieving an 84% reduction in computation time. We refer to this approach as position invariant video processing.

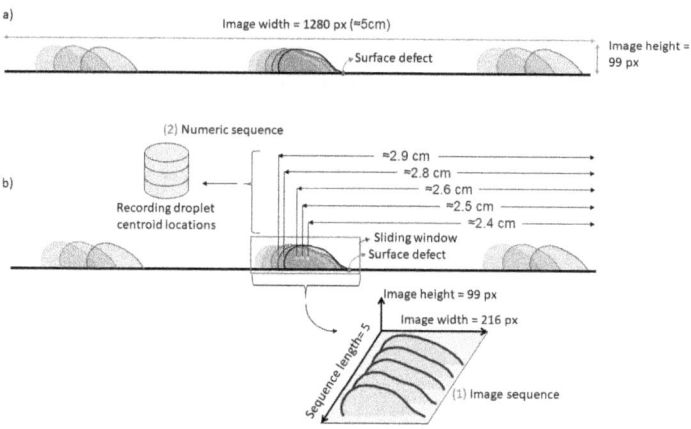

Fig. 2. Data preparation and pipeline for formatting input for the model. a) Initial approach: Cropping the full sliding path (1280×99) results in extensive empty space and positional bias due to the drop's varying location. b) Improved method: Using a SSW of size 216 × 99 pixels, matching the maximum drop dimensions. For demonstration, a 5-frame sequence is shown, while the model utilizes 20 frames for effective drop analysis.

3.4 Spatiotemporal Model Architecture

The model begins with a VGG-style 2D CNN to extract spatial features from consecutive video frames (Fig. 3). The architecture is adapted for smaller datasets and images with lower informational density. It is inspired by VGG8, but replaces standard pooling layers with BlurPooling and employs the Gaussian Error Linear Unit (GELU) as the activation function. BlurPooling improves shift-equivariance, leading to better generalization [36]. It consists of four convolutional blocks with 64, 128, 256, and 512 filters, each featuring a 3×3 convolution (padding $= 1$). We refer to this architecture as BlurVGG8. The extracted spatial features are reshaped to align with the temporal data. Velocity from the 4S-SROF method [19] is processed through a fully connected layer for dimensional consistency before being integrated element-wise with spatial features. The position invariant video processing method stacks consecutive drop images, but to retain relative positional information, it requires integrating the velocity to preserve temporal dynamics.

The velocity encoded data is processed by the ConvTran architecture, starting temporal convolutional layers that refine short-term dependencies, followed by spatial convolutional layer. The embedding size is set to 64, followed by temporal convolutional layers that refine short-term dependencies. Next, position encoding is applied to enhance temporal awareness. We introduce an improved Absolute Position Encoding (APE), called low-dimensional Absolute Position Encodings (ldAPE), to enhance the model's capability. Simultaneously, efficient Relative Position Encoding (eRPE) captures relative frame distances. Since transformers process data in parallel, explicitly encoding temporal order is essential [38]. Next, the transformer encoder was applied with self-attention to capture long-range dependencies, analyzing frame interactions and tracking drop behavior. The number of heads was set to 4, and the feed-forward dimension was adjusted to 128 for our specific task.

We set the learning rate to 0.0001, used the AdamW optimizer with a weight decay of 1×10^{-5}, and selected a batch size of 16. We split the dataset into training, testing, and validation sets with a 60%/20%/20% distribution. The model was trained to minimize the Mean Squared Error (MSE) loss between predicted and actual widths. Performance was evaluated using the Root Mean Squared Error (RMSE) metric on the test set to maintain consistent units. To mitigate overfitting, the maximum training epochs were set to 400, with early stopping triggered by validation loss. All experiments were performed on a high-performance computing system with a single node featuring 36 CPU cores, 250 GB of memory, and an Nvidia A100 GPU.

3.5 Low-Dimensional Absolute Position Encodings

In transformer architectures, the self-attention mechanism alone cannot capture the natural order of sequential data. However, preserving the order of the sequence is crucial for accurate analysis, especially when dealing with time-series data. To overcome this limitation, transformer-based models introduce positional encoding, which injects order-related information into the input representation. The positional encoding ensures that the model can distinguish between different positions in the sequence and maintain the relationships. There are different

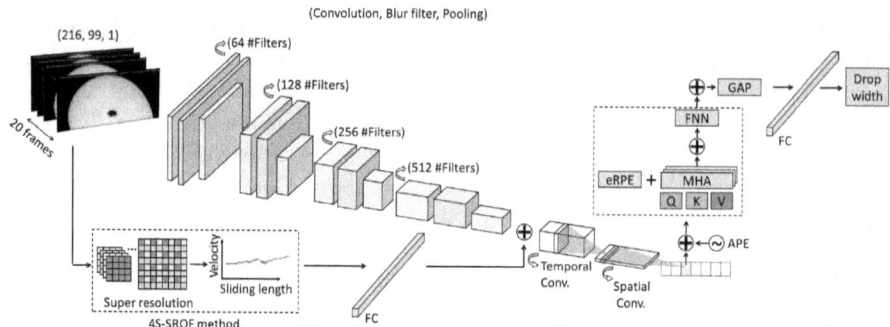

Fig. 3. Architecture of the spatiotemporal model. BlurVGG8 extracts spatial features using four convolutional blocks. Temporal dynamics are preserved by integrating velocity data with spatial features. The ConvTran architecture refines these features with additional convolutions, position encoding (APE and eRPE), and a Transformer encoder to capture long-range dependencies.

types of positional encoding such as absolute positional encoding (APE) and relative positional encoding (RPE) as the most common techniques [39,40].

In the APE method, absolute position information is directly incorporated into the input embedding. This is achieved by adding a position-specific encoding to each input vector, formulated as:

$$x_i = x_i + p_i \qquad (6)$$

Here, $p_i \in R^{d_{\text{model}}}$ represents the positional embedding corresponding to position i, and x_i denotes the input embedding at that position. d_{model} refers to the dimension of the model's hidden representations. The positional embedding is typically defined using sine and cosine functions as follows:

$$p_i(2k) = \sin(i\omega_k), \quad p_i(2k+1) = \cos(i\omega_k) \qquad (7)$$

where

$$\omega_k = 10000^{-2k/d_{\text{model}}} \qquad (8)$$

While i and k are both indices, i corresponds to the feature dimension, and k is the index of the frequency components. This method (called Sin-APE) has been widely used in transformer-based architectures [38]. Sin-APE was originally proposed for language modeling, where high embedding dimensions such as 512 or 1024 are typically used. However, it exhibits limitations when applied to time series data. In low embedding dimensions, the dot product between position encodings does not consistently decrease with increasing positional distance, leading to the loss of the distance awareness property. To address this issue, time Absolute Positional Encoding (tAPE) has been introduced [32]. This method modifies the frequency term to account for both the embedding dimension d_{model} and the sequence length L, ensuring a more balanced frequency distribution:

$$\omega_k^{\text{tAPE}} = \omega_k \cdot \frac{d_{\text{model}}}{L} \qquad (9)$$

Here, L is the total length of the time series.

We modified the absolute positional encoding by adjusting the frequency term to improve accuracy. The new formulation is given by:

$$\omega_k^{\text{ldAPE}} = 35^{-2k/d_{\text{model}}} \cdot \frac{2\sqrt{d_{\text{model}}}}{L} \qquad (10)$$

This adjustment introduces a scaling factor that accounts for both d_{model}, and L. By modifying ω_k, the encoding achieves a more balanced frequency distribution, and enhancing the model's ability to distinguish between positional embeddings. We refer to this method as low-dimensional Absolute Positional Encoding (ldAPE). The dot product between positional embeddings at a fixed reference position reflects their similarity. Compared to other methods, ldAPE produces a broader and more distinct, yet smooth and noise-free, distribution of similarity scores across positions (Fig. 4a), enhancing the model's ability to differentiate between them. Also, in ldAPE, the positional encodings for positions 2 and 20 show minimal overlap, indicating that ldAPE enhances position distinguishability more effectively than other methods (Fig. 4b-d). The ldAPE demonstrates a better dot product than the other mentioned APEs for dimensions below 128, SI Section S.4.

4 Results and Discussion

We tested LSTM models with 64, 128, and 256 units, as well as Bi-LSTM models with the same configurations. The Bi-LSTM models consistently outperformed the LSTM models, prompting us to use Bi-LSTM architectures for further experiments.

Initially, we tested transformer models and the VGG16 architecture, known for their effectiveness in capturing complex patterns and features across various tasks [34,35]. However, due to the limited amount of training data available and low information density image frames, these models did not perform as well as expected (Table 1). The concept of low information density has been used to compare information density in computer vision and Natural Language Processing (NLP), suggesting that pixels in computer vision contain less information than words in NLP [37]. Additionally, different regions of an image contribute unequally to its overall meaning. Based on this, we argue that our images have even lower information density than typical computer vision images, as only the drop contour is relevant while the rest of the image holds minimal significance. To address this, we switched to VGG8, a streamlined version of the VGG architecture with lower complexity. This change achieved an RMSE of 63.54 μm, surpassing earlier studies that used features based on domain knowledge (RMSE of 67.6 μm [12]).

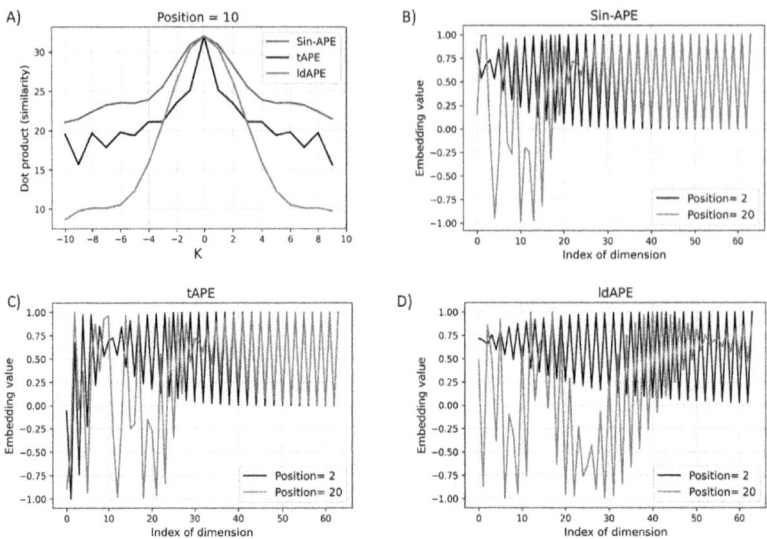

Fig. 4. Comparing different absolute positional embeddings. a) Dot product of absolute positional embeddings, demonstrating the wider similarity axis coverage in ldAPE with reduced fluctuations. K represents the relative distance between two positions b–d) Embedding values for positions 2 and 20 in a sequence of length 20 for Sin-APE, tAPE, and ldAPE, respectively, highlighting the improved position distinguishability in ldAPE.

Performance improved even more after modifying VGG8, replacing standard pooling with BlurPooling, utilizing Gaussian Error Linear Unit (GELU) activation, and adding self-attention after the Bi-LSTM layer, achieving an RMSE of 54.13 μm.

The modified VGG8 (BlurVGG8) was retained because it yielded better results, while ConvTran was used for the temporal component. To conduct an ablation study, three different APE variants were evaluated: Sin-APE, tAPE, and the proposed ldAPE (see Sect. 3.5). The ldAPE achieved the best performance, reaching an RMSE of 48.4μm (Table 2). To further assess the contribution of input velocity and the proposed BlurVGG8 architecture, we removed the velocity input and replaced BlurVGG8 with the original VGG8 in the best-performing configuration, observing the corresponding performance drop in each case.

Surface defects and their larger geometry create more complex time series patterns, increasing the error rate. One defect-free sample (I) and three samples with a block defect (800 μm thick) from the test set are visualized in Fig. 5a: sample II (1000 × 106 μm), sample III (2000 × 74 μm), and sample IV (3000 × 174 μm). In nearly all cases, the error rate decreased compared to the previous study that used predefined features. Specifically, the error changed from 30.8 μm to 33.9 μm for sample I, from 56.2 μm to 21.9 μm for sample II, from 50.4 μm to 49.3 μm for sample III, and from 82.8 μm to 57.1 μm for sample IV [12].

Table 1. Model comparison based on RMSE. Results are repeated over three independent runs for reliability.

Model Configuration	RMSE Avg.	RMSE std.
ViT + transformer encoder	148.2	3.6
VGG16 + BiLSTM	204.1	2.8
Pre-trained VGG16 + BiLSTM	81.9	9.1
VGG8 + BiLSTM	63.5	2.8
Pre-trained VGG8 + BiLSTM	86.1	4.0
BlurVGG8 + BiLSTM + Self attention	54.1	4.0
BlurVGG8 + ConvTran (ours)	**48.4**	2.4

Table 2. Ablation study on the effects of BlurVGG8, velocity input, and different APE variants.

Configuration	RMSE Avg.	RMSE std.
BlurVGG8 + ConvTran (Sin-APE)	53.8	6.1
BlurVGG8 + ConvTran (tAPE)	50.2	4.3
BlurVGG8 + ConvTran (ldAPE)	**48.4**	2.4
BlurVGG8 + ConvTran (ldAPE) without velocity	61.1	4.9
VGG8 + ConvTran (ldAPE)	57.5	4.1

Additionally, to evaluate the generalization capability, we compared their results on a sliding drop example that was not part of the training dataset. This experiment was performed on a hydrophobic surface (PFOTS_Si) with a block defect (800 μm thick, 3000 μm long, 23 μm high). While PFOTS_Si surfaces were in the training videos, this specific defect size was not. During the experiment, the drop stuck to the defect and detached very slowly, which had not occurred in the dataset. The model with predefined features based on domain knowledge produced an RMSE of 112.5 μm [12], while the model utilizing auto-extracted features achieved a significantly lower RMSE of 66.6 μm (Fig. 5b). We hypothesized that deep learning models with automated feature extraction would better capture complexities than those using predefined features. The RMSE improvement confirmed this. We altered the frames by adjusting illumination and introducing blurriness and artifacts, simulating challenging real-world conditions. The results indicated that the model's estimations remained robust under these perturbations, exhibiting minor fluctuations and slight deviations in the drop width measurements (Fig. 5c).

Feature Sensitivity. To evaluate how the model identifies key features for drop width estimation, we applied the Grad-CAM algorithm to visualize the Regions of Interest (ROIs) in the input images (Fig. 6). The figure presents seven middle frames from a sequence of 20, focusing on estimating the width of

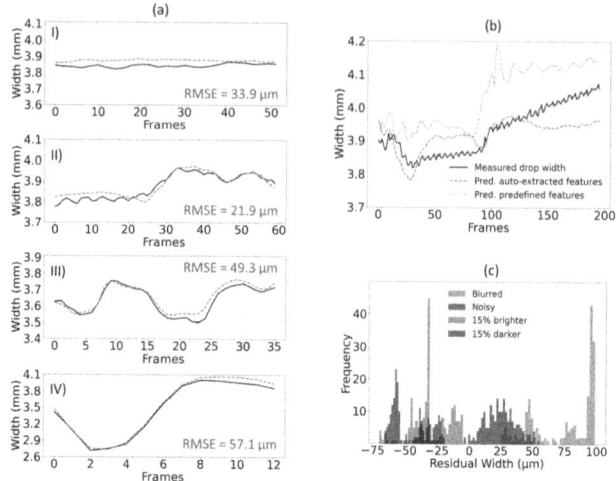

Fig. 5. a) Drop width measurements while sliding over a defect-free surface and three samples with defect, all 800 μm thick: sample II (length 1000 μm, height 106 μm), sample III (2000 × 74 μm), and sample IV (3000 × 174 μm). b) Comparison of the predefined features model and the automated feature extraction model on a sample outside the training dataset, with RMSEs of 112.5 μm and 66.6 μm, respectively. c) Effect of data augmentations (illumination changes, blurriness, and artifacts) on estimation diagrams using the automated feature extraction model. Distribution of residual errors (predicted - measured width) under different data augmentations. Each individual bar corresponds to the frequency of a specific residual value range.

the central frame (frame 10). Each row represents a different time step in the video sequence, illustrating how the model's attention dynamically shifts as the sliding drop interacts with the surface.

The sequence captures the critical moment when the advancing edge of the drop encounters a surface defect (Fig. 6, frame 7) and its subsequent response. The heatmaps in the middle column are spatially normalized between 0 and 1, ensuring that the most significant regions within each frame are distinctly highlighted. These visualizations reveal that the model consistently focuses on the drop's contour. The heatmaps in the left column remain unnormalized, preserving absolute activation values to capture spatiotemporal dependencies across frames. This enables a direct comparison of activation patterns over time. Notably, frames 8 and 9 exhibit the strongest activations, suggesting they provide the most critical information for accurately estimating the width of frame 10. This experiment demonstrates that the model effectively identifies key features aligned with established domain knowledge, such as drop length, height, and receding. Additionally, the Grad-CAM visualizations highlight the model's dynamic attention shifts, particularly at critical interaction points, reinforcing its ability to capture spatiotemporal dependencies. This opens the door for fur-

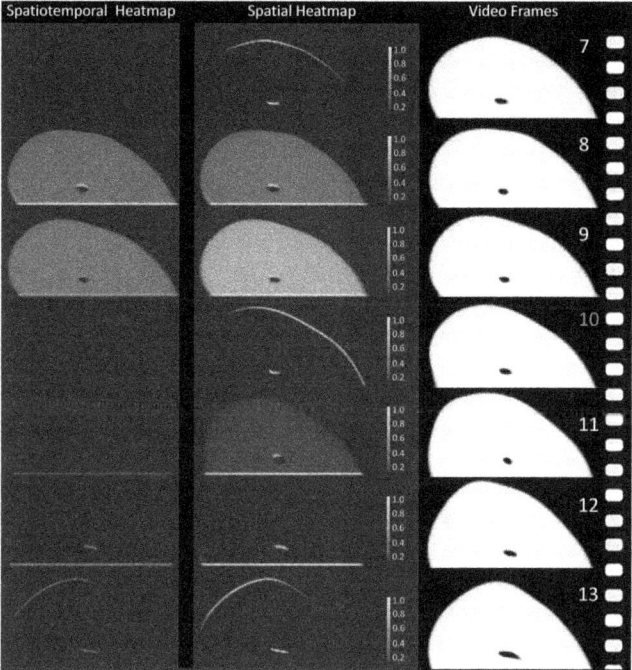

Fig. 6. Grad-CAM visualization of key regions influencing drop width estimation. The normalized heatmaps (middle column) emphasize critical spatial features, primarily the drop's edges, while the unnormalized heatmaps (left column) preserve absolute activation values, capturing spatiotemporal dependencies across frames.

ther studies to explore deeper feature correlations and refine automated methods for analyzing sliding drops.

5 Conclusions

In this study, we introduced a novel position invariant video processing method that effectively prevents overfitting to object location while reducing computation time by 84%. This is achieved by introducing the sliding spatiotemporal window (SSW) concept and incorporating the first derivative of the position of the region of interest into an architecture capable of processing both spatial and temporal data. The approach is scalable and can be extended to higher-dimensional cases, such as 2D object motion. Our approach, which leverages both a specialized VGG8-inspired architecture and the novel ldAPE representation, is well-suited for addressing spatiotemporal challenges with low information density, such as drop motion analysis. This method can effectively address challenges in drop and soft matter research. It is also applicable to scientific domains involving video sequences where the temporal contour evolution of small objects of interest is critical and data availability is limited, such as in biomedical video analysis. Moreover, it integrates with interpretability techniques like Grad-CAM, offering deeper insights into model behavior by highlighting the most influential video features. The interpretability and performance of our method pave the way for uncovering new correlations. For example, we observed that subtle reflections within drops, although seemingly insignificant, may carry meaningful information about drop geometry. Our dataset includes variations in drop viscosity, surface chemistry, wettability, sliding angle, and surface defect geometry, enabling our research to address a broad range of physical conditions and support generalization. However, the current scope does not include phenomena such as slide electrification or extreme wetting regimes (e.g., superhydrophobic or superhydrophilic surfaces), which are left for future investigation. This approach is currently being applied in experimental workflows at the Max Planck Institute for Polymer Research to support automated drop analysis in surface science experiments. To support further research, we have made our code and dataset publicly available.

6 Supplementary Information

Several related works and additional implementation details are discussed in the Supplementary Information document, where the following references are also cited [12,33,44].

Acknowledgments. We thank Geoff Webb for the valuable scientific discussions. We acknowledge financial support from the European Research Council (ERC) under the European Union's Horizon 2020 research and innovation programme (Grant Agreement No. 883631) (S.S., F.D., H.-J.B.). Additional support was provided by the Priority Programme 2171 Dynamic Wetting of Flexible, Adaptive, and Switchable Surfaces (Grant Nos. BU 1556/36 and BE 3286/6-1: H.-J.B., R.B.), and by the German Research Foundation (DFG) through the Collaborative Research Center (CRC) 1194 Interaction between Transport and Wetting Processes (Project-ID 265191195), project C07N and T02 (R.B., H.-J.B.).

Disclosure of Interests. The authors declare no competing interests.

References

1. Sbragaglia, M., et al.: Sliding drops across alternating hydrophobic and hydrophilic stripes. Phys. Rev. E **89**(1), 012406 (2014)
2. Yonemoto, Y., Suzuki, S., Uenomachi, S., Kunugi, T.: Sliding behaviour of water-ethanol mixture droplets on inclined low-surface-energy solid. Int. J. Heat Mass Transf. **1**(120), 1315–24 (2018)
3. Li, X., Bodziony, F., Yin, M., Marschall, H., Berger, R., Butt, H.J.: Kinetic drop friction. Nature Commun. **14**(1), 4571 (2023)
4. Extrand, C.W., Kumagai, Y.: Liquid drops on an inclined plane: the relation between contact angles, drop shape, and retentive force. J. Colloid Interface Sci. **170**(2), 515–21 (1995)

5. Furmidge, C.G.: Studies at phase interfaces. I. The sliding of liquid drops on solid surfaces and a theory for spray retention. J. Colloid Sci. **17**(4), 309–324 (1962)
6. Larkin, B.K.: Numerical solution of the equation of capillarity. J. Colloid Interface Sci. **23**(3), 305–12 (1967)
7. Frenkel, Y.I.: On the behavior of liquid drops on a solid surface. 1. The sliding of drops on an inclined surface. arXiv preprint physics/0503051 (2005)
8. Buzágh, A., Wolfram, E.: Bestimmung der Haftfähigkeit von Flüssigkeiten an festen Körpern mit der Abreißwinkelmethode. II. Kolloid-Zeitschrift. **157**, 50–3 (1958)
9. Extrand, C.W., Gent, A.N.: Retention of liquid drops by solid surfaces. J. Colloid Interface Sci. **138**(2), 431–42 (1990)
10. Gao, N., Geyer, F., Pilat, D.W., Wooh, S., Vollmer, D., Butt, H.J., Berger, R.: How drops start sliding over solid surfaces. Nat. Phys. **14**(2), 191–6 (2018)
11. Li, X., et al.: Spontaneous charging affects the motion of sliding drops. Nat. Phys. **18**(6), 713–9 (2022)
12. Shumaly, S., et al.: Estimating sliding drop width via side-view features using recurrent neural networks. Sci. Rep. **14**(1), 12033 (2024)
13. Yancheshme, A.A., Hassantabar, S., Maghsoudi, K., Keshavarzi, S., Jafari, R., Momen, G.: Integration of experimental analysis and machine learning to predict drop behavior on superhydrophobic surfaces. Chem. Eng. J. **1**(417), 127898 (2021)
14. Zhang, J., Lin, G., Yin, X., Zeng, J., Wen, S., Lan, Y.: Application of artificial neural network (ANN) and response surface methodology (RSM) for modeling and optimization of the contact angle of rice leaf surfaces. Acta Physiol. Plant. **42**, 1–5 (2020)
15. Kokalis, C.C., Tasakos, T., Kontargyri, V.T., Siolas, G., Gonos, I.F.: Hydrophobicity classification of composite insulators based on convolutional neural networks. Eng. Appl. Artif. Intell. **1**(91), 103613 (2020)
16. Roy, S.S., Paramane, A., Singh, J., Chatterjee, S.: Accurate hydrophobicity grade detection of polymeric insulators in extremely wetted and humid environments using Bi-LSTM neural network classifier. In: 2022 IEEE Power & Energy Society General Meeting (PESGM), pp. 1–5. IEEE (2022)
17. Rabbani, A., Sun, C., Babaei, M., Niasar, V.J., Armstrong, R.T., Mostaghimi, P.: DeepAngle: fast calculation of contact angles in tomography images using deep learning. Geoenergy Sci. Eng. **1**(227), 211807 (2023)
18. Kabir, H., Garg, N.: Machine learning enabled orthogonal camera goniometry for accurate and robust contact angle measurements. Sci. Rep. **13**(1), 1497 (2023)
19. Shumaly, S., et al.: Deep learning to analyze sliding drops. Langmuir **39**(3), 1111–22 (2023)
20. Ismail Fawaz, H., Forestier, G., Weber, J., Idoumghar, L., Muller, P.A.: Deep learning for time series classification: a review. Data Min. Knowl. Disc. **33**(4), 917–63 (2019)
21. Faouzi, J.: Time series classification: a review of algorithms and implementations. In: Machine Learning (Emerging Trends and Applications) (2022)
22. Lim, B., Zohren, S.: Time-series forecasting with deep learning: a survey. Phil. Trans. R. Soc. A **379**(2194), 20200209 (2021)
23. Torres, J.F., Hadjout, D., Sebaa, A., Martínez-Álvarez, F., Troncoso, A.: Deep learning for time series forecasting: a survey. Big data. **9**(1), 3–21 (2021)
24. Benidis, K., et al.: Deep learning for time series forecasting: tutorial and literature survey. ACM Comput. Surv. **55**(6), 1–36 (2022)
25. Tan, C.W., Bergmeir, C., Petitjean, F., Webb, G.I.: Time series extrinsic regression: predicting numeric values from time series data. Data Min. Knowl. Disc. **35**(3), 1032–60 (2021)

26. Sammut, C., Webb, G.I., (eds.) Encyclopedia of Machine Learning. Springer (2011)
27. Reiss, A., Indlekofer, I., Schmidt, P., Laerhoven, K.: Deep PPG: large-scale heart rate estimation with convolutional neural networks. Sensors **19**(14), 3079 (2019)
28. Zhang, Z., Pi, Z., Liu, B.: TROIKA: a general framework for heart rate monitoring using wrist-type photoplethysmographic signals during intensive physical exercise. IEEE Trans. Biomed. Eng. **62**(2), 522–31 (2014)
29. Dempster, A., Petitjean, F., Webb, G.I.: ROCKET: exceptionally fast and accurate time series classification using random convolutional kernels. Data Min. Knowl. Disc. **34**(5), 1454–95 (2020)
30. Ismail Fawaz, H., et al.: InceptionTime: finding alexnet for time series classification. Data Min. Knowl. Disc. **34**(6), 1936–62 (2020)
31. Mohammadi Farsani, R., Pazouki, E.: A transformer self-attention model for time series forecasting. J. Electr. Comput. Eng. Innovations (JECEI) **9**(1), 1 (2020)
32. Foumani, N.M., Tan, C.W., Webb, G.I., Salehi, M.: Improving position encoding of transformers for multivariate time series classification. Data Min. Knowl. Disc. **38**(1), 22–48 (2024)
33. Canny, J.: A computational approach to edge detection. IEEE Trans. Pattern Anal. Mach. Intell. **6**, 679–98 (1986)
34. Wen, Q., et al.: Transformers in time series: a survey. arXiv preprint arXiv:2202.07125 (2022)
35. Jiang, Z.P., Liu, Y.Y., Shao, Z.E., Huang, K.W.: An improved VGG16 model for pneumonia image classification. Appl. Sci. **11**(23), 11185 (2021)
36. Zhang, R.: Making convolutional networks shift-invariant again. In: International Conference on Machine Learning, pp. 7324–7334 (2019)
37. He, K., Chen, X., Xie, S., Li, Y., Dollár, P., Girshick, R.: Masked autoencoders are scalable vision learners. In: Proceedings of the IEEE/CVF Conference on Computer Vision and Pattern Recognition, pp. 16000–16009 (2022)
38. Vaswani, A., et al.: Attention is all you need. In: Advances in Neural Information Processing Systems, p. 30 (2017)
39. Wu, K., Peng, H., Chen, M., Fu, J., Chao, H.: Rethinking and improving relative position encoding for vision transformer. In: Proceedings of the IEEE/CVF International Conference on Computer Vision, pp. 10033–10041 (2021)
40. Dufter, P., Schmitt, M., Schütze, H.: Position information in transformers: an overview. Comput. Linguist. **48**(3), 733–63 (2022)
41. Boinovich, L.B., Emelyanenko, A.M.: Recent progress in understanding the anti-icing behavior of materials. Adv. Coll. Interface. Sci. **1**(323), 103057 (2024)
42. Ghasemlou, M., et al.: Self-lubricated, liquid-like omniphobic polymer brushes: advances and strategies for enhanced fluid and solid control. Prog. Polym. Sci. **19**, 101933 (2025)
43. Zhou, X., et al.: Thickness of nanoscale poly (Dimethylsiloxane) layers determines the motion of sliding water drops. Adv. Mater. **36**(29), 2311470 (2024)
44. Darvish, F., et al.: Control of spontaneous charging of sliding water drops by plasma-surface treatment. Sci. Rep. **14**(1), 10640 (2024)

Open Access This chapter is licensed under the terms of the Creative Commons Attribution 4.0 International License (http://creativecommons.org/licenses/by/4.0/), which permits use, sharing, adaptation, distribution and reproduction in any medium or format, as long as you give appropriate credit to the original author(s) and the source, provide a link to the Creative Commons license and indicate if changes were made.

The images or other third party material in this chapter are included in the chapter's Creative Commons license, unless indicated otherwise in a credit line to the material. If material is not included in the chapter's Creative Commons license and your intended use is not permitted by statutory regulation or exceeds the permitted use, you will need to obtain permission directly from the copyright holder.

Personalized Contest Recommendation in Fantasy Sports

Madiraju Srilakshmi[(✉)], Kartavya Kothari, and Kamlesh Marathe

Dream11, Mumbai, India
{madiraju.srilakshmi,kartavya.kothari}@dream11.com

Abstract. In daily fantasy sports, players enter into "contests" where they compete against each other by building teams of athletes that score fantasy points based on what actually occurs in a real-life sports match. For any given sports match, there are a multitude of contests available to players, with substantial variation across 3 main dimensions: entry fee, number of spots, and the prize pool distribution. As player preferences are also quite heterogeneous, contest personalization is an important tool to match players with contests. This paper presents a scalable contest recommendation system, powered by a Wide and Deep Interaction Ranker (WiDIR) at its core. We productionized this system at our company, one of the large fantasy sports platforms with millions of daily contests and millions of players, where online experiments show a marked improvement over other candidate models in terms of recall and other critical business metrics.

Keywords: recommender systems · deep learning · fantasy sports

1 Introduction

Over the past decade, fantasy sports have grown remarkably. The global market is estimated to exceed \$37 billion in 2025 and is projected to continue to grow by 14% annually through 2030 [4]. The majority of this growth is driven by daily fantasy sports (DFS), where players create teams of athletes and compete against each other on a match-by-match basis. To enter into these competitions–typically referred to as "contests"–players pay an entry fee which contributes to a shared prize pool. Once a contest concludes, this prize pool is then divided across the top-performing entries according to a predetermined prize distribution.

In this paper, we focus on the contest recommendation problem at our company, one of the large fantasy sports platforms globally with millions of players. For a real-life sports match, our platform hosts a wide variety of different contests for players to join, ranging from small head-to-head clashes to extremely vast competitions that involve millions of teams. Beyond just size (number of spots), contests also principally differ across two other key dimensions: entry

---

K. Marathe—Work done while at Dream11.

fees and prize distributions. Player preferences are also quite diverse, meaning that personalized recommendations can be critical in directing players to contests that best align with their tastes, and can generate substantial lifts in player conversions and entry amounts for the platform [3].

To solve this problem, we built what we call a Wide and Deep Interaction Ranker (WiDIR), which builds upon the architecture developed to rank apps on the Google Play store [2]. WiDIR similarly integrates a wide linear branch, which excels at "generalization", and a deep neural network branch, which specializes in "memorization".

In the context of fantasy sports, generalization in contest recommendation refers to the ability to recommend relevant contests to new players or recommend newer or less popular contests that may still be a good fit to the existing players. Memorization, however, focuses on recommending popular contests to players who have previously shown a preference for them. Our recommendation model is designed to achieve both of these capabilities.

We further enhance the deep network by explicitly modelling contest-player interactions and by dividing it into three specialized sub-branches: one dedicated to player features, another to contest features, and a third focused specifically on interaction features. Our offline experiments show that WiDIR achieves better precision and recall compared to other candidate models on out of sample test data. Moreover, online experiments showed that significantly more lift on player engagement and other key business metrics against other candidates.

The primary contributions of our paper are listed below;

- We introduce WiDIR (Wide and Deep Interaction Ranker), a personalized recommendation system specifically tailored for daily fantasy sports (DFS) contests.
- Through extensive experimentation on a large-scale DFS platform involving millions of players, WiDIR achieves a significant uplift in key player engagement and business metrics such as contest joins and gross gaming revenue (GGR).
- We present a fully operational and scalable inferencing pipeline designed to deliver personalized contest recommendations within milliseconds, effectively handling millions of players and contests daily.

The rest of the paper is organized as follows; Sect. 2 provides additional context on fantasy sports as well as a brief overview of our platform. Section 3 presents our data and methodology. Section 4 describes our overall system. Section 5 discusses the experimental results and analysis. Finally, Sect. 6 concludes the paper.

2 Context

Fantasy sports involve creating virtual teams composed of real-life athletes, where the performance of these athletes in actual sporting events determines the success of the fantasy team. Players draft athletes, manage rosters, and

(a) Contest categories listed   (b) *Specially For You* Section

Fig. 1. Some of the contests on our platform for Delhi (DEL-W) vs Mumbai (MUM-W) TATA WPL match

compete based on the accumulated statistical metrics of their athletes, such as runs scored in cricket, touchdowns in football, or goals in soccer. These metrics have an equivalent "fantasy score", for example in cricket:

- Run Scored: 1 point per run
- Wicket Taken: 25 points per wicket
- Catch: 8 points per catch
- Stumping/Run-out: 12 points per dismissal
- Boundary Bonus: 1 point for each boundary (4 runs), 2 points for each six (6 runs)

Traditional fantasy sports competitions last an entire season, requiring long-term strategic planning, regular engagement, and active management of team rosters. However, in recent years, daily fantasy sports have become increasingly popular due to their shorter contest durations, typically spanning a single day. Unlike traditional fantasy sports, where teams remain relatively stable throughout a season, DFS participants create new teams for each contest. DFS's appeal lies primarily in its immediate outcomes and reduced time commitment, attracting a broader range of participants. On our platform, after entering into a contest, players will construct a team from the athletes who are competing in the corresponding real-life sports match.

We host three types of contests: Public, Special, and Mega (or Grand). "Public contests" are non-guaranteed, with spots ranging from 2 to over 1,500. These contests are regenerated each time an instance fills up. "Special contests" offer guaranteed prize pools, often featuring highly attractive top-prize templates.

These contests provide significant business benefits and are among the most appealing on the platform. "The Mega (or Grand) contest" is a special contest with the largest prize pool, standing out as the most prestigious and high-value contest available.

Our proposed WiDIR excels in Daily Fantasy Sports (DFS) by effectively leveraging dynamic player-contest interactions and rapidly adapting to evolving player preferences. Unlike traditional season-long fantasy sports, DFS's highly dynamic contest environment and immediate feedback loop allow WiDIR to continuously adapt recommendations, utilising interaction features to enhance player engagement and business metrics.

Figure 1a depicts the player interface after selecting a specific cricket match (Delhi (DEL-W) vs Mumbai (MUM-W) TATA WPL match) on our mobile app. At the top is the "Mega Contest", the largest and most lucrative contest, offering significant prize pools that attract up to millions of players. Directly below are contest bundles, known as "Combo Contests". Allowing players to conveniently join multiple contests simultaneously at discounted entry fees, enhancing the overall playing experience and value proposition.

Further down, players encounter the "Specially For You" section, illustrated in greater detail in Fig. 1b. This section leverages advanced personalization algorithms, recommending contests tailored to individual player preferences and historical playing behaviour, thereby increasing engagement and player satisfaction. As much of the rest of the first page is more business-optimized, this section is explicitly optimizing for player engagement, ensuring a more balanced experience. Players benefit from organic engagement driven by personal preferences while maintaining visibility for key business offerings.

2.1 Problem Definition

Our contest recommendation model aims to predict which contests a user is most likely to join in future rounds, leveraging their historical join behavior and the features of available contests.

Our primary objective is to generate personalized contest recommendations that align closely with individual player preferences. By improving the relevance of contest recommendations, we aim to enhance user engagement, increase contest participation, and ultimately support long-term player retention and platform revenue growth.

3 Data and Methodology

3.1 Primary Data and Feature Engineering

Our primary data comprises two main components: the player contest join history and contest characteristics. The join history records contain `player_id`, `contest_id`, `match_id`, and `joining_time`, while the contest characteristics include `entry_fee`, `prize_money`, `contest_size`, `prize_distribution`, `guaranteed`, `contest_type`, and `multi_entry`.

Among these, `contest_size`, `contest_type`, `prize_distribution`, `guaranteed`, and `multi_entry` are categorical variables, whereas `entry_fee` and `prize_money` are numerical. Below is a brief description of each feature:

- `player_id`: Unique identifier for each player.
- `contest_id`: Unique identifier for each contest. Multiple instances of the same contest can exist; once one contest is filled, a new contest with identical features is dynamically created and assigned a different `contest_id`.
- `match_id`: Unique identifier for the sports event associated with the contest.
- `joining_time`: Timestamp indicating when a player joined a contest.
- `entry_fee`: Amount required to participate in a contest.
- `prize_money`: Total prize pool for a contest.
- `contest_size`: Maximum number of participants allowed in a contest.
- `contest_type`: Type of contest (e.g., public, special, mega).
- `prize_distribution`: Template identifier representing the prize distribution among winners.
- `guaranteed`: Indicates whether the contest is guaranteed (i.e., the prize money remains fixed even if the contest is not fully filled).
- `multi_entry`: Indicates whether a contest allows multiple team entries from the same player.

From our primary data, we engineered three distinct sets of features: player features, contest features, and interaction features.

- **Player Features**: These features characterize a player's behaviour based on their historical contest participation. For each player, we compute statistics over the contests joined in the last k days. The goal is to capture current player behavior ($k = 3$) alongside historical preferences ($k \in (7, 30)$).
  The features include:
    - *Contest Join Behavior*: Counts of distinct contest types, contest sizes, and entry fees encountered.
    - *Spending Patterns*: Average and maximum entry fees paid.
    - *Winning Proportion*: Average and maximum prize money won.
    - *Diversity Level*: Count of distinct types of contests played.
- **Contest Features**: These features describe the intrinsic attributes of a contest, as outlined above.
- **Interaction Features**: These capture the current affinity between a player and a contest by aggregating player behavior over recent time windows. Specifically, we compute features over the contests the player participated in over the previous day and the last k days (with $k = 5$).
  Examples include the count of contests with the same type as the target contest, count of contests with the same entry fee as the target contest, and number of contests with the same prize pool as the target contest.

This final dataset is then split into training ($\sim$ 12 months), validation ($\sim$ 2 months) and test sets ($\sim$ 6 months). Table 1 summarizes key data statistics, including the duration of the training and test periods, contest join counts, and the number of unique players and contests.

Table 1. Train and Test Data Statistics

Property	Train	Test
Contest joins	~ 1 Billion	~ 0.5 Billion
Total players	~ 100 thousand	~ 100 thousand
Unique contests	~ 1.5 thousand	~ 1.1 thousand
Total contests	~ 1.5 Million	~ 0.9 Million

3.2 Methodology

Our contest recommendation system aims to predict the ranking of contests that a player is most likely to join in future matches, given their contest transaction history. Let i index the set of players $\mathcal{P}$, t index the set of matches $\mathcal{M}$, and c index the set of contests $\mathcal{C}$. We construct training samples at the player-match level as the active set of contests varies from match to match: for each player $i \in \mathcal{P}$ and match $t \in \mathcal{M}$, we construct an ordered list of contests:

$$\mathcal{O}_{it} = \left(c_{it}^{(1)}, c_{it}^{(2)}, \ldots, c_{it}^{(L_{it})} \right)$$

where $c_{it}^{(1)}$ denotes the most frequently joined contest by player i in match t to $c_{it}^{(L_{it})}$ which denotes the least. This list is then fixed to 100 entries, either trimmed down or padded by randomly appending contests that weren't joined to the end of $\mathcal{O}_{it}$. We set this value based on our experiments with $(50, 100, 200)$. From $\mathcal{O}_{it}$, we can form the set of contest pairs:

$$\Theta_{it} = \left\{ (c, c') \in \mathcal{O}_{it} \times \mathcal{O}_{it} \mid c \succ c' \right\},$$

where $c \succ c'$ indicates that contest c was joined more frequently than contest c' by u_i. These pairs are constructed to train our ranking model, WiDIR using a pairwise hinge loss [5]. A ranking loss was chosen since we aim to rank the contests based on their relative relevance rather than accurately predicting the affinity score of each contest.

WiDIR produces an affinity score $\hat{s}_{ic}$ for each player i, each match t, and each contest c. This model is then trained using pairwise hinge loss as mentioned above.

$$\mathcal{l}_{it}(c, c') = \max\{0, \ 1 - \hat{s}_i(c) + \hat{s}_i(c')\}. \tag{1}$$

which penalizes situations where a less preferred contest c' is scored higher than a more preferred contest c. The overall loss is given by

$$\mathcal{L} = \sum_{i \in \mathcal{P}} \sum_{t \in \mathcal{M}} \sum_{(c,c') \in \mathcal{O}_{it}} \mathcal{l}_{it}(c, c'). \tag{2}$$

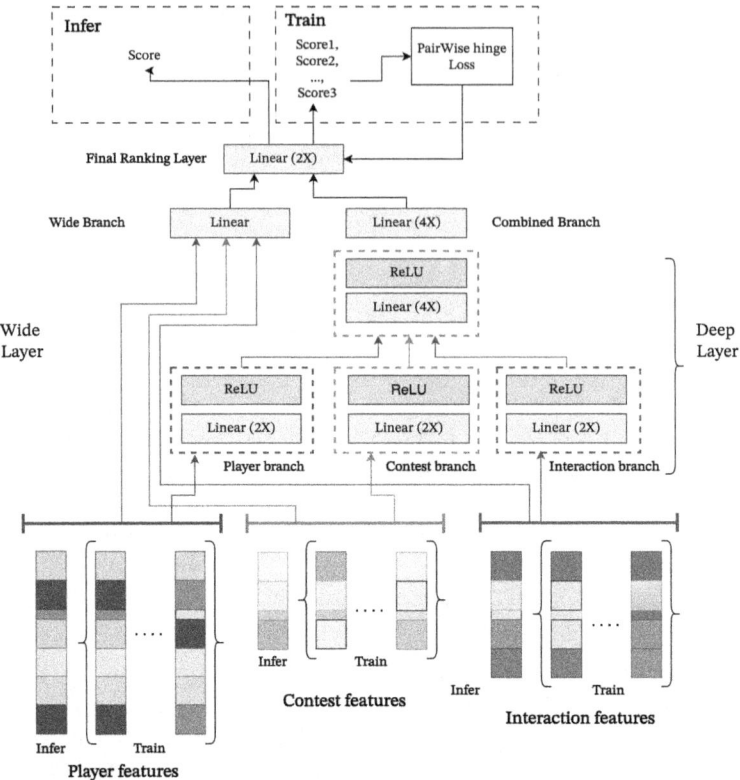

Fig. 2. WiDIR architecture showing both training and inference flow

WiDIR is built on a wide and deep neural architecture to leverage both memorization and generalization capabilities (see Fig. 2). Unlike [2], our model employs three separate deep branches to model the embeddings for players, contests, and their interactions. This approach allows each component to be represented more effectively. The embeddings are then combined in a final branch to model the correlations between them. The training process is described below:

- Embed the player, contest, and interaction features into dense representations.
- Concatenate these embeddings and pass them through multiple fully connected layers (the deep component).
- In parallel, combine the raw features into a wide layer.
- Merge the wide and deep components, then feed the result into a final linear layer to predict contest scores.
- Compute the pairwise hinge loss from Eq. (1) over all contest pairs and backpropagate the error.

Table 2 summarizes the layer flow and parameter counts in each branch. Here, d_p, d_c, and d_i denote the dimensionalities of the player, contest, and interaction

Table 2. Model Architecture and Parameter Counts (Symbolic)

Component	Layer Flow	Parameter Count
Player Branch (PB)	$P \to 64 \to 64$	$64 * d_p + 4224$
Contest Branch (CB)	$C \to 64 \to 64$	$64 * d_c + 4224$
Interaction Branch (IB)	$I \to 16 \to 16$	$16 * d_i + 560$
Wide Branch (WB)	$P + C + I \to 1$	$d_p + d_c + d_i + 1$
Deep Branch (DB)	$(64 + 64 + 16) \to 128$ (4X)	68096
Combined Layer	$128 \to 64 \to 64 \to 32 \to 8 \to 4$	14796
Final Ranking	$(4 + 1) \to 4 \to 1$	29
Total		$\mathbf{65 * d_p + 65 * d_c + 17 * d_i + 91930}$

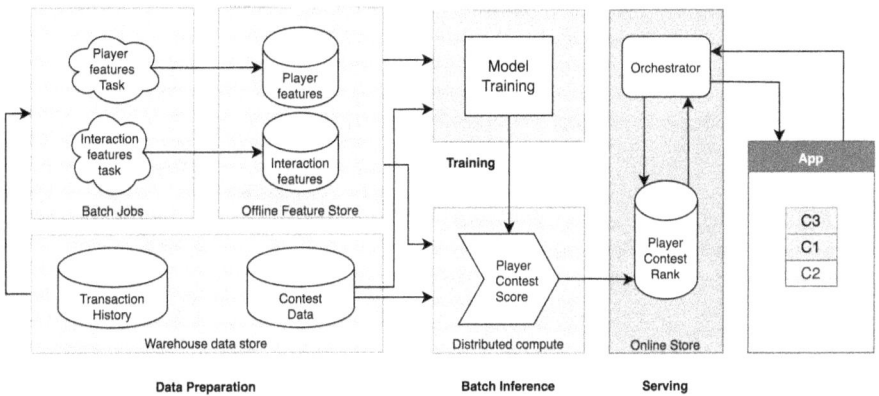

Fig. 3. Data flow and Inference architecture

features, respectively (our raw feature set dimensions were 107, 11, and 9 in our experiments).

During inference, the model scores all contests available in a match based on their features. The top-h contests, as determined by their predicted scores, are then recommended to the player. Since the model relies on high-level contest features (e.g., `contest_type`, `entry_fee`) rather than contest-specific identifiers, it can generalize effectively to new contests.

4 System Architecture and Data Flow

This section describes the architecture of the personalized contest recommendation system implemented in our fantasy gaming platform. The system integrates the following key phases as shown in Fig. 3. The following sections provide details on each phase.

1. Data Preparation
2. Training
3. Inference
4. Serving

4.1 Data Preparation

We use player transaction history and contest features to generate our recommendations. This data is stored in a data warehouse which is maintained and gets updated with any real-time changes via data engineering stream/ETL pipelines.

We fetch the data from the warehouse and compute player features, and interaction features using distributed pyspark jobs viz. *Player features task* and *Interaction features task*. Section 3.1 describes our feature engineering.

This data is then processed into model-expected formats and stored in the *Offline Feature Store*, serving as a repository for the processed feature data. Features are created and updated once a day since our feature aggregation granularity is day-level.

4.2 Training

For model training, *player features* and *interaction features* are fetched from the offline feature store, and *contest features* are fetched from the data warehouse. Our baseline system, Light GBM ranker, is trained using synapseML[1] to efficiently process large datasets stored in PySpark dataframes. For WiDIR, we use tensorflow [1] with petastorm data loaders[2]. The pair wise loss implementation is sourced from tensorflow-ranking.

The entire training process is managed through run identifiers enabling us to reproduce any component specific to a given run. We track those run-ids, model artefacts, hyperparameters, data statistics and evaluation metrics using MLflow [7][3].

4.3 Batch Inference

During inference also, we fetch *player features* and *interaction features* from the offline feature store, and *contest features* from the data warehouse and input them to our *trained ranking model*. The model outputs a player-contest affinity score for all available contests and we rank them in decreasing order of their scores.

To optimize the balance between providing recommendations and minimizing the cost of running inference on players who may not engage with the app, inference is performed only for players who have been active in the past month.

4.4 Serving

To ensure that player rankings remain dynamic with contests currently live, we maintain a relative ranking of all available contests in our Sylla DB-based Online Feature Store. The orchestration layer performs the following operations:

---

[1] https://microsoft.github.io/SynapseML/.
[2] https://github.com/uber/petastorm.
[3] https://mlflow.org/docs/latest/.

- Whenever a player is active on the app and selects a gaming match, it gathers all live contests and requests the online feature store for the relative ranking of these contests.
- The ranking is then served back to the app, all within 10 milliseconds. Each subsequent refresh or update, including specific triggers such as a contest being filled and needing replacement, involves a fresh call from the orchestrator.

5 Experiments

To select the optimal modelling strategy, we employ a two-stage experimentation process that includes both offline and online A/B testing. This approach ensures thorough testing before production deployment. In this section, we outline our evaluation metrics, the baselines used for comparison, the experimental setup, and the results from both online and offline settings.

5.1 Baseline Systems

We compare WiDIR with the following baseline systems.

- ML-based model: tree-based Light GBM ranker (LGB) [6] with same input features as WiDIR.
- Popularity-based ranker: This approach ranks contests by the prize amount.

5.2 Evaluation Metrics

Our offline experiments are evaluated using precision@h and recall@h, where $h \in (1, 3, 5, 10)$.

$$\text{Precision@h} = \frac{|\text{recommended contests@h} \cap \text{actual contests joined}|}{h}$$

$$\text{Recall@h} = \frac{|\text{recommended contests@h} \cap \text{actual contests joined}|}{|\text{actual contests joined}|}$$

We evaluate online simulations / AB tests using the following gameplay business metrics. Each metric is aggregated and then we compute the delta between the control group CG and each target group TG_i for the entire test period.

$$\Delta = \frac{M_{TG_{post}} - M_{CG_{post}}}{M_{CG_{post}}} - \frac{M_{TG_{pre}} - M_{CG_{pre}}}{M_{CG_{pre}}}$$

where Δ is delta and M is the aggregated metric, one of the below. CG_{pre} and TG_{pre} are the pre-treatment start aggregates, and CG_{post} and TG_{post} are the post-treatment start aggregates.

- CJ - denotes the total *contest joins*.
- CEA - denotes the cumulative *entry amounts*.
- GGR - denotes the *gross gaming revenue*.

Table 3. Hyperparameter Configurations for WiDIR and LGB Models

Hyperparameter	WiDIR	LGB ranker
Embedding Dimensions	64	–
Epochs	100	30
Learning Rate (LR)	0.001	0.1
Batch Size	2^{12} (4096)	64
Validation Batch Size	2^{14} (16384)	–
Loss Function	pw_hinge	lambdarank (application)
Ranking Sort Order	–	player_id, match_id, join_count
Boosting	–	dart
Num Leaves	–	64
Early Stopping rounds	15	10
Eval at	–	1, 3, 5, 10

Table 4. Experiment Details: Here TG_i refers to the different cohorts on which we exposed the mentioned treatment. The cohorts were sampled from monthly active players, stratified randomly

Group	Treatment	player Count	Duration
CG	None	1M	6 Weeks
TG_1	Popular	1M	6 Weeks
TG_2	LGB	1M	6 Weeks
TG_3	WiDIR	1M	6 Weeks

5.3 Experimental Setup

The process starts with trained models viz. tree-based light gbm, WiDIR. Table 3 reports the details of hyperparameters for both systems. The parameter tuning was conducted using a hold-out validation set.

Stage 1: Offline Experiments. We evaluated modelling strategies through offline experiments on a year's worth of player transactional data. The recommendation models were evaluated using precision and recall.

Stage 2: Online A/B Testing. Promising models based on offline results undergo A/B testing and deployed to a subset of players while a control group gets no treatment. We record player interactions and business impact before full deployment and record the business metrics after the experiment. Refer to Table 4 for details.

5.4 Results and Analysis

The online and offline results of our wide and deep recommendation model and the baselines are shown in Fig. 4 and Fig. 5. From the results, it is evident that

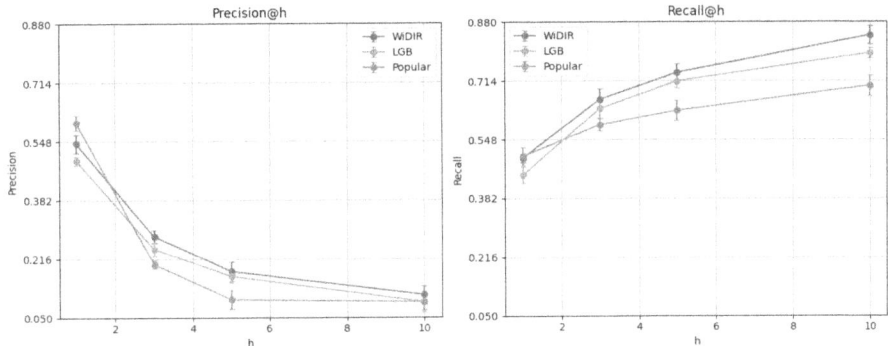

Fig. 4. Comparing Precision@h and Recall@h of WiDIR against popular and LGB ranker

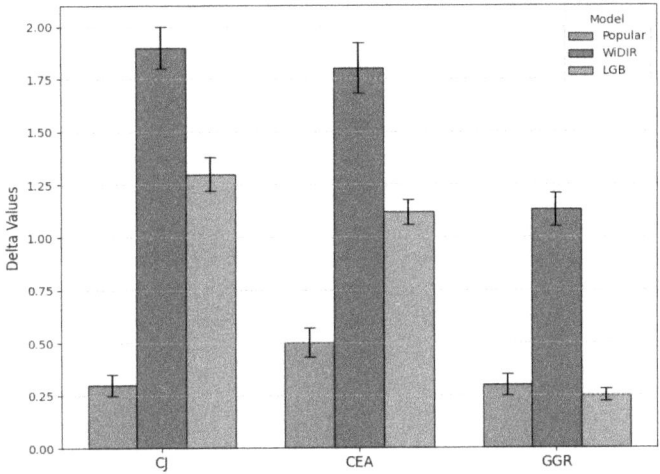

Fig. 5. Comparing our online metrics (CJ delta, CEA delta and GGR delta)

WiDIR performs better than popular and LGB ranker in all but one case. The popular performs better at position 1 as the most popular contest is one that most players join anyway as it is attractive and strategically priced.

Offline experiments indicate that, as number of recommended contests (h) increases, precision decreases while recall increases for all models. This is because most players join only one or two contests in a given match, fewer than h. This doesn't negatively impact recall, as recall is measured by the percentage of actual contest joins that the model successfully recommends.

The online results show that WiDIR significantly outperforms other systems in terms of business metrics. By effectively learning player preferences, it drives an increase in contest joins, which subsequently improves CEA and GGR. While the LGB ranker also performs better than Popular in the CJ and CEA metrics, it performs poorly in GGR.

6 Conclusion and Future Scope

We presented our model-wide and deep interaction ranker for recommending personalized contests at scale. Our online and offline experiments demonstrate that the model significantly improves key player relevance metrics, such as precision and recall, alongside critical business metrics like CJ, CEA, and GGR.

The proposed WiDIR (Wide and Deep Interaction Ranker) has demonstrated strong performance in personalized contest recommendations; however, several avenues remain for further enhancement. Future work will integrate edge models to optimize last-mile inference and incorporate session-based features, enabling real-time personalization closer to the player. The model's interaction features provide inherent flexibility to adapt to evolving playing patterns. Additionally, we aim to explore multi-armed bandits to facilitate richer dynamic exploration-exploitation strategies, ensuring contest recommendations continuously evolve in response to changing player behaviour.

Beyond ranking optimization, multi-task learning presents an opportunity to extend WiDIR beyond a single-task ranker, making it adaptable to multiple personalization objectives. To further enhance representation learning, we plan to capture higher-order relationships in player-contest interactions by investigating graph modelling approaches, which could uncover deeper structural dependencies and improve recommendation diversity. Additionally, scalable online learning techniques will be explored to maintain efficiency while dynamically adjusting to the ever-changing contest landscape.

Acknowledgments. We would like to express our sincere gratitude to Nilesh Patil, Hitesh Kapoor, Michael Zhao, and Vedavyas Chigurupati for their insightful feedback and guidance throughout this work. We also acknowledge the foundational contributions of Aditya Narisetty, Sriram Mudunuri, and others who laid the groundwork for this project. Special thanks to the Dream11 engineering teams for their assistance in setting up the inference layer, online feature store, and frontend integration, which were critical to the deployment and evaluation of our system.

References

1. Abadi, M., et al.: TensorFlow: large-scale machine learning on heterogeneous systems (2015). https://www.tensorflow.org/, software available from tensorflow.org
2. Cheng, H.T., et al.: Wide & deep learning for recommender systems. In: Proceedings of the 1st Workshop on Deep Learning for Recommender Systems, pp. 7–10 (2016)
3. Chugh, V., Kretz, W., Rosa, S., Beckelman, B., Tong, H., Mitkovski, D.: Ready for the big game: how fanduel boosts conversions and revenue at scale with a real-time recommender system for daily fantasy sports. In: 2023 IEEE International Conference on Big Data (BigData), pp. 1677–1686. IEEE (2023)

4. Intelligence, M.: Fantasy sports market: growth, trends, covid-19 impact, and forecasts (2023–2028). Online (2023). https://www.mordorintelligence.com/industry-reports/fantasy-sports-market. Accessed 13 Mar 2025
5. Joachims, T.: Optimizing search engines using clickthrough data. In: Proceedings of the Eighth ACM SIGKDD International Conference on Knowledge Discovery and Data Mining (KDD), pp. 133–142 (2002)
6. Ke, G., et al.: Lightgbm: a highly efficient gradient boosting decision tree. Adv. Neural Inf. Process. Syst. **30** (2017)
7. Zaharia, M., et al.: Accelerating the machine learning lifecycle with mlflow. IEEE Data Eng. Bull. **41**(4), 39–45 (2018)

Talk is Cheap, Energy is Not: Towards a Green, Context-Aware Metrics Framework for Automatic Speech Recognition

Maria Ulan[1(✉)], Erik Johannes Husom[2], and Jeriek Van den Abeele[3]

[1] RISE Research Institutes of Sweden, Gothenburg, Sweden
maria.ulan@ri.se
[2] SINTEF Digital, Oslo, Norway
erik.johannes.husom@sintef.no
[3] Telenor Research and Innovation, Fornebu, Norway
jeriek-van-den.abeele@telenor.com

Abstract. Automatic Speech Recognition (ASR) systems are increasingly deployed across diverse computing environments, from cloud servers to edge devices. While accuracy has traditionally been the primary evaluation metric, the inference efficiency of these systems, including energy consumption, memory usage, and hardware utilisation, significantly impacts their practical usability. This paper introduces a novel benchmarking framework that assesses ASR models during inference from both performance and sustainability perspectives. We introduce a multi-metric evaluation approach quantifying Word Error Rate (WER), Real-Time Factor (RTF), Energy Per Audio Second (EPAS), inference latency, GPU Memory Efficiency (GME), and Hardware Utilisation Rate (HUR). Our framework includes configurable weighting schemes tailored for various deployment scenarios: balanced general-purpose evaluation, resource-constrained environments, high-throughput batch inference, and real-time processing. To demonstrate the utility of the framework, we benchmark several state-of-the-art ASR architectures (Whisper, Wav2Vec2, HuBERT, WavLM, UniSpeech, and SpeechT5) in both FP16 and FP32 precision on NVIDIA Jetson AGX Orin hardware. The proposed methodology supports researchers and practitioners in making informed model selection decisions based on context-specific inference requirements. By illuminating performance–consumption trade-offs, the metrics framework can help to reduce computational costs and the carbon footprint of ASR systems, while maintaining acceptable accuracy.

Keywords: Green Machine Learning · Sustainability · Automatic Speech Recognition · Benchmarks

1 Introduction

Automatic speech recognition (ASR), the conversion of acoustic speech signals to text, is key for enhancing human–machine interaction. Advances in hardware, algorithms, and data have given rise to ASR models with impressive accuracy, as typically measured by the Word Error Rate (WER). Consequently, a variety of speech-based applications is nowadays deployed across the edge–cloud continuum, from cloud-hosted virtual customer service agents and large-scale transcription services, to on-device applications like offline voice translation on smartphones and voice command recognition in smart speakers, and increasingly, in wearables and ultralow-power IoT devices. The deployment of AI models closer to the edge is driven by a growing demand for enhanced privacy, reduced latency, and increased energy efficiency.

The surging popularity of Large Language Models (LLMs) and Large Multimodal Models (LMMs) has increased scrutiny to the energy consumption of AI systems [9,40]. While most Green AI research efforts focus on the training phase [39], Google data from 2019 to 2021 indicated that about 60% of the energy consumption for their machine learning systems came from the inference phase [30], and this was before the boost in public LLM adoption triggered by OpenAI's ChatGPT release. Although a typical ASR inference task may not require as much energy as, for instance, image generation or captioning [22], when performed at scale, the environmental impact can become substantial. For example, transcribing a whole workday's worth of calls for every agent in a customer service centre accumulates a considerable energy cost. After all, ASR pipelines are computationally demanding: they typically consist of an acoustic model for inferring phoneme sequences from audio signals, a lexical model describing word pronunciations, and a language model estimating the probability of word sequences for enhanced transcription accuracy.

While various ASR model architectures reach high WER scores on benchmark datasets [36], in practice model selection requires a holistic view, going beyond accuracy. Real-world ASR deployment requires considering often underemphasised factors like inference latency, computational efficiency, memory usage, and energy consumption. As ASR systems become gradually more embedded in resource-constrained and environment-sensitive contexts, these dimensions of inference efficiency directly impact the practical usability, sustainability, and operational costs of ASR solutions. Therefore, understanding and balancing trade-offs between performance and resource use is essential to select the appropriate ASR models for specific deployment scenarios.

This paper presents a new multi-metric framework for evaluating the ASR systems in the inference phase, aiming to provide practitioners with a straightforward methodology for assessing which ASR model is most suitable for deployment in specific usage contexts. Our approach considers WER accuracy alongside sustainability- and efficiency-oriented metrics: Real-Time Factor, Inference Latency, Energy Per Audio Second, GPU Memory Efficiency and Hardware Utilisation Rate. We introduce metric weighting schemes to accommodate diverse deployment scenarios, including resource-constrained environments, and real-time or batch processing. Finally, we benchmark several state-of-the-art ASR architectures (Whisper, Wav2Vec2, HuBERT, WavLM, UniSpeech, and SpeechT5) on NVIDIA Jetson AGX Orin hardware, illustrating how the framework supports informed, context-aware model selection that balances accuracy, performance, and sustainability.

2 Related Work

The environmental impact of artificial intelligence has gained significant attention following seminal research by Strubell et al. [37], which documented the substantial carbon emissions associated with training large neural networks. Schwartz et al. [34] introduced the concept of "Green AI" to contrast "Red AI," which prioritises accuracy and capability over efficiency. They argue for incorporating energy usage and computational cost as primary evaluation metrics alongside traditional performance measures, introducing a more holistic evaluation paradigm. These studies were some of the first of a growing body of research on sustainable computing practices within AI development.

While many studies focused primarily on the training stage [25,29,30,37], large-scale deployment and use of AI models may lead to substantially larger inference costs due to the cumulative impact of numerous inference requests over the lifetime of a deployed model. Wu et al. [44] demonstrated that both training and inference phases contribute significantly to the overall carbon footprint of machine learning applications, with relative proportions varying across different use cases and implementation scenarios. This variability highlights the importance of context-specific energy analyses rather than generalised approaches to environmental impact assessment. Luccioni et al. [20] called for expanding the analysis of environmental impacts across the entire ML lifecycle to include the costs during deployment and inference. Investigations into the inference phase have identified that task-specific models typically demonstrate better energy efficiency compared to multi-purpose alternatives used for the same tasks, encouraging the use of specialised models over general-purpose large models when task requirements permit [21].

The quantification of AI systems' energy usage requires robust monitoring frameworks, which have evolved considerably in recent years. Henderson et al. [12] made important contributions by establishing a framework for environmental accountability through systematic documentation of energy consumption throughout the AI development process. Several additional teams [1,4,10,18,19] have developed methodologies to estimate or track the energy consumption of AI. These approaches vary in granularity, hardware compatibility, and methodology, often yielding inconsistent results that complicate systematic comparisons between models and systems.

The hardware compatibility constraints of energy monitoring tools present significant challenges for comprehensive energy assessment. Most tools for energy monitoring of a system's internal components only support Intel CPUs and NVIDIA graphics cards [1,4,10], as they rely on the manufacturers' proprietary monitoring interfaces, RAPL and NVML/`nvidia-smi`, respectively. While these represent common hardware choices, this dependency limits applicability across deployment scenarios such as edge computing. Moreover, Yang et al. [45] identified significant limitations in `nvidia-smi`'s accuracy, showing a ±5% error margin (versus the claimed ±5W), which can lead to substantial measurement discrepancies on high-power GPUs. Their study also revealed that newer GPU architectures only sample power during 25% of runtime, leaving most power fluctuations unmonitored. Software-based methods additionally have the inherent limitation of relying on power models for providing their metrics [16], meaning that they provide estimates rather than direct measurements.

The AI Energy Score Leaderboard [22] is a benchmarking initiative evaluating models based on standardised power efficiency metrics. While important for promoting transparency in AI energy consumption and a useful high-level benchmark, it has notable methodological limitations. First, the AI Energy Score focuses exclusively on GPU power consumption, without accounting for significant system-wide energy factors—a shortcoming shared with other energy assessment studies [33]. The creators of the benchmark acknowledge that "CPU and RAM usage was found to be approximately 30% greater than GPU energy use," yet these components remain excluded from their primary metrics. Second, given nvidia-smi's aforementioned accuracy limitations and sampling gaps, these GPU-centric measurement approaches may compound measurement errors with incomplete system coverage, potentially leading to significant underestimation of actual energy consumption. Finally, such benchmarks typically isolate energy efficiency from other critical performance indicators, and the AI Energy Score creators note that users should independently consider "throughput, accuracy, and latency" alongside efficiency metrics.[1]

Despite the growing focus on Green AI, relatively few studies have specifically addressed energy consumption in Automatic Speech Recognition (ASR) systems. Parcollet et al. [28] investigated the carbon footprint of training end-to-end speech recognisers, quantifying CO_2 emissions during model training and highlighting how minimal performance improvements often come at extremely high environmental costs. However, their work focused primarily on the training phase rather than inference.

Chakravarty [7] conducted one of the few studies examining ASR inference energy consumption, specifically for edge deployment. This work measured energy consumption for various ASR models on the NVIDIA Jetson Orin Nano, analysing the effects of model quantisation, precision levels, and noise on performance and energy efficiency. The study found that changing precision from FP32 to FP16 halved energy consumption across different models with minimal performance degradation, and that larger model size does not necessarily predict better noise resilience or energy consumption patterns.

While these studies provide valuable insights into ASR energy consumption, they lack a cohesive method evaluating both performance and sustainability. Most existing work focuses either on single-metric evaluations or fails to provide context-specific evaluations tailored to different deployment scenarios. Additionally, many studies do not adequately address the trade-offs between energy efficiency, accuracy, and other performance metrics that practitioners must navigate when deploying ASR systems.

---

[1] Thus, while the AI Energy Score offers meaningful ratings, our objective is to enable the level of granularity needed for deployment-specific trade-off analysis across various performance and sustainability factors. Differences in energy measurement methodology preclude direct comparison with our framework.

3 Benchmark Framework

Recent ASR models perform remarkably well, reaching accuracy levels comparable to human annotations [36]. However, these advances often come with significant computational and energy costs. Our benchmarking framework addresses this fundamental trade-off by providing a comprehensive evaluation approach that integrates both traditional performance metrics and sustainability considerations. We design the framework around four key principles: *(1)* moving beyond accuracy-only assessment to encompass efficiency metrics, *(2)* recognising that different deployment scenarios prioritise different aspects of performance, *(3)* ensuring consistent and reliable measurements across test runs, and *(4)* providing insights that are actionable for researchers and practitioners.

Moreover, our approach acknowledges that ASR deployment occurs across diverse computing environments, from cloud servers to edge devices. Each environment has unique constraints and different evaluation criteria for different priorities. For edge deployment, specifically, where battery life and thermal management are critical concerns, energy efficiency plays a crucial role.

The framework follows a modular pipeline architecture with four main components. The *Inference Engine* executes ASR models on audio inputs while measuring computational metrics such as inference time, latency, and accuracy. It ensures that the model's real-world performance is evaluated effectively. The *Power Monitoring module* collects data on the power consumption in real time during inference. By tracking energy usage, it helps to assess the efficiency of ASR models and optimise them for deployment on various hardware platforms. The *Metrics Aggregator* collects and combines performance and efficiency metrics from multiple sources. Collect data related to ASR accuracy, processing speed, and power consumption, providing a comprehensive evaluation of the effectiveness of each model. The *Weighted Scoring System* applies context-specific weightings to different performance metrics to generate deployment-optimised scores. This enables informed decision-making by prioritising models that best meet the specific requirements of a given use case.

3.1 Metrics Definition

The framework measures six key metrics that comprehensively characterise ASR system performance.

Word Error Rate (WER) is a standard accuracy metric for ASR that measures the edit distance between the reference and hypothesised transcripts [24,43]. The ASR model inference output is a text file, each corresponding to a single audio input file. To ensure consistency between characters in prediction and ground truth datasets, we apply a normalisation process where punctuation marks, special characters, and capitalisation are removed. WER is expressed as a percentage, and calculated as: $WER = \frac{Substitutions + Deletions + Insertions}{Number\ of\ Words\ in\ Reference}$.

Real-Time Factor (RTF) is the dimensionless ratio of the processing time to the audio duration, indicating how much faster (or slower) the system operates compared to real-time [23]. This metric is crucial for assessing whether an ASR system can keep up with live audio input.

Energy Per Audio Second (EPAS) is a metric that quantifies the energy required to process one second of audio, measured in joules per second. This metric was inspired by the energy-per-token metric used for profiling energy consumption in LLM inference [15,33]. EPAS is calculated as the ratio of total energy consumption to total audio duration.

Inference Latency (in milliseconds) is computed as the 95th percentile of the processing times of all audio segments, providing insight into the worst-case responsiveness. The 95th percentile is more useful than the maximum latency, because it filters out rare outliers, while still representing worst-case scenarios. It is also known as tail latency [46].

GPU Memory Efficiency (GME) is the ratio of active GPU memory to total allocated GPU memory, expressed as a percentage.

Hardware Utilisation Rate (HUR) is a measure for the average utilisation of the compute resources (CPU and GPU), providing insight into balanced resource usage. The HUR is expressed as a percentage, and is calculated by taking the mean of the average GPU utilisation and average CPU utilisation.

Lower WER indicates better accuracy, and lower RTF indicates more efficient processing. When RTF < 1, the system processes audio faster than it would take to play it. Lower EPAS and Inference Latency values are desirable. Higher GME values are better, values close to 100% indicate effective use of allocated GPU memory. Balanced, high HUR (60–90%) is ideal: lower values suggest underutilisation, higher HUR may indicate bottlenecks and high energy usage.

3.2 Weights and Aggregation

We use min–max normalisation to transform the raw metrics to a 0–1 scale where 1 represents the best performance. For metrics where lower values are better (WER, RTF, EPAS, Latency), we invert the normalised values. For HUR, we use a piecewise normalisation that assigns optimal scores (0.8–1.0) to the balanced utilisation range (60–90%), with lower scores for both underutilisation (<60%) and overutilisation (>90%). This approach rewards efficient resource usage while penalising potential bottlenecks and wasteful underutilisation.

We define a green score as a weighted sum of normalised metrics:

$$\text{Green Score} = \mathbf{w} \cdot \mathbf{m}_{\text{norm}} = \sum_{i=1}^{6} w_i \cdot m_i,$$

where $\mathbf{w} = [w_{\text{WER}}, w_{\text{RTF}}, w_{\text{EPAS}}, w_{\text{lat}}, w_{\text{GME}}, w_{\text{HUR}}]$ and the components of $\mathbf{m}_{\text{norm}}$ are ordered analogously.

In our framework we use configurable weighting schemes that adapt the evaluation to different deployment contexts. Rather than providing a single score, we define four weighting schemes, shown in Table 1, that reflect common ASR deployment scenarios:

Table 1. Weighting scheme coefficients reflecting different deployment contexts

Scenario	w_{WER}	w_{RTF}	w_{EPAS}	w_{lat}	w_{GME}	w_{HUR}
Balanced	0.25	0.20	0.20	0.15	0.10	0.10
Mobile	0.15	0.20	0.30	0.05	0.25	0.05
Real-time	0.25	0.25	0.10	0.30	0.05	0.05
Server	0.25	0.10	0.35	0.00	0.20	0.10

Balanced General-Purpose Evaluation (Balanced) is designed for general-purpose applications with balanced requirements. In this scenario, accuracy is always important; processing speed matters in most cases; energy efficiency is highly beneficial across all cases; responsiveness is crucial mostly in interactive systems; and memory efficiency and efficient hardware utilisation are beneficial but less critical.

Resource-Constrained Environments (Mobile) is optimised for battery-powered and edge devices with limited resources. In this scenario, accuracy still matters, but some degradation is acceptable; responsiveness is essential despite limited resources; energy efficiency is critical for battery-powered devices; latency is less important than overall energy efficiency; memory constraints are significant; and balanced utilisation is important, but not a primary concern.

Real-Time Processing (Real-Time) is optimised for applications requiring immediate responses, like voice assistants and interactive systems. In this scenario, high accuracy for user experience is important; the system must process faster than real-time; energy matters but is secondary to responsiveness; immediate response is critical; memory efficiency is less critical for devices with sufficient RAM; and hardware utilisation is a minor concern.

High-Throughput Batch Inference (Server) is optimised for large-scale cloud deployments. In this scenario, accuracy is still important; throughput matters, but time sensitivity is lower; energy efficiency is crucial for managing operational costs; per-request latency is irrelevant for batch jobs; memory efficiency determines how many models fit on a server; and balancing CPU/GPU load enhances computational performance.

4 Experimental Setup

We conducted experiments on several ASR models obtained from Hugging Face. We evaluated the models with half- and single-precision settings, and measured and aggregated metrics from the proposed benchmark framework. We used high-quality English speech recordings from public-domain readings and a diverse, crowdsourced voice collection with broad demographic coverage. To assess robustness, we also injected synthetic noise into the clean speech samples.

Table 2. Technical hardware specifications

Component	Specification
GPU	NVIDIA Ampere architecture (cores: 2048 NVIDIA CUDA, 64 Tensor)
CPU	12-core Arm Cortex-A78AE v8.2 64-bit CPU 3MB L2 + 6MB L3, 2.2GHz max frequency
Memory	32GB LPDDR5 RAM
Storage	64GB eMMC 5.1 Flash Storage
Power	Configurable TDP from 15W to 60W
Dimensions	100mm × 79mm × 21mm

4.1 Hardware Platform

All experiments were conducted on the NVIDIA Jetson AGX Orin Developer Kit, which represents a high-performance edge computing platform, Table 2 shows its technical specifications. The Jetson AGX Orin was chosen for its ability to represent both edge and small server deployment scenarios, with sufficient computational power to run all the evaluated models, while still being constrained enough to reveal meaningful differences in efficiency metrics. Its lightweight design allows for seamless integration into smaller devices, while still providing the computational capabilities necessary to handle complex loads without relying on cloud computing resources.

The device was interfaced through wired keyboard and mouse, with the JetPack 6.2 [L4T 36.4.3] OS providing the graphical user interface. For power measurements, we utilised the built-in INA3221 power monitors [38] on the Jetson platform, which provide accurate measurements of system-on-chip (SoC) and memory subsystem power consumption.

4.2 Implementation Details

Our framework is implemented as a collection of Python modules that can be easily extended to accommodate new models and metrics. It includes *ASR engine wrappers*: custom scripts for each model architecture, providing a unified interface for model loading, inference, and metrics collection; a *power monitoring daemon*: a background process that collects power consumption data using platform-specific utilities; and a *metrics aggregator*: a data processing pipeline that combines metrics from various sources, handles normalisation, and applies weighting schemes.

The entire framework is designed to be portable across different computing environments, with currently optimised support for NVIDIA Jetson platforms. The source code is publicly available[2], allowing researchers to replicate our experiments and enhance the framework to suit their specific needs.

We employ continuous sampling of power consumption using the NVIDIA `tegrastats` utility [26] at 200 ms intervals, which provides fine-grained power measurements for Jetson platforms. Baseline measurements of RAM and power

---
[2] https://github.com/ulmarise/asr-green-metrics-framework.

are first established during device inactivity, and these values are subtracted from the total consumption to calculate the specific resources allocated to ASR tasks. Moreover, we utilise PyTorch's built-in CUDA memory tracking capabilities combined with system-level memory monitoring to calculate memory efficiency. We track both allocated and active memory to understand utilisation patterns.

For consistent and reliable metrics collection, our framework implements the following methodology. For WER calculation, we use the `jiwer` library [17] with a custom normalisation procedure to handle punctuation, capitalisation, and spacing consistently. This ensures fair comparisons across different model architectures and output styles. We set up model inference to capture the exact start and end times for each audio segment, ensuring the accurate calculation of RTF and Inference Latency metrics. Each audio file is processed separately to provide per-file metrics for statistical analysis. For EPAS calculations, we isolated the incremental energy consumption attributable to the ASR model by subtracting baseline power draw. GME and HUR metrics were calculated from memory usage statistics and from CPU and GPU percentages in `tegrastats` output.

4.3 ASR Model Selection

To demonstrate the utility of our framework, we selected six state-of-the-art ASR architectures representing a diverse range of model families:

1. **Whisper**, a transformer-based encoder–decoder model trained on a massive multilingual dataset. We used the distilled version [11], which maintains performance with reduced computational requirements. Specifically, we used a compact version optimised for English speech recognition with reduced parameters yet similar performance ; a medium-sized version that balances computational efficiency and transcription accuracy ; and the largest variant in the Distil-Whisper family, offering high-quality speech recognition with significantly fewer parameters than the original Whisper Large-v2 model.
2. **Wav2Vec2** [5], a self-supervised model that learns representations directly from raw audio, using a convolutional feature encoder followed by a transformer. We used Facebook Wav2Vec2 Large 960h, a self-supervised speech recognition model pre-trained on 960 h of data, featuring robust performance on diverse speech inputs.
3. **HuBERT** [14], a hidden-unit BERT model that learns representations from clustered audio features, with a mask prediction objective. We used Facebook HuBERT Large LS960 FT, a model pre-trained on unlabelled audio and fine-tuned on 960 h of labelled speech for improved representation learning.
4. **WavLM** [8], an evolution of the HuBERT approach incorporating masked language modeling and denoising objectives. We used WavLM Libri-Clean 100h Base Plus, an enhanced audio representation model that builds upon the Wav2Vec framework, fine-tuned on 100 h of clean data.
5. **UniSpeech** [42], a unified pre-training framework that combines self-supervised and supervised learning. We used Microsoft UniSpeech-SAT Base 100h

Libri FT, a speech representation model leveraging self-supervised and semi-supervised training approaches, fine-tuned on 100 h of data.
6. **SpeechT5** [2], a unified-modal encoder-decoder framework that handles both speech and text. We used Microsoft SpeechT5 ASR, a unified text-to-speech and speech-to-text transformer model based on the T5 architecture, specifically optimised for automatic speech recognition tasks.

For each model, we utilised the implementations available through the Hugging Face library, which provides consistent APIs and optimised CUDA support. Each model was tested in both FP32 (full precision) and FP16 (half precision) to evaluate the performance–efficiency trade-offs of reduced precision. Each model's inference code was configured to capture timing and resource utilisation metrics, with detailed logs generated for subsequent analysis.

4.4 Dataset Characteristics

We used the benchmark framework to evaluate two speech datasets. The first is a smaller benchmark: a subset of the LibriSpeech dataset [27], consisting of 70 audio tracks from the test-clean partition. The second dataset is larger and more diverse, is an English subset of the Common Voice dataset [3], comprising 3995 audio tracks from the valid-test partition.

The LibriSpeech audio data is stored in FLAC-encoded (lossless), sampled at 16 kHz with a mono channel. Each segment lasts 3–5 s, totaling approximately 328 s. The recordings feature high signal-to-noise ratio speech, balanced gender distribution, and native English speakers reading public domain audiobooks. The dataset size was chosen to be large enough to provide statistically significant results while remaining manageable for repeated evaluations across multiple models and configurations.

To evaluate the model's ability to handle acoustic interference, we considered a noisy version of the dataset. It was created using Gaussian white noise with a mean of zero and a standard deviation of one, ensuring it matched the length of each audio track. The noise amplitude was reduced by 10 dB to limit its impact on the original signal. Then the noise was combined with the audio signal to produce a composite track that simulates real-world audio corruption in noisy environments. This approach allowed us to systematically evaluate performance degradation under consistent noise conditions.

In addition to LibriSpeech, we include the Common Voice dataset to introduce greater variability in speaker demographics, recording conditions, and background noise levels. This enables evaluation under more realistic, less controlled conditions. The audio files are in MP3 format, sampled at 48 kHz mono. Segments range 1–28 s, totalling around 5 h of audio. Recordings are crowd-sourced with moderate noise levels, covering global English speakers with balanced gender distribution, reading from open-domain text prompts. Audio files were used as-is, but downsampled to 16 kHz.

4.5 Evaluation Details

Our evaluation followed these steps for each model and precision configuration. First, each model was loaded into memory with the specified precision (FP16 or FP32). Loading time was measured but not included in the inference metrics. Second, ten audio samples (not part of the dataset) were processed to prime the model and stabilise GPU memory allocation. Third, during the inference phase, each audio file was processed sequentially with the following measurements: processing time for each audio sample, memory utilisation tracked at 200 ms intervals, power consumption recorded continuously, and output transcriptions saved for subsequent WER calculation. Fourth, raw measurements were processed to calculate the six core metrics (see Sect. 3.1). Fifth and finally, the four weighting schemes were applied to generate context-specific Green Scores.

To ensure reliability, each experiment was conducted three times, and the median values were used for the final results. The ambient temperature was maintained at 22°C ± 1°C to minimise thermal variability. The Jetson AGX Orin was configured in MAXN power mode to ensure consistent maximum performance across all tests.

5 Results and Analysis

We first examine the overall performance trends under clean conditions, followed by an analysis of noise robustness, where artificial noise is added. This is then complemented by an evaluation under natural conditions using real-world noisy speech. Table 3 presents the evaluation metrics, and Table 4 shows the corresponding green scores computed with various weighting schemes for ASR models evaluated on clean and artificially noisy speech. Table 5 presents the metrics and green scores for ASR models evaluated on speech with real-world noise.

On clean LibriSpeech data, HuBERT yields the best transcription accuracy, while Distil Whisper Large excels with noise. Precision format (FP16 vs. FP32) minimally impacts accuracy but greatly affects performance metrics. UniSpeech is fastest overall, with Distil Whisper Small/Medium (FP16) being the most efficient among transformer models. FP16 models consistently outperform FP32 in speed and energy use, with WavLM, UniSpeech, and Wav2Vec2 (FP16) showing the highest energy efficiency. Larger models are predictably less memory-efficient, with Distil Whisper Large (FP32) achieving the most balanced hardware utilisation.

HuBERT FP32 achieves the highest balanced green score on clean LibriSpeech data, challenging the notion that FP16 models are always more efficient. Distil Whisper FP16 models offer good accuracy–efficiency balance, while SpeechT5 and WavLM rank lowest. For mobile/edge deployment, UniSpeech and HuBERT FP32 excel. In real-time scenarios, UniSpeech FP16 and HuBERT FP32 perform best. Server-side applications favour HuBERT FP32 and Distil Whisper Large FP16, with the latter providing strong WER performance. Green scores remain consistent between clean and noisy LibriSpeech data, suggesting the aggregation approaches may underweight audio quality sensitivity.

On Common Voice data, Distil Whisper Large achieves the best transcription accuracy, followed by Distil Whisper Medium and Small. UniSpeech has the fastest processing speed overall, while WavLM and traditional transformer models (Wav2Vec2, HuBERT) show moderate performance. FP16 models consistently show superior energy efficiency, with UniSpeech, WavLM, and SpeechT5 showing the lowest energy consumption per audio second. FP32 variants of Wav2Vec2, HuBERT, and WavLM achieve lower latency, while Distil Whisper models exhibit higher latency but maintain competitive speed-accuracy trade-offs. Larger Distil Whisper models predictably consume more GPU memory, with the Large variant (FP32) reaching the highest memory utilisation, while UniSpeech and WavLM maintain more balanced resource use across precisions.

HuBERT FP32 dominates on Common Voice data with the highest balanced green score, demonstrating that FP32 models can be more efficient despite their higher precision. Wav2Vec2 FP32 and Distil Whisper Medium FP16 also perform strongly in balanced scenarios. For mobile/edge deployment, HuBERT (both precisions) and Wav2Vec2 FP32 excel, while UniSpeech maintains consistent performance across precision types. In real-time scenarios, HuBERT FP32 performs the best, with Wav2Vec2 FP32 and Distil Whisper Medium FP16 close behind. Server-side applications favour HuBERT models. SpeechT5 consistently ranks lowest across all categories, with particularly poor real-time performance.

Comparing results across both datasets shows consistent patterns in model performance. HuBERT FP32 demonstrates superior efficiency-accuracy trade-offs, achieving the highest balanced green scores on both LibriSpeech and Common Voice. UniSpeech FP16 maintains the lowest energy consumption and processing time across datasets, while Distil Whisper Large offers the best accuracy on Common Voice but is outperformed by HuBERT on LibriSpeech. The relative performance ranking of models remains largely consistent across datasets, suggesting that our green score metrics robustly capture model characteristics rather than dataset-specific features.

Given a specific precision format, our results may help identify the most economical model for various deployment scenarios. For FP16 precision, UniSpeech offers optimal resource efficiency, Distil Whisper models provide the best accuracy–efficiency balance for real-time applications, and HuBERT delivers superior server performance. For FP32 precision, HuBERT consistently demonstrates the best overall performance, particularly for real-time scenarios, while UniSpeech and WavLM maintain excellent resource efficiency. These findings challenge the common assumption that lower precision formats always yield more efficient models, as demonstrated by HuBERT FP32's exceptional performance across both datasets. It is important to note that these recommendations are specific to the hardware platform and dataset characteristics used in the experiments. Performance may vary with different hardware configurations, audio conditions, or application requirements.

Table 3. LibriSpeech metrics for various ASR models with different precision formats—for clean and, in parentheses, for noisy speech data

Model	Prec.	WER	RTF	EPAS	Latency	GME	HUR
Distil-Whisper-S	FP16	3.48 (17.19)	0.127 (0.125)	0.79 (0.64)	0.83 (0.79)	12.67 (12.45)	31.60 (22.68)
	FP32	3.70 (17.19)	0.182 (0.181)	3.29 (3.10)	0.91 (0.90)	12.64 (12.47)	29.45 (33.40)
Distil-Whisper-M	FP16	4.13 (14.25)	0.123 (0.120)	1.58 (1.38)	0.65 (0.64)	15.62 (15.25)	28.75 (26.86)
	FP32	3.92 (14.25)	0.248 (0.253)	11.36 (11.11)	1.18 (1.18)	18.04 (17.80)	36.94 (35.81)
Distil-Whisper-L	FP16	4.03 (12.40)	0.152 (0.152)	3.26 (3.56)	0.85 (0.86)	20.48 (20.27)	34.30 (30.68)
	FP32	4.03 (12.40)	0.417 (0.418)	23.46 (23.83)	1.97 (2.00)	27.09 (26.90)	39.92 (40.80)
Wav2Vec2	FP16	4.13 (38.96)	0.378 (0.380)	0.23 (0.25)	1.81 (1.83)	20.71 (20.32)	6.02 (16.55)
	FP32	4.13 (39.17)	0.094 (0.096)	1.91 (1.73)	0.29 (0.30)	19.74 (19.52)	18.50 (19.03)
HuBERT	FP16	2.39 (10.88)	0.387 (0.394)	0.26 (0.23)	1.86 (1.86)	20.10 (19.99)	10.02 (3.83)
	FP32	2.39 (10.88)	0.093 (0.098)	1.97 (1.85)	0.33 (0.32)	19.49 (19.24)	29.28 (21.52)
WavLM	FP16	12.5 (63.76)	0.32 (0.332)	0.18 (0.23)	1.79 (1.78)	20.70 (20.51)	5.72 (15.66)
	FP32	12.5 (63.76)	0.07 (0.063)	0.68 (0.65)	0.16 (0.15)	19.87 (19.88)	17.30 (25.06)
UniSpeech	FP16	6.31 (31.23)	0.054 (0.052)	0.26 (0.23)	0.08 (0.07)	20.10 (19.77)	12.87 (26.86)
	FP32	6.31 (31.23)	0.058 (0.061)	0.53 (0.68)	0.13 (0.12)	19.27 (19.11)	23.62 (12.71)
SpeechT5	FP16	11.9 (27.31)	0.351 (0.356)	0.34 (0.37)	2.88 (2.88)	20.59 (20.25)	14.18 (13.94)
	FP32	11.9 (27.31)	0.360 (0.361)	0.80 (0.79)	2.98 (3.00)	20.10 (19.83)	26.15 (18.13)

6 Discussion

Our evaluation across LibriSpeech and Common Voice datasets reveals significant insights for ASR model selection. While FP16 models generally offer better energy efficiency and speed, some FP32 models achieve better overall green scores due to superior accuracy and balanced hardware utilisation. HuBERT FP32 consistently demonstrates exceptional efficiency-accuracy balance across both datasets, while UniSpeech FP16 excels in resource-constrained scenarios. For practical deployments, UniSpeech FP16 is optimal for energy and latency constraints, HuBERT FP32 delivers the best balanced performance, and Distil Whisper models offer strong accuracy with reasonable efficiency. Precision-specific analysis directly addresses which model is most economical given particular constraints, challenging the assumption that energy efficiency necessarily compromises accuracy. These findings emphasise the importance of multi-dimensional ASR evaluation frameworks, as the traditional focus on WER alone fails to capture the complex trade-offs in real-world deployments, particularly for resource-constrained environments and large-scale use, where energy considerations are increasingly critical.

Limitations. While our evaluation provides valuable insights into ASR model performance, some limitations should be noted. Firstly, while our green scoring system provides a useful aggregated metric for model comparison, we acknowledge that such aggregation approaches may potentially mask poor performance in individual metrics. The relative importance of different metrics also varies according to specific application requirements. Users should always examine indi-

Table 4. LibriSpeech green scores—for clean and, in parentheses, for noisy speech data

Model	Prec.	Balanced	Mobile	Realtime	Server
Distil-Whisper-S	FP16	0.73 (0.72)	0.64 (0.64)	0.76 (0.76)	0.69 (0.67)
	FP32	0.67 (0.68)	0.58 (0.58)	0.70 (0.71)	0.62 (0.64)
Distil-Whisper-M	FP16	0.74 (0.76)	0.68 (0.70)	0.77 (0.80)	0.70 (0.72)
	FP32	0.59 (0.61)	0.53 (0.54)	0.61 (0.63)	0.56 (0.59)
Distil-Whisper-L	FP16	0.74 (0.76)	0.73 (0.74)	0.75 (0.78)	0.74 (0.77)
	FP32	0.41 (0.45)	0.42 (0.44)	0.39 (0.42)	0.46 (0.50)
Wav2Vec2	FP16	0.55 (0.47)	0.61 (0.56)	0.49 (0.40)	0.69 (0.61)
	FP32	0.78 (0.69)	0.76 (0.71)	0.84 (0.74)	0.74 (0.66)
HuBERT	FP16	0.59 (0.58)	0.62 (0.62)	0.52 (0.51)	0.72 (0.72)
	FP32	0.84 (0.82)	0.79 (0.78)	0.88 (0.87)	0.80 (0.79)
WavLM	FP16	0.37 (0.39)	0.51 (0.52)	0.31 (0.32)	0.49 (0.51)
	FP32	0.61 (0.62)	0.67 (0.68)	0.66 (0.68)	0.56 (0.58)
UniSpeech	FP16	0.77 (0.79)	0.78 (0.79)	0.84 (0.85)	0.72 (0.74)
	FP32	0.77 (0.76)	0.76 (0.75)	0.83 (0.82)	0.72 (0.70)
SpeechT5	FP16	0.33 (0.48)	0.49 (0.58)	0.20 (0.36)	0.51 (0.66)
	FP32	0.33 (0.47)	0.48 (0.57)	0.19 (0.35)	0.51 (0.66)

vidual metric values alongside green scores to ensure that models meet specific requirements for their deployment scenarios. The green scores are intended as a complementary decision-making tool rather than a replacement for detailed metric analysis. Future work could explore the incorporation of minimum performance thresholds or weighted penalty functions to address scenarios where certain metrics are considered critical for specific applications.

Secondly, in our experiments, we utilised power measurements obtained from the built-in sensors of NVIDIA Jetson devices. Although the accuracy of these measurements may pose a threat to construct validity, previous studies demonstrated that such measurements are quite accurate and can be further calibrated to develop more realistic energy consumption models [35]. Moreover, we illustrated our framework on a limited selection of eight ASR models and two speech recording datasets. Implementing our framework on other hardware with more models and data would reduce this threat to external validity, and is a matter for future work.

Finally, we emphasise that our framework does not cover the total energy cost over the full AI system lifecycle, and that improved AI efficiency may still lead to higher overall energy consumption due to increased demand (Jevons paradox). Also, the framework does not consider potential biases in the ASR training data and models, which may disproportionately affect underrepresented user groups.

Table 5. Common Voice metrics and green scores

Model	Prec.	WER	RTF	EPAS	Latency	GME	HUR	Balanced	Mobile	Realtime	Server
Distil-Whisper-S	FP16	6.16	0.074	0.514	433.07	14.20	36.96	0.77	0.67	0.81	0.71
	FP32	6.15	0.106	2.995	558.52	13.94	41.70	0.73	0.62	0.77	0.67
Distil-Whisper-M	FP16	5.78	0.071	1.558	386.33	17.79	41.06	0.80	0.73	0.84	0.76
	FP32	5.77	0.192	11.147	933.02	19.83	41.66	0.63	0.56	0.64	0.61
Distil-Whisper-L	FP16	4.81	0.096	3.232	516.20	22.70	20.72	0.78	0.76	0.81	0.78
	FP32	4.82	0.360	23.972	1671.79	28.82	48.12	0.46	0.45	0.43	0.51
Wav2Vec2	FP16	9.84	0.053	0.307	1799.57	24.25	15.19	0.69	0.78	0.63	0.78
	FP32	9.84	0.030	1.816	190.39	21.75	48.70	0.82	0.79	0.86	0.78
HuBERT	FP16	6.19	0.056	0.412	1812.83	25.24	16.99	0.74	0.82	0.67	0.84
	FP32	6.17	0.033	1.945	212.09	22.46	50.24	0.87	0.83	0.90	0.83
WavLM	FP16	22.36	0.048	0.229	1371.85	25.66	18.90	0.58	0.73	0.54	0.65
	FP32	22.39	0.018	0.709	93.74	23.78	42.18	0.69	0.75	0.73	0.66
UniSpeech	FP16	18.45	0.011	0.197	64.14	24.09	42.46	0.75	0.80	0.79	0.72
	FP32	18.46	0.014	0.654	76.47	23.26	45.64	0.74	0.78	0.78	0.71
SpeechT5	FP16	24.59	0.292	0.237	2407.59	25.05	18.87	0.33	0.53	0.19	0.54
	FP32	24.60	0.286	0.452	2369.41	24.58	22.12	0.34	0.53	0.20	0.54

7 Conclusions and Outlook

We presented a multi-metric framework for ASR systems that extends beyond traditional accuracy metrics to incorporate energy efficiency and deployment considerations. Evaluation across both controlled (LibriSpeech) and real-world (Common Voice) speech datasets demonstrates that our findings are robust across different speech conditions. Our results highlight that ASR model selection involves complex trade-offs between accuracy, speed, energy consumption, and hardware utilisation. We found that HuBERT and UniSpeech models achieve the best overall efficiency across different deployment scenarios, while Distil Whisper models offer an excellent balance between accuracy and efficiency, particularly in noisy environments. Importantly, our analysis challenges the assumption that energy efficiency necessarily compromises accuracy, as evidenced by models like HuBERT FP32 that excel in both dimensions. The green scoring system introduced in this work provides stakeholders with a practical tool for making informed decisions based on their specific deployment requirements. By quantifying the environmental impact of ASR models, we contribute to the growing effort to develop more sustainable AI systems without sacrificing performance.

Several limitations and promising directions for future research emerge from this work. Our evaluation was conducted on read speech datasets, which do not fully represent real-world conditions. Future work should extend this analysis to more challenging datasets, such as those involving conversational speech with overlapping speakers (e.g., CHiME [6]), realistic noise and reverberation conditions (e.g., Rev16 [32]), semi-spontaneous speech (e.g., TED-LIUM [13]), and multilingual domain-specific content (e.g., VoxPopuli [41]). Additionally, our model selection could be expanded to include non-transformer architectures like KALDI [31], which employs lightweight Hidden Markov Models. These models may offer competitive accuracy on clean speech, while potentially delivering superior efficiency metrics compared to transformer-based approaches. Beyond traditional metrics, future evaluations should consider incorporating semantic similarity measures as complementary accuracy metrics. Semantically-aware evaluation would provide a more nuanced understanding of model performance, especially in applications where precise wording is less critical than conveying the correct meaning. Finally, as ASR systems are deployed in increasingly diverse settings—from edge devices to large data centres—research on domain-specific optimisation techniques will be increasingly important. This includes exploring quantisation methods beyond FP16, model pruning, and architecture-specific optimisations that can further improve the balance between accuracy and efficiency. By advancing holistic evaluation approaches for ASR systems, we hope to encourage the development of models that not only recognise speech accurately, but do so in an environmentally responsible manner across the spectrum of deployment contexts.

Acknowledgments. This research is supported by the European Union's HORIZON Research and Innovation Programme under grant agreement No. 101120657, project ENFIELD (European Lighthouse to Manifest Trustworthy and Green AI).

References

1. Anthony, L.F.W., et al.: Carbontracker: tracking and predicting the carbon footprint of training deep learning models. arXiv preprint arXiv:2007.03051 (2020)
2. Ao, J., et al.: SpeechT5: unified-modal encoder-decoder pre-training for spoken language processing. ACL Anthol. **1**, 5723–5738 (2022). https://doi.org/10.18653/v1/2022.acl-long.393 https://doi.org/10.18653/v1/2022.acl-long.393 https://doi.org/10.18653/v1/2022.acl-long.393 https://doi.org/10.18653/v1/2022.acl-long.393
3. Ardila, R., et al.: Common voice: a massively-multilingual speech corpus. ACL Anthol., 4218–4222 (2020). https://aclanthology.org/2020.lrec-1.520
4. Argerich, M.F., et al.: Measuring and improving the energy efficiency of large language models inference. IEEE Access **12**, 80194–80207 (2024). https://doi.org/10.1109/ACCESS.2024.3409745
5. Baevski, A., et al.: wav2vec 2.0: a framework for self-supervised learning of speech representations. NeurIPS **33**, 12449–12460 (2020). https://proceedings.neurips.cc/paper/2020/hash/92d1e1eb1cd6f9fba3227870bb6d7f07-Abstract.html
6. Barker, J., et al.: The fifth 'CHiME' speech separation and recognition challenge: dataset, task and baselines. In: Interspeech 2018, pp. 1561–1565 (2018). https://doi.org/10.21437/Interspeech.2018-1768
7. Chakravarty, A.: Deep learning models in speech recognition: measuring GPU energy consumption, impact of noise and model quantization for edge deployment. arXiv preprint arXiv:2405.01004 (2024)

8. Chen, S., et al.: WavLM: large-scale self-supervised pre-training for full stack speech processing. IEEE J. Sel. Top. Sig. Process. **16**(6), 1505–1518 (2022). https://doi.org/10.1109/JSTSP.2022.3188113
9. Chen, S.: How much energy will AI really consume? The good, the bad and the unknown. Nature **639**, 22–24 (2025). https://doi.org/10.1038/d41586-025-00616-z
10. Courty, B., et al.: mlco2/codecarbon: v2.4.1 (2024). https://doi.org/10.5281/zenodo.11171501
11. Gandhi, S., et al.: Distil-whisper: robust knowledge distillation via large-scale pseudo labelling. arXiv preprint arXiv:2311.00430 (2023)
12. Henderson, P., et al.: Towards the systematic reporting of the energy and carbon footprints of machine learning. J. Mach. Learn. Res. **21**(1), 10039–10081 (2020). https://doi.org/10.5555/3455716.3455964
13. Hernandez, F., et al.: TED-LIUM 3: twice as much data and corpus repartition for experiments on speaker adaptation. In: Speech and Computer, pp. 198–208. Springer, Cham (2018). https://doi.org/10.1007/978-3-319-99579-3_21
14. Hsu, W.N., et al.: HuBERT: self-supervised speech representation learning by masked prediction of hidden units. IEEE/ACM Trans. Audio Speech Lang. Process. **29**, 3451–3460 (2021). https://doi.org/10.1109/TASLP.2021.3122291
15. Husom, E.J., et al.: The price of prompting: profiling energy use in large language models inference. arXiv preprint arXiv:2407.16893 (2024)
16. Jay, M., et al.: An experimental comparison of software-based power meters: focus on CPU and GPU. In: Proceedings of the IEEE/ACM CCGrid 2023, pp. 106–118. IEEE (2023). https://doi.org/10.1109/CCGrid57682.2023.00020
17. Jitsi: JiWER (2025). https://github.com/jitsi/jiwer
18. Lacoste, A., et al.: Quantifying the carbon emissions of machine learning. arXiv preprint arXiv:1910.09700 (2019)
19. Lannelongue, L., et al.: Green algorithms: quantifying the carbon footprint of computation. Adv. Sci. **8**(12), 2100707 (2021)
20. Luccioni, A.S., et al.: Counting carbon: a survey of factors influencing the emissions of machine learning. arXiv preprint arXiv:2302.08476 (2023)
21. Luccioni, S., et al.: Power hungry processing: watts driving the cost of AI deployment? In: FAccT '24 Proceedings, pp. 85–99. ACM (2024). https://doi.org/10.1145/3630106.3658542
22. Luccioni, S., et al.: AI energy score leaderboard - February 2025 (2025). https://huggingface.co/spaces/AIEnergyScore/Leaderboard
23. Microsoft Corporation: Measuring the real-time factor on your device. https://learn.microsoft.com/en-us/azure/ai-services/speech-service/embedded-speech-performance-evaluations
24. Morris, A.C., et al.: From WER and RIL to MER and WIL: improved evaluation measures for connected speech recognition. In: Interspeech 2004, pp. 2765–2768 (2004). https://doi.org/10.21437/Interspeech.2004-668
25. Naidu, R., et al.: Towards quantifying the carbon emissions of differentially private machine learning. arXiv preprint arXiv:2107.06946 (2021)
26. NVIDIA Corporation: NVIDIA DRIVE OS 5.2 Linux SDK developer guide: tegrastats utility (2023). https://docs.nvidia.com/drive/drive-os-5.2.0.0L/drive-os/index.html#page/DRIVE_OS_Linux_SDK_Development_Guide/Utilities/util_tegrastats.html

27. Panayotov, V., et al.: Librispeech: an ASR corpus based on public domain audio books. In: 2015 IEEE International Conference on Acoustics, Speech and Signal Processing (ICASSP), pp. 19–24. IEEE (2015). https://doi.org/10.1109/ICASSP.2015.7178964
28. Parcollet, T., et al.: The energy and carbon footprint of training end-to-end speech recognizers. In: Interspeech 2021, pp. 4583–4587 (2021). https://doi.org/10.21437/Interspeech.2021-456
29. Patterson, D., et al.: Carbon emissions and large neural network training. arXiv preprint arXiv:2104.10350 (2021)
30. Patterson, D., et al.: The carbon footprint of machine learning training will plateau. Then Shrink. Comput. **55**(7), 18–28 (2022). https://doi.org/10.1109/MC.2022.3148714
31. Povey, D., et al.: The Kaldi speech recognition toolkit. In: Proceedings of the IEEE ASRU 2011. IEEE Signal Processing Society, Catalog No.: CFP11SRW-USB. IEEE (2011)
32. Radford, A., et al.: Robust speech recognition via large-scale weak supervision. In: ICML, pp. 28492–28518. PMLR (2023). https://proceedings.mlr.press/v202/radford23a.html
33. Samsi, S., et al.: From words to Watts: benchmarking the energy costs of large language model inference. In: 2023 IEEE High Performance Extreme Computing Conference (HPEC), pp. 25–29. IEEE (2023). https://doi.org/10.1109/HPEC58863.2023.10363447
34. Schwartz, R., et al.: Green AI. Commun. ACM **63**(12), 54–63 (2020). https://doi.org/10.1145/3381831
35. Shalavi, N., et al.: Accurate calibration of power measurements from internal power sensors on NVIDIA Jetson devices. In: Proceedings IEEE EDGE 2023, pp. 166–170. IEEE (2023)
36. Srivastav, V., et al.: Open automatic speech recognition leaderboard (2023). https://huggingface.co/spaces/hf-audio/open_asr_leaderboard
37. Strubell, E., et al.: Energy and policy considerations for modern deep learning research. AAAI **34**(09), 13693–13696 (2020). https://doi.org/10.1609/aaai.v34i09.7123
38. Texas Instruments: INA3221 data sheet, product information and support | TI.com (2016). https://www.ti.com/product/INA3221
39. Verdecchia, R., et al.: A systematic review of Green AI. WIREs Data Min. Knowl. Discov. **13**(4), e1507 (2023). https://doi.org/10.1002/widm.1507
40. Vries, A.: The growing energy footprint of artificial intelligence. Joule **7**(10), 2191–2194 (2023). https://doi.org/10.1016/j.joule.2023.09.004
41. Wang, C., et al.: VoxPopuli: a large-scale multilingual speech corpus for representation learning, semi-supervised learning and interpretation. ACL Anthol., 993–1003 (2021). https://doi.org/10.18653/v1/2021.acl-long.80
42. Wang, C., et al.: UniSpeech: unified speech representation learning with labeled and unlabeled data. In: ICML, pp. 10937–10947. PMLR (2021). https://proceedings.mlr.press/v139/wang21y.html
43. Woodard, J., et al.: An information theoretic measure of speech recognition performance. In: Workshop on Standardisation for Speech I/O Technology, Naval Air Development Center, Warminster, PA (1982)

44. Wu, C.J., et al.: Sustainable AI: environmental implications, challenges and opportunities. PMLS **4**, 795–813 (2022)
45. Yang, Z., et al.: Accurate and convenient energy measurements for GPUs: a detailed study of NVIDIA GPU's built-in power sensor. In: SC '24 Proceedings, pp. 1–17 (2024). https://doi.org/10.1109/SC41406.2024.00028
46. Yang, Z., et al.: Quality at the tail of machine learning inference. arXiv preprint arXiv:2212.13925 (2022)

Sequential Rule Analysis of ICU Patient Vital Signals and Alarms

Michela Venturini[1,2(✉)], Len Feremans[3], Wouter De Corte[4], and Celine Vens[1,2]

[1] Department of Public Health and Primary Care, KU Leuven, Campus KULAK, Leuven, Belgium
michela.venturini@kuleuven.be
[2] ITEC - IMEC, Kortrijk, Belgium
[3] Department of Computer Science, University of Antwerp, Antwerp, Belgium
[4] Department of Anesthesiology and Intensive Care Medicine, AZ Groeninge Hospital, Kortrijk, Belgium

Abstract. In Intensive Care Units (ICUs), excessive medical alarms can cause alarm fatigue and desensitization, compromising patient safety. Alarm management is typically based on manual threshold adjustments, while advanced algorithmic solutions remain underused due to the complexity of patient conditions, dynamic environments, and missing contextual data. Our goal is to investigate the diagnostic utility of combining multiple signals and alarms to enhance relevance and minimize false alarms. A major challenge is integrating heterogeneous data sources, as vital signs are continuously sampled while alarms are event-driven. To bridge this gap, we encode the ICU data into a discretized symbolic representation, reducing dimensionality and improving pattern discovery. We propose a methodology for extracting sequential rules from multivariate datasets, structuring data into a sequence database using a sliding window transformation to capture temporal dependencies. To improve robustness, we introduce a rule ensemble approach, integrating patterns discovered across multiple representations. We applied our method to ICU data from 604 patients, incorporating continuous vital signs and alarm logs. Our findings reveal interpretable sequential rules, analyzed with clinical experts, including patterns highly relevant to intubation events. Our results highlight the potential of data-driven approaches to refine alarm management and improve patient monitoring in critical care settings.

Keywords: Rule Mining · Time Series Analysis · ICU · Alarm fatigue

1 Introduction

An Intensive Care Unit (ICU) is a specialized hospital department dedicated to providing intensive care and treatment to patients who are severely ill or critically injured. ICUs are furnished with advanced medical equipment that allows close monitoring of patients, provision of life support, and prompt intervention to stabilize their condition and prevent further deterioration. Such medical devices produce alarms designed to alert caregivers to any change in the condition of patients. This is particularly important in the ICU, as patients are often physiologically unstable and their condition can change very suddenly, requiring immediate action. However, with increasing patient parameters to be monitored, concerns have been raised about excessive and inappropriate alarm triggers. ICU alarms are a broad term that encompasses several types of alarm, classified into three groups: clinical, technical, and caused by intervention. Clinical alarms are the ones we are interested in and generally rely on a hard coded threshold for each physiological parameter separately, e.g., a "low saturation" alarm is triggered whenever the detected blood oxygen saturation (S_pO_2) falls below 88%. Unfortunately, these fixed alarm settings may not be appropriate for all ICU patients. For example, a patient with a respiratory condition may have a completely different saturation level considered normal compared to a young person admitted to the ICU for trauma. Technical alarms mostly refer to device malfunction or low battery. Finally, alarms caused by intervention are clinical alarms that are not triggered by actual changes in the patient state but rather by external factors (e.g., the patient is being transported or changed position in bed) [14,15]. It has been extensively shown that the proportion of actionable alarms is extremely low ranging from 1% to 26% in adult ICU settings [23], with an average of 771 alarms per bed per day [16], leading to alarm fatigue [5], desensitization to alarms [10], and ultimately impacting the safety of patients [2].

Current literature on managing clinical alarms can be broadly classified into two main strategies: customization of alarm settings and automated algorithms. The former strategy involves tailoring alarm settings based on patient-specific profiles, requiring nurses to manually adjust monitor settings according to the patient's current condition, and it is the most widely adopted in clinical practice. The latter approaches operate on signal acquisition, alarm validation, and alarm generation [13], in order to reduce false alarms. However, a limitation of both these methodologies is their specificity toward a single type of alarm. Others have studied the use of composite alarms, arguing that the correlation of multiple sensors provides a more accurate reflection of the state of a patient than single threshold alarms [3,12]. Despite these advancements, most alarm systems are designed to signal immediate concerns, overlooking longer-term alarm patterns. Moreover, strategies applied in the ICU setting did not show sufficient effectiveness in reducing the number of alarms [11].

Investigating sequential patterns of signals, alarms, and events may provide valuable insights for improving clinical alarms and reducing alarm fatigue. Identifying patterns that occur in close temporal proximity can help assess the usefulness of existing threshold alarms, uncover non-trivial patterns that anticipate meaningful changes in a patient's status, and ultimately avail the introduction of composite alarms that integrate multiple signals for a more accurate representation of the patient's condition. This approach could streamline alarm management, reduce the overall number of alarms, and enhance clinical efficiency.

This work retrospectively explores and quantifies sequential rules in vital signs and alarms originating from ICU monitoring devices. Based on previous work, we hypothesize that alarm patterns exist and can be used to reduce the number of alarms [17]. We propose an approach that extracts non-redundant sequential rules from Mixed-Type Multivariate Time Series (MXT-MTS), consisting of multiple vital signs and alarm logs [6]. Our method allows us to identify and visualize such relationships for large volumes of signals and alarm data. We applied our method to previously collected data from the ICU of AZ Groeninge Secondary Care Hospital in Belgium. Our dataset comprises raw physiological signals and alarm logs generated from ICU monitors for hundreds of patients.

2 Sequential Rule Mining in MTS

2.1 MTS in Medical Time Series

Figure 1 contextualizes the concept of MXT-MTS in the medical field and depicts a realistic scenario of a patient showing signs of respiratory failure. At time T_0, the patient is in a stable state. At time T_1, S_pO_2 drops, triggering an alarm for mild hypoxia (red band). In response, the body reacts by increasing cardiac output through an increase in heart frequency (HF) to compensate for reduced oxygen availability, leading to a tachycardia alarm. If no action is taken, as the cardiovascular system begins to struggle and it is impossible for the body to further increase the cardiac output, at time T_2, the mean arterial blood pressure (ABP_m) gradually decreases but remains within a range that does not yet trigger an alarm (blue band). As stated previously, sequential rules could be used to trigger early interventions before deterioration, and build clinically relevant composite alarms based on multiple signals, potentially less sensitive to false positives.

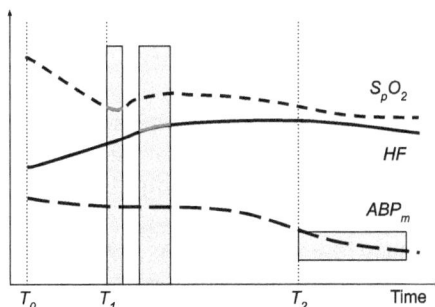

Fig. 1. Example of multivariate time series of a patient with alarms. S_pO_2 oxygen saturation, HF heart frequency, ABP_m arterial blood pressure.

2.2 Sequential Rule Mining

Rule mining is a set of analytical techniques used in data mining to uncover interesting patterns, associations, or relationships among a set of items in large databases [1]. It finds application in several areas, including medicine, where it was used, for example, to extract diagnosis patterns from medical health records [18]. These rules can help identify common co-occurrences of symptoms, laboratory results, or treatments that frequently appear together, aiding in clinical decision-making. Sequential Rule Mining focuses on finding relationships between sequences of events, where the order of occurrence matters. It aims to predict subsequent events based on preceding events [9]. The problem of mining sequential rules common to several sequences is defined as follows [8]. A sequence database T consists of a set of sequences $Q = \{q_1, q_2, ..., q_n\}$ built from a set of items $I = \{i_1, i_2, ..., i_m\}$, where i_j is an atomic element such as an alarm or an event. Each sequence q is an ordered list of itemsets $q = \langle I_1, I_2, ..., I_k \rangle$ such that each itemset I_j is a subset of I, i.e., $I_j \subseteq I$. A sequential rule $X \rightarrow Y$ is defined as a relationship between two itemsets $X, Y \subseteq I$ such that $X \cap Y = \emptyset$ and X, Y are not empty. The interpretation of a rule $X \rightarrow Y$ is that if the items of X occur in some itemsets of a sequence, the items in Y will occur in some itemsets afterwards in the same sequence. Notably, there is no ordering restriction between the items within X (or Y).

2.3 MTS Applications

The above definition usually refers to sequences of events of the same type (or of a single time series). Despite its importance, few studies attempted to discover rules in multivariate time series data. Nguyen et al. [22] approached the problem by separately finding rules in each single time series, by using the Apriori algorithm, and then scanning them to find inter-patterns. Park et al. [24] created symbolic baskets from the MTS and then applied the Apriori algorithm to such encoding. Karaca et al. [19] introduced temporal abstractions and applied a modified version of the Prefix-Span algorithm to mine frequent patterns. A prevalent challenge in the applications mentioned above, as well as in mining patterns or rules in MTS generally, is the issue of rule explosion. This phenomenon, where conventional mining algorithms generate an excessive number of redundant rules, complicates the process due to the overwhelming volume of data to analyze. In this study, our focus shifts towards identifying non-redundant sequential rules rather than merely frequent ones. In addition, we explore a methodology that allows for the simultaneous analysis of multiple time series and alarm logs. The usefulness of such approach can easily be motivated by considering the example depicted in Fig. 1 where the corresponding sequential rule might look like:

$$(S_pO_2 \downarrow, HF \uparrow) \Rightarrow (ABP_m \downarrow)$$

where $S_pO_2 \downarrow$ is the mild hypoxia alarm, $HF \uparrow$ is the tachycardia alarm, and $ABP_m \downarrow$ indicates that the patient's blood pressure is within a certain range, considered low. A single signal or alarm is insufficient to accurately assess the patient's status. A fluctuation in a single parameter, or an alarm triggered by an isolated change, could simply result from minor variations or patient movement rather than a clinically significant event. In contrast, analyzing multiple signals together provides a more comprehensive view, enabling a deeper understanding of the patient's condition.

3 Our Approach

We propose a novel approach for identifying sequential rules within MXT-MTS derived from ICU data and alarm logs. Our approach is based on a representation that combines occurrences of discrete alarms with continuous vital signals discretized in time and value. A discretized representation of time series is crucial as it allows for dimensionality reduction and more efficient data manipulation. Additionally, we need to consolidate different vital signs that are sampled at different fixed rates and alarm logs that are event-driven and recorded only when predefined thresholds are exceeded. The steps of our approach are depicted in Fig. 2 and are explained in more detail in the next subsections. In the initial phase, data preprocessing converts the raw multivariate time series data into a symbolic representation in the form of letters, a format suitable for rule discovery, using Symbolic Aggregate approXimation (SAX) [21]. Subsequently, the encodings for each physiological variable and alarm are merged into a unified tabular representation. The tabular representation is then transformed into a sequence database using a sliding window transformation. Next, we use a state-of-the-art method to efficiently extract the top-k non-redundant sequential rules [9]. Our approach depends on several parameters, and we analyze their sensitivity. We propose an ensemble of rules discovered in multiple representations in Sect. 4.

3.1 Time Series Representation

SAX is a data-adaptive technique that transforms a time series into a symbolic sequence. It is used to effectively represent time series, as it allows dimensionality reduction of data while maintaining their original characteristics. The SAX procedure comprises three steps, depicted in Fig. 2. The first step involves applying Piecewise Aggregate Approximation (PAA) [20] to the original time series. PAA reduces the dimensionality of the time series by dividing it into segments of a predefined length W and representing such segments with their average value. Given the time series $\mathbf{S} = [s_0, s_1, ..., s_N]$, the resulting approximation is $\bar{\mathbf{S}} = [\bar{s}_0, \bar{s}_1, ..., \bar{s}_{N/W}]$, and the i_{th} element $\bar{s}_i$ of $\bar{\mathbf{S}}$ is obtained as follows:

$$\bar{s}_i = \frac{1}{W} \sum_{j=i \times W}^{(i+1) \times W} s_j. \tag{1}$$

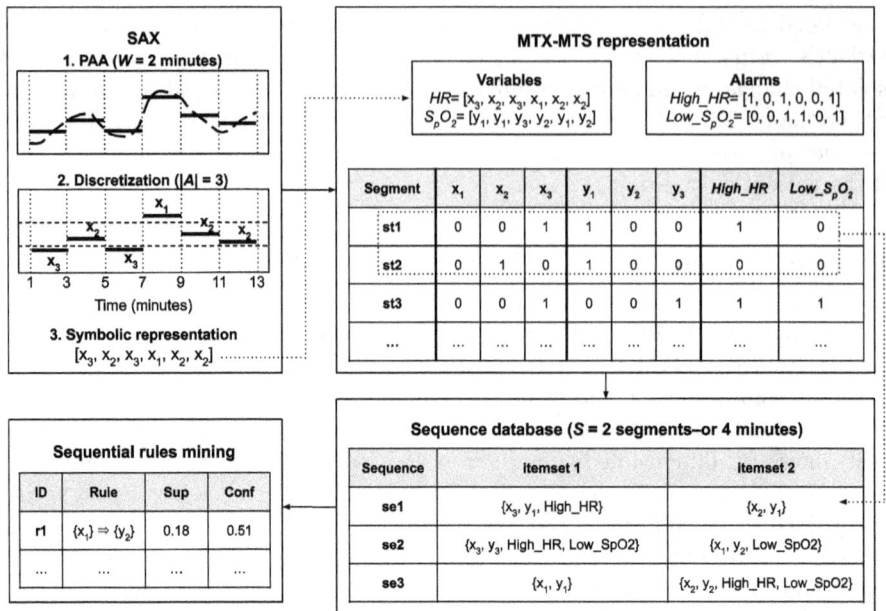

Fig. 2. Overview of our approach. The first step is a modified version of SAX to obtain a symbolic representation of each physiological time series. The second step consists of creating a joined tabular representation of physiological variables and alarms. The third steps consists of translating this representation into a sequence database, the proper input for rule mining (fourth step). The final result is a set of sequential rules. We vary the parameters for preprocessing, i.e. the segment length (W), alphabet size ($|\mathcal{A}|$), and sequence length (S).

W, which in Fig. 2 is 2 min, significantly affects the level of data compression and fidelity. The second step is the discretization of the time series, which consists of mapping the continuous values obtained from the PAA to an alphabet $\mathcal{A}$ with a given set of discrete symbols. Each average value from the PAA step is then assigned to a symbol based on its value. This mapping is performed using breakpoints that divide the distribution of the data into intervals, corresponding to each symbol in the alphabet. The canonical version of SAX partitions data into bins based on the assumption of a normal distribution. However, when data are not normally distributed, this can result in some value ranges being assigned more symbols than others, distorting the data structure. To avoid this, we used quantiles, ensuring that each interval contains the same number of observations. In this way, all parts of the signal contribute equally to the symbolic representation, preventing high-density regions from dominating the encoding and low-density regions from being overlooked. The final step in the SAX process involves converting the discretized values into a symbolic sequence. Each segment's symbol from the discretization step is concatenated to form a symbolic representation of the original time series. The resulting approximation is $\hat{\mathbf{S}} = [\hat{s}_0, \hat{s}_1, ..., \hat{s}_{N/W}]$. The symbolic representation significantly reduces the size and complexity of the data. Within the framework of encoding MTS, the SAX technique is applied individually to each variable. However, the parameters selected for the transformation are kept consistent across all variables. It is worth mentioning that we apply normalization across all patients rather than per patient to ensure that SAX binning captures meaningful patterns at the population level. This allows the sequential pattern mining algorithm to detect trends that are globally relevant rather than patient-specific variations.

3.2 Alarm Log Representation

The encoding of the alarm logs follows a similar method, without the need for SAX representation. Since alarms occur irregularly and can be triggered multiple times in short intervals, the most reasonable way to reduce the dimensionality of alarm logs is to divide them into segments of a predefined length W and represent each segment using a binary indicator that denotes whether at least one alarm of a given type occurred within that segment. Consider the original alarm logs for a specific alarm type, represented by $\mathbf{Z} = [z_0, z_1, ..., z_N]$, where z_t represents the presence (1) or absence (0) of this alarm type at time t. For each time segment of length W, we denote the presence/absence of alarms, regardless of the number of identical alarm occurrences, obtaining the approximation $\hat{\mathbf{Z}} = [\hat{z}_0, \hat{z}_1, ..., \hat{z}_{N/W}]$.

3.3 MXT-MTS Representation

Given our objective to analyze sequential rules in both alarms and patterns collectively, we need a unified encoding that represents all signals and alarms. Upon deriving the SAX representation for each variable individually, we transform the MTS into a unified representation. For each variable, a dummy version of the SAX representation is generated as a matrix, with rows representing time segments and columns indicating symbols. This approach facilitates the encoding of the presence (1) or absence (0) of symbols in each time segment, thereby enabling straightforward concatenation of multiple variables and alarms into a symbolized MXT-MTS (sMXT-MTS). The resulting representation consists of $\frac{N}{W}$ rows and $|M_v| \cdot |\mathcal{A}| + |M_a|$ columns, where M_v is the set of variables, $\mathcal{A}$ is the alphabet, and M_a is the set of alarm types. In Fig. 2, these sets are defined as $M_v = \{HF, S_pO_2\}$, $\mathcal{A} = \{x_1, x_2, x_3, y_1, y_2, y_3\}$, and $M_a = \{High\_HF, Low\_S_pO_2\}$. The notation $|\cdot|$ symbolizes the cardinality of a set. This representation is an intermediate step to summarize the data in intervals and reduce dimensionality. The following section illustrates the steps to obtain the final data format.

3.4 Encoding MTS and Alarm Logs into a Sequence Database

Sequential rule mining algorithms require a sequence database for input. As such, we need to convert the sMXT-MTS to a proper representation. The sequence database is organized temporally, with each row corresponding to a sequence of length S and containing itemsets representing subsequent segments of length W. Each itemset contains symbols of the sMXT-MTS present in the time frame of the corresponding segment. Within each itemset, symbols are treated as concurrent, lacking temporal precedence, yet the sequence of itemsets is crucial, as their order is instrumental in identifying sequential rules. Figure 2 shows the resulting sequence database. In the example, $S = 2$ segments (or 4 min), so we obtain sequences of two itemsets (representing 2 segments), where the events of itemset 1 happen before those of itemset 2, and each itemset can contain information about multiple signals (HF, S_pO_2) and alarms ($High\_HF$, $Low\_S_pO_2$). Intuitively, if the original data contain signals and events from multiple individuals, the final sequence database contains multiple sequences for each individual, where the number of sequences per individual depends on the number of recorded time points and S.

3.5 Sequential Rule Mining

We use a sequential rule mining technique that focuses on mining the top-K most frequent occurring non-redundant rules. This reduces the risk of rule explosion and enables control of the number of generated sequential rules. First, we define two representative measures to evaluate the candidate rules.

Definition 1. *The support of a rule $X \to Y$ is the relative frequency of the co-occurrence of X and Y, and is calculated by dividing the number of transactions containing both X and Y by the total number of transactions $|T|$.*

$$sup(X \to Y) = \frac{|\{q = [I_1, I_2, \ldots, I_n] \in T \mid X \subseteq I_{k_1} \wedge Y \subseteq I_{k_2} \wedge k_1 < k_2\}|}{|T|} \quad (2)$$

Definition 2. *The confidence of a rule measures the likelihood of the occurrence of the consequent event Y in all transactions that contain the antecedent event X.*

$$conf(X \to Y) = \frac{sup(X \cup Y)}{sup(X)}. \quad (3)$$

To discover sequential rules, we used TNS [9], an algorithm for discovering the top-K non-redundant sequential rules appearing in a sequence database. The problems of top-K sequential rule mining and redundancy are defined as follows.

Definition 3. *A rule mining algorithm discovers a set $\mathcal{L}$ containing K rules in transaction database $\mathcal{D}$ such that:*

$$\forall r \in \mathcal{L} : conf(r) \geq minconf$$
$$\forall r \in \mathcal{L} : \nexists s \in \mathcal{L} : conf(s) \geq minconf \wedge sup(s) > sup(r). \quad (4)$$

This is in contrast to most rule mining algorithms that require that the user set a minimum support threshold parameter that is hard to set, i.e., usually users set it by trial and error. In addition, we avoid many redundant rules, with potentially thousands of variations of rules having the same support and confidence. The following definition eliminates redundancy in results by keeping similar rules that have a smaller antecedent and a larger consequent.

Definition 4. *A rule $r_a : X \to Y$ is redundant with respect to another rule $r_b : X_1 \to Y_1$ if and only if $conf(r_a) = conf(r_b) \wedge sup(r_a) = sup(r_b) \wedge X_1 \subseteq X \wedge Y \subseteq Y_1$.*

The TNS algorithm is based on a depth-first search procedure. TNS is an approximate algorithm that generates non-redundant rules, which might not always be the exact top-K non-redundant rules. TNS depends on a parameter δ, which can be used to improve the chance that the result is exact (the higher the delta value, the higher the chance that the result will be exact), i.e., it allows to make a trade-off between accuracy and runtime performance. In our setting δ was left to default, in all experiments approximate rule mining took less than 1 h.

4 Case Study: Multivariate Time Series and Alarm Logs Form ICU

4.1 Data Collection

We collected data from Philips hospital monitors installed in the Intensive Care Unit (ICU) of AZ Groeninge Secondary Care Hospital in Kortrijk, Belgium, over a seven month period in 2021, for more than 1000 patients. The hospital server stored all monitor signals and alarm logs from bedside patient monitors with a sampling rate of 0.2 Hz. These logs contained the timestamp, ID, alarm category, and nature of the alarm. As for the monitoring signals, we focused on Heart Frequency (HF), Respiratory Frequency (RF), systolic, diastolic, and mean Arterial Blood Pressure (ABP_s, ABP_d, ABP_m), end-tidal carbon dioxide ($etCO_2$), and oxygen saturation (S_pO_2). The alarm categories belong to physiological or technical monitor alarms. Physiological alarms included mainly threshold alarms such as $High\_HR$ or $Low\_S_pO_2$. The physiological thresholds for generating these alarms could be a standard set of values or modified by the medical team based on the specific clinical profile of the patients, but this information was not available to us. The medical data used in this study are confidential and cannot be shared due to privacy regulations.

4.2 Data Preprocessing

We sampled signals and alarm logs with a frequency of 2 measurements per minute (0.033 Hz). Furthermore, we excluded patients with less than 6 h of recording, patients with less than 5 variables recorded among HF, RF, ABP_s, ABP_d, ABP_m, $etCO_2$ and SpO_2. Moreover, since we were specifically interested in alarms, we excluded patients without alarms recorded, and included only time frames within five minutes before and after the alarm. Finally, we excluded all alarms that occurred in the same time frame as technical alarms to exclude potential biases in the discovered rules. Since sequential rule mining techniques naturally handle missing values, and all signals had a percentage of missing values lower than 6% (except $etCO2$), we did not impute the data set. We decided to binarize the variable $etCO2$ in present/absent as it is an indicator of intubation. The final cohort comprised 604 patients, 7 signals, and 31 alarm types, totaling more than 3700 h of recorded data, 16 million data points, and 3 million alarms.

4.3 Discovering Sequential Rules

We applied our method to the preprocessed dataset. We run the experiments in Python 3.10 on a laptop with a 2.60 GHz 6 cores CPU with 32 GB of memory. The operating system used in this machine is Ubuntu 20.04.6 LTS. We used the TNS Java implementation from the SPMF library [7][1], available through a Python wrapper[2]. The code is available upon request to the corresponding author.

Table 1. Parameter ranges for pre-processing. For sequential rule mining we use default values.

Parameter	Description	Value(s)
$|\mathcal{A}|$	Alphabet size for SAX	[3, 5, 7]
W	Segment length for SAX and alarm grouping (minutes)	[1, 3, 5]
S	Length sliding window (minutes)	[20, 40, 60]
min_conf	Minimum confidence threshold	0.5
K	# of sequential rules	1000

Hyper-parameters. Table 1 lists the parameters for preprocessing and sequential rule mining. We used all parameter combinations to perform a sensitivity analysis and extract different rule variants. The size of the alphabet $|\mathcal{A}|$ determines the granularity of the representation of time series. The length of the sequence S affects the capacity to capture long-term dependencies within the data. Longer sequences work as upper bound for identifying patterns, allowing us to identify both patterns close to each other and patterns that span in a longer time period. The choice of segment length W is important to capture the trend of the signal correctly. W is also relevant to the representation of alarm logs, as often alarms of the same type occur in clusters, close to each other, and choosing a small W would capture redundant patterns. For sequential rule mining we use default values for min_conf and K.

---

[1] http://www.philippe-fournier-viger/spmf/.
[2] https://pypi.org/project/spmf/.

Sensitivity Analysis Parameters. There is an inherent trade-off between timeliness and accuracy when selecting S. Although increasing S increases confidence, it can reduce the clinical utility of the rules discovered. For example, an algorithm might detect events that repeat in the same order over a 24-h sequence, but their apparent co-occurrence might be due to their high prevalence in the dataset, rather than a true temporal relationship. As expected, the sensitivity analysis revealed that the confidence was proportional to S and inversely proportional to W. Furthermore, the effect of $|\mathcal{A}|$ is not negligible. With increasing alphabet size, the number of observed patterns containing alarms increases and confidence decreases.

4.4 Rule Interpretation

We extracted 1000 rules for each combination of parameter values. To evaluate the extracted rules, we selected the 50 rules with highest support and directly inspected them. We report a selection of both trivial and interesting rules and discuss their medical relevance in Table 2. First, we discuss our ensemble approach, since the reported rules are discovered using different representations of the data, i.e. using a combination of values for preprocessing parameters as shown in Table 1.

Ensemble of Sequential Rules. We use multiple parameter values for preprocessing, thereby reporting rules spanning both short and long periods and considering different granularities of physiological variables. That is, we mined sequential rules using all combinations of $|\mathcal{A}|$, W and S, and aggregated the resulting rules. It is important to note that multiple rules or similar variations were found for different combinations of the parameters we tested. Intuitively, the support and confidence changed slightly as the parameters affected the itemset construction. We discuss the effect of each parameter independently:

- By varying S we discover sequential rules in a varying time horizon. Existing sequential rule mining algorithms enable a temporal constraint that is enforced on the maximal duration of a rule [4]. In contrast, by varying S we enable domain-experts to inspect both short-term and long-term rules that are of interest. Moreover, we can filter redundant rules automatically, i.e., rules discovered in a short window are also discovered using a longer window, while the opposite is not true. In our case we discover rules where the gap between the condition and consequent event is at most 60 min.
- The choice of binning strategy for continuous signals is determined by $|\mathcal{A}|$ and has a direct impact on the extracted rules in two key ways. First, it influenced the granularity and relevance of the rules: using a coarse binning (e.g., 3 bins for heart frequency) captures broad trends but may miss finer physiological variations, whereas a finer binning (e.g., 7 bins) allows for more specific conditions but increases rule set complexity. Second, binning affected support and confidence: rules derived from higher granularity bins tend to be more specific and potentially more clinically meaningful, but they also

become rarer in the dataset, leading to lower support and confidence. These rules may apply only to specific subgroups of patients or reflect less frequent but highly relevant clinical conditions.
- W determines the smoothing of continuous vital signs and has a similar effect on granularity to $|\mathcal{A}|$ but in the time domain. With lower values of W we detect peaks and sudden changes, while with higher values we focus on increasing and decreasing trends. Using W_{min}, i.e. 1 min, we take the average of 2 values, while using W_{max} we take the average of 10 raw time series measurements.

Table 2. Selection of trivial and rules of interest for the intubation alarm. We run our method with different combinations of $|\mathcal{A}|$, W, and S. Event codes are HF (heart frequency), RF (respiratory frequency), and systolic, diastolic and mean arterial blood pressure (ABP_s, ABP_d, ABP_m). Conf. confidence, Sup. support.

ID	Rule	Conf.	Sup.
(a)	$\{HF\_low\} \rightarrow \{HF < 60\}$	0.62	0.11
(b)	$\{ABP_s < 100\} \rightarrow \{ABP_s\_low\}$	0.61	0.30
(c)	$\{S_pO_2 < 91\} \rightarrow \{S_pO_2\_low\}$	0.57	0.30
(d)	$\{ABP_m > 93, ABP_s > 156\} \rightarrow \{ABP_s\_high\}$	0.50	0.13
(e)	$\{HF < 60, 28 < RF < 31\} \rightarrow \{intubation\}$	0.55	0.02
(f)	$\{74 < HF < 86, RF > 30\} \rightarrow \{intubation\}$	0.53	0.03
(g)	$\{ABP_d < 47, RF > 30\} \rightarrow \{intubation\}$	0.52	0.05
(h)	$\{ABP_d < 45, ABP_m < 64, RF > 31\} \rightarrow \{intubation\}$	0.51	0.02
(i)	$\{intubation, ABP_d < 45, 91 < S_pO_2 < 93\} \rightarrow \{ABP_m < 64\}$	0.51	0.02

We make a distinction between medically trivial and interesting rules, specific to intubation, and provide the following interpretation explaining their prevalence and medical significance.

Trivial Rules. Rules (b), (c), and (d) are trivial, as they reflect the standard response to vital signs that cross a predefined threshold and are commonly embedded in the ICU monitor, to alert physicians to possible clinical deterioration. The low confidence can be explained by two main reasons: the possibility for physicians to manually change the threshold to make it more suitable for specific patient profiles and the possibility to turn off an alarm if it is not needed. Rule (a) depicts a scenario where the alarm goes off first and subsequently the vital sign is still low. Rules such as this one were found relatively often, and although they might appear counterintuitive, multiple reasons could contribute to their presence with a relatively high confidence. First, the vital sign can still vary after the alarm goes off, and even if doctors take action, it might take time before the value returns to normal ranges. Moreover, the threshold can be set differently after the alarm goes off or the alarm can be switched off.

Interesting Rules. In addition, we inspected patterns that include *intubation* for mechanical ventilation, which was chosen as an event because it is one of the highest-risk procedures in the ICU and was straightforward to extrapolate from the data. Intubation is an intervention performed when a patient cannot maintain adequate gas exchange and it can be planned or unforeseen. In the latter case, it can lead to negative consequences for the patient and ultimately to increased mortality if not performed in a timely manner. Intubation is usually required in cases of acute respiratory failure, shock, or neurological deterioration. The scenarios that can lead to intubation can be, for example, severe hypoxia (low S_pO_2) in patients with worsening oxygenation despite oxygen therapy; hypercapnic respiratory failure (elevated CO_2 levels and high RF) in conditions such as COPD exacerbation; cardiogenic or septic shock, usually accompanied by low ABP in addition to elevated HF as a compensatory response to hypoxia, hypotension, or metabolic acidosis. Rules (e) to (i) were selected and assessed to determine whether our method could extract clinically plausible patterns and thus hold potential utility for future applications. Rule (e) associates intubation with a combination of bradycardia and mild tachypnea, which could indicate early respiratory failure. Rule (g) indicates hypotension in combination with tachypnea, which could be related to shock or respiratory distress. Both rules (e) and (g) could be improved in clinical relevance and usefulness if included information regarding blood gases, which were not available in the dataset, or oxygen saturation (S_pO_2). Rule (f) describes patients with normal HF and moderate tachypnea and is too broad to be useful to predict intubation. Rule (h) indicates more severe hypotension and tachypnea, which could be representative of septic and cardiogenic shock with respiratory distress and is associated with a higher likelihood of intubation. Finally, rule (i) suggests that intubated patients have a low ABP_m when they are still mildly hypoxic, but it is an observational rule rather than a predictive rule. Surprisingly, patterns related to the event of intubation lack oxygeneation in favor of HF, RF and ABP. Moreover, due to limitations related to available data, we missed important markers such as $PaCO_2$, pH, and information about neurological condition such as the Glasgow coma scale.

Sequential Rule Clusters. Finally, we examined how frequently sequential rules (without and with alarms) appeared within individual patients and across multiple patients. To achieve this, we first extracted the top-50 rules, obtained with constant $|\mathcal{A}| = 7$, while exploring all the possible combinations of parameter values for W and S. To simplify the calculation of rule occurrences per patient and across patients, we focused on a single parameter configuration ($W = 5$, $S = 60$), ensuring consistency in how the patients were encoded into a sequential database. For each rule, we counted the number of patients where the rule appeared at least once, and, for these patients only, also the average number of times the rule appeared in each patient. Figure 3 shows the distribution of the rules in terms of the number of patients and the average number of occurrences per patient. The figure allows to distinguish "general" and "cluster-specific" rules, where the former apply to the majority of the population but are less specific, while the latter apply to specific sub-populations. The presence of "cluster-specific" rules suggests that patients might be categorized into subgroups with different temporal patterns, potentially relevant for clinical decision support. In our setting, rules exclusively containing signals are more general, while rules containing alarms tend to appear in fewer patients but with a higher number of occurrences per patient, and might be of interest to personalize alarm settings to specific patient profiles.

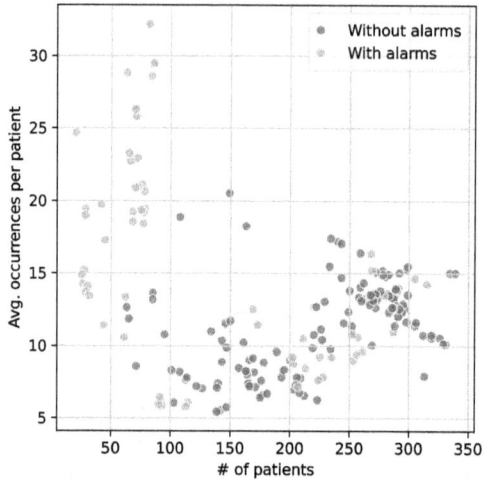

Fig. 3. Each dot represents a rule. The x-axis represents the number of patients for which the sequential rule holds, and the y-axis represents the average rule occurrences within each of these patients.

5 Limitations

Despite the potential usefulness of our framework and the relevance of the application, we must acknowledge multiple limitations of this work. First, ICU monitors generate high-frequency data that are susceptible to sensor artifacts and noise. Although the data were smoothed during preprocessing, this may not have been sufficient to prevent outliers from affecting the extracted rules. Moreover, although one of our core motivations was to address the problem of false alarms, our dataset could not be linked to clinically verified alarm annotations. Thus, we were unable to quantify false alarms directly. In addition, the framework was applied to a retrospective single-center cohort of patients from a Belgian hospital, limiting its generalizability to other ICU settings with different monitoring systems, patient populations, and clinical protocols. Due to privacy constraints, we are currently unable to publicly release the dataset. While we filtered rules using support and confidence thresholds, their interpretation still relied on expert review. Furthermore, although our approach identifies frequent and clinically plausible sequential rules, it does not establish causal relationships between physiological signals and alarms or events. Finally, the nature of the alarms based on thresholds that are predefined but easily changed by clinicians to fit the patient profile, could introduce biases into the discovered alarms. Future work should include the use of multiple cohorts of patients from different hospitals. Efforts should also focus on linking signals and alarms with clinically valid annotations to enable verification of false alarms and to quantify the usefulness of the proposed rules. In addition, future studies should investigate the use of additional interestingness metrics and domain-specific constraints to automatically prioritize informative rules.

6 Conclusions

In this work, we introduce a novel framework for mining patterns in multivariate ICU signals and alarms, providing a data-driven approach to understanding alarm triggers and physiological trends. By applying the framework to a case study from a Belgian hospital, we demonstrate its potential to extract clinically meaningful patterns that may help reduce alarm fatigue, optimize the early warning system, and support the decision-making process in the ICU. The extracted patterns are consistent with clinical expectations, but also highlight potential limitations of current ICU alarm systems, such as false positive alarms and threshold-based dependencies. This work serves as a basis for further refinement of ICU alarm systems by integrating multiple signals and creating alarms that provide a meaningful indication of the overall state of the patient.

Acknowledgments. M.V. and L.F. are funded through the Research Fund Flanders (project G0A2120N and grant 12B0V24N, respectively). The authors also acknowledge the Flemish Government (AI Research Program).

Declaration of Competing Interest. The authors have no competing interests to declare that are relevant to the content of this article.

References

1. Agrawal, R.: Fast algorithms for mining association rules. VLDB (1994)
2. Alsuyayfi, S., Alanazi, A.: Impact of clinical alarms on patient safety from nurses' perspective. Inf. Med. Unlocked **32**, 101047 (2022)
3. Bitan, Y., O'Connor, M.F.: Correlating data from different sensors to increase the positive predictive value of alarms: an empiric assessment. F1000Research **1** (2012)
4. Cule, B., Feremans, L., Goethals, B.: Efficiently mining cohesion-based patterns and rules in event sequences. Data Min. Knowl. Disc. **33**(4), 1125–1182 (2019). https://doi.org/10.1007/s10618-019-00628-0
5. Cvach, M.: Monitor alarm fatigue: an integrative review. Biomed. Instrum. Technol. **46**(4), 268–277 (2012)

6. Feremans, L., Vercruyssen, V., Cule, B., Meert, W., Goethals, B.: Pattern-based anomaly detection in mixed-type time series. In: Brefeld, U., Fromont, E., Hotho, A., Knobbe, A., Maathuis, M., Robardet, C. (eds.) ECML PKDD 2019. LNCS (LNAI), vol. 11906, pp. 240–256. Springer, Cham (2020). https://doi.org/10.1007/978-3-030-46150-8_15
7. Fournier-Viger, P., et al.: The SPMF open-source data mining library version 2. In: Berendt, B., et al. (eds.) ECML PKDD 2016. LNCS (LNAI), vol. 9853, pp. 36–40. Springer, Cham (2016). https://doi.org/10.1007/978-3-319-46131-1_8
8. Fournier-Viger, P., Nkambou, R., Tseng, V.S.M.: RuleGrowth: mining sequential rules common to several sequences by pattern-growth. In: Proceedings of the 2011 ACM Symposium on Applied Computing, pp. 956–961 (2011)
9. Fournier-Viger, P., Tseng, V.S.: TNS: mining top-K non-redundant sequential rules. In: Proceedings of the 28th Annual ACM Symposium on Applied Computing, pp. 164–166 (2013)
10. Frankenthal, H., et al.: Perceived reliability of medical device alarms–a major determinant of medical errors driven by frozen medical thinking. Int. J. Qual. Health Care **34**(1), mzac009 (2022)
11. Gul, G., Intepeler, S.S., Bektas, M.: The effect of interventions made in intensive care units to reduce alarms: a systematic review and meta-analysis study. Intensive Crit. Care Nurs. **75**, 103375 (2023)
12. Hever, G., Cohen, L., O'Connor, M.F., Matot, I., Lerner, B., Bitan, Y.: Machine learning applied to multi-sensor information to reduce false alarm rate in the ICU. J. Clin. Monit. Comput. **34**, 339–352 (2020)
13. Huo, J., Wung, S., Roveda, J., Li, A.: Reducing false alarms in intensive care units: a scoping review. Exploratory Res. Hypothesis Med. **8**(1), 57–64 (2023)
14. Imhoff, M., Kuhls, S.: Alarm algorithms in critical care monitoring. Anesth. Analg. **102**(5), 1525–1537 (2006)
15. Imhoff, M., Kuhls, S., Gather, U., Fried, R.: Smart alarms from medical devices in the or and ICU. Best Pract. Res. Clin. Anaesthesiol. **23**(1), 39–50 (2009)
16. Jones, K.: Alarm fatigue a top patient safety hazard (2014)
17. Joshi, R., Pul, C., Atallah, L., Feijs, L., Huffel, S., Andriessen, P.: Pattern discovery in critical alarms originating from neonates under intensive care. Physiol. Meas. **37**(4), 564–579 (2016)
18. Kang, S.M., Wagacha, P.W.: Extracting diagnosis patterns in electronic medical records using association rule mining. Int. J. Comput. Appl. **108**(15) (2014)
19. Karaca, M., Alvarado, M.M., Gahrooei, M.R., Bihorac, A., Pardalos, P.M.: Frequent pattern mining from multivariate time series data. Expert Syst. Appl. **194**, 116435 (2022)
20. Keogh, E., Chakrabarti, K., Pazzani, M., Mehrotra, S.: Dimensionality reduction for fast similarity search in large time series databases. Knowl. Inf. Syst. **3**, 263–286 (2001)
21. Lin, J., Keogh, E., Wei, L., Lonardi, S.: Experiencing sax: a novel symbolic representation of time series. Data Min. Knowl. Disc. **15**, 107–144 (2007)
22. Nguyen, D.T., Khuat, B.D.L.: Discovery of temporal association rules in multivariate time series. Int. J. Appl. Eng. Res. **14**(1), 79–84 (2019)
23. Paine, C.W., et al.: Systematic review of physiologic monitor alarm characteristics and pragmatic interventions to reduce alarm frequency. J. Hosp. Med. **11**(2), 136–144 (2016)
24. Park, H., Jung, J.Y.: SAX-ARM: deviant event pattern discovery from multivariate time series using symbolic aggregate approximation and association rule mining. Expert Syst. Appl. **141**, 112950 (2020)

Continuous Learning of Ordinal User Preferences on Wearable Devices

Simón Weinberger[1,2(✉)], Jairo Cugliari[2], and Aurélie Le Cain[1]

[1] affiliate of EssilorLuxottica, Essilor International, 39 Building Jean Baptiste Oudry, 94000 Créteil, France
weinbes@essilor.fr
[2] Laboratoire ERIC, Pierre Mendès France, 5 Avenue, 69500 Bron, France
jairo.cugliari@univ-lyon2.fr

Abstract. Wearable devices allow collecting data at an individual level, which can be used to propose an unseen degree of personalization for a broad domain of applications. For instance, we focus on electrochromic frames that allow to manually change the lens' tint, or automatically, based on an ambient light sensor. We aim to use the user's interactions with his frame to adapt this automatic mode to better consider his preferences. From a technical standpoint, this is a difficult task, as prediction and estimation cannot be done separately. That is why we approach this industrial problem from a reinforcement learning perspective: a policy must control the tint class in such a way that the number of user interactions is minimized. A particularity of this problem is that there is an inherent notion of order between the finite proposed tint classes, as some are darker than others. The usual Boltzmann parametrization does not account for this. Thus, we develop and implement policy gradient methods for ordinal policies. Using a simulation setting, we show that ignoring the ordinal structure of the response variables yields a suboptimal strategy. Additionally, we tested this technique with real users in controlled conditions; as the tint-control mode updated, the number of user interactions decreased. At last, using ordinal policies can be adapted to a deep reinforcement learning context, solving classic problems with continuous actions using discretization of this space.

Keywords: Reinforcement Learning · On-policy Policy Gradient Methods · Ordinal regression · Wearables

1 Introduction

Wearable devices have revolutionized the way we interact with technology, offering personalized experiences tailored to individual preferences and needs [16]. From tracking fitness goals [8] to monitoring health metrics [13], wearables

Supplementary Information The online version contains supplementary material available at https://doi.org/10.1007/978-3-032-06118-8_5.

have become indispensable companions in our daily lives. However, the dynamic nature of user preferences and habits presents a challenge in maintaining optimal performance over time. As users' needs evolve, the effectiveness of pre-defined models and algorithms may diminish, highlighting the necessity for continuous learning mechanisms.

Traditional machine learning approaches often struggle to adapt to the changing preferences observed in wearable device users; moreover, the inherent constraints of wearable devices, such as limited computational resources and battery life, further exacerbate this challenge [17]. In industrial applications, where reliability and robustness are paramount, the need to fortify decision-making processes becomes even more pronounced.

In this research, we propose leveraging Reinforcement Learning (RL) techniques to facilitate continuous learning of ordinal user preferences on wearable devices. By formulating the learning problem as one of policy optimization, we aim to capture the nuanced ranking of user preferences. To accommodate the constraints of wearable devices, we integrate a generalized vectorial linear model that accounts for resource limitations and computational efficiency.

Additionally, our proposed framework can also be used in a Deep Reinforcement Learning (DRL) context to solve classical continuous action RL problems by discretizing the set of actions into a finite and ordered set of actions. Doing so yields similar results than using continuous actions.

1.1 A General Learning Setting for Ordinal User Preferences

Let us consider a system that pilots automatically a setting of a wearable device, using the wearable's sensors. In addition, let us suppose that there are $K \in \mathbb{N}$ settings and there exists an order relationship between these categories. The particular setting will be called level. Additionally, the user may interact with the wearable and manually adjust the setting at any moment.

Ideally, the system pilots the setting in a way that provides the best user experience. As a measure of user experience, it is reasonable to use the number of interactions or the eventual difference between the system-chosen and user-chosen levels. Indeed, if the system is well adapted for the user, the user should not manually choose a level often, and inversely if the system is ill-adapted.

We formulate this problem in a RL setting. The state space $\mathcal{S}$ corresponds to the measures of the wearable device, the action space $\mathcal{A}$ corresponds to the possible setting levels and the reward space $\mathcal{R}$ is either a penalty if the user manually changed the level or the eventual absolute value difference between the system-proposed and user-chosen levels.

The data collection process would be as follows: the wearable's sensors collect a measure *(state)*. Based on that measure, the system proposes a new level to the user *(action)*. Then the user would either accept the proposed level or choose another level *(reward)*. The objective is to have a system that proposes levels that are often accepted by the user or would be close to the levels the user prefers. This process would be repeated at each instant for a certain amount of time (for example, a day), creating an episode τ of length $T \in \mathbb{N}$,

$$\tau = (s_t, a_t, r_t)_{t=0}^T \quad ; \quad s_t \in \mathcal{S},\, a_t \in \mathcal{A},\, r_t \in \mathcal{R}.$$

As in standard RL [21], we suppose the state-reward transitions are governed by the distribution defined by

$$p(s', r|s, a) = \mathbb{P}(S_{t+1} = s', R_{t+1} = r | S_t = s, A_t = a).$$

And episodes verify the Markov hypothesis:

$$\mathbb{P}(S_{t+1} = s', R_{t+1} = r | S_t = s, A_t = a, \ldots, S_0, A_0) = p(s', r|s, a).$$

The tuple $(\mathcal{S}, \mathcal{A}, \mathcal{R}, p)$ is a Markov Decision Process (MDP) [21]. Let us note $\mathcal{P}(\mathcal{A})$ the set of probability distributions over the action space $\mathcal{A}$, at each step, actions are taken by according to a policy: $\pi(\cdot|s_t) \in \mathcal{P}(\mathcal{A})$. For a given discount factor $\gamma \in [0, 1[$, action $a \in \mathcal{A}$ and state $s \in \mathcal{S}$ and a policy π, we define the state-action value function, $Q^\pi(s, a)$ and state value function $V^\pi(s)$:

$$Q^\pi(s,a) = \mathbb{E}_\pi \left(\sum_{t=0}^T \gamma^t R_t | S_0 = s, A_0 = a \right) ; \quad V^\pi(s) = \mathbb{E}_\pi \left(\sum_{t=0}^T \gamma^t R_t | S_0 = s \right).$$

Additionally, we suppose that the policy belongs to a given parametric space:

$$\pi \in \{\pi_\theta : \mathcal{S} \to \mathcal{P}(\mathcal{A}) | \theta \in \Theta \subset \mathbb{R}^d\}.$$

In this article, the policy families of interest are the Boltzmann distribution, also known as softmax or multinomial distribution, and policies defined by the cumulative ordinal model. Both of these allow a policy to choose a level, the first family does not consider the order between levels, the latter does. Let ν be any initial state distribution, the goal of policy optimization is to find the maximum of the objective function $J(\cdot)$:

$$J(\theta) = \mathbb{E}_{\substack{a_t \sim \pi_\theta(\cdot|s_t) \\ s_0 \sim \nu}} \left(\sum_{t=0}^T \gamma^t R_t \right) ; \quad \theta \in \Theta.$$

It is worth noting that the problem of parametrizing policies is orthogonal to the method used for policy optimization. Most policy-based methods, or actor-critic methods, can be adapted for different types of policies.

1.2 Electrochromic Adaptative Automatic Mode

In our industrial application, we chose to work with smart lenses, which admits some kind of customization. EssilorLuxottica is developing a smart eyewear equipped with electrochromic lenses. The tint of this eyewear can change by passing an electric signal, allowing the user to choose one tint among four: C_0, C_1, C_2, C_3. There is an inherent order relationship between these classes, as some are clearer than others. There exists an automatic mode for these frames that controls the tint by using measures from an Ambient Light Sensor (ALS) and comparing these values to three predefined, ordered thresholds $\rho_1 < \rho_2 < \rho_3$. If the ALS measure is below ρ_1, the clearest tint (C_0) is chosen, if the value lays between ρ_1 and ρ_2, C_1 is chosen, if the value is between ρ_2 and ρ_3, C_2 is chosen and if the value is greater than ρ_3 the darkest tint (C_3) is chosen. This tint control could be used to create a *hybrid mode*: the tint is controlled as previously described, except when the user manually changes the frame's tint, when this happens the automatic control is disabled for a certain amount of time or until the situation changes.

In previous work, we studied how to personalize the tint control mode using labeled data issued from the manual usage of these smart lenses, adopting a supervised approach [26]. In contrast, this article is about how to personalize this hybrid mode so that the user's preferences are considered using observations collected while in hybrid mode. We do so applying the RL paradigm, as described in Sect. 1.1.

For this particular problem, we use only the ALS measures, and because the eye reacts to light on a logarithmic scale [24], we consider the state space as the log 10 of the ALS measures (which are between 0 and 5). The set of actions is the set of tint classes. The reward is -1 if there was a user interaction and 0 otherwise. Concretely:

$$\mathcal{S} = [0, 5] \; ; \; \mathcal{A} = \{C_0, C_1, C_2, C_3\} \; ; \; \mathcal{R} = \{-1, 0\}.$$

1.3 Main Contributions

We introduce a family of policies taking actions on a finite, totally ordered action space. These policies are an adaptation of linear ordinal regression models [3] and CORAL neural networks [4] into a RL setting.

We provide necessary conditions assuring that the policy has a form of smoothness. We reparametrize the parameters of this model, allowing to optimize in an unconstrained space. This is done in a way that guarantees the smoothness of the policy and respects constraints over the parameters of the policy. We use this to implement policy optimization using REINFORCE, NPG, TRPO and PPO for this policy.

We demonstrate that, in certain scenarios where there is a notion of order among actions, using an ordinal policy converges faster to better policies than using a softmax distribution (Sect. 3.1). This suggests that considering the notion of order among action can be beneficial for tackling real-world problems.

We tested this method with real electrochromic prototypes worn by real users, in a controlled setting (Sect. 3.2). The results of this study are positive: as the tint control parameters are updated, the number of user interactions diminishes.

We show that using an ordinal policy instead of a continuous action policy can perform as well as a traditional continuous action policy in standard RL benchmark environments (Sect. 3.3).

1.4 Related Work

In a supervised context, ordinal regression models were introduced by McCullagh [15]; those models belong to the more general family of Vector Generalized Additive Models (VGAM), which were introduced by Yee and Wild [28]. This approach can be extended in even a more general setting: the predictor can, in fact, be parametrized by a neural network. Indeed, ordinal regression can be achieved using binary extended classification, as explained by Li and Lin [14], allowing to perform ordinal regression using any binary classification algorithm. This was used to implement COnsistent RAnk Logits (CORAL) in neural networks [4] and Conditional Ordinal Regression for neural networks (CORN) [20]. Both methods augment the training data set to encode an ordinal regression problem as a binary classification problem, and then train a neural network using a particular loss function that assures that the obtained rank logits are ordered.

In a RL context, the parametrization of policies taking action or ordered sets has received little to no attention. Although there are some articles that tackle solving continuous actions by using discretization, for example, this was done by Seyde et al. [19] and Tang and Agrawal [22] to solve environments with continuous actions, which achieved state-of-the-art convergence rates in different benchmark environments. The first article used a dichotomous action space, using higher and lower actions as actions; the latter used a discretization with more classes by implementing a policy inspired by "stick-breaking" [12]. Both approaches rely on defining neural networks outputting logits to take actions, the latter article then accordingly defines a notion of order between classes (Eq. 4 of [22]). Although not directly linked to ordinal actions, efforts have been made to consider policies taking actions on structured continuous actions spaces, as presented by Wu et al. [27], or considering monotonic policies as explained by Feng et al. [6], relying on monotonic neural networks [25]. Either way, using monotonic or structured policies, yielded more stable numerical results.

We propose using a different parametrization over ordinal actions, based on a thresholded model [14], which is a latent variable model relying on a scalar predictor and ordered thresholds. Unlike the method proposed by Tang and Agrawal [22], our parametrization enforces the notion of order among actions, which is desirable for our industrial application. For instance, if the state space is defined by ALS measurements, the scalar predictor is proportional to these. As a result, the predicted classes will follow an ordered structure: if the proportionality coefficient is positive, an increase in ALS values will correspond to the prediction of progressively darker classes.

2 Theory: Ordinal Policies

For simplicity, in this section, we first present an ordinal policy for one-dimensional actions, present some results and finally extend it to multivariate ordinal actions, by factorizing across dimensions.

2.1 Definitions

We consider the situation where the action space has a finite number of elements $\mathcal{A} = \{a_k\}_{k=1}^{K}$, with K being a natural number greater or equal than three, and there exists an order relationship between actions:

$$a_1 < a_2 < \ldots < a_{K-1} < a_K. \tag{1}$$

For any natural numbers $a, b \in \mathbb{N}$, let us note $[\![a, b]\!]$ the set of whole numbers between a and b. Without losing generality, we suppose $\mathcal{A} = [\![1, K]\!]$. In the general discrete setting, the only way to parametrize a distribution is to use the discrete probability distribution, using a multinomial model over logits for each class, for example. In the ordinal context, there is another possible parametrization: using the cumulative distribution function, which is well-defined. Let us consider a function $g_\omega : \mathcal{S} \to \mathbb{R}$, parametrized by a weight, $\omega \in \Omega$, and consider $K - 1$ ordered thresholds $(\tau_k)_{k=1}^{K-1}$:

$$\tau_1 < \tau_2 < \ldots < \tau_{K-2} < \tau_{K-1}.$$

Let $\sigma(x) = (1 + \exp(-x))^{-1}$ be the sigmoid function. A policy π over the set $\mathcal{A}$ is defined by the relation:

$$\sigma^{-1}\left(\mathbb{P}(A \leq j | S = s)\right) = \tau_j - g_\omega(s). \tag{2}$$

Indeed, using the convention $\tau_0 = -\infty$ and $\tau_K = \infty$, Eq. (2) induces a probability distribution on the action space $\mathcal{A}$:

$$\pi(a|s) = \sigma(\tau_a - g_\omega(s)) - \sigma(\tau_{a-1} - g_\omega(s)) \quad ; \quad a \in \mathcal{A}.$$

It is worth noting that because the thresholds $(\tau_j)_{j=1}^{K-1}$ are ordered, the obtained cumulative probabilities are assured to be ordered:

$$\mathbb{P}(A \leq 0 \, S = s) < \mathbb{P}(A \leq 1 \, S = s) < \ldots < \mathbb{P}(A \leq K - 1 \, S = s).$$

Definition (2) is equivalent to the following latent variable relationship:

$$\begin{cases} A^* = g_\omega(s) + e \quad ; \quad e \sim \text{Logistic}(0, 1), \\ A = j \quad \Leftrightarrow \quad \tau_{j-1} < A^* \leq \tau_j. \end{cases} \tag{3}$$

This latter definition is more interpretable: the function g_ω is a map between the state space and $\mathbb{R}$, when it is high, the policy will often take high actions, when low, the policy will take low actions. Let us note $\Delta_{K-1} \subset \mathbb{R}^{K-1}$ the set of ordered thresholds:

$$\Delta_{K-1} = \left\{ (x_1, \ldots, x_{K-1}) \in \mathbb{R}^{K-1} | x_{i+1} - x_i > 0, \quad \forall i \in [\![1, K-1]\!] \right\}.$$

Definition 1. *A policy π is said to be an ordinal policy if it verifies Eq. (2). This parametric family is parametrized by $\Theta = \Omega \times \Delta_{K-1}$.*

It is worth noting that unlike normal and multinomial distributions, this ordinal distribution is not in the exponential family, and therefore it is not straightforward that usual policy improvement methods work with this ordinal policy.

Definition 2. *Let β be a positive real number and a function $f\colon \mathbb{R}^p \to \mathbb{R}$, f is said to be β-smooth, if its gradient is β-Lipschitz. Namely, $\forall a, b \in \mathbb{R}^p$:*

$$\|\nabla f(a) - \nabla f(b)\|_2 \leq \beta \|a - b\|_2.$$

In general, a suitable condition for gradient optimization techniques is that the function to optimize must be β-smooth. For instance, in the RL context, the improvement of policies with NPG, depends on the logarithm of the probability density function of the policy being β-smooth (Theorem 20 in [2]).

Definition 3. *A policy is said to be β-smooth if $\theta \mapsto \log \pi_\theta(.|s)$ is β-smooth for every $s \in \mathcal{S}$.*

It is straightforward to prove that a policy is β-smooth if it belongs in the exponential family. Yet, the introduced ordinal policy is neither in the exponential family nor β-smooth, even with a linear predictor. To have a β-smooth ordinal policy, it is necessary to assure that the distance between thresholds is sufficiently large. Let $\varepsilon > 0$, let us introduce the set Δ^ε_{K-1}:

$$\Delta^\varepsilon_n = \{(x_1, \ldots, x_n) \in \mathbb{R}^n | x_{i+1} - x_i > \varepsilon,\ \forall i \in [\![1, n]\!]\}.$$

In Proposition 1, we provide sufficient conditions that guarantee that the ordinal policy is β-smooth, when the predictor, g_ω, belongs to a large class of functions, such as some neural networks. When the predictor is a linear function, the obtained policy is β-smooth as long as the feature mapping is bounded (Corollary 1).

2.2 Linear Prediction

If the function g_ω is a linear function, in ω, then the obtained policy is exactly equal to the cumulative ordinal regression model, presented by Agresti [3]. Indeed, let us suppose $\Omega = \mathbb{R}^p$ and let us consider a feature mapping $\phi\colon \mathcal{S} \to \mathbb{R}^p$, then suppose the function $g_\omega(\cdot)$ is a linear function: $g_\omega(s) = \langle \phi(s), \omega \rangle_{\mathbb{R}^p}$. Then, with Eq. 2, we obtain:

$$\mathbb{P}(A \leq j) = \sigma\left(\tau_j - \langle \phi(s), \omega \rangle_{\mathbb{R}^d}\right),$$

which is the definition of a logistic cumulative ordinal regression model [3].

2.3 Thresholded Model

The presented ordinal policy does not need the predictor $g_\omega(\cdot)$ to be a linear function. Indeed, in its more general form, the presented ordinal in an instance of thresholded model [14]. To use it with policy gradient methods, the predictor g_ω should be differentiable in its parameter ω, and preferable somehow "smooth" in its parameter. For instance, it could be parametrized by any neural network, this would allow solving complex tasks using DRL techniques. The obtained policy is then the same as a CORAL or CORN neural networks [4,20].

2.4 Sufficient Conditions for β-Smoothness on Ordinal Policies

We now present sufficient conditions to guarantee that an ordinal policy is β-smooth. This is important because theoretical results [1] then ensure that policy gradient methods can be applied to improve the policy.

Proposition 1. *Let $s \in \mathcal{S}$, if:*

- *The function $\omega \mapsto g_\omega(s)$ is L_Ω-Lipschitz*
- *The function $\omega \mapsto \nabla_\omega g_\omega(s)$ is C_Ω-Lipschitz function and bounded by M_Ω*

Then the function:

$$\Omega \times \Delta^\varepsilon_{K-1} \to \mathbb{R}$$
$$(\omega, \tau) \mapsto \log \pi_{(\tau,\omega)}(a, s)$$

is β-smooth, with $\beta = \sqrt{2D_\varepsilon^2 + C_\varepsilon^2}$, where $C_\varepsilon = (1 + \exp(-\varepsilon))^{-2}$ and $D_\varepsilon = \sqrt{2}\max(C_\Omega + \sqrt{2}M_\Omega C_\varepsilon L_\Omega, M_\Omega)$.

We provide a proof of Property 1 as supplementary material

As a direct consequence of Property 1, we obtain sufficient conditions assuring that an ordinal policy with a linear predictor is β-smooth. We present these condition in Corollary 1.

Corollary 1. *If $g_\omega(.) = \langle \phi(.), \omega \rangle_{\mathbb{R}^p}$ and $\|\phi(s)\| \leq M_\phi$, then the ordinal policy π_θ is β-smooth with $\beta = \sqrt{2D_\varepsilon^2 + C_\varepsilon^2}$, where $C_\varepsilon = (1+\exp(-\varepsilon))^{-2}$ and $D_\varepsilon = \sqrt{2}\max(\sqrt{2}M_\phi^2 C_\varepsilon, M_\phi)$.*

2.5 Implementation Details

It is difficult to use policy optimization methods over the set Δ^ε_K because there are constraints that must be respected to remain over this parametric set: the thresholds must remain ordered and the difference between thresholds must be controlled, this guarantees stability (Proposition 1). We tackle this by using a reparametrization $\xi = (\xi_1, \xi_2, \ldots, \xi_{K-1})$ of $\tau = (\tau_1, \tau_2, \ldots, \tau_{K-1})$, with:

$$\xi_1 = \tau_1 \quad ; \quad \xi_{k+1} = \log(\tau_{k+1} - \tau_k - \varepsilon), \quad k \in [\![1, K-2]\!].$$

Thus, policy improvement can be done on (ω, ξ) which belong to the unconstrained space $\Omega \times \mathbb{R}^{K-1}$. Then the corresponding thresholds, $(\tau_k)_{k=1}^{K-1}$, can be computed using the inverse of this reparametrization.

Additionally, using log-probabilities instead of probabilities is numerically more stable. Let $a \in [\![2, K-1]\!]$ and $\eta_k = \tau_k - g_\omega(s)$, for ordinal policies we can use the exact expression of log-probabilities given by:

$$\log \pi_\theta(1\,s) = \log \sigma(\eta_1), \quad \log \pi(K|s) = \log \sigma(-\eta_{K-1}),$$
$$\log \pi(a|s) = g_\omega(s) + \log(\exp(-\tau_{a-1}) - \exp(-\tau_a)) + \log \sigma(\eta_a) + \log \sigma(\eta_{a-1}),$$

2.6 Multivariate Ordinal Actions

It is straightforward to extend univariate ordinal actions to multivariate ordinal actions, by factorizing across action dimensions. Indeed, let $d \in \mathbb{N}$, let us consider a d-dimensional continuous action space $\mathcal{A} = [\![1, K]\!]^d$. We define a predictor function $g_\omega: \mathcal{S} \to \mathbb{R}^d$ and consider a parameter $\tau \in (\Delta_K^\varepsilon)^d$. Then for a given state $s \in \mathcal{S}$, let us note:

$$g_\omega(s) = (g_\omega^{(1)}(s), \ldots, g_\omega^{(d)}(s)) \quad ; \quad \tau = \left(\tau_k^{(j)}\right)_{k \in [\![1,K]\!], j \in [\![1,d]\!]}.$$

Let $(k^{(1)}, \ldots k^{(d)}) \in \mathcal{A}$, we define the multivariate cumulative distribution function of a policy by the following relationship:

$$\mathbb{P}(A_1 \leq k^{(1)}, \ldots, A \leq k^{(d)}) = \prod_{j=1}^d \sigma\left(\tau_{k^{(j)}}^{(j)} - g_\omega^{(j)}(s)\right),$$

Which induces a conditional probability distribution over $\mathcal{A}$. It is worth noting that actions are not drawn independently across dimensions because the distribution depends on the multivariate predictor g_ω.

3 Applications

3.1 A Simple Simulation Setting

A key point to consider is that the presented ordinal policy is more restrictive than the usual softmax policy. As an alternative to an ordinal policy, the policy may be parametrized by a univariate softmax distribution, but then the prediction zones for the different classes may not be ordered. In this section, we study numerically if this has an impact on the rate of improvement or quality of the policies in a simple simulation setting. This simulation setting is similar to the scenario we expect to observe when facing the problem described in Sect. 1.2.

We simulate the ALS of one episode by sampling from a Gaussian process, which is then squished into the set $[0, 5]$ using a sigmoid function. Additionally, we simulate the user response using a fixed, but unknown ordinal model π_U. Let us suppose that at a given instant, for a given state measure s_t, the class a_t is proposed. We keep track of a "discomfort" score Z_t, which is updated:

$$Z_{t+1} = (1 - \pi_U(a_t|s_t))^{\gamma_{\text{reaction}}} + \gamma_{\text{discomfort}} Z_t.$$

Then, with probability $\sigma(Z_{t+1})$, the user reacts, if he does, a tint class is drawn accordingly to $\pi_U(.|s_t)$. The term $(1 - \pi_U(a_t|s_t))$ measures the discrepancy between the proposed class and user preferred class. The environment parameter $\gamma_{\text{reaction}} \in \mathbb{R}^+$ determines the "laziness" of the user: if it is low, the user often reacts, if it is high, the user only reacts if the proposed class is unlikely to be drawn by π_U. At last, the environment parameter $\gamma_{\text{discomfort}} \in [0, 1]$ determines the memory of the user, if this parameter is zero, the user only reacts to the current proposed class.

Using this simulation setting, we compare the performances of ordinal policies against the performances of softmax policies using as updates: REINFORCE, NPG and TRPO. For every policy and every method, the hyperparameters are tuned, to provide a fair comparison among parametrizations.

We use $\gamma_{\text{reaction}} = 0.5$, $\gamma_{\text{discomfort}} = 1$ and a discount rate of 0.9. We simulate episodes of length sixty, at the end of each episode the policy is updated. For a given update strategy and policy, we simulate four hundred episodes. This process gives one learning trajectory, and we simulate ten learning trajectories per update strategy and policy combinations. We present the simulation results in Fig. 1.

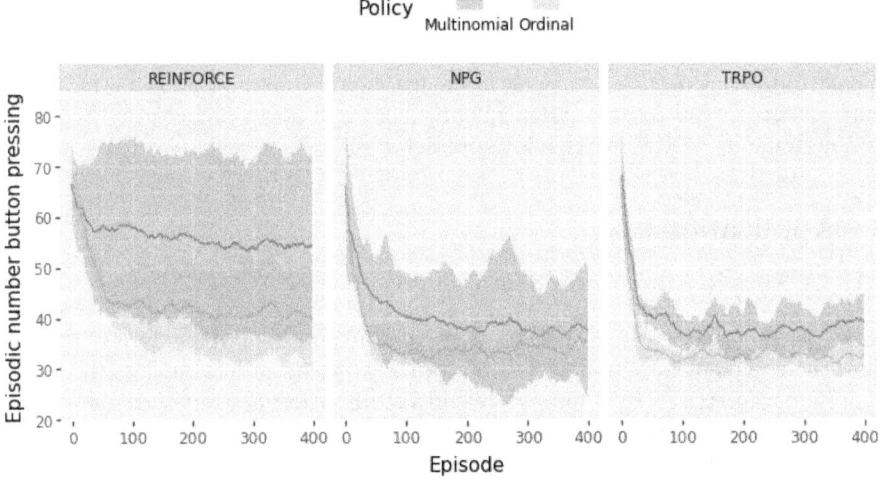

Fig. 1. Total episodic reward vs episode, for different policy gradient methods and policies. Average curves are calculated using mean of ten random seeds, calculated on learning curves after a rolling mean with a window of twenty episodes. Shaded areas show mean ± one standard deviation.

Similarly to how using ordinal information provides better predictions in a supervised setting [7], we find that using ordinal policies improves the performance of policy gradient methods, independently of the method that is used. This suggests that using an ordinal policy, when there is a notion of order among actions.

Indeed, convergence seems faster and towards a better policy for ordinal policies than for multinomial policies, and this parametrization seems more stable: the standard deviation is smaller when an ordinal policy is used (see Fig. 1).

Among the six studied methods, updating an ordinal policy using TRPO yield the best results. Indeed, it provides a faster improvement rate than REINFORCE while being slightly more stable than NPG, this is consistent with numerical experiments presented by Schulman et al. [18].

We should stress that the simulation setting may favor ordinal policies, as tints are chosen from an ordinal model. Nevertheless, the setting reflects what is expected in a real setting: users tend to prefer clear tints for low luminosity and darker ones for high luminosity, while the thresholds are unknown.

3.2 A Real Life Study

A study was done to test adapting the parameters of the hybrid tint control, described in Sect. 1.2, using an ordinal policy updated with TRPO.

We used an electrochromic prototype for this study, which was equipped with an ALS and two buttons in the branches of the frame. We implemented the hybrid mode controlling the tint using only the ALS values; the tint was automatically controlled by default, but at any moment the user could manually change the tint by using the buttons. After a user interaction, the automatic control was deactivated for ten seconds, and afterward the tint was again automatically controlled.

Nine users were recruited for this study; these reported using sunglasses in all seasons of the year and did not work at EssilorLuxottica nor in any optic-related company. All the participants consented to participate in the study, and a safety assessment validated the use of this electrochromic prototype in a controlled environment.

A walking circuit was created for this study, allowing users to experience various real-life light situations: indoor/outdoor transitions, reading and far vision situations, etc. The same circuit was used for all participants, and participants walked the circuit one at a time. Participants were free to walk the circuit at their rhythm; on average, the circuit was completed after 10 min. Each user was asked to walk the circuit four times while wearing the electrochromic frames in the hybrid tint control. At the end of each circuit, the parameters controlling the hybrid mode were updated using TRPO. The same maximum Kullback-Leibler divergence was used for every participant after every circuit.

The objective of this study was to assess whether the number of user interactions decreases as the model parameters are updated.

For one of the nine users, the model parameters could not be updated; the TRPO algorithm proposed the old parameters after each episode. We discuss why this is so later in this section. We present the results obtained with the eight remaining participants in Fig. 2.

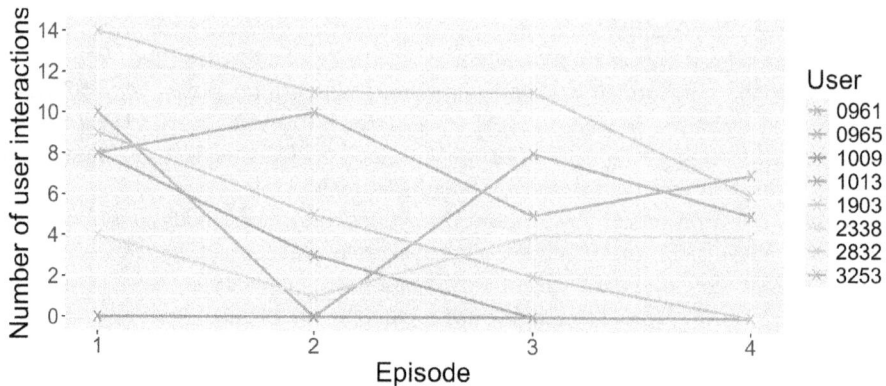

Fig. 2. Number of button pressings, per episode and user. Button pressings corresponding to a darker (resp. lighter) tint when current tint is C_3 (resp. C_0) were removed

Two participants did not press the button at any moment of the study; after the four circuits were done, they reported that the proposed tint was well adapted for them. At first glance, the number of button presses seems to decrease as the model is updated, for the remaining participants.

To assess if there was a significant decrease in the number of user interactions, we analyzed the trend using a Poisson regression, modeling the link between the number of button pressings per episode Y *(count response)* in function of the episode number X *(numeric covariate)* with an additive interaction for the user j *(categorical covariate)* to account for the differences between users. Concretely, we consider the statistical model:

$$Y \sim \text{Poisson}(\lambda); \; \log(\lambda) = \alpha \cdot X + F_j,$$

where the slope $\alpha \in \mathbb{R}$ and user effects $\{F_j\}_{j=1}^{6}$ are model parameters. We present the observed and fitted number of button pressings as well as 95% confidence prediction intervals in Fig. 3. The estimated slope α is statistically significantly negative (point estimation: -0.28 and 95% confidence interval: $[-0.43, -0.13]$). To address possible overfitting issues caused by the observed sparse dataset, we calculate a confidence interval for α using a leave-one-out procedure, the *jackknife* method [5], and obtain a point estimation of -0.28 and a 95% confidence interval of $[-0.49, -0.06]$. Since the slope α is statistically significantly negative, the number of button pressings diminishes as circuits go by.

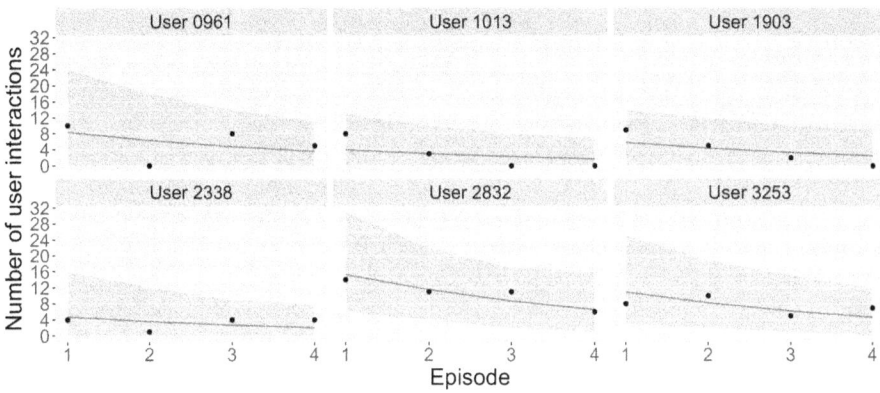

Fig. 3. Observed number of user interaction, fitted average (red line) and 95% prediction intervals, per user and episode. (Color figure online)

These are encouraging results for this exploratory study, yet because no control group was used, we cannot claim causality; we cannot claim that users interact less often *because* the model parameters are updated. A confirmatory study with more users and a control group should be done to confirm this.

After a close inspection of the data of the participant for whom the model did not update, we noticed an unexpected behavior: instead of reacting to the proposed tints, this participant tried different tints and then chose the most adapted one. This behavior is not well described by the RL formulation of Sect. 1.2. For instance, when ALS was high, the tint C_3 was proposed, and then the user tried all the tints and then manually selected the tint C_3. Thus, proposing the tint C_3 was a good choice in reality. Instead, with our RL approach, proposing the tint C_3 would be judged as a bad action because it yields low rewards: ALS would be high, the tint C_3 would be proposed, and then the user would successively press the button six times. This is likely the reason for which TRPO could not update the model parameters.

A simple solution to align the RL formulation with this behavior is to adapt the reward signal. For example, instead of having a reward of -1 when there is a user interaction, the reward could be the opposite of the eventual difference between the user selected and automatically proposed tints.

3.3 Discretizing Continuous State Space

Ordinal actions may arise from the discretization of a continuous action space. Indeed, let us consider a bounded continuous action space $\mathcal{A} = [m, M]$. Let us consider the following discretization of the action space:

$$\mathcal{A}_K = \{a_k\}_{k=1}^{K} \quad ; \quad a_k = m + k\frac{M-m}{K}.$$

The set $\mathcal{A}_K$ is an ordinal set: there is an immediate order relationship between actions, Eq. 1, and there is a finite number of actions. Hence, we may take actions on $\mathcal{A}_K$ using ordinal policies.

When multivariate continuous are considered, the same discretization may be applied dimension-wise and then use the multivariate ordinal extension presented in Sect. 2.6. We implement this approach, using an ordinal policy with 17 classes (per dimension) to solve different Mujoco [23] and other benchmark RL environments. To improve the policy we use PPO, as implemented for PPO for continuous actions by Huang et al. [10], with the same hyperparameters. We use the same neural network parametrizing PPO for continuous actions implemented by Huang et al. [10], which uses a two layer MLP to parametrize $g_\omega(\cdot)$ and uses a learnable standard deviation per action dimension, independent of the state, as suggested by Huang et al. [9]. We run experiments in the environments of the Table 1, using a learning rate of $3 \cdot 10^{-4}$ and a discount factor of $\gamma = 0.99$ for both continuous action PPO and ordinal PPO, in all the environments. We obtain the results presented in Fig. 4

Table 1. Continuous action environments where ordinal actions were used by discretization

Environment	State dimensions	Action Dimensions
Ant-v4	105	8
BipedalWalker-v3	24	4
HalfCheetah-v4	17	6
Hopper-v4	11	3
Humanoid-v4	348	17
InvertedDoublePendulum-v4	9	1
Pusher-v4	23	7
Walker2d-v4	17	6

We find that using ordinal policies for classic RL problems with continuous actions yields similar performances than using a continuous policy. This is coherent with results from the literature [19,22].

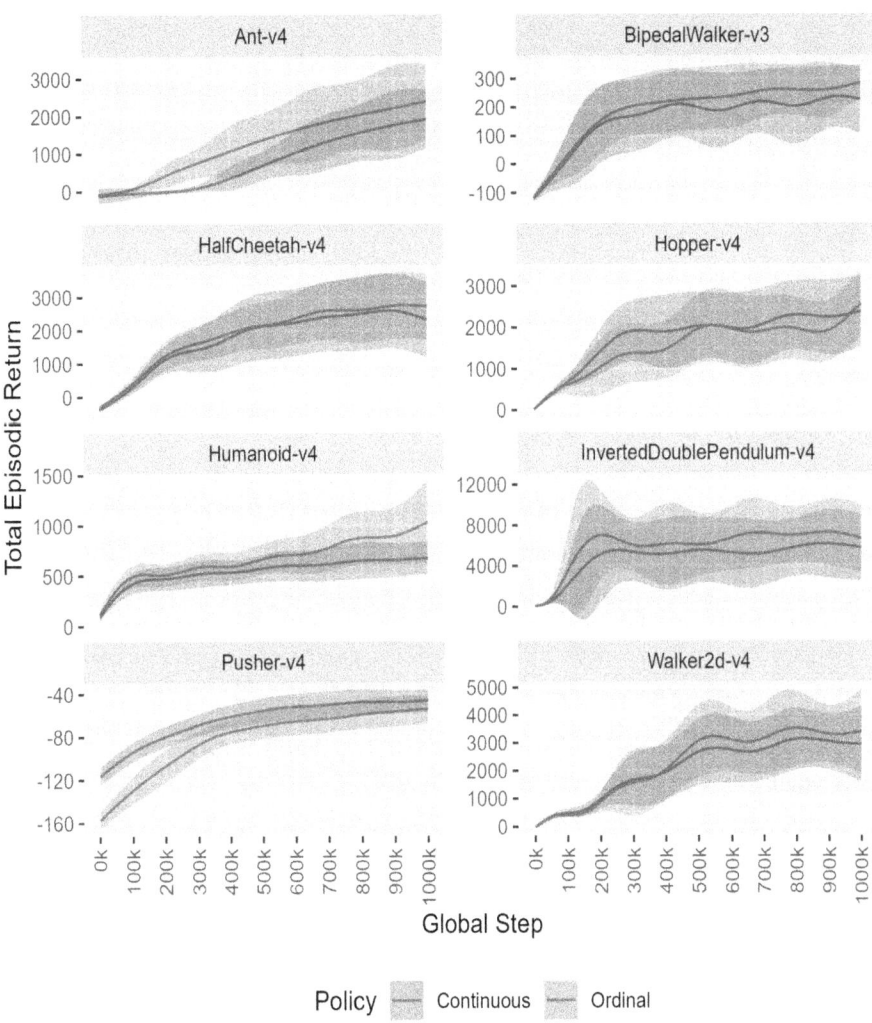

Fig. 4. Learning curves for different policies across different environments. Mean and 95% confidence prediction interval, fitted using a location-scale Gaussian GAM on data generated using five different random seeds per environment.

4 Conclusion Discussion

Satisfying every user, using one predefined model with fixed parameters, is challenging since each user's preferences are unique and may vary and evolve. Thanks to today's highly configurable wearable devices, we may tailor a model to answer each individual's needs. In this article, we present a method to do this in an online manner using the RL paradigm. This opens a door for a wide range of real applications, but in a real-world setting, it is important to do so robustly. For instance, when the system pilots an ordinal setting, using an adapted policy provides this robustness: no matter how the user interacts with the wearable, the policy will always be an ordinal model, thus the notion of order between levels is assured.

Furthermore, the studied simulation setting suggests that considering the notion of order, when there is one, is beneficial. And the proposed method can be directly applied in a real-world setting (Sect. 3.2) and a deep learning approach may also be used (Sect. 3.3).

There are two main axes for future work. For the industrial application, it is of great importance to converge fast to a "good" model. Indeed, a method that would require thousands of episodes to improve would be pointless for any real-life application: the user may simply stop wearing the device before there are enough episodes. Thus, a solution would be to use simple models, such as the one used in Sect. 3.2, or leverage off-policy methods, which are known to be more sample-efficient than on-policy methods. Secondly, ALS collected during a time window could better explain user context and thus allow for better policies than the ones that use only the instantaneous ALS. This temporal covariate could be used with an adapted ordinal model, such as the one proposed by Jacques and Samardžić [11].

Acknowledgments. We thank Walid M'Zough, Khalil BEN GHORBEL, Carole NADOLNY, Armel JIMENEZ, Alexandre GOURRAUD and Jean SAHLER for their collaboration and support for the study presented in this article.

Disclosure of Interests. The authors have no competing interests to declare that are relevant to the content of this article.

References

1. Agarwal, A., Kakade, S.M., Lee, J., Mahajan, G.: On the theory of policy gradient methods: optimality, approximation, and distribution shift. J. Mach. Learn. Res. **22**, 98:1–98:76 (2019)
2. Agarwal, A., Kakade, S.M., Lee, J.D., Mahajan, G.: Optimality and approximation with policy gradient methods in markov decision processes. In: Abernethy, J., Agarwal, S. (eds.) Proceedings of Thirty Third Conference on Learning Theory. Proceedings of Machine Learning Research, vol. 125, pp. 64–66. PMLR (2020)
3. Agresti, A.: Analysis of Ordinal Categorical Data, vol. 656. John Wiley & Sons (2010)
4. Cao, W., Mirjalili, V., Raschka, S.: Rank consistent ordinal regression for neural networks with application to age estimation. Pattern Recogn. Lett. **140**, 325–331 (2020)
5. Efron, B., Tibshirani, R.J.: An Introduction to the Bootstrap. Chapman and Hall/CRC (1994)
6. Feng, J., Shi, Y., Qu, G., Low, S.H., Anandkumar, A., Wierman, A.: Stability constrained reinforcement learning for decentralized real-time voltage control. IEEE Trans. Control Netw. Syst. **11**(3), 1370–1381 (2024). https://doi.org/10.1109/TCNS.2023.3338240

7. Gutiérrez, P.A., Pérez-Ortiz, M., Sánchez-Monedero, J., Fernández-Navarro, F., Hervás-Martínez, C.: Ordinal regression methods: survey and experimental study. IEEE Trans. Knowl. Data Eng. **28**(1), 127–146 (2016)
8. Henriksen, A., et al.: Using fitness trackers and smartwatches to measure physical activity in research: analysis of consumer wrist-worn wearables. J. Med. Internet Res. **20**(3), e110 (2018)
9. Huang, S., Dossa, R.F.J., Raffin, A., Kanervisto, A., Wang, W.: The 37 implementation details of proximal policy optimization. In: ICLR Blog Track (2022)
10. Huang, S., et al.: CleanRL: high-quality single-file implementations of deep reinforcement learning algorithms. J. Mach. Learn. Res. **23**(274), 1–18 (2022). http://jmlr.org/papers/v23/21-1342.html
11. Jacques, J., Samardžić, S.: Analyzing cycling sensors data through ordinal logistic regression with functional covariates. J. Roy. Stat. Soc. Ser. C Appl. Stat. (2022). https://hal.archives-ouvertes.fr/hal-03107427
12. Khan, M., Mohamed, S., Marlin, B., Murphy, K.: A stick-breaking likelihood for categorical data analysis with latent gaussian models. In: Lawrence, N.D., Girolami, M. (eds.) Proceedings of the Fifteenth International Conference on Artificial Intelligence and Statistics. Proceedings of Machine Learning Research, vol. 22, pp. 610–618. PMLR, La Palma, Canary Islands (2012)
13. Kim, J., Campbell, A.S., de Ávila, B.E.F., Wang, J.: Wearable biosensors for healthcare monitoring. Nat. Biotechnol. **37**(4), 389–406 (2019)
14. Li, L., Lin, H.t.: Ordinal regression by extended binary classification. In: Schölkopf, B., Platt, J., Hoffman, T. (eds.) Advances in Neural Information Processing Systems, vol. 19. MIT Press (2006)
15. McCullagh, P.: Regression models for ordinal data. J. Roy. Stat. Soc. Ser. B (Methodological) **42**(2), 109–142 (1980). http://www.jstor.org/stable/2984952
16. Mukhopadhyay, S.C.: Wearable sensors for human activity monitoring: a review. IEEE Sens. J. **15**, 1321–1330 (2015)
17. Sabry, F., Eltaras, T., Labda, W., Alzoubi, K., Malluhi, Q.: Machine learning for healthcare wearable devices: the big picture. J. Healthc. Eng. **2022**(1), 4653923 (2022). https://doi.org/10.1155/2022/4653923, https://onlinelibrary.wiley.com/doi/abs/10.1155/2022/4653923
18. Schulman, J., Levine, S., Moritz, P., Jordan, M.I., Abbeel, P.: Trust region policy optimization. CoRR arXiv:1502.05477 (2015)
19. Seyde, T., et al.: Is bang-bang control all you need? Solving continuous control with bernoulli policies. In: Ranzato, M., Beygelzimer, A., Dauphin, Y., Liang, P., Vaughan, J.W. (eds.) Advances in Neural Information Processing Systems, vol. 34, pp. 27209–27221. Curran Associates, Inc. (2021)
20. Shi, X., Cao, W., Raschka, S.: Deep neural networks for rank-consistent ordinal regression based on conditional probabilities (2021)
21. Sutton, R.S., Barto, A.G.: Reinforcement Learning: An Introduction. A Bradford Book, Cambridge, MA, USA (2018)
22. Tang, Y., Agrawal, S.: Discretizing continuous action space for on-policy optimization. CoRR arXiv:1901.10500 (2019)
23. Todorov, E., Erez, T., Tassa, Y.: Mujoco: a physics engine for model-based control. In: 2012 IEEE/RSJ International Conference on Intelligent Robots and Systems, pp. 5026–5033. IEEE (2012). https://doi.org/10.1109/IROS.2012.6386109
24. Tranchina, D., Gordon, J., Shapley, R.: Retinal light adaptation–evidence for a feedback mechanism. Nature **310**(5975), 314–316 (1984)
25. Wehenkel, A., Louppe, G.: Unconstrained monotonic neural networks. In: Advances in Neural Information Processing Systems, vol. 32 (2019)

26. Weinberger, S., Cugliari, J., Cain, A.: Ordinal regression for preference learning in wearables using sensor data. Expert Syst. Appl. **281**, 127616 (2025)
27. Wu, Z., Khan, N.M., Gao, L., Guan, L.: Deep reinforcement learning with parameterized action space for object detection. In: 2018 IEEE International Symposium on Multimedia (ISM), pp. 101–104 (2018). https://doi.org/10.1109/ISM.2018.00025
28. Yee, T.W., Wild, C.J.: Vector generalized additive models. J. Roy. Stat. Soc. Ser. B (Methodological) **58**(3), 481–493 (1996). https://doi.org/10.1111/j.2517-6161.1996.tb02095.x

7. Gutiérrez, P.A., Pérez-Ortiz, M., Sánchez-Monedero, J., Fernández-Navarro, F., Hervás-Martínez, C.: Ordinal regression methods: survey and experimental study. IEEE Trans. Knowl. Data Eng. **28**(1), 127–146 (2016)
8. Henriksen, A., et al.: Using fitness trackers and smartwatches to measure physical activity in research: analysis of consumer wrist-worn wearables. J. Med. Internet Res. **20**(3), e110 (2018)
9. Huang, S., Dossa, R.F.J., Raffin, A., Kanervisto, A., Wang, W.: The 37 implementation details of proximal policy optimization. In: ICLR Blog Track (2022)
10. Huang, S., et al.: CleanRL: high-quality single-file implementations of deep reinforcement learning algorithms. J. Mach. Learn. Res. **23**(274), 1–18 (2022). http://jmlr.org/papers/v23/21-1342.html
11. Jacques, J., Samardžić, S.: Analyzing cycling sensors data through ordinal logistic regression with functional covariates. J. Roy. Stat. Soc. Ser. C Appl. Stat. (2022). https://hal.archives-ouvertes.fr/hal-03107427
12. Khan, M., Mohamed, S., Marlin, B., Murphy, K.: A stick-breaking likelihood for categorical data analysis with latent gaussian models. In: Lawrence, N.D., Girolami, M. (eds.) Proceedings of the Fifteenth International Conference on Artificial Intelligence and Statistics. Proceedings of Machine Learning Research, vol. 22, pp. 610–618. PMLR, La Palma, Canary Islands (2012)
13. Kim, J., Campbell, A.S., de Ávila, B.E.F., Wang, J.: Wearable biosensors for healthcare monitoring. Nat. Biotechnol. **37**(4), 389–406 (2019)
14. Li, L., Lin, H.t.: Ordinal regression by extended binary classification. In: Schölkopf, B., Platt, J., Hoffman, T. (eds.) Advances in Neural Information Processing Systems, vol. 19. MIT Press (2006)
15. McCullagh, P.: Regression models for ordinal data. J. Roy. Stat. Soc. Ser. B (Methodological) **42**(2), 109–142 (1980). http://www.jstor.org/stable/2984952
16. Mukhopadhyay, S.C.: Wearable sensors for human activity monitoring: a review. IEEE Sens. J. **15**, 1321–1330 (2015)
17. Sabry, F., Eltaras, T., Labda, W., Alzoubi, K., Malluhi, Q.: Machine learning for healthcare wearable devices: the big picture. J. Healthc. Eng. **2022**(1), 4653923 (2022). https://doi.org/10.1155/2022/4653923, https://onlinelibrary.wiley.com/doi/abs/10.1155/2022/4653923
18. Schulman, J., Levine, S., Moritz, P., Jordan, M.I., Abbeel, P.: Trust region policy optimization. CoRR arXiv:1502.05477 (2015)
19. Seyde, T., et al.: Is bang-bang control all you need? Solving continuous control with bernoulli policies. In: Ranzato, M., Beygelzimer, A., Dauphin, Y., Liang, P., Vaughan, J.W. (eds.) Advances in Neural Information Processing Systems, vol. 34, pp. 27209–27221. Curran Associates, Inc. (2021)
20. Shi, X., Cao, W., Raschka, S.: Deep neural networks for rank-consistent ordinal regression based on conditional probabilities (2021)
21. Sutton, R.S., Barto, A.G.: Reinforcement Learning: An Introduction. A Bradford Book, Cambridge, MA, USA (2018)
22. Tang, Y., Agrawal, S.: Discretizing continuous action space for on-policy optimization. CoRR arXiv:1901.10500 (2019)
23. Todorov, E., Erez, T., Tassa, Y.: Mujoco: a physics engine for model-based control. In: 2012 IEEE/RSJ International Conference on Intelligent Robots and Systems, pp. 5026–5033. IEEE (2012). https://doi.org/10.1109/IROS.2012.6386109
24. Tranchina, D., Gordon, J., Shapley, R.: Retinal light adaptation–evidence for a feedback mechanism. Nature **310**(5975), 314–316 (1984)
25. Wehenkel, A., Louppe, G.: Unconstrained monotonic neural networks. In: Advances in Neural Information Processing Systems, vol. 32 (2019)

26. Weinberger, S., Cugliari, J., Cain, A.: Ordinal regression for preference learning in wearables using sensor data. Expert Syst. Appl. **281**, 127616 (2025)
27. Wu, Z., Khan, N.M., Gao, L., Guan, L.: Deep reinforcement learning with parameterized action space for object detection. In: 2018 IEEE International Symposium on Multimedia (ISM), pp. 101–104 (2018). https://doi.org/10.1109/ISM.2018.00025
28. Yee, T.W., Wild, C.J.: Vector generalized additive models. J. Roy. Stat. Soc. Ser. B (Methodological) **58**(3), 481–493 (1996). https://doi.org/10.1111/j.2517-6161.1996.tb02095.x

Iterative Corpus Refinement for Materials Property Prediction Based on Scientific Texts

Lei Zhang[✉] and Markus Stricker

Interdisciplinary Centre for Advanced Materials Simulation, Ruhr-University Bochum, Universitätsstraße 150, 44780 Bochum, Germany
{lei.zhang-w2i,markus.stricker}@rub.de

Abstract. The discovery and optimization of materials for specific applications is hampered by the practically infinite number of possible elemental combinations and associated properties, also known as the 'combinatorial explosion'. By nature of the problem, data are scarce and all possible data sources should be used. In addition to simulations and experimental results, the latent knowledge in scientific texts is not yet used to its full potential. We present an iterative framework that refines a given scientific corpus by strategic selection of the most diverse documents, training Word2Vec models, and monitoring the convergence of composition-property correlations in embedding space. Our approach is applied to predict high-performing materials for oxygen reduction (ORR), hydrogen evolution (HER), and oxygen evolution (OER) reactions for a large number of possible candidate compositions. Our method successfully predicts the highest performing compositions among a large pool of candidates, validated by experimental measurements of the electrocatalytic performance in the lab. This work demonstrates and validates the potential of iterative corpus refinement to accelerate materials discovery and optimization, offering a scalable and efficient tool for screening large compositional spaces where reliable data are scarce or non-existent.

Keywords: text mining · materials informatics · corpus refinement

1 Introduction

The discovery of new materials has traditionally relied on experimental intuition and trial-and-error methods, where researchers manually combined and tested materials, guided by experience and theoretical knowledge [6,7,25]. These methods have led to significant breakthroughs, such as platinum-based electrocatalysts for fuel cells [5] and advanced alloys for aerospace applications [4]. However, they are time-consuming, resource-intensive, and difficult to scale, particularly as material systems containing more than one or two principle elements become more complex. *Modern* material systems, such as high-entropy alloys [15] or oxides [26], multi-principal element compounds [9], involve a large number of possible and tunable compositions, which represents a possibility to use them as 'discovery platforms' [2]. However, the sheer number of possible compositions makes experimental searches impractical or even impossible. Furthermore, global challenges such as the switch to renewable energy and sustainability require faster and more efficient ways to discover new and optimize existing materials [11,17].

In recent years, computational methods have become powerful tools for materials discovery. Simulation techniques such as density functional theory (DFT) can predict material properties, reducing the need for extensive experimental trials at the cost of the energy spent in high performance computing centers [10,18,19]. Machine learning has added another dimension by finding patterns in structured datasets and predicting properties for unexplored compositions [13,16]. Although these methods have been successful in narrowing the search space, they have limitations. DFT simulations are computationally expensive, in particular when small ≤ 1 atom-% compositional changes require many calculation to achieve a statistically correct property prediction for one composition point due to the different random distributions of elements and their impact on material properties. Supervised machine learning models to substitute expensive DFT simulations require high-quality datasets that are available at scale and variety to match the parameter space of technologically interesting materials.

The scientific literature offers an alternative resource for material discovery. Research articles and patents contain hidden knowledge encoded in text about composition-property relationships from experimental results and theoretical approaches [24]. Natural language processing (NLP) methods like Word2Vec [14] and Doc2Vec [12] can extract this knowledge by turning textual data into vector representations. These vectors capture relationships and correlations between words, which allows to link 'material dimensions', such as composition, to properties, e.g. electrocatalytic performance, and to develop models for the prediction of new high-performing candidate compositions. Unlike simulations or structured datasets, text mining can leverage unstructured data, providing access to this latent knowledge.

Despite its potential, using the scientific literature effectively presents challenges. Not all text sources are equally relevant, and including too many irrelevant or redundant sources can reduce the predictive quality of the models. The increasing volume of scientific literature, including artificial intelligence (AI)-generated content, makes this issue even more pressing. Many AI-generated texts are repetitive or inaccurate, introducing noise into the dataset, and if repetitively used to retrain the models eventually leading to their *collapse* [20]. Effective methods are therefore needed to filter out 'low-quality content' to ensure that models are trained on the most meaningful information.

Another challenge is scalability. NLP models can process large datasets, but training them on massive corpora is expensive and it is unclear if more data actually results in a better model. Static, corpus-based models also struggle to adapt to specific tasks. For instance, a model trained on a broad corpus may not effectively capture the relationships required to predict material properties for a specific system accurately. The term 'material system' here refers to a fixed set of elements which can be mixed in an arbitrary proportion. To address these challenges, there is a need for methods that allow to tailor a training corpus w.r.t. specific prediction tasks.

In this work, we propose an iterative framework to address these challenges. First we start with a broad collection of abstracts from scientific papers, further on referred to as 'documents', and use Doc2Vec embeddings [3] to create a *map* of abstracts. This map allows us to then derive an ordered list based on greedy selection which represents the most diverse documents to avoid information duplication and information fuzziness. From this list, we use batches of 50 documents to train Word2Vec [8,14] models. In their respective embedding space, we measure the change of the centroid of the embeddings w.r.t. our specific prediction task and stop adding new document batches once a convergence criterion is met. The resulting Word2Vec model then constitutes our material system-optimized model which we use to predict reaction-specific high-performance candidate compositions for electrocatalysis. To demonstrate the effectiveness of our approach, we predict highest performing compositions from three different material systems for three different electrocatalytic reactions: oxygen reduction (ORR), hydrogen evolution (HER), and oxygen evolution (OER) and validate them against experimental measurements. While electrocatalysts are used as a case study, our framework is general and can be applied to a wide range of materials discovery tasks.

2 Experiments

All code and data needed to reproduce our workflow are available. The code can be found in [28], references to all datasets are provided when they are introduced further below.

2.1 Corpus Collection and Preprocessing

Figure 1 shows a schematic overview of our methodology. First, we collect a relevant corpus of documents using the `PaperCollector` module in `MatNexus` [27]. As source for the documents we use the application programming interfaces (APIs) of Scopus and limit ourselves to use open access-only publications up to including the year 2023 which results in 6506 papers. The retrieved abstracts and metadata are stored in a structured comma-separated values (CSV) file. Text preprocessing is performed using the `TextProcessor` module, which removes licensing statements, filters common English stopwords, and retains domain-specific terms, such as chemical element symbols. Tokenization is applied to prepare the text for embedding generation.

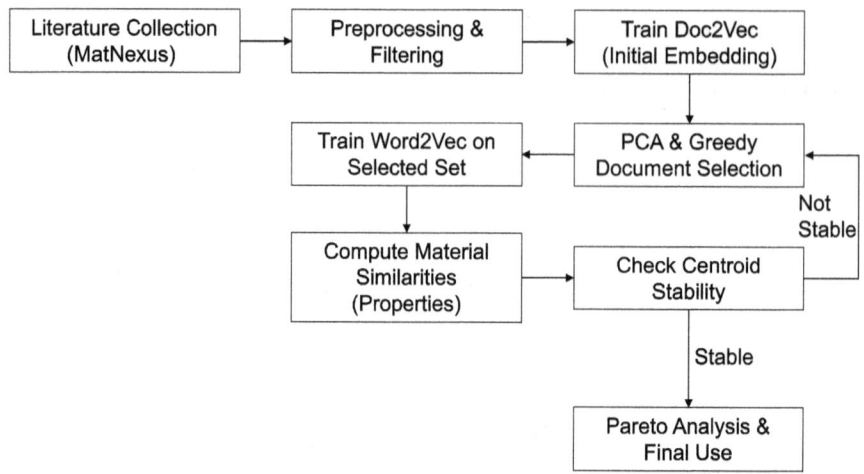

Fig. 1. Schematic overview for iterative corpus refinement framework from literature collection, document selection, Word2Vec model training to final predictions based on Pareto front analysis.

2.2 Embedding Generation and Greedy Selection

The initial document embeddings are generated using a Doc2Vec model trained on the full corpus containing 6506 documents. The embeddings capture the semantic content of each document, mapping the tokens into a 200-dimensional vector space, which offers a balanced trade-off between computational efficiency and representational capacity for capturing domain-specific linguistic nuances. A greedy selection algorithm is then applied to iteratively refine the subset of documents for analysis.

Initialization: We initialize the greedy selection algorithm with the central document in embedding space. This ensures that the starting point is representative of the corpus's overall thematic distribution, i.e. an "average abstract" w.r.t. the Doc2Vec embedding space.

Iterative Expansion: Subsequent documents are selected by identifying the farthest (in cosine distance) from all previously selected documents. It is a classic greedy farthest point sampling except the initial point is selected always the central document in embedding space instead of a random starting point. To improve computational efficiency and focus on principal directions of variance, the 200-dimensional Doc2Vec embeddings are reduced to two dimensions using principal component analysis (PCA) before distance calculations. The selection process continues until a predetermined batch size of 50 additional documents is reached, which serves as a heuristic balance between introducing sufficient diversity in each iteration and maintaining computational manageability. This process results in an ordered list of the most different documents in batches of 50 and constitutes the basis for subsequent analysis and optimization.

A selected subset is then used to train a Word2Vec [8,14] model via the `Vec-Generator` module of MatNexus [27]. The skip-gram architecture is used with a vector size of 200, a window size of 5, and hierarchical softmax. The vector size of 200 provides sufficient capacity to capture nuanced relationships between terms while maintaining training efficiency. A window size of 5 is used to reflect a moderate contextual range, allowing the model to learn meaningful co-occurrence patterns without overextending semantic connections. Hierarchical softmax is chosen for its effectiveness in handling large vocabularies with improved training speed over full softmax.

Material Similarity Calculation: We create the representation of 'a material' w.r.t. its composition by a linearly weighted superposition of the embeddings for pure elements, e.g. 'Pt' for platinum, 'Pd' for palladium, etc. The linear weights model the composition. That is, the representation of a composition of 20% element A and 80% element B means to linearly superpose the word embeddings R_i of elements A and B $R_{A_{20}B_{80}} = 0.2R_A + 0.8R_B$. We then calculate the similarity scores of each composition to the embedding vectors of the two properties 'dielectric' and 'conductivity' using cosine similarity which we denote $S_{\text{dielectric}}$ and $S_{\text{conductivity}}$. Given a composition space and concentration resolution for a given material system containing several elements, we can use the two-dimensional similarity scores to calculate a centroid of the based on N different compositions in the material system as follows:

$$\text{centroid} = \frac{1}{N} \sum_{i=1}^{N} \begin{bmatrix} S_{\text{dielectric}}(i) \\ S_{\text{conductivity}}(i) \end{bmatrix}. \tag{1}$$

Convergence Criterion: The previous step is then iterated with an increasing corpus size in batches of 50 documents. With each increase, we monitor the change of the centroid coordinates using Euclidean distance. If the distance between the previous and current centroid falls below a heuristically determined threshold of 0.03, we stop adding more documents and define the word embedding model *converged*. Our rationale is that when an additional batch of 50 documents does not significantly change the word embeddings, adding more documents is unnecessary or even detrimental to predictive performance.

2.3 Pareto Optimization for Candidate Selection

With the converged Word2Vec model for a given material system, Pareto optimization is applied to identify optimal trade-offs between material properties for three electrochemical reactions. For the Pareto front optimization we follow [29] which was shown to be very effective in identifying high-performing regions.

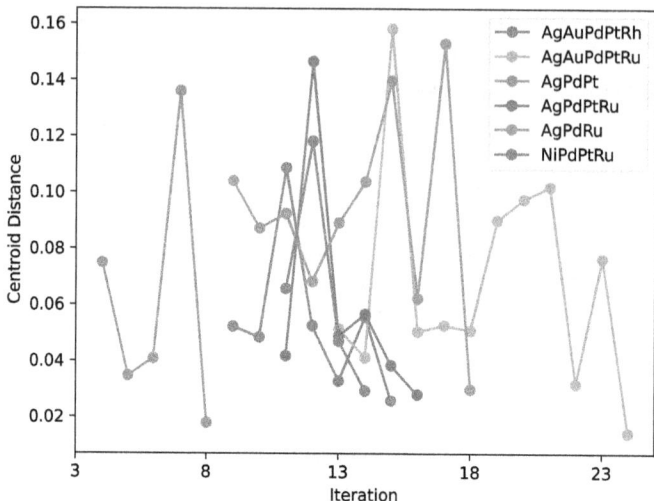

Fig. 2. Centroid distance as a function of iterations for different material systems.

- For HER and ORR, the objective was to maximize similarity to *conductivity* while minimizing similarity to *dielectric*.
- For oxygen evolution OER, the objective was to maximize similarity to *dielectric* while minimizing similarity to *conductivity*.

Compositions on the reaction-specific Pareto fronts in similarity space defined by S_i constitute our predictions for high-performing materials.

3 Results

3.1 Centroid Convergence Over Iterations

Figure 2 shows the changes in centroid distance during each iteration for the six material systems we tested: AgPdPt, AgPdRu, AgPdPtRu (for ORR) [1], AgAuPdPtRh, AgAuPdPtRu (for HER) [21], and NiPdPtRu (for OER) [22]. The centroid distance measures the *shift* in the embedding space between iterations, and serves as a quantitative indicator of convergence. The first iteration constitutes the initialization and, therefore, does not have a previous iteration to compare against. Additionally, not all systems have values for every iteration because the embedding space is only defined when a trained Word2Vec model provides representations for all required elements as well as the target properties *dielectric* and *conductivity*. In other words, for some compositions, the first few batches of documents do not contain all tokens required to compute the word embeddings as well as their similarity scores. If the selected corpus for a given iteration lacks such similarities, the similarity space representation can not be established and, consequently, the centroid cannot be calculated. The number of iterations required to reach the convergence threshold of 0.03 for each material system is as follows:

- **AgPdPt:** Converged after 8 iterations, indicating steady refinement and early stabilization.
- **AgPdRu:** Required 18 iterations to stabilize, reflecting a gradual and extended refinement process.
- **AgPdPtRu:** Achieved convergence in 16 iterations, suggesting moderate complexity in refining its embedding space.
- **AgAuPdPtRh:** Stabilized after 15 iterations, indicating consistent refinement with gradual improvement.
- **AgAuPdPtRu:** Required 24 iterations to reach the threshold, showing a more extended effort to refine the embedding space.
- **NiPdPtRu:** Converged after 14 iterations, balancing between moderate refinement complexity and stabilization.

These results for different material systems exhibit a large variability in convergence behavior. AgPdPt has relatively fast convergence, while AgAuPdPtRu requires the largest number of iterations, reflecting the challenges of establishing a complex embedding space. Again, once the centroid distance falls below a user-defined, heuristically obtained threshold of 0.03, we consider the embedding space converged.

3.2 Pareto Analysis with Full Corpus vs. Selected Subset

After centroid convergence, we perform Pareto analysis following the method presented in [29] on each reaction type (ORR, HER, OER) using the final Word2Vec model for each material system. We compare the prediction of the candidate materials of the converged representations with predictions based on a model trained on all documents. This reference full-corpus model is the same for all three materials systems. Figures 3, 4 and 5 summarize the prediction metrics, highlighting the models' ability to predict high-performing materials in very different material systems and reaction types.

For ORR (Fig. 3), the selected-corpus model identified high-performing materials with subsequently measured minimum current densities at 850 mV of -0.50, -0.67, and $-0.37\,\mathrm{mA/cm^2}$ for the AgPdPt, AgPdRu, and AgPdPtRu systems, respectively. These predictions align closely with best-performing experimentally measured electrocatalytic response, which recorded -0.58, -0.67, and $-0.37\,\mathrm{mA/cm^2}$, respectively. The full-corpus model, while also successful in identifying high-performing materials, predicted slightly less optimal values of -0.44, -0.67, and $-0.37\,\mathrm{mA/cm^2}$. This difference demonstrates the effectiveness of the selected-corpus model in refining the search space and focusing on the most relevant documents for a given composition space.

Figure 4 shows the performance for the AgAuPdPtRh and AgAuPdPtRu systems for HER. The selected-corpus model achieved minimum current densities at $-300\,\mathrm{mV}$ of -1.13 and $-1.44\,\mathrm{mA/cm^2}$, closely matching the best measured electrocatalytic response of -1.13 and $-1.49\,\mathrm{mA/cm^2}$. The full-corpus model predicts values of -1.11 and $-1.41\,\mathrm{mA/cm^2}$, which, while accurate, do not represent the actual highest-performing compositions. These results further validate the ability of the selected-corpus model to identify optimal candidates effectively.

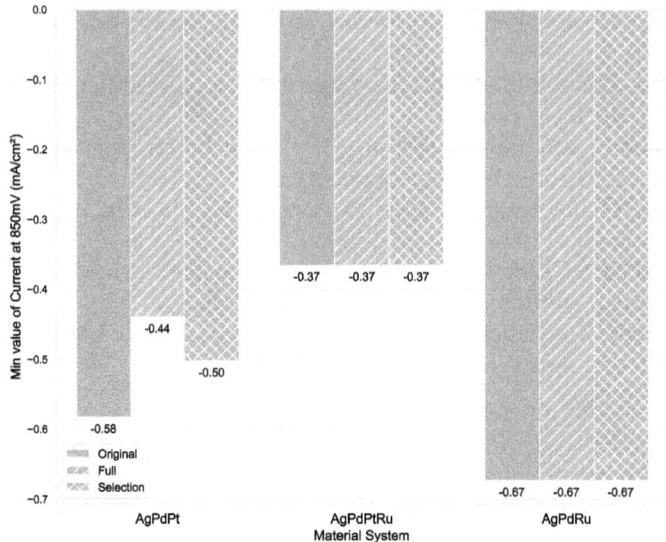

Fig. 3. Comparison of minimum current density values at 850 mV for ORR systems (AgPdPt, AgPdRu, AgPdPtRu) derived from the original performance data, the full-corpus model, and the selected-corpus model.

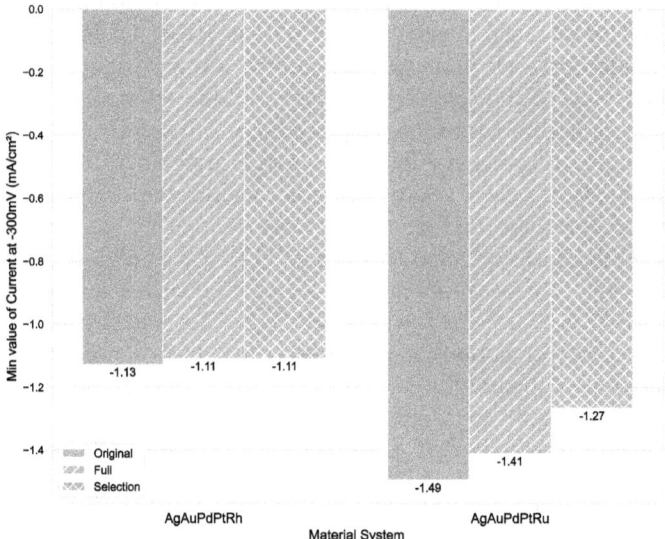

Fig. 4. Comparison of minimum current density values at −300 mV for HER systems (AgAuPdPtRh, AgAuPdPtRu) derived from the original performance data, the full-corpus model, and the selected-corpus model.

For HER, Fig. 4 presents the performance for the AgAuPdPtRh and AgAuPdPtRu systems. The selected-corpus model predicts minimum current densities at $-300\,\mathrm{mV}$ of -1.11 and $-1.27\,\mathrm{mA/cm^2}$. For the AgAuPdPtRu system, the value is slightly less optimal than the full-corpus model predictions of $-1.41\,\mathrm{mA/cm^2}$. Despite this, the selected-corpus model captures essential information from the full corpus, demonstrating its ability to approximate high-performing materials with a significantly smaller number of documents.

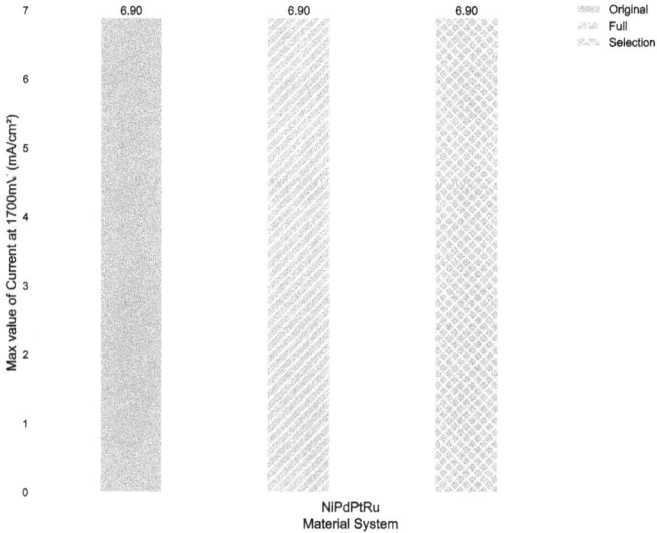

Fig. 5. Comparison of maximum current density values at 1700 mV for the OER system (NiPdPtRu) derived from the original performance data, the full-corpus model, and the selected-corpus model.

For OER, as shown in Fig. 5, the maximum current density at 1700 mV for the NiPdPtRu system is identical across all models, including the selected-corpus model, the full-corpus model, and the best measured data performance: 6.90 $\mathrm{mA/cm^2}$. This, again, confirms the consistency of our approach in capturing the best-performing materials using much fewer documents for creation of the representations.

All results collectively demonstrate that both the full-corpus and selected-corpus models successfully predict high-performing materials across all reaction types. Notably, the selected-corpus models achieve this with a much smaller number of documents. By refining the training corpus to only the most diverse documents measured by a combination of Doc2Vec embeddings, greedy selection and convergence threshold based on the centroid change, the iterative selection process improves the predictive power of the model without compromising performance across very different scenarios.

Table 1. Statistical details for electrocatalysts under specified potentials. Abbreviations: Entries (Ori), the original number of possible compositions before text-mining selection; Entries (Full), number of compositions on the Pareto front for the Word2Vec model based on the full corpus; Entries (Selection), number of compositions on the Pareto front based on the converged model with iterative greedy selection; Selected Documents, the total number of documents used in the final iteration to train the selected-corpus model.

Material Systems	Potential (mV)	Entries (Ori)	Entries (Full)	Entries (Selection)	Selected Documents
AgPdPt	850	341	11	63	400
AgPdRu	850	342	15	10	900
AgPdPtRu	850	341	27	4	800
AgAuPdPtRh	−300	327	16	29	750
AgAuPdPtRu	−300	335	23	3	1200
NiPdPtRu	1700	4026	374	168	700

Table 2. Minimum and maximum current densities (mA/cm^2) for electrocatalysts under specified potentials. Abbreviations: Min/Max (Ori, Full, Selection), the minimum and maximum current densities for each of the three scenarios (original data, full corpus model, selected-corpus models).

Material Systems	Min (Ori)	Min (Full)	Min (Selection)	Max (Ori)	Max (Full)	Max (Selection)
AgPdPt	−0.58	−0.44	−0.50	−0.06	−0.16	−0.06
AgPdRu	−0.67	−0.67	−0.67	−0.07	−0.36	−0.36
AgPdPtRu	−0.37	−0.37	−0.37	−0.06	−0.06	−0.34
AgAuPdPtRh	−1.13	−1.11	−1.11	−0.69	−0.73	−0.72
AgAuPdPtRu	−1.49	−1.41	−1.27	−0.79	−1.14	−1.06
NiPdPtRu	0.24	0.60	0.53	6.90	6.90	6.90

3.3 Current Density Measurements and Statistical Overview

Tables 1 and 2 present the statistical details and measured current densities (in mA/cm^2) for each system at its corresponding potential.

ORR Systems (AgPdPt, AgPdRu, AgPdPtRu at 850 mV):

- In **AgPdPt**, the selection-based model retains 63 entries compared to 11 in the full-corpus model. The minimum current density shifts from −0.44 mA/cm^2 in the full model to −0.50 mA/cm^2 in the selection model, while the maximum rises to −0.06 mA/cm^2.
- In **AgPdRu**, the minimum and maximum current densities remain the same across selection-based model and full-corpus model, at −0.67 mA/cm^2 and −0.36 mA/cm^2, respectively, with 10 entries retained in the selection model compared to 15 in the full model.
- In **AgPdPtRu**, the selection-based model retains 4 entries compared to 27 in the full model. The minimum current density remains −0.37 mA/cm^2, while

the maximum is lower at -0.34 mA/cm^2 compared to -0.06 mA/cm^2 in the full model.

HER Systems (AgAuPdPtRh, AgAuPdPtRu at -300 mV):

- In **AgAuPdPtRh**, the selection-based model retains 29 entries compared to 16 in the full model. The minimum current density is consistent at -1.11 mA/cm^2, while the maximum slightly increases from -0.72 mA/cm^2 in the selection model to -0.73 mA/cm^2 in the full model.
- In **AgAuPdPtRu**, the selection-based model retains 3 entries compared to 23 in the full model. The minimum current density slightly increases from -1.41 mA/cm^2 in the full model to -1.27 mA/cm^2 in the selection model, while the maximum decreases from -1.14 mA/cm^2 to -1.06 mA/cm^2.

OER System (NiPdPtRu at 1700 mV):

- **NiPdPtRu** starts with a large set of 4026 candidate compositions. The selection-based model retains 168 entries compared to 374 in the full-corpus model. The minimum current density decreases from 0.60 mA/cm^2 in the full model to 0.53 mA/cm^2 in the selection model, while the maximum remains consistent at 6.90 mA/cm^2.

All these results demonstrate that the iterative selection-based approach effectively narrows the dataset while preserving or even improving the ability to predict high-performing electrocatalysts from a large list of possible candidate compositions. The evidence in Table 2 supports the conclusion that a focused corpus can adequately capture and even surpass predicting the key characteristics of the full-corpus dataset.

4 Discussion

Our iterative selection approach consistently results in models that match or exceed the performance of the model built using the full corpus. For ORR and HER systems, the method identifies more negative (better) current densities, indicating higher catalytic performance. For OER, the selected-corpus model suggests the same high-performing compositions as the full corpus model. These results confirm that reducing the training set—when done strategically—does not compromise, and even improves the capability to predict high-performance compositions.

4.1 Advantages of Iterative Corpus Selection

A feature of our approach is the *stability criterion* that checks whether adding more information significantly changes the model's representation of materials. Once the difference between subsequent centroids in embedding space stays below a user-defined, heuristically found threshold, we stop adding more information. Note, all models use the same threshold. This ensures:

1. **Reduced Noise:** Unnecessary or very similar information is left out, preventing additional fuzziness of key semantic signals related to electrocatalytic properties.
2. **Computational Efficiency:** Fewer documents result in faster training and analysis.
3. **Focus:** The final Word2Vec embeddings capture terminology tailored to the studied compositions, reactions, and the properties *dielectric* and *conductivity*.

4.2 Practical Impact on Electrocatalyst Screening

By identifying fewer yet relevant documents for training, this approach can speed up the overall pipeline of electrocatalyst design in particular for scenarios where experimental data are scarce and simulation-based data prove computationally intractable. Fewer experimental tests are needed because the Pareto analysis, driven by these tailored embeddings, allows to narrow down a large pool of candidate compositions to a much small, experimentally accessible likely high-performing compositions.

4.3 Mitigating the Growing Volume of AI-Generated Text

The rise of AI-generated information, specifically texts, poses new challenges. Large language models sometimes produce repetitive, paraphrased, or even wrong content by hallucination [30]. On a large scale, if generative AI models which are retrained on recursively generated output (meaning their own output), the resulting models become defective – they start producing noise [20]. Our iterative selection loop, which operates in the embedding space and discards information that does not shift the centroid meaningfully, offers a possibility to filter noise or at least avoid duplicated information: our framework avoids documents which contribute little new information. As AI-generated content continues to grow, such filtering mechanisms may become essential to maintaining reliable text-based models.

4.4 Limitations and Potential Extensions

While the proposed framework demonstrates significant strengths in refining training corpora and often even improves predictive performance, it is not without limitations. A critical challenge lies in balancing coverage and specificity. If the initial subset of documents is too small or biased, it risks omitting important details, potentially reducing the general applicability of the model. Additionally, reliance on predefined target properties, such as *dielectric* and *conductivity* as in our case require domain knowledge to be defined. Such terms might be difficult to find for other prediction scenarios and broader applicability of our method. Future work will address these challenges by exploring the following extensions:

- **Human in the loop:** Involve domain experts to review and validate the selected documents, ensuring that important topics or underrepresented domains are not overlooked. For example, experts could identify emerging areas or validate key materials that align with research objectives.
- **Hybrid Models:** Integrate advanced NLP methods, such as transformer-based encoders (e.g., MatBERT [23]), to complement the iterative selection process. These models may provide additional layers of semantic evaluation or help identify nuanced relationships that Word2Vec with fixed representations might miss.
- **Property Expansion:** Extend the framework to incorporate a broader range of material properties or performance metrics. For instance, multi-objective optimization could include properties like catalytic efficiency, stability under reaction conditions, or environmental impact, enabling more targeted materials discovery and optimization pipelines.

5 Conclusion

Our contribution introduces an iterative framework for refining scientific corpora to create word2vec representations of with a minimal set of documents for specific prediction scenarios. By dynamically selecting a subset of 'most diverse' documents sampled in Doc2Vec embedding space with a greedy selection strategy and subsequently training Word2Vec models, our approach results in representations with minimal noise w.r.t. user-defined composition spaces and target properties as well as their relationships. Applied to material systems for ORR, HER, and OER, our framework reliably identifies high-performing compositions from a large candidate pool using fewer training documents, matching or exceeding the performance of models trained on full corpora. Our predictions are verified with experimental data. This verification demonstrates the ability of our framework to efficiently use text-based knowledge for composition-property correlations.

Acknowledgments. The authors gratefully acknowledge the financial support provided by the China Scholarship Council (CSC, CSC number: 202208360048) and funding by the Deutsche Forschungsgemeinschaft (DFG, German Research Foundation) through CRC 1625, project number 506711657, subprojects INF, A05.

Disclosure of Interests. The authors have no competing interests to declare.

References

1. Banko, L., Krysiak, O., Schumann, W., Ludwig, A.: Electrochemical activity of several compositions in the system AG-PD-PT-RU for the oxygen reduction reaction in 0.05 m koh solution ph 12.5 (2024). https://doi.org/10.5281/zenodo.13992986
2. Batchelor, T.A., Pedersen, J.K., Winther, S.H., Castelli, I.E., Jacobsen, K.W., Rossmeisl, J.: High-entropy alloys as a discovery platform for electrocatalysis. Joule **3**(3), 834–845 (2019). https://doi.org/10.1016/j.joule.2018.12.015

3. Bilgin, M., Sentürk, I.F.: Sentiment analysis on twitter data with semi-supervised doc2vec. In: 2017 International Conference on Computer Science and Engineering (UBMK), pp. 661–666 (2017). https://doi.org/10.1109/UBMK.2017.8093492
4. Ezugwu, E., Bonney, J., Yamane, Y.: An overview of the machinability of aero-engine alloys. J. Mater. Process. Technol. **134**(2), 233–253 (2003). https://doi.org/10.1016/S0924-0136(02)01042-7
5. Ferreira, P., et al.: Instability of Pt/C electrocatalysts in proton exchange membrane fuel cells: a mechanistic investigation. J. Electrochem. Soci. **152**(11), A2256–A2271 (2005). https://doi.org/10.1149/1.2050347
6. Fujishima, A., Rao, T.N., Tryk, D.A.: Titanium dioxide photocatalysis. J. Photochem. Photobiol., C **1**(1), 1–21 (2000). https://doi.org/10.1016/S1389-5567(00)00002-2
7. Geim, A., Novoselov, K.: The rise of graphene. Nat. Mater. **6**(3), 183–191 (2007). https://doi.org/10.1038/nmat1849
8. Goldberg, Y., Levy, O.: word2vec explained: deriving Mikolov et al.'s negative-sampling word-embedding method (2014). https://arxiv.org/abs/1402.3722
9. Huang, P.K., Yeh, J.W., Shun, T.T., Chen, S.K.: Multi-principal-element alloys with improved oxidation and wear resistance for thermal spray coating. Adv. Eng. Mater. **6**(1-2), 74–78 (2004). https://doi.org/10.1002/adem.200300507
10. Jain, A., Shin, Y., Persson, K.A.: Computational predictions of energy materials using density functional theory. Nature Rev. Mater. **1**(1) (2016). https://doi.org/10.1038/natrevmats.2015.4
11. Larcher, D., Tarascon, J.M.: Towards greener and more sustainable batteries for electrical energy storage. Nat. Chem. **7**(1), 19–29 (2015). https://doi.org/10.1038/nchem.2085
12. Le, Q., Mikolov, T.: Distributed representations of sentences and documents (2014)
13. Liu, Y., Zhao, T., Ju, W., Shi, S.: Materials discovery and design using machine learning. J. Materiomics **3**(3), 159–177 (2017). https://doi.org/10.1016/j.jmat.2017.08.002
14. Mikolov, T., Chen, K., Corrado, G., Dean, J., Sutskever, L., Zweig, G.: word2vec **22**, 795 (2013). https://code.google.com/p/word2vec
15. Miracle, D., Senkov, O.: A critical review of high entropy alloys and related concepts. Acta Materialia **122**, 448 – 511 (2017). https://doi.org/10.1016/j.actamat.2016.08.081
16. Raccuglia, P., et al.: Machine-learning-assisted materials discovery using failed experiments. Nature **533**(7601), 73–76 (2016). https://doi.org/10.1038/nature17439
17. Ragauskas, A.J., et al.: The path forward for biofuels and biomaterials. Science **311**(5760), 484–489 (2006). https://doi.org/10.1126/science.1114736
18. Saal, J.E., Kirklin, S., Aykol, M., Meredig, B., Wolverton, C.: Materials design and discovery with high-throughput density functional theory: the open quantum materials database (OQMD). JOM **65**(11), 1501–1509 (2013). https://doi.org/10.1007/s11837-013-0755-4
19. Schmidt, J., et al.: Improving machine-learning models in materials science through large datasets. Mater. Today Phys. **48**, 101560 (2024). https://doi.org/10.1016/j.mtphys.2024.101560
20. Shumailov, I., Shumaylov, Z., Zhao, Y., Papernot, N., Anderson, R., Gal, Y.: AI models collapse when trained on recursively generated data. Nature **631**(8022), 755–759 (2024). https://doi.org/10.1038/s41586-024-07566-y

21. Thelen, F., Zehl, R., Limani, N., Schuhmann, W., Ludwig, A.: High-throughput SECCM and EDX data for the hydrogen evolution reaction in ag-au-pd-pt-ru and ag-au-pd-pt-rh thin-film materials libraries (2025). https://doi.org/10.5281/zenodo.14959252
22. Thelen, F., Zehl, R., Zerdoumi, R., Bürgel, J.L., Schuhmann, W., Ludwig, A.: Dataset - accelerating combinatorial electrocatalyst discovery with Bayesian optimization: a case study in the quaternary system ni-pd-pt-ru for the oxygen evolution reaction (2025). https://doi.org/10.5281/zenodo.14891704
23. Trewartha, A., et al.: Quantifying the advantage of domain-specific pre-training on named entity recognition tasks in materials science. Patterns **3**(4), 100488 (2022). https://doi.org/10.1016/j.patter.2022.100488
24. Tshitoyan, V., et al.: Unsupervised word embeddings capture latent knowledge from materials science literature. Nature **571**(7763), 95–98 (2019). https://doi.org/10.1038/s41586-019-1335-8
25. Yeh, J.W., et al.: Nanostructured high-entropy alloys with multiple principal elements: novel alloy design concepts and outcomes. Adv. Eng. Mater. **6**(5), 299–303 (2004). https://doi.org/10.1002/adem.200300567
26. Zerdoumi, R., Ludwig, A., Schuhmann, W.: High entropy intermetallic compounds: a discovery platform for structure–property correlations and materials design principles in electrocatalysis. Curr. Opin. Electrochem. **48**, 101590 (2024). https://doi.org/10.1016/j.coelec.2024.101590
27. Zhang, L., Stricker, M.: MatNexus: a comprehensive text mining and analysis suite for materials discovery. SoftwareX **26**, 101654 (2024). https://doi.org/10.1016/j.softx.2024.101654
28. Zhang, L., Stricker, M.: Code for "iterative corpus refinement for materials property prediction based on scientific texts" (2025). https://github.com/lab-mids/word_embedding_paper_selection
29. Zhang, L., Stricker, M.: Electrocatalyst discovery through text mining and multi-objective optimization (2025). https://arxiv.org/abs/2502.20860
30. Zhang, Y., et al.: Siren's song in the AI ocean: a survey on hallucination in large language models. arXiv:2309.01219 (2023)

CARIS: Cache Affinity-Aware Reinforced Intelligent Strategy

Yu Zuo and Yanlei Shang(✉)

Beijing University of Posts and Telecommunications, Beijing, China
shangyl@bupt.edu.cn

Abstract. The cache is a critical component that directly impacts the computational system's performance and Quality of Service (QoS), with its effectiveness determined by the caching policy in use. An ideal caching policy must adapt to diverse workloads while approximating the optimal strategy. Recent advancements in caching strategies have focused on two paradigms: user access pattern prediction based on supervised learning and policy search methods based on Reinforcement Learning (RL). Supervised learning approaches often suffer from predictive inaccuracies. RL methods face challenges with large state spaces and insufficient exploration. Both paradigms lead to suboptimal performance and unbearable complexity in the decision making process. In this paper, we propose CARIS, a novel caching policy that integrates cache affinity estimation with a deep reinforcement learning agent. CARIS estimates the cache affinity of each user access, and focuses the agent's exploration on accesses with higher predicted cache affinity, effectively reducing unnecessary exploration and addressing the limitations of both paradigms. Additionally, to reduce complexity in decision making, CARIS introduces an "empty action" mechanism during cache hits to reduce noise from irrelevant actions. Through comprehensive experiments with multiple datasets, CARIS achieves an improvement more than 294% in the average cache hit rates compared to the SOTA learning-based caching policies under the tested scenarios. Our results highlight CARIS's potential to advance both theoretical understanding and practical efficiency in modern caching systems.

Keywords: Caching Strategy · Reinforcement Learning · Storage

1 Introduction

The cache system is widely deployed in computer systems across various domains, greatly affecting their performance and quality of experience (QoE). The fundamental principle of the cache system is to store the frequently accessed data objects in a smaller but quicker-to-access medium, to reduce the access frequency on the larger but slower-to-access medium, so that the average access time is minimized. We find caches in networking systems, large databases, and micro systems on chips (SoCs).

Although caching greatly improves the system's performance in general, the key to its optimization is to find the most appropriate caching policy for the scenario under specific workloads. The classic heuristic-based caching policies are studied in depth, including Least-recently-used (LRU), Least-frequently-used (LFU), First-in-first-out (FIFO), and Greedy-dual-size-frequency (GDSF) [1]. They are simple to understand and implement, integrated in the commonly deployed cache systems (e.g. Redis [3], Memcached [7]). However, the storage system's access pattern is often complex and hard to predict, while these policies can only stick to their predetermined rules, not adapting to the evolving access pattern. The next step to developing better caching policies is to employ machine learning (ML) techniques.

Recently, many learning-based caching policies are proposed (e.g. [8,10,21, 22,27]). Most of these works are based on the idea of predicting the user access pattern so as to approximate the globally optimal policy. For instance, the Belady's replacement policy always chooses the object that is accessed furthest to the future to replace when the cache is full and a cache load operation is imminent, making the key to its approximation the prediction of an object's revisit time from the current moment. The recently proposed models predict patterns required by the theoretically optimal policies to invoke the ideal policies with confidence in their predictions. However, since all ML models suffer from inevitable limitations in their predicting abilities, these caching policies based on user access pattern prediction are always suboptimal.

Other policies based on reinforcement learning are also studied in depth (e.g. [12,15]). Unlike the methods based on user access pattern predictions, the RL-based policies employ an agent to explore the cache system's state space and search for the optimal policy. By deciding on an objective such as maximizing object hit rate and using an RL training method (e.g. DQN [17], Actor-Critic [13], PPO [19]), the policy is learned in an end-to-end fashion, fulfilling the designated objective. The major limitation in the RL-based policies is that the state space is too large to be sufficiently explored for an RL agent with a policy network that has a limited number of parameters in during the training phase. The agent is highly likely to spend an excessive amount of time on unimportant states and actions, resulting in its underperformance compared to the policies based on the user access pattern prediction.

For the problem of caching strategy optimization, the main challenges are (1) how the RL agent's exploration can be effectively simplified and (2) how cache affinity prediction can aid the agent's exploration. In this paper, we propose CARIS, a cache admission policy based on reinforcement learning and the cache affinity prediction on the user access, to address the aforementioned challenges. We summarize the key contributions of this work as follows:

1. CARIS introduces an "empty action" during cache hits. For a cache admission policy, the action taken in the event of a cache hit cannot actually influence the cache system's state, and the agent always receives a higher immediate reward. CARIS forces the agent to take the empty action on cache hit during training, not taking any irrelevant actions.

2. CARIS merges the concept of cache affinity into the RL policy. CARIS first estimates the cache affinity of each user access. Then the access deemed cache-averse is rejected to be admitted by the agent without consulting the major policy network. By filtering the cache-averse objects beforehand, the exploration focuses on objects that are more likely to generate cache hits in the near future.
3. We constructed datasets with real-world workloads to test CARIS and compare it with existing SOTA methods, and prove its superiority in terms of cache hit rate.

2 Related Works

This section introduces some basic concepts related to the following major sections, and recent research development concerning these concepts.

2.1 Deep Reinforcement Learning

A decision process is a sequence of states and actions of an agent, denoted as $\{(S_t, a_t)\}_{t=0}^{t=\infty}$. An agent is capable of making decisions at each step. If the state's probability distribution at time $t+1$ solely depends on the state and action taken at the previous moment t, we call the decision process Markovian, or a Markov Decision Process (MDP). That is, the state transition kernel has the form of $p(S_{t+1}|S_t, a_t)$.

At each moment in an MDP, an immediate reward depending on the state and action taken of the moment can be sampled by the agent, denoted as r_t and has the distribution of the form $p(r_t|S_t, a_t)$.

The agent must decide upon an action at each time t by some learned distribution $p(a_t|S_t)$ called policy, so the discounted sum of the rewards across all time steps is maximized. To learn such a policy, reinforcement learning methods are often employed. Common RL training methods based on deep learning (DL) includes DQN [4], Actor-Critic [13], TRPO, PPO [19], DDPG [25].

2.2 Caching Policies Based on Access Pattern Prediction

Caching policies based on user access pattern prediction approximate the optimal policy by having the model predict a key variable derived from the user access sequences, that indirectly leads to optimality.

Multiple papers try to approximate the Belady's replacement policy. LRB [21] predicts the reuse time of each user-accessed object to meet Belady's requirement with GBM [11], and produce a cache replacement policy. LHR [27] predicts the hazard rate of the user-accessed objects, an upper bound of the reuse time, to do the same thing as in LRB [21]. Raven [8] does the estimation with a mixed-density neural network (MDN) [23].

Cache affinity of the user accesses has also been favored as a key to optimality. Hawkeye [10] trains a model to find the cache-averse objects, and replace them with a higher priority. HR-Cache [22] employs the hazard rate estimation from LHR [27] as a measure of cache affinity, as in Hawkeye [10], and replaces them as in Hawkeye [10].

Methods based on user access pattern prediction have 2 major issues. (1) It requires explicit feature selection and engineering. (2) It suffers from prediction inaccuracy.

CARIS resolves these issues by introducing an RL agent that is feature-agnostic and trained end-to-end. The agent explores in depth the cache system's state space induced by the accesses to the cache-friendly objects to mitigate the impact of the inaccurate predictions.

2.3 Caching Policies Based on RL

The RL-based caching policies train an RL agent that outputs the action's probability distribution at each time step. Parrot [15] tries to approximate the Belady's cache replacement policy by imitation learning. RL-Cache [12] maximizes the discounted sum of the number of cache hits by Monte-Carlo sampling.

Different from Parrot [15] or RL-Cache [12], other studies do not present a caching policy for the general case, but for problems encountered in the specific fields. [2,14,26] constructed RL-based policy models for caching problems for networking in device-to-device scenarios, vehicles, video streaming and mobile edge respectively.

RL-based caching policies underperform policies based on access pattern prediction in general, due to the inefficiency of the agent's exploration. The more successful applications focus on special case scenarios, rather than the general cache system optimization problem.

CARIS resolves the exploration problem (1) by introducing an empty action during cache hits, and (2) by filtering away the cache-averse objects before the agent is invoked. By applying these two techniques, CARIS outperforms the existing RL-based methods without sharing any of their defectiveness.

3 The Caching Problem Analysis

This section first proves the caching policy optimization problem CARIS means to solve is equivalent to an RL problem in Sect. 3.1. Then, Sects. 3.2, 3.3 introduces the techniques used in solving the problem of interest.

3.1 The Cache Admission Process as an MDP

Consider a storage system with cache that receives user access requests as time progresses. Denote the user-accessed data object at time t as e_t, and the cache table as c_t, that is the set of all objects in cache. We further consider a cache system with an admission policy, that decides whether the accessed object should be loaded into cache in the event of a cache miss. Denote the admission decision as a_t, with $a_t = 1$ meaning the object should be loaded into cache. Denote the replaced data object in cache at time t as u_t. The cache behaviour can be described as Eq. 1, with the cache state unchanged when the admission policy rejects the object.

$$c_{t+1} = \begin{cases} c_t \cup \{e_t\} \setminus \{u_t\} & (a_t = 1) \\ c_t & (a_t = 0) \end{cases} \quad (1)$$

Let us first show that any caching decision process is Markovian. At any given time t, denote the sequence of the cache table c_t in Eq. 1 before time t as $C_t = \{c_\tau\}_{\tau=t}^{\tau=\infty}$, the cache admission action at time t as a_t, the user accessed object at time t as e_t, and the user's access sequence before time t as $U_t = \{e_\tau\}_{\tau=t}^{\tau=\infty}$. The cache table at time $t+1$ is determined by the cache table at time t according to Eq. 1. Consider the cache system's state as $S_t = (C_t, U_t)$. The next state S_{t+1} is determined once the current state S_t and action a_t is given, making the caching decision process Markovian.

Note that cache admission policy must be accompanied by a cache replacement policy, as in Eq. 1 u_t must be given when the cache is full. Any cache replacement policy can work in general.

The caching policy optimization problem can be formulated as an optimization problem of MDP. The cache system's state transition kernel is explicitly given in Eq. 2, where $p(C_{t+1}|C_t, e_{t+1}, U_t)$ is the δ function equivalent to Eq. 1.

$$p(S_{t+1}|S_t, a_t) = p(U_{t+1}, C_{t+1}|C_t, U_t, a_t) = p(e_{t+1}|U_t)p(C_{t+1}|C_t, e_{t+1}, U_t) \quad (2)$$

Denote $X_t = 1$ in the event of a cache hit, and $X_t = 0$ in the event of a cache miss. The optimization objective is to maximize the discounted number of cache hits, which is the discounted sum of X_t by a factor of γ less than 1, as in Eq. 3.

$$H_T = \sum_{t \geq T} \gamma^{t-T} X_t \quad (3)$$

Since the caching decision process can be considered Markovian, we propose to maximize the objective H_T in Eq. 3 by reinforcement learning methods for all choices of T. At any moment t, treat S_t as the agent's state, $a_t \in \{0, 1\}$ as the agent's action, and X_t sampled at time t as the immediate reward r_t. Denote the state space as $\mathbf{S}$, which is constructively formed by all possible values that S_t might take at any given moment t. H_T's expectation given the observed state at the same moment T is the state value function $V(S_T)$ by definition. By solving the reinforcement learning problem, CARIS finds the expected optimal H_T for all T of interest and the accompanied optimal caching policy.

Different from the general MDP problems, the decision process we consider yields immediate rewards regardless of the action taken at the moment, since whether the access attains a cache hit is not determined by whether the cache admits the accessed object. Therefore, during training, the agent can first sample states and rewards, then decides upon an action.

3.2 Focus on Cache Misses

The cache admission policy agent is not active when there is a cache hit. Only when there is a cache miss, is the policy's decision actually affecting the objective in Eq. 3. Based on this observation, CARIS introduces the empty action, denoted as $a_t = 2$. The empty action is equivalent to the no-admit action when there is a cache miss. CARIS is forced to take the empty action when there is a cache hit in training, as in Eq. 4, where $h_t = 0$ represents a cache miss at time t and $h_t = 1$ represents a cache hit.

$$p(a_t = 2 | h_t = 0) = 0, p(a_t = 2 | h_t = 1) = 1 \qquad (4)$$

By the definition of the MDP optimization problem, if the action is either admit or no-admit, the immediate rewards and state transitions at that moment should be statistically dependent on the action, as in Eq. 2. By introducing the empty action, this assumption is satisfied for the admit and no-admit actions, and misleading exploration induced by actions during cache hits is avoided.

3.3 Focus on Cache-Friendly Objects

Many objects are rarely revised by the users within a short period of time, according to the dataset statistics in Table 1a. As in Fig. 2, the number of accesses for an object within one sequence is below 10 for the datasets used in the experiments. Generally speaking, the cache admission policy should adopt the behaviour that it admits with a higher probability the objects that are more likely to be repeatedly accessed by the users.

Denote $p_{T,T+L}^{m,R}$ for object m in some given time interval $[T, T + L)$ as the probability of the object being accessed R times in the given time interval, provided that the object is not replaced, as in Eq. 5. $\mathbf{M}_{T,T+L}^m$ is a collection of sequences that is composed of 0's and 1's and sums to R. $M \in \mathbf{M}_{T,T+L}^m$ is a sequence in the collection, and M_i denotes the ith object of the sequence. p_t^m is the probability of the accessed object e_t being object m. $p_{T,T+L}^{m,R}$ is small for most m, R, L.

$$p_{T,T+L}^{m,R} = \sum_{M \in \mathbf{M}_{T,T+L}^m} \prod_{t=T}^{T+L} (p_t^m)^{M_{t-T}} \qquad (5)$$

To simplify the exploration, CARIS introduces the concept of cache affinity as in [10] and [27]. It considers an object m cache-friendly at time T if $p_{T,T+L}^{m,R} > \rho$ holds for some predetermined constants ρ, L, R, and the object is cache-averse if otherwise.

When there is a cache miss and CARIS is deciding whether it admits the accessed object, CARIS first evaluates its cache affinity. If the object is cache-averse, reject the object. If the object is cache-friendly, CARIS then consults the policy model trained as a reinforcement learning agent. By filtering out the cache-averse objects before the major reinforcement learning agent is taken into account, the agent is protected from learning to decide on rarely revised objects. The exploration is significantly simplified, and focuses only on the decisions concerning cache-friendly objects. The input space of the agent's policy distribution function $p(a_t|S_t)$ is reduced since the potential U_t in S_t is partially filtered away.

In Sect. 4.2, we propose the cache affinity predictor as a part of CARIS to implement the aforementioned decision plan. In Sect. 4.3, we adopt the maskable action from [9] to force the agent to perform a no-admit action in the event of the accessed object being cache-averse.

4 The CARIS Policy Model

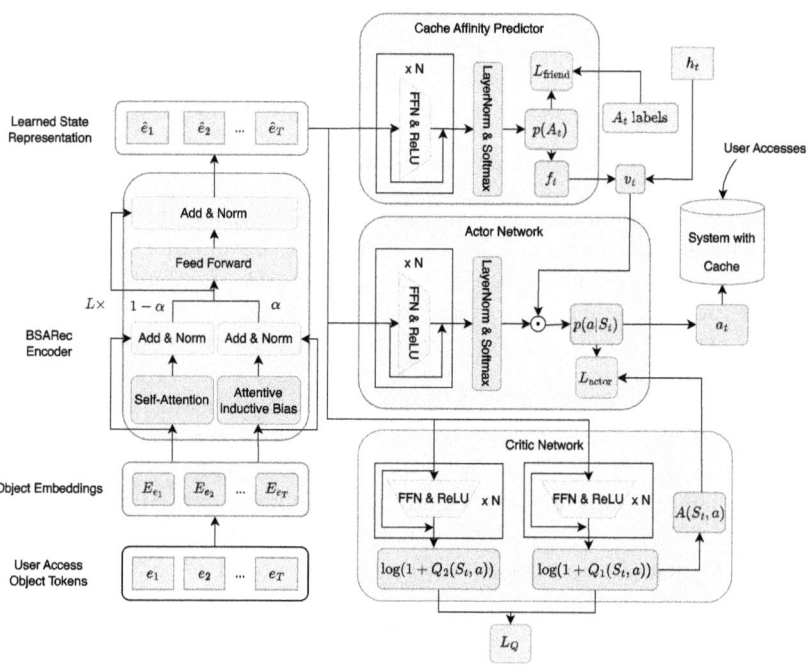

Fig. 1. Cache Affinity-aware Reinforced Intelligent Strategy Model

This section describes CARIS's internal structure in depth. CARIS is composed of a user access sequence encoder and multiple feed-forward neural networks, as in Fig. 1, estimating the cache affinity, the state value function and the policy distribution. The hyper parameters used for model building and training are listed in Table 2 in the appendix Sect. A.

4.1 The Object Access Sequence Encoder

This subsection introduces the object access sequence encoder which learns the user-accessed objects' representation.

As in the cases of NLP and CV, the transformer family does a good job in learning the sequence representation for inputs from various domains. In our case, CARIS uses BSARec [20], a transformer-like architecture, to encode the object access sequence. The vanilla transformer suffers from information loss in the high-frequency spectrum of the representation computed at each of its layers. BSARec introduces a high-pass filter against this background to mitigate the problem.

As in Fig. 1, the encoder based on BSARec takes the user access sequence tokens $e_1, ..., e_T$ as input, and produces vectors $\hat{e}_t$ as the representation $\hat{e}_t$ of the cache system state S_t.

4.2 The Cache Affinity Predictor

In this subsection, we propose to estimate the cache affinity from Sect. 3.3. CARIS estimates $\hat{p}_{T,T+L}^m$ given by Eq. 6, an upper bound of $p_{T,T+L}^{m,R} \cdot \hat{p}_{T,T+L}^m$ is the probability that object m is accessed at least 2 times between time T and $T+L$, so it satisfies 6. Since $p_{T,T+L}^{m,R} > 0$ for any m, R, T, L, we have $\hat{p}_{T,T+L}^m > p_{T,T+L}^{m,R}$, which is a tight bound when the probability that an object is revised by a user is relatively small.

$$\hat{p}_{T,T+L}^m = 1 - \prod_{t=T}^{T+L}(1 - p_t^m) = \sum_{R \geq 2} p_{T,T+L}^{m,R} \qquad (6)$$

For some predetermined constants $\rho \in (0,1)$ and L, CARIS considers the object e_t accessed at time t cache-friendly if $\hat{p}_{T,T+L}^{e_t} \geq \rho$, and cache-averse if otherwise. At time t, denote the event that the object e_t is accessed in $(t, t+L)$ as $A_t = 1$, and $A_t = 0$ if otherwise. A_t's probability distribution is computed according to Eq. 7 based on the representation learned by the sequence encoder.

$$p(A_t = 1|\hat{e}_t) = \text{softmax}(\text{FFN}_{\text{affinity}}(\hat{e}_t)) \qquad (7)$$

The loss function for the cache affinity predictor's training is Eq. 8, where we use i to differentiate the training experiences. Denote the number of state transitions in the training sequence l as $N_l^{(i)}$, and denote the number of experiences used in training as N_L.

$$L_{\text{affinity}} = -\frac{1}{N_L}\sum_i \frac{1}{N_l^{(i)}} \sum_t [A_t^{(i)} \log p(A_t^{(i)} = 1) + (1 - A_t^{(i)}) \log p(A_t^{(i)} = 0)] \qquad (8)$$

4.3 The Actor Learner

This subsection describes the actor network and the computation of $p(a_t|S_t)$.

The policy distribution is computed based on the representation $\hat{e}_t$ given by the sequence encoder, as the actor network in Fig. 1 and Eq. 9. The actor network outputs a 3 dimensional vector, representing the no-admit, admit, and empty actions respectively as $p(a_t|S_t)$.

$$p(a_t|S_t) = \mathrm{softmax}(\mathrm{FFN}_{\mathrm{policy}}(\hat{e}_t)) \tag{9}$$

A valid action is the action that can be taken by the agent. CARIS computes the action validity indicators, with which the policy rules described in Sects. 3.2, 3.3 are enforced. When there is a cache miss and $\hat{p}^m_{T,T+L} \geq \rho$, $a_t = 0$ is an invalid action, while other actions are valid. When there is a cache hit, the only valid action is $a_t = 2$. Denote the event that the action i at time t is valid as $v_t^i = 1$, and as $v_t^0 = 0$ if otherwise. Denote the event that there is a cache hit at time t as $h_t = 1$, and $h_t = 0$ if otherwise. Denote the event that $\hat{p}^{et}_{T,T+L} < \rho$ as $f_t = 1$, and $f_t = 0$ if otherwise. The validity indicators v_t^i for each of the actions i can be computed as in Eq. 10.

$$\begin{cases} v_t^0 = (1 - h_t) f_i \\ v_t^1 = 1 - h_t \\ v_t^2 = h_t \end{cases} \tag{10}$$

CARIS adopts action masks [9] to implement the action constraints. To avoid taking an invalid action, the input logits to the softmax function in Eq. 9 is set to a very small negative constant (CARIS uses -10^8) to represent $-\infty$, so that the component produce 0 probability. Reformulate Eqs. 9, 10 and 11, where $\odot$ is the vector's element-wise product.

One may consider enforcing Eq. 4 by assigning negative rewards to invalid actions during training. However, the agent would still have to spend time exploring by taking invalid actions and might not come to the right conclusion after lots of efforts. This is explained in [9] in detail. By using the action masks, we help the agent skip the exploring part.

$$p(a_t|S_t) = \mathrm{softmax}(v_t \odot \mathrm{FFN}_{\mathrm{policy}}(\hat{e}_t) + (1 - v_t) \cdot (-\infty)) \tag{11}$$

CARIS uses the PPO algorithm to train the policy network. Once a state transition from S_t to S_{t+1} by action a_t is observed, the loss is given by Eq. 12, where $R_t = \frac{p(a_t|S_t^{(i)})}{\mathbf{sg}[p(a_t|S_t^{(i)})]}$, and $\mathbf{sg}$ is the stop-gradient operator in the computation graph. $A(S_t, a_t)$ is the estimate of the advantage, which is discussed in Sect. 4.4 in depth. CARIS introduces a penalty on the policy's entropy $\mathbf{H}[p(\cdot|S_t^{(i)})]$, preventing the policy from collapsing onto a single action too early.

$$(L_{actor})_t^{(i)} = -\min\left[R_t A(S_t^{(i)}, a_t), \mathrm{clip}\left(R_t, 1 + \epsilon, 1 - \epsilon\right)\right] - \beta_1 \mathbf{H}[p(\cdot|S_t^{(i)})] \tag{12}$$

4.4 The Critic Learner

This subsection describes the estimation of $A(S_t, a_t)$ required by Eq. 12. For any possible state S_t and action a, CARIS estimates the state value function $V(S_t)$ and state-action value function $Q(S_t, a)$, then derives the advantage estimate by computing $A(S_t, a) = Q(S_t, a) - V(S_t)$. The state value function can be estimated by Q's estimate, as $V(S_t) = \max_a Q(S_t, a)$.

The Q function is estimated by the critic network part in Fig. 1. Like DreamerV3 [5], the multilayered feed-forward network's output is set to be the symlog value of Q's estimate, as in Eq. 14, where the symlog function and its inverse symexp is given in Eq. 13.

$$\text{symlog}(x) = \log(1+x), \text{symexp}(x) = \exp(x) - 1 \tag{13}$$

$$\text{symlog}(Q(S_t, a)) = \text{FFN}_Q(\hat{e}_t) \tag{14}$$

The critic network's parameters are trained in the double DQN fashion. The critic network is composed of 2 multilayered feed-forward networks, denoted as the training and target critics respectively, as in Fig. 1. Denote the output of the training critic as $Q_1(S_t, a)$ and the output of the target critic as $Q_2(S_t, a)$. Once a state transition from S_t to S_{t+1} by action a_t is observed, the loss given by Eq. 16 is computed and accumulated into the total loss. In Eq. 15, r_t is the immediate reward yielded by the state transition, and **sg** is the stop-gradient operator in the computation graph, so no parameter update would be performed on its input.

$$\hat{Q}(S_t, a_t) = r_t + \gamma \mathbf{sg}[Q_2(S_{t+1}, \arg\max_a Q_1(S_{t+1}, a))] \tag{15}$$

$$L_Q = \frac{1}{N_L} \sum_{i,t} \frac{1}{2} \left[\text{symlog}(Q_1(S_t^{(i)}, a_t^{(i)})) - \text{symlog}(\hat{Q}(S_t^{(i)}, a_t^{(i)})) \right]^2 \tag{16}$$

Combining Eqs. 8,16,12, the total loss is the weighted sum of the 3 losses, as in Eq. 17, where β_2, β_3 are the predetermined weights.

$$L = L_{actor} + \beta_2 L_Q + \beta_3 L_{\text{affinity}} \tag{17}$$

4.5 Offline Training and Online Inference

CARIS is trained in the same way as the vanilla PPO algorithm, in an on-policy manner with a replay buffer as in [4]. Training experiences are generated by a cache system simulation and fed into the replay buffer. The training process samples experiences from the replay buffer and performs parameter updates.

When using a trained CARIS model for online inference, CARIS splits the user access sequence into 2 subsequencesses by picking a separating time step. The moments before the separating time step t is denoted as the history window, while the moments after the separating time step t is denoted as the inference window. After an inference operation is performed, the cache system performs cache loading operations according to the inference results of the items in the inference window. Then, user access records in the inference window are merged into the history window, and the inference window is cleared. New user access records are added to the empty inference window, before the next inference operation clears it again. When the history window grows larger than a predetermined limit, the window removes the oldest user access records each time new records are added. By adjusting the window sizes, the trade-off between inference time and system performance is addressed.

To simulate the data distribution in inference, the training dataset is expanded. For each sequence $\{e_t\}_{t=0}^{t=N^{(i)}}$ used during training, the expanded sequences are created according to $\{\{e_t\}_{t=0}^{t=l} | \forall l \in [1, N^{(i)}]\}$, to form a step-by-step scenario. All training sequences are expanded in this fashion to construct an expanded sequence set. The sequences used to generate experiences are sampled from the expanded sequence set.

Our model deployed in an real world application system is updated every hour. Newly received user access records are appended to the ever-growing training dataset, which is then used to incrementally train the model.

5 Experiments

Our experiments on CARIS were conducted with the PyTorch library [18]. A cache system simulator was built to evaluate various kinds of caching policies. Our code and dataset is publicly available at GitHub[1].

5.1 Datasets and Cache System Settings

We used the datasets enumerated in Table 1a for simulation and policy evaluation. The datasets have diverse characteristics. (1) The ML-1M [6] dataset contains user rating records on movies. We sort the rating records with respect to their timestamp for each user. Consider the movies as data objects and the rating records as a user's access to that object. The dataset is reformulated as a collection of user access sequences. (2) The Wiki dataset [24] is the access log of the Wikipedia website's server. We extract from it the requests to the main pages in Wikipedia, and divide the log into subsequences of length no larger than 550 to form a dataset of user access sequences. (3) The Twitter dataset [28] is the access log of Twitter's cache server. We sort the access records with respect to the access time for each user, like that is done with the ML-1M dataset. The dataset is reformed into a collection of user access sequences. We also tested CARIS with real-world workloads. While the results supported our work, these details cannot be disclosed due to commercial privacy and proprietary restrictions.

---

[1] https://github.com/Anarion-zuo/caris_repo.

Table 1. Datasets

(a) Datasets Statistics

Dataset		ML-1M	Wiki	Twitter
#Items		3416	12236	8280
Frequency	Avg	292.63	101.24	1207.73
	P50	146	104	50
	P90	765	138	2406
#Distinct	Avg	624.74	467.2	770.38
	P50	563	467	772
	P90	874.6	478	927
LEN	Avg	751.59	549.08	1665.83
	P50	677	549	1618
	P90	1040.6	549	2290.8
OHWR		0.69	0.81	0.25

(b) Cache Item Capacity

Dataset	Cache Capacity
ML-1M	17, 34, 68, 102
Wiki	13, 25, 50, 75
Twitter	75, 100, 125, 150

Table 1a includes some statistics of these datasets. The meaning of each of the statistics is listed here. (1) #Items is the total number of data objects accessed by the user. (2) Frequency is the number of accesses to each data object. (3) Distinct is the number of distinct data objects in each user access sequence. (4) LEN is the length of each user access sequence. (5) OHWR is the ratio between the number of data objects that are accessed only once in each user access sequence, and the number of user accesses in that same sequence.

Figure 2 depicts the distribution of the number of accesses for each data object within one sequence. Most objects are rarely accessed more than 10 times within one sequence.

A good caching strategy must perform well under difficult conditions, so the simulated cache capacities were chosen to be no more than 3% of the number of all data objects in each dataset, as given in Table 1b.

5.2 Experimental Methodology

Compared Caching Policies. We compared CARIS with 10 different caching policies, including Random, FIFO, LRU, LRU-4, LFU, GDSF [1], PredMarker [16], LRB [21], Raven [8], HR-Cache [22]. Random is the random replacement policy, which randomly selects an object in the cache to replace when the cache is full. PredMarker [16], LRB [21], Raven [8], HR-Cache [22] are policies based on machine learning, while others are based on heuristic rules.

Evaluation Metrics. For each dataset, randomly pick 64 sequences for performance evaluation, and use the rest for training. For each of the sequences used in evaluation, the last 100 user accesses were used as the inference window, as in Sect. 4.5. We used the cache object hit rate (OHR) in the inference window as

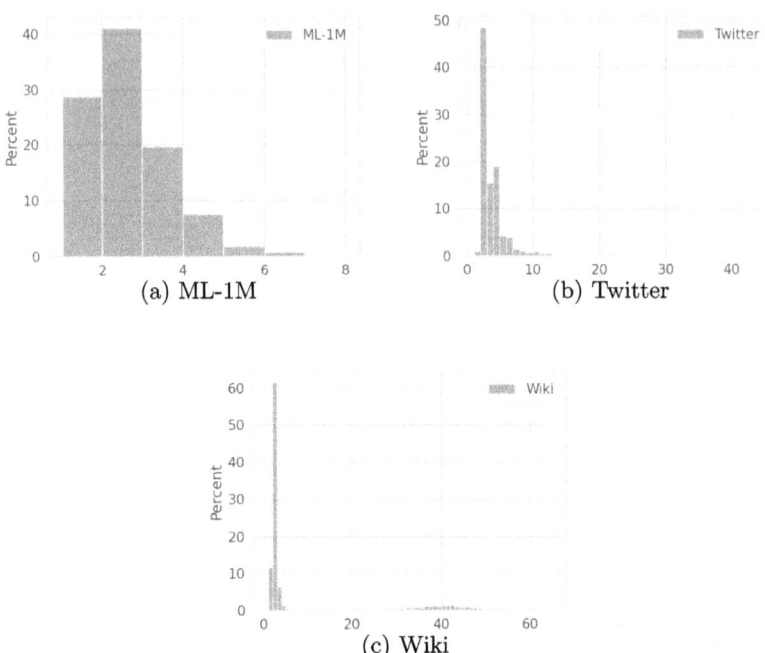

Fig. 2. Histograms of the Objects' #Accesses within One Sequence

the performance metric of a evaluation sequence. To enable comparison across datasets, we used the OHR of the Random policy as a baseline value and computed the normalized metric score with $x_r = \frac{x}{x_{\text{base}}} - 1$. x_{base} was set to be the OHR of the Random policy given the testing conditions if not specified otherwise.

5.3 Main Results

Figure 3 depicts the CARIS's OHR (not normalized) on the 3 datasets we used under various simulated cache capacities from Table 1b. Figure 4 depicts the normalized OHR of other policies compared to CARIS's, with the Random policy's OHR as the baseline value x_{base}.

Under all experimented conditions, CARIS outperformed all other policies consistently. Compared to the learning-based methods, CARIS achieved an improvement of more than 294% on average. CARIS's advantage differed on the various datasets, with ML-1M being the most victorious. Note that CARIS's normalized OHR did not monotonically increase with the simulated cache capacity, while its OHR did.

The compared learning-based methods (PredMarker, LRB, Raven, HR-Cache) exhibited apparent drawbacks. They are policies based on user access pattern predictions, whose performance is largely affected by the dataset's one

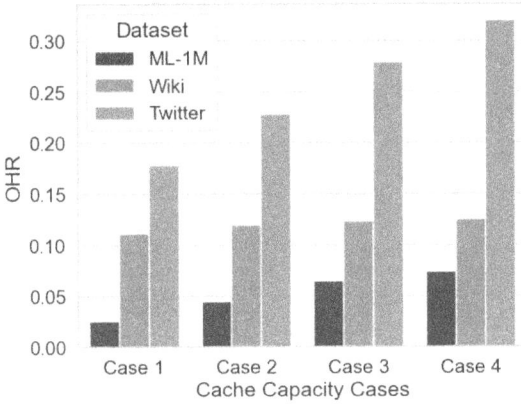

Fig. 3. CARIS OHR under Various Dataset and Cache Capacities

hit wonder ratio. When the one hit wonder ratio was large, wrong predictions were less harmful, since a right prediction hardly pays off when objects are rarely revised. The Wiki dataset has the largest one hit wonder ratio, and these policies performed the best and were closest to CARIS on Wiki.

However, when the cache capacity was relatively small, the prediction-based methods suffered more from a bad decision, since cache hits were relatively rare. Therefore they were even outperformed by the Random policy. CARIS has an RL agent to mitigate the damage caused by prediction errors.

5.4 Ablation Study

Consider the ablation study results in Fig. 5. Denote the CARIS without the empty action as RL+PredAffinity, and the case without the affinity predictor as RL+Nop. Denote the CARIS without the RL agent as PredAffinity, using solely the affinity predictor for object admission decisions. The PredAffinity CARIS admits objects when the access is considered cache-friendly. Figure 5 depicts the normalized OHR of CARIS when these key features were removed from it. The simulated cache capacity for the 3 datasets were 34, 100, 100 for these ablation studies. The baseline value x_{base} used in score rescaling was the OHR of the original CARIS. As is demonstrated by Fig. 5, any removal of the key components in CARIS damaged it.

A simple observation showed the importance of the cache affinity predictor in CARIS. Degradation was worst in the RL+Nop case on datasets Wiki and Twitter, where their OHR was so small compared to the original CARIS that the normalized scores were close to -1. However, since Twitter had its one hit wonder ratio smaller than Wiki's, and RL+Nop degraded almost equally on both datasets, the cache affinity is equally important for user access patterns with both larger or smaller probability of revisiting the previously accessed objects.

We further investigated the impact of the cache affinity predictor's accuracy on CARIS's performance. We tested on the datasets ML-1M, Wiki and Twitter

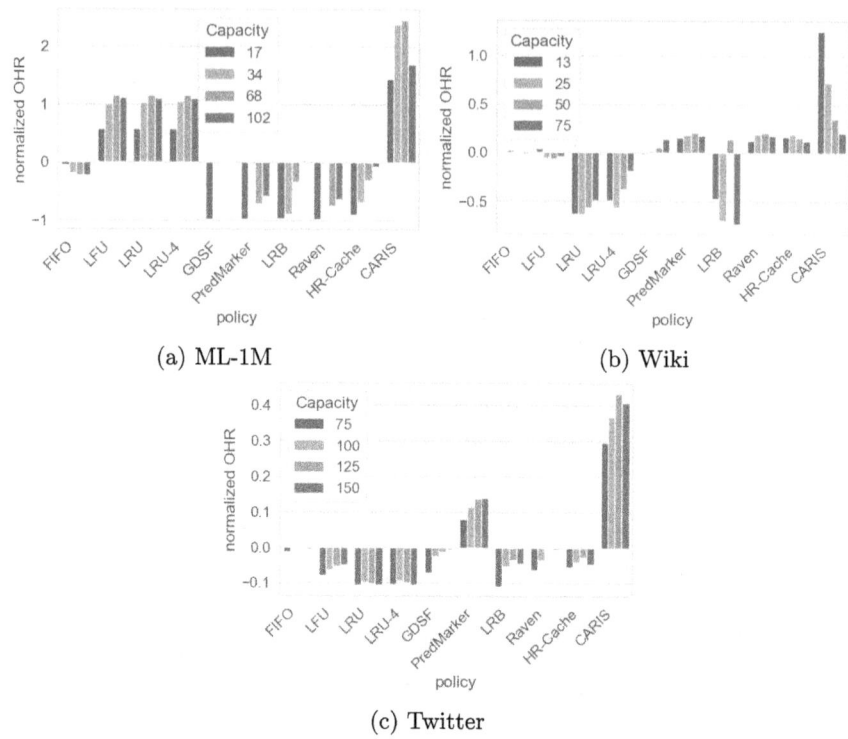

Fig. 4. CARIS OHR Compared with Other Policies

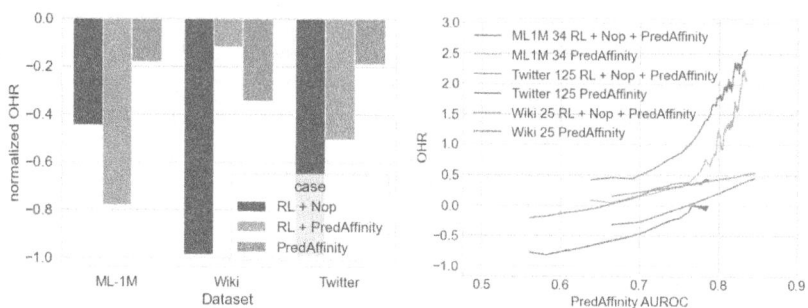

(a) OHR when Key Features are Removed (b) PredAffinity AUROC vs OHR during Training

Fig. 5. Ablation Study Results

with simulated cache capacities 34, 25, 125, and depict the relation between the prediction's AUROC score and the achieved OHR of CARIS during the training process in Fig. 5. As before, the PredAffinity case was outperformed by the fully equipped CARIS throughout the training process. Obviously, OHR got higher as the AUROC got larger and the prediction became more accurate.

6 Conclusions

In this paper, we introduce the caching admission policy model CARIS, based on RL for the most part, and aided by cache affinity estimation. CARIS uses a Transformer-like encoder [20] to learn the sequence item representation, based on which it computes the predicted cache affinity and the policy. By focusing the exploration on the cache-friendly user accesses, CARIS's training process is significantly simplified. Besides, CARIS is forced to take an empty action in the event of a cache hit, addressing the problem of useless caching actions. To the best of our knowledge, CARIS is the first caching policy model that incorporates RL with prediction methods based on supervised learning.

Presently, the CARIS model is deployed in our web application servers. We are looking to generalize its application to other systems such as CDN and edge computing, so as to verify its ability across diverse fields.

A Parameters Used for Model and Training

Table 2. Model & Training Parameters

Parameter Name	Chosen Value
Learning rate	0.0005
Random seed	42
BSARec α	0.7
BSARec c	5
Batch size	16
BSARec attention #heads	4
BSARec hidden #layers	6
Representation hidden size	64
Adam beta 1	0.9
Adam beta 2	0.999
Adam weight decay	0.1
Actor network #layers	2
Critic network #layers	2
BSARec hidden layers dropout	0.5
BSARec attention dropout	0.5
Actor network dropout	0.5
Critic network dropout	0.5
Discount ratio γ	0.99
Replay buffer size	1024
Entropy loss weight β_1	1
Q loss weight β_2	1
Cache affinity loss weight β_3	1
Affinity threshold ρ	0.3
Cache affinity range L	400
PPO clip tolerance ϵ	0.1

Table 2 lists the parameters used in deep learning model building and training. The parameters prefixed with "BSARec" are for the encoder part of the model based on BSARec [20].

References

1. Arlitt, M., Cherkasova, L., Dilley, J., Friedrich, R., Jin, T.: Evaluating content management techniques for web proxy caches. SIGMETRICS Perform. Eval. Rev. **27**(4), 3–11 (2000)
2. Cui, L., et al.: Towards real-time video caching at edge servers: a cost-aware deep q-learning solution. IEEE Trans. Multimedia **25**, 302–314 (2023)
3. Eddelbuettel, D.: A brief introduction to redis (2022)
4. Hafiz, A.M.: A survey of deep q-networks used for reinforcement learning: state of the art. In: Intelligent Communication Technologies and Virtual Mobile Networks, pp. 393–402 (2023)
5. Hafner, D., Pasukonis, J., Ba, J., Lillicrap, T.: Mastering diverse domains through world models (2024)
6. Harper, F.M., Konstan, J.A.: The movielens datasets: History and context. ACM Trans. Interact. Intell. Syst. **5**(4) (2015)
7. Hei, W., Sun, B., Wang, Q.: A memcached cache-based approach to fast response for large language models in power systems. In: Proceedings of the 2024 International Conference on Computer and Multimedia Technology, pp. 547–553. ICCMT 2024 (2024)
8. Hu, X., Ramadan, E., Ye, W., Tian, F., Zhang, Z.L.: Raven: belady-guided, predictive (deep) learning for in-memory and content caching. In: Proceedings of the 18th International Conference on Emerging Networking EXperiments and Technologies, pp. 72–90. CoNEXT 2022 (2022)
9. Huang, S., Ontañón, S.: A closer look at invalid action masking in policy gradient algorithms. In: The International FLAIRS Conference Proceedings, vol. 35 (2022)
10. Jain, A., Lin, C.: Back to the future: Leveraging belady's algorithm for improved cache replacement. In: 2016 ACM/IEEE 43rd Annual International Symposium on Computer Architecture (ISCA), pp. 78–89 (2016)
11. Ke, G., et al.: LightGBM: a highly efficient gradient boosting decision tree. In: Advances in Neural Information Processing Systems, vol. 30 (2017)
12. Kirilin, V., Sundarrajan, A., Gorinsky, S., Sitaraman, R.K.: Rl-cache: learning-based cache admission for content delivery. In: Proceedings of the 2019 Workshop on Network Meets AI & ML, pp. 57–63. NetAI 2019 (2019)
13. Kumar, H., Koppel, A., Ribeiro, A.: On the sample complexity of actor-critic method for reinforcement learning with function approximation. Mach. Learn. **112**(7), 2433–2467 (2023)
14. Li, L., et al.: Deep reinforcement learning approaches for content caching in cache-enabled D2D networks. IEEE Internet Things J. **7**(1), 544–557 (2020)
15. Liu, E., Hashemi, M., Swersky, K., Ranganathan, P., Ahn, J.: An imitation learning approach for cache replacement. In: Proceedings of the 37th International Conference on Machine Learning. Proceedings of Machine Learning Research, vol. 119, pp. 6237–6247 (2020)
16. Lykouris, T., Vassilvtiskii, S.: Competitive caching with machine learned advice. In: Proceedings of the 35th International Conference on Machine Learning. Proceedings of Machine Learning Research, vol. 80, pp. 3296–3305 (2018)

17. Mnih, V., Kavukcuoglu, K., Silver, D., Rusu, A.A., Veness, J., Bellemare, M.G., Graves, A., Riedmiller, M., Fidjeland, A.K., Ostrovski, G., Petersen, S., Beattie, C., Sadik, A., Antonoglou, I., King, H., Kumaran, D., Wierstra, D., Legg, S., Hassabis, D., Mnih, V., et al.: Human-level control through deep reinforcement learning. Nature **518**(7540), 529–533 (2015)
18. Paszke, A., et al.: PyTorch: an imperative style, high-performance deep learning library. Curran Associates Inc. (2019)
19. Rio, A.d., Jimenez, D., Serrano, J.: Comparative analysis of A3C and PPO algorithms in reinforcement learning: a survey on general environments. IEEE Access **12**, 146795–146806 (2024)
20. Shin, Y., Choi, J., Wi, H., Park, N.: An attentive inductive bias for sequential recommendation beyond the self-attention (2024)
21. Song, Z., Berger, D.S., Li, K., Lloyd, W.: Learning relaxed belady for content distribution network caching. In: 17th USENIX Symposium on Networked Systems Design and Implementation (NSDI 20), pp. 529–544 (2020)
22. Torabi, H., Khazaei, H., Litoiu, M.: A learning-based caching mechanism for edge content delivery. In: Proceedings of the 15th ACM/SPEC International Conference on Performance Engineering, pp. 236–246. ICPE 2024, ACM (2024)
23. Tosi, F., Liao, Y., Schmitt, C., Geiger, A.: SMD-Nets: Stereo mixture density networks. In: Proceedings of the IEEE/CVF Conference on Computer Vision and Pattern Recognition (CVPR), pp. 8942–8952 (2021)
24. Urdaneta, G., Pierre, G., van Steen, M.: Wikipedia workload analysis (2007)
25. Miao, Q.: Deep reinforcement learning: a survey. IEEE Trans. Neural Netw. Learn. Syst. **35**(4), 5064–5078 (2024)
26. Wu, Q., Zhao, Y., Fan, Q., Fan, P., Wang, J., Zhang, C.: Mobility-aware cooperative caching in vehicular edge computing based on asynchronous federated and deep reinforcement learning. IEEE J. Sel. Top. Sig. Process. **17**(1), 66–81 (2023)
27. Yan, G., Li, J., Towsley, D.: Learning from optimal caching for content delivery. In: Proceedings of the 17th International Conference on Emerging Networking EXperiments and Technologies, pp. 344–358. CoNEXT 2021 (2021)
28. Yang, J., Yue, Y., Rashmi, K.V.: A large scale analysis of hundreds of in-memory cache clusters at twitter. In: 14th USENIX Symposium on Operating Systems Design and Implementation (OSDI 20), pp. 191–208 (2020)

Finance, Economy, Management or Marketing

Better Capturing Interactions Between Products in Retail: Revisited Negative Sampling for Basket Choice Modeling

Jules Désir[1], Vincent Auriau[1,2(✉)], Martin Možina[3], and Emmanuel Malherbe[1]

[1] Artefact Research Center, Paris, France
{jules.desir,vincent.auriau,emmanuel.malherbe}@artefact.com
[2] MICS, CentraleSupélec Université Paris-Saclay, Gif-sur-Yvette, France
[3] Fortenova Group, Zagreb, Croatia
martin.mozina@mercator.si

Abstract. Brick-and-mortar retailers face many different challenges that involve understanding thoroughly its products catalog and customer preferences. In particular, assortment optimization - proposing the ideal mix of products - and promotion planning hold a pivotal role in their strategy. By leveraging sales data, retailers can make informed decisions on which products to sell and how to manage inventory, based on customer preferences as well as regional and seasonal trends. It is especially crucial to capture interactions between products, in order to minimize the number of items that cannibalize each other's sales and to ensure that complementary products, which are often purchased together, are conjointly available and sold across all stores. In this paper, we propose a model of shopping basket that learns embeddings to represent interactions between products, prices and stores. Our model is built to uncover sales patterns from very large transaction datasets. In particular, the optimization loss is computed with random negative samples in order to overcome the computational bottlenecks that arise with large number of items. Our experiments on synthetic data show the efficiency of drawing such negative samples based on the actual assortment of available products, with better results than approaches from the literature. We also validate our approach by training and evaluating our model on a dataset composed of millions of transactions from *Fortenova Group*, one of the leading retail company in Southeast Europe. Our model showcases promising applications in the sector of retail, with enriched interfaces to efficiently support category managers.

Keywords: Basket · Choice Modeling · Assortment · Retail · Representation Learning · Negative Sampling

1 Introduction

Choosing the optimal combination of products to sell at the right price is a crucial stake for retailers. It is needed to select which products, among the hundreds of thousands offered by various suppliers, should be offered for sale in each store, or should be under promotion. This decision can be taken using insights such as past revenues or current trends.

It is also highly crucial to take into consideration the different products synergies. Indeed, a customer planning to bake a cake should be able to purchase all the necessary ingredients or he may choose to shop at another supermarket. This notion of complementarity between products should be carefully considered, along with cannibalization, where the presence of two similar items lead to a reduction in each other's sales. Historically, this assortment selection has been done manually by the category managers, based on their business experience. With thousands of daily customers in its different stores, a supermarket company typically records hundreds of millions of purchases per year. This data - baskets of co-purchased items - conveys rich patterns, especially compared to assortments which remain relatively stable due to logistical reasons. Gathering statistical insights from these data can greatly help category managers make informed decisions on the assortment selection.

Choice modeling is a common approach that leverages purchase datasets to understand customers preferences. Each product is assigned a utility, a latent value that reflects its probability to be purchased. Common models use a linear representation of utility [2,10], while more recent work has shown that incorporating non-linear effects can help in better capturing the heterogeneity in the different customer behaviors. In particular, neural networks [6,8] have shown promising performances. Besides, estimating and leveraging product interactions is a problem yet to be tackled. Indeed, the exponentially growing number of interactions to take into account leads to difficulties in using classical methods [7,11] with a large number of products. Another approach, the nested logit model [4], requires the modeler to decide a priori the sets of substitutable items, which is on the contrary what we want the model to learn.

In this paper, we propose a neural-network choice model that learns latent representations of items, shops and baskets, with a structure capable of capturing product interactions from a large dataset of purchase receipts. It enables to interpret the choice probabilities predicted by the model, and has promising applications for enriching interfaces used by category managers. Such interfaces are used to plan promotion campaigns or select the assortment of a shop and would be more informative if the interactions between products were displayed.

Our contributions in this paper are the following. First, we propose a choice model capturing interactions between products, able to be learned on large-scale data with no or few features to describe items, shops or customers. Second, we propose to leverage the assortment of available products in a soft manner within the negative sampling during the training procedure. Last, we present experiments on synthetic data and a real-world retailer dataset, confirming the benefits of our approach when compared to existing models. Our code is publicly available on GitHub[1].

---

[1] The different Python implementations can be found in the Choice-Learn package at https://github.com/artefactory/choice-learn.

2 Related Work

Our paper relates to two strands of the literature: discrete choice models and representation learning, with similarities with word embeddings.

2.1 Discrete Choice Models

Discrete choice models try to explain or predict choice decisions made by humans from a set of alternatives, called an assortment. They have been widely adopted for a large range of applications, usually involving a customer decision, such as choice of transportation mode or products purchases. The discrete choice framework based on Random Utility Maximization [10] considers that an individual attributes a utility to the different options and chooses the one that maximizes this utility. The objective of discrete choice modeling is to estimate this latent utility function harnessing data with past choices or preferences. The classical conditional logit model [2] formulates a linear utility function leveraging the different available features of the problem. Recent works use more complex functions that introduce nonlinearities, using for example neural networks [3,5,6,35] or tree-based models [31,34].

Discrete choice models are designed to handle the variations of options availability within the assortment. This is particularly important in a retail context where products might be out of stock or simply not sold in specific locations. However, they are usually built to model a single choice and still face challenges when modeling bundles of options, like we observe in retail. These challenges result in limited methods for estimating interactions between these choices. Interaction terms can be introduced within the utility function [7,11], but such formulations are typically restricted to a small number of distinct options. Indeed, the number of possible bundles grows exponentially with the number of available items, which can be very high in applications such as retail.

2.2 Representation Learning

Object representation in machine learning has significantly evolved with the advent of neural networks [19]. Unlike traditional machine learning methods, which could mainly transform pre-existing features, neural networks can learn continuous representations when the data is categorical and comes with no features [20]. Traditionally, such categorical data is represented using one-hot vectors [21] that have the size of the set of possible values. In comparison, learned embeddings provide a continuous representation that replaces these vectors in a generally much lower dimension. One may note that the term "embedding" sometimes refers to a transformed object's features after multiple operations [15], but in this paper it will only refer to categorical data representation.

One of the primary data structures that have greatly benefited from embeddings is word representation [18]. Traditionally, words were represented using sparse vectors [16], similar to weighted one-hot vectors. [9] proved the efficiency to train a neural network where each word in the vocabulary is associated with a learned dense continuous vector. This training process typically requires large-scale data and is often conducted in a self-supervised manner using natural data [14], i.e. an unlabeled corpus of documents. In this case, negative sampling [17] is commonly employed to complement the positive cases derived from the natural data. This involves randomly sampling words from the vocabulary, under the assumption that they are likely to be implausible outputs.

Embeddings have also found applications beyond words. They can be used for any categorical data, typically the labels of a multiclass classification [22,23], the nodes of a graph [24], or the rows of tabular data represented as graphs [25]. In a scenario similar to choice modeling, collaborative filtering for recommender systems, matrix factorization or neural networks aim at building embeddings for each user and product [26,27]. In this case, the model is generally trained on the scores given by users on products, such as movies [28]. To our knowledge, limited research has proposed embedding structures for neural network-based choice models. Among existing work, [8,36] embeddings are fed directly into the softmax function and thus do not model any interaction. [37] incorporates interaction terms with respect to the items in the assortments, but focuses solely on single-choice modeling, which does not fully leverage the rich information provided by bundles of items purchased together. [1] presents a closer approach to our work; however, their method requires heavy computing since their neural network is Bayesian and they need to generate all subsets of items within a bundle, both during training and inference.

3 Model

3.1 Context and Objectives

We build a model with the following characteristics in mind:

- Only a few or no features are available to characterize the items other than their price and whether they are on promotion. The main signals come from co-purchase patterns.
- The model should capture complementarity and cannibalization between products – i.e. respectively the tendency for items to be purchased together within a single basket and the reduction of sales when items are both available in the assortment.
- The model is designed to efficiently handle large datasets, both in terms of the number of items considered as well as the volume of purchases.

This setup corresponds to our retail scenario and would apply to other sectors with brick-and-mortar stores.

3.2 Notations

The data we consider consists of a collection of purchases, each representing a basket of items bought by a customer. Additional contextual information includes the store where the purchases took place, the list of items that were available at that time, and their prices. More formally, we write $\mathcal{I}$ the set of items sold in the set $\mathcal{S}$ of stores. The observed purchases correspond to a tuple $(\mathcal{B}, \mathcal{A}, s, p)$ with:

- $\mathcal{B} \subseteq \mathcal{I}$ the basket of purchased items;
- $\mathcal{A} \subseteq \mathcal{I}$ the products assortment available at the time of the purchase (by definition, $\mathcal{B} \subseteq \mathcal{A}$);
- $s \in \mathcal{S}$ the store in which the purchase happened;
- p the prices for all the items in $\mathcal{A}$ at the time of the purchase. In particular, p_i is the price of item i.

We decide not to consider duplicated items in the basket. This choice reflects our objective of capturing interactions between items of the catalog.

3.3 Conditional Definition of the Utility

We propose a conditional formulation of the utility. Considering an already chosen basket of items $\mathcal{B}$, we write the utility of an additional item as $V(i|\mathcal{B}, s, p)$, modeled as two independent contributions:

$$V(i|\mathcal{B}, s, p) = V^{pref}(i|s, p) + V^{inter}(i|\mathcal{B}) \quad (1)$$

where V^{pref} represents the intrinsic utility (or "preference") attributed to the item and the interaction utility V^{inter} depends on the other items that will also be purchased. V^{pref} can be understood as the popularity of an item, regardless of the other items for sale. In our case, it would only depend on the item, its price and the store where it is purchased. Following classical formulations of the utility, we define V^{pref} as an itemwise intercept, a logarithmic contribution of the price and an elasticity that depends on the item and the store:

$$V^{pref}(i|s, p) = \alpha_i + \boldsymbol{\beta}_i \cdot \boldsymbol{\delta}_s \log p_i \quad (2)$$

where $\cdot$ denotes the scalar product and variables in bold are vectors. We have $\alpha_i \in \mathbb{R}$ and $\boldsymbol{\beta}_i, \boldsymbol{\delta}_s \in \mathbb{R}^K$, with $K \in \mathbb{N}^*$ the size of the latent representation to be chosen. $\boldsymbol{\delta}_s$ captures that each store has a different population with its own elasticities. The formulation of $V^{pref}(i|s, p)$ can be easily modified to introduce multiple underlying factors governing customer choice.

For the interaction term, we use a formulation inspired by methods such as Word2Vec [9], where, in a similar fashion, the probability that a word matches its surrounding words is estimated. In our case, the context is given by items in the basket $\mathcal{B}$, so that V^{inter} is expressed as:

$$V^{inter}(i|\mathcal{B}) = \boldsymbol{\gamma}_i \cdot \boldsymbol{E}_\mathcal{B} \quad (3)$$

with $\boldsymbol{\gamma}_i \in \mathbb{R}^K$ a learned representation of item i and $\boldsymbol{E}_\mathcal{B}$ the representation for basket $\mathcal{B}$. Different formulations of such basket embedding could be used, we have opted for: $\boldsymbol{E_B} = \frac{1}{|\mathcal{B}|}\sum_{j\in\mathcal{B}} \boldsymbol{\gamma}_j$. One notes that it would be possible to learn different items embeddings for $\boldsymbol{E_B}$ than the $\boldsymbol{\gamma}_j$ ("encoding-decoding" structure).

We assume that the customer behaves rationally and will maximize their utility during a shopping session. Following Discrete Choice Models formulation, we consider that the final utility U is the sum of the deterministic part V as well as a random contribution, ϵ_i:

$$U(i|\mathcal{B},s,p) = V(i|\mathcal{B},s,p) + \epsilon_i$$

from which we can derive probabilities, as described in the following section.

3.4 Purchase Probability

The random variable ϵ_i is assumed to be independent across items and to follow a zero-mean Gumbel distribution (generalized type I extreme value). Consequently, the conditional choice probability of choosing an item $i \in \mathcal{A}$ that is not yet in the basket is a softmax over the remaining items in the assortment $\mathcal{A}$:

$$\mathbb{P}(i|\mathcal{B},s,p) = \mathbb{P}\Big(U(i|\mathcal{B},s,p) > U(j|\mathcal{B},s,p) \;\; \forall j \in \mathcal{A}\setminus\mathcal{B}, j\neq i\Big) \quad (4)$$

$$= \frac{e^{V(i|\mathcal{B},s,p)}}{\sum_{j\in(\mathcal{A}\setminus\mathcal{B})} e^{V(j|\mathcal{B},s,p)}} \quad (5)$$

where $\mathbb{P}(i|\mathcal{B},s,p)$ is the probability to add the item i to the basket $\mathcal{B}$ at the store s with the prices p and is estimated with the latent parameters $\Theta = \{\alpha,\beta,\delta,\gamma\}$. We set this probability to zero when $i\notin\mathcal{A}$ or $i\in\mathcal{B}$.

4 Implementation for Large-Scale Data

Given a large dataset of N shopping sessions $\{(\mathcal{B}_k,\mathcal{A}_k,s_k,p_k)\}_{k=1}^N$, our goal is to infer the latent parameters $\Theta \subset \{\alpha,\beta,\delta,\gamma\}$ which are the trainable weights of our model. We now describe how to learn the optimal Θ^* from the dataset.

4.1 Training Procedure

The model parameters Θ^* are estimated by leveraging all baskets data. To this end, similarly to [11,29] (Chap. 12), we aim at maximizing the quantity:

$$\Theta^* = \underset{\Theta}{\operatorname{argmax}} \prod_{k=1}^N \prod_{i\in\mathcal{B}_k} \mathbb{P}(i|\mathcal{B}_k\setminus i, s_k, p_k)$$

which can be seen as a form of self-supervision similar to text, where the missing word is predicted based on the remaining words of its context sentence. One notes that it differs from [1] where they maximize the probability of the baskets, which is not explicitly defined in our model. Besides, for this purpose they generate all possible sub-baskets $\mathcal{B}' \subseteq \mathcal{B}$, which we believe is not always informative and makes computation exponentially costly as the basket size grows.

One also notes that the formula of $\mathbb{P}(i|\mathcal{B}_k \setminus i, s_k, p_k)$ (Eq. 5) is computationally heavy too, since $\mathcal{A}$ can be very large. Instead, we normalize $e^{V(i|\mathcal{B},s,p)}$ over a set of randomly drawn negative samples, formally written $\mathcal{NS}$ (whose size $|\mathcal{NS}|$ is a hyperparameter). We thus approximate $\mathbb{P}(i|\mathcal{B}_k \setminus i, s_k, p_k)$ with:

$$f(i, \mathcal{B}_k \setminus i, s_k, p_k) = \frac{e^{V(i|\mathcal{B}_k, s_k, p_k)}}{e^{V(i|\mathcal{B}_k, s_k, p_k)} + \sum_{j \in \mathcal{NS}} e^{V(j|\mathcal{B}_k, s_k, p_k)}}$$

Such negative sampling has also been used in [9,30], and can be shown to approximate well the log probabilities of the softmax. This strategy is particularly important in a large-scale environment with thousands of different products.

In practice, we maximize a lower bound of $\prod_{k=1}^{N} \prod_{i \in \mathcal{B}_k} f(i|\mathcal{B}_k \setminus i, s_k, p_k)$:

$$\prod_{k=1}^{N} \prod_{i \in \mathcal{B}_k} f(i|\mathcal{B}_k \setminus i, s_k, p_k) \geq \prod_{k=1}^{N} \prod_{i \in \mathcal{B}_k} \frac{e^{V(i|\mathcal{B}_k, s_k, p_k)}}{(1 + e^{V(i|\mathcal{B}_k, s_k, p_k)}) \prod_{j \in \mathcal{NS}} (1 + e^{V(j|\mathcal{B}_k, s_k, p_k)})}$$

which gives us the final loss to be minimized during our training, that is the opposite of the log of the lower bound:

$$\mathcal{L} = -\sum_{k=1}^{N} \sum_{i \in \mathcal{B}_k} \left(\log \sigma[V(i|\mathcal{B}_k \setminus i, s_k, p_k)] + \sum_{j \in \mathcal{NS}} \log(1 - \sigma[V(j|\mathcal{B}_k \setminus i, s_k, p_k)]) \right) \tag{6}$$

where $\sigma[x] = \frac{e^x}{1+e^x}$ is the sigmoid function. One notes that this loss corresponds to a binary cross-entropy where the $V(i|\mathcal{B}_k \setminus i, s_k, p_k)$ are associated to the positive labels and the negative samples $V(j|\mathcal{B}_k \setminus i, s_k, p_k)$ to the negative labels.

This loss is minimized during a stochastic gradient descent. At each batch of baskets, the negative samples $\mathcal{NS}$ are randomly drawn, with a different sampling for each epoch in the case of multiple epochs on the dataset. In the following, we describe our method to randomly sample $\mathcal{NS}$.

4.2 Negative Sampling

In scenarios involving a fixed set of options, such as the vocabulary in the context of natural language [9], negative samples $\mathcal{NS}$ are uniformly sampled from all other options, excluding the true option. In our choice modeling scenario, however, there are several key differences. First, we exclude items already present in basket $\mathcal{B}_k$, as our context does not allow for duplicated items (see Sects. 3.1 and 3.2). Second, we propose to draw negative samples $\mathcal{NS}$ exclusively from items within the available assortment $\mathcal{A}_k$. Formally, we enforce the condition:

$$\mathcal{NS} \subset \mathcal{A}_k \setminus \mathcal{B}_k \tag{7}$$

Implicitly, the negative samples are generated depending on both $\mathcal{A}_k$ and $\mathcal{B}_k$ on the data point k. It could be explicitly written $\mathcal{NS}(\mathcal{A}_k, \mathcal{B}_k)$. Practically, it means that $\mathcal{A}_k$ must be provided as information during the training process. In contrast, [1] draws their negative samples from the entire item catalog outside the considered basket, that is to say $\mathcal{I}\backslash\mathcal{B}_k$.

The rationale for the use of the assortment during negative sampling is that it prevents the model from considering that two items are cannibalizing each other just because they are not available both at the same time in the training data. Indeed, when item $j \in \mathcal{I}\backslash\mathcal{B}_k$ is drawn as a negative sample of item $i \in \mathcal{B}_k$, then the conditional utility $V(j|\mathcal{B}_k\backslash i, s_k, p_k)$ will be reduced during the gradient descent that minimizes the loss $\mathcal{L}$ (see Eq. 6). Imposing item j to be in the assortment $\mathcal{A}_k$ means that such reduction of a conditional probability during the gradient descent will happen only to items that could have been bought with item i but had not, leaving items outside of the assortment untouched and thus enabling the model to learn a difference between items that are in the assortment and items that are not. In other words, drawing a negative sample $j \in \mathcal{I}\backslash\mathcal{B}_k$ that is not in assortment $\mathcal{A}_k$ amounts to assuming that j would have been cannibalizing item i if j were in assortment $\mathcal{A}_k$, which is not necessarily true.

We consider this method of incorporating assortment $\mathcal{A}_k$ in the estimation of $\mathbb{P}(i|\mathcal{B}_k\backslash i, s_k, p_k)$ to be simple yet sufficient and effective, with significant benefits, as demonstrated in the following section.

5 Experiments

We have conducted several types of experiments that validate the relevance of our approach. First, synthetic experiments let us showcase how it behaves on a smaller and controlled environment. Second, we share results obtained on a large real-world industrial dataset issued from Fortenova Group's supermarkets.

5.1 Synthetic Experiments

Dataset. We build a synthetic dataset for which the catalog has 8 items, $\mathcal{I} = \{1, \ldots, 8\}$, with the following interactions:

- **Cannibalization:** $\{1, 2, 3\}$ on the one hand and $\{4, 5, 6\}$ on the other hand form groups of items cannibalizing each other.
- **Complementarity:** each of the items in $\{1, 2, 3\}$ are complementary to each of the items in $\{4, 5, 6\}$;
- **Neutral:** 7 and 8 are neutral in the sense that they don't have specific interaction with other items.

As a concrete example, we can consider that items $\{1, 2, 3\}$ are badminton shuttlecocks, items $\{4, 5, 6\}$ are badminton rackets while items $\{7, 8\}$ are a t-shirt and a short. We implemented a routine that, given an assortment $\mathcal{A} \subseteq \mathcal{I}$, generates a dataset $\mathcal{D}$ of purchased baskets. These baskets are generated following the interactions described above, without price or shop effect (apart from its assortment). The details of this implementation are in Appendix A[2]. In the left of Fig. 1, we illustrate the simulated interactions by computing $\mathbb{P}(i \in \mathcal{B} | j \in \mathcal{B})$ on baskets generated by our routine for a full assortment $\mathcal{A} = \mathcal{I}$. A train dataset $\mathcal{D}_{train}$ and a test dataset $\mathcal{D}_{test}$, illustrated in Fig. 2, are constituted by sampling baskets for the different following assortments:

- Training set $\mathcal{D}_{train}$:
  - Store 1: $\mathcal{A}_1 = \{1, 2, 4, 5, 7, 8\} = \mathcal{I} \backslash \{3, 6\}$ yields $\mathcal{D}_1$;
  - Store 2: $\mathcal{A}_2 = \{1, 3, 5, 6, 7, 8\} = \mathcal{I} \backslash \{2, 4\}$ yields $\mathcal{D}_2$;
  - Store 3: $\mathcal{A}_3 = \{2, 3, 4, 6, 7, 8\} = \mathcal{I} \backslash \{1, 5\}$ yields $\mathcal{D}_3$;
- Test set $\mathcal{D}_{test}$:
  - Store 4: $\mathcal{A}_4 = \{1, 2, 5, 6, 7, 8\} = \mathcal{I} \backslash \{3, 4\}$ yields $\mathcal{D}_4$;
  - Full Assortment: $\mathcal{A}_{full} = \mathcal{I}$, i.e. all items yields $\mathcal{D}_{full}$.

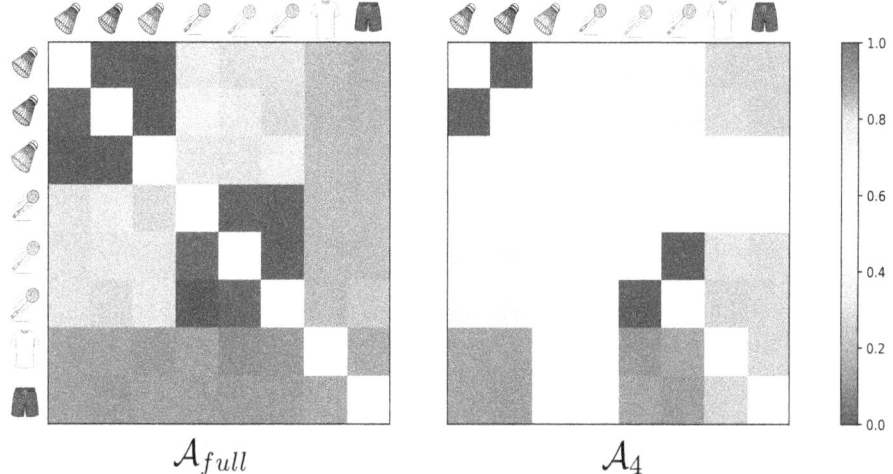

Fig. 1. $\mathbb{P}(i \in \mathcal{B} | j \in \mathcal{B})$ for all item pairs (i, j), computed on the synthetic baskets $\mathcal{D}_{full}$ on the left and $\mathcal{D}_4$ on the right. Low values correspond to cannibalization and high values to complementarity.

Protocol. We compare several versions of our approach with other state of the art models:

- Shopper [1]: A choice model that iteratively builds the most probable basket. It models the probability to add an item to an already partially built basket with price and interactions effects. The main difference lies in the expression of the basket probability that is computed by summing over all the possible ordered permutations of the basket.

---
[2] Appendix can be found in the GitHub repository at https://github.com/artefactory/alea-carta-est.

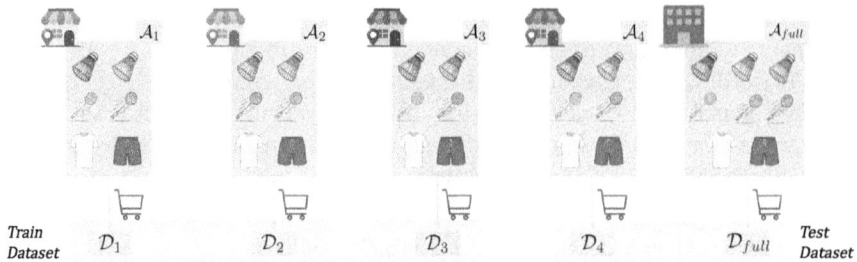

Fig. 2. Illustration of the synthetic data assortments. The full set of items $\mathcal{I}$ is in $\mathcal{A}_{full}$.

- Basket-MVL [11]: This choice model assumes the utility of a basket $\mathcal{B}$ to be the additive contributions of the marginal linear utilities of each item within the basket along with a symmetrical interaction term between those items: $U(\mathcal{B}) = \sum_{i \in \mathcal{B}} \beta \log p_i + \sum_{i,j \in \mathcal{B}} \gamma_i \cdot \gamma_j$. Finally, the probability for $\mathcal{B}$ to be purchased is computed with the softmax function over all possible baskets.
- Translation-Based Recommendation (TBR) [38]: It models a customer next choice as a translation from its previous choices with learned item-item interactions.
- Ours: Our model trained on $\mathcal{D}_{train}$ with negative samples drawn following Eq. 7.
- Ours$_{\mathcal{I}}$: Our model trained on $\mathcal{D}_{train}$, however any item can be a negative sample as long as it is not in the basket. For this model, $\mathcal{NS} = \mathcal{I} \backslash \mathcal{B}_k$.
- Ours$_{full}$: Our model, trained on $\mathcal{D}_{full}$. This idealistic version of the model has been trained on the true underlying distribution. The two negative sampling strategies are the same for this model since $\mathcal{A} = \mathcal{I}$ in $\mathcal{D}_{full}$.

Except for Ours$_{full}$, all models are trained with basket data $\mathcal{D}_{train}$ issued from the three assortment $\mathcal{A}_1, \mathcal{A}_2$ and $\mathcal{A}_3$, and evaluated on the test dataset $\mathcal{D}_{test}$. The differences between the models can be easily analyzed by comparing the co-purchase probabilities $\mathbb{P}(i \mid \mathcal{B} = \{j\})$ in Fig. 3 with the ground truth on $\mathcal{D}_{full}$ in Fig. 1. Similarly, Fig. 4 presents a new product combination with assortment $\mathcal{A}_4$, which is not part of the training set. In both cases, we observe that our model, Ours$_{\mathcal{A}}$ better captures the product interactions. We also evaluate the models with two metrics, the conditional Negative Log-Likelihood NLL and the Mean Reciprocal Rank MRR computed as:

$$NLL(\mathcal{D}) = - \sum_{\mathcal{B} \in \mathcal{D}} \sum_{i \in \mathcal{B}} \log \mathbb{P}(i \mid \mathcal{B} \backslash i) \qquad (8)$$

$$MRR(\mathcal{D}) = \sum_{\mathcal{B} \in \mathcal{D}} \sum_{i \in \mathcal{B}} \frac{1}{rank\left[V(i \mid \mathcal{B} \backslash i)\right]} \qquad (9)$$

with $rank[.]$ being the ranking function over the available options.

The metrics, reported in Table 1, show that taking well into account the assortment while drawing the negative samples is key to capture the proper

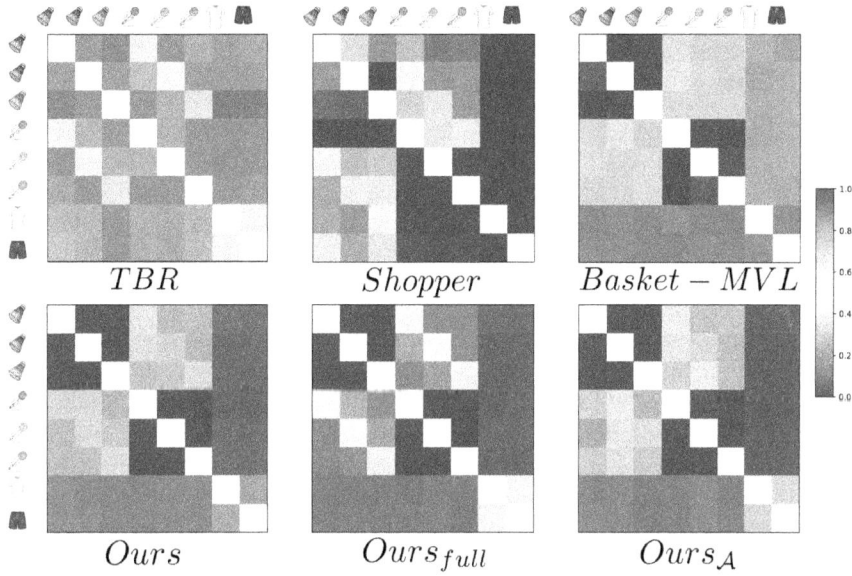

Fig. 3. Conditional probabilities $\mathbb{P}(i|\mathcal{B} = \{j\})$ for $i \neq j$ as estimated by the different models on $\mathcal{D}_{full}$. These probabilities are to be compared with the left of Fig. 1.

Fig. 4. Conditional probabilities $\mathbb{P}(i|\mathcal{B} = \{j\})$ for $i \neq j$ as estimated by the different models on the test data $\mathcal{D}_4$. These probabilities are to be compared with the right of Fig. 1.

Table 1. Negative Log-Likelihood NLL (lower is better) and Mean Reciprocal Rank MRR (higher is better) for the different models on the test set.

Model	Shopper	Basket-MVL	TBR	Ours$_{full}$	Ours$_\mathcal{I}$	Ours
$NLL(\mathcal{D}_{full})$	1.75	1.69	1.82	**1.25**	1.43	1.26
$NLL(\mathcal{D}_4)$	1.49	1.41	1.55	0.97	1.07	**0.95**
$MRR(\mathcal{D}_{full})$	0.32	0.41	0.28	**0.42**	0.39	0.41
$MRR(\mathcal{D}_4)$	0.45	0.60	0.45	**0.62**	0.59	0.61

patterns. Our proposition of negative sampling Ours$_\mathcal{A}$ better learns the true underlying distribution, and better generalizes on new assortment variations. A first explanation can be found using the conditional probabilities illustrated in Fig. 3. Indeed, the difference is particularly visible for some pairs of complementary items, such as items $(1, 6)$ and $(2, 6)$ that have not always been sold at the same time. The models resulting from the naive negative sampling tend to underestimate the complementarity between such items (or equivalently overestimate cannibalization). Except few surprising outliers with high values, Shopper appears to worsen this effect, that we interpret as an impact of its encoding-decoding structure as well as the use of all sub-baskets during its training. Taking into account the assortment is thus beneficial to capture well the different product interactions. While this notion might not be necessary for settings such as language [9] or online retail [1], it definitely should not be overlooked for brick-and-mortar retailers.

5.2 Large Scale Experiments: Computation Time and Memory Usage

Computation time and memory usage are critical when dealing with basket choice models, particularly in real-world applications where models need to process large-scale sales data efficiently. While some open-source packages offer optimized processes for data storage and discrete choice models estimation [12,13], it is still a challenge when considering bundles of products.

For this experiment, we compare the processing time for a single epoch of training with a dataset of one million purchases, with respectively 100 and $1,000$ items considered. We compare our approach implemented in Python with TensorFlow [32] with the two other models. Shopper [1], has a C++ codebase publicly available. Additionally, we have re-implemented in Python a deterministic version of the model[3], reproducing the training procedure for a non-Bayesian neural network. We also use our own Python implementation for the basket-MVL model, whose estimation uses a composite conditional likelihood function described in [11], and the Translation-Based Recommendation [38]. The exper-

---

[3] The code for the experiments can be found at https://github.com/artefactory/aleacarta-est.

Table 2. Comparison of computation time and RAM usage for different models

	100 Items		1000 Items	
	Process Time	Fits in RAM	Process Time	Fits in RAM
Shopper	100 s	✓	-	✗
Python-Shopper	110 s	✓	620 s	✓
Basket-MVL	3,000 s	✓	-	✗
TBR	550 s	✓	1020 s	✓
Ours	80 s	✓	360 s	✓

Table 3. Description of our retail dataset. Numbers are rounded for confidentiality reasons.

#Referenced Items	#Shops	#Baskets	#Assortments	Avg Basket Size
6,000+	600+	100,000,000+	10,000+	12.4

iment is conducted on a single AMD Ryzen PRO 5955WX CPU and 250GB of RAM.

The results are reported in Table 2. First, we can observe that our approach as well as our Python implementation of Shopper scale way better in terms of dataset size, while it is competitive with the C++ implementation in terms of training speed. Our approach is also faster than the Shopper re-implementation, mainly because it does not need to consider permutations of the basket. Following these results, we discarded Shopper and Basket-MVL models for our large scale real-world dataset, with experiments described below.

5.3 Experiments on Real-World Retail Data

We consider a dataset of purchases collected through hundreds of different supermarkets of the European retail company *Fortenova Group* during four years, from 2017 to 2021 that we describe in Table 3. Restraining the dataset to food related products that have been sold at least 1,000 times, we count more than 6,000 different products purchased. We consider a train/test temporal split to evaluate our model. The train data covers purchases from 2017 to 2020 and test data $\mathcal{D}_{2021}$ covers year 2021. In Table 4 we share some metrics results, stressing again the need for a negative sampling adapted to the assortment. The results were obtained with the same latent size $K = 128$ for all embeddings and $|\mathcal{NS}| = 20$ negative samples. We share more details of the implementation in Appendix B.

In Fig. 5, we provide a T-SNE [33] projection of a subset of the learned γ_i embeddings of our model, colored according to product i's category. We observe that while the model is not provided with any type of information about the different products beside their price, it successfully creates clusters that corre-

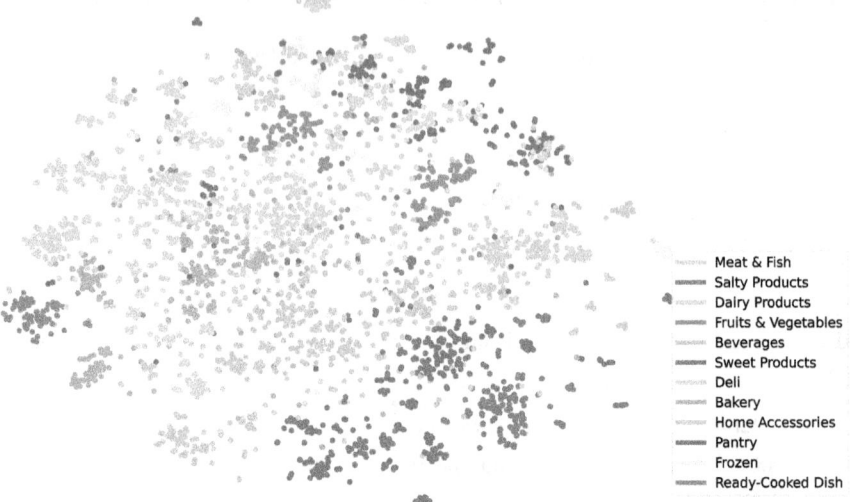

Fig. 5. T-SNE projection of the learned γ_i embeddings

Table 4. Conditional Negative Log-Likelihood (lower is better) and Mean Reciprocal Rank (higher is better) on the retail test set.

Model	Ours$_\mathcal{I}$	Ours
$NLL(\mathcal{D}_{2021})$	3.03	**2.48**
$MRR(\mathcal{D}_{2021})$	0.015	**0.018**

spond to products categories. It showcases that the model is able to learn a logical hierarchy of the products using the basket information.

5.4 Application: Highlighting Complementary Products

The main purpose of such models is to assist a category manager when planning the future assortment or promotion campaign for different stores. One basic experiment is to infer for each product a short list of the most complementary items. With such knowledge provided, the category manager can decide to make sure that complementary items are integrated within the same assortments. We propose to measure the following quantity $C(i,j) \in \mathbb{R}$ in order to rank the items j according to their complementarity with item i:

$$C(i,j) = \sum_{\mathcal{B} \in \mathcal{D}} \mathbb{P}(i \mid \mathcal{B} \cup \{j\}) + \mathbb{P}(j \mid \mathcal{B} \cup \{i\}) - \mathbb{P}(i \mid \mathcal{B}\backslash\{j\}) - \mathbb{P}(j \mid \mathcal{B}\backslash\{i\}) \quad (10)$$

which is symmetrical w.r.t i and j. The top 10 products j in terms of $C(i,j)$ values are shown in Table 5, for 4 examples of products i. In the case of tomato sauce

Table 5. Examples of top-10 complementary products according to our model, ranked w.r.t $C(i,j)$ (Eq. 10) for the product i displayed on top. The products are referenced by their nature and brand names, replaced by a letter for anonymity. For each product displayed on top, the first-ranked complementary product is on the top left and the tenth-ranked complementary product is on the bottom right.

Soda A **0.5L**		Soda A **2L**	
Water A **0.5L**	Water B **1L**	Soda B **2L**	Soda C **2L**
Soda B **0.5L**	Water C **0.5L**	Water A **1.5L**	Sweets A **500g**
Soda C **0.5L**	Energy Drink **0.5L**	Soda D **1.5L**	Water B **1L**
Soda D **0.5L**	Strong Alcohol **0.1L**	Light Alcohol **0.5L**	Soda E **2L**
Water D **0.5L**	Ice Cream **0.16L**	Sweets B **100g**	Soda F **2L**
Tomato sauce A		Vanilla powder A	
Pasta A	Pasta B	Margarin A	Chocolate A
Bread A	Pizza Dough A	Chocolate B	Chocolate C
Pasta C	Other Sauce A	Baking Powder A	Sugar A
Toasts A	Other Sauce B	Baking Powder B	Margarin B
Bread B	Other Sauce C	Whipped Cream A	Margarin C

and vanilla powder, the model outlines products that do appear highly complementary. We obtain respectively pasta, bread and pizza dough with tomato sauce and diverse ingredients to bake a cake with the vanilla powder, thus recovering meaningful ingredients together. The example of the soda bottles is also particularly interesting. Indeed, the model has understood packaging size interactions. The large soda bottle has other large bottles as complementary items, while the small soda bottles has smaller formats as top complementary products and also a single portion, to-go ice cream. It may correspond to two types of purchasing behaviors, one optimizing the price/quantity ratio with larger packages and the other one corresponding to instant consumption.

Following these promising results, we are currently conducting a survey with the company's category managers in order to confirm the relevancy of our top complementary items. They are asked to give feedback on different lists of items inferred by our model. Following these feedbacks, we plan to deploy the model as an API that would be called by several user interfaces used by category managers in their daily work. The model would regularly be trained on the sales data in order to keep up-to-date patterns.

6 Conclusion

In this work, we introduced a machine learning model for basket choice modeling that learns embeddings of items in order to capture interactions between them. By leveraging negative sampling techniques, we addressed the computational challenges posed by large transaction datasets, ensuring efficient and scalable learning. Our experiments on synthetic data demonstrated the added value of our model and of its negative sampling method that better captures interactions between products in retail. The large-scale evaluation on more than one million transactions from a leading European retailer validated the practical applicability of our approach, with notably very promising top complementary items. Besides, our approach shows competitive predictive performances and computing scalability, in particular when compared to the models from the literature.

The results confirm the potential of our model to enhance retail decision-making, particularly in helping category managers with assortment optimization and promotion campaign planning. Beyond the direct applications by enriching user interfaces in retail, our model can be extended to other domains involving large-scale consumer choice modeling. Future work will explore the integration of additional features, such as spatial proximity between products in the store shelves and personalized customer profiles. The former will enable the identification of product interactions with respect to their distance in store, while the latter will reveal how these interactions vary across different customer segments.

References

1. Ruiz, Francisco J.R. and Athey, Susan and Blei, David M.: SHOPPER: a probabilistic model of consumer choice with substitutes and complements. Ann. Appl. Stat. **14**(1), 1–27 JSTOR (2020)
2. McFadden, D.: Conditional logit analysis of qualitative choice behavior. Front. Econ., 105–142 (1974)
3. Wang, S., Mo, B., Zhao, J.: Deep neural networks for choice analysis: architecture design with alternative-specific utility functions. Transport. Res. Part C: Emerg. Technol. **112**, 234–251 (2020)
4. McFadden, Daniel et al.: Modelling the choice of residential location. Institute of Transportation Studies, University of California California (1978)
5. Han, Y., Pereira, F.C., Ben-Akiva, M., Zegras, C.: A neural-embedded discrete choice model: learning taste representation with strengthened interpretability. Transport. Res. Part B: Methodol. **163**, 166–186 (2022)
6. Aouad, A., Désir, A.: Representing random utility choice models with neural networks. arXiv preprint arXiv:2207.12877 (2022)
7. Sobolewski, M., Kopczewski, T.: Estimating demand for fixed-line telecommunication bundles. Telecommun. Policy **41**(4), 227–241 (2017)
8. Arkoudi, I., Krueger, R., Azevedo, C.L., Pereira, F.C.: Combining discrete choice models and neural networks through embeddings: formulation, interpretability and performance. Transport. Res. Part B: Methodological **175**, 102783 (2023)
9. Mikolov, T., Sutskever, I., Chen, K., Corrado, G.S., Dean, J.: Distributed representations of words and phrases and their compositionality. In: Advances in Neural Information Processing Systems, vol. 26 (2013)
10. McFadden, D., Train, K.: Mixed MNL models for discrete response. J. Appl. Econ. **15**(5), 99–110 (2000)
11. Caputo, V., Lusk, J.L.: The basket-based choice experiment: a method for food demand policy analysis. Food Policy **109**, 102252 (2022)
12. Auriau, V., Aouad, A., Désir, A., Malherbe, E.: Choice-learn: large-scale choice modeling for operational contexts through the lens of machine learning. J. Open Source Softw. **9**(101), 6899 (2024)

13. Du, T., Kanodia, A., Athey, S.: Torch-choice: a PyTorch package for large-scale choice modelling with Python. arXiv preprint arXiv:2304.01906 (2023)
14. Balestriero, R., et al.: A cookbook of self-supervised learning. arXiv preprint arXiv:2304.12210 (2023)
15. Gong, Y., Ke, Q., Isard, M., Lazebnik, S.: A multi-view embedding space for modeling internet images, tags, and their semantics. Int. J. Comput. Vis. **106**(2), 210–233 (2013). https://doi.org/10.1007/s11263-013-0658-4
16. Liu, C.Z., Sheng, Y.X., Wei, Z.Q., Yang, Y.Q.: Research of text classification based on improved TF-IDF algorithm. In: IEEE International Conference of Intelligent Robotic and Control Engineering (IRCE), pp. 218–222 (2018)
17. Yang, Z., et al.: Does negative sampling matter? A review with insights into its theory and applications. IEEE Trans. Pattern Anal. Mach. Intell. **46**, 5692–5711 (2024)
18. Pilehvar, M.T., Camacho-Collados, J.: Embeddings in Natural Language Processing: Theory and Advances in Vector Representations of Meaning. Morgan & Claypool Publishers (2020)
19. LeCun, Y., Bengio, Y., Hinton, G.: Deep learning. Nature **521**, 436–444 (2015)
20. Guo, C., Berkhahn, F.: Entity embeddings of categorical variables. arXiv preprint arXiv:1604.06737 (2016)
21. Seger, C.: An investigation of categorical variable encoding techniques in machine learning: binary versus one-hot and feature hashing (2018)
22. Rodríguez, P., Bautista, M.A., Gonzalez, J., Escalera, S. et al.: Beyond one-hot encoding: lower dimensional target embedding. Image Vis. Comput. **75**, 21–31 (2018)
23. Akata, Z., Perronnin, F., Harchaoui, Z., Schmid, C.: Label-embedding for image classification. IEEE Trans. Pattern Anal. Mach. Intell. **38**(7), 1425–1438 (2015)
24. Xu, M.: Understanding graph embedding methods and their applications. SIAM Rev. **63**(4), 825–853 (2021)
25. Kim, M.J., Grinsztajn, L., Varoquaux, G.: CARTE: pretraining and transfer for tabular learning. arXiv preprint arXiv:2402.16785 (2024)
26. Koren, Y., Rendle, S., Bell, R.: Advances in collaborative filtering. In: Recommender Systems Handbook, 91–142, Springer (2021). https://doi.org/10.1007/978-1-0716-2197-4_3
27. Li, S., et al.: MBedding compression in recommender systems: a survey. ACM Comput. Surv. **56**(5), 1–21 (2024)
28. The Netflix recommender system: Algorithms, business value, and innovation. ACM Trans. Manage. Inf. Syst. (TMIS) **6**(4), 1–19 (2015)
29. Molenberghs, G., Verbeke, G., et al.: Models for discrete longitudinal data. Springer (2005)
30. Gutmann, M.U., Hyvärinen, A.: AAPO: Noise-contrastive estimation of unnormalized statistical models, with applications to natural image statistics. J. Mach. Learn. Res. **13**(1), 307–361 (2012)
31. Salvadé, N., Hillel, T.: RUMBoost: gradient boosted random utility models. Transport. Res. Part C: Emerg. Technol. **170**, 104897 (2025)
32. Abadi, M., et al.: TensorFlow: large-scale machine learning on heterogeneous distributed systems. arXiv preprint arXiv:1603.04467 (2016)
33. Maaten, L.V.D., Hinton, G.: Visualizing data using t-SNE. J. Mach. Learn. Res. **9**(11), 2579–2605 (2008)
34. Aouad, A., Elmachtoub, A.N., Ferreira, K.J., McNellis, R.: Market segmentation trees. Manuf. Serv. Oper. Manage. **25**(2), 648–667 (2023)

35. Sifringer, B., Lurkin, V., Alahi, A.: Enhancing discrete choice models with neural networks. In: 18th Swiss Transport Research Conference, pp. 1–3 (2018)
36. Pereira, F.C.: Rethinking travel behavior modeling representations through embeddings. arXiv preprint arXiv:1909.00154 (2019)
37. Ko, J., Li, A.A.: Modeling choice via self-attention. arXiv preprint arXiv:2311.07607 (2023)
38. He, R., Kang, W.C., McAuley, J.: Translation-based recommendation. In Proceedings of the Eleventh ACM Conference on Recommender Systems (RecSys 2017). Association for Computing Machinery, New York, NY, USA, pp. 161–169 (2017). https://doi.org/10.1145/3109859.3109882

Transaction Categorization with Relational Deep Learning in QuickBooks

Kaiwen Dong[1,2], Padmaja Jonnalagedda[1], Xiang Gao[1], Ayan Acharya[1], Maria Kissa[1], Mauricio Flores[1], Nitesh V. Chawla[2], and Kamalika Das[1]($\boxtimes$)

[1] Mountain View, Intuit, CA 94043, USA
{kaiwen_dong,saisri_jonnalagedda,Xiang_Gao,maria_kissa, mauricio_flores,Kamalika_Das}@intuit.com
[2] University of Notre Dame, Notre Dame, IN 46556, USA
{nchawla,mus,kdong2mus}@nd.edu

Abstract. Automatic transaction categorization is crucial for enhancing the customer experience in QuickBooks by providing accurate accounting and bookkeeping. The distinct challenges in this domain stem from the unique formatting of transaction descriptions, the wide variety of transaction categories, and the vast scale of the data involved. Furthermore, organizing transaction data in a relational database creates difficulties in developing a unified model that covers the entire database. In this work, we develop a novel graph-based model, named `Rel-Cat`, which is built directly over the relational database. We introduce a new formulation of transaction categorization as a link prediction task within this graph structure. By integrating techniques from natural language processing and graph machine learning, our model not only outperforms the existing production model in QuickBooks but also scales effectively to a growing customer base with a simpler, more effective architecture without compromising on accuracy. This design also helps tackle a key challenge of the cold start problem by adapting to minimal data.

Keywords: Transaction Categorization · Relational Deep Learning · Financial Applications

1 Introduction

QuickBooks offers essential bookkeeping and accounting capabilities tailored to the needs of small and medium-sized businesses. It enables them to efficiently manage critical aspects of their business operations, including accounting, payroll, payments, and inventory. A key feature of QuickBooks is its ability to categorize financial activities captured through invoice descriptions, bank statements, etc. flexibly to enhance insights into business performance and to streamline tax compliance. By automating labor-intensive and error-prone tasks, QuickBooks allows business owners to focus on driving growth and increasing revenue.

At the core of QuickBooks's functionality is its advanced bookkeeping experience. Most business transactions today are processed through financial institutions, and QuickBooks integrates seamlessly with these institutions, enabling businesses to link their accounts and synchronize data. This connectivity triggers an influx of transactions—approximately 6.2 billion annually into QuickBooks. Having business owners or accountants manually review transactions would be an ineffective use of their time. Automating the processing of such a vast volume of transactions is crucial.

To facilitate its sophisticated accounting features, QuickBooks organizes transactions into specific categories or accounts. For example, a fuel purchase at an ExxonMobil station might be categorized under "Transportation", while an electricity bill could be classified as "Utilities". This paper addresses QuickBooks's transaction categorization challenge, employing state-of-the-art methods in natural language processing [4] and graph machine learning [3] to solve this as a link prediction problem [5] within a relational database. Drawing inspiration from Relational Deep Learning [8], we propose a unified approach to effectively model the transaction database through interconnected relational tables, introducing modifications specific to the unique challenges and practical requirements of QuickBooks.

1.1 Problem Statement

In QuickBooks, effective bookkeeping relies on the accurate categorization of transactions into specific accounts. Businesses have unique needs and preferences for how transactions are categorized. QuickBooks facilitates this by allowing customization of account names. This feature enables different companies to maintain both common and distinct account names based on their individual requirements. To further refine the organization of financial data and support compliance with tax regulations, QuickBooks allows users to classify these account names into a structured hierarchy of more abstract account types. This system not only personalizes the accounting experience for each business but also guarantees the accurate recording of financial activities. The more abstract account type, referred to as *Code*, corresponds to the IRS tax code, while the more granular account name, *Category*, is user-defined. For example, *Category* "Airfare" and "Internet" can both be grouped into a more abstract *Code* "Business Expenses".

The primary task we address in this paper is predicting the appropriate *Category* for any new transaction imported into QuickBooks. In addition to delivering the most likely categorization for a new transaction, we explore providing the Top-5 probable Categories. This approach is predicated on the likelihood that the company's preferred *Category* is more often found within the Top-5 predictions rather than solely the top prediction. Offering a selection of probable *Category* can significantly enhance user trust in QuickBooks's capabilities, fostering a stronger reliance on QuickBooks for critical financial management tasks.

The data supporting this transaction categorization task is managed within a relational database, where various tables are interconnected through primary and foreign keys. The database schema, detailed in Fig. 1a, includes the following critical tables:

1. **Transaction table**: Stores records of all transactions across different companies.
2. *Category* **table**: Contains all specific account names used by QuickBooks users.
3. *Code* **table**: Includes the abstract account types aligned with overarching tax codes, that facilitate the organization of *Category*.
4. **Company table**: Contains information about companies utilizing QuickBooks.

1.2 Related Works

Transaction categorization is fundamental to the user experience in QuickBooks. There are several ways to solve and productionize transaction categorization in accounting systems. To date, two major approaches have been deployed to effectively solve the task in QuickBooks.

The first approach, known as IRIS [12], categorizes incoming transactions based solely on a company's historical data. It begins by extracting business entity names from transaction descriptions using a rule-based normalization process that includes case folding and digit folding. IRIS then queries the company's historical transactions for similar business entities, defining similarity via Jaccard similarity—entities are considered similar if they are frequently categorized together. A weighted voting mechanism is then employed to determine the most likely *Category* for the new transaction. While IRIS is an efficient system capable of managing large datasets and ensuring quick database queries, its reliance on a company's historical data limits its utility, especially for new users with little to no transaction history.

The second methodology is embodied in the work by [13] in QuickBooks. This work addresses the limitations of IRIS by enhancing performance for users new to the system (cold-start users) with a populational model. It utilizes a Word2Vec-based [14] encoding for transactions and *Category*, and applies a contrastive learning framework to maximize the matching pairs of transaction-*Category* and minimize the non-matching pairs. It also employs a logistic regression classifier to enable personalized categorization for each company. During inference, the calibrated population and personalized model is applied to predict the category of a new transaction. Although this method has demonstrated effective performance in practice, maintaining an individual logistic regression classifier for each company introduces significant overhead and risks of overfitting. Additionally, calibrating two models can lead to suboptimal performance due to challenges in effectively leveraging strengths of both models.

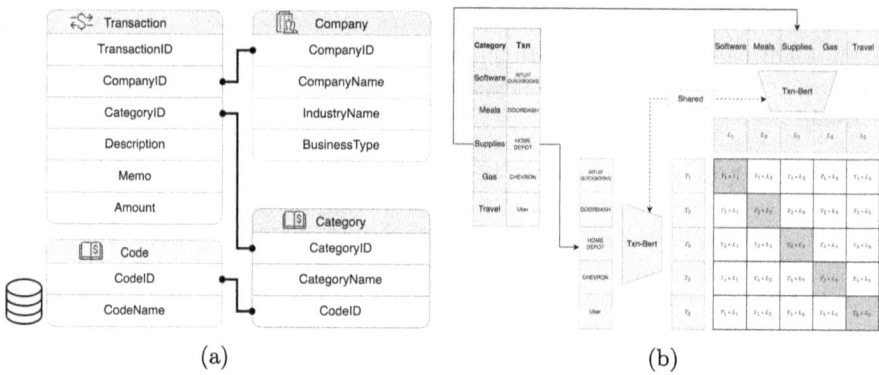

Fig. 1. (a) The schema of the relational database of QuickBooks transactions. (b) Training paradigm of `Txn-Bert`.

1.3 Challenges and Contributions

Challenges. The transaction categorization task in QuickBooks presents several core challenges. Firstly, transaction data is stored in a relational database composed of multiple tables, making it difficult to effectively apply a single unified machine learning model without explicitly engineering features to consolidate the tables. Secondly, the transaction description field, crucial for identifying the semantic meaning of a transaction, often follows the formatting standards of financial institutions rather than natural language. This necessitates an effective method to encode transaction data, capturing nuances such as business entity names and financial acronyms. Thirdly, the vast scale and skewed distribution of *Category* labels result in a highly imbalanced learning scenario. The categorization is highly personalized so that one transaction can be put into different *Category* by different users. Traditional multi-class classifiers can struggle with effectiveness and generalizability on this task. Last but not the least, the large volume of transactions processed by QuickBooks requires a balance between model capability and computational efficiency to ensure real-time performance.

Contributions. The design choices of the proposed pipeline are geared towards tackling one or more of these challenges. The salient contributions are summarized as follows:

1. To model the relational database of the transaction data, we transform the database to a heterogeneous graph and apply a unified graph model, `Rel-Cat`, to effectively represent the relationships within the data and support both new and old users of QuickBooks.
2. To encode the transaction data with unique linguistic characteristics, we integrate a trained-from-scratch text encoder `Txn-Bert` into `Rel-Cat`, which effectively captures the semantics of the transaction data.

3. To handle large-scale transaction data efficiently, we introduce practical techniques to improve Rel-Cat's scalability, including a similarity-based neighbor sampling, edge direction dropping, and Top-K Nearest Neighbor early exit.

2 Txn-Bert: Text Encoder Trained from Scratch

In this section, we introduce Txn-Bert, a text encoder developed specifically for encoding transaction descriptions into fixed-length embeddings. The entire encoder is trained from scratch, recognizing the unique linguistic patterns found in transaction data. We begin with the rationale behind pretraining a new language model, followed by the detailed process of the training of the transformer model.

2.1 Unique Linguistic Characteristics of Transaction Data

To effectively convert transaction text data into embeddings, it is essential to first examine the unique characteristics of this data.

Transaction descriptions, found in banking statements, serve as crucial identifiers for financial activities within businesses. These descriptions adhere to formatting standards set by financial institutions. For instance, Visa mandates that business entity names in transaction descriptions be no longer than 25 characters, requiring abbreviations as necessary.[1].

Such descriptions, therefore, consist predominantly of abbreviated business names, a feature markedly distinct from the more fluid and expansive natural language. This distinctiveness necessitates a specialized approach for encoding transaction. The conventional language models, typically pretrained on generic natural language datasets, do not suffice for capturing the nuances of transaction descriptions. This inadequacy forms the core motivation for developing Txn-Bert from the ground up, ensuring it is finely tuned to the specific lexicon and syntax of transaction language.

2.2 Training the Transformer Model

We start by building a custom tokenizer to fit the specific vocabulary of transaction descriptions. Once we have built the custom tokenizer, the next step is to train our text encoder. We train the model to classify new transactions into specific *Category* solely based on the information from that transaction—like its description, amount, and any additional memo—without considering the historical patterns of the company. We model our training approach after Sentence-Bert [17], treating it as a sentence pair matching problem to match transactions to *Category*. The training paradigm of Txn-Bert is shown in Fig. 1b. We adopt a Siamese network architecture, where a shared text encoder independently processes a pair of a transaction and its corresponding *Category*.

---

[1] https://usa.visa.com/content/dam/VCOM/download/merchants/visa-merchant-data-standards-manual.pdf.

We format each transaction by combining its key fields into a single sentence. We include the <description>, <amount>, and <memo>. We also add a <polarity> field, which labels the transaction as "received" if the amount is positive or "paid" if it's negative. The complete transaction text looks something like this: "Transaction <polarity> $ <amount> for: <description> <memo>." For the *Category* labels, we use them just as they are.

The text encoder is a transformer [18], which will refine the representation of each token iteratively through the transformer blocks. After processing through these layers, we take a mean pooling strategy to get a single representation for the whole sentence.

The training objective mirrors the CLIP approach [16], optimizing for high cosine similarity between matched transaction-*Category* pairs and low similarity for unmatched pairs. We use a symmetric cross-entropy loss. Specifically, given a batch of N transaction-*Category* pairs $\{(T_i, L_i) | 1 \leq i \leq N\}$, and our text encoder $f(\cdot)$, the training loss is:

$$\mathcal{L} = -\frac{1}{N} \sum_{i=1}^{N} \log \left(\frac{e^{\text{Sim}(f(T_i), f(L_i))}}{\sum_{j=1}^{N} e^{\text{Sim}(f(T_i), f(L_j))}} \right) + \log \left(\frac{e^{\text{Sim}(f(T_i), f(L_i))}}{\sum_{j=1}^{N} e^{\text{Sim}(f(T_j), f(L_i))}} \right)$$

where $\text{Sim}(v, w) = \frac{v \cdot w}{|v| \cdot |w|}$ represents the cosine similarity. This method leverages all non-matching pairs within a batch for contrastive learning, thus eliminating the need for explicit negative sampling. This effective training allows `Txn-Bert` to robustly encode transaction and *Category* data for use in downstream tasks.

3 Rel-Cat: Modeling Relations Within Database

In this section, we introduce `Rel-Cat`. We outline our approach for preprocessing a relational database into a heterogeneous graph, thereby redefining the transaction categorization task as a link prediction problem within this graph. We then describe `Rel-Cat`, a hybrid method combining rule-based early exit (`TopK NN`) with a robust heterogeneous graph neural network (GNN). The overview pipeline can be found in Fig. 2.

3.1 Build a Heterogeneous Graph from a Relational Database

The transaction data in QuickBooks is organized within a relational database comprising multiple interconnected tables, each representing different facets of the transaction data. To unify modeling across this multi-table architecture, we employ the concept of Relational Deep Learning [8], transforming the relational database into a heterogeneous graph. We provide an overview of this transformation process with a conversion diagram depicted in Fig. 3.

Conversion Overview. Referencing Fig. 1a, the relational database for transaction data consists of four key components:

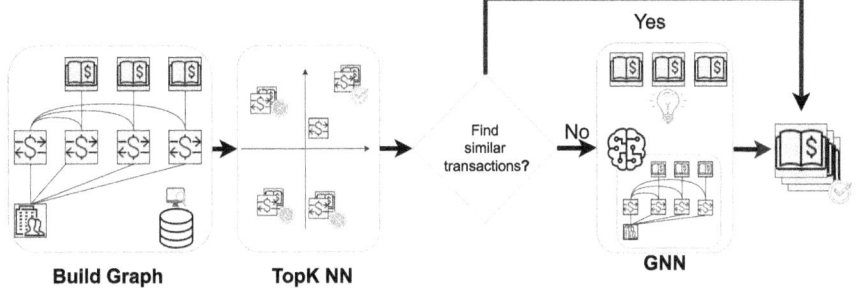

Fig. 2. The overview pipeline of Rel-Cat.

1. **Multiple tables**: The database is structured into several tables, each detailing a specific aspect of the transactions.
2. **Rows within tables**: Each table comprises multiple rows, each row encapsulating a distinct transaction or fact.
3. **Foreign-primary key relationships**: Rows across different tables are interconnected via foreign-primary key associations, facilitating relational references among them.
4. **Row attributes**: Each row includes attributes that describe its elements, such as the transaction description in the transaction table or the company name in the company table.

These elements of the relational database are mapped to the components of a heterogeneous graph as follows:

1. **Node types**: Each table in the database is treated as a distinct node type within the graph.
2. **Nodes**: Individual rows within a table are represented as nodes with the node type corresponding to their table.
3. **Edges**: Connections between rows (nodes) across tables, facilitated by foreign-primary key pairs, are represented as edges in the graph.
4. **Node attributes**: Attributes of each row, particularly textual data, are utilized as node attributes in the graph.

Following the method described in [8], we convert a relational database $(\mathcal{T}, \mathcal{L})$ into a heterogeneous graph $G = (\mathcal{V}, \mathcal{E}, \phi, \psi)$. The relational database consists of tables $\mathcal{T} = \{T_i\}$, each containing rows that become graph nodes $v \in \mathcal{V}$, with node types assigned by table origin via ϕ. Attributes x_v of each row v are encoded using Txn-Bert embeddings. Edges $\mathcal{E}$ between nodes represent primary-foreign key relationships across tables defined by links $\mathcal{L}$, with relation types $\mathcal{R} = \mathcal{L} \cup \mathcal{L}^{-1}$ accounting for both original and inverse relations via ψ.

Transform to a Link Prediction Task. In the heterogeneous graph we've constructed, historical transaction nodes $v \in T_{\text{transaction}}$, that have already been categorized form links with corresponding *Category* nodes, such that $p_{v'} \in \mathcal{K}_v$ where $v' \in T_{Category}$. However, new transactions that have not yet been categorized enter the graph without any existing links to *Category* nodes ($p_{v'} \notin \mathcal{K}_v$ where $v' \in T_{Category}$). This scenario redefines the transaction categorization task. Instead of assigning a *Category* to each new transaction, our task shifts to predicting which *Category* node in the graph should be linked to the new transaction node. Essentially, the categorization challenge is transformed into a link prediction task as shown in Fig. 3a, where the objective is to determine the most appropriate connections for uncategorized transaction nodes based on the graph's existing structure and the attributes of its nodes. This design also allows us to address the cold start problem, a key challenge for our task, by mapping a transaction from a new user to a relevant *Category* based on the historical similarity from other similar businesses.

3.2 Model the Heterogeneous Graph

This section details how Rel-Cat models the heterogeneous graph G. We employ a message-passing Graph Neural Network (GNN) [10], specifically a variant of GraphSAGE [11], to encode node representations. Given the graph's diverse node and edge types, we adapt our approach to model message-passing along different edge types separately. Each message type is initially processed through a homogeneous GNN. Messages from various edge types are then combined using a second-level aggregation function to get a comprehensive node representation:

$$\mathbf{h}_v^{(i+1)} = t_{\phi(v)}\Big(\mathbf{h}_v^{(i)}, \text{AGG}_{\text{Heter}}(\{\text{AGG}_{\text{Homo}}(\{g_R(\mathbf{h}_w^{(i)}) \mid \quad (1)$$
$$w \in \mathcal{N}_R(v)\}) \mid \forall R = (T, \phi(v)) \in \mathcal{R}\})\Big),$$

where $\mathcal{N}_R(v) = \{w \in \mathcal{V} \mid (w,v) \in \mathcal{E} \text{ and } \psi(w,v) = R\}$ is the neighborhood of node v under the specific edge type R. Here, AGG_{Homo} employs a mean operator to normalize message contributions within the same type, while $\text{AGG}_{\text{Heter}}$ uses attention mechanism [18] to dynamically weight the importance of different message types, improving the model's prioritization of relevant messages

Two-Hop Connections for Transaction Nodes. Our initial node representation learning framework in Rel-Cat, as outlined in Eq. 1, aggregates messages from immediate neighbors within the graph G. While effective, this approach can introduce issues inherent in GNNs such as over-squashing [1] and limited expressiveness [20], which we address through graph data augmentation.

Graph Data Augmentation. When GNNs learn the node representation of the target transaction in Fig. 3b, they have to propagate at least two rounds of message passing to receive the information from the historical transactions of the same company. To enhance node representation, especially for the target transaction node, we introduce an additional type of edge within transaction nodes,

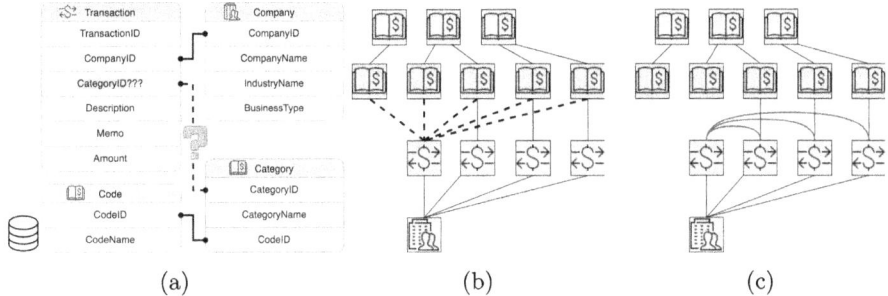

Fig. 3. Transformation of a relational database into a heterogeneous graph for transaction categorization. (a) A new transaction enters the system without a foreign key connection to the *Category* table. (b) The heterogeneous graph is built from the relational database, where transaction categorization is formulated as a link prediction task. (c) Two-hop connections for transaction nodes mitigate over-squashing and improve model expressiveness.

effectively making historical transactions direct neighbors of the target transaction. This adjustment allows the target transaction to aggregate messages from historical transactions in just one message-passing iteration. The augmented graph with these new connections is shown in Fig. 3c. For this new edge type (transaction to transaction), we utilize the GATv2 [2] as the aggregation operator (AGG_{Homo}). While applying GATv2 to all edge types can lead to GPU memory issues, using it for this specific edge type does not significantly increase memory requirements.

Specifically, we introduce an extra set of edges $\mathcal{E}_{aug}$ into the original graph:

$$\mathcal{E}_{aug} = \{(v_1, v_2) \in \mathcal{V} \times \mathcal{V} \mid v_1, v_2 \in T_{transaction}, \exists v_c \in T_{company}, p_c \in \mathcal{K}_{v_1} \cap \mathcal{K}_{v_2}\}.$$

The edge set $\mathcal{E}_{aug}$ is the set of transaction pairs if they are from the same company. Next, we discuss how this modification can mitigate the two issues.

Addressing Over-Squashing. GNNs learn the node representation iteratively from the local neighborhood. However, due to this recurrent learning paradigm, GNNs often face a challenge where the information from a growing receptive field is compressed into a fixed-length vector, potentially losing valuable information. This phenomenon is prevalent in the transaction graph G. For the target transaction in Fig. 3b, the message from its historical transactions is equally compressed into one fixed-length vector. Since this message is not conditioned on the target transaction, it cannot adjust itself so that the signals more important to the target transaction are preserved. By rewiring the graph and applying a weighted message aggregator like GATv2, it can effectively enable the target transaction's incoming message to keep the most relevant information [1], enhancing the effectiveness of the prediction.

Enhancing Expressiveness. GNNs essentially simulate the Weisfeiler-Lehman graph isomorphism algorithm [20]. This limits their expressiveness in terms of distinguishing non-isomorphic graphs. By directly connecting two-hop neighbors (historical transactions) as immediate neighbors to the target transaction in graph G, our model approximates a K-hop GNN approach [7]. This augmentation not only improves expressiveness but does so without significantly increasing computational costs, thus maintains a balance between accuracy and efficiency.

3.3 Training Objective

The transformation of the relational database into the heterogeneous graph G redefines our task as a link prediction challenge. In essence, link prediction in this context is a ranking problem where the model is expected to rank the correct node pair (the ground truth link) higher than other node pairs (non-connected links). Specifically, for a transaction node v_i and its corresponding *Category* node v_j in graph G, the score of (v_i, v_j) should be higher than that of any other *Category* node pair (v_i, v_k), where v_k represents any *Category* node not connected to v_i. We utilize the inner product as the scoring function between transaction and *Category* nodes, employing AUCLoss [19], a surrogate for AUC, as the training objective of Rel-Cat:

$$\mathcal{L} = \sum_{(v_i,v_j)\in\mathcal{E}^+, (v_i,v_k)\in\mathcal{E}^-} (1 - (\mathbf{h}_i * \mathbf{h}_j) + (\mathbf{h}_i * \mathbf{h}_k))^2, \qquad (2)$$

where $\mathbf{h}_v$ denotes the final representation of either a transaction or *Category* node from Eq. 1. The set of positive node pairs $\mathcal{E}^+$ is chosen as:

$$\mathcal{E}^+ \subseteq \{(v_i, v_j) \in T_{\text{transaction}} \times T_{Category} \mid p_{v_j} \in \mathcal{K}_{v_i}\}. \qquad (3)$$

The set of negative node pairs, $\mathcal{E}^-$, includes non-connected links, defined as:

$$\mathcal{E}^- \subseteq \{(v_i, v_k) \in T_{\text{transaction}} \times T_{Category} \mid p_{v_j} \notin \mathcal{K}_{v_i}\}. \qquad (4)$$

Weighted Negative Sampling. The set of negative node pairs, $\mathcal{E}^-$, consists of non-connected links. Due to the impracticality of enumerating all potential negative pairs, we employ a negative sampling strategy. For a transaction node v_i and its corresponding positive *Category* node v_j, simple uniform sampling from $T_{Category} \setminus \{v_j\}$ would be suboptimal due to the long-tail distribution of *Category*. This could prevent effective learning if those *Category* nodes v_k, which rarely appear as positives, are sampled as negatives. To address this, we employ a weighted multinomial distribution for negative sampling, where weights are assigned proportional to the normalized frequency of *Category* appearances, enhancing the relevance and challenge of the sampled negatives.

Selective Loss Computation via Diversity Filtering. During the loss computation and backpropagation over a batch - not all samples contribute equally to learning, some being too easy (providing little gradient signal) or redundant (leading to inefficient updates). Thus, we propose a selective loss computation strategy, where all samples undergo a forward pass, but only a subset of challenging or informative samples contribute to the loss and gradient computation, i.e., a full-forward partial-backward strategy. This strategy retains the benefits of large-batch inference while ensuring that gradient updates focus on samples that are most challenging and diverse. Since all samples contribute to feature extraction during the forward pass, the model benefits from seeing a broader distribution of the data. This results more accurate hard sample identification, targeted gradient updates, and improved generalization. To select the subset of diverse samples, we compute the dot product similarity of transaction feature representation. From this distribution, we gradually refine the selection over epochs, choosing samples with lower similarity scores and only use those for loss computation. Initially, we utilize 100% of the samples, then gradually decrease this proportion in stages until reaching 40%, maintaining a core set of diverse samples throughout training. Experiments show that this provides us with the optimal diversity samples for loss computation in a batch, providing highest gradient signals during back-propagation.

3.4 Scalability and Practical Designs

In this section, we detail several scalability improvements to Rel-Cat, designed to effectively manage the extensive volume of transaction data encountered in real-world applications. We discuss practical designs to reduce neighborhood sizes for transaction and *Category* nodes during node representation encoding and introduce a rule-based early exit method, Top-K Nearest Neighbor, to efficiently manage the workload on GNNs.

Reducing Neighborhood Size. Given that GNNs encode node representations by aggregating features from local neighborhoods, large neighborhoods can pose significant scalability challenges, particularly in terms of memory consumption. To address this, we implement a node-wise neighbor sampling strategy. Different from existing methods [9,11,21], we further take node types into consideration to optimize the receptive field of the GNNs. We employ distinct strategies for transaction nodes and *Category* nodes:

Similarity-Based Neighbor Sampling for Transaction Nodes. For transaction nodes, $\{v \mid v \in T_{\text{transaction}}\}$, the local neighborhood typically includes all historical transactions associated with the company, which can be extensive. For example, there are companies owning over 2000 transactions within just one year. To manage this, we utilize similarity-based neighbor sampling, which reduces neighborhood size while preserving relevant information.

We compute the cosine similarity between the text embeddings of the target transaction node and its historical counterparts. Historical transactions are then sampled based on their similarity scores, prioritizing those most relevant to the target. This approach not only constrains computational overhead but also ensures that the most informative connections are maintained in Rel-Cat's neighborhood. Techniques like Faiss [6] can be employed to enhance the efficiency of these computations.

Edge Direction Dropping for Category Nodes. Category nodes, $\{v \mid v \in T_{Category}\}$, often have neighborhoods that include a huge set of transaction nodes linked to them. The popularity of some *Category* can lead to extremely large neighborhood sizes, which are not only impractical to process, but also ineffective to model.

To mitigate this, we discard all incoming edge connections from transaction to *Category* nodes. This adjustment significantly reduces the computational load by limiting the receptive field to exclude transaction nodes, while outgoing connections from *Category* to transaction nodes are kept. This approach not only simplifies the computation required to encode *Category* node but also ensures consistency in *Category* node representation during inference, as the computational graph remains unchanged regardless of new transactions being added.

Top-K Nearest Neighbor. Despite the sophisticated capabilities of Rel-Cat, equipped with GNNs to perform predictions based on graph structure G, real-world scenarios often present varying degrees of prediction difficulty [15]. Many transactions imported into QuickBooks by users are very similar or even identical to past entries due to routine business activities. In such cases, users frequently reuse the same *Category* as in previous transactions. Consequently, a significant portion of transactions could be accurately categorized without necessitating full GNN processing. To capitalize on this, we utilize the streamlined and effective early exit method through Top-K Nearest Neighbor (TopK NN).

Upon the arrival of a new transaction, while we still prepare the graph G for subsequent GNN processing, we first assess if sufficiently similar historical transactions might already provide reliable predictions. Utilizing the similarity scores computed during the similarity-based neighbor sampling of transaction nodes, we identify a subset of historical transactions that exhibit a similarity score exceeding a cutoff, set at 0.8 for our experiments.

From this subset, we directly derive *Category* from the top-K most similar transactions. Given that our categorization task aims to predict the 5 most likely categories, Rel-Cat will output these labels directly if 5 distinct *Category* are available from this subset. If fewer than 5 categories are available, the graph G is then processed by the GNNs to generate the remaining predictions.

4 Experiments

4.1 Experimental Setup

Dataset. To evaluate the performance of Rel-Cat comprehensively, we curated a dataset from active QuickBooks users as of November 2023. We randomly selected $7.5K$ companies and used their two most recent transactions with

labeled *Category* post-November 2023 as our test set, resulting in a total of $15K$ transactions. The training set consisted of $3000K$ transactions having $100K$ *Category* across $15K$ companies reflecting a wide range of user preferences and patterns.

Experimental Settings. We benchmark the performance of Rel-Cat against the current production models in QuickBooks, namely Shorthair and Lynx. Shorthair is a population model that employs contrastive learning and Word2Vec embeddings, whereas Lynx, built on top of Shorthair is a logistic regression model customized to a company. We assess the models using the metrics of Top-1, Top-2, and Top-5 accuracy, which measure whether the correct label is among the Top-k predictions of the model, ranked by the *Category* scores. We conduct evaluations under two distinct settings:

Zero Shot: In this setting, categorization is based solely on the information from the new transaction itself, without any contextual data from the owning company or its historical transactions. Both Shorthair and Txn-Bert are evaluated under this setting.

Few Shot: This setting incorporates not only the data from the new transaction but also contextual information from the owning company and its historical data. Lynx, TopK NN, and Rel-Cat are assessed under this framework.

4.2 Results

The experimental results are presented in Table 1. In the Zero Shot setting, Txn-Bert outperforms the production Shorthair model significantly. The Txn-Bert model with 6 layers achieves a Top-1 accuracy boost of 7.76% and a Top-5 accuracy of 74.12%, indicating that our trained-from-scratch text encoder effectively captures the semantics of transaction descriptions and maps them accurately to the corresponding *Category*. The 12-layer Txn-Bert model shows only marginal improvement over the 6-layer model, suggesting that a lightweight language model pretrained from scratch is sufficient for encoding transaction data.

In the Few Shot setting, Rel-Cat demonstrates substantial performance advantages. It achieves a Top-1 accuracy of 68.67% and a Top-5 accuracy of 88.04%, significantly outperforming the Lynx model. Additionally, the TopK NN method, which uses text embeddings from Txn-Bert, achieves a Top-1 accuracy of 65.80%, surpassing the performance of Rel-Cat with GNNs alone. This result highlights the effectiveness of TopK NN in identifying recurring transactions in a user's history, thereby enhancing Top-1 accuracy of Rel-Cat.

However, when the transaction categorization must be inferred beyond the user's most similar historical transactions, the GNN component of Rel-Cat exhibits superior generalizability, achieving nearly 85% in Top-5 accuracy. This demonstrates that while TopK NN is highly effective for repeated transactions, the GNN module of Rel-Cat provides a broader and more accurate categorization capability for diverse transaction scenarios.

Table 1. Transaction categorization evaluated by accuracy under Zero Shot and Few Shot settings.

Methods	Top-1	Top-2	Top-5
Zero Shot			
Shorthair	36.07	-	-
Txn-Bert (6 layers)	43.83	57.96	74.12
Txn-Bert (12 layers)	**45.52**	**59.47**	**75.46**
Few Shot			
Lynx	62.49	-	-
TopK NN	65.80	73.63	78.55
Rel-Cat (GNNs only)	63.38	74.60	84.89
Rel-Cat	**68.67**	**78.97**	**88.04**
Ablation Study			
Rel-Cat (GNNs only)	63.38	74.60	84.89
w/o Txn-Bert	55.46	64.02	73.16
w/o two-hop connections	47.07	61.16	76.58
w/o similarity sampling	56.39	67.89	80.63
w/o diversity filtering	61.74	73.18	83.85

Table 2. Performance breakdown in different scenarios. **Acc** is the overall Top-1 accuracy, **HS** is the accuracy on Historical Seen subset, and **HU** is the accuracy on Historical Unseen subset.

Methods	Acc	HS	HU
TopK NN	65.80	**79.72**	0.16
Rel-Cat (GNNs only)	63.38	72.25	**22.05**
Rel-Cat	**68.67**	78.64	20.84
Methods (GNNs only)	**Acc**	**HS**	**HU**
Rel-Cat (GNNs only)	63.38	72.25	22.05
w/o Txn-Bert	55.46	66.24	4.83
w/o two-hop connections	47.07	51.36	26.93
w/o similarity sampling	56.39	65.26	14.73
w/o diversity filtering	61.74	70.46	20.75

4.3 Seen vs Unseen Category in a Company's History

In this section, we discuss why Rel-Cat is designed as a hybrid model, namely a combination of TopK NN and GNNs. In Table 2, we not only report our overall accuracy, but further break down the performance of Rel-Cat into Historical Seen and Historical Unseen scenarios. For Historical Seen, we choose the test samples such that their ground-truth *Category* is present within the company's own history as context. For Historical Unseen, we choose the samples whose *Category* are present in the overall dataset but unseen to that company's history.

We note that TopK NN, while having the best performance at repeated labels, has no predictive power for unseen labels. For this subset, Rel-Cat's GNN is able to detect the labels with over 22% accuracy, highlighting its generalizable ability. Given that most transactions in production systems belong to the historical seen category, Rel-Cat has the best overall performance, balancing between both the subsets, thereby demonstrating the need for GNN and TopK NN hybrid model. Furthermore, analyzing these trends over the ablation studies, we note that each design choice adds to the overall accuracy, augmenting performance for either or both the seen and unseen subsets.

4.4 Ablation Studies

In this section, we delve deeper into the validation of the effectiveness of various design choices in Rel-Cat.

In Table 1, we report ablation studies to validate if the proposed components in Rel-Cat can enhance the predictive power of transaction categorization. For the ablation studies, we only include the GNNs module for Rel-Cat.

w/o Txn-Bert *(Sect. 2)*: Replacing Txn-Bert with off-the-shelf Sentence-Bert [17], we observe a decrease in performance, underscoring the necessity of a trained-from-scratch text encoder tailored to transaction data. We further note the steep drop in performance for the unseen subset.

w/o Two-Hop Connections (Sect. 3.2): This ablation study emphasizes the critical role of explicit graph augmentation. It demonstrates that directly connecting the target and historical transactions as neighbors significantly enhances performance. This finding underscores that merely converting a relational database to a heterogeneous graph without strategic modifications is inadequate for maximizing the model's effectiveness. While this setting has the best performance for the unseen subset, it comes at the expense of significant decline in overall performance.

w/o Similarity Sampling (Sect. 3.4): Testing the impact of neighbor sampling based on semantic similarity, we find that sampling similar historical transactions in GNN's computation graphs allows Rel-Cat to leverage relevant information effectively for accurate predictions. We note that this setting also suffers from lack of generalizability.

w/o Diversity Filtering (Sect. 3.3): here we report the results without the diversity filtering, when all samples pass through the backward pass during GNN training throughout the training. We note that while the drop in the unseen subset performance is to be expected without this filtering, we also note a drop across all metrics, suggesting the effectiveness of selective backpropagation.

4.5 Time Complexity

We have assessed the processing time for various components within Rel-Cat, with the results detailed in Table 3. We report the processing time as time taken in milliseconds (ms) per $1,000$ transactions. The entire pipeline of Rel-Cat is designed to operate effectively on both CPU and GPU environments, catering to different production system requirements.

Table 3. Inference times for $1,000$ transactions.

Walltime (ms)	CPU	GPU
Txn-Bert	1400	67
Rel-Cat	6808	843
- TopK NN	333	-
- Rel-Cat (GNNs only)	6614	324
Total	8208	910

On a CPU, the lightweight text encoder Txn-Bert processes $1,000$ transactions in just 1400 milliseconds. To deliver the Top-5 predictions, Rel-Cat requires approximately 8 seconds for $1,000$ transactions. In contrast, utilizing a GPU significantly reduces the processing time to under 1 second for outputting the Top-5 predictions. This efficiency demonstrates `Rel-Cat`'s capability to scale and meet the demands of real-world transaction volumes effectively.

4.6 Prediction Cascade

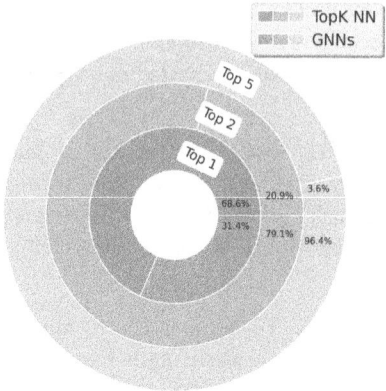

Fig. 4. Cascade process in `Rel-Cat`. TopK NN efficiently resolves 68% of transactions when only a Top-1 prediction is needed. However, for more comprehensive Top-5 predictions, over 96% of transactions necessitate processing by GNNs.

In the `Rel-Cat` pipeline shown in Fig. 2, the processed graph initially enters the TopK NN module, which serves as an early exit strategy to identify similar transactions via text embeddings. If this step does not yield sufficient *Category* predictions, the pipeline advances to the GNNs for additional predictions.

Our analysis of this cascade, shown in Fig. 4, reveals that for Top-1 predictions, TopK NN alone efficiently handles over 68% of transactions. This high percentage underscores the prevalence of similar transactions within the database. However, to generate the Top-5 predictions, more than 96% of transactions require processing by the GNNs, indicating the need for a more in-depth computation to fulfill broader prediction requirements.

This flexible approach in `Rel-Cat` demonstrates the system's adaptability, allowing for a balance between efficiency and thoroughness in prediction based on system demands and user experience considerations.

5 Conclusion

In this study, we introduce `Rel-Cat`, a unified model designed for transaction categorization within QuickBooks. Recognizing the unique linguistic characteristics of transaction data, we train, from scratch, a `Txn-Bert` text encoder, to grasp the semantic nuances of financial transaction descriptions. Subsequently, we employ a GNN-based model to capture the relationships among the tables in a relational database, redefining transaction categorization as a link prediction task over a heterogeneous graph. To address the challenges posed by the high volume of transactions and the specific demands of the categorization task, we integrate several innovative components that significantly boost `Rel-Cat`'s predictive capabilities. Our experimental results demonstrate that `Rel-Cat` not only surpasses previous production models in terms of performance but also offers remarkable scalability and efficiency, making it well-suited for handling large-scale transaction data in real-world settings. Having proved its merit in offline testing, our approach is currently in the process of being implemented for deployment in production due to its improved metrics, improved customer experience providing multiple options for categories to choose from (top-k), and the simplified overall architecture allowing the company to move away from running and maintaining million plus models in production for supporting personalized transaction categorization.

Acknowledgments. We thank the anonymous reviewers for their insightful comments and helpful discussions. We are also grateful to Byron Tang, Heather Simpson, Jocelyn Lu, and Hilaf Hasson for their assistance in retrieving the dataset and providing constructive feedback on this project.

References

1. Alon, U., Yahav, E.: On the Bottleneck of Graph Neural Networks and its Practical Implications. arXiv:2006.05205 (2021). arXiv: 2006.05205
2. Brody, S., Alon, U., Yahav, E.: How Attentive are Graph Attention Networks? (2022). arXiv:2105.14491
3. Bronstein, M.M., Bruna, J., LeCun, Y., Szlam, A., Vandergheynst, P.: Geometric deep learning: going beyond Euclidean data. IEEE Signal Process. Mag. **34**(4), 18–42 (2017). arXiv: 1611.08097
4. Devlin, J., Chang, M.W., Lee, K., Toutanova, K.: BERT: pre-training of deep bidirectional transformers for language understanding. In: Burstein, J., Doran, C., Solorio, T. (eds.) Proceedings of the 2019 Conference of the North American Chapter of the Association for Computational Linguistics: Human Language Technologies, Volume 1 (Long and Short Papers), pp. 4171–4186. Association for Computational Linguistics, Minneapolis, Minnesota (2019)
5. Dong, K., Guo, Z., Chawla, N.V.: Pure Message Passing Can Estimate Common Neighbor for Link Prediction (2023). arXiv:2309.00976
6. Douze, M., et al.: The Faiss library (2024). _eprint: 2401.08281
7. Feng, J., Chen, Y., Li, F., Sarkar, A., Zhang, M.: How Powerful are K-hop Message Passing Graph Neural Networks (2023). arXiv:2205.13328
8. Fey, M., et al.: Position: Relational Deep Learning - Graph Representation Learning on Relational Databases (2024)
9. Frasca, F., Rossi, E., Eynard, D., Chamberlain, B., Bronstein, M., Monti, F.: SIGN: Scalable Inception Graph Neural Networks (2020). arXiv:2004.11198
10. Gilmer, J., Schoenholz, S.S., Riley, P.F., Vinyals, O., Dahl, G.E.: Neural Message Passing for Quantum Chemistry. CoRR (2017)

11. Hamilton, W.L., Ying, R., Leskovec, J.: Inductive Representation Learning on Large Graphs. arXiv:1706.02216 (2018). arXiv: 1706.02216
12. Lesner, C., Ran, A., Rukonic, M., Wang, W.: Large scale personalized categorization of financial transactions. In: Proceedings of the AAAI Conference on Artificial Intelligence, vol. 33, no. 01, pp. 9365–9372 (2019)
13. Liu, J., Pei, L., Sun, Y., Simpson, H., Lu, J., Ho, N.: Categorization of financial transactions in QuickBooks. In: Proceedings of the 27th ACM SIGKDD Conference on Knowledge Discovery & Data Mining, KDD 2021, pp. 3299–3307. Association for Computing Machinery, New York (2021)
14. Mikolov, T., Sutskever, I., Chen, K., Corrado, G.S., Dean, J.: Distributed representations of words and phrases and their compositionality. In: Burges, C.J.C., Bottou, L., Welling, M., Ghahramani, Z., Weinberger, K.Q. (eds.) Advances in Neural Information Processing Systems, vol. 26. Curran Associates, Inc. (2013)
15. Panda, P., Sengupta, A., Roy, K.: Conditional deep learning for energy-efficient and enhanced pattern recognition. In: Proceedings of the 2016 Conference on Design, Automation & Test in Europe, DATE 2016, pp. 475–480. EDA Consortium, San Jose, CA, USA (2016)
16. Radford, A., et al.: Learning transferable visual models from natural language supervision. In: Proceedings of the 38th International Conference on Machine Learning, pp. 8748–8763. PMLR (2021). iSSN: 2640-3498
17. Reimers, N., Gurevych, I.: Sentence-BERT: sentence embeddings using siamese BERT-networks. In: Inui, K., Jiang, J., Ng, V., Wan, X. (eds.) Proceedings of the 2019 Conference on Empirical Methods in Natural Language Processing and the 9th International Joint Conference on Natural Language Processing (EMNLP-IJCNLP), pp. 3982–3992. Association for Computational Linguistics, Hong Kong, China (2019)
18. Vaswani, A., et al.: Attention is all you need. In: Advances in Neural Information Processing Systems, vol. 30. Curran Associates, Inc. (2017)
19. Wang, Z., Zhou, Y., Hong, L., Zou, Y., Su, H., Chen, S.: Pairwise Learning for Neural Link Prediction. arXiv:2112.02936 (2022). arXiv: 2112.02936
20. Xu, K., Hu, W., Leskovec, J., Jegelka, S.: How Powerful are Graph Neural Networks? CoRR abs/1810.00826 (2018). arXiv:1810.00826
21. Ying, R., He, R., Chen, K., Eksombatchai, P., Hamilton, W.L., Leskovec, J.: Graph convolutional neural networks for web-scale recommender systems. In: Proceedings of the 24th ACM SIGKDD International Conference on Knowledge Discovery & Data Mining, KDD 2018, pp. 974–983. Association for Computing Machinery, New York (2018)

Attribute-Aware Sequential Recommendation Model for Used Car Auctions

Shereen Elsayed[1], Ngoc Son Le[1(✉)], Ahmed Rashed[2], Lukas Hestermeyer[2], Radoslaw Wlodarczyk[2], Maximilian Stubbemann[1], and Lars Schmidt-Thieme[1]

[1] Information Systems and Machine Learning Lab (ISMLL) & VWFS Data Analytics Research Center (VWFS DARC), University of Hildesheim, Hildesheim, Germany
{elsayed,sle,schmidt-thieme}@ismll.uni-hildesheim.de
[2] Volkswagen Financial Services AG, Braunschweig, Germany
{ahmed.galal.ahmed.rashed,Lukas.Hestermeyer,Radoslaw.Wlodarczyk}@vwfs.com

Abstract. In used cars auction systems, users can buy vehicles through fixed-price rounds or participate in auction rounds where they place bids, with each item typically awarded to the highest bidder. This auction setup presents a challenge for recommender systems, as it involves sequential recommendation of unique items, where each item is available for sale only once in both fixed-price and auction rounds. Although this scenario is highly relevant, it has received limited attention in existing sequential recommendation research. Moreover, this challenge relates to the cold start problem encountered by many recommendation models. In this work, we aim to address the unique item sequential recommendation problem by developing an attribute-aware model for next-item prediction. Specifically, we introduce the **A**ttribute-**A**ware **S**equential **R**ecommendation Model (**ASRM**), which is designed to handle unique item data and effectively leverage item attributes in the absence of item IDs. To further enhance performance in this context, we propose an improved version, **ASRM++**. Our experiments, conducted on a dataset from Volkswagen Financial Services' used car center, demonstrate that ASRM significantly outperforms existing state-of-the-art models for unique item recommendation. Additionally, we present A/B test results from the deployed ASRM model to validate its effectiveness.

Keywords: Attribute-aware recommendation · Auction systems · Sequential recommendation

1 Introduction

Recommender systems have become essential for nearly all online platforms today. Over the past decade, the number of recommender system models

---

S. Elsayed, N. S. Le and A. Rashed—All three authors contributed equally to this work.

© The Author(s), under exclusive license to Springer Nature Switzerland AG 2026
I. Dutra et al. (Eds.): ECML PKDD 2025, LNAI 16021, pp. 161–177, 2026.
https://doi.org/10.1007/978-3-032-06118-8_10

has grown rapidly, including various types such as sequential recommendation [2,11,12], context-aware recommendation, and attribute-aware recommendation [7,10]. Auction platforms raise unique challenges due to their specific characteristics. In business-to-business (B2B) used car auction systems, users can purchase vehicles in two types of rounds: a fixed-price round or a bidding round, where users place bids and the item is sold to the highest bidder. Once sold, an item is removed from the platform, meaning each item is unique and becomes unavailable after the sale in both fixed-price and bidding rounds. As a result, relying on item IDs in such systems is not possible, as it is similar to the cold start problem with constantly unseen items. In this context, item attributes are essential for learning user preferences, as each item must be represented by its attributes rather than a persistent ID.

Sequential recommendation models have rapidly advanced due to their significance. Early approaches relied on convolutional neural networks (Caser) [12] and Gated Recurrent Units (GRU4Rec) [2]. A pivotal model, SASRec [4], uses a transformer encoder to build a simple yet effective recommendation model that is trained in an autoregressive manner. Several models have since built upon SASRec, such as S^3Rec [13], which incorporates pre-training to improve learning, and TiSASRec [5], which accounts for time intervals between interactions. Other methods integrate item or user attributes, including NOVA [6] that enhances BERT4Rec [11] to leverage the side information in the data, CARCA [7] which is an attribute and context-aware model that applies cross-attention for item scoring and ProxyRCA [10] further refines CARCA by enhancing the training protocol and introducing proxy-based item embeddings, allowing less frequently observed items to benefit from the information of more frequent ones.

Although many sequential recommendation models have been developed, few address the challenge of unique item settings. In this work, we aim to leverage a sequential recommendation model that focuses on item attributes instead of item IDs. Inspired by the CARCA model architecture, we propose an attribute-aware sequential recommendation model specifically designed for car auction systems, which can learn user preferences based on the features of historical items. Additionally, our model integrates both sales and bid interactions within a multi-task learning framework. The main contributions of the paper can be summarized as follows:

- We introduce an attribute-aware sequential recommendation model (ASRM) tailored for recommending unique items in auction systems. The model utilizes both bids and sales interactions for training, where user bids serve as an auxiliary task.
- We enhance several components of the proposed model and present an improved version called ASRM++.
- We demonstrate superior offline results compared to several state-of-the-art models, highlighting the effectiveness of our approach in unique item recommendation scenarios.
- We present online A/B test results, showcasing the real-world impact of our approach when deployed for actual users.

2 Related Work

2.1 Attribute and Context-Aware Recommendation

Attribute and context-aware recommendations aim at enhancing the quality of recommendations by leveraging both item features and contextual information, moving beyond mere item IDs. This is especially crucial in certain domains where all the item IDs are unique, such as in the cases of auctions. Early works introduced Factorization Machines (FM) [9], which models contextual feature interactions between every pair of variables in the dataset. Later, DeepFM [1] unified FM with deep learning to enable higher-order feature interactions. Attention-based methods, such as NOVA [6], proposed to incorporate item attributes and interaction contexts in a non-invasive way, by separating the embeddings of the item IDs and its contextual information, thus preserving the integrity of the original item embeddings. S^3Rec [13] captured the correlation between items and their attributes more effectively by modeling these relationships during both the pre-training and fine-tuning stages of its self-supervised learning protocol. Most recently, CARCA [7] and ProxyRCA [10] achieved state-of-the-art performance in recommendation tasks by adopting a holistic method that incorporate the contextual and attribute-based information deeply within the collaborative filtering process. ProxyRCA further addresses the cold start problem by allowing the less frequent items to benefit from the well-trained proxy embeddings.

2.2 Sequential Recommendation

Sequential recommendation focuses on predicting the next item that the user is supposed to interact with, given the sequence of his historical interactions. In contrast to traditional collaborative filtering methods that do not consider the order of interactions, sequential recommendation methods aim to model evolving user preferences over time. Earlier methods, such as FM [9], were based on Markov Chains and modeled item-item transitions based on the last item interaction. The emergence of deep learning techniques has allowed more complex user-item interactions to be modeled. Recurrent Neural Networks (RNNs) based models, particularly Gated Recurrent Units (GRU) [2,3], were used to capture longer-term dependencies of the user behavior. With the early success of self-attention mechanisms and the transformer architecture in sequence encoder tasks, such as machine translation, it has naturally been extended to sequential recommendation tasks. SASRec [4] was one of such early examples and its extension SASRec$_F$ [13] that further incorporated the item attributes by fusing it together with the item ID (Fig. 1).

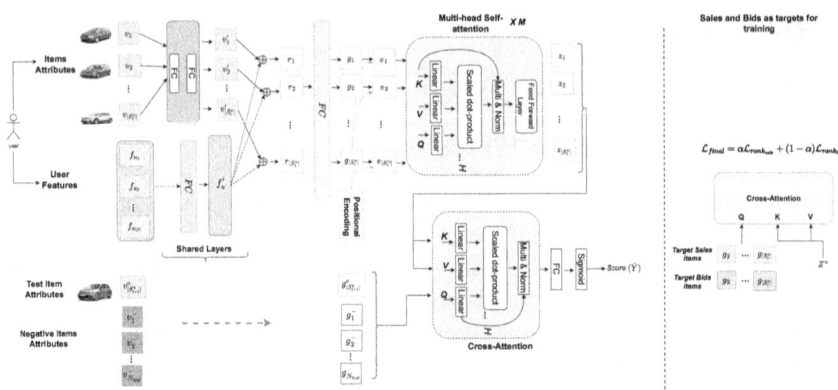

Fig. 1. Illustration of the deployed Attribute-aware Model Architecture

3 Attribute-Aware Unique-Item Recommendation Problem Formulation

In this paper, we address the following problem: Given a set of *items* $\mathcal{I} = \{i_1, \ldots, i_{|\mathcal{I}|}\}$, where each item $i \in \mathcal{I}$ is represented by an *attribute-vector* $v_i \in \mathbb{R}^A$, and a set of users $\mathcal{U} = \{u_1, \ldots, u_{|\mathcal{U}|}\}$, where each user $u \in \mathcal{U}$ has an *feature-vector* $f_u \in \mathbb{R}^F$. Each user u has a sequence of sales interactions $S^u = (S^u_1, \ldots, S^u_{|S^u|})$ and a sequence of bids interactions $B^u = (B^u_1, \ldots, B^u_{|B^u|})$. The objective is to predict the likelihood scores for a set of target items $\mathcal{T}^o = \{t^o_1, \ldots, t^o_{|\mathcal{T}^o|}\}$ for each user u. The model parameters are optimized by maximizing the log-likelihood (or minimizing cross-entropy) of the observed target item over all users. The bidding behavior serves as auxiliary information to help more accurately model user actions over time. In the context of auction systems, our problem is distinct from typical sequential recommendation scenarios in that each item in every interaction is unique. Formally, for any two interactions S^u_i and $S^{u'}_j$, where $u, u' \in U$ and $(u, i) \neq (u', j)$, we have $S^u_i \neq S^{u'}_j$.

4 ASRM: The Deployed Attribute-Aware Sequential Model for Unique Item Recommendation

4.1 Input Encoding

To form the item latent representation, we first embed item attributes in the input sequence using two fully connected layers to obtain the initial embeddings as:

$$v'_j = (v_j W + b) W' + b' \tag{1}$$

where $W \in \mathbb{R}^{A \times d'}, W' \in \mathbb{R}^{d' \times d}$ are the weight matrices $b \in \mathbb{R}^{d'}, b' \in \mathbb{R}^d$ are the bias vectors and d is the items embedding dimension.

For user features, we apply a fully connected layer to encode the user's features as:

$$f'_u = f_u W_f + b_f \qquad (2)$$

where $W_f \in \mathbb{R}^{F \times d}$ is a weight matrix, F is the number of user features, and d is the items embedding dimension and b_f is the bias term. Notice that in this case, user features are the same for all items in the input sequence.

Afterward, we concatenate items, and user embeddings to get the combined item encoding r_j. Then, feed it to another fully connected layer for a refined representation:

$$r_j = \text{concat}_{col}\left(v'_j, f'_u\right), \qquad g_j = r_j W_r + b_r \qquad (3)$$

where $W_r \in \mathbb{R}^{2d \times d}$ is the weight matrix, d is the layer embedding dimension, and b_r is the bias term. For simplicity, we use the **same dimension** d for all embedding layers. Finally, a learnable positional embedding $p_j \in \mathbb{R}^d$ is added to the final embedding to indicate the position in the input interactions sequence:

$$e_j = g_j + p_j \qquad (4)$$

4.2 Multi-head Self-attention Block

The ASRM model leverages a multi-head self-attention mechanism applied across the latent embeddings of all items. Let $\mathcal{E}^u := (e_1, \ldots, e_{|S^u|}) \in (\mathbb{R}^d)^{|S^u|}$ be the encoded sequence. In the following, we interpret this sequence as a matrix $\mathcal{E}^u \in \mathbb{R}^{|S^u| \times d}$. The first layer in the MHA block is a linear projection on each of the *Query*, *Keys*, and *Values* as follows:

$$Q, K, V = LeakyReLU(\mathcal{E}^u W_Q), LeakyReLU(\mathcal{E}^u W_K), \\ LeakyReLU(\mathcal{E}^u W_V) \qquad (5)$$

where $\mathbf{W}^Q, \mathbf{W}^K, \mathbf{W}^V \in \mathbb{R}^{d \times d}$ represent the linear projection matrices. Then each of the output embedding is split over the number of heads H to obtain $\mathbf{W}_h^Q$, $\mathbf{W}_h^K, \mathbf{W}_h^V \in \mathbb{R}^{d \times \frac{d}{H}}$ of the head at index h. A multi-head self-attention is applied afterward to get the attention across all items in the sequence. This allows the model to capture dependencies between different items in the sequence, resulting in a latent representation for each item:

$$C^u = \text{SA}(\mathcal{E}^u) = \text{concat}_{col}\left(\text{Att}(Q_h, K_h, V_h)\right)_{h=1:H} \qquad (6)$$

Here, $C^u \in \mathbb{R}^{|S^u| \times d}$ represents the column-wise concatenation of the attention heads. Afterward, a multiplicative residual is applied between C^u and Q, then we apply a normalization layer to obtain the output $C^{u'}$ as follows:

$$C^{u'} = Normalize(C^u * \mathcal{E}^u) \qquad (7)$$

Finally, we have the row-wise feed-forward layers to obtain the component's output representations $Z^u \in \mathbb{R}^{|S^u| \times d}$ as follows. For all $i \in \{1, \ldots, |S^u|\}$ we have:

$$\begin{aligned} Z_i^u &= \text{FFN}(C_i^{u'}) \\ &= LeakyReLU(C_i^{u'}W^Z + b^Z)W^{Z'} + b^{Z'} \end{aligned} \quad (8)$$

where $W^Z, W^{Z'} \in \mathbb{R}^{d \times d}$ are the weight matrices of the two feed-forward layers, while b^Z and $b^{Z'} \in \mathbb{R}^d$ are their bias row-vectors. **LeakyReLU** is the activation function applied after the first layer.

4.3 Next Item Prediction with ASRM

Given Z^u, we predict for a given a set of target items represented by the attribute-matrix $\mathcal{T}^o$ the likelihood via cross-attention.

Cross Attention. To derive the latent embedding G^o for the target items, their attribute vectors are passed through the shared item encoding layers up to Eq. 3. However, the fully connected layer applied after concatenating the user features is skipped on the target branch. For item ranking, we apply cross-attention between Z^u and G^o as follows: We get a linear projection on each of the $Query$, $Keys$ and $Values$ similar to the input MHA block, as follows:

$$\begin{aligned} Q, K, V = LeakyReLU(G^o W_Q), LeakyReLU(Z^u W_K), \\ LeakyReLU(Z^u W_V) \end{aligned} \quad (9)$$

where $\mathbf{W}^Q, \mathbf{W}^K, \mathbf{W}^V \in \mathbb{R}^{d \times d}$ represent the linear projection matrices. Then each of the output embedding is split over the number of heads H to obtain $\mathbf{W}_h^Q$, $\mathbf{W}_h^K, \mathbf{W}_h^V \in \mathbb{R}^{d \times \frac{d}{H}}$ of the head at index h. A multi-head self-attention is applied afterward to get the attention across all items in the sequence. This allows the model to capture dependencies between different items in the sequence, resulting in a latent representation for each item:

$$X^o = \text{CA}(Z^u, G^o) = \text{concat}_{col}\left(\text{Att}(Q_h, K_h, V_h)\right)_{h=1:H} \quad (10)$$

Here, $X^o \in \mathbb{R}^{|\mathcal{T}^o| \times d}$ represents the column-wise concatenation of the attention heads. Afterward, a multiplicative residual is applied between X^o and Q, then we apply a normalization layer to obtain the output $X^{o'}$ as follows:

$$X^{o'} = Normalize(X^o * G^o) \quad (11)$$

To reduce the output dimension, we apply a fully connected layer with output dimension 1 followed by a sigmoid function to compute a probability score between $[0, 1]$:

$$\hat{Y}_k^o = \sigma(X^{o'}{}_k W_o + b_o) \quad (12)$$

for all $k \in \{1, \ldots, |\mathcal{T}^o|\}$, where σ is the sigmoid function, $W_o \in \mathbb{R}^{d \times 1}$ is the weight matrix of the output layer to reduce the output dimension to one value and $b \in \mathbb{R}$ is the bias term.

In the context of used-car recommendations, we have given a sequence of used-cars bought by a dealer and the main task is to rank a sequence of used cars based on their likelihood to be bought by this dealer.

4.4 ASRM Model Optimization

Bids and Sales as Model Targets. Given a sequence of positive sales target items from the user's input and an equally long set of negative items sampled from a pool excluding the user's input sequence, we define the binary cross-entropy objective as follows:

$$\mathcal{L}_{Sales} = - \sum_{\mathcal{T}^o \in \mathcal{S}} \sum_{t=0}^{|\mathcal{T}^o|} [log(\hat{Y}_t^{o^{(+sale)}}) + (log(1 - \hat{Y}_t^{o^{(-)}}))] \tag{13}$$

As previously discussed, positive target items can also be selected from the user's bid sequence, as these reflect additional items of interest. Thus, we define the auxiliary loss for bids as follows:

$$\mathcal{L}_{Bids} = - \sum_{\mathcal{T}^o \in \mathcal{S}} \sum_{t=0}^{|\mathcal{T}^o|} [log(\hat{Y}_t^{o^{(+bid)}}) + (log(1 - \hat{Y}_t^{o^{(-)}}))] \tag{14}$$

where $\hat{Y}_t^{o^{(+)}}$ are the output scores for the positive samples (sales or bids) and $\hat{Y}_t^{o^{(-)}}$ are the output scores for the negative samples, $\mathcal{S}$ is the set of all sequences, and $|\mathcal{T}^o|$ is the length of the target sequence.

The final model loss is computed as a weighted sum of the sales and bids losses:

$$\mathcal{L} = \alpha \mathcal{L}_{Sales} + (1 - \alpha) \mathcal{L}_{Bids} \tag{15}$$

Training Protocol. Following the CARCA [7] and SASRec [4] models training protocol, we define a fixed sequence length L in which we select the input sequence as the most recent L items for each user, the sequence length can be obtained by truncation or padding in some cases. The target positive items sequence has the same sequence length L and is formed once using the shifted sequence of the sales items $[v_{|S_t^u|-L+1}, \ldots, v_{|S_t^u|}]$ and once using the most recent L bidding items to have this multi-task learning paradigm between the sales and the bids and positive target items. On the other hand, the negative sequence is formed as random unseen items of sequence length L, thus the number of negative samples N_{train} is L in this case (Fig. 2).

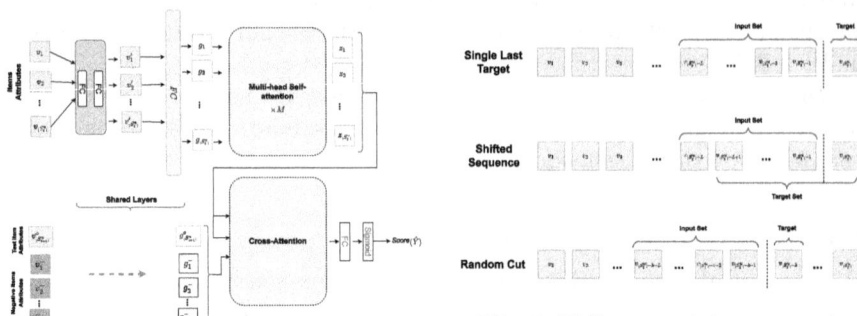

Fig. 2. Illustration of ASRM++ model

Fig. 3. Different training protocols

5 Enhanced ASRM for Unique Item Recommendation (ASRM++)

5.1 Input Encoding

To form the item latent representation, we first embed item attributes in the input sequence using two fully connected layers and GeLU activation to obtain the initial embeddings as:

$$v_j^{'} = GeLU(v_j W + b)W^{'} + b^{'} \qquad (16)$$

where $W \in \mathbb{R}^{A \times d^{'}}, W^{'} \in \mathbb{R}^{d^{'} \times d}$ are the weight matrices $b \in \mathbb{R}^{d^{'}}, b^{'} \in \mathbb{R}^{d}$ are the bias vectors and d is the items embedding dimension.

Then, feed it to another two fully connected layers for a deeper representation:

$$g_j = v_j^{'} W_{v^{'}} + b_{v^{'}} \qquad (17)$$

where $W_{v^{'}} \in \mathbb{R}^{d \times d}$ is the weight matrix, d is the layer embedding dimension, and $b_{v^{'}}$ is the bias term. For simplicity, we use the **same dimension** d for all embedding layers.

Multi-head Self-attention. Similar to the ASRM model a multi-head self-attention is applied across the latent embeddings of all items. Let $G^u := (g_1, \ldots, g_{|S^u|}) \in (\mathbb{R}^d)^{|S^u|}$ be the encoded sequence. In the following, we interpret this sequence as a matrix $G^u \in \mathbb{R}^{|S^u| \times d}$. A normalization layer is applied on G^u before it is fed into the multi-head self-attention as follows:

$$G^{u^{'}} = Normalize(G^u) \qquad (18)$$

We utilize multi-head self-attention to apply attention across all items in the sequence. This allows the model to capture dependencies between different items in the sequence, resulting in a latent representation for each item.:

$$C^u = \text{SA}(G^{u'}) = \text{concat}_{col} \left(\text{Att}(G^{u'} \mathbf{W}_h^Q, G^{u'} \mathbf{W}_h^K, G^{u'} \mathbf{W}_h^V) \right)_{h=1:H} \mathbf{W}^P \quad (19)$$

where $\mathbf{W}_h^Q, \mathbf{W}_h^K, \mathbf{W}_h^V \in \mathbb{R}^{d \times \frac{d}{H}}, \mathbf{W}^P \in \mathbb{R}^{d \times d}$ represent the linear projection matrices of the head at index h, and H is the number of heads. Here, $C^u \in \mathbb{R}^{|S^u| \times d}$ represents the column-wise concatenation of the attention heads.

Then additive residual is applied between C^u and Q to obtain the output $C^{u'}$:

$$C^{u'} = C^u + G^u \quad (20)$$

Lastly, we have the row-wise feed-forward layers to obtain the component's output representations $Z^u \in \mathbb{R}^{|S^u| \times d}$ as follows. For all $i \in \{1, \ldots, |S^u|\}$ we have:

$$\begin{aligned} Z_i^u &= \text{FFN}(C^{u'}{}_i) \\ &= GeLU(C^{u'}{}_i W^Z + b^Z) W^{Z'} + b^{Z'} \end{aligned} \quad (21)$$

where $W^Z, W^{Z'} \in \mathbb{R}^{d \times d}$ are the weight matrices of the two feed-forward layers, while b^Z and $b^{Z'} \in \mathbb{R}^d$ are their bias row-vectors. **GeLU** is the activation function applied after the first layer.

5.2 Next Item Prediction with ASRM++

Given Z^u, and the latent embedding G^o of the target item attribute vector. We predict the likelihood via cross-attention.

Cross Attention. Simply here the item scoring is calculated similarly to the original ASRM model, where we apply cross attention between the input sequence and target items. Finally, the output layer is a fully connected layer of output 1 followed by a *Sigmoid* function to limit the output scores between $[0, 1]$, as in Eq. 12. However, in this case the scores are of size $(N_{train} + 1)$ as we have one positive item and N_{train} negative items, which is explained in detail in the next section.

5.3 ASRM++ Model Optimization

Unlike the original ASRM, we removed the multi-task learning part that was previously employed. As it is shown in later sections, we show that employing the different training protocol was more effective in learning the model and outperformed the added benefit cause by using the bids information. Thus in this enhanced version we eliminated that part. The binary cross-entropy objective can be defined as follows:

$$\mathcal{L} = - \sum_{T^o \in \mathcal{S}} [log(\hat{Y}^{o(+)}) + \sum_{t=0}^{N_{train}} (log(1 - \hat{Y}_t^{o(-)}))] \quad (22)$$

where $\hat{Y}^{o(+)}$ are the output scores for the positive sale sample and $\hat{Y}_t^{o(-)}$ are the output scores for the negative samples N_{train} in our case we set N_{train} to 100. $\mathcal{S}$ is the set of all sequences.

Enhanced Training Protocol. There exist multiple ways to conduct training protocols in recommendation systems. Specifically, the original ASRM followed a shifted sequence training protocol (as shown in Fig. 3). In this approach, during training the training sequence $[v_{|S_t^u|-L}, \ldots, v_{|S_t^u|-1}]$ is shifted to form the target sequence $[v_{|S_t^u|-L+1}, \ldots, v_{|S_t^u|}]$. This technique has also been implemented in previous works [4,13], with the main difference being that the ASRM model uses cross-attention and does not enforce a causality constraint during both the training and inference phases, allowing bidirectionality in both cases. Despite not leveraging autoregressive tasks due to leakage, the ASRM training protocol has significantly outperformed the training protocol that uses only the last item in the sequence as the target, as well as the case where causality is enforced during the training phase. A newly introduced training protocol, as proposed by [10], addresses the discrepancies between training and inference by using only the final item of a randomly cut sequence as the target. We chose this approach to further increase the variety of target items that appear during training, which has shown to be particularly advantageous for long interaction sequences in the VWFS dataset.

Hard Negative Training Sampling. To ensure a realistic assessment of model performance at deployment, during evaluation we would sample 2,000 negative samples that occurred close in time to the test item. This approach mirrors the scenario in auction datasets with unique items, where only unsold items still available for bidding are considered for recommendation during deployment. The original ASRM, however, employed a standard random negative sampling protocol during training, which led to a mismatch between the training and evaluation phases. To address this, one of the key improvements introduced was to apply the same time-aware hard negative sampling protocol during training to align it with the test phase. Specifically, during the training phase the negative items are being chosen to be the ones sold within the same month as the target item.

6 Deployment Infrastructure

To deploy the ASRM model in production, we utilized the AWS step functions to build our training and inference pipelines. Those pipelines are called every weekend to train and deploy a new model using the recent sales and bids data. We also cache the recommendation scores for all expected dealers-vehicle pairs for faster retrieval during the following weekdays.

6.1 Online Training Pipeline

In the training pipeline shown in Fig. 4, we first retrieve the latest sales, bids, and dealer data from AWS-Athena. Afterward, we feed this data to a SageMaker pre-processing job that filters and converts the vehicle raw features, sales, and bids data to interaction tuples, and numerical features. Once the data is pre-processed we spawn a SageMaker training job that trains the model on the pre-processed data using the best-found hyperparameters at that time and it saves the model artifact in AWS S3. Once the model is trained we initiate the inference step function which pre-computes and caches the recommendation scores for all expected dealer-vehicle pairs of the upcoming week. It is worth noting that we employ multiple intermediary validation steps in our training pipeline that check the correctness of the generated preprocessed data, whether the model performance is above a predefined accuracy threshold, and whether the inference job finished successfully or not.

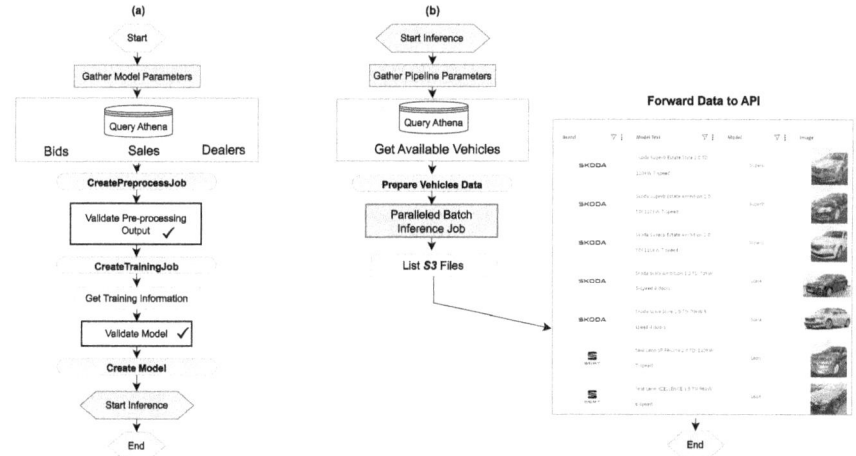

Fig. 4. AWS Training (a) and Inference Pipeline (b)

6.2 Online Inference Pipeline

In our setup, the vehicles that we expect to show on our website are known at least one month beforehand. This allows our inference pipeline shown in Fig. 4 to retrieve, preprocess, and utilize the AWS SageMaker batch inference to pre-compute all the possible dealer-vehicle pairs that can exist in the next upcoming week. These scores are stored as a per-dealer binary file on S3 that contains vehicle scores. This file is then retrieved by our API gateway once it receives a recommendation request from the frontend for a specific dealer.

Table 1. Model performance and comparison against baselines on VWFS dataset. Where ASRM is the deployed model which we later illustrate A/B test results, and ASRM ++ is the improved version of the model. The best results are reported in red and the second best in blue.

Method	Components			HR@10	NDCG@10
	Multi-task	Random-cut	Cross-Att.		
MultiRec [8]	✓	✗	✗	$0.1329 \pm {\scriptstyle 2.3e-3}$	$0.0917 \pm {\scriptstyle 4e-4}$
SASRec [4]	✗	✗	✗	$0.1556 \pm {\scriptstyle 6e-4}$	$0.0740 \pm {\scriptstyle 3e-4}$
CARCA [7]	✗	✗	✓	$0.1808 \pm {\scriptstyle 7e-4}$	$0.0966 \pm {\scriptstyle 1.1e-3}$
ProxyRCA [10]	✗	✓	✓	$0.2135 \pm {\scriptstyle 9.2e-3}$	$0.1168 \pm {\scriptstyle 2.8e-3}$
ASRM (deployed)	✓	✗	✓	$0.2027 \pm {\scriptstyle 3.4e-3}$	$0.1052 \pm {\scriptstyle 5e-4}$
ASRM++ (ours)	✓	✓	✓	$0.2321 \pm {\scriptstyle 3.6e-3}$	$0.1289 \pm {\scriptstyle 6e-4}$
Improv.(%)				8.71%	10.36%

HR@25	NDCG@25	HR@50	NDCG@50
$0.2153 \pm {\scriptstyle 2.7e-3}$	$0.0917 \pm {\scriptstyle 8e-4}$	$0.2941 \pm {\scriptstyle 4.3e-3}$	$0.1068 \pm {\scriptstyle 1.4e-3}$
$0.2751 \pm {\scriptstyle 1.5e-3}$	$0.1031 \pm {\scriptstyle 4e-4}$	$0.3750 \pm {\scriptstyle 1.3e-3}$	$0.1223 \pm {\scriptstyle 1e-4}$
$0.2892 \pm {\scriptstyle 3.4e-3}$	$0.1229 \pm {\scriptstyle 4e-4}$	$0.3742 \pm {\scriptstyle 6.2e-3}$	$0.1393 \pm {\scriptstyle 3e-4}$
$0.3396 \pm {\scriptstyle 8e-4}$	$0.1475 \pm {\scriptstyle 6e-4}$	$0.4477 \pm {\scriptstyle 2.9e-3}$	$0.1683 \pm {\scriptstyle 1e-3}$
$0.3185 \pm {\scriptstyle 3.9e-3}$	$0.1332 \pm {\scriptstyle 6e-4}$	$0.4221 \pm {\scriptstyle 1.3e-2}$	$0.1532 \pm {\scriptstyle 2.4e-3}$
$0.3581 \pm {\scriptstyle 3e-3}$	$0.1595 \pm {\scriptstyle 1.4e-3}$	$0.4605 \pm {\scriptstyle 1.1e-3}$	$0.1792 \pm {\scriptstyle 1e-3}$
5.45%	8.14%	2.86%	6.48%

7 Experiments

7.1 Experimental Settings

Dataset. The dataset captures a B2B setting where vehicles are sold to dealers. Collected between January 1, 2016, and December 31, 2023, it includes data from 5,916 users/dealers and records 1,224,364 interactions, each corresponding to a unique vehicle. Each vehicle is described by 109 distinct features, including model, brand, color, and gear type. Additionally, the dataset includes 11,573,971 bid interactions, which provide supplementary information for each user. It is essential to note that all user/dealer data is anonymized, with confidentiality ensured in compliance with GDPR requirements.

Implementation Details. The ASRM and ASRM++ models were optimized using binary cross-entropy loss through AdamW, and with the weight decay tuned between the range of 0.0 and 1.0. The learning rate was tuned within the range of 1e-6 and 0.1, dropout rate between 0.0 and 0.5 and the random cut probability between 0.0 and 1.0. The number of heads was searched among the set of {2, 4, 8}, hidden dimension {64, 128, 256} and the batch size was kept at 128. The tuning job was performed with the AWS SageMaker Hyperparameter-

Tuner using Bayesian optimization. The implementation is publicly available in our code repository[1].

7.2 Evaluation Protocol

We use a leave-one-out mechanism, training and validating the model with the entire sequence except the last interaction, which is used for testing. We sample 2000 negative items N_{test} within the same month of the corresponding positive item date and assess model performance with Hit Ratio (HR@N) and Normalized Discounted Cumulative Gain (NDCG@N). Higher HR and NDCG values indicate better performance. We report the mean and standard deviation of results from three separate runs to ensure statistical robustness.

Baselines. We compare our proposed method against various attribute-aware sequential recommendation methods, that can rely only on items attributes and remove the items ids.

- **MultiRec** [8]: A multi-relational model built for unique item recommendation in auction systems, that can leverage items attributes and bids interactions.
- **SASRec** [4]: A model that applies multi-head self-attention to capture the sequential pattern in the users' history, then applies dot product for calculating the items scores. In this case we replace the items ids in the original model to be only items attributes to be applicable in unique item setting.
- **CARCA** [7]: A context-aware sequential recommendation approach employing cross-attention between user profiles and items for score prediction. For this experiment we removed the items ids part from the model.
- **ProxyRCA** [10]: A state-of-the-art attribute-aware model that introduced using proxy-based embedding to allow less frequent items to benefit from more-frequent ones. For this experiment we removed the items ids part from the model.

8 Offline Results

8.1 Model Performance Against Baselines

The experimental results in Table 1 demonstrate that the ASRM model, specifically designed for the unique item recommendation task, surpasses the original CARCA [7], as well as SASRec [4] and MultiRec [8]. Furthermore, the results indicate that the improved model ASRM++ achieves state-of-the-art performance, outperforming the second-best model ProxyRCA [10] by up to 10%, and significantly improves upon the currently deployed ASRM model by more than 20%. This shows the effectiveness of the applied methods in the ASRM model within auction systems, as well as the substantial performance gains achieved by ASRM++ following the applied enhancements.

[1] https://github.com/sonngocl22/ASRM-improved/.

Table 2. The table illustrates the effect of different model components

Model	HR@10	NDCG@10	Model	HR@10	NDCG@10
w/o Random cut	0.1581	0.0854	ASRM w/ bids	**0.2027**	**0.1052**
w/o Round type	0.1995	0.1096	ASRM w/o bids	0.1750	0.0916
w/o Hard sampling	0.2194	0.1206	ASRM++ w/ bids	0.2172	0.1206
ASRM++	**0.2321**	**0.1289**	ASRM++ w/o Bids	**0.2321**	**0.1289**

8.2 Ablation Studies

Effect of Negative Sampling (Having Negative Items in the Same Month). The first ablation experiment was to test the effect of hard negative sampling during training. This approach involves using negative items from the same month as the target item during the training phase, which better aligns with the real workings of the auction bidding system. As demonstrated in Table 2, there is a notable performance improvement of approximately 7%, with HR@10 increasing from 0.2194 to 0.2321 when hard sampling is incorporated into the implementation.

Effect of Different Training Protocols (Random Cut Training Protocol). This study aims to examine the impact of the random cut training protocol. When the random cut method is removed, in this case it means only a single target item—the last item in the sequence is considered during training. As shown in Table 2, this has a substantial effect on the performance of the model, changing the HR@10 from 0.2321 to 0.1581.

A useful comparison is shown in the main results in Table 1, highlighting a key difference between ASRM and ASRM++. Specifically, ASRM adopts the training protocol used in SASRec [4] and CARCA [7], which sets the target sequence as a shifted sequence of the input sequence, while ASRM++ adopts the random-cut protocol. Results indicate that by sampling multiple cuts throughout the entire user sequence, the model learns more effectively than when trained solely on the most recent items.

Effects of Adding Sales Round Type. As previously mentioned, the auction system consists of two different sales round types: the fixed-price round and the bidding round. Although this distinction was known, the deployed version of ASRM did not utilize this information during training. By incorporating the sales round type as a feature both during training and evaluation phases, we were expecting a performance boost. The results of the ablation study, shown in Table 2, confirm that by including the round type information into the model we can significantly increase the model performance. It is important to note that the sales round type will be known during deployment, aligning with whether the user is in a fixed-price or bidding round.

Effect of Adding Bids as Auxiliary Behavior on the Target Side. In our approach, we included bids in the target set during training, allowing them to serve as potential targets for users. As shown in Table 2, for the ASRM model this strategy increased the HR@10 from 0.195 to 0.205, reflecting a 5% improvement and demonstrating the effectiveness of this multi-task learning approach in leveraging auxiliary information. However, for the case of ASRM++ including the bids as targets hurt the performance. This could be due to the fact that the inclusion of random cut in ASRM++ helped expose the model to a broader coverage of unique items, compensating for the effects of using bids as targets in the original ASRM.

Impact of Random Cut Frequency on Performance. The experimental results and ablation study clearly demonstrate the significant impact of the random cut training protocol. This effect is attributed to the broader coverage of the unique items in the input sequences and target items. However, because some users have very long interaction histories and only recent interactions have a strong impact on the final prediction, the frequency of using uniformly randomly chosen items as training targets may affect the final outcomes. To examine this hypothesis, we conducted experiments across varying probabilities that a sequence is cut during training. The results, shown in Fig. 5, confirm our hypothesis, with overall performance steadily increasing and peaking at a cut probability of 0.8, while cutting sequences 100% of the time led to a slight decrease in the performance. Further experiments with different sequence lengths and the optimal random cut probability revealed that, given adequate item coverage, sequence length has a minimal effect on model performance.

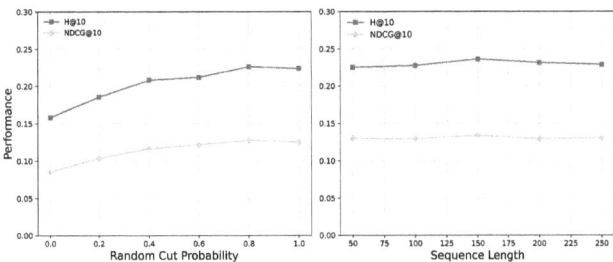

Fig. 5. Performance evaluation across different random cut probabilities and sequence lengths

9 Online A/B Test Results

We evaluated our ASRM model using an online ab test that ran between 26.6.2023 and 17.10.2023. We employed our recommendation model as a new

Table 3. AB Test statistics

KPI	Mean			Median			P-Value
	Group B	Group A	improv.	Group B	Group A	improv.	
CTR	**0.7780**	0.7600	2.36%	**0.7500**	0.7450	0.67%	0.6560
CTR on top 25 vehicles	**0.0960**	0.0688	39.53%	**0.0320**	0.0240	33.33%	**0.0007**
Bid-TR	**0.0079**	0.0063	25.39%	0.0	0.0	-	0.1629
Bid-TR on top 25 vehicles	**0.0046**	0.0007	557%	0.0	0.0	-	0.3580
Buy-TR	**0.0005**	0.0003	66.67%	0.0	0.0	-	0.9890
Buy-TR on top 25 vehicles	**4.071e-6**	3.162e-6	28.75%	0.0	0.0	-	0.8229
Adjusted Bid-Buy actions							
Bid-TR on top 25 vehicles	**0.0159**	0.0098	62.24%	0.0	0.0	-	**0.0352**
Buy-TR on top 25 vehicles	**0.0005**	0.0001	400%	0.0	0.0	-	**0.0195**

option for sorting the main vehicles list on our website stock list page and we compared that behavior against the default behavior of sorting by date. We split the dealers into two groups randomly and tracked the sample mismatch ratio during the test. We tracked multiple KPIs such as clicks, bids, and buy-through rates. Although dealers can directly bid or buy a vehicle from the main list without clicking on the vehicle record to view its detailed information, this is usually rare and dealers prefer to buy or bid on the vehicle after they open its details page. To measure the bid and buy-through rates in such scenarios we included adjusted bid and buy metrics that also track actions on the vehicles pages and link them to their corresponding main list view. Additionally, we measured the differences between the two groups and the statistical significances were computed using Mann-Whitney-U-Tests as most metrics had non-normal distributions. Results in Table 3, show that in general, the treatment group B's KPIs have higher metric values but the effect is statistically significant if we focus on actions on the top 25 records of the main list.

References

1. Guo, H., Tang, R., Ye, Y., Li, Z., He, X.: Deepfm: a factorization-machine based neural network for CTR prediction. arXiv preprint arXiv:1703.04247 (2017)
2. Hidasi, B.: Session-based recommendations with recurrent neural networks. arXiv preprint arXiv:1511.06939 (2015)
3. Jannach, D., Ludewig, M.: When recurrent neural networks meet the neighborhood for session-based recommendation. In: Proceedings of the Eleventh ACM Conference on Recommender Systems, pp. 306–310 (2017)
4. Kang, W.C., McAuley, J.: Self-attentive sequential recommendation. In: 2018 IEEE International Conference on Data Mining (ICDM), pp. 197–206. IEEE (2018)
5. Li, J., Wang, Y., McAuley, J.: Time interval aware self-attention for sequential recommendation. In: Proceedings of the 13th International Conference on Web Search and Data Mining, pp. 322–330 (2020)

6. Liu, C., Li, X., Cai, G., Dong, Z., Zhu, H., Shang, L.: Noninvasive self-attention for side information fusion in sequential recommendation. In: Proceedings of the AAAI Conference on Artificial Intelligence, vol. 35, pp. 4249–4256 (2021)
7. Rashed, A., Elsayed, S., Schmidt-Thieme, L.: Context and attribute-aware sequential recommendation via cross-attention. In: Proceedings of the 16th ACM Conference on Recommender Systems, pp. 71–80 (2022)
8. Rashed, A., Jawed, S., Schmidt-Thieme, L., Hintsches, A.: Multirec: a multi-relational approach for unique item recommendation in auction systems. In: Fourteenth ACM Conference on Recommender Systems, pp. 230–239 (2020)
9. Rendle, S.: Factorization machines. In: 2010 IEEE International Conference on Data Mining, pp. 995–1000. IEEE (2010)
10. Seol, J., Gang, M., Lee, S.G., Park, J.: Proxy-based item representation for attribute and context-aware recommendation. In: Proceedings of the 17th ACM International Conference on Web Search and Data Mining, pp. 616–625 (2024)
11. Sun, F., et al.: Bert4rec: sequential recommendation with bidirectional encoder representations from transformer. In: Proceedings of the 28th ACM International Conference on Information and Knowledge Management, pp. 1441–1450 (2019)
12. Tang, J., Wang, K.: Personalized top-n sequential recommendation via convolutional sequence embedding. In: Proceedings of the Eleventh ACM International Conference on Web Search and Data Mining, pp. 565–573 (2018)
13. Wu, L., Li, S., Hsieh, C.J., Sharpnack, J.: SSE-PT: sequential recommendation via personalized transformer. In: Fourteenth ACM Conference on Recommender Systems, pp. 328–337 (2020)

Attribute and Context-Aware Multi-Behavior Model for Unique-Item Recommendation

Shereen Elsayed[1]([✉]), Ngoc Son Le[1], Ahmed Rashed[2], and Lars Schmidt-Thieme[1]

[1] Information Systems and Machine Learning Lab (ISMLL) and VWFS Data Analytics Research Center (VWFS DARC), University of Hildesheim, Hildesheim, Germany
{elsayed,sle,schmidt-thieme}@ismll.uni-hildesheim.de
[2] Volkswagen Financial Services AG, Braunschweig, Germany
{ahmed.galal.ahmed.rashed}@vwfs.com

Abstract. In the context of sequential recommendation, incorporating auxiliary information has consistently shown improvements in several scenarios. Some models focus on integrating item and user features, other approaches include context information. A notable area of growth is the multi-behavior recommendation, which considers the different user's behaviors to indicate their preferences. Current methods rely on graph-based models while other sequential multi-behavior models use transformers. However, none of these models take items or user features into consideration which causes a limited understanding of user preferences through different actions and item characteristics. In this paper, we propose an **A**ttribute and **C**ontext-aware **M**ulti-**B**ehavior model (**ACMB**) for unique item recommendation. This not only accounts for users' varying behaviors but also integrates the relevant attributes of items to enhance the understanding of user preferences. ACMB encodes the items with the respective attributes then it applies a hierarchical attention over the different behaviors separately, followed by attention across the entire input sequence to generate a comprehensive deep sequence representation. Extensive experiments on real-world Volkswagen Financial Services (VWFS) dataset demonstrate the significance of our proposed model over the current state-of-the-art attribute-aware sequential recommendation methods.

1 Introduction

In Volkswagen Financial Services (VWFS) Business-to-Bussiness (B2B) settings, vehicles are sold to dealers through auctions. Auction systems possess unique characteristics as items are sold in a fixed-price round followed by several bidding rounds. These items are considered unique because each can be sold only once within the auction system. This scenario can be framed as a sequential recommendation problem. However, it presents a significant challenge that items (vehicles) are not identified by fixed IDs but rather by their attributes (features). This makes the problem highly relevant to attribute-aware sequential models.

Modern platforms increasingly leverage not only transactional data but also auxiliary information to capture user preferences, enabling the creation of more accurate recommendation systems. These systems, often referred to as multi-relational or multi-behavior recommendation models, integrate additional behavioral data to improve performance. For instance, in retail platforms, incorporating behaviors such as "add to cart" or "clicks" enhances model accuracy. Similarly, auction systems provide rich auxiliary information beyond sales data, such as bid histories and user click interactions. Incorporating these additional behaviors is crucial for accurately capturing user preferences in such complex environments. However, existing state-of-the-art multi-behavior recommendation methods [2,21,22] rely heavily on fixed item IDs, which makes them unsuitable for unique item recommendation scenarios like auction systems. Addressing this limitation requires adapting models to work effectively in attribute-based settings without relying on item IDs.

To address these challenges, we propose an attribute- and context-aware multi-behavior framework for unique item recommendation. Unlike earlier approaches to multi-behavior recommendation [7,19], which depend on item IDs for item representation, our method eliminates this dependency. Instead, it leverages rich item attributes to construct item representations. Additionally, our framework integrates interaction context, such as time and user behavior type to provide a comprehensive understanding of user preferences. This combination enables our model to effectively tackle the challenges posed by unique item recommendation in auction systems. Our contributions can be summarized as follows:

- We propose the first attribute- and context-aware multi-behavior model, which employs hierarchical attention to capture comprehensive behavioral representations.
- We introduce a novel approach that leverages item attributes and auxiliary behaviors to effectively learn user preferences in auction systems.
- Extensive experiments on a VWFS real-world dataset demonstrate that our proposed model, ACMB, significantly outperforms state-of-the-art attribute-aware sequential recommendation models.

2 Related Work

In our work, we focus mainly on the three branches of research, consisting of attribute and context-aware recommendation, sequential recommendation, and multi-behavior recommendation.

Attribute and Context-Aware Models is a substantial sector in recommendation systems that seek to improve the quality of recommendations by leveraging both item features and contextual information, moving beyond mere item IDs. Early approaches utilizing contextual features are the factorization machine-based methods such as FM [13]. Later the neural factorization machine (NFM) utilized deep neural networks for learning non-linear feature interactions [5]. Furthermore, DeepFM [4] is a popular context-aware method that combines the FM and DNNs for extracting latent representations. More recent approaches benefit from incorporating the time-aspect, which allows learning the sequential pattern in the data along with the contextual features. More recent state-of-the-art attribute and context-aware sequential methods is CARCA model [11], which includes contextual information and item attributes. The sequence of profile items and the target items passes through a cross-attention mechanism to get the final items' scores. Additionally, ProxyRCA [14] further improves upon CARCA, by improving the items encoding method.

Sequential Recommendation is a prevalent task in recommender systems that utilizes the historical interactions of each user to predict the next item the user will most likely interact with. GRU4Rec [6] is one of the early approaches that utilize RNNs for mining the sequential behavior in a session-based recommendation scenario. Another sequential model is Caser [16], which applies convolutional filters on the time and item embeddings to capture the latent sequential behavior of users. Additionally, more recent approaches started to employ transformer architectures such as the SASRec [8] model, which feeds the item embedding sequence into a multi-head self-attention block to capture the sequential correlation between historical items. Another method that improves upon SASRec is BERT4Rec [15], which uses a Bi-directional self-attention mechanism to better model the sequential behaviors. Other recent approaches tried to extend the SASRec model are SSE-PT [23], TiSASRec [10] and S^3Rec [17].

With the current massive data sources available for recommender systems, recent models started not only to employ the user-item primary interaction relation such as purchases but also to use other available click data. Employing auxiliary information has different namings in the existing prior work: relation-aware recommender systems, multi-relation recommendation, and multi-behavior recommendation.

Many recent **multi-behavior recommendation** approaches rely on convolutional graph networks by treating the different behaviors as a global heterogeneous graph, such as the MB-GCN [7] and MB-GMN [20] models. Additionally, other methods tried to employ transformer encoders in their architecture for better representation learning. One such example is the memory-augmented transformer networks (MATN) [18], which uses a transformer encoder followed by a cross-behavior aggregation layer to model the different behaviors. Moreover, KHGT [19] is a graph transformer method that captures user-item interaction characteristics; also, a graph attention layer is employed to understand the item-item relation further. State-of-the-art advancements include MBHT [21], which utilizes low-rank self-attention coupled with a hyper-graph neural architecture to model long- and short-term dependencies. MB-STR [22] introduces a multi-behavior sequential transformer layer to simultaneously learn sequential patterns across various historical behaviors. Furthermore, MBSRec [3] learns all behaviors via a multi-head self-attention block while maintaining the behavior contibution using weighted binary cross-entropy loss. A dditionally, HMAR [2] employs a hierarchical attention mechanism to capture dependencies within items of the same behavior and encode cross-behavior relationships in the input sequence.

Building on these advancements, we propose an attribute- and context-aware multi-behavioral sequential model that effectively leverages multi-behavior data in a sequential manner. Our model goes beyond traditional methods by integrating item attributes and contextual information, achieving superior performance in unique item recommendation scenarios.

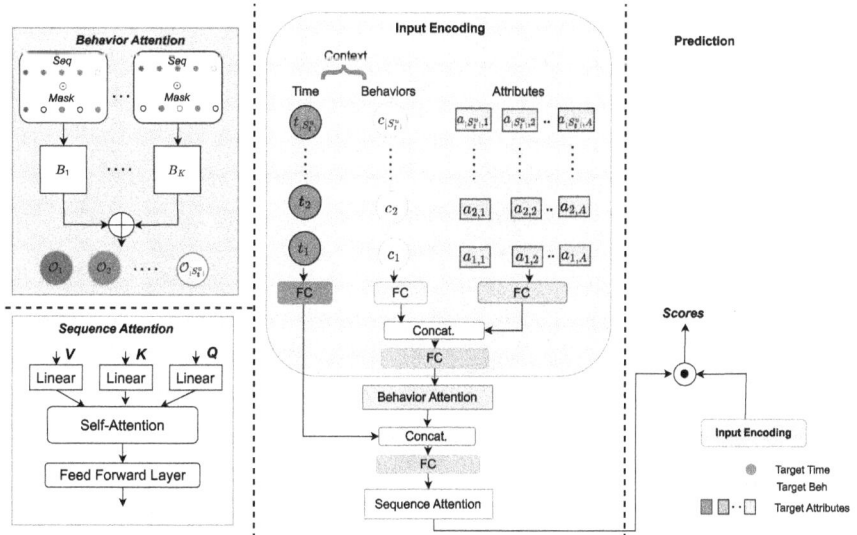

Fig. 1. Attribute and Context-aware Model Architecture

3 Methodology

In this section, we elaborate on the model components, describe the training protocol, model optimization, and provide implementation details.

3.1 Problem Formulation

In the context of unique item sequential recommendation, consider a set of items $\mathcal{I} = 1, \ldots, I$ and a set of users $\mathcal{U} = 1, \ldots, U$. For each user $u \in \mathcal{U}$, there exists a chronologically ordered sequence of item interactions, denoted as $S^u = v_1^u, \ldots, v_{|S^u|}^u$. Each item v is characterized by a set of attributes $\mathcal{A} = 1, \ldots, A$.

Users may engage in up to K distinct behaviors, with each interaction in the sequence corresponding to a specific behavior type. For example, in auction systems, behaviors might include buying, bidding and navigate/click. Each interaction in the sequence is also associated with contextual information, such as the interaction time, denoted as $t_1^u, \ldots, t_{|S^u|}^u$, and the behavior type, represented as $c_1^u, \ldots, c_{|S^u|}^u$.

The primary objective is to predict the next item a user is likely to interact with, focusing specifically on the main behavior. In this case, the buy/sale behavior is considered is the target behavior. Other behaviors act as auxiliary signals to provide a richer representation of user activity over time, enabling more accurate modeling of user preferences.

3.2 Attribute and Context-Aware Multi-Behavior Recommendation (ACMB)

Inspired by the multi-behavior recommendation model HMAR [2], we adapt a hierarchical attention mechanism to effectively model diverse user behaviors. Figure 1 illustrates the architecture of the proposed model, which comprises three main components: input encoding, hierarchical masked attention, and prediction for calculating item scores.

Input Encoding. In auction systems, items are unique since each is sold only once, making it impractical for the model to rely on item IDs. Instead, each item is represented by its attributes. The input, therefore, consists of two key components; item attributes and interaction context (time and behavior). To derive the latent representation of an item, we first process its attributes vector v_j. The attributes vector of each item in the input sequence are passed through a fully connected layer to generate embeddings as:

$$v'_j = v_j W_v + b_v \qquad (1)$$

where $W_v \in \mathbb{R}^{|\mathcal{A}| \times d}$ is the weight matrix, $|\mathcal{A}|$ is the number of items attributes, and d is the items embedding dimension and b_v is the bias term.

A fully connected layer is used for encoding the one-hot vector representing the interaction behavior as follows:

$$c'_j = c_j W_{beh} + b_{beh} \qquad (2)$$

where $W_{beh} \in \mathbb{R}^{K \times d_{beh}}$ is the weight matrix, K is the number of behaviors, d_{beh} is the embedding dimension and b_{beh} is the bias term.

Next, items attributes embedding and behavior embeddings are concatenated to form a combined representation q_j. This combined representation is then passed through another fully connected layer to capture a deeper encoding:

$$q_j = \text{concat}_{col}\left(v'_j, c'_j\right), \qquad g_j = q_j W_q + b_q \qquad (3)$$

where $W_q \in \mathbb{R}^{(d+d_{beh}) \times d}$ is the weight matrix, d is the layer embedding dimension, and b_q is the bias term. For simplicity, we use the **same dimension** d for all embedding layers.

Attention Within Behavior. Recent approaches often employ graph-based models to capture multi-behavior information. However, this can come at the cost of losing the sequential patterns inherent in the input data. To preserve the chronological order of items while generating latent representations, we draw inspiration from the model proposed in [2] and employ a hierarchical attention mechanism on the input sequence.

The first attention block is designed to encode items associated with a specific behavior. To achieve this, we construct a mask M_b^u from the sequence of items, filtering out items not corresponding to the aimed behavior b. The item sequence embedding $G^u := [g_1, g_2, ..., g_{|S_t^u|}]$ is then multiplied element-wise with the behavior-specific mask $M_b^u := [m_1^b, m_2^b, ..., m_{|S_t^u|}^b]$ as shown in Fig. 1.

Ideally, the model employs one behavior encoder block per behavior, resulting in K blocks where K is the number of behaviors. However, when the input sequence includes a large number of behaviors, creating attention blocks for each behavior can lead to excessive memory and computational overhead. To address this, we combine relevant behaviors and process them together through shared behavior attention blocks. The buy-related behaviors are processed through a dedicated attention block, while bid-related behaviors are handled separately in another attention block. Finally, a distinct attention block is assigned to click-related behaviors, ensuring each behavior type is effectively modeled.

Once the input sequence is masked based on behavior type, the masked latent embeddings are passed through a fully connected layer to produce $E_b^u := \{e_1^b, \ldots, e_{|S_t^u|}^b\}$, computed as follows:

$$e_j^b = \left(g_j \odot m_j^b\right) W_e + b_e, \quad W_e \in \mathbb{R}^{d \times d}, \quad b_e \in \mathbb{R}^d \tag{4}$$

Here, $\odot$ denotes element-wise multiplication, W_e is the weight matrix, and b_e is the bias term.

The output embeddings E_b^u, are then fed into a multi-head self-attention block. This block consists of a multi-head attention mechanism followed by a feedforward layer, enabling the sequential encoding of items with the same behavior. The hierarchical attention mechanism ensures that behavior-specific patterns are captured effectively while maintaining the temporal structure of the input sequence.

$$X_b^u = \text{SA}(E_b^u) = \text{concat}_{col}\left(\text{Att}(E_b^u \mathbf{W}_h^{Q^b}, E_b^u \mathbf{W}_h^{K^b}, E_b^u \mathbf{W}_h^{V^b})\right)_{h=1:H} \tag{5}$$

where $\mathbf{W}_h^{Q^b}, \mathbf{W}_h^{K^b}, \mathbf{W}_h^{V^b} \in \mathbb{R}^{d \times \frac{d}{H}}$ represent the linear projection matrices of the head at index h, and H is the number of heads. X_b^u represents the column-wise concatenation of the attention heads.

Finally, we have the point-wise feed-forward layers to obtain the component's final output representations $F_b^u \in \mathbb{R}^{|S_t^u| \times d}$ as follows:

$$F_b^u = FFN(X_b^u) = \text{concat}_{row}\left(ReLU(X_{b,j}^u \mathbf{W}^{(1)^b} + b^{(1)^b})\mathbf{W}^{(2)^b} + b^{(2)^b}\right)_{j=1:|S_t^u|} \tag{6}$$

where $\mathbf{W}^{(1)^b}$, $\mathbf{W}^{(2)^b} \in \mathbb{R}^{d \times d}$ are the weight matrices of the two feed-forward layers, and $b^{(1)^b}, b^{(2)^b} \in \mathbb{R}^d$ are their bias vectors. The initial embedding sequence is added via a ReZero [1] residual connection to the behavior encoder output to obtain as:

$$L_b^u = F_b^u + \gamma \left(G^u \odot M_b^u \right) \tag{7}$$

where γ is a learnable weight initialized with zero to adjust the contribution of $(G^u * M_b^u)$. The output is multiplied by the behavior mask again to mask the positions of the other behaviors as follows:

$$O_b^u = L_b^u \odot M_b^u \tag{8}$$

We combine the output sequences of each behavior $O_b^u := [o_1^b, o_2^b, ..., o_{|S_t^u|}^b]$ by summing them element-wise to generate the first stage multi-behavioral latent sequence embeddings $\mathcal{O}^u$ as follows:

$$\mathcal{O}^u = \sum_{b=0}^{N_{Blocks}} O_b^u \tag{9}$$

where N_{Blocks} is the number of behavior specific attention blocks, O_b^u is the output of the corresponding block.

As previously mentioned, the contextual component of the data consists of two elements: interaction behavior and interaction time. Before applying the behavior-specific attention block, we incorporate the behavior type due to its importance in distinguishing between different behaviors at this stage. To model relationships across the entire sequence and capture interactions between various behaviors, we include time information to indicate the sequential order and provide additional contextual details. Specifically, we extract multiple time-related features from the date, including **year, month, day, week of the year, and day of the year**. These extracted features enrich the sequence representation by providing temporal context.

The time features are encoded using a fully connected layer, producing embeddings that are concatenated with the output of the behavior-specific attention layer. This combined representation is then processed through another fully connected layer, as defined below:

$$t'_j = t_j W_t + b_t \tag{10}$$

$$r_j = LeakyReLu \left(\text{concat}_{col} \left(O_j, t'_j \right) W_r + b_r \right) \tag{11}$$

where $W_t \in \mathbb{R}^{T \times d_t}$ is the weight matrix, T is the number of time extracted details, d_t is the embedding dimension and b_t is the bias term. $W_r \in \mathbb{R}^{(d+d_t) \times d}$ is the weight matrix, d is the layer embedding dimension, and b_r is the bias term. For consistency, we use the same embedding dimension d across all layers. Once the combined representation is obtained, it is passed through the second part of the hierarchical attention mechanism, which models the relationships across different behaviors in the sequence.

Attention Across Behaviors. Once the sequence comprising all behaviors is constructed, denoted as $\mathcal{R}^u$, the sequence encoder applies attention mechanisms across all items in the sequence. This approach allows the model to capture both intra- and inter-behavioral dependencies, producing a multi-behavior latent representation for each item. The self-attention mechanism is defined as follows:

$$J^u = \text{SA}(\mathcal{R}^u) = \text{concat}_{col}\left(\text{Att}(\mathcal{R}^u\mathbf{W}_h^Q, \mathcal{R}^u\mathbf{W}_h^K, \mathcal{R}^u\mathbf{W}_h^V)\right)_{h=1:H} \quad (12)$$

where $\mathbf{W}_h^Q, \mathbf{W}_h^K, \mathbf{W}_h^V \in \mathbb{R}^{d \times \frac{d}{H}}$ represent the linear projection matrices of the head at index h, and H is the number of heads. A^u represents the column-wise concatenation of the attention heads. Additionally, for the model stability, we add a residual connection between sequence attention output J^u and sequence items G^u:

$$J^{u'} = J^u + G^u \quad (13)$$

Finally, we have the point-wise feed-forward layers to obtain the component's output representations $Z^u \in \mathbb{R}^{|S_t^u| \times d}$ as follows:

$$Z^u = \text{FFN}(J^{u'}) = \text{concat}_{row}\left(\text{ReLU}(J^{u'}\mathbf{W}^{(1)^Z} + b^{(1)^Z})\mathbf{W}^{(2)^Z} + b^{(2)^Z}\right)_{j=1:|S_t^u|} \quad (14)$$

where $\mathbf{W}^{(1)^Z}, \mathbf{W}^{(2)^Z} \in \mathbb{R}^{d \times d}$ are the weight matrices of the two feed-forward layers, and $b^{(1)^Z}, b^{(2)^Z} \in \mathbb{R}^d$ are their bias vectors.

3.3 Model Prediction and Training Protocol

For item ranking, we calculate the final score by taking the dot product of the last item embedding $z_{|S_t^u|}$ from the sequence encoder and the target item embedding $q^o_{|S_{t+1}^u|}$ as follows:

$$\hat{Y}_{t+1} = \sigma(z_{|S_t^u|} \cdot q^o_{|S_{t+1}^u|}) \quad (15)$$

where σ is a sigmoid function.

In multi-behavior datasets, interactions have varying importance for next-item recommendation. To handle this, we introduce weighting factors α_b in the loss function, one for each behavior. The number and values of α_b may differ based on the dataset's behavior count and their importance. Thus, our weighted binary cross-entropy objective for multi-behavior recommendation is as follows:

$$\mathcal{L}_{rank} = -\sum_{S^u \in \mathcal{S}} \sum_{t=0}^{|S^u|} [\alpha_b log(\hat{Y}_t^{O^{(+)}}) + (log(1 - \hat{Y}_t^{O^{(-)}}))] \quad (16)$$

where $\hat{Y}_t^{O^{(+)}}$ are the output scores for the positive samples and $\hat{Y}_t^{O^{(-)}}$ are the output scores for the negative samples, $\mathcal{S}$ is the set of all sequences, α_b indicate the behaviors weights.

Model Training. Following the training protocols established by the SASRec [8] and CARCA [11] models, we define a fixed sequence length L for the input sequence. The input sequence is randomly selected [14] from the user's entire item sequence $|S_t^u|$. Depending on the length of the user's sequence, truncation or padding is applied to ensure the sequence length matches L. The target positive item sequence is constructed with the same fixed length L by shifting the input sequence by one position. In contrast, the negative item sequence is generated by randomly sampling L unseen items from the dataset.

3.4 Implementation Details

To deploy the training pipeline, we utilize the AWS Step Functions service for seamless automation. The data on sales, dealers, and auxiliary behaviors is pulled directly from AWS Athena for pre-processing, after which structured interaction tuples and numerical features are formed. Afterwards, the training job is deployed using the previously determined best hyperparameters and the model is then saved on AWS S3. To ensure reliability, we include multiple validation checks at each step of the pipeline. Figure 2 provides an overview of the entire training pipeline.

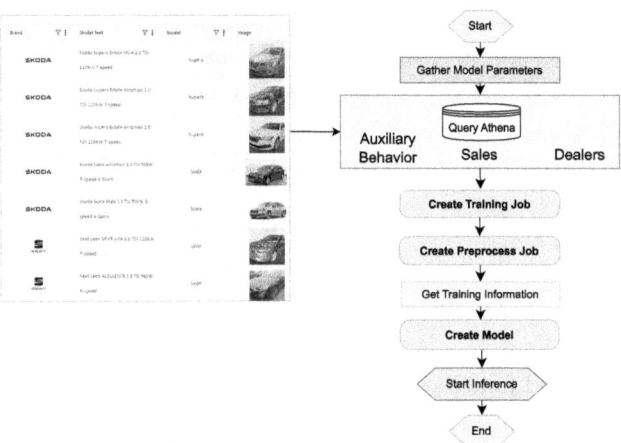

Fig. 2. Model Training Pipeline

Our proposed model is scheduled for deployment in the near future, leveraging AWS SageMaker to precompute all dealer-vehicle scores, which will be stored in Amazon S3 on a weekly basis. When a recommendation request is initiated from the front end for a specific dealer, the API gateway will facilitate the retrieval of the corresponding precomputed scores. Additionally, we intend to conduct a comparative performance analysis between the newly developed ACMB model and the currently deployed CARCA-based model using A/B testing methodologies. Key performance indicators (KPIs) such as buy-through rate, bid-through rate, and click-through rate will be systematically monitored and evaluated to assess the efficacy of the models.

4 Experiments

In this section, we present the offline evaluation results of our model, including ablation studies to assess the effectiveness of our approach and the importance of individual model components. This analysis aims to address the following research questions:

- RQ1: How does the ACMB model perform compared to attribute-aware sequential recommendation models?
- RQ2: How do auxiliary behaviors impact the model's performance?
- RQ3: How does each model component contribute to overall performance?
- RQ4: How do hyper-parameters influence the model performance?

4.1 Experimental Settings

Dataset. The dataset represents a B2B setting where vehicles are sold to dealers. Collected between January 1, 2016, and December 31, 2023, it includes data from 5,916 users (dealers) and documents 1,224,364 sales interactions, each corresponding to a unique vehicle. Each vehicle is characterized by 109 distinct features, such as model, brand, color, and gear type.

In addition to sales data, the dataset contains 4,949,049 bid interactions, which serve as supplementary information for each user. As shown in Table 1, the dataset also includes front-end interaction data collected between December 31 2022 and December 31, 2023 that captures various behaviors within the framework. These behaviors include sale-dialog, which represents a dialog displayed before a sale is finalized, similar to the bid-dialog for bidding interactions. The certificate behavior indicates that the user accessed detailed vehicle information. Furthermore, bookmark behavior, denotes vehicles were saved by users for future reference. Finally, navigate behavior, refers to click interactions on specific vehicles.

All user and dealer data has been anonymized, ensuring confidentiality and compliance with GDPR regulations.

4.2 Evaluation Protocol

We employ a leave-one-out evaluation strategy, where the model is trained and validated using the full interaction sequence, except for the final interaction, which is reserved for testing. To assess performance, we sample 2,000 negative items (N_{toot}) from the same month as the corresponding positive item. Model effectiveness is measured using Hit Ratio (HR@N) and Normalized Discounted Cumulative Gain (NDCG@N), with higher values indicating superior performance. To ensure statistical robustness, we report the mean and standard deviation from three independent runs.

Table 1. Dataset statistics

Behavior	Interactions	date
Sale	1,224,362	01.01.2016–31.12.2023
Bid	4,949,049	
Sale Dialog	171,612	31.12.2022–31.12.2023
Bid Dialog	523,191	
Certificate	1,213,960	
Bookmark	450,186	
Navigate	4,662,995	
$\sum$ Sum	**13,195,355**	-

Table 2. Model performance and comparison against baselines on VWFS dataset. The best results are reported in bold and the second best in underlined.

Method	Model type		HR@10	NDCG@10
	Multi-behavior	Sequential		
MultiRec [12]	✓	✗	$0.1329 \pm _{2.3e-3}$	$0.0917 \pm _{4e-4}$
SASRec [8]	✗	✓	$0.1556 \pm _{6e-4}$	$0.0740 \pm _{3e-4}$
CARCA [11]	✗	✓	$0.1808 \pm _{7e-4}$	$0.0966 \pm _{1.1e-3}$
ProxyRCA [14]	✗	✓	$\underline{0.2135 \pm _{9.2e-3}}$	$\underline{0.1168 \pm _{2.8e-3}}$
ACMB (ours)	✓	✓	$\mathbf{0.3304 \pm _{1.5e-3}}$	$\mathbf{0.1918 \pm _{3e-4}}$
Improv.(%)			54.75%	64.21%
HR@25	NDCG@25		HR@50	NDCG@50
$0.2153 \pm _{2.7e-3}$	$0.0917 \pm _{8e-4}$		$0.2941 \pm _{4.3e-3}$	$0.1068 \pm _{1.4e-3}$
$0.2751 \pm _{1.5e-3}$	$0.1031 \pm _{4e-4}$		$0.3750 \pm _{1.3e-3}$	$0.1223 \pm _{1e-4}$
$0.2892 \pm _{3.4e-3}$	$0.1229 \pm _{4e-4}$		$0.3742 \pm _{6.2e-3}$	$0.1393 \pm _{3e-4}$
$\underline{0.3396 \pm _{8e-4}}$	$\underline{0.1475 \pm _{6e-4}}$		$\underline{0.4477 \pm _{2.9e-3}}$	$\underline{0.1683 \pm _{1e-3}}$
$\mathbf{0.4742 \pm _{5.7e-3}}$	$\mathbf{0.2268 \pm _{1.1e-3}}$		$\mathbf{0.5857 \pm _{3.3e-3}}$	$\mathbf{0.2483 \pm _{9e-4}}$
39.63%	53.76%		30.82%	47.53%

Baselines. We evaluate our proposed method against several attribute-aware sequential recommendation models that rely solely on item attributes, without utilizing item IDs.

- **MultiRec [12]**: A multi-relational model designed specifically for unique item recommendation in auction systems. It leverages item attributes and bid interactions to enhance recommendation accuracy.
- **SASRec [8]**: A self-attention-based model that captures sequential patterns in user interactions. In our setting, we modify the original model by replacing item IDs with item attributes to adapt it for unique item recommendations.
- **CARCA [11]**: A context-aware sequential recommendation model that employs cross-attention between user profiles and item representations for

score prediction. For this experiment, we remove item IDs from the model to make it applicable to unique item settings.
- **ProxyRCA** [14]: A state-of-the-art attribute-aware model that introduces proxy-based embeddings, enabling less frequent items to benefit from representations of more frequently occurring ones. In our setup, we exclude item IDs to align with the unique item recommendation scenario.

4.3 Results

Model Performance Against Baselines. The unique-item recommendation task is fundamentally challenging, with limited prior research addressing this problem. One notable work is MultiRec [12], a multi-task model that leverages both sales and bid interactions. However, as shown in Table 2, our proposed ACMB model significantly outperforms MultiRec by not only utilizing sales and bid data but also incorporating auxiliary user behaviors through an efficient hierarchical attention mechanism.

Additionally, we compare our model to SASRec [8], a highly effective sequential recommendation model capable of integrating item attributes instead of item IDs. While SASRec focuses solely on the primary behavior, our ACMB model outperforms SASRec, highlighting the importance of incorporating multi-behavioral information to enhance user preference learning.

Furthermore, we evaluate our model against state-of-the-art attribute-aware sequential models, including CARCA [11] and ProxyRCA [14]. While these models effectively leverage item attributes, they lack the ability to incorporate auxiliary behaviors. As demonstrated by our results, ACMB achieves an HR@10 of 0.3304, significantly outperforming CARCA (0.180) and ProxyRCA (0.213). This clearly illustrates the effectiveness and superiority of our proposed model in addressing the attribute- and context-aware multi-behavior recommendation problem.

The Effect of Auxiliary Behaviors on the Model Performance. Auxiliary behaviors provide valuable insights into user preferences; however, their contribution to model performance varies. As shown in Table 3, certain behaviors, such as sale dialog and bid dialog, have a negligible impact, with their effects falling within the standard deviation of the model's results. In contrast, behaviors like bidding and navigation play a more significant role in enhancing performance. This is further supported by their frequency, as bids and navigation interactions are the most dominant behaviors, making them crucial for capturing user intent and improving preference learning.

The Effect of Model Components on the Model Performance. Table 4 highlights the importance of including time information in the input sequence. When time information is excluded, the performance drops to 0.3167, underscoring the critical role of temporal data in capturing interaction patterns. Additionally, the model employs attention blocks to capture dependencies between items

Table 3. Auxiliary behaviors effect on the model performance

Model	HR@10
ACMB w/o Bids	0.3103
ACMB w/o Sale Dialog	0.3273
ACMB w/o Bid Dialog	0.3292
ACMB w/o Certificate	0.3231
ACMB w/o Bookmark	0.3167
ACMB w/o Navigate	0.3127
ACMB w/ Only Sale&Bid	0.2794
ACMB w/ Only Sale	0.2480
ACMB	**0.3304**

within the same behavior. Removing these attention blocks leads to a noticeable decline in performance, with the metric decreasing from 0.3304 to 0.3213. This demonstrates the importance of modeling intra-behavior dependencies for optimal performance.

Finally, we examine the effect of incorporating one-hot encoding of the behavior type as contextual information (BehCxt). While the impact of this component is less pronounced compared to factors like time, it still results in a relative performance drop of 1.8%. This indicates that while behavior type encoding contributes to the model's performance, its influence is relatively minor compared to other components.

Table 4. Model components effect on the model performance

Model	HR@10
ACMB w/o Time	0.3167
ACMB w/o BehCxt	0.3243
ACMB w/o BehAtt	0.3213
ACMB	**0.3304**

The Influence of Hyper-Parameters on the Model Performance. Model hyperparameters play a critical role in determining the performance of a machine learning model. In this work, we investigate the sensitivity of the model to two key hyperparameters: sequence length and embedding size. As illustrated in Fig. 3, the sequence length significantly impacts model performance, especially when including several behaviors. Increasing the sequence length allows the model to capture more historical information from the user's behavior, leading to improved performance. However, this comes at a cost: longer sequences increase the computational complexity and resource requirements of the model. On the other hand, the embedding size is another crucial hyperparameter, as shown in Fig. 4. In our dataset, each vehicle is represented by 109 distinct features. A larger embedding size enables the model to better encode these features, enhancing its ability to capture complex patterns. In our experiments, an embedding size of 650 yielded the best results. However, reducing the embedding size to 600 only slightly decreased performance, with the metric dropping from 0.3337 to 0.3275. This suggests that the model is relatively robust to moderate changes in embedding size, allowing for some flexibility in tuning this parameter to balance performance and computational efficiency.

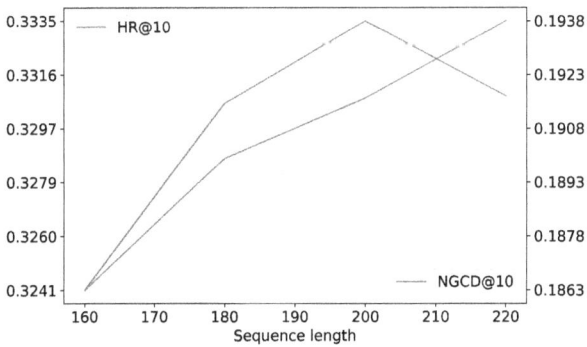

Fig. 3. Effect of sequence length on the HR@10 and NDCG@10

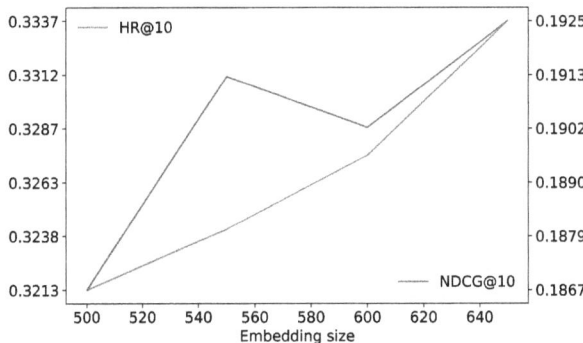

Fig. 4. Effect of embedding size on the HR@10 and NDCG@10

5 Hyperparameters Settings

Our experiments were conducted on an AWS EC2 P3.8xlarge instance equipped with an NVIDIA Tesla V100 GPU, an Intel Xeon E5 CPU, and 244 GB of RAM.

We implemented the models using TensorFlow[1]. For hyperparameter optimization, we leveraged AWS Bayesian optimization across the following ranges: latent embedding size [50–700], learning rate [0.000005–0.000025], maximum sequence length [50–250], number of attention heads [1–3], number of blocks [1–3], and dropout rate [0.2–0.6]. The best performance was achieved with a batch size of 128, two attention blocks, and one attention head. The optimal embedding dimension was 667, with a learning rate of 0.0000146, dropout rate of 0.11, and a maximum sequence length of 194. We trained the model for 3,400 epochs. Additionally, we performed a grid search to tune the α_b parameter for different behaviors within the range [0,1]. The optimal values were: 0.8 for sale/buy behavior, 0.5 for sale dialog, 0.2 for bid and bid dialog, and 0.1 for certificate, bookmark, and navigate behaviors. Finally, we used the Adam optimizer [9] for model optimization.

6 Conclusion

In this work, we proposed an attribute- and context-aware multi-behavior (ACMB) recommendation model designed specifically for unique item recommendation in auction systems. Unlike traditional approaches that rely on item IDs, our model leverages item attributes for representation learning. The ACMB model employs a hierarchical attention mechanism, first capturing dependencies among items within the same behavior group, followed by cross-behavior attention to model sequential patterns and auxiliary user behaviors. This approach enhances user preference learning by incorporating richer behavioral context. Experiments on the real-world VWFS dataset demonstrate the superiority of our model compared to state-of-the-art attribute-aware sequential recommendation methods.

References

1. Bachlechner, T., Majumder, B.P., Mao, H., Cottrell, G., McAuley, J.: Rezero is all you need: fast convergence at large depth. In: Uncertainty in Artificial Intelligence, pp. 1352–1361. PMLR (2021)
2. Elsayed, S., Rashed, A., Schmidt-Thieme, L.: Hmar: hierarchical masked attention for multi-behaviour recommendation. In: Pacific-Asia Conference on Knowledge Discovery and Data Mining, pp. 131–143 (2024)
3. Elsayed, S., Rashed, A., Schmidt-Thieme, L.: Multi-behavioral sequential recommendation. In: Proceedings of the 18th ACM Conference on Recommender Systems, pp. 902–906 (2024)
4. Guo, H., Tang, R., Ye, Y., Li, Z., He, X.: Deepfm: a factorization-machine based neural network for CTR prediction. arXiv preprint arXiv:1703.04247 (2017)
5. He, X., Chua, T.S.: Neural factorization machines for sparse predictive analytics. In: Proceedings of the 40th International ACM SIGIR Conference on Research and Development in Information Retrieval, pp. 355–364 (2017)

---

[1] https://www.tensorflow.org.

6. Jannach, D., Ludewig, M.: When recurrent neural networks meet the neighborhood for session-based recommendation. In: Proceedings of the Eleventh ACM Conference On Recommender Systems, pp. 306–310 (2017)
7. Jin, B., Gao, C., He, X., Jin, D., Li, Y.: Multi-behavior recommendation with graph convolutional networks. In: Proceedings of the 43rd International ACM SIGIR Conference on Research and Development in Information Retrieval, pp. 659–668 (2020)
8. Kang, W.C., McAuley, J.: Self-attentive sequential recommendation. In: 2018 IEEE International Conference on Data Mining (ICDM), pp. 197–206. IEEE (2018)
9. Kingma, D.P., Ba, J.: Adam: a method for stochastic optimization. arXiv preprint arXiv:1412.6980 (2014)
10. Li, J., Wang, Y., McAuley, J.: Time interval aware self-attention for sequential recommendation. In: Proceedings of the 13th International Conference on Web Search and Data Mining, pp. 322–330 (2020)
11. Rashed, A., Elsayed, S., Schmidt-Thieme, L.: Context and attribute-aware sequential recommendation via cross-attention. In: Proceedings of the 16th ACM Conference on Recommender Systems, pp. 71–80 (2022)
12. Rashed, A., Jawed, S., Schmidt-Thieme, L., Hintsches, A.: Multirec: A multi-relational approach for unique item recommendation in auction systems. In: Fourteenth ACM Conference on Recommender Systems, pp. 230–239 (2020)
13. Rendle, S.: Factorization machines. In: 2010 IEEE International Conference on Data Mining, pp. 995–1000. IEEE (2010)
14. Seol, J., Gang, M., Lee, S.G., Park, J.: Proxy-based item representation for attribute and context-aware recommendation. In: Proceedings of the 17th ACM International Conference on Web Search and Data Mining, pp. 616–625 (2024)
15. Sun, F., et al.: Bert4rec: sequential recommendation with bidirectional encoder representations from transformer. In: Proceedings of the 28th ACM International Conference on Information and Knowledge Management, pp. 1441–1450 (2019)
16. Tang, J., Wang, K.: Personalized top-n sequential recommendation via convolutional sequence embedding. In: Proceedings of the Eleventh ACM International Conference on Web Search and Data Mining, pp. 565–573 (2018)
17. Wu, L., Li, S., Hsieh, C.J., Sharpnack, J.: SSE-PT: sequential recommendation via personalized transformer. In: Fourteenth ACM Conference on Recommender Systems, pp. 328–337 (2020)
18. Xia, L., Huang, C., Xu, Y., Dai, P., Zhang, B., Bo, L.: Multiplex behavioral relation learning for recommendation via memory augmented transformer network. In: Proceedings of the 43rd International ACM SIGIR Conference on Research and Development in Information Retrieval, pp. 2397–2406 (2020)
19. Xia, L., et al.: Knowledge-enhanced hierarchical graph transformer network for multi-behavior recommendation. In: Proceedings of the AAAI Conference on Artificial Intelligence, vol. 35, pp. 4486–4493 (2021)
20. Xia, L., Xu, Y., Huang, C., Dai, P., Bo, L.: Graph meta network for multi-behavior recommendation. In: Proceedings of the 44th International ACM SIGIR Conference on Research and Development in Information Retrieval, pp. 757–766 (2021)
21. Yang, Y., Huang, C., Xia, L., Liang, Y., Yu, Y., Li, C.: Multi-behavior hypergraph-enhanced transformer for sequential recommendation. In: Proceedings of the 28th ACM SIGKDD Conference on Knowledge Discovery and Data Mining, pp. 2263–2274 (2022)

22. Yuan, E., Guo, W., He, Z., Guo, H., Liu, C., Tang, R.: Multi-behavior sequential transformer recommender. In: Proceedings of the 45th International ACM SIGIR Conference on Research and Development in Information Retrieval, pp. 1642–1652 (2022)
23. Zhou, K., et al.: S3-rec: self-supervised learning for sequential recommendation with mutual information maximization. In: Proceedings of the 29th ACM International Conference on Information & Knowledge Management, pp. 1893–1902 (2020)

On the Performance of LLMs for Real Estate Appraisal

Margot Geerts[1(✉)], Manon Reusens[1], Bart Baesens[1,3], Seppe vanden Broucke[1,2], and Jochen De Weerdt[1]

[1] LIRIS, KU Leuven, Leuven, Belgium
margot.geerts@kuleuven.be
[2] Department of Business Informatics and Operations Management, Ghent University, Ghent, Belgium
[3] Department of Decision Analytics and Risk, University of Southampton, Southampton, UK

Abstract. The real estate market is vital to global economies but suffers from significant information asymmetry. This study examines how Large Language Models (LLMs) can democratize access to real estate insights by generating competitive and interpretable house price estimates through optimized In-Context Learning (ICL) strategies. We systematically evaluate leading LLMs on diverse international housing datasets, comparing zero-shot, few-shot, market report-enhanced, and hybrid pro-mpting techniques. Our results show that LLMs effectively leverage hedonic variables, such as property size and amenities, to produce meaningful estimates. While traditional machine learning models remain strong for pure predictive accuracy, LLMs offer a more accessible, interactive and interpretable alternative. Although self-explanations require cautious interpretation, we find that LLMs explain their predictions in agreement with state-of-the-art models, confirming their trustworthiness. Carefully selected in-context examples based on feature similarity and geographic proximity, significantly enhance LLM performance, yet LLMs struggle with overconfidence in price intervals and limited spatial reasoning. We offer practical guidance for structured prediction tasks through prompt optimization. Our findings highlight LLMs' potential to improve transparency in real estate appraisal and provide actionable insights for stakeholders.

Keywords: Large Language Models · Real Estate Appraisal · In-Context Learning

1 Introduction

Global real estate, valued at $379.7 trillion in 2022, represents the world's largest wealth store, with residential properties constituting the majority[1]. The real

---

[1] https://www.savills.com/impacts/market-trends/the-total-value-of-global-real-estate-property-remains-the-worlds-biggest-store-of-wealth.html.

Supplementary Information The online version contains supplementary material available at https://doi.org/10.1007/978-3-032-06118-8_12.

estate market plays a crucial role in economies worldwide, impacting homeowners, investors, and governments. Accurate price estimations are vital for all stakeholders, from home buyers facing affordability challenges in Europe[2] and the U.S.[3] to China's slowing market[4]. Access to reliable price data helps ensure informed decision-making and supports a stable and sustainable market across regions. Nevertheless, real estate valuation remains opaque and unevenly accessible, contributing to information asymmetry between buyers and sellers [16]. Sellers inherently have superior knowledge of the local market and the property's condition as opposed to buyers. While potential buyers can call upon a real estate broker or other experts, this asymmetry is difficult to eliminate. Some argue that a data-driven house price prediction approach can help real estate stakeholders, including buyers, by informing their decisions [1, 18]. However, this approach requires advanced Machine Learning (ML) expertise, extensive manual data processing and access to a substantial dataset, which may not be readily available to the average home buyer. Large Language Models (LLMs) present a promising solution to address this information asymmetry [34]. Trained on vast and diverse datasets encompassing a significant portion of Internet knowledge [5], these models have the potential to uncover meaningful insights and patterns, including those relevant to real estate [9]. Recently, LLMs have been proven to excel in structured prediction tasks with In-Context Learning (ICL), enabling them to approximate regression problems without explicit training [32]. This makes them a promising tool for ad hoc house price prediction, reducing the barriers to data-driven real estate insights. By leveraging their extensive training, LLMs could bridge knowledge gaps, offering nuanced perspectives and data-driven guidance in this complex domain. This marks a key step towards democratizing access to real estate appraisal insights and enhancing transparency for a diverse range of stakeholders. Reducing information asymmetry improves price accuracy, benefiting both buyers, who avoid overpaying, and sellers, who experience faster sales due to improved liquidity and as such receiving fair market value [16]. Additionally, investors, financial institutions, and policymakers can make more informed decisions, leading to improved investment strategies, risk assessments, and more effective tax and policy frameworks.

In this paper, we assess LLMs' potential for improving accessibility to real estate appraisal, or valuation, by answering four Research Questions (RQs):

RQ1 How effectively can prompt engineering techniques optimize LLM performance for house price prediction and what is the most effective prompt?

RQ2 Can LLMs generate sufficiently accurate house price estimates to serve as viable alternatives to traditional ML models?

RQ3 How reliably do LLMs estimate price intervals for real estate appraisal, and how does this compare to traditional ML approaches?

---

[2] https://ec.europa.eu/eurostat/web/interactive-publications/housing-2023.
[3] https://www.forbes.com/advisor/mortgages/real-estate/housing-market-predictions/predictions/.
[4] https://www.imf.org/en/News/Articles/2024/02/02/cf-chinas-real-estate-sector-managing-the-medium-term-slowdown.

RQ4 What features do LLMs prioritize in their house price prediction processes, and how do these align with traditional valuation methodologies?

To address these questions, we investigate different prompting approaches with ICL and evaluate a wide range of pre-trained LLMs on various housing datasets worldwide. In the context of the house price prediction task, we scrutinize the capabilities of LLMs in three dimensions: the accuracy of price predictions, the delineation of price intervals, and their explanatory capacity. Our contributions can be summarized as follows:

1. We demonstrate that optimizing prompt design significantly improves LLM performance in house price prediction. Carefully selecting in-context examples based on feature similarity and geographic proximity enhances accuracy and adaptability across different housing markets.
2. We show that LLMs can generate sufficiently accurate house price estimates, approaching the performance of traditional ML models. While they do not surpass ML models in predictive accuracy, their accessibility, interpretability, and flexibility make them valuable for real estate stakeholders.
3. We identify overconfidence in price intervals as a key limitation of LLM-based valuation. LLMs consistently underestimate price uncertainty, producing narrower prediction ranges that fail to capture real market values.
4. We find that LLMs prioritize hedonic property features effectively but struggle with spatial and temporal reasoning. Despite leveraging variables like property size and amenities, they undervalue the role of location and time.
5. We help reduce information asymmetry in the real estate market by providing concrete guidelines for harnessing LLMs to support informed decision-making among buyers, sellers, financial institutions and policymakers.

2 Related Work

House price prediction is typically framed as a supervised learning problem involving tabular data. Automated Valuation Models (AVMs) are trained on datasets $D = \{(X_i, y_i)\}_{i=1}^{n}$ where $X_i \in \mathbb{R}^m$ are the m-dimensional features of property i, and $y_i \in \mathbb{R}$ is its price. The objective is to minimize prediction error $L(\hat{y}, y)$, using loss functions like mean squared error (MSE). Features are broadly categorized into hedonic attributes, i.e. structural attributes (e.g., size, number of rooms), and locational factors (e.g., coordinates, proximity to amenities). Recent research has shifted from hedonic regression models [2] to modern ML and deep learning approaches [7,17,18], with increasing focus on interpretability, including Shapley values [29] and uncertainty quantification techniques such as conformal prediction for prediction intervals [1,12].

LLMs for data science have revolutionized predictive modeling with unstructured textual data. In house price prediction, Natural Language Processing (NLP) extracts insights from property descriptions, market reports, and reviews, converting them into structured features [30,40]. Building on recent advancements in NLP, pre-trained LLMs are increasingly used in data science applications with tabular data [35], such as geospatial interpolation [24], Point of Interest recommendation [6], and time series analysis [14]. Despite their growing adoption, research on LLMs for real estate appraisal remains limited, with a recent study focusing only on rental price prediction [3]. Our work addresses this gap by examining more robust prompting strategies, evaluating diverse datasets, and integrating interpretability, thereby offering new insights into real estate appraisal with LLMs.

In-Context Learning (ICL) is an inference-time technique where the model, without updating its parameters, generalizes from provided examples. Specifically, LLMs are provided with K examples as context and are then tasked with completing a new example by leveraging the patterns and information from the preceding ones [22]. [32] show how LLMs can perform regression tasks when provided in-context examples. LLMs' ability to handle tabular data is demonstrated through frameworks like TabLLM for data-efficient classification [11], while the Meta-ICL framework further enhances ICL efficiency [4].

3 Methodology

3.1 Large Language Models for House Price Prediction

To effectively prompt LLMs with tabular housing data, we follow the guidelines set by [11] for manual data serialization in zero- and few-shot learning settings. Our goal is not to replace traditional ML models but to evaluate LLMs' capabilities in estimating house prices and identify the optimal prompt.

Figure 1 illustrates the prompting strategy used in the experiments. To determine the optimal prompt for house price prediction, we evaluate twelve different strategies combining various building blocks. Specifically, we incorporate market reports and in-context examples on top of the zero-shot baseline containing the task definition and property description. Our prompting optimization strategy uses ICL to enforce two pillars that are relevant in real estate: regional real estate market dynamics, which are often accounted for in AVMs by explicitly modeling temporal effects [17], and comparable property valuation examples [18], essentially delineating housing submarkets [2]. The market reports provide context on regional house price indices from the preceding month or quarter. The labeled examples from the training data are selected based on either haversine distance (geographic proximity) or cosine distance (similar hedonic features) and limited to three or ten examples. Finally, we test a combination of ten examples evenly split between geographic and hedonic neighbors. This combination of geographic and characteristic-based similarity has been shown to be effective in hedonic price modeling in prior work [27]. Based on these results, we extend the interaction with the LLM by maintaining the conversation history. Using the best-ranked prompt configuration across datasets and LLMs, the LLM generates a price interval with a 90% target coverage. While methods like conformal

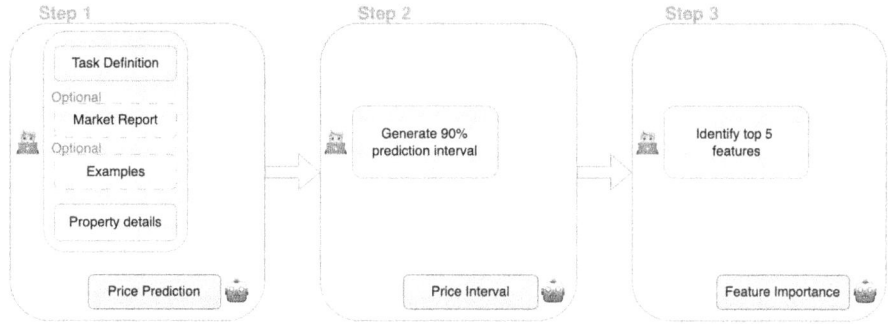

Fig. 1. Overview of the LLM prompting methodology for house price prediction. Step 1: The model receives a structured prompt containing the task definition, an optional market report, optional ICL examples, and details of the target property-forming the basis for prompt optimization. It then predicts the property price. Step 2: The model generates a 90% prediction interval. Step 3: The model identifies the five most important features. This approach enables price estimation, uncertainty quantification, and interpretability in real estate appraisal.

prediction require access to the internal LLM structure, which is unavailable in standard API interactions, direct prompting aligns with how real estate practitioners would use LLMs. Finally, we assess explainability by asking the model to identify the top five features influencing its prediction. The full prompt template is shown in Appendix A.

Since LLMs struggle with raw geographic coordinates due to tokenization of prompts, we follow [24] in reverse geocoding the coordinates into full addresses using the Nomatim API[5] to OpenStreetMap[6], incorporating both representations into the prompt.

Given the importance of accessibility in this study, we include a range of the most recent pre-trained LLMs comprising both open-source and closed-source models of varying sizes and architectural design. In our experiments, we use Llama 3.2:3B [25], Llama 3.1:70B [5], and GPT-4o-mini [26]. These models were selected to balance scale (number of parameters), provider diversity, and accessibility constraints. All models were prompted with a seed of 0 and temperature of 0 to ensure reproducibility. All code and data used for the experiments is available via https://github.com/margotgeerts/LLM4RealEstate. More information on the checkpoints and computing environment used can be found in Appendix B.

3.2 ML Baselines

We consider two common house price prediction baselines: k Nearest Neighbor (kNN) regression and Gradient Boosted Trees (GBT). These baselines are cho-

---
[5] https://nominatim.org/.
[6] https://www.openstreetmap.org/.

sen based on their conceptual relevance to our LLM-approach and their strong empirical performance in real estate appraisal. First, kNN serves as a natural baseline because it predicts a property's price based on an interpolation of its nearest neighbors. This aligns well with our LLM prompting strategy, which provides the model with similar properties as context. Comparing LLMs to kNN allows us to determine whether LLMs can extract deeper insights beyond simple interpolation. To ensure a fair comparison, we match the LLM prompt settings with $k = \{3, 10\}$ neighbors, using haversine distance (geographic proximity), cosine distance (hedonic similarity), or a combination of both for ten examples. Second, we include GBTs—specifically LightGBM (LGBM) [15]—as they remain the state-of-the-art (SOTA) choice for structured tabular data and have consistently outperformed deep learning methods in house price prediction tasks [8]. Unlike kNN, LGBM learns complex, nonlinear relationships in data, allowing us to benchmark whether LLMs can approach fully optimized ML models that have access to structured training data. We use LGBM with default parameters to ensure a fair, out-of-the-box comparison that mirrors how practitioners might deploy an ML model without extensive hyperparameter tuning. Other ML methods, such as linear regression or support vector machines (SVMs), were excluded as they generally underperform compared to GBTs on tabular data. Similarly, deep learning models such as Graph Neural Networks, while promising, have not yet demonstrated consistent superiority over GBTs in house price prediction [8].

To compare prediction intervals between LLMs and LGBM, we use Conformal Prediction (CP). CP is a framework that provides valid prediction intervals without assuming any specific model, offering a distribution-free method for uncertainty quantification in ML tasks [33]. This approach works by using the observed data to "conform" the model's predictions, ensuring that the true value lies within the predicted interval with a specified confidence level. Since house prices exhibit temporal trends that violate the assumption of data exchangeability (i.e., the data distribution is not independent and identically distributed over time), we apply a CP procedure designed to handle such distribution shifts, known as EnbPI [37], via the MAPIE library [31]. Finally, we use the SHapley Additive exPlanations (SHAP) values [20] to compare the LLM and LGBM explanations. Considering that the LLMs are provided with both coordinates and address, we adjust for this by aggregating the SHAP values corresponding to the two coordinate features (X-Y). Subsequently, we rank all features based on the mean absolute SHAP value computed across the test instances.

3.3 Evaluation Metrics

To evaluate predictive performance, we report the Mean Absolute Percentage Error (MAPE), consistent with prior work [18], due to space limitations, and the standard deviation of the Percentage Error (PE) across test observations. Prediction intervals are assessed based on actual coverage (percentage of instances where the true price is within the predicted interval) and the Mean Prediction Interval Width (MPIW), which measures precision. Valid intervals should achieve coverage close to 90%, with narrower MPIWs indicating higher precision. Feature importance is compared by evaluating the top five features prioritized by LLMs and SHAP-based rankings from LGBM. With this comparison, we do not attempt to evaluate the ground truth correctness of these explanations. Our objective is to examine the degree of alignment between two distinct paradigms: LLMs and GBTs. Validating the intrinsic accuracy or faithfulness of the LLM explanations would require expert assessments or adversarial testing, which guide important directions for future work.

3.4 Datasets

To generalize LLM performance for real estate appraisal, we selected four real-world housing datasets located in various geographic areas. The datasets from King County, USA (from Kaggle[7]), Flanders, Belgium (proprietary), and Beijing, China (from Kaggle[8]) contain property transactions, while the dataset from Barcelona, Spain [28] contains property listings. Despite the subtle distinction between listings and transactions, we treat them similarly. A 60:20:20 train-validation-test split is used, and results are reported based on a random subset of 1000 test examples per dataset. Table 1 summarizes key statistics.

Table 1. Summary statistics of the housing datasets used for evaluation.

	King County	Flanders	Barcelona	Beijing
Train size	12914	174135	25714	117349
Validation size	4349	59188	12339	37045
Test size	3569	55125	23295	41301
No. variables	14	16	35	17
Min. price	$75 000	€34 280	€37 000	¥1 270 021
Max. price	$7 700 000	€970 512	€4 866 000	¥11 000 094
Min. date	2014-05-02	2015-01-04	2018-03-01	2015-01-01
Max. date	2015-05-27	2023-05-24	2018-12-01	2017-12-31

4 Results and Discussion

This section examines the effectiveness of large language models (LLMs) in house price prediction, focusing on both prompt optimization and comparisons with traditional ML approaches. First, we analyze the impact of different prompt engineering strategies on LLM performance, identifying the most effective techniques for improving prediction accuracy (**RQ1**). Next, we compare LLM-based predictions with traditional ML baselines, evaluating their absolute accuracy,

---

[7] https://www.kaggle.com/datasets/astronautelvis/kc-house-data.
[8] https://www.kaggle.com/datasets/ruiqurm/lianjia.

interval estimates, and feature prioritization (**RQ2–RQ4**). Finally, we synthesize these findings into practical guidelines, offering insights on when and how LLMs can be effectively deployed for real estate appraisal.

4.1 Optimizing LLMs with Prompt Engineering

Figure 2 summarizes the MAPE scores across all prompting strategies, models, and datasets. Generally, prompting strategies with more labeled examples lead to more accurate predictions, with ten mixed examples (`10 ex. mixed`) emerging as the best-performing strategy in most datasets and models. This suggests that combining geographically near and hedonic similar properties provides a balanced context that enhances LLM predictions. This approach aligns with prior work in hedonic price modeling, where integrating geographic and characteristic-based similarity has been shown to effectively capture local housing market dynamics [27]. Ten-shot prompting strategies consistently outperform three-shot prompts, independent of the selection method, indicating that LLMs benefit from comprehensive contextual information. Only for the Beijing dataset, the performance is sensitive to the specific method for example selection.

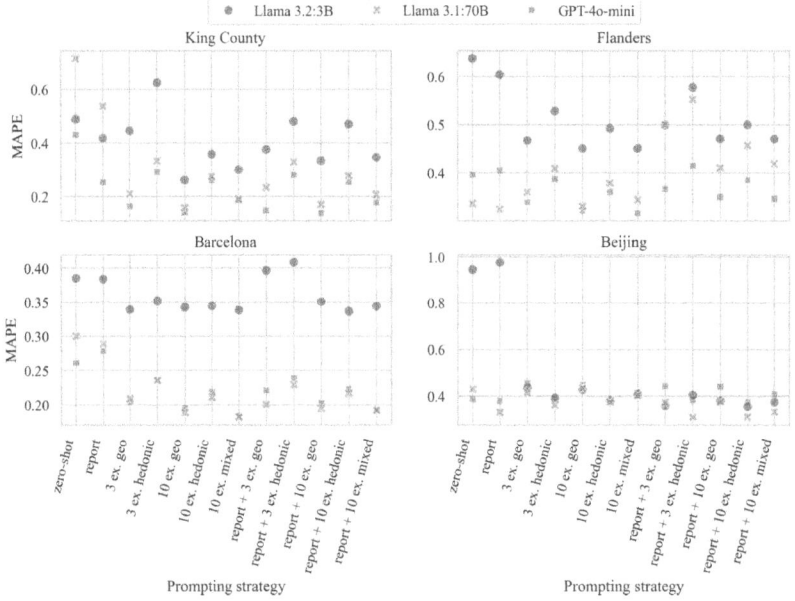

Fig. 2. Including 10 mixed examples (geographic and hedonic similarity) provides the best results overall and zero-shot prompting the worst. GPT-4o-mini generally outperforms the other models. This figure shows the results for the twelve different prompting strategies across all four datasets.

While 10 ex. mixed performs best on average, the optimal strategy can vary by dataset. King County benefits from combining market reports with ten geographic neighbors (report + 10 ex. geo), Flanders and Barcelona favor ten mixed examples (10 ex. mixed), and Beijing performs best with market reports and three hedonic examples (report + 3 ex. hedonic). While a mixed example selection approach generally ranks best, geographic neighbors provide typically more useful contextual information than hedonic examples. Again, the Beijing dataset deviates from this observation and ranks hedonic examples higher. In most regions, spatial correlations in house prices are prominent, while Beijing's market may be influenced by higher levels of heterogeneity leading to property characteristics being more important in combination with broader economic trends. Another reason could be that the spatial structure in Beijing's house prices may be more complex than geographic proximity.

While market reports consistently improve zero-shot prompting, they are rarely effective on their own. Notably, in Beijing, monthly, city-specific reports (≈ 501 characters in length) improve results across all prompting strategies, reinforcing the importance of market trends in this region and underscoring the value of fine temporal and spatial resolution. In the King County dataset, its US-wide, monthly market reports (≈ 987 characters), which include quarterly sub-regional breakdowns of market trends, also benefit price prediction in most cases. In contrast, Barcelona and Flanders see limited or no gains: for both regions, quarterly, country-level reports ($\approx 1\,817$ characters for Barcelona, $\approx 1\,566$ characters for Flanders) are available, with Flanders additionally comparing neighboring countries and Barcelona highlighting only regions with the largest changes. This pattern suggests that higher temporal granularity (monthly vs. quarterly), tighter geographic specificity (city vs. national), and even concise report length materially enhance an LLM's ability to incorporate dynamic market trends. Given that the King County and especially the Beijing dataset present significant temporal trends in house prices, these results show that market reports provide essential context for LLMs to capture temporal dynamics and thereby improve predictive performance.

Ranking the LLMs across datasets and prompting strategies reveals that GPT-4o-mini outperforms the other models, with Llama 3.1:70B as a close second. While GPT-4o-mini still achieves reasonable results with zero-shot prompts, Llama 3.2:3B consistently performs worst. This might be due to low-parameter models containing less world knowledge compared to high-parameter models, making them more dependent on prompts with richer context for accurate predictions. While larger models, Llama 3.1:70B and GPT-4o-mini, generally outperform smaller models, LLM performance also slightly varies across datasets. Llama 3.2:3B performs comparably to larger models on the Beijing dataset. This anomaly could be again due to the volatile market dynamics which makes all LLMs struggle equally. GPT-4o-mini performs best in King County and Flanders, whereas Llama 3.1:70B outperforms it in Barcelona and Beijing. This performance disparity could be attributed to GPT-4o-mini's stronger tailoring to the US and Western European contexts, where its training data and fine-tuning are more focused [10]. In contrast, Llama 3.1, designed for multilingual text generation, appears to perform better for non-English or geographically diverse contexts, making it more adept at handling the varied linguistic and cultural features found in regions such as Beijing and Barcelona [25]. Furthermore, GPT-4o-mini exhibits the least variability across prompting strategies, making it the most stable performer overall. While its advantage over Llama models is not always substantial, it consistently follows structured formatting, reducing output inconsistencies. Llama models, particularly Llama 3.2:3B, sometimes struggle to conform to the output format, which can contribute to higher prediction errors.

Despite some dataset-specific variations, `10 ex. mixed` emerges as the most robust prompting strategy, ranking the highest when averaged over models and datasets. This approach effectively balances geographic and hedonic information, making it a strong default choice when selecting prompting strategies for house price estimation. While market reports may further enhance performance in markets with strong temporal trends, their usefulness varies by region. Therefore, a hybrid approach—prioritizing mixed examples and potentially incorporating market reports when relevant—offers the most generalizable strategy.

4.2 Positioning LLM Performance Relative to ML Baselines

Prediction Accuracy. Table 2 compares the performance of LLMs with baseline methods using MAPE across datasets. The table shows the LLM results for the best-ranked prompt strategy `10 ex. mixed` and corresponding setting for kNN, alongside a SOTA GBT model with (LGBM) and without coordinates (LGBM ∅ XY). Generally, high-parameter LLMs outperform kNN, indicating they leverage labeled examples through ICL more effectively than kNN's simple interpolation. The Beijing dataset presents a particular challenge, with all LLMs performing worse than kNN. This is due to the strong temporal trends as established earlier, and can be mitigated with a market report (`report + 10 ex. mixed`) which results in a decrease in MAPE from 0.4022 to 0.3322 for Llama 3.1:70B, effectively outperforming kNN (0.3810).

Table 2. LLMs generally outperform kNN and get competitive to SOTA models. Comparison of MAPE and PE Standard Deviation between LLMs with `10 ex. mixed` prompt and baseline models.

	King County	Flanders	Barcelona	Beijing
Llama 3.2:3B	0.2995 ± 0.3282	0.4511 ± 0.5828	0.3383 ± 0.4211	0.4092 ± 0.1320
Llama 3.1:70B	0.1905 ± 0.2072	0.3440 ± 0.4997	<u>0.1825</u> ± 0.2044	<u>0.4022</u> ± 0.1108
GPT-4o-mini	<u>0.1861</u> ± 0.1925	<u>0.3170</u> ± 0.4782	0.1842 ± 0.2004	0.4125 ± 0.1117
kNN	0.2105 ± 0.2113	0.3207 ± 0.4380	0.2638 ± 0.4070	0.3810 ± 0.1292
LGBM ∅ XY	0.2391 ± 0.3220	0.3136 ± 0.4988	0.1936 ± 0.2825	0.2427 ± 0.2031
LGBM	**0.1378** ± 0.1611	**0.2625** ± 0.4170	**0.1556** ± 0.1780	**0.1056** ± 0.0840

Comparing LLMs with LGBM ∅ XY, we see that LLMs show comparable performance. This indicates that LLMs are effective in extracting hedonic patterns from real estate pricing data. Finally, comparing LLMs with the SOTA LGBM models, we do not expect LLMs to perform better, but we see that LLMs can get relatively close without having access to the full dataset. In Flanders and Barcelona, GPT-4o-mini's MAPE is around 20% higher than LGBM, while in King County the difference is 35%. However, with the optimal strategy (`report + 10 ex. geo`), the MAPE in King County improves to 0.1390, completely matching LGBM's performance.

Interestingly, the Beijing dataset deviates in the baseline performance opposed to other datasets as well. It sees a great decrease in MAPE between kNN and LGBM ∅ XY, likely due to LGBM's ability to take advantage of temporal features. In addition, adding the geographic coordinates as predictors to LGBM reduces the MAPE from 0.2427 to 0.1056 for Beijing. While LLMs struggle with incorporating spatial relationships through neighboring examples, LGBM succeeds in deciphering the spatial structure in the dataset and significantly improves predictions. This strengthens our findings that LLMs can learn hedonic pricing patterns, but require more advanced techniques when the dataset is characterized by unconventional spatial structures and strong temporal dynamics.

The PE Standard Deviation shows LLMs have error variability comparable to baselines, though Llama 3.2 exhibits greater fluctuation. Overall, LLMs surpass kNN and show competitive performance compared to SOTA models, particularly in extracting hedonic patterns from real estate pricing data.

Price Intervals. To address **RQ3**, we assess LLM prediction intervals using the `10. mixed` prompt. Table 3 reports two metrics: coverage (percentage of true prices within intervals) and MPIW (Mean Prediction Interval Width).

Table 3. Prediction interval quality measured by Coverage (Cov.), percentage of true prices in test sample within intervals, and MPIW, Mean Prediction Interval Width. As we enforce LLMs to produce intervals around their predicted price, we included respectively 949, 872, 960, and 945 intervals for Llama 3.2:3B and 998 for Llama 3.1:70B on the Flanders dataset and 999 on the Beijing dataset.

	King County		Flanders		Barcelona		Beijing	
	Cov.	MPIW	Cov.	MPIW	Cov.	MPIW	Cov.	MPIW
Llama 3.2:3B	39.6	220 289	36.7	193 447	46.8	262 199	10.8	1 625 475
Llama 3.1:70B	57.5	182 823	51.4	156 658	64.0	151 641	3.6	1 093 476
GPT-4o-mini	35.5	**98 319**	25.8	**65 488**	40.3	**74 444**	1.2	**514 394**
LGBM	**90.5**	316 293	**90.5**	317 476	**86.2**	210 681	**85.1**	1 900 473

LLMs generate narrower intervals but often miss the 90% coverage target, showing overconfidence [36]. In contrast, conformal prediction enables LGBM to achieve near-target coverage but with wider intervals, illustrating the trade-off between coverage and precision. GPT-4o-mini produces the narrowest intervals but consistently underperforms on coverage, while Llama 3.1 offers the best balance across datasets. The Beijing dataset proves particularly difficult, with LLMs showing extremely low coverage and LGBM struggling despite conformal adjustments, likely due to the dataset's temporal trends. Despite adjusting for this distribution shift, this still influences predictions. LLMs may also lack geographical knowledge or show regional biases in Beijing [23]. Overall, it is clear that LLMs struggle with producing calibrated prediction intervals, but advanced techniques like conformal prediction or iterative prompting [38,39] that would be necessary to mitigate this problem, make it less evident for real estate practitioners to leverage LLM-based solutions.

Feature Importance. We compare LLM-generated feature explanations to SHAP values from LGBM in Fig. 3, which shows the Venn diagrams of the top five features for all datasets. GPT-4o-mini generally aligns with LGBM on hedonic features, supporting their ability to extract property-related pricing patterns. This alignment suggests that LLM-generated explanations are not only consistent with established ML models but also offer a degree of trustworthiness, as they reflect key predictive drivers identified through robust, model-agnostic interpretability methods like SHAP.

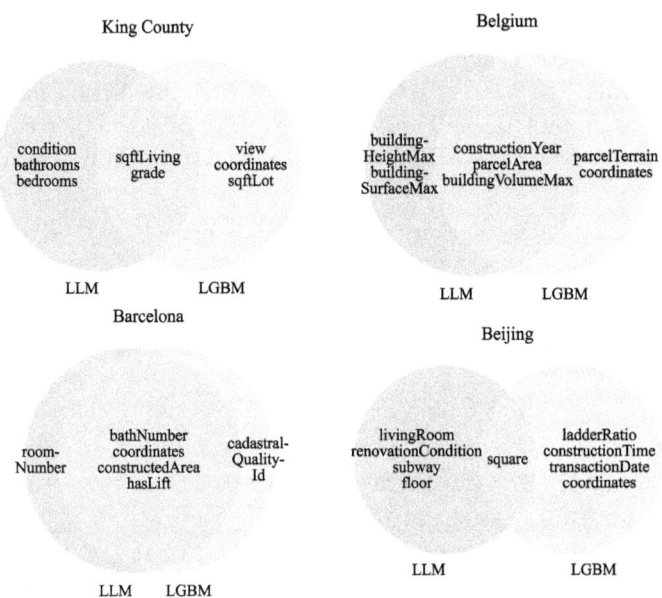

Fig. 3. LLMs generally align with LGBM on the importance of hedonic variables. Comparison of top five features between GPT-4o-mini and LGBM.

However, LGBM consistently ranks locational features, particularly coordinates, among its top predictors, while LLMs do not prioritize them, despite receiving full addresses and coordinates. The only exception is in the Barcelona dataset. This suggests that LLMs struggle with spatial reasoning, likely due to tokenization issues with coordinates and difficulty mapping addresses to house price patterns [19,24]. Additionally, in accordance with the previous analyses, LGBM prioritizes temporal features in the Beijing dataset, while GPT-4o-mini does not. Similar to LLMs' issues with interpreting coordinates, LLMs might struggle with dates and generalizing temporal trends in the data. Recent research has focused on improving temporal generalization of LLMs [13]. Although these limitations in spatial and temporal reasoning may explain the performance gap, caution is warranted since LLM self-explanations are not always reliable [21]. Appendix C confirms the findings for Llama3.1:70b.

4.3 Practical Implications

Our findings indicate that LLMs offer a low-barrier alternative to traditional ML solutions for real estate appraisal. With as few as ten examples, LLMs can provide reasonable price estimates, making them valuable for quick, accessible, and interactive valuations. We recommend structuring prompts with ten properties that are geographically near and share similar hedonic characteristics, while incorporating a market report in cases with strong temporal trends. LLMs are particularly suited for decision-support systems, especially for non-technical users and low-data environments. Private buyers and sellers, for instance, can use LLMs to gain insight into fair market prices, while creditors, real estate agents, and investors may rely on them for preliminary valuations that can later be refined with expert assessments or ML-based approaches.

Table 4 summarizes the key advantages and limitations of LLMs compared to ML models. While LLMs work out of the box, we identify three main limitations: they struggle with spatial reasoning, failing to properly integrate location effects; they exhibit weak temporal understanding, making it difficult to learn price trends over time; and they are overconfident in uncertainty estimation, often producing narrow and unreliable price intervals. Though market reports improve temporal generalization capabilities, fully addressing these weaknesses requires more advanced techniques, such as retrieval-augmented generation or fine-tuning [41]. These approaches introduce additional complexity that can undermine the accessibility and immediacy that make LLMs attractive alternatives to traditional ML methods. Similarly, reliable uncertainty estimation requires post-processing techniques that are challenging, especially with closed-source models [38,39]. Given these trade-offs, LLMs are best suited for fast, accessible valuations rather than high-accuracy, large-scale appraisals where calibrated uncertainty estimates are essential.

Table 4. Comparison of LLMs and ML models for real estate appraisal

Aspect	LLMs	ML Models
Accessibility		
Ease of Use	Works out of the box	Requires training & tuning
User Input	Natural Language via interface	Structured data through code
Data Requirements		
Data Needs	Few examples needed	Large structured dataset
Feature Handling	Implicit understanding	Manual selection required
Unstructured Data	Can use reports & text	Limited to structured inputs
Model Capabilities		
Accuracy	Competitive, slightly below ML	State-of-the-art
Geospatial Data	Limited handling	Explicitly modeled
Temporal Trends	Struggles with time patterns	Can model time effects
Prediction Intervals	Often overconfident	More calibrated
Explainability	Text-based, intuitive	SHAP & feature importance
Practical Deployment		
Interactivity	Can take user feedback	Static predictions
Computation	Free/low-cost web, API, local	Local CPU/GPU
Best Use Case	Quick, flexible valuations	Accurate, large-scale modeling

5 Conclusion

This study investigated how prompt engineering techniques optimize LLM performance for real estate appraisal (**RQ1**) and whether LLMs can serve as viable alternatives to traditional ML models (**RQ2-4**). Our results show that LLMs, when prompted using In-Context Learning with just ten real estate examples selected based on geographic and hedonic similarity (**RQ1**), can generate competitive price estimates (**RQ2**), making them a practical tool for real estate valuation. However, their spatial reasoning and temporal generalization capabilities remain limited, affecting the reliability of predicted price intervals (**RQ3**) compared to structured ML models. Nevertheless, LLMs align with ML models in explaining predictions based on property characteristics (**RQ4**), reinforcing their ability to capture hedonic valuation patterns.

By improving accessibility to property appraisal, LLMs help reduce information asymmetry in real estate transactions. While ML models remain more accurate in structured, large-scale applications, LLMs provide an interactive and intuitive alternative, particularly for non-technical users who need quick and interpretable price estimates. These findings align with **RQ2** and **RQ4**, highlighting that while LLMs can extract meaningful hedonic features, they require further refinement to fully capture spatial and temporal trends.

In summary, LLMs show potential for accurate and explainable price predictions. Future work should explore more recent LLMs with enhanced reasoning capabilities, alongside diverse prompting techniques such as chain-of-thought and self-consistency, or retrieval-augmented generation to further improve performance and robustness. Additionally, a systematic investigation into scaling LLMs with large-scale datasets is needed to provide deeper insights into data efficiency and generalization, though our results indicate that larger model sizes generally yield better accuracy. Exploring alternative geographic encoding strategies could also address current spatial reasoning limitations. Collectively, these directions offer a clear roadmap to enhance LLM trustworthiness and reliability, advancing their practical application in real estate appraisal.

Disclosure of Interests. The authors have no competing interests to declare that are relevant to the content of this article.

References

1. Bastos, J.A., Paquette, J.: On the uncertainty of real estate price predictions. J. Prop. Res. 1–19 (2024). https://doi.org/10.1080/09599916.2024.2403998
2. Bourassa, S.C., Hoesli, M., Peng, V.S.: Do housing submarkets really matter? J. Hous. Econ. **12**, 12–28 (2003). https://doi.org/10.1016/S1051-1377(03)00003-2
3. Chen, T., Si, S.: Predicting rental price of lane houses in shanghai with machine learning methods and large language models. arXiv preprint arXiv:2405.17505 (2024)
4. Coda-Forno, J., Binz, M., Akata, Z., Botvinick, M., Wang, J., Schulz, E.: Meta-in-context learning in large language models. In: Advances in Neural Information Processing Systems, vol. 36, pp. 65189–65201 (2023)
5. Dubey, A., et al.: The llama 3 herd of models. arXiv preprint arXiv:2407.21783 (2024)
6. Feng, S., Lyu, H., Li, F., Sun, Z., Chen, C.: Where to move next: Zero-shot generalization of llms for next poi recommendation. In: IEEE Conference on Artificial Intelligence (2024). https://doi.org/10.1109/CAI59869.2024.00277
7. Geerts, M., vanden Broucke, S., De Weerdt, J.: A survey of methods and input data types for house price prediction. ISPRS Int. J. Geo-Inf. **12**, 200 (2023). https://doi.org/10.3390/ijgi12050200
8. Geerts, M., vanden Broucke, S., De Weerdt, J.: Graph neural networks for house price prediction: do or don't? Int. J. Data. Sci. Anal. (2024). https://doi.org/10.1007/s41060-024-00682-y
9. Gloria, B., Melsbach, J., Bienert, S., Schoder, D.: Real-GPT: efficiently tailoring LLMs for informed decision-making in the real estate industry. J. Real Estate Portf. Manag. (2024). https://doi.org/10.1080/10835547.2024.2372748
10. Guo, H., et al.: Hey GPT, can you be more racist? analysis from crowd-sourced attempts to elicit biased content from generative AI. arXiv preprint arXiv:2410.15467 (2024)
11. Hegselmann, S., Buendia, A., Lang, H., Agrawal, M., Jiang, X., Sontag, D.: Tabllm: few-shot classification of tabular data with large language models. In: 26th International Conference on Artificial Intelligence and Statistics, vol. 206, pp. 5549–5581. PMLR (2023)

12. Hjort, A., Williams, J.P., Pensar, J.: Clustered conformal prediction for the housing market. In: 13th Symposium on Conformal and Probabilistic Prediction with Applications. Proceedings of Machine Learning Research, vol. 230, pp. 366–386. PMLR (2024)
13. Jin, M., et al.: Time-LLM: Time series forecasting by reprogramming large language models. In: 12th International Conference on Learning Representations (2023)
14. Jin, R., et al.: LLM-based knowledge pruning for time series data analytics on edge-computing devices. arXiv preprint arXiv:2406.08765 (2024)
15. Ke, G., et al.: Lightgbm: a highly efficient gradient boosting decision tree. In: 31st International Conference on Neural Information Processing Systems, vol. 30, pp. 3146–3154 (2017)
16. Kurlat, P., Stroebel, J.: Testing for information asymmetries in real estate markets. Rev. Financ. Stud. **28**, 2429–2461 (2015). https://doi.org/10.1093/rfs/hhv028
17. Lee, H., Jeong, H., Lee, B., Lee, K.D., Choo, J.: ST-rap: a spatio-temporal framework for real estate appraisal. In: 32nd ACM International Conference on Information and Knowledge Management, pp. 4053–4058 (2023)
18. Li, C., Wang, W., Du, W., Peng, W.: Look around! a neighbor relation graph learning framework for real estate appraisal. In: Advances in Knowledge Discovery and Data Mining (2024). https://doi.org/10.1007/978-981-97-2238-9_1
19. Li, F., Hogg, D.C., Cohn, A.G.: Advancing spatial reasoning in large language models: an in-depth evaluation and enhancement using the stepgame benchmark. In: AAAI Conference on Artificial Intelligence, vol. 38, pp. 18500–18507 (2024). https://doi.org/10.1609/aaai.v38i17.29811
20. Lundberg, S.M., Lee, S.I.: A unified approach to interpreting model predictions. In: 31st International Conference on Neural Information Processing Systems, vol. 30, pp. 4768–4777 (2017)
21. Madsen, A., Chandar, S., Reddy, S.: Are self-explanations from large language models faithful? In: Findings of the Association for Computational Linguistics. pp. 295–337 (2024). https://doi.org/10.18653/v1/2024.findings-acl.19
22. Manikandan, H., Jiang, Y., Kolter, Z.: Language models are weak learners. In: Advances in Neural Information Processing Systems, vol. 36, pp. 50907–50931 (2023)
23. Manvi, R., Khanna, S., Burke, M., Lobell, D., Ermon, S.: Large language models are geographically biased. arXiv preprint arXiv:2402.02680 (2024)
24. Manvi, R., Khanna, S., Mai, G., Burke, M., Lobell, D.B., Ermon, S.: GeoLLM: extracting geospatial knowledge from large language models. In: 12th International Conference on Learning Representations (2024)
25. Meta: Llama 3.2: revolutionizing edge AI and vision with open, customizable models (2024). https://ai.meta.com/blog/llama-3-2-connect-2024-vision-edge-mobile-devices/
26. OpenAI: Hello gpt-4o (2024). https://openai.com/index/hello-gpt-4o/
27. Ozhegov, E.M., Ozhegova, A.: Distance in geographic and characteristics space for real estate pricing. Int. J. Hous. Mark Anal. **15**, 938–952 (2022). https://doi.org/10.1108/IJHMA-04-2021-0041
28. Rey-Blanco, D., Arbues, P., Lopez, F., Paez, A.: A geo-referenced micro-data set of real estate listings for spain's three largest cities. Environ. Plan B: Urban Anal. City Sci. **51**, 1369–1379 (2024). https://doi.org/10.1177/23998083241242844
29. Rico-Juan, J.R., de La Paz, P.T.: Machine learning with explainability or spatial hedonics tools? an analysis of the asking prices in the housing market in Alicante, Spain. Expert Syst. Appl. **171** (2021). https://doi.org/10.1016/j.eswa.2021.114590

30. Shen, L., Liu, Q., Chen, G., Ji, S.: Text-based price recommendation system for online rental houses. Big Data Min. Anal. **3**, 143–152 (2020). https://doi.org/10.26599/BDMA.2019.9020023
31. Taquet, V., Blot, V., Morzadec, T., Lacombe, L., Brunel, N.: Mapie: an open-source library for distribution-free uncertainty quantification. arXiv preprint arXiv:2207.12274 (2022)
32. Vacareanu, R., Negru, V.A., Suciu, V., Surdeanu, M.: From words to numbers: your large language model is secretly a capable regressor when given in-context examples. arXiv preprint arXiv:2404.07544 (2024)
33. Vovk, V., Gammerman, A., Shafer, G.: Algorithmic Learning in a Random World. Springer, Cham (2005). https://doi.org/10.1007/978-3-031-06649-8
34. Weiss, M., et al.: Redesigning information markets in the era of language models. In: First Conference on Language Modeling (2024)
35. Wu J., Hou M.: An efficient retrieval-based method for tabular prediction with LLM. In: 31st International Conference on Computational Linguistics, pp. 9917–9925 (2025)
36. Xiong, M., et al.: Can LLMs express their uncertainty? an empirical evaluation of confidence elicitation in LLMs. In: 12th International Conference on Learning Representations (2024)
37. Xu, C., Xie, Y.: Conformal prediction for time series. IEEE Trans. Pattern Anal. Mach. Intell. **45**, 11575–11587 (2023). https://doi.org/10.1109/TPAMI.2023.3272339
38. Yadkori, Y.A., Kuzborskij, I., György, A., Szepesvari, C.: To believe or not to believe your LLM: iterative prompting for estimating epistemic uncertainty. In: Advances in Neural Information Processing Systems, vol. 37, pp. 58077–58117 (2024)
39. Ye, F., et al.: Benchmarking LLMs via uncertainty quantification. In: Advances in Neural Information Processing Systems, vol. 37, pp. 15356–15385 (2024)
40. Zhang, H., Li, Y., Branco, P.: Describe the house and i will tell you the price: house price prediction with textual description data. Nat. Lang. Eng. **30**, 661–695 (2024). https://doi.org/10.1017/S1351324923000360
41. Zhang, Y., et al.: BB-GEOGPT: a framework for learning a large language model for geographic information science. Inf. Process Manag. **61** (2024). https://doi.org/10.1016/J.IPM.2024.103808

InterDiff: Synthesizing Financial Time Series with Inter-Stock Correlations via Classifier-Free Guided Diffusion

Hou-Wan Long[1], Zhoufei Tang[2], Jianhui Zhang[2], Zhuoyang Zhan[2], Tao Lu[3], and Xiaoquan Michael Zhang[4](✉)

[1] Department of Statistics, The Chinese University of Hong Kong, Shatin, Hong Kong, China
houwanlong@link.cuhk.edu.hk
[2] Super Quantum Capital Management, Hong Kong, China
{tangzhoufei,jianhui,zhanzhuoyang}@superquant.fund
[3] College of Business, Southern University of Science and Technology, Shenzhen, China
lut@sustech.edu.cn
[4] Department of Management Science and Engineering, Tsinghua University, Beijing, China
zhangxiaoquan@sem.tsinghua.edu.cn

Abstract. Stock prediction is hindered by data scarcity, and although existing data augmentation techniques have made significant strides, they often overlook the dynamic inter-stock interactions crucial for robust modeling. To address these challenges, we propose **InterDiff**, a diffusion-based framework that synthesizes realistic financial time series by dynamically modeling both intra- and inter-stock correlations. Inter-Diff employs hierarchical transformers to learn these correlations, encoding them into a guidance vector that steers a diffusion model via classifier-free guidance. This approach ensures that the synthetic data preserves fidelity while introducing controlled variability. Evaluations on CSI300 and CSI800 show that models trained on InterDiff-augmented data boost the information coefficient by 1.13–4.70% on CSI300 and 40.15–49.60% on CSI800, while delivering cumulative return improvements of 0.57–13.87% on CSI300 and 28.72–51.33% on CSI800 under 0.1% per-trade cost. The framework outperforms alternatives such as DiffsFormer and Quant GAN. Ablation studies reveal a fidelity-diversity tradeoff: while larger guidance strength improves synthetic data fidelity, it does not necessarily enhance prediction performance. Visualizations confirm the preservation of inter-stock correlations and a reduction in overfitting. These results demonstrate InterDiff's ability to enhance robustness and profitability in real-world trading environments and mitigate data scarcity.

Keywords: Data Augmentation · Diffusion Model · Stock Forecasting

1 Introduction

Stock prediction, which involves forecasting future trends and prices based on historical stock prices and factor time series, is a crucial technique for making profitable investment decisions [1–4]. Numerous machine learning models, such as the State Frequency Memory (SFM) [5], have been proposed for this task. However, the effectiveness of these models heavily depends on the availability of high-quality data. A full year of stock price records typically contains only about 252 daily prices [6]. Furthermore, stock prices exhibit high volatility and are influenced by numerous external factors, leading to a low signal-to-noise ratio (SNR) [7]. These challenges—data scarcity and low SNR—complicate stock prediction, making it difficult to extract meaningful signals and train robust models. As a result, models often suffer from overfitting and poor generalization. A widely adopted approach to mitigate these issues is data augmentation, which generates synthetic sequences to expand the input space while preserving correct labels. This process helps prevent overfitting and improves model generalization [8–10]. Traditional time series augmentation methods rely on transformations in the time, frequency, and time-frequency domains [11–14]. More advanced techniques incorporate decomposition-based methods and statistical generative models [15,16]. Although these approaches can produce diverse samples, they often struggle to fully capture the complex characteristics of real-world stock data. Recently, deep generative models (DGMs) have gained popularity for time series data augmentation, particularly generative adversarial networks (GANs) and variational autoencoders (VAEs). GAN-based methods, such as TimeGAN [17] and Quant GAN [18], employ an adversarial framework in which a generator and a discriminator compete to produce realistic synthetic data that closely mimics the underlying distribution [19,20]. Similarly, VAEs, such as TimeVAE [21], use a probabilistic encoder-decoder architecture to learn latent representations, generating synthetic data that maintains temporal dependencies. The most recent advancement in this domain is the application of diffusion models (DMs) for time series augmentation [22]. Methods like Diffsformer [7] leverage a forward and reverse diffusion process to iteratively denoise data, generating high-quality synthetic samples.

A major limitation of existing DGM-based methods is their tendency to treat stocks as independent entities. While these models effectively capture temporal dependencies within individual stocks (intra-stock correlations), they often overlook relationships between different stocks (inter-stock correlations), which contain valuable predictive signals about market behavior [23–28]. For instance, stocks within the same sector or industry frequently exhibit similar long-term trends. Ignoring these relationships can lead to synthetic data that disrupts the statistical dependencies between inter-stock correlations and future returns, ultimately impairing the performance of models trained on such data. A notable exception is DiffsFormer [7], a state-of-the-art model that attempts to incorporate inter-stock correlations by conditioning the data generation process on static industry-sector classifications. This approach assumes that stocks within the same sector behave similarly. However, such a rigid classification oversimplifies real-world market dynamics [29]. In reality, sector-based relationships are fluid and complex—firms within the same industry can respond asymmetrically to market shocks (e.g., competing companies reacting differently to supply chain disruptions), experience intra-sector competition, or even redefine their industry alignment over time (e.g., traditional companies pivoting to AI-driven business models). This raises a critical question: **How can we dynamically capture both intra- and inter-stock correlations to improve financial time series augmentation?**

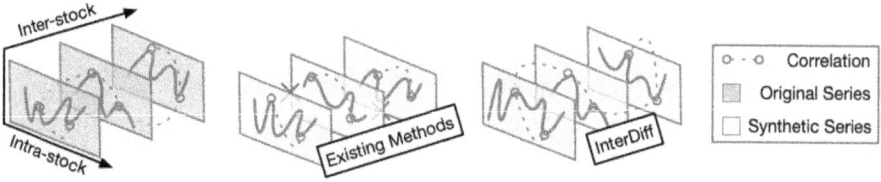

Fig. 1. A comparison of existing methods and InterDiff for financial time series augmentation.

To address this limitation, we present InterDiff, a diffusion-based framework that synthesizes financial time series with dynamic correlations across stocks. InterDiff employs hierarchical transformers to first capture intra-stock correlation and then model inter-stock correlation. These transformers produce a guidance vector that encodes real-world evolving market logic. This vector then steers a diffusion model via classifier-free guidance. During training, InterDiff learns to denoise data by optimizing two objectives: (1) a diffusion loss to match the statistical properties of real data and (2) a supervised loss to align guidance vector with predictive signals for future returns. At inference, InterDiff blends guided predictions (informed by the learned correlations) with unguided predictions, ensuring synthetic data retains realistic inter-stock correlations while introducing controlled variability to avoid overfitting (Fig. 1).

This paper makes the following contributions:

(i) **Hierarchical Correlation Learning:** We design a process to dynamically model intra-stock correlations and inter-stock correlations through transformers, encoding these correlations into a guidance vector.
(ii) **InterDiff Framework:** We introduce a diffusion-based method using classifier free guidance, conditioned on learned correlations, to synthesize financial time series that balance fidelity to real data with controlled variability.
(iii) **Empirical Validation:** We demonstrate the framework's effectiveness via comprehensive evaluations on real world datasets (CSI300/CSI800), ablation studies, and visualizations showing preserved market dynamics and improved prediction robustness.

2 Related Work

Deep generative models (DGMs) have demonstrated superior performance over traditional augmentation techniques in capturing the complex characteristics of real data. A pivotal work in this domain is TimeGAN [17], which integrates a generative adversarial network (GAN) with a supervised autoregressive model to preserve temporal dependencies while synthesizing realistic time series data. Another notable model, Quant GAN [18], is specifically designed for financial time series, effectively capturing long-range dependencies such as volatility clustering. Its data-driven approach makes it particularly suited for modeling continuous sequential data with long-term dependencies. A comprehensive review of GAN-based time series synthesis can be found in [30]. Beyond GANs, variational autoencoders (VAEs) offer a probabilistic framework that explicitly models the data distribution, resulting in stable and diverse synthetic samples [34]. TimeVAE [21] enhances this framework by incorporating seasonality and trend modules, improving both model performance and interpretability.

The state-of-the-art model in this field is DiffsFormer [7], which leverages diffusion models (DMs) for stock factor augmentation. Unlike previous methods that generate synthetic data from scratch, DiffsFormer employs transfer learning to refine existing samples. Additionally, it conditions the generation process on static industry classifications, aiming to incorporate inter-stock relationships into the synthetic data. However, we argue that static industry classification is insufficient to capture dynamic inter-stock correlation. Therefore, we propose to condition the generation process on a learned vector that encodes dynamic inter-stock relationships and market trends for realistic synthesis in InterDiff.

3 Background

In this section, we will introduce some definitions in our work and the problem of stock price forecasting.

3.1 Problem Formulation

Stock forecasting aims to predict future normalized returns of stocks based on historical factor data. For each stock $u \in S$, quantifiable factors such as momentum, volatility and liquidity are collected over a historical lookback window of T days, forming a 2-D factor vector $x^u \in \mathbb{R}^{T \times F}$, where F denotes the number of factors. The prediction target is the normalized return ratio r_u, defined as:

$$r_u = \frac{\text{Price}^u_{t+i} - \text{Price}^u_t}{\text{Price}^u_t},$$

where t is the current time and i is the forecast horizon (in days). To mitigate data scarcity, a DGM synthesizes realistic sequences $\hat{x}^u$, augmenting the original dataset with synthetic data that preserves market dynamics. The task requires jointly predicting $\{r_u\}_{u \in S}$ for all stocks using their augmented factors $\{\hat{x}^u\}_{u \in S}$.

3.2 Denoising Diffusion Probabilistic Model

Denoising Diffusion Probabilistic Models (DDPMs) have demonstrated exceptional performance and outperformed Generative Adversarial Networks (GANs) in several areas, particularly in text-to-image generation tasks. The training of a diffusion model involves two main processes: diffusion and denoising.

Diffusion Process: Starting with a data point $x_0 \sim q(x_0)$[1], the diffusion process progressively adds noise to create a sequence of step-dependent variables, $\{x_k\}_{k=1}^{K}$. This process can be described as a Markov chain:

$$q(x_{1:K}|x_0) = \prod_{k=1}^{K} q(x_k|x_{k-1}) \quad (1)$$

where $q(x_k|x_{k-1}) = \mathcal{N}(x_k; \sqrt{\alpha_k}x_{k-1}, \beta_k \mathbf{I})$. Here, $\mathcal{N}$ represents a Gaussian distribution, α_k controls the signal retention strength, and β_k governs the scale of the noise added. These scalars, α_k and β_k, are predefined for each step k. A common setting is the variance-preserving process where $\alpha_k = 1 - \beta_k$.

Denoising Process: The goal of the denoising process is to reconstruct the original data by reversing the transformations introduced in the diffusion process. This is accomplished by another Markov chain:

$$p_\theta(x_{0:K}) = p(x_K) \prod_{k=1}^{K} p_\theta(x_{k-1}|x_k), \quad (2)$$

where $x_K \sim \mathcal{N}(0, \mathbf{I})$. The distribution p_θ is an approximation of the true distribution q. Specifically, $p_\theta(x_{k-1}|x_k) = \mathcal{N}(x_{k-1}; \mu_\theta(x_k, k), \sigma_\theta(x_k, k)\mathbf{I})$, where μ_θ and σ_θ are learned functions of the noisy input x_k and the step k. For each sample in a batch, a time step k is randomly selected from $1, 2, \ldots, K$, and the noise is adjusted accordingly at step k.

Inference Process: Once θ is well-trained, the DM generates samples by initializing $x_K \sim \mathcal{N}(0, \mathbf{I})$ and iteratively denoising through $x_K \to \cdots \to x_k \to x_{k-1} \to \cdots \to x_0$ using $p_\theta(x_{k-1}|x_k)$.

3.3 Classifier and Classifier-Free Guidance

DMs utilize two primary conditioning strategies to incorporate information from a guidance variable c: classifier guidance and classifier-free guidance. Classifier guidance relies on training an auxiliary classifier to estimate $p(c|x_k, k)$. During inference, the gradient $\nabla_{x_k} \log p(c|x_k, k)$ from this classifier is used to steer

---

[1] x_0 denotes the initial (non-noised) step, with the total diffusion steps K set to 500 in our work (or say in the experiment section).

the synthesis process. Specifically, the predicted noise at each step is adjusted according to

$$\bar{\epsilon} = \epsilon_\theta(x_k, k) - \sqrt{1-\bar{\alpha}_k}\omega \nabla_{x_k} \log p(c|x_k, k) \qquad (3)$$

where ω scales the guidance strength.

In contrast, classifier-free guidance eliminates the need for a separate classifier by jointly training a conditional DM and an unconditional DM. These two components are combined during inference using a weighted interpolation of their predicted noise:

$$\hat{\epsilon}_\theta = (1 + \omega_{\text{free}})\epsilon_\theta(x_k, c, k) - \omega_{\text{free}}\epsilon_\theta(x_k, \emptyset, k) \qquad (4)$$

where ω_{free} controls the trade-off between conditioning fidelity and sample diversity.

We opt for classifier-free guidance due to a critical limitation inherent to classifier guidance: gradient instability. When classifier gradients are injected into the denoising process, they can behave adversarially. This instability disrupts the generation process, as erratic gradient updates degrade output quality and consistency. Empirical results from [31] confirm that this sensitivity to adversarial-like gradients often renders classifier-guided synthesis inferior to classifier-free approaches.

4 Methodology

The InterDiff framework generates synthetic stock data that balances diversity with correlation-consistency through two key stages. First, for each stock u, a guidance vector e_u is learned to capture its intra-stock correlation and inter-stock correlations through a 3-stage hierarchical transformer (Intra-, Inter-stock and Temporal Aggregation). Next, e_u guides a DM in the denoising and inference process by classifier-free approach (Fig. 2).

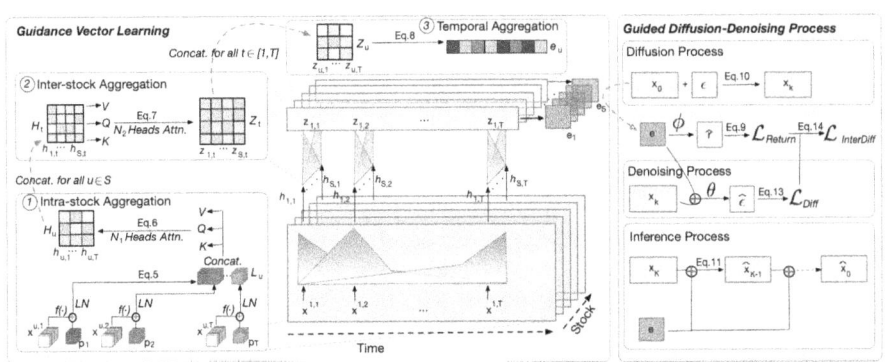

Fig. 2. The Pipeline for InterDiff

4.1 Guidance Vector Learning Through Hierarchical Transformer

The guidance vector learning process begins by splitting the set of stock factors $\{x^u\}_{u \in S}$ into $\{x^{u,t}\}_{u \in S, t \in [1,T]}$, where each stock's data is associated with factors at each time step. The learning process proceeds as follows:

Intra-Stock Aggregation: For each stock, the factors at each time step $\{x^{u,t}\}_{u \in S, t \in [1,T]}$ are first encoded into embeddings $l_{u,t} = f(x^{u,t})$ via a linear layer $f(\cdot)$. A transformer encoder then processes these embeddings with sinusoidal positional encodings p_t to preserve chronological order:

$$L_u = ||_{t \in [1,T]} LN(f(x^{u,t}) + p_t) \tag{5}$$

where $||$ denotes concatenation and LN is layer normalization. Multi-head attention (N_1 heads) and feed-forward networks (FFNs) then aggregate intra-stock correlations across time steps. The transformer computes query (Q_u^1), key (K_u^1) and value (V_u^1) matrices from L_u producing local embeddings $h_{u,t}$ enriched with cross-time signals:

$$\begin{aligned} Q_u^1 = W_Q^1 L_u, \quad K_u^1 = W_K^1 L_u, \quad V_u^1 = W_V^1 L_u \\ H_u^1 = ||_{t \in [1,T]} h_{u,t} = FFN^1(MHA^1(Q_u^1, K_u^1, V_u^1) + L_u) \end{aligned} \tag{6}$$

These embeddings retain local temporal details while integrating global historical context, ensuring the learned intra-stock correlations reflect both short-term fluctuations and long-term trends.

Inter-Stock Aggregation: At each time step t, local embeddings $\{h_{u,t}\}_{u \in S}$ from all stocks are combined to model inter-stock correlations. Another multi-head attention layer (N_2 heads) computes cross-stock interactions:

$$\begin{aligned} Q_t^2 = W_Q^2 H_t, \quad K_t^2 = W_K^2 H_t, \quad V_t^2 = W_V^2 H_t \\ Z_t = ||_{u \in S} z_{u,t} = FFN^2(MHA^2(Q_t^2, K_t^2, V_t^2) + H_t^2) \end{aligned} \tag{7}$$

where $H_t^2 = ||_{u \in S} h_{u,t}$. The temporal embedding $z_{u,t}$ for stock u at time t encodes both its intrinsic features and dependencies on other stocks.

Temporal Aggregation: To summarize the obtained temporal embeddings and obtain a comprehensive stock embedding e_u, we employ a temporal attention layer along the time axis. We use the latest temporal embedding $z_{u,T}$ as the query vector, and compute the attention score $\lambda_{u,t}$ in a hidden space with transformation matrix W_λ,

$$\lambda_{u,t} = \frac{exp(z_{u,t}^T W_\lambda z_{u,T})}{\sum_{i \in [1,T]} exp(z_{u,i}^T W_\lambda z_{u,T})}, \quad e_u = \sum_{t \in [1,T]} \lambda_{u,t} z_{u,t} \tag{8}$$

Return Calibration: For stock forecasting, each input requires a label, but rather than directly generating label as an additional dimension, using ground truth labels to guide data generation and keep the original label is more effective [7]. Therefore, we introduce an auxiliary predictor ϕ that maps the learned guidance vector e_u to the stock return r_u. This ensures e_u captures the dependencies critical for forecasting while allowing us to use the original return as a label through a mean squared error (MSE) loss:

$$\mathcal{L}_{\text{return}} = \mathbb{E}_{u \in S}[||r_u - \phi(e_u)||_2^2] \tag{9}$$

4.2 Classifier-Free Correlation Guided Diffusion-Denoising Process

The InterDiff framework synthesizes stock data with realistic intra- and inter-stock correlations by integrating a DM conditioned on the learned guidance vector e_u. For clarity, we omit the stock-specific superscript u in this section (e.g., $x_0^u \equiv x_0, e_u \equiv e$), as the diffusion and denoising processes operate identically for each stock. The process follows a diffusion-denoising pipeline.

Diffusion Process: The forward process gradually corrupts x_0 over K steps by adding Gaussian noise. At step k, the noised state x_k follows $q(x_k|x_0) = \mathcal{N}(x_k; \sqrt{\overline{\alpha}_k}x_0, (1-\overline{\alpha}_k)\mathbf{I})$, where $\overline{\alpha}_k = \prod_{m=1}^{k} \alpha_m$ and $\alpha_k = 1 - \beta_k$. This allows direct sampling of x_k via reparameterization:

$$x_k = \sqrt{\overline{\alpha}_k}x_0 + \sqrt{1-\overline{\alpha}_k}\epsilon, \quad \text{where } \epsilon \sim \mathcal{N}(0, \mathbf{I}) \tag{10}$$

Denoising Process: The denoising process iteratively removes noise from x_k to reconstruct $\hat{x}_0 \sim q(x_0)$. To enable classifier-free guidance, we stochastically mask the guidance vector e with a null token $\emptyset$ with probability p during training, enabling the model to learn both conditional and unconditional denoising. Formally:

$$p_\theta(x_{k-1}|x_k, e) = \mathcal{N}(x_{k-1}; \mu_\theta(x_k, k, e), \Sigma_q(k)\mathbf{I}) \tag{11}$$

with:

$$\mu_\theta(x_k, k, e) = \begin{cases} \frac{1}{\sqrt{\alpha_k}}\left(x_k - \frac{\beta_k}{\sqrt{1-\overline{\alpha}_k}}\epsilon_\theta(x_k, k, e)\right), & \text{with probability } (1-p) \\ \frac{1}{\sqrt{\alpha_k}}\left(x_k - \frac{\beta_k}{\sqrt{1-\overline{\alpha}_k}}\epsilon_\theta(x_k, k, \emptyset)\right), & \text{with probability } p \end{cases} \tag{12}$$

The mean square error between the true noise ϵ and the predicted noise ϵ_θ is computed across all timesteps and incorporated into the InterDiff loss function to ensure accurate noise estimation and effective denoising.

$$\mathcal{L}_{\text{diff}} = \mathbb{E}_{x_0 \sim q(x_0), \epsilon \sim \mathcal{N}(0,\mathbf{I}), k \sim \text{Uniform}(1,K)}[||\epsilon - \epsilon_\theta||_2^2] \tag{13}$$

Loss Function: InterDiff employs an uncertainty-aware loss [32] that dynamically weights the denoising and return calibration tasks to balance the dual objectives of generating relationally consistent stock data and preserving return-predictive signals. The total loss integrates the DM's noise prediction error $\mathcal{L}_{\text{diff}}$ and the return calibration error $\mathcal{L}_{\text{return}}$ through learnable variance parameters σ^2_{diff} and σ^2_{return}, which quantify the intrinsic uncertainty of each task:

$$\mathcal{L}_{\text{InterDiff}} = \frac{1}{2\sigma^2_{\text{diff}}}\mathcal{L}_{\text{diff}} + \frac{1}{2\sigma^2_{\text{return}}}\mathcal{L}_{\text{return}} + \frac{1}{2}(\log \sigma^2_{\text{diff}} + \log \sigma^2_{\text{return}}) \qquad (14)$$

The first two terms adaptively scale each loss based on task difficulty, where volatile tasks (higher σ^2) receive lower weights. The third term penalizes excessive uncertainty. This mechanism eliminates manual loss weighting, critical in financial applications where market volatility and return scales vary widely across stocks and time periods.

Inference Process: Synthetic data generation begins with Gaussian noise x_K and a guidance vector e. The model iteratively denoises x_K to $\hat{x}_0$ over K steps. During inference, the predicted noise $\hat{\epsilon}_\theta$ combines conditional and unconditional predictions using a guidance strength ω_{free}:

$$\hat{\epsilon}_\theta = (1 - \omega_{\text{free}}) \cdot \epsilon_\theta(x_k, k, \emptyset) + \omega_{\text{free}} \cdot \epsilon_\theta(x_k, k, e) \qquad (15)$$

This blended prediction guides the denoising trajectory, ensuring outputs align with the correlation patterns encoded in e while maintaining statistical diversity. The final synthetic data $\hat{x}_0$ is sampled by progressively refining $\hat{x}_{k-1}$ from $p_\theta(x_{k-1}|x_k, e)$.

5 Experiment

We conduct experiments to address three key questions. **RQ1 (Compatibility)**: Does InterDiff generalize across diverse backbone models while improving their forecasting performance? **RQ2 (Component Efficacy)**: How do key design choices, such as guidance variable and critical parameters like guidance strength, influence the quality of synthetic data and the overall performance of the model? **RQ3 (Correlation Preservation)**: Can InterDiff synthesize data that retains realistic intra- and inter-stock correlations observed in real markets?

5.1 Dataset

We evaluate InterDiff on CSI300 and CSI800—datasets comprising the 300 and 800 largest stocks by market capitalization from the Shanghai and Shenzhen exchanges. Following [7,33], we use daily data spanning 2008–2023, partitioned into training (Q1 2008–Q1 2021), validation (Q2 2021), and test (Q3 2021–Q4 2023) sets. Stock features are obtained from the Alpha158 factor suite in Qlib[2], with a lookback window $T = 8$ days and prediction horizon $i = 5$ days, consistent with [29].

---

[2] https://github.com/microsoft/qlib.

5.2 Reproducibility

We implement InterDiff using Python 3.8.5 and PyTorch 1.11.0, running on NVIDIA RTX 3090 GPUs and AMD EPYC 7532 CPUs. To facilitate reproducibility, we outline the key techniques used in our implementation.

First, we use Robust Z-score Normalization, which replaces the mean and standard deviation with the median (MED) and median absolute deviation (MAD). This approach ensures scale-invariant features and reduces sensitivity to outliers:

$$\tilde{x}^u = \frac{|x^u - \text{MED}(X)|}{\text{MAD}(X)}, \tag{16}$$

Second, we apply Extreme Label Filtering, which removes the top and bottom 2.5% of returns. This step mitigates distortions caused by limit-up and limit-down events, preventing extreme values from biasing the model. Third, we employ the "train on synthetic, test on real" (TSTR) strategy to evaluate the effectiveness of the synthetic data generated by InterDiff. This approach involves training the model on the augmented, synthetic dataset and testing it on real-world data, allowing us to assess the generalization of the model when faced with actual market conditions. Lastly, we optimize hyperparameters such as guidance vector size, attention heads and guidance strength through grid search. The best-performing values are highlighted in Table 1.

Table 1. Hyper-parameters and the search range, the optimal parameters are indicated in boldface.

Parameters	Search Range
layers in DM	{3, **6**}
stop loss thred	{0.6, 0.8, 0.9, 0.95, **0.965**, 1}
Guidance Vector Size	{128, **256**, 512}
Guidance Strength ω_{free}	{1.5, **2**, 3, 4, 5}
Attention Heads N_1	{2, 3, **4**, 5}
Attention Heads N_2	{**2**, 3, 4, 5}

5.3 Experimental Setup

To evaluate our framework's performance in stock forecasting, we use five widely adopted models as backbones: Multi-Layer Perceptron (MLP), Long Short-Term Memory (LSTM) [36], Gated Recurrent Unit (GRU) [37], State Frequency Memory (SFM) [5], and a Transformer-based model [35]. These models serve as forecasting backbones, allowing us to compare their effectiveness in predicting stock movements. Each experiment is repeated 10 times, with results averaged for robust model evaluation and statistical reliability. Training follows a daily batch strategy: each batch comprises all stock data for a single day, enabling gradient updates based on return prediction errors per day. The model minimizes the Pearson Loss:

$$\mathcal{L}_{\text{Pearson}} = 1 - \frac{\text{COV}\left(r, r^{\text{pred}}\right)}{\text{SD}(r) \cdot \text{SD}\left(r^{\text{pred}}\right)}, \tag{17}$$

where $r, r^{\text{pred}} \in \mathbb{R}^{|S|}$ denote ground-truth and predicted daily returns for all stocks, respectively. Each r_u represents the normalized daily return of stock u.

We assess model performance using both ranking metrics and portfolio-based metrics. The ranking metrics include Information Coefficient (IC) [38], which measures the Pearson correlation between predictions and labels, and Rank Information Coefficient (RankIC) [39], which computes the Spearman rank correlation. These metrics provide insights into the model's ability to generate accurate stock rankings. For portfolio-based evaluation, we use cumulative return to measure investment profitability. We simulate stock trading using a 'top30-drop30' strategy under two scenarios: with and without transaction cost. The strategy retains the top 30 stocks with the highest predicted return ratios, while any stock that falls out of the top 30 is dropped, regardless of its previous ranking. For the cost-inclusive scenario, a transaction cost of 0.1% per trade is applied to both entry (buy) and exit (sell) transactions. This dual evaluation helps assess both the theoretical potential and practical viability of forecasting models in real trading environments.

5.4 Performance Comparison (RQ1)

To answer RQ1, we conduct a thorough comparison of key metrics for backbones trained on both original and augmented data. InterDiff consistently enhances cumulative returns across all models and datasets. For CSI300 (Fig. 3a), improvements from synthetic data range from 4.46% to 13.66% without transaction cost. When incorporating a 0.1% per-trade cost, improvements persist but vary by model: the Transformer retains nearly all gains (13.87%), while GRU's improvement drops sharply to 0.57%, reflecting sensitivity to turnover. MLP and SFM exhibit moderate erosion, highlighting model-specific cost tolerance. For CSI800 (Fig. 3b), improvements are far more pronounced, with cost-free gains spanning 50.34% to 76.48%. Transaction costs reduce returns but preserve significant margins. These improvements underscore InterDiff's capability to generate correlation-aware synthetic financial time series that enhance model robustness and profitability across diverse market conditions.

Table 2a and Table 2b show that ranking metrics such as IC and RankIC also improve universally with the augmented data. The sharper increase in performance for CSI800 (40.15–49.60% for IC and 39.8–68.91% for RankIC) underscores the ability of InterDiff to adapt to markets with more noise and variation. This suggests that InterDiff not only improves predictive accuracy but also enhances the model's ability to handle the complexities of broader, more volatile markets. What sets InterDiff apart from DiffsFormer [7] is its ability to capture dynamic inter-stock correlations, making it highly scalable. By incorporating evolving relationships between stocks, InterDiff amplifies predictive signals in

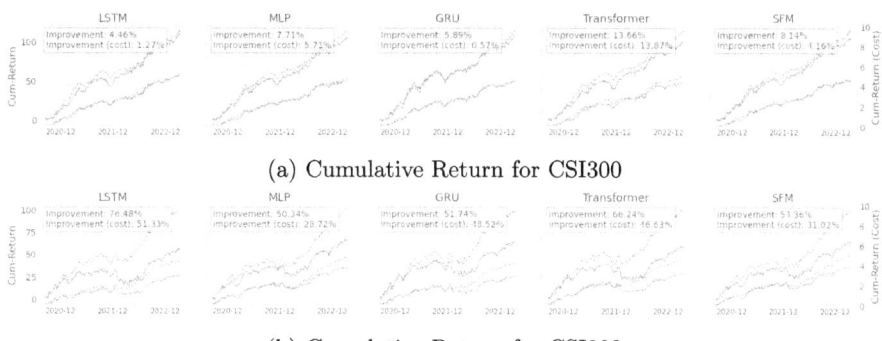

(a) Cumulative Return for CSI300

(b) Cumulative Return for CSI800

Fig. 3. Cumulative returns (in %) for CSI300 and CSI800. Purple lines exclude a 0.1% transaction cost; dashed lines represent models trained on InterDiff-augmented data. Solid lines denote original data. (Color figure online)

Table 2. Performance Comparison of Different Backbones on CSI300 and CSI800 with Original and Augmented Data

Methods	CSI300					
	IC			RankIC		
	original	augmentation	↑	original	augmentation	↑
MLP	0.0512±0.0005	**0.0535±0.0008**	4.49%	0.0458±0.0011	**0.0464±0.0005**	1.31%
LSTM	0.0496±0.0012	**0.0519±0.0011**	4.64%	0.0365±0.0012	**0.0389±0.0021**	6.58%
GRU	0.0480±0.0003	**0.0502±0.0006**	4.58%	0.0334±0.0001	**0.0351±0.0005**	5.09%
SFM	0.0511±0.0005	**0.0535±0.0008**	4.70%	0.0455±0.0009	**0.0458±0.0011**	0.66%
Transformer	0.0530±0.0008	**0.0536±0.0008**	1.13%	0.0451±0.0010	**0.0454±0.0006**	0.67%

(a) Performance comparison on CSI300. The better results are indicated in boldface.

Methods	CSI800					
	IC			RankIC		
	original	augmentation	↑	original	augmentation	↑
MLP	0.0269±0.0005	**0.0377±0.0003**	40.15%	0.0334±0.0007	**0.0467±0.0005**	39.80%
LSTM	0.0241±0.0008	**0.0348±0.0008**	44.4%	0.0256±0.0013	**0.0409±0.0012**	59.77%
GRU	0.0231±0.0006	**0.0330±0.0014**	42.86%	0.0231±0.0009	**0.0363±0.0017**	57.14%
SFM	0.0270±0.0008	**0.0379±0.0025**	40.37%	0.0331±0.0011	**0.0471±0.0029**	42.30%
Transformer	0.0250±0.0005	**0.0374±0.0007**	49.60%	0.0267±0.0007	**0.0451±0.0012**	68.91%

(b) Performance comparison on CSI800. The better results are indicated in boldface.

markets with greater volatility and complexity, thereby offering a substantial advantage over traditional methods that rely on static assumptions and data.

5.5 Ablation Study (RQ2)

To answer RQ2, we focus on the impact of guidance strength and the choice of guidance variable on the fidelity and diversity of synthetic data generated by InterDiff. Fidelity refers to how closely the synthetic data mirrors real data, while diversity refers to the model's ability to generalize by introducing variation in the synthetic data. To evaluate fidelity, we use the Fréchet Inception Distance (FID), a metric commonly used to assess the similarity between distributions of real and generated data. Diversity, on the other hand, is assessed through model performance in terms of Information Coefficient (IC), following [7].

As shown in Fig. 4, we observe that as the guidance strength increases, the FID decreases, indicating that the synthetic data becomes more faithful to the original data. Specifically, InterDiff is able to achieve an FID as low as 0.5004, which suggests a high degree of fidelity in the generated data. This finding highlights the effectiveness of the correlation guidance mechanism employed by InterDiff. Furthermore, Fig. 4 reveals a fidelity-diversity tradeoff: Beyond a certain point ($\omega_{\text{free}} > 2$), the performance starts to degrade. This may occurs due to over-specialization, where the model becomes too focused on specific patterns and fails to capture the broader, more diverse dynamics of the market. This highlights the importance of finding the right balance between fidelity and diversity to ensure that the synthetic data is both accurate and generalizable.

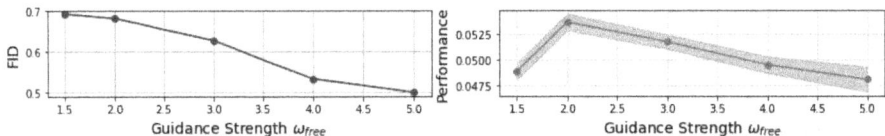

Fig. 4. Synthetic data quality (FID) and model performance (IC).

We compare InterDiff with two variants of DiffsFormer [7] guided by return labels (DiffsFormer-R) and another guided by static industry classifications (DiffsFormer-I), as well as Quant GAN [18]. As shown in Fig. 5, InterDiff achieves improvements of 4.30% and 5.42% in IC over DiffsFormer-R and DiffsFormer-I respectively, showing the effectiveness of InterDiff's correlation guidance mechanism for generating synthetic data that enhances predictive performance. Quant GAN degrades IC performance compared to training on original data, reflecting the instability in financial applications. This instability aligns with our rationale for adopting diffusion models in InterDiff.

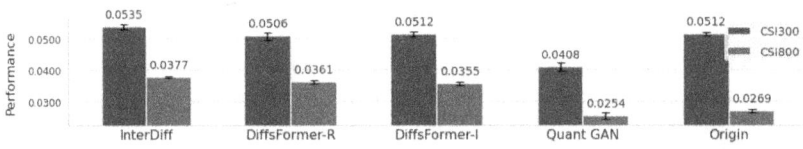

Fig. 5. Comparison of InterDiff with DiffsFormer variants and Quant GAN.

5.6 Visualization (RQ3)

To analyze the learned inter-stock correlations, we visualize attention maps from the inter-stock aggregation transformer in Fig. 6. The figure depicts attention scores across three trading dates for two target stocks (SH601857 and SH601398) and 100 randomly sampled stocks. The red box shows regions where attention weights weaken over time, signaling shifting trend patterns, while the green box marks persistent trends with consistently high attention. These observations confirm that the intra-stock aggregation module effectively captures temporal relationships within individual stocks. Notably, in the blue box, SH601857 exhibits sparse correlations, whereas SH601398 shows strong dependencies with multiple stocks, validating Inter-stock aggregation module's ability to dynamically capture asymmetric and evolving market relationships.

To evaluate InterDiff's ability to maintain inter-stock correlations, we compare real and synthetic data from the CSI300 on a randomly selected date (December 30, 2022). Figure 7 (top row) shows pairwise correlation heatmaps, where denoising progressively removes noise while retaining correlation structures. The histogram (bottom-left) confirms synthetic data's correlation distribution increasingly aligns with real data during denoising. The t-SNE plots (bottom-right) visualize overall data distribution alignment by showing how synthetic samples gradually converge to real data manifolds while maintaining controlled variability, demonstrating InterDiff's capacity to generate realistic yet diverse sequences that generalize to out-of-sample scenarios.

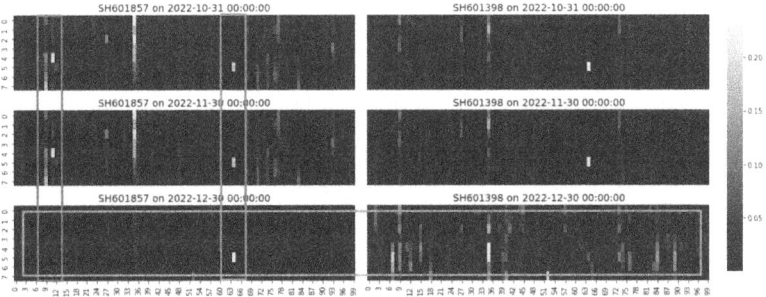

Fig. 6. Attention Map for target stocks SH601857 (left) and SH601398 (right) across three dates, with source stocks (x-axis) and timesteps (y-axis). (Color figure online)

5.7 Discussion

To examine how InterDiff helps mitigate overfitting caused by data scarcity, we plot the training loss over time in Fig. 8. The three subplots represent training loss curves for models trained on (1) original data, (2) data augmented with random noise, and (3) data augmented by InterDiff. Random noise addition is a simple augmentation method used to improve model robustness.

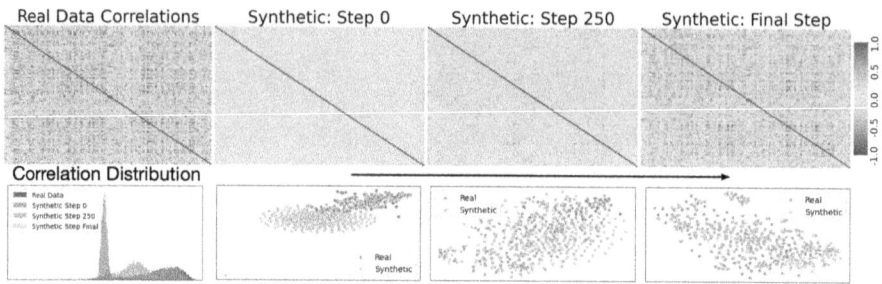

Fig. 7. Synthetic vs. real data distributions visualized via t-SNE, pair-wise correlation heatmaps, and histograms across denoising steps (0–500).

During the 2020 stock market crash[3] triggered by the COVID-19 pandemic, stock forecasting loss was notably low. We attribute this to the market's temporary simplification, where price movements were dominated by a few strong factors, as highlighted by the red dots in Fig. 8. However, a model that overfits to this period may struggle to generalize in later years when market patterns become more complex. Simply removing these data points is not an ideal solution, as it would further exacerbate data scarcity. As shown in Fig. 8, models trained on InterDiff-augmented data exhibit smoother and more stable loss curves compared to those trained with random noise augmentation. This suggests that InterDiff effectively reduces overfitting while preserving essential market patterns, leading to a more generalizable forecasting model.

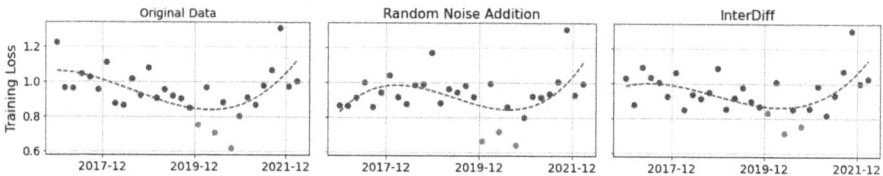

Fig. 8. Training loss for original, noise-augmented, and InterDiff-augmented data. (Color figure online)

6 Conclusion

This paper introduces InterDiff, a diffusion-based framework that synthesizes financial time series by dynamically modeling intra- and inter-stock relationships through hierarchical transformers. By encoding these correlations into a guidance vector and leveraging classifier-free guidance during diffusion, InterDiff generates synthetic data that preserves realistic market dynamics while

---

[3] https://en.wikipedia.org/wiki/2020_stock_market_crash

introducing controlled variability. Empirical evaluations on CSI300 and CSI800 datasets demonstrate that InterDiff-augmented data consistently improves forecasting performance across diverse backbone models. Ablation studies confirm the effectiveness of InterDiff's correlation guidance mechanism, demonstrating its ability to balance fidelity and diversity in synthetic financial time series data, while visualizations validate its capacity to capture evolving market correlations. InterDiff mitigates overfitting, as evidenced by smoother training loss curves compared to baseline augmentation methods. These results highlight the importance of dynamic correlation modeling in financial data augmentation, offering a robust solution to enhance stock prediction models in real-world scenarios.

Acknowledgments. This research was supported in part by the Department of Statistics and New Asia College at The Chinese University of Hong Kong, by Super Quantum Capital Management, and by the Young Scientists Fund of the National Natural Science Foundation of China (Grant number 72301125). The research was carried out during Hou-Wan Long's internship at Super Quantum Capital Management.

References

1. Nugroho, F.X., Satriyo, D., Adji, T.B., Fauziati, S.: Decision support system for stock trading using multiple indicators decision tree. In: 2014 The 1st International Conference on Information Technology, Computer, and Electrical Engineering, pp. 291–296. IEEE (2014)
2. Kamble, R.A.: Short and long term stock trend prediction using decision tree. In: 2017 International Conference on Intelligent Computing and Control Systems (ICICCS), pp. 1371–1375. IEEE (2017)
3. Xie, B., Passonneau, R., Wu, L., Creamer, G.G.: Semantic frames to predict stock price movement. In: Proceedings of the 51st Annual Meeting of the Association for Computational Linguistics, pp. 873–883 (2013)
4. Li, Q., Jiang, L.L., Li, P., Chen, H.: Tensor-based learning for predicting stock movements. In: Proceedings of the AAAI Conference on Artificial Intelligence, vol. 29, no. 1 (2015)
5. Zhang, L., Aggarwal, C., Qi, G.-J.: Stock price prediction via discovering multi-frequency trading patterns. In: Proceedings of the 23rd ACM SIGKDD International Conference on Knowledge Discovery and Data Mining, pp. 2141–2149 (2017). Association for Computing Machinery
6. Cetingoz, A.R., Lehalle, C.-A.: Synthetic Data for Portfolios: A Throw of the Dice Will Never Abolish Chance. arXiv preprint (2025)
7. Gao, Y., et al.: DiffsFormer: A diffusion transformer on stock factor augmentation. arXiv preprint (2024)
8. Shorten, C., Khoshgoftaar, T.M.: A survey on image data augmentation for deep learning. J. Big Data **6**(1), 1–48 (2019). Springer
9. Um, T.T., et al.: Data augmentation of wearable sensor data for Parkinson's disease monitoring using convolutional neural networks. In: Proceedings of the 19th ACM International Conference on Multimodal Interaction, pp. 216–220 (2017)
10. Guennec, L.A., Malinowski, S., Tavenard, R.: Data augmentation for time series classification using convolutional neural networks. In: ECML/PKDD Workshop on Advanced Analytics and Learning on Temporal Data (2016)

11. Yang, W., Yuan, J., Wang, X.: SFCC: data augmentation with stratified fourier coefficients combination for time series classification. Neural Process. Lett. **55**(2), 1833–1846 (2023). Springer
12. Li, Y., Lu, X., Wang, Y., Dou, D.: Generative time series forecasting with diffusion, denoise, and disentanglement. Adv. Neural Inf. Process. Syst. **35**, 23009–23022 (2022)
13. Gao, Z., Liu, H., Li, L.: Data Augmentation for Time-Series Classification: An Extensive Empirical Study and Comprehensive Survey. arXiv preprint (2023)
14. Takahashi, S., Chen, Y., Tanaka-Ishii, K.: Modeling financial time-series with generative adversarial networks. Phys. A: Stat. Mech. Appl. **527**, 121261 (2019). Elsevier
15. Wen, Q., et al.: Time Series Data Augmentation for Deep Learning: A Survey. arXiv preprint arXiv:2002.12478 (2020)
16. Ho, J., et al.: Cascaded diffusion models for high fidelity image generation. J. Mach. Learn. Res. **23**(47), 1–33 (2022)
17. Yoon, J., Jarrett, D., Van der Schaar, M.: Time-series generative adversarial networks. Adv. Neural Inf. Process. Syst. **32** (2019)
18. Wiese, M., Knobloch, R., Korn, R., Kretschmer, P.: Quant GANs: deep generation of financial time series. Quant. Finance **20**(9), 1419–1440 (2020). Taylor & Francis
19. Lee, T.E.K.M., Kuah, Y.L., Leo, K.-H., Sanei, S., Chew, E., Zhao, L.: Surrogate rehabilitative time series data for image-based deep learning. In: 2019 27th European Signal Processing Conference (EUSIPCO), pp. 1–5. IEEE (2019)
20. Kollovieh, M., et al.: Predict, refine, synthesize: self-guiding diffusion models for probabilistic time series forecasting. Adv. Neural Inf. Process. Syst. **36** (2024)
21. Desai, A., Freeman, C., Wang, Z., Beaver, I.: TimeVAE: A Variational Auto-Encoder for Multivariate Time Series Generation. arXiv preprint (2021)
22. Ho, J., Jain, A., Abbeel, P.: Denoising diffusion probabilistic models. Adv. Neural Inf. Process. Syst. **33**, 6840–6851 (2020)
23. Huynh, T.T., et al.: Efficient integration of multi-order dynamics and internal dynamics in stock movement prediction. In: Proceedings of the Sixteenth ACM International Conference on Web Search and Data Mining, pp. 850–858 (2023)
24. Wang, H., Li, S., Wang, T., Zheng, J.: Hierarchical adaptive temporal-relational modeling for stock trend prediction. In: IJCAI, pp. 3691–3698 (2021)
25. Liu, J., et al.: Transformer-based capsule network for stock movement prediction. In: Proceedings of the First Workshop on Financial Technology and Natural Language Processing, pp. 66–73 (2019)
26. Ding, Q., Wu, S., Sun, H., Guo, J., Guo, J.: Hierarchical multi-scale gaussian transformer for stock movement prediction. In: IJCAI, pp. 4640–4646 (2020)
27. Yoo, Jaemin., Soun, Y., Park, Y., Kang, U.: Accurate multivariate stock movement prediction via data-axis transformer with multi-level contexts. In: Proceedings of the 27th ACM SIGKDD Conference on Knowledge Discovery & Data Mining, pp. 2037–2045 (2021)
28. Feng, F., et al.: Temporal relational ranking for stock prediction. ACM Trans. Inf. Syst. (TOIS) **37**(2), 1–30 (2019). ACM New York, NY, USA
29. Li, T., Liu, Z., Shen, Y., Wang, X., Chen, H., Huang, S.: MASTER: market-guided stock transformer for stock price forecasting. In: Proceedings of the AAAI Conference on Artificial Intelligence, vol. 38, no. 1, pp. 162–170 (2024)
30. Brophy, E., Wang, Z., She, Q., Ward, T.: Generative adversarial networks in time series: a systematic literature review. ACM Comput. Surv. **55**(10), 1–31 (2023). ACM New York, NY

31. Nichol, A., et al.: Glide: Towards Photorealistic Image Generation and Editing with Text-Guided Diffusion Models. arXiv preprint (2021)
32. Kendall, A., Gal, Y., Cipolla, R.: Multi-task learning using uncertainty to weigh losses for scene geometry and semantics. In: Proceedings of the IEEE Conference on Computer Vision and Pattern Recognition, (pp. 7482–7491) (2018)
33. Xu, W., et al.: HIST: A graph-based framework for stock trend forecasting via mining concept-oriented shared information. arXiv preprint (2021)
34. Long, Q., et al.: Practical synthetic human trajectories generation based on variational point processes. In: Proceedings of the 29th ACM SIGKDD Conference on Knowledge Discovery and Data Mining, pp. 4561–4571 (2023)
35. Vaswani, A.: Attention is all you need. Advances in Neural Information Processing Systems (2017)
36. Hochreiter, S.: Long Short-term Memory. MIT Press, Neural Computation (1997)
37. Chung, J., Gulcehre, C., Cho, K., Bengio, Y.: Empirical evaluation of gated recurrent neural networks on sequence modeling. arXiv preprint (2014)
38. Lin, H., Zhou, D., Liu, W., Bian, J.: Learning multiple stock trading patterns with temporal routing adaptor and optimal transport. In: Proceedings of the 27th ACM SIGKDD Conference on Knowledge Discovery & Data Mining, pp. 1017–1026 (2021). Association for Computing Machinery
39. Li, Z., Yang, D., Zhao, L., Bian, J., Qin, T., Liu, T.-Y.: Individualized indicator for all: stock-wise technical indicator optimization with stock embedding. In: Proceedings of the 25th ACM SIGKDD International Conference on Knowledge Discovery & Data Mining, pp. 894–902. Association for Computing Machinery (2019)

Evaluating Transfer Learning Methods on Real-World Data Streams: A Case Study in Financial Fraud Detection

Ricardo Ribeiro Pereira[1,2(✉)], Jacopo Bono[1], Hugo Ferreira[1], Pedro Ribeiro[2], Carlos Soares[2], and Pedro Bizarro[1]

[1] Feedzai, Coimbra, Portugal
ricardo.ribeiro@feedzai.com
[2] University of Porto, Porto, Portugal

Abstract. When the available data for a target domain is limited, transfer learning (TL) methods leverage related data-rich source domains to train and evaluate models, before deploying them on the target domain. However, most TL methods assume fixed levels of labeled and unlabeled target data, which contrasts with real-world scenarios where both data and labels arrive progressively over time. As a result, evaluations based on these static assumptions may not reflect how methods perform in practice. To support a more realistic assessment of TL methods in dynamic settings, we propose an evaluation framework that (1) simulates varying data availability over time, (2) creates multiple domains via resampling of a given dataset and (3) introduces inter-domain variability through controlled transformations, e.g., including time-dependent covariate and concept shifts. These capabilities enable the systematic simulation of a large number of variants of the experiments, providing deeper insights into how algorithms may behave when deployed. We demonstrate the usefulness of the proposed framework by performing a case study on a proprietary real-world suite of card payment datasets. To support reproducibility, we also apply the framework on the publicly available Bank Account Fraud (BAF) dataset. By providing a methodology for evaluating TL methods over time and in different data availability conditions, our framework supports a better understanding of model behavior in real-world environments, which enables more informed decisions when deploying models in new domains.

Keywords: Evaluation Framework · Transfer Learning · Fraud Detection

1 Introduction

Machine learning (ML) models often require large volumes of labeled data to achieve strong predictive performance. However, in many real-world applications, obtaining sufficient labeled data can be difficult and costly. Transfer learning

(TL) addresses this challenge by leveraging knowledge from one or more source domains to improve performance on a target domain with limited data. Most TL methods and evaluation protocols assume fixed conditions regarding the availability of labeled and unlabeled data, such as having a large labeled source dataset and only unlabeled target data. However, in many real-world industry settings, these conditions are not permanent, as data from the various domains is progressively collected and labeled over time.

One example of this setting is financial fraud detection. This task involves monitoring streams of financial transactions from different financial institutions, *domains* in the TL terminology, and classifying each transaction as fraudulent or legitimate. New institutions may initially lack historical data, but typically the volume of financial transactions quickly increases over time. However, labeling a transaction as fraudulent often depends on customer complaints and/or manual reviews by analysts, leading to a delay between the moment a transaction is recorded and when it is labeled. This delay can range from several days to a few months, affecting the training and evaluation of ML models. While TL can in principle help mitigate the issues of having insufficient data at the onset, and insufficient labeled data at a later stage, the evolving nature of the data availability itself presents an additional challenge. TL methods are designed for fixed conditions and their performance is expected to change significantly when those conditions are violated. However, they are typically evaluated under those fixed (and favorable) conditions, which would lead to unrealistic expectations concerning their performance in real world settings. The problem therefore remains on how to evaluate TL methods in a way that reflects these dynamic data constraints, such as those encountered in fraud detection.

To address this challenge, we propose an evaluation framework that captures the dynamic nature of data streams in real-world applications. Our framework provides three key capabilities: (1) creating multiple domains from a given dataset through resampling, enabling systematic TL evaluation even when few datasets are available; (2) applying transformations to the data, hence reproducing realistic data shifts over time and across domains, while also introducing controlled variability across experiments; and (3) simulating the gradual arrival of data and labels over time, mimicking the evolving nature of industry environments. These combined features enable our framework to systematically generate a large number of experiments, making it possible to assess TL methods across a wide range of realistic scenarios.

We perform a case study using our framework on a suite of proprietary real-world datasets containing payment events from multiple financial institutions. This case study demonstrates how insights derived from our evaluation framework can inform practical decisions, such as model selection, deployment timing, and the prioritization of data collection efforts. Given the confidential nature of the case study dataset, we perform a similar analysis on the publicly available Bank Account Fraud (BAF) dataset [13], which consists of synthetic examples of account opening applications. The source code that implements the evaluation framework, along with the configurations used for the experiments on the public dataset, are available at https://github.com/feedzai/tred.

The remainder of this paper is structured as follows: Sect. 2 formalizes our problem setting and compares it with traditional TL setups studied in academia; Sect. 3 introduces the design of our evaluation framework and its key components; Sect. 4 describes how we apply the framework in practice, detailing the datasets, experimental setup, and TL methods evaluated; Sect. 5 presents the results and their practical implications in an industry setting; and Sect. 6 summarizes our contributions and highlights the broader impact of our work.

2 Background and Related Work

In this section, we formalize the problem setting and introduce the notation used throughout the paper (Sect. 2.1). We then review traditional TL paradigms, highlighting their assumptions and differences from our use case (Sect. 2.2). Finally, we discuss common evaluation strategies for TL and motivate the need for a new framework that better captures real-world data dynamics (Sect. 2.3).

2.1 Problem Definition

We consider the machine learning setting where data is collected from multiple domains over time, with labels becoming available after a delay. This is a common scenario in many real-world applications, such as fraud detection, where instances (e.g., transactions) are initially unlabeled and only later confirmed as fraudulent or legitimate. To formalize this problem, we assume there are m source domains $\mathcal{D}_{S_1}, \ldots, \mathcal{D}_{S_m}$ and a target domain $\mathcal{D}_T$. Each domain $\mathcal{D}_d$ (including the target) is associated with a dataset $D_d = \{(x_i, y_i, t_i^x, t_i^y) \mid i = 1, \ldots, n_d\}$, where $x_i \in \mathcal{X}_d$ is a feature vector, $y_i \in \mathcal{Y}_d$ is the label, t_i^x is the timestamp when x_i is collected, and $t_i^y \geq t_i^x$ is the timestamp when y_i becomes available.[1] At any given time t, D_d can be decomposed into a labeled dataset $D_d^L(t) = \{(x_i, y_i) \mid t_i^y \leq t\}$ which consists of all instances that have already received their labels by time t, and an unlabeled dataset $D_d^U(t) = \{x_i \mid t_i^x \leq t < t_i^y\}$ which consists of instances that have been observed but their labels are still unavailable at time t.

Eventually, at some time t_a, the target domain $\mathcal{D}_T$ is introduced, initially without any data ($D_T^L(t_a) = D_T^U(t_a) = \emptyset$), and target domain data and labels begin to be collected from that point on. Our goal is to leverage $D_{S_1}, \ldots, D_{S_m}$ and D_T to learn a predictive function $f_T : \mathcal{X}_T \to \mathcal{Y}_T$ that approximates $P_T(Y|X)$. Over time, as more data and labels become available, f_T can be updated to improve its approximation of $P_T(y \mid x)$.

2.2 Transfer Learning Paradigms

Different TL paradigms have been explored, each making different assumptions about the datasets used to train the ML models. All these paradigms assume

---

[1] To simplify notation, we will sometimes use the letter i to index the entries of the dataset without explicitly stating $i = 1, \ldots, n_d$.

that a large volume of labeled data is available from the source domains. Their main difference relates to the available target domain data at training time.

In Domain Generalization (**DG**) [24,28], the goal is to use the source domain datasets to learn a predictive function f that generalizes to the target domain without access to any data from $\mathcal{D}_T$. As such, at training time, $D_T^L = D_T^U = \emptyset$. In Unsupervised Domain Adaptation (**UDA**) [26], in addition to the source domain datasets, there is an unlabeled target domain dataset that can be used to adapt the predictive function f_T to the target domain $\mathcal{D}_T$. This means that, at training time, $|D_T^U| > 0$ while $D_T^L = \emptyset$. In Supervised Domain Adaptation (**SDA**) [25], in addition to the source domain datasets, there is both a large unlabeled dataset and a small labeled dataset from the target domain, which are used to adapt the predictive function f_T to the target domain $\mathcal{D}_T$. As such, at training time, $|D_T^U| \gg |D_T^L| > 0$. In Multi-Domain Learning (**MDL**) [27], the goal is to use datasets from multiple domains to learn a single predictive function f that performs well across all observed domains simultaneously. Here, at training time, labeled data is available from all domains, i.e., $\forall d, |D_d^L| \gg 0$.

Each of these paradigms operates under specific assumptions about data availability, but none of them account for the progressive collection of data and possible label delay. In contrast, our problem setting requires a framework that can systematically model the evolving availability of data and labels over time.

2.3 Evaluation of TL Methods

Various datasets have been used to evaluate TL methods, under the different paradigms discussed in the previous section. Most TL benchmarks focus on image classification, including datasets such as Office-31 [21], Office-Caltech10 [8], Office-Home [23], DomainNet [19], and PACS [17]. Beyond computer vision, the Amazon Reviews dataset [1] is often used for sentiment analysis.

Another common strategy is to evaluate TL methods across different datasets of the same task. Examples include: digit classification (USPS [12], MNIST [16], SVHN [18]); large-scale image recognition (ImageNet [5], Caltech [9], CiFAR [15]); and semantic segmentation (CityScapes [4], GTA5 [20]).

Additionally, some tools have been developed to facilitate the evaluation of TL methods in specific fields. One example is DomainATM [10], an open-source MATLAB package for domain adaptation in medical data analysis. It provides dataset management functionalities, visualization tools, and a collection of domain adaptation methods with built-in evaluation capabilities.

However, both DomainATM and traditional TL benchmarks assume a static evaluation setting, where data availability conditions remain fixed. This assumption overlooks the temporal dynamics present in real-world applications, such as fraud detection, where data and labels arrive progressively over time. As a result, existing evaluation strategies are insufficient for assessing TL methods in dynamic environments. Addressing this gap requires a framework that systematically models the evolving availability of data and labels, enabling more realistic evaluations that reflect real-world deployment scenarios.

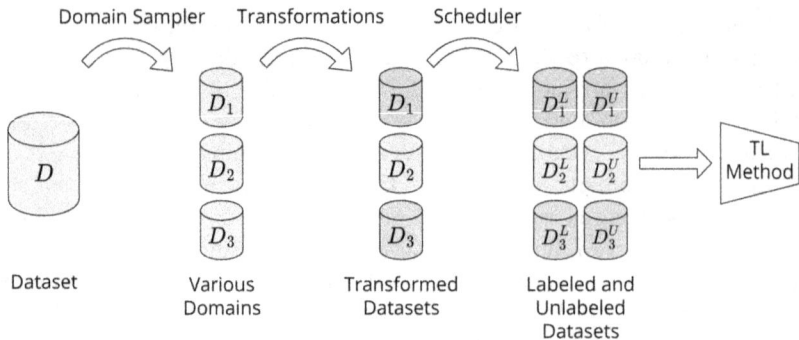

Fig. 1. The evaluation framework is composed of three sequential components: domain sampler, transformations, and scheduler. The number of domains depicted in the diagram is just an example.

3 Method

Our evaluation framework consists of three components (Fig. 1). First, the *domain sampler* builds multiple domains from a single dataset, enabling systematic TL evaluation even when few datasets are available. Next, the *transformations* introduce controlled variations to each domain, to reproduce real-world data shifts over time and across domains. Finally, the *scheduler* simulates the progressive arrival of data and labels, enabling the evaluation of TL methods under diverse data availability conditions. We describe each component with more detail in the following subsections.

3.1 Domain Sampler

The *domain sampler* creates domains from a dataset by randomly selecting anchor instances, followed by resampling the events according to the distance to these anchors, as illustrated in Fig. 2.

More formally, the *domain sampler* is a stochastic process that receives a dataset $D = \{(x_i, y_i, t_i^x, t_i^y)\}$, a distance function δ, a real number λ, and a positive integer k, and outputs a set of datasets $\{D_1, \ldots, D_k\}$ where $D_d \subseteq D$ for all $d \in \{1, \ldots, k\}$. To extract each D_d, the *domain sampler* first selects an instance x_{anchor}. Then, each instance x_i is assigned a probability of being included in this domain, which decreases exponentially with its distance to x_{anchor},

$$P(x_i | x_{\text{anchor}}) = e^{-\lambda \delta(x_i, x_{\text{anchor}})}.$$

The decay rate of the exponential is controlled by the scaling factor λ, which regulates the expected domain size. Finally, instances are sampled randomly according to their respective probability.

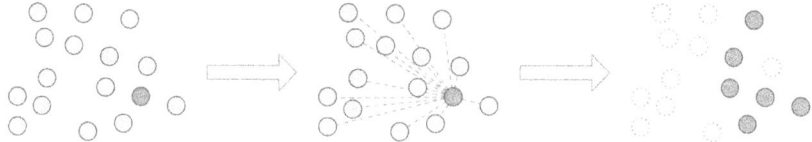

Fig. 2. Toy example of sampling a domain from dataset. First, an anchor instance is selected (purple point). Then, the distances to all other instances are computed. Lastly, the instances are sampled with probability decreasing as distance increases.

3.2 Transformations

The *transformations* apply controlled modifications to the datasets. These transformations are defined by the user to better suit their setting. For example, transformations that may make sense in the image domain would not be suitable for tabular data and vice-versa. Each *transformation* should ideally be parameterized differently for each domain, provoking some level of domain shift. Furthermore, they can be designed to depend on the timestamp of the instance, which effectively simulates data drift over time or seasonalities.

Each *transformation* can be described as a function $\Phi_\theta : (x, y, t^x, t^y) \mapsto (x', y', t'^x, t'^y)$, parameterized by θ. This general formulation allows the instantiation of various types of changes, for example:

- covariate shift (change in $P(X)$): $x' = \phi(x; \theta)$;
- concept shift (change in $P(Y|X)$): $y' = \phi(x, y; \theta)$;
- data drift (change in $P(X)$ over time): $x' = \phi(x, t^x; \theta)$.

If the transformations are parameterized differently for each experiment, the results will express a distribution of each methods' performance on related settings, increasing the robustness of the results. We describe a set of *transformations* for tabular data in detail in Sect. 4.3 (as well as making them available with our code) and provide a toy example in Fig. 3.

3.3 Scheduler

The *scheduler* orchestrates two processes: (1) the progressive arrival of instances and labels over time and (2) the performance estimation over time.

The first process (progressive data arrival) is achieved by discretizing the time range of the target dataset in contiguous periods. At each step, the test period advances, while the training set expands to include all data up to that point. More formally, the *scheduler* receives datasets $D_{S_1}, \ldots, D_{S_m}, D_T$ and a sequence of user-defined timestamps $t_1, \ldots, t_l$ s.t. $\min(t_i^x) \leq t_1 < \ldots < t_l \leq \max(t_i^x)$ for $t_i^x \in D_T$. At each time step t_a for $a = 1, \ldots, l-1$, it decomposes all source and target domain datasets D_d into $D_d^L(t_a)$ and $D_d^U(t_a)$, as described in Sect. 2.1.

The second process (performance estimation) is achieved by leveraging the data splits that result from the first process to train the TL methods under study and evaluate them on the target domain instances s.t. $t_a \leq t_i^x < t_{a+1}$.[2]

---

[2] Notice that the label delay is ignored for the purpose of evaluating the methods.

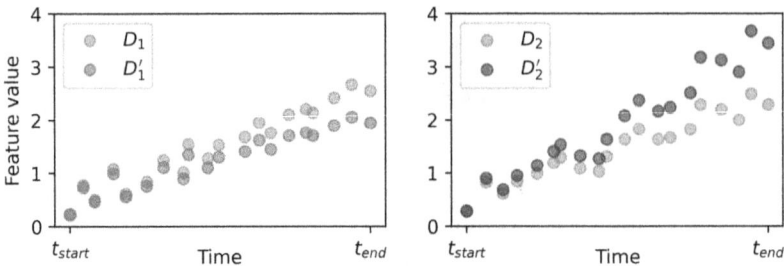

Fig. 3. Toy example showing how applying the same transformation with different parameters affects the same feature of datasets from two domains.

Since this process is repeated for each time step t_a, every model is evaluated multiple times throughout the evolving target dataset. This allows for an analysis of performance trends over time, highlighting how different TL methods adapt to increasing data availability. Figure 4 presents an example of this scheduling.

4 Experimental Setup

In the previous section, we introduce the general architecture of the framework, which is designed to be broadly applicable to many real-world scenarios. In this section, we detail how we apply this framework to our specific use case, including a description of the datasets that we use, the methods that we test and other design decisions that are specific to our experimental setup.[3]

4.1 Datasets

In this section, we provide details about the dataset used in our case study, but due to confidentiality constraints, we can only share general metrics. The Acquirers is a real-world proprietary dataset, containing payment events from 4 different financial institutions (*domains*) over a period of 41 weeks ($\approx$ 9 months). Each domain has $\approx$ 5M events, but their fraud rates (relative frequency of the positive class) vary between $\approx 0.01\%$ and $\approx 0.4\%$. Each instance has 58 features (52 numerical and 6 categorical), the event timestamp and the fraud label.

Because the above dataset is confidential, we also perform experiments on the publicly available Bank Account Fraud (BAF) dataset [13]. BAF is a publicly available synthetic bank account fraud dataset.[4] It contains one million examples of account opening applications, some of which are fraudulent, from February through September. Each instance has 28 features (24 numerical and 4 categorical), the time information and the label.

---

[3] Implementation details and code are available at https://github.com/feedzai/tred.
[4] In fact, the authors published 6 different variations of this dataset, but we just use the "Base" variant without device_fraud_count and device_os features.

In both experiments, each numerical feature from each domain is standardized to have 0 mean and 1 standard deviation. Also, each categorical feature is label encoded [2], i.e. each category is mapped to an integer starting from 0, to enable the use of embedding layers. Furthermore, to address class imbalance, we oversample the minority class during training by constructing batches with a fixed 10% positive class ratio. For evaluation, the original proportion is used.

4.2 Domain Sampler

The BAF dataset does not contain any explicit separation of domains. As such, in our experiments, we use the *domain sampler* to the create 4 domains: 3 sources and 1 target. Since the domains are randomly sampled, without loss of generality, we always select the first one to be the target. Given that BAF is a tabular dataset, we define a distance function δ to compare rows containing a set of numerical features $\mathcal{N}$ and a set of categorical features $\mathcal{C}$. For numerical features, we compute the squared difference between their standardized values. For categorical features, we use an indicator function that returns 0 if the values are the same, and 1 otherwise. The distance function is then given by

$$\delta(x_i, x_j) = \sum_{f \in \mathcal{N}} \left(\frac{x_{i,f} - x_{j,f}}{\sigma_f} \right)^2 + \sum_{f \in \mathcal{C}} \mathbb{I}[x_{i,f} \neq x_{j,f}],$$

where $x_{i,f}$ is the value of feature f in the feature vector x_i and σ_f is the standard deviation of feature f computed over the dataset from which samples are drawn.

The Acquirers dataset already contains 4 distinct domains, so we decided not to use the domain sampler. However, a user may decide to apply it even when multiple domains are available, to simulate a wider variety of settings.

4.3 Transformations

We define three types of operations that can be applied to features of tabular datasets:

- ϕ_1 rescales numerical features by a time-dependent factor, with scaling parameter $\alpha \in \mathbb{R}^+$,

$$\phi_1(x_{i,j}, t_i^x; \theta) = x_{i,j} \cdot \alpha^{\tau(t_i^x)}, \text{ where } \theta = (\alpha, \tau). \quad (1)$$

- ϕ_2 computes a weighted average between a numerical feature and a certain anchor value β, with $\beta \in \mathbb{R}$ and a mixing coefficient $\gamma \in [0, 1]$,

$$\phi_2(x_{i,j}, t_i^x; \theta) = (1 - \gamma \cdot \tau(t_i^x)) \cdot x_{i,j} + (\gamma \cdot \tau(t_i^x)) \cdot \beta, \text{ where } \theta = (\beta, \gamma, \tau). \quad (2)$$

- ϕ_3 resamples values of a categorical feature, approximating its relative frequencies to some marginal distribution $P(X_j')$,

$$\phi_3(x_{i,j}, t_i^x; \theta) \sim (1 - \tau(t_i^x)) P(X_j) + \tau(t_i^x) P(X_j'), \text{ where } \theta = (\tau, P(X_j')). \quad (3)$$

Here, τ is a user-defined function that controls the magnitude of the transformation as a function of t_i^x. We use three versions of τ (not in a one-to-one correspondence with the transformations): (1) a constant function equal to 1, simulating fixed changes between domains (e.g., currency changes); (2) a linear function that goes from 0 to 1 over the dataset's time span, simulating gradual drifts (e.g., inflation effects); (3) a sinusoidal function with a configurable period, simulating seasonal patterns (e.g., weekly fluctuations in consumer behavior).

We combine these three types of transformations with the different τ functions to implement various transformations based on domain knowledge relevant to our use case. Each transformation is applied to a subset of features, and we define sensible ranges for the parameters θ to ensure that the resulting transformations are plausible. For each domain in each experiment, we independently sample the transformation parameters from their respective ranges. This approach ensures that the resulting shifts mimic realistic behavior while also introducing controlled variability across experiments, and thus increasing the robustness and generality of our conclusions.

4.4 Scheduler

For each experiment, given a set of source and target datasets with time span $[t_s, t_e)$, we define t_α and t_β as the start times for using source and target domain data respectively in the experiment, and t_γ as the end time of the experiment, such that $t_s \leq t_\alpha < t_\beta < t_\gamma \leq t_e$. The target domain data in the interval $[t_\alpha, t_\beta]$ is ignored to ensure that the first training split contains only source domain data, mimicking real-world deployment scenarios where historical target data is unavailable at launch. We define the time interval between model updates Δ_t, which is also the duration of each test split. Lastly, since neither dataset contains a label timestamp, we define a fixed label delay Δ_l such that $t_i^y = t_i^x + \Delta_l$. Using these parameters, the *scheduler* simulates the progressive arrival of data as described in Sect. 3.3, generating a sequence of timestamps $t_1, \ldots, t_l$ s.t.

$$t_1 = t_\beta, \quad t_{a+1} = t_a + \Delta_t, \text{ for } a = 1, \ldots, l-1$$

where t_l it the largest timestamp satisfying $t_l \leq t_\gamma$.

For the Acquirers dataset, we use the time unit of one week, with timestamps indexed in the range $[0, 41)$, and set $\Delta_t = 2$ and $\Delta_l = 4$. In each experiment, t_α is randomly selected from $\{0, \ldots, 7\}$ to introduce variability while ensuring the framework leverages the entire data range. Then, t_β is set as $t_\alpha + 16$, ensuring 16 weeks of available source domain data before the target appears, and t_γ is set as $t_\alpha + 34$, resulting in 9 contiguous test periods.

For the BAF dataset, we use the time unit of one month with timestamps indexed in the range $[0, 8)$. We set $t_\alpha = 0$, $t_\beta = 3$, $t_\gamma = 8$ and $\Delta_t = \Delta_l = 1$. The resulting schedule for this dataset is depicted in Fig. 4.

4.5 TL Methods

We implemented and tested representative methods from each of the four TL paradigms discussed in Sect. 2.2: Multi-Task Autoencoder (**MTAE**) [7] for DG;

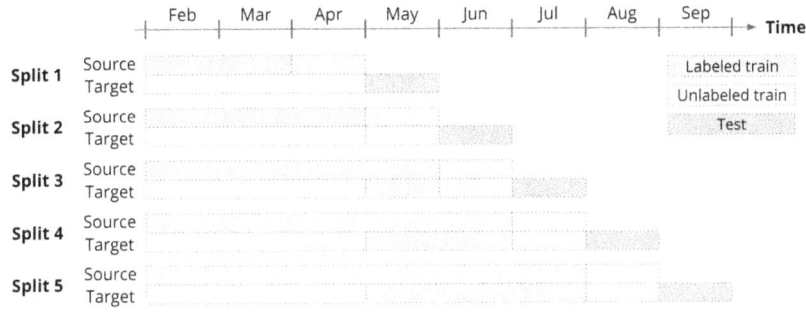

Fig. 4. Schedule of the splits used for the BAF experiments.

Domain Adaptation Neural Networks (**DANN**) [6] for UDA; Minimax Entropy (**MME**) [22] for SDA; and Multinomial Adversarial Networks (**MAN**) [3] for MDL. We selected these well-established methods, which represent a variety of modeling techniques, not to conduct an exhaustive benchmark but to illustrate how our framework enables the comparison of diverse TL algorithms under evolving data availability conditions. Additionally, we tested three MLP baselines, differing only in their training data: **BL-S** is trained only with labeled source domain data; **BL-T** is trained only with labeled target domain data; and **BL-A** is trained using all labeled data available.

We also tested Kernel Mean Matching (**KMM**) [11] to reweight labeled training data for a LightGBM [14] classifier. The training data is obtained by sampling (with replacement) an equal number of labeled instances from each available domain, which means it may or may not include target domain instances, depending on their availability at that point in time. Due to the computational complexity of solving the optimization problem of the KMM method, the size of the training set was tuned to match the training time of the deep learning methods.

4.6 Evaluation

For all deep learning methods, we use the latest 30% of the labeled training data from each domain as a holdout validation set for early stopping. To ensure a consistent stopping criterion, even when labels are scarce, we measure the average predicted performance across all domains, measured as Recall at 1% False Positive Rate (FPR), which is a standard metric in fraud detection tasks.

For each experiment, we compute paired t-tests for each pair of methods at every data split, to assess the statistical significance of the observed performance differences. Given the substantial number of comparisons, we controlled the False Discovery Rate (FDR) at 1% using the Benjamini Hochberg procedure, which reduces the risk of identifying spurious effects.

4.7 Pre-training and Hyperparameter Tuning

Many TL methods use pre-trained state-of-the-art models to initialize the parameters of their deep learning components. In our experiments, we pre-train an MLP-based autoencoder using the first three months of source domain data, using a typical encoder-decoder architecture with reconstruction loss defined per feature type: we use mean squared error for numerical features (after standardization) and cross-entropy loss for categorical features. This self-supervised learning phase enables the networks to learn robust feature representations before applying specific transfer learning methods.

To optimize the autoencoder architecture, we conduct a hyperparameter search over 200 randomly sampled configurations. The search space includes variations in the number and size of hidden layers, the size of the latent space, the learning rate, regularization techniques (dropout, normalization), and the inclusion of skip connections. For method-specific hyperparameters, we primarily followed the values recommended in the respective papers. The details of the search space and best hyperparameters are provided in the code repository.

The encoder block of the best-performing autoencoder, selected based on validation loss, is then used to initialize the feature extractors of the TL methods. For their classifier components, we used a simple architecture with a single hidden layer followed by the output layer.

5 Results

In this section, we first present the results from our case study on the proprietary Acquirers dataset, and then the results on the publicly available BAF dataset. Finally, we discuss the practical implications of these findings and describe how industry practitioners could use them to guide their decision-making process.

5.1 Acquirers Dataset Case Study

We conducted 64 experiments on the Acquirers dataset, following the schedule described in Sect. 4.4. Figure 5 depicts the results of these experiments, showing the evolution of predictive performance over time for various baselines and TL methods. The x-axis represents the time elapsed since the target domain appeared, while the y-axis depicts the recall percentage at 1% FPR, which is a standard evaluation metric for the fraud detection problem.

There is a clear distinction between methods that leverage labeled target domain data and those that do not. As such, we identify three groups of methods:

- MTAE, DANN and BL-S, which do not use any target domain labels to train, maintain relatively stable performance throughout, but are consistently surpassed by the other methods.
- MAN, BL-A and BL-T, despite requiring target labels before their initial deployment, immediately outperform the other methods, and continue to improve as more data becomes available, with an average gain of approximately 4% points of recall per model update.

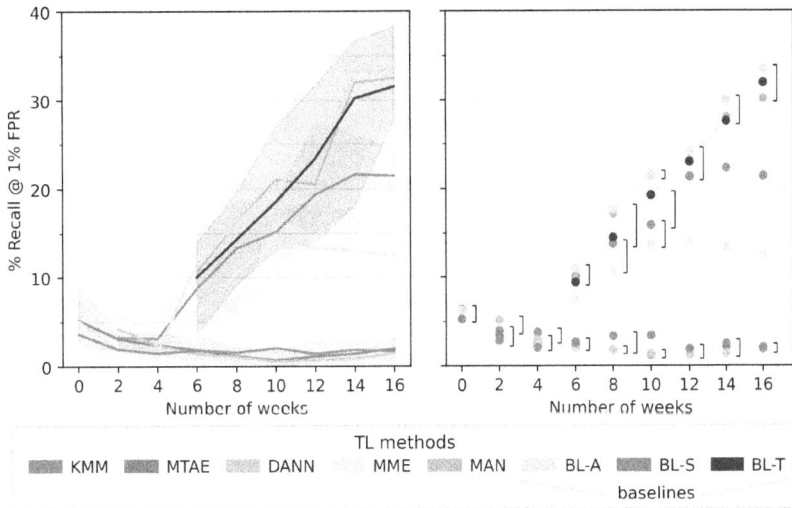

Fig. 5. Predictive performance (recall at 1% FPR) of each method over time on the Acquirers dataset. The left panel shows the median recall per method across experiments (solid lines) and their interquartile ranges (shaded). The right panel presents statistical comparisons at each time step, where each point represents the average recall across experiments, and brackets group methods that are not significantly different, after correcting for multiple comparisons.

– KMM and MME initially follow the trend of the previous group, but plateau earlier. We hypothesize that the sampling we use to run KMM limits the training of LightGBM, while the semi-supervised approach of MME offers diminishing returns as more labels become available.

The statistical tests confirm that, as soon as labeled target domain data becomes available, the methods that leverage it achieve significantly better performance. Furthermore, these tests help to identify the point in time when MME and KMM methods are overtaken by the second group.

5.2 BAF Dataset

We conducted 128 independent experiments on the BAF dataset. In each experiment, we sampled four domains from the dataset, applied domain transformations (described in Sect. 4.3), and followed the schedule depicted in Fig. 4 to train and evaluate the methods. Figure 6 depicts the results of these experiments, in the same format of Fig. 5.

Similar to the previous experiments, the statistical tests allow us to identify three groups of methods.

– MTAE, DANN, BL-A and BL-S show similar levels of recall, maintaining a stable distribution of predictive performance over time. This suggests that there is a limited benefit from the additional target domain data and labels.

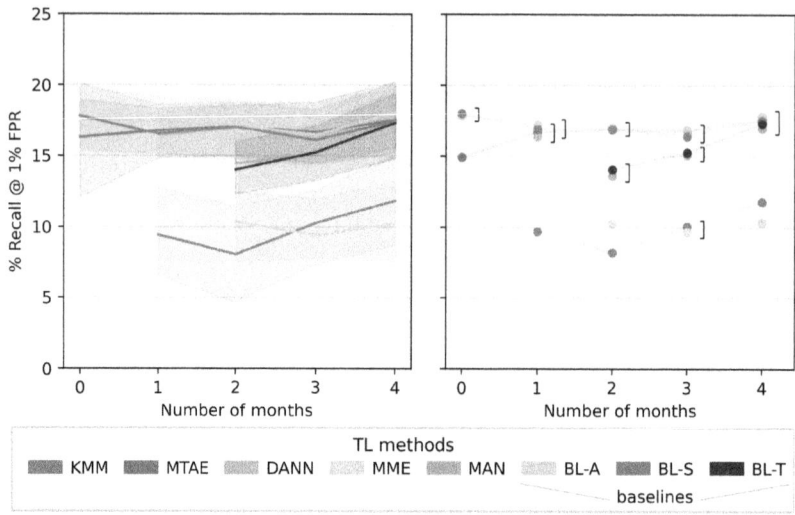

Fig. 6. Predictive performance (recall at 1% FPR) of each method over time on the BAF dataset. The left panel shows the median recall per method across experiments (solid lines) and their interquartile ranges (shaded). The right panel presents statistical comparisons at each time step, where each point represents the average recall across experiments, and brackets group methods that are not significantly different, after correcting for multiple comparisons.

- MAN and BL-T begin to perform significantly worse than the previous group of methods, but they improve steadily over time (gaining on average 2% points of recall per model update) and eventually reaching the same level of performance. This improvement is not surprising, since both methods use exclusively labeled data from the target domain to train their classifiers.
- KMM and MME are consistently surpassed by the other methods. While MME maintains a relatively stable performance throughout, KMM is improving at the same rate as the previous group.

Furthermore, we observe that the performance of methods such as MTAE and BL-S, which do not use any target data during training, is similar to the performance of BL-T, which follows the traditional ML approach of only using in-domain data to train. This suggests that the source and target domains in the BAF dataset are relatively similar, which means that there is great potential for sharing knowledge across domains. Alternatively, we could adapt the transformation ranges to simulate a setting with more differences between domains.

5.3 Practical Implications

Our experimental results highlight how the performance of different TL methods is affected by the evolving data availability conditions. In general, methods

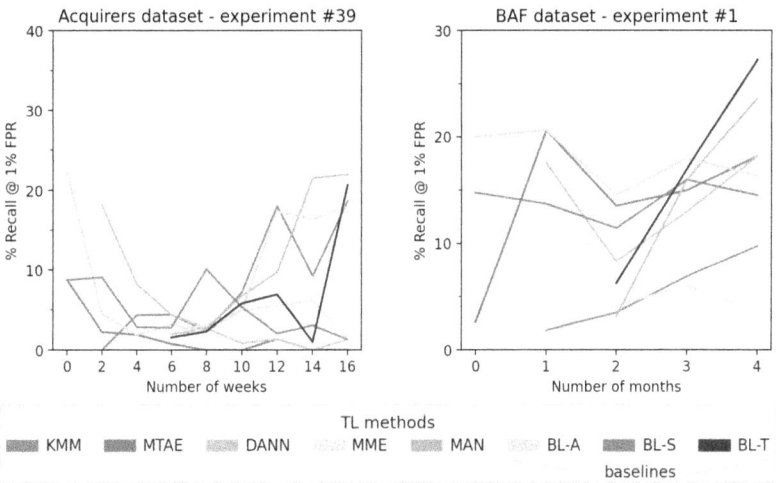

Fig. 7. Predictive performance (recall at 1% FPR) of each method over time. These panels show the results from two specific experiments (one from each dataset) that conflict with the general insights derived from the general analysis.

that do not require target domain labels maintain stable but potentially limited performance, while methods that leverage target labels tend to noticeably improve as more data becomes available. However, the extent and timing of this improvement vary across settings, meaning that both the effectiveness of these methods and the value of target labels depend on the specific characteristics of the dataset. Recognizing these trends is essential for guiding real-world deployment decisions, helping practitioners select methods that align with their specific constraints and assess the cost-benefit of target labeling efforts.

For example, as seen in our Acquirers case study, practitioners may observe a clear performance gap between methods that leverage labeled target data and those that do not. This gap suggests significant domain drift, making it difficult to share knowledge between domains. In such cases, ML practitioners may decide to conduct a thorough exploratory data analysis to detect potential issues in the data collection pipeline. They may also explore data pre-processing techniques, such as feature normalization, to mitigate domain discrepancies. If the performance gap persists, deploying a DG-based solution initially can be a viable approach, but obtaining labeled target domain data should remain a priority to improve model performance.

Additionally, our results from Acquirers show that MDL methods (such as MAN and BL-A), which optimize performance across multiple domains simultaneously, perform comparably to domain-specific solutions. In those cases, practitioners can benefit from these centralized solutions by minimizing the number of models that need to be developed and maintained. Conversely, as seen in the BAF dataset experiments, practitioners may find that models trained exclusively on source domain data achieve performance levels similar to traditional in-domain models. In those scenarios, DG methods can be confidently deployed for new domains without requiring immediate target domain labels, significantly reducing early labeling efforts and accelerating model deployment timelines.

Finally, we highlight the importance of repeating multiple variants of the experiments to ensure robust conclusions. Figure 7 illustrates two specific cases that deviate from the general trends observed in our main analysis. In the left panel, the results show that methods leveraging labeled target domain data, such as MAN and BL-A, only begin to outperform the other methods 12 weeks after the target domain appears, which is twice as long as observed in Sect. 5.1. In the right panel, the results show that MAN and BL-T improve steeply over time, eventually surpassing all other methods, whereas the aggregated results in Sect. 5.2 indicate no significant performance advantage for these methods. These inconsistencies demonstrate the risk of drawing misleading conclusions from isolated experiments, which our evaluation framework helps to mitigate.

Beyond predictive performance, robustness over time is crucial for real-world deployment. Some methods may maintain more stable performance, while others can exhibit a larger variance. In high-risk applications such as fraud detection, consistency may be preferable to occasional peaks in performance. Another important factor when comparing ML methods is computationally efficiency, as highlighted by the KMM method. Evaluating methods in terms of training time or resource usage could provide further insights, and integrating such metrics into the framework is a promising direction for future work. Other practical trade-offs, such as model update complexity or explainability, may also be considered when selecting a TL method for real-world use.

6 Conclusion

In this paper, we introduce an evaluation framework designed to assess transfer learning methods under evolving data availability conditions. Unlike traditional static benchmarks, our framework simulates the progressive arrival of data and labels, allowing for a more realistic and comprehensive evaluation of TL approaches in dynamic settings. Additionally, by generating multiple realistic domain variations from the same dataset and applying controlled transformations, the framework enables systematic testing across diverse and realistic scenarios. We demonstrate the capabilities of our framework through a case study on a proprietary dataset of card payment transactions, and perform an analogous study on the publicly available BAF dataset for reproducibility. Our results illustrate how practitioners can leverage the framework to analyze TL performance trends over time, identify promising methods under varying data availability scenarios, and make informed decisions regarding deployment.

A natural concern with evaluation methodologies is how much the observed results depend on specific design decisions. To address this, we use the framework to systematically conduct a large number of experiments with diverse and realistic variations, and report distributions of performance metrics and statistical significance to highlight trends that are consistent across the different settings.

Nonetheless, we do not claim that our results generalize to all possible real-world conditions. Rather, the framework is designed to support this type of studies: by modifying transformation types, parameter ranges, or scheduling strategies, users can tailor experiments to reflect domain-specific assumptions and assess method performance under conditions relevant to their application. Future work may extend this by systematically analyzing sensitivity to each design component or by exploring generalization across broader use cases.

Overall, our framework improves upon traditional evaluations to address practical industry needs, providing a valuable tool for developing robust and adaptable machine learning solutions in dynamic real-world environments.

Disclosure of Interests. The authors have no competing interests to declare that are relevant to the content of this article.

References

1. Blitzer, J., Dredze, M., Pereira, F.: Biographies, Bollywood, boom-boxes and blenders: domain adaptation for sentiment classification. In: Proceedings of the 45th Annual Meeting of the Association of Computational Linguistics (2007)
2. Borisov, V., Leemann, T., Seßler, K., Haug, J., Pawelczyk, M., Kasneci, G.: Deep neural networks and tabular data: a survey. IEEE Transactions on Neural Networks and Learning Systems (2022)
3. Chen, X., Cardie, C.: Multinomial adversarial networks for multi-domain text classification. In: Proceedings of the 2018 Conference of the North American Chapter of the Association for Computational Linguistics: Human Language Technologies, Volume 1 (Long Papers), pp. 1226–1240 (2018)
4. Cordts, M., et al.: The cityscapes dataset for semantic urban scene understanding. In: Proceedings of the IEEE Conference on Computer Vision and Pattern Recognition, pp. 3213–3223 (2016)
5. Deng, J., Dong, W., Socher, R., Li, L.J., Li, K., Fei-Fei, L.: ImageNet: a large-scale hierarchical image database. In: 2009 IEEE Conference on Computer Vision and Pattern Recognition, pp. 248–255. IEEE (2009)
6. Ganin, Y., et al.: Domain-adversarial training of neural networks. J. Mach. Learn. Res. **17**(59), 1–35 (2016)
7. Ghifary, M., Kleijn, W.B., Zhang, M., Balduzzi, D.: Domain generalization for object recognition with multi-task autoencoders. In: Proceedings of the IEEE International Conference on Computer Vision, pp. 2551–2559 (2015)
8. Gong, B., Shi, Y., Sha, F., Grauman, K.: Geodesic flow kernel for unsupervised domain adaptation. In: 2012 IEEE Conference on Computer Vision and Pattern Recognition, pp. 2066–2073. IEEE (2012)
9. Griffin, G., Holub, A., Perona, P., et al.: Caltech-256 object category dataset. Tech. rep., Technical Report 7694, California Institute of Technology Pasadena (2007)
10. Guan, H., Liu, M.: DomainATM: domain adaptation toolbox for medical data analysis. Neuroimage **268**, 119863 (2023)
11. Huang, J., Gretton, A., Borgwardt, K., Schölkopf, B., Smola, A.: Correcting sample selection bias by unlabeled data. Adv. Neural Inf. Process. Syst. **19** (2006)
12. Hull, J.J.: A database for handwritten text recognition research. IEEE Trans. Pattern Anal. Mach. Intell. **16**(5), 550–554 (1994)

13. Jesus, S., et al.: Turning the tables: biased, imbalanced, dynamic tabular datasets for ML evaluation. Adv. Neural. Inf. Process. Syst. **35**, 33563–33575 (2022)
14. Ke, G., et al.: LightGBM: a highly efficient gradient boosting decision tree. Adv. Neural Inf. Process. Syst. **30** (2017)
15. Krizhevsky, A., Hinton, G., et al.: Learning multiple layers of features from tiny images (2009)
16. LeCun, Y., Bottou, L., Bengio, Y., Haffner, P.: Gradient-based learning applied to document recognition. Proc. IEEE **86**(11), 2278–2324 (1998)
17. Li, D., Yang, Y., Song, Y.Z., Hospedales, T.M.: Deeper, broader and artier domain generalization. In: Proceedings of the IEEE International Conference on Computer Vision, pp. 5542–5550 (2017)
18. Netzer, Y., et al.: Reading digits in natural images with unsupervised feature learning. In: NIPS Workshop on Deep Learning and Unsupervised Feature Learning. vol. 2011, p. 4. Granada (2011)
19. Peng, X., Bai, Q., Xia, X., Huang, Z., Saenko, K., Wang, B.: Moment matching for multi-source domain adaptation. In: Proceedings of the IEEE/CVF International Conference on Computer Vision, pp. 1406–1415 (2019)
20. Richter, S.R., Vineet, V., Roth, S., Koltun, V.: Playing for data: ground truth from computer games. In: Computer Vision–ECCV 2016: 14th European Conference on Computer Vision, pp. 102–118. Springer (2016)
21. Saenko, K., Kulis, B., Fritz, M., Darrell, T.: Adapting visual category models to new domains. In: Computer Vision–ECCV 2010: 11th European Conference on Computer Vision, pp. 213–226. Springer (2010)
22. Saito, K., Kim, D., Sclaroff, S., Darrell, T., Saenko, K.: Semi-supervised domain adaptation via minimax entropy. In: Proceedings of the IEEE/CVF International Conference on Computer Vision, pp. 8050–8058 (2019)
23. Venkateswara, H., Eusebio, J., Chakraborty, S., Panchanathan, S.: Deep hashing network for unsupervised domain adaptation. In: Proceedings of the IEEE Conference on Computer Vision and Pattern Recognition, pp. 5018–5027 (2017)
24. Wang, J., et al.: Generalizing to unseen domains: a survey on domain generalization. IEEE Trans. Knowl. Data Eng. **35**(8), 8052–8072 (2022)
25. Wang, M., Deng, W.: Deep visual domain adaptation: a survey. Neurocomputing **312**, 135–153 (2018)
26. Wilson, G., Cook, D.J.: A survey of unsupervised deep domain adaptation. ACM Trans. Intell. Syst. Technol. (TIST) **11**(5), 1–46 (2020)
27. Yang, Y., Hospedales, T.M.: A unified perspective on multi-domain and multi-task learning. arXiv preprint arXiv:1412.7489 (2014)
28. Zhou, K., Liu, Z., Qiao, Y., Xiang, T., Loy, C.C.: Domain generalization: a survey. IEEE Trans. Pattern Anal. Mach. Intell. **45**(4) (2022)

Harnessing Mixed Features for Imbalance Data Oversampling: Application to Bank Customers Scoring

Abdoulaye Sakho[1,2]([✉]), Emmanuel Malherbe[1], Carl-Erik Gauthier[3], and Erwan Scornet[2]

[1] Artefact Research Center, Paris, France
{abdoulaye.sakho,emmanuel.malherbe}@artefact.com
[2] Laboratoire de Probabilités, Statistique et Modélisation Sorbonne Université and Université Paris Cité, CNRS, 75005 Paris, France
erwan.scornet@polytechnique.edu
[3] Société Générale, Paris, France
carl-erik.gauthier@socgen.com

Abstract. This study investigates rare event detection on tabular data within binary classification. Standard techniques to handle class imbalance include SMOTE, which generates synthetic samples from the minority class. However, SMOTE is intrinsically designed for continuous input variables. In fact, despite SMOTE-NC—its default extension to handle mixed features (continuous and categorical variables)—very few works propose procedures to synthesize mixed features. On the other hand, many real-world classification tasks, such as in banking sector, deal with mixed features, which have a significant impact on predictive performances. To this purpose, we introduce MGS-GRF, an oversampling strategy designed for mixed features. This method uses a kernel density estimator with locally estimated full-rank covariances to generate continuous features, while categorical ones are drawn from the original samples through a generalized random forest. Empirically, contrary to SMOTE-NC, we show that MGS-GRF exhibits two important properties: (i) the coherence i.e. the ability to only generate combinations of categorical features that are already present in the original dataset and (ii) association, i.e. the ability to preserve the dependence between continuous and categorical features. We also evaluate the predictive performances of LightGBM classifiers trained on data sets, augmented with synthetic samples from various strategies. Our comparison is performed on simulated and public real-world data sets, as well as on a private data set from a leading financial institution. We observe that synthetic procedures that have the properties of coherence and association display better predictive performances in terms of various predictive metrics (PR and ROC AUC...), with MGS-GRF being the best one. Furthermore, our method exhibits promising results for the private banking application, with development pipeline being compliant with regulatory constraints.

Keywords: Imbalanced data · Classification · Mixed features · Tabular data · Scoring · Banking

1 Introduction

Addressing class imbalance in binary classification presents a significant challenge across various machine learning applications [27,30], such as medical diagnosis, customer churn prediction or anomaly detection [14,23,30]. In particular, detecting fraud is a prime issue in banking [11,19]: the vast majority of customers make legitimate transactions, while the fraudulent ones represent only a minority but have a significant operational, regulatory, and reputational impact.

Several seminal works have introduced rebalancing strategies in order to improve the predictive performances of generic classifiers [5,22]. These strategies can be divided into two categories [25]: model-level strategies, that aim at adapting an existing algorithm, for example by weighting classes or minimizing a specific loss function [4,20]; and data-level strategies, that act on the original data set by oversampling or undersampling the observations, and are thus model agnostic. A subclass of data-level strategies, named synthetic procedures, generates new samples in the minority class, with many variants introduced in the literature [5,10,12]. Data-level synthetic procedures handle class imbalance by generating new informative samples. This contrasts with model-level approaches (which do not add or lose information), data-level undersampling (which entails information loss), and data-level oversampling via duplication (which does not introduce novel information). One key characteristic of synthetic procedure is that most of them are primarily designed to handle numerical features and thus do not handle categorical features [7,27]. In practice, categorical features are very common in tabular data (e.g. job category, country, gender), and can represent a relevant signal for improving the predictive performances of the learning tasks, such as those described in [8,9]. This highlights the importance of handling mixed features when generating samples for imbalance data. Besides, combination of several categorical variables need to be generated in a coherent way with each other and with respect to the continuous variables.

When properly designed for tabular data sets, synthetic methods have the potential to yield superior predictive performance compared to other rebalancing approaches. Accordingly, in the following, we focus on synthetic rebalancing strategies for tabular data, with the main objective of handling mixed features. We emphasize that when generating categorical features, a major aspect is to ensure their intrinsic coherence and their association with continuous features. The notion of coherence aims at expressing that a combination of categorical variables can be judged as plausible by some business owner, such as a bank analyst. Indeed, generating samples that do not seem credible may lead to a reluctance to apply subsequent machine learning analyses, without mentioning the potential negative impact on the predictive performances. We define formally coherent combinations as the ones existing in the original samples. On the other hand, the association level measures the dependence between continuous and categorical features, via the accuracy of a given model trained to predict the categorical variables based on continuous variables. Thus, preserving the level of association between original and synthetic data ensures that the distribution of categorical variables conditional on continuous variables remains similar.

An augmented data set that is coherent and preserves the association level compared to the original data has a distribution close to the original data set. Our main contributions are:

- We introduce MGS-GRF, a strategy for mixed features, with a kernel density estimation for continuous ones and a generalized forest for categorical ones.
- On simulated data, we prove that SMOTE-NC, probably the most widely used synthetic rebalancing strategy, is not coherent and does not preserve association, thus creating unplausible samples. On the contrary, our method satisfies these properties, thus creating more realistic samples.
- We also show that both notions of coherence and association are positively correlated with predictive performances. Thus, creating implausible samples not only makes the models less trustworthy, but also reduces the performances.
- We compare our proposed method with other rebalancing strategies on two banking public data sets and one private data set from a major financial institution. We show that our proposed strategy, MGS-GRF, which is both coherent and preserves association, has the best predictive performances.

2 Related Work

Notations. We consider a data-set $\{(X^i, Y^i)\}_{i=1}^{N}$ constituted of N independent pairs, each one distributed as (X, Y). The random variable X takes values in $\mathbb{R}^d \times \mathcal{X}^p$ while $Y \in \{0, 1\}$, where $\mathcal{X}$ is the space of categorical features. Here, without loss of generality, we assume that the first d features of X, denoted $X_{1:d}$, are continuous, while the p others, denoted $X_{d:}$, are categorical. Similarly, we suppose that the n first samples are labeled $Y = 1$, denoted $\{X^i\}_{i=1}^{n}$, verifying $n << N - n$ since we work in an imbalanced data setting.

Algorithm 1 All rebalancing strategies in the literature are divided into two parts, the first one handling the continuous features and the second one handling the categorical ones. Accordingly, we encompass all oversampling strategies in Algorithm 1, which describes the generation of a single synthetic example. Algorithm 1 may be run as many times as necessary to obtain the desired number of minority samples. The procedure starts by selecting uniformly at random $c \in \{1, \ldots, n\}$ and the corresponding minority sample X^c. Let $\text{NN}_{K,L}(X^c)$ be the set of the $K \in \mathbb{N}^*$ nearest neighbors of X^c among minority samples w.r.t. to a given norm L. Finally, ContinuousSampler and CategoricalSampler functions are applied if necessary. We present below the state-of-the art procedures using Algorithm 1.

SMOTE [5] is the most common synthetic procedure for generating continuous new samples in the minority class. Thus, SMOTE does not have a CategoricalSampler in Algorithm 1. To generate a new synthetic sample, an observation X^k is drawn uniformly at random among the K nearest neighbors of X^c w.r.t. the L_2 norm. The synthetic sample generation is the following

$$\texttt{ContinuousSampler}\left(X_{1:d}^c, \text{NN}_{K,L_2}(X^c)\right) = X_{1:d}^c + w X_{1:d}^k,$$

Algorithm 1. OverSampler: One iteration for generating a new sample.
***
Require: $X^1, \ldots, X^n$, ContinuousSampler and CategoricalSampler, d, p.
Select uniformly X^c among $X^1, \ldots, X^n$.
Derive $\text{NN}_{K,L}(X^c)$ the set composed of the K nearest-neighbors of X^c.
if $d > 0$: then
    $Z_{1:d} \leftarrow$ ContinuousSampler $(X_{1:d}^c, \text{NN}_{K,L}(X^c))$.
end if
if $p > 0$: then
    $Z_{d:} \leftarrow$ CategoricalSampler $(\text{NN}_{K,L}(X^c))$.
end if
return $Z = [Z_{1:d}, Z_{d:}]$, new minority class synthetic sample.
***

where $w \sim \mathcal{U}([0,1])$ and with $\mathcal{U}$ the uniform distribution. Note that SMOTE has several variants [10,12], but, to the best of our knowledge, these variants are also originally designed for continuous input features only.

SMOTE-N is presented in the original paper introducing SMOTE [5]. This methodology is designed only for categorical input. SMOTE-N uses a version of the Value Difference Metric [28], denoted L_{VDM}, as norm. More precisely, for two categorical vectors $u, v \in \mathcal{X}^p$ we have,

$$L_{\text{VDM}}(u_j, v_j) = \sum_{j=1}^{p} \delta(u_j, v_j),$$

where $\delta(u_j, v_j) = 2|p_n(Y = 0|X_j = u_j) - p_n(Y = 0|X_j = v_j)|$. The value $p_n(Y = 0|u_j)$ is the empirical conditional probability that the output class is $Y = 0$ given that the feature j has the value u_j. Note that, in order to compute L_{VDM}, the majority class samples are necessary. To generate a new observation, a sample is drawn uniformly among the minority samples. Then, its nearest neighbors according to L_{VDM} are computed. Finally, the new minority sample is generated by a vote among the previous nearest neighbors along each variable. With Algorithm 1 notations :

$$\text{CategoricalSampler}\,(\text{NN}_{K,L_{\text{VDM}}}(X^c)) = \text{Vote}\,(\text{NN}_{K,L_{\text{VDM}}}(X^c)),$$

where $\text{Vote}\,(\text{NN}_{K,L_{\text{VDM}}}(X^c))_j$, is a vote among the nearest-neighbors for the categorical feature $j \in \{1, \ldots, p\}$.

SMOTE-NC is designed to handle data sets containing both continuous and categorical features, and is also presented in the original SMOTE paper [5]. The main idea is to define a distance metric, denoted L_{NC}, that takes into account the categorical features. To this aim, the median $C \in \mathbb{R}$ of standard deviations of all continuous features for the minority class is computed. The L_{NC} takes the form

$$L_{\text{NC}}(X, X') = \sqrt{\sum_{j=1}^{d}(X_j' - X_j)^2 + C^2 \sum_{j=d+1}^{d+p} \mathbb{1}_{X_j \neq X_j'}}.$$

Then, continuous features are generated using SMOTE interpolation while categorical one are based on a nearest neighbors vote. For SMOTE-NC we have:

$$\texttt{ContinuousSampler}\left(X_{1:d}^c, \text{NN}_{K,L_{\text{NC}}}(X^c)\right) = X_{1:d}^c + w X_{1:d}^{k_c},$$
$$\texttt{CategoricalSampler}\left(\text{NN}_{K,L_{\text{NC}}}(X^c)\right) = \text{Vote}\left(\text{NN}_{K,L_{\text{NC}}}(X^c)\right),$$

SMOTE-ENC [22] applies the same procedure as SMOTE-NC except that L_{NC} is replaced by

$$L_{\text{ENC}}(X, X') = \sqrt{\sum_{j=1}^{d} (X'_j - X_j)^2 + \sum_{j=d+1}^{d+p} C_j^2 \mathbb{1}_{X_j \neq X'_j}}.$$

However, to the best of our knowledge, SMOTE-ENC has no implementation agnostic to the data-set, and in the original repository the computation of C_j differs for each data-set.

Regarding the theoretical perspectives, [25] demonstrated that when used with default parameters on continuous features, SMOTE tends to copy the original minority samples. In such a setting, SMOTE is also unable to regenerate the original distribution of the minority class near the density support boundary. The authors of [25] also showed that CTGAN, a GAN-based procedure [32], has slightly lower predictive performances compared to SMOTE. In fact, [15] showed that, empirically, SMOTE remains competitive even compared to recent diffusion models [15, see Table 4 and Table 5]. Besides, GAN-based and diffusion-based strategies are computationally expensive [25, for details]. In our real-world high-dimensional application with millions of rows, we choose not to apply such expensive (GAN-based and diffusion-based) methodologies.

3 Our Proposed Algorithm: MGS-GRF

In this section, we describe our new algorithm to handle mixed data. It is organized similarly to Algorithm 1, so that we first describe our procedure to generate continuous features before detailing the categorical variables methodology.

3.1 Handling Continuous Features

Numerous studies have proposed Kernel Density Estimator (KDE) for generating synthetic samples within the minority class for continuous input features. Actually, SMOTE itself can be seen as a KDE with uniform kernel piece by piece [29]. For instance, [17,18] introduce an oversampling strategy that, based on original samples, adds centered Gaussian noise with a unique diagonal scale matrix to original samples to generate new observations. [21] develops ROSE, a KDE based oversampling strategy which is associated to a unique scale matrix for the whole minority class. Later, [31] proposes a weighted sample KDE oversampling strategy with fixed diagonal scale matrix, thus isotropic, of the form $h \times I$ with $h \in \mathbb{R}$ and I the identity matrix. h is as in Adasyn [12]: higher weights are given to original minority samples surrounded mostly by majority class samples.

Multivariate Gaussian SMOTE (MGS) is a synthetic procedure for continuous features introduced by [25]. MGS is presented as a variant of SMOTE that generate new samples from multivariate Gaussian distributions and no longer with a linear interpolation. We analyzed the MGS procedure and reformulate it as a Gaussian KDE from the sample smoothing estimator family [26], i.e. with several different full-rank local scale matrices. Furthermore, MGS does not assume the covariance matrix to be diagonal, thus not isotropic, which allows a better adaptivity to the unknown minority class distribution. We choose to generate the continuous features of synthetic samples, $Z_{1:d} \in \mathbb{R}^d$, according to the following density $\hat{f}_{MGS}(Z_{1:d})$ fitted on the original minority samples $\{X^i\}_{i=1,\ldots,n}$:

$$\hat{f}_{MGS}(Z_{1:d}) = \frac{1}{n} \sum_{i=1}^{n} \frac{1}{(2\pi)^{d/2}|\hat{\Sigma}^i|} \exp\left(-\frac{1}{2}(Z_{1:d} - \hat{\mu}^i)^T (\hat{\Sigma}^i)^{-1} (Z_{1:d} - \hat{\mu}^i)\right), \tag{1}$$

where $|\hat{\Sigma}^i|$ denotes the determinant of $\hat{\Sigma}^i$ and

$$\hat{\mu}^i = \frac{1}{K} \sum_{X \in NN_{K,L_2}(X^i)} X_{1:d}, \quad \hat{\Sigma}^i = \frac{1}{K} \sum_{X \in NN_{K,L_2}(X^i)} (X_{1:d} - \hat{\mu}^i)(X_{1:d} - \hat{\mu}^i)^T$$

are estimated for each minority class sample using its K nearest-neighbors from the minority class, w.r.t. to L_2 norm. We choose a value of $K = d + 1$ in order to possibly obtain full-rank covariance matrices. Besides, Σ^i can be estimated using shrinkage [6,16] or simply the sample covariance matrix estimate [25], but empirically we got better results with the latter one.

One notes that the underlying distribution of this sampling is a n Gaussian mixture with equal weights. We also remark that ROSE [21] corresponds to the special case where all Σ^i are equal.

3.2 Handling Categorical Data via Generalized Random Forests

Now, we introduce our selected procedure for generating synthetic categorical features. A first remark when looking at Algorithm 1 is that multi-output classifiers, such as nearest neighbors, can be used to generate the categorical features. Indeed, such models can be trained using only minority samples, aiming at predicting the categorical features $\{X_{d:}^i\}_{i=1}^n$ based on the continuous features $\{X_{1:d}^i\}_{i=1}^n$. Denoting by $\hat{g}$ such trained classifier, based on Algorithm 1, one can repeatedly generate categorical samples as

$$\texttt{CategoricalSampler}(Z_{1:d}) = \hat{g}(Z_{1:d}).$$

Our selected methodology to generate categorical variables relies on Generalized Random Forests (GRF) [1]. The main difference between a random forest [3] and a GRF, is that, given the new point, GRF assigns a probability to each training

Algorithm 2. Prediction procedure of GRF

Require: Forest composed of T trees $\mathcal{T}_1, \ldots, \mathcal{T}_T$. A new unlabeled sample $Z_{1:d}$.
$\forall k = 1..T$, $\mathcal{L}_k(Z_{1:d}) \leftarrow$ set of training samples which end up in the same leaf as $Z_{1:d}$ in the tree $\mathcal{T}_k$
for $i \in [1, \ldots, n]$ **do**
$$w_{(Z_{1:d})}(X^i) \leftarrow \frac{1}{T} \sum_{k=1}^{T} \frac{\mathbf{1}_{\{X^i \in \mathcal{L}_k(Z_{1:d})\}}}{|\mathcal{L}_k(Z_{1:d})|}$$
end for
$Z_{d:} \leftarrow$ Sample $\{X_{d:}^1, \ldots, X_{d:}^n\}$ based on $\{w_{(Z_{1:d})}(X_{1:d}^1), \ldots, w_{(Z_{1:d})}(X_{1:d}^n)\}$.
return $Z_{d:}$

---

sample. These probabilities are derive from the frequency of the training samples to fall in the same leaf as the predicted sample. Finally, GRF can be used to estimate any quantity identified via local moment conditions.

We implemented our own version of GRF from the *RandomForestClassifier* class of scikit-learn [24]. In our algorithm, the derivate probabilities are used to draw predicted target from training target vectors (Y^i). The predict procedure of our GRF is detailed in Algorithm 2. Besides, we try several default hyperparameters for our GRF and finally we keep the default values from *RandomForestClassifier* class of scikit-learn for the tree building. Furthermore, we do not apply the principle of honesty [2], and neither scale the target variables.

3.3 MGS-GRF

Now we detail MGS-GRF, our new procedure that combines MGS and GRF which are described in the previous sections. MGS-GRF follows the three following steps. First, MGS is applied to generate the continuous features of the new synthetic samples. Then, a Generalized Random Forest (GRF) denoted by $\hat{g}_{GRF}$ is trained on all the original minority samples with the continuous features $\{X_{1:d}^i\}_{i=1}^n$ as inputs and the categorical features $\{X_{d:}^i\}_{i=1}^n$ as outputs. Finally, the trained GRF is used to build the categorical features based on the continuous ones generated in the first step. Using Algorithm 1 notations we have,

$$\texttt{ContinuousSampler}(\{X_{1:d}^i\}_{i=1}^n) = Z_{1:d} \sim \hat{f}_{\text{MGS}}$$
$$\texttt{CategoricalSampler}(Z_{d:}) = \hat{g}_{\text{GRF}}(Z_{1:d}).$$

Our proposed method enjoys the following properties: (*i*) GRF generates combinations of categorical features that are all from the original minority class. (*ii*) Due to tree building procedure, GRF may be able to use only the few continuous variables that are relevant to generate the categorical variables, thus ensuring a better correlation between continuous and categorical variables. (*iii*) The categorical features are generated directly from the continuous ones of the new sample. Thus, they are no longer based on the neighborhood of the central point.

4 Illustrations on Simulated Data

In the following, we describe our baselines before defining both coherence and associations. We illustrate these notions through numerical simulations.[1]

4.1 Baselines

Now, we introduce different strategies to preprocess the original imbalanced data set. We denote by None strategy the procedure where no rebalancing strategy is applied. CW is the class-weighting strategy while Random Oversampling strategy (ROS) and Random Undersampling Strategy (RUS) are data-level approaches. We also include the synthetic procedure SMOTE-NC, with the default number of nearest neighbors equal to 5. There is no generic implementation of SMOTE-ENC, thus we do not include this strategy (see Sect. 2).

Besides, we introduce 3 synthetic baselines for our comparison. MGS-NC selects a central point X^c uniformly over minority samples. MGS distribution is used (see Eq. 1) with $\hat{\Sigma}^i$ and $\hat{\mu}^i$ computed on the K nearest neighbors $NN_{L_{NC},K}(X^c)$ of X^c w.r.t. the L_{NC} norm. Then, each categorical variable is generated separately via a vote among the same neighbors. The second baseline, MGS-5NN, applies MGS on the continuous features, and builds the categorical ones using a $k = 5$ nearest neighbors w.r.t. L_2 norm as multi-output classifier $\hat{g}$ (see Sect. 3.2). Similarly, MGS-1NN is the same procedure with $k = 1$.

All strategies (except None) resample or generate observations so that each of the two classes contains the same number of observations (balanced data set).

4.2 Numerical Illustrations of Non-coherence Notion

In our first experimental protocol, we want to analyze the distribution of categorical variables via the notion of coherence defined below.

Definition 1. *We denote by $\mathcal{C}$ the set of combinations of categorical features in the original data set. We denote by $\mathcal{C}_{Y=1}$ the combination present in the original minority class $Y = 1$. We say that a synthetic oversampling strategy is coherent, with respect to the minority class, if all combinations of generated categorical features belong to $\mathcal{C}_{Y=1}$. Accordingly, we say that a minority sample is coherent if its categorical vector belongs to $\mathcal{C}_{Y=1}$.*

Our main objectives are to detect non-coherent synthetic procedures and assess whether incoherent samples harm predictive performances. We define the coherence value, denoted Coh, by the proportion of coherent synthetic observations generated by a strategy, over all the synthetic data. If we denote by n_g the number of generated samples $Z_{d:}^\ell$, we have

$$Coh = \frac{1}{n_g} \sum_{\ell=1}^{n_g} \mathbb{1}_{\{Z_{d:}^\ell \in \mathcal{C}_{Y=1}\}}.$$

---

[1] All our experiments are available at https://github.com/artefactory/mgs-grf.

We note that strategies that generate categorical features one by one with a vote are not coherent, as they can mix original combinations. This applies to SMOTE-NC, MGS-NC and MGS-5NN. However, MGS-1NN copies the features of the nearest neighbor from the minority class, thus leading the combination to be originally present in the minority class. Similarly, GRF is coherent because it draws randomly a combination of categorical features from the minority class.

Protocol. We simulate a binary classification task data set such that class 0 is overrepresented, with $d = 9$ continuous features and $p = 2$ categorical ones. We denote by $\mathcal{C} = \mathcal{D} \times \mathcal{E}$ the set of combinations of categorical features where $\mathcal{D}$ (resp. $\mathcal{E}$) is the set of possible modalities for the first (resp. second) categorical features. Each categorical feature is composed of m modalities, i.e. $|\mathcal{D}| = |\mathcal{E}| = m$ and $|\mathcal{C}| = m^2$, and only m (out of m^2) combinations of categorical features are present in the minority class, written $\mathcal{C}_{Y=1} = m$. Only the 3 informative continuous features and the categorical features are used for generating the target Y. Our procedure consists of the following steps :

1. Draw 5000 samples composed of d continuous features as follows $X_{1:d} = (X_1, \ldots, X_d) \sim \mathcal{N}(0, I_d)$.
2. Draw $Z \in \mathcal{C}$ such that

$$\mathbb{P}[Z = c | X_{1:d}] = \frac{\exp(-\theta_c^\top X_{1:3})}{\sum_{\ell \in \mathcal{C}} \exp(-\theta_\ell^\top X_{1:3})},$$

with $c \in \mathcal{C}$. The set of parameters $\Theta = \{\theta_c, c \in \mathcal{C}\}$, verify, for all $c \in \mathcal{C}$, $\theta_c \in \mathbb{R}^3$. $X_{1:3}$ are the 3 informative components of X, while other X_j values ($j > 3$) do not impact Z value.

3. Draw the target variable Y such that

$$Y | X_{1:d}, Z = c \sim \mathcal{B}(\sigma(\alpha^\top X_{1:3} + \gamma_c)),$$

where $\mathcal{B}$ is the Bernoulli distribution, σ is the logistic function and $\alpha \in \mathbb{R}^3$. The set of parameters $\Gamma = \{\gamma_c, c \in \mathcal{C}\}$ verify, for all $c \in \mathcal{C}$, $\gamma_c \in \mathbb{R}$. In order to limit the number of coherent combinations present in the minority class, we set high γ_c values only for m different combinations $c \in \mathcal{C}$. Besides, we choose α and all γ_c values such that the class $Y = 1$ is underrepresented.

4. Return $[X_1, \ldots, X_d, Z_1, Z_2, Y]$, where $Z_1 \in \mathcal{D}, Z_2 \in \mathcal{E}$ satisfy $Z = (Z_1, Z_2)$.

One Combination of Θ, α, Γ. We fix the values of Θ, α and Γ once and for all and run the above protocol 50 times. Thus, we produce 50 data sets (with different random seeds), that we split into train and test set. We preprocess the train set with the different rebalancing strategies and train a LightGBM classifier on it. Predictive performances on the test set are displayed in Table 1.

In Table 1, we see that MGS-GRF and MGS-1NN have a coherence value $Coh = 100\%$, which is expected for these two coherent strategies. On the contrary, the non-coherent strategies (SMOTE-NC, MGS-NC and MGS-5NN) have coherence values lower than 100%, as they can generate minority samples whose

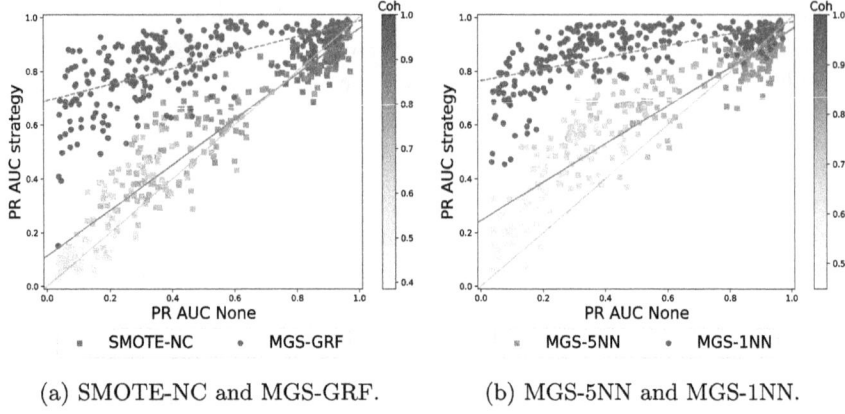

Fig. 1. *PR AUC* of coherence simulations. Points color reflect their *Coh* value.

categorical vectors are not found in the original data set. We observe that strategies with low *Coh*, i.e. creating non-coherent combinations of categorical features deteriorate the predictive performances of the final classifier. This is particularly visible for MGS-5NN and MGS-1NN, while being very similar models. In contrast, MGS-GRF achieves the best predictive performances in terms of both PR AUC and ROC AUC, with a computation time (for oversampling and LightGBM training) only 50% longer than SMOTE-NC. Finally, we remark that MGS-NC leads to better predictive performances than SMOTE-NC, indicating that MGS seems to better regenerate the distributions of the minority class than SMOTE.

Different Combination of Θ, α *and* Γ. We run our protocol with 6 configuration values for Θ, α, Γ. For each configuration, we apply the protocol above, so that we obtain in total 300 datasets. The PR AUC of the LightGBM classifier for each rebalancing strategy and for each data set is displayed in Figs. 1a and 1b, where each point corresponds to one of the 300 data sets. We display the PR AUC of a given rebalancing strategy in y-axis and the PR AUC of the None strategy in x-axis. Circles points are all associated to coherent strategies (MGS-1NN and our proposed strategy MGS-GRF), while the squares ones are associated to non-coherent ones (SMOTE-NC, MGS-5NN). We plot linear fitting curves and also add the first bisector in gray (line $y = x$).

Table 1. LightGBM trained on simulated data from experimental protocol.

Strategy	None	CW	ROS	RUS	SMOTE-NC	MGS-NC	MGS-5NN	MGS-1NN	MGS-GRF
PR AUC	0.903	0.903	0.893	0.699	0.860	0.922	0.870	0.952	**0.954**
ROC AUC	0.975	0.977	0.975	0.935	0.962	0.984	0.970	**0.993**	**0.993**
Coh		100%	100%	100%	100%	90%	90%	83%	100%	100%
Time (s)	0.55	0.56	0.74	0.27	1.01	1.23	1.04	1.00	1.43

In both figures, we remark that the points (both squares and circles) are above the first bisector, thus the rebalancing strategies lead to improvement of PR AUC. However, the average coherent strategies achieve higher PR AUC than the non-coherent ones. This difference is the highest when the PR AUC of the None strategy is the lowest (left side of the figures), which corresponds to more complex classification settings. In such difficult scenarios, non-coherent strategies have low Coh values, which may in turn explain their low PR AUC, close to that of the None strategy. When the learning task is easier, all strategies have similar performance (right side of the figures). All in all, this experiment shows that coherent strategies should be preferred to non-coherent ones, especially in more difficult classification problems.

4.3 Numerical Illustrations of Association Notion

In the following, we define and present our numerical experiments on association.

Definition 2. *The association level of a multi-output classifier is its predictive performance when inferring categorical features with respect to continuous ones. This performance is measured as the empirical excess risk w.r.t. Bayes error.*

We choose to measure the association level of a classifier via its accuracy on a leave-one-out validation on original minority samples. More precisely, if we write $\hat{Z}_{d:}^{\ell}$ the prediction for $X_{1:d}^{\ell}$ of a given classifier trained on $\{X^i\}_{i \neq \ell}$ (leave-one-out prediction), the association level $Asso$ of this classifier is

$$Asso = 1 - \left(\frac{1}{n} \sum_{\ell=1}^{n} \mathbb{1}_{\{X_{d:}^{\ell} \neq \hat{Z}_{d:}^{\ell}\}} - \frac{1}{n} \sum_{\ell=1}^{n} \mathbb{1}_{\{X_{d:}^{\ell} \neq h^*(X_{1:d}^{i})\}} \right),$$

where h^* is the Bayes classifier whose predictions are defined by $h^*(X_{1:d}) = \arg\max_{c \in \mathcal{C}} \mathbb{P}(X_{d:} = c | X_{1:d})$, with $\mathcal{C}$ the set of combination of categorical features. In practice, we do not have access to the Bayes classifier, and thus to the association level. In such situations, the association level can also be estimated without the last term, that is with the classifier accuracy. Another point is that we focus on original minority points for which we have a ground truth $X_{d:}^{i}$. While measuring on generated continuous features would be ideal given our oversampling objective (see Sect. 3.1), we do not have the ground truth for the categorical values of those points, and all reference data for measuring association are with the minority points.

In this second numerical experiments, we generate an imbalance binary classification data based on four input variables: 3 of them are continuous and the remaining one is categorical, with 3 modalities. We add $d - 3$ continuous noise variables, which are independent of all previous variables. More precisely:

1. Draw 5000 samples as a mixture of 3 Gaussian in $\mathbb{R}^3$: $(X_1, X_2, X_3) \sim \sum_{w=1}^{3} \pi_w \mathcal{N}(\mu_w, \Sigma_w)$, with $\sum_{w=1}^{3} \pi_w = 1$ and $\pi_w \geq 0$. Let $W \in \{1, 2, 3\}$ be the latent variable of the mixture s.t. $(X_1, X_2, X_3)|W \sim \mathcal{N}(\mu_W, \Sigma_W)$.

2. Draw $d-3$ noise features: $(X_4, \ldots, X_d) \sim \mathcal{N}(\mu_2, \lambda I_{d-3})$ with $\lambda \in \mathbb{R}^*$.
3. Draw $Z \in \{\text{``A''}, \text{``B''}, \text{``C''}\}$ such that,

$$\mathbb{P}[Z = c | X_{1:d}, W = w] = \frac{\exp(-\zeta_c^\top X_{1:3} + \chi_{w,c})}{\sum_{\ell \in \mathcal{C}} \exp(-\zeta_\ell^\top X_{1:3} + \chi_{w,\ell})},$$

where $\zeta_c \in \mathbb{R}^3$ and $\chi_{w,c} \in \mathbb{R}$. For each Gaussian, that is for each $w \in \{1, 2, 3\}$, we choose $\chi_{w,c}$ such that one modality is associated to the minority class. We emphasize that the notion of *association* between categorical and continuous features occurs at this step, where Z depends only on the 3 informative values $X_{1:3}$ (W is a confounding variable) while others $X_j (j > 3)$ are pure noise.
4. Draw the target variable Y such that

$$Y|X_{1:d}, W = w, Z = c \sim \mathcal{B}(\sigma(\beta^\top X_{1:3} + \eta_w + \phi_c)),$$

where $\beta \in \mathbb{R}^3$, and $\eta_w, \phi_c \in \mathbb{R}$. One notes that Y depends on $X_{1:3}$, while other X_j ($j > 3$) are non-informative.
5. Return $[X_1, X_2, X_3, X_4, \ldots, X_d, Z, Y]$.

Following this protocol, we generate 8 data sets with increasing number of non-informative features $d - 3$. On each of these 8 data sets, we estimate the association level of 3 multi-output classifiers: 1NN, 5NN and GRF. Since we are in a simulation setting, we have access to the Bayes predictor (see Sect. A.2 for details), which allows us to compute the association level. We observe in Fig. 2a, that the association level of nearest neighbors (1NN and 5NN) decreases with increasing dimension, contrary to that of GRF which remains constant, and close to 1, this more accurately generating categorical features. As it is a known behavior for supervised tasks with many noisy uninformative features, nearest neighbors do not predict well the categorical feature.

We now study how the initial prediction task (predicting $Y \in \{0, 1\}$ based on continuous and categorical features) is impacted by the categorical feature generation. On each data set, we apply rebalancing strategies followed by Light-GBM (with default hyperparameters) and compute its PR AUC. Results are depicted in Fig. 2b. We observe that all methods have the same performance for low dimensions. In this setting, the problem can be considered as easy (since the None strategy has good performances) and all rebalancing strategies are roughly equivalent, similarly to experiments implemented in Sect. 4.2.

As expected due to the curse of dimensionality, all performances degrade when the dimension increases, with the notable exception of our proposed method MGS-GRF, whose performances remain unaffected by the addition of noise variables. In fact, we see that the use of GRF compared to nearest neighbors (MGS-1NN or MGS-5NN) for generating categorical variables improves the final predictive performances. This finds explanation in the splitting procedure at work in GRF, which selects the variables that are the most predictive of the output (here the categorical input vector). On the contrary, nearest neighbors are unable to detect relevant variables for splitting, which explains their poor performances in high-dimensional settings.

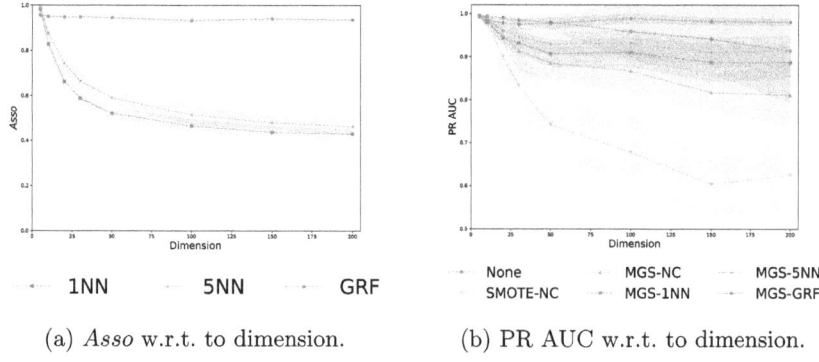

(a) *Asso* w.r.t. to dimension. (b) PR AUC w.r.t. to dimension.

Fig. 2. Association experiments in high dimensional setting with noisy features.

We also note that SMOTE-NC, probably the default synthetic rebalancing strategy, is the worst in high dimensions, both in terms of mean value and standard deviation. On the opposite, our proposed method MGS-GRF exhibits the best performances with a small standard deviation. This seems to indicate that a good generation of categorical features (via GRF) leads to good predictive performance on the initial binary classification task.

5 Experiments on Real-World Data Sets

In this section, we describe all our numerical experiments on real-world data sets. We describe our protocol before commenting our results.

5.1 Data Sets

We use two open source banking-related data sets, Bankmarketing [22] and Bankchurners [33], described in Table 2, both about bank customer behavior prediction. The first data set objective is to predict if a client subscribes to a banking offer after a phone marketing campaign. The second data set aims at predicting customer attrition from a financial institution. Both data set covariates contain historical records of the customers. To be closer to the challenge encountered in the private sector, we undersample the open source data set to have an imbalance ratio of 1%.

We also have a private data set, from a major bank, that contains clients information from one country in Europe. The purpose is to predict if a customer meets some criterion from historical records. The target criterion is beyond the scope of this paper. Positive cases predicted by the model are pushed to analysts, with corresponding explainability results, and the analysts have to make a decision based on the model output. Furthermore, analysts give feedbacks on the pertinence of pushed cases to the data science team, who retrain the model several times per year. A version from the ML-based system has been deployed.

Table 2. Data sets.

	N samples	n/N imbalance	d continuous	p categorical
Private	$\simeq 10^7$	<1%	>200	<10
BankMarketing	40325	1%	16	10
BankChurners	8585	1%	19	5

The data set contains millions of *anonymized* customers and we recall that all process is done in compliance with the country's regulatory requirements.

5.2 Evaluation

We evaluate the public data sets with the following protocol. For an iteration, the data set is evaluated through a 5-fold cross validation, with Z-score scaling of the train set. We stress on the fact that each strategy is applied on the same training set. We run this protocol 20 times and averaged the metrics from each run. The private data set is evaluated through a temporal train/test split, with the test set covering year 2023 and no overlap of clients between train and test sets. Tree-based models produce state-of-the-art performances on tabular data sets [9] and we choose LightGBM [13] as classifier due to its computational efficiency.

We introduce an evaluation metric, the precision at recall, denoted Pr-at-rec(x), which equals the precision associated to a recall of at least x, for any $x \in [0,1]$. This metric aims at representing an industrial or operational trade-off between precision and recall. After discussions with the analyst, we choose a recall $x = 0.2$. We also use two usual aggregated metrics, the ROC AUC and the PR AUC. Results are displayed in Table 3.

5.3 Results

In Table 3, we first observe that oversampling strategies that preserve coherence (MGS-1NN and MGS-GRF) leads to better predictive performances than the non-coherent ones (SMOTE-NC, MGS-NC, MGS-5NN). Besides, we remark that SMOTE-NC induces the greatest deterioration of predictive performances, for example −28% of PR AUC on the private data set. Furthermore, MGS-NC strategy leads to better predictive performances than SMOTE-NC for all three data sets, reinforcing conclusions of [25]: the MGS KDE is better suited than SMOTE linear interpolation for minority class continuous features regeneration. We also see that our proposed method MGS-GRF has the best predictive performances for BankChurners and BankMarketing in Table 3 for all metrics, with a running time (for oversampling and LightGBM training) close to that of SMOTE-NC.

For the private data set, we observe that MGS-GRF and CW are the two best strategies (in italics). Those are promising results for our method and validate our findings of Sect. 4.2 and Sect. 4.3 on association and coherence. To take

Table 3. BankChurners, BankMarketing and Private data sets. For confidentiality motivations, private data set metrics are relative gains compared to None strategy and no running time is provided. Standard deviations are available in Table 4.

Metric	Data	Strategy									
		None	CW	ROS	RUS	SMOTE-NC	MGS-NC	MGS-5NN	MGS-1NN	MGS-GRF	CW×MGS-GRF
Pr-at-rec (0.2)	Churn	0.894	0.870	0.847	0.632	0.850	0.908	0.910	0.913	**0.930**	–
	Mark.	0.119	0.118	0.115	0.106	0.093	0.128	0.126	0.128	**0.129**	–
	Private	Ref.	9%	2%	9%	−34%	7%	9%	9 %	9%	**13%**
PR AUC	Churn	0.622	0.608	0.576	0.394	0.595	0.655	0.653	0.663	**0.664**	–
	Mark.	0.092	0.090	0.090	0.082	0.076	0.099	0.099	0.098	**0.100**	–
	Private	Ref.	11%	7%	10%	−28%	8%	8%	10%	11%	**15%**
ROC AUC	Churn	0.977	0.971	0.963	0.941	0.975	0.983	0.983	**0.984**	**0.984**	–
	Mark.	0.890	0.882	0.878	0.881	0.861	**0.899**	**0.899**	**0.899**	0.898	–
	Private	Ref.	0%	0%	0%	−2%	0%	0%	0%	0%	0%
Time (s)	Churn.	0.296	0.333	0.494	0.060	0.852	2.158	1.245	1.217	0.893	–
	Mark	1.294	1.338	1.919	0.288	4.214	16.274	8.050	7.767	5.869	–

advantage of both strategies, we built an ensemble learning model CW×MGS-GRF combining the two LightGBM obtained after CW and MGS-GRF strategies. This methodology obtains the best results by far, highlighting the fact that samples generated via MGS-GRF procedure are informative for the learning task.

6 Conclusion and Perspectives

In this paper, we propose an oversampling strategy, MGS-GRF which synthesizes continuous features with a kernel density estimator and categorical ones by a GRF. We show through our first experimental protocol with simulated data (Sect. 4.2), that coherent strategies (MGS-1NN and MGS-GRF) lead to better predictive performances in terms of PR AUC and ROC AUC. Then, in Sect. 4.3, we show that nearest-neighbor based oversampling strategies are not well suited to handle categorical variables, since they do not preserve the association of generated samples in the presence of noisy features.

We performed numerical experiments on two real-world open source data sets and an industrial private data set from a financial institution which is used in production. Our results show that MGS-GRF is the most promising strategy for real-world applications, achieving the best predictive performances. Thus, we recommend designing strategies are coherent and preserve association and, among those, we recommend the use of our proposed method MGS-GRF, which achieves the best predictive performances on real-world data sets.

Acknowledgments. We would like to express our gratitude to the following individuals for their valuable help and feedbacks : Vincent AURIAU, Mohamed CHTIBA, Jean-Baptiste JANVIER, Martin KLIEBER and Benjamin BOSCH.

A Details on protocols

A.1 Numerical Illustrations of Non-coherence Phenomenon

The protocol from Sect. 4.2 with 6 configuration values for Θ, α, Γ. For each configuration, 50 different data sets (with different seeds) are generated. All in all, we obtain 300 datasets. Finally, each data set is composed of 5000 samples with an imbalance ratio less than 10%. For each data set, we apply different rebalancing strategies and apply a LightGBM classifier on the rebalanced data set.

A.2 Protocol: High Dimensional Setting

The protocol from Sect. 4.3 is executed with the following dimensions values $d : [5, 10, 20, 30, 50, 100, 150, 200]$. All the dimensions share the same parameter values. Each dimension simulation is executed 20 times in order to be able to compute standard deviations. Regarding the generation of the samples, let π_1, π_2, π_3 be the proportions of these three Gaussians, we have $\pi_1 = \pi_2 \gg \pi_3$.

Details on Fig. 2a. The Bayes Classifier for the *Asso* of Fig. 2a is derived empirically from a LightGBM trained on continuous features to predict the categorical feature. This latter model is trained on a different simulated data sets with millions of samples. We make this choice because we predict only one categorical feature and because LightGBm is a consistent estimator.

B Supplementary Materials

Table 4. Table 3 with standard deviations. For confidentiality motivations, all metrics of the private data set are relative gains compared to None strategy.

Metric	Data	Strategy									
		None	CW	ROS	RUS	SMOTE-NC	MGS-NC	MGS-5NN	MGS-1NN	MGS-GRF	CWxM GS-GRF
Pr-at-rec (0.2)	Churn	0.894	0.870	0.847	0.632	0.850	0.908	0.910	0.913	**0.930**	–
	std	±0.051	±0.056	±0.061	±0.123	±0.053	±0.057	±0.048	±0.050	±0.052	
	Mark.	0.119	0.118	0.115	0.106	0.093	0.128	0.126	0.128	**0.129**	–
	std	±0.009	±0.009	±0.011	±0.012	±0.007	±0.014	±0.008	±0.012	±0.008	
	Private	Ref.	9%	2%	9%	−34%	7%	9%	9 %	9%	13%
PR AUC	Churn	0.622	0.608	0.576	0.394	0.595	0.655	0.653	0.663	**0.664**	–
	std	±0.024	±0.026	±0.024	±0.043	±0.021	±0.026	±0.024	±0.022	±0.025	
	Mark.	0.092	0.090	0.090	0.082	0.076	0.099	0.099	0.098	**0.100**	–
	std	±0.008	±0.005	±0.006	±0.006	±0.004	±0.005	±0.005	±0.006	±0.006	
	Private	Ref.	11%	7%	10%	−28%	8%	8%	10%	11%	15%
ROC AUC	Churn	0.977	0.971	0.963	0.941	0.975	0.983	0.983	**0.984**	**0.984**	–
	std	±0.005	±0.005	±0.006	±0.008	±0.004	±0.002	±0.003	±0.003	±0.002	
	Mark.	0.890	0.882	0.878	0.881	0.861	**0.899**	**0.899**	**0.899**	0.898	–
	std	±0.003	±0.004	±0.003	±0.004	±0.004	±0.003	±0.002	±0.003	±0.003	
	Private	Ref.	0%	0%	0%	−2%	0%	0%	0%	0%	0%
Time (s)	Churn.	0.296	0.333	0.494	0.060	0.852	2.158	1.245	1.217	0.893	–
	std	±0.015	±0.022	±0.032	±0.003	±0.069	±0.051	±0.038	±0.056	±0.033	
	Mark	1.294	1.338	1.919	0.288	4.214	16.274	8.050	7.767	5.869	–
	std	±0.022	±0.033	±0.088	±0.010	±0.054	±0.563	±0.086	±0.203	±1.342	

References

1. Athey, S., Tibshirani, J., Wager, S.: Generalized random forests (2019)
2. Biau, G.: Analysis of a random forests model. J. Mach. Learn. Res. **13**(1), 1063–1095 (2012)
3. Breiman, L.: Random forests. Mach. Learn. **45**, 5–32 (2001)
4. Cao, K., Wei, C., Gaidon, A., Arechiga, N., Ma, T.: Learning imbalanced datasets with label-distribution-aware margin loss. Adv. Neural Inf. Process. Syst. **32** (2019)
5. Chawla, N.V., Bowyer, K.W., Hall, L.O., Kegelmeyer, W.P.: SMOTE: synthetic minority over-sampling technique. Journal of Artificial Intelligence Research (2002)
6. Chen, Y., Wiesel, A., Eldar, Y.C., Hero, A.O.: Shrinkage algorithms for MMSE covariance estimation. IEEE Trans. Sig. Process. **58**(10) (2010)
7. Fernández, A., García, S., Galar, M., Prati, R.C., Krawczyk, B., Herrera, F.: Learning from imbalanced data sets, vol. 10. Springer (2018)
8. Garchery, M., Granitzer, M.: On the influence of categorical features in ranking anomalies using mixed data. Procedia Comput. Sci. **126**, 77–86 (2018)
9. Grinsztajn, L., Oyallon, E., Varoquaux, G.: Why do tree-based models still outperform deep learning on typical tabular data? Adv. Neural. Inf. Process. Syst. **35**, 507–520 (2022)
10. Han, H., Wang, W.Y., Mao, B.H.: Borderline-smote: a new over-sampling method in imbalanced data sets learning. In: International Conference on Intelligent Computing, pp. 878–887. Springer (2005)
11. Hassan, A.K.I., Abraham, A.: Modeling insurance fraud detection using imbalanced data classification. In: Advances in Nature and Biologically Inspired Computing: Proceedings of the 7th World Congress on Nature and Biologically Inspired Computing (NaBIC2015) in Pietermaritzburg, South Africa, held December 01-03, 2015, pp. 117–127. Springer (2016)
12. He, H., Bai, Y., Garcia, E.A., Li, S.: ADASYN: adaptive synthetic sampling approach for imbalanced learning. In: 2008 IEEE International Joint Conference on Neural Networks (IEEE World Congress on Computational Intelligence). IEEE (2008)
13. Ke, G., et al.: LightGBM: a highly efficient gradient boosting decision tree. Adv. Neural Inf. Process. Syst. **30** (2017)
14. Khalilia, M., Chakraborty, S., Popescu, M.: Predicting disease risks from highly imbalanced data using random forest. BMC Med. Inform. Decis. Mak. **11**, 1–13 (2011)
15. Kotelnikov, A., Baranchuk, D., Rubachev, I., Babenko, A.: TabDDPM: modelling tabular data with diffusion models. In: International Conference on Machine Learning, pp. 17564–17579. PMLR (2023)
16. Ledoit, O., Wolf, M.: A well-conditioned estimator for large-dimensional covariance matrices. J. Multivar. Anal. **88**(2), 365–411 (2004)
17. Lee, S.S.: Regularization in skewed binary classification. Comput. Stat. **14**, 277–292 (1999)
18. Lee, S.S.: Noisy replication in skewed binary classification. Comput. Stat. Data Anal. **34**(2), 165–191 (2000)
19. Li, K., et al.: SEFraud: graph-based self-explainable fraud detection via interpretative mask learning. In: Proceedings of the 30th ACM SIGKDD Conference on Knowledge Discovery and Data Mining, pp. 5329–5338 (2024)
20. Lin, T.Y., Goyal, P., Girshick, R., He, K., Dollár, P.: Focal loss for dense object detection. In: Proceedings of the IEEE International Conference on Computer Vision, pp. 2980–2988 (2017)

21. Menardi, G., Torelli, N.: Training and assessing classification rules with imbalanced data. Data Min. Knowl. Disc. **28**, 92–122 (2014)
22. Mukherjee, M., Khushi, M.: SMOTE-ENC: a novel smote-based method to generate synthetic data for nominal and continuous features. Appl. Syst. Innovation **4**(1), 18 (2021)
23. Nguyen, N.N., Duong, A.T.: Comparison of two main approaches for handling imbalanced data in churn prediction problem. J. Adv. Inf. Technol. **12**(1) (2021)
24. Pedregosa, F., et al.: Scikit-learn: machine learning in Python. J. Mach. Learn. Res. **12**, 2825–2830 (2011)
25. Sakho, A., Malherbe, E., Scornet, E.: Do we need rebalancing strategies? A theoretical and empirical study around smote and its variants. arXiv:2402.03819 (2024)
26. Scott, D.W.: Multivariate density estimation: theory, practice, and visualization. John Wiley & Sons (2015)
27. Spelmen, V.S., Porkodi, R.: A review on handling imbalanced data. In: 2018 international conference on current trends towards converging technologies (ICCTCT), pp. 1–11. IEEE (2018)
28. Stanfill, C., Waltz, D.: Toward memory-based reasoning. Commun. ACM **29**(12), 1213–1228 (1986)
29. Stocksieker, S., Pommeret, D., Charpentier, A.: Generalized oversampling for learning from imbalanced datasets and associated theory: Application in regression
30. Sun, Y., Wong, A.K., Kamel, M.S.: Classification of imbalanced data: a review. Int. J. Pattern Recogn. Artif. Intell. **23**(04) (2009)
31. Tang, B., He, H.: KernelADASYN: kernel based adaptive synthetic data generation for imbalanced learning. In: IEEE Congress on Evolutionary Computation (2015)
32. Xu, L., Skoularidou, M., Cuesta-Infante, A., Veeramachaneni, K.: Modeling tabular data using conditional GAN. Adv. Neural Inf. Process. Syst. **32** (2019)
33. Zhyli: Prediction of churning credit card customers [data set] (2020)

Proactive Detection of Model Degradation in Financial Fraud Prediction with Delayed Labels

Akshay Sethi[✉], Priyanshi Gupta, Sparsh Kansotia, Kamal Kant, and Nitish Srivasatava

AI Garage, Mastercard, Gurugram, India
{akshay.sethi,priyanshi.gupta,sparsh.kansotia,
kamal.kant,nitish.srivasatava}@mastercard.com

Abstract. Financial fraud detection systems rely on machine learning models, but their performance degrades over time due to concept and covariate drift. A critical challenge is the delayed label problem: ground truth labels (confirming fraud) often arrive 1–6 months after the initial prediction. This creates a "blind period" where models can silently deteriorate, leading to substantial financial losses. Existing monitoring approaches, relying on delayed labels or statistical drift detection, are often too slow or insensitive. To address this, we propose PRODEM (PROactive DEtection of Model degradation), a framework that detects model degradation without immediate ground truth. PRODEM uses a meta-modeling technique: a sophisticated "meta-model" learns to predict when the deployed "primary" fraud model will make errors. We use a reverse distillation approach, where the meta-model specifically targets error prediction in out-of-time scenarios typical of fraud detection. Experiments on two proprietary datasets from a payment network show that PRODEM significantly improves degradation detection compared to statistical methods and recent drift detection techniques. Importantly, PRODEM identifies failing models before ground truth labels become available, mitigating the financial impact of model degradation in high-stakes decision-making. We also demonstrate PRODEM's effectiveness at identifying increases in false positive rates, a crucial but often overlooked aspect of fraud model monitoring.

Keywords: Fraud Detection · Delayed Labels · Model Degradation · Drift Detection · Meta-modeling · Reverse Distillation

1 Introduction

Financial fraud presents a significant threat to the global economy, with total losses soaring to approximately $485.6 billion in 2023 [7]. Fraud detection systems are essential for minimizing these financial losses and protecting institutions from evolving threats. However, a major challenge in this domain is the

delayed label problem: ground truth labels confirming fraud often arrive 1–6 months after a transaction is processed [9]. This delay is due to factors such as lengthy investigations, customer dispute processes, and chargeback periods. This "blind period" creates a significant vulnerability where machine learning models, commonly used for fraud prediction, can degrade silently due to covariate drift (changes in the input feature distribution while the relationship between features and target remains stable) and concept drift (changes in the relationship between features and the target variable).

These distribution shifts are driven by the constantly evolving landscape of financial fraud. Fraudsters adapt their tactics, new attack vectors emerge, and seasonal variations, economic fluctuations, changes in customer behavior all contribute to shifts in the underlying data distribution [38]. This makes the problem *increasingly critical* as fraud attacks become more sophisticated and regulatory scrutiny intensifies. Without timely feedback, a model trained on historical data can quickly become outdated and ineffective. The combination of sophisticated fraud techniques and stringent regulatory requirements necessitates effective monitoring systems.

Existing model monitoring approaches are inadequate for addressing this challenge effectively. Methods relying on delayed ground truth are, by definition, too late; significant losses can accumulate before any action is triggered. Statistical drift detection techniques, such as Kolmogorov-Smirnov tests [2], Population Stability Index (PSI) [6], and Wasserstein distance metrics [40] often struggle to distinguish between harmless covariate drift and performance-impacting concept drift. This can lead to either excessive false alarms, reducing operational efficiency by prompting unnecessary investigations, or, worse, missed degradation signals. More recent approaches integrate machine learning with statistical testing [20], but still exhibit similar limitations.

To address these shortcomings, we introduce PRODEM (PROactive DEtection of Model degradation), a framework that detects model degradation *before* ground truth labels become available. PRODEM employs a meta-modeling approach, where a sophisticated "meta-model" is trained to predict the errors of the deployed "primary" fraud prediction model. We leverage a **reverse distillation** technique, where, unlike traditional knowledge distillation—where a smaller model learns from a larger one—our meta-model is *more complex* than the primary model. This design choice, driven by production constraints on the primary model, enables the meta-model to capture subtle patterns indicative of future errors, particularly in out-of-time scenarios common in fraud detection with delayed feedback. The meta-model learns, in essence, the "failure modes" of the primary model. This proactive approach enables timely intervention – such as model retraining, feature re-engineering, or adjustments to decision thresholds – mitigating the financial impact of model degradation and preventing a prolonged period of increased losses.

A particularly overlooked aspect of monitoring financial fraud detection is the importance of identifying false positives, cases where legitimate transactions are incorrectly flagged as fraudulent. In label-delayed environments, a silent increase in false positive rates can go undetected for months, resulting in significant customer friction when legitimate transactions are declined and eventual loss of confidence in the automated system. PRODEM addresses this challenge by outperforming existing methods in detecting increases in false positive rates with greater accuracy and timeliness.

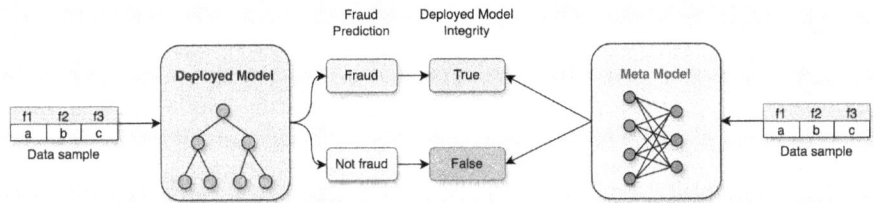

Fig. 1. The PRODEM framework architecture. The deployed model generates fraud predictions on transaction data, while the meta-model analyzes the same inputs to predict the likelihood of the deployed model making errors. This enables early detection of model degradation during periods of label unavailability.

Our key contributions are:

- A framework, PRODEM, for the proactive detection of model degradation in financial fraud detection systems operating under delayed label conditions, enabling timely intervention and risk mitigation.
- A meta-modeling approach leveraging reverse distillation to predict the errors of a deployed fraud model, specifically designed to handle the out-of-time challenges inherent in this domain. This allows the meta-model to learn complex patterns that the primary model misses.
- Demonstrated superior performance on two real-world financial fraud datasets from a payment network, significantly outperforming existing statistical and drift detection methods in identifying errors and model degradation.

The remainder of this paper is organized as follows: Sect. 2 reviews related work in model monitoring and drift detection. Section 3 describes our PRODEM framework in detail. Section 4 presents our experimental setup. Section 5 evaluates PRODEM's degradation detection capabilities and analyzes error prediction performance. Finally, Sect. 6 concludes the paper and outlines directions for future research.

2 Related Work

Model degradation from temporal distribution shifts presents a fundamental challenge in machine learning, particularly in dynamic domains like financial fraud detection. This section reviews relevant literature, highlighting limitations of existing approaches when confronted with delayed label availability.

2.1 Drift Detection

Drift detection methods identify changes in data distributions that may impact model performance [8]. These methods typically address two primary types of drift: covariate drift and concept drift. Traditional statistical approaches include the Kolmogorov-Smirnov test [2], Population Stability Index (PSI) [6,40], and Wasserstein distance metric [6,40], which compare reference and current distributions. However, these methods often fail to distinguish harmful concept drift from benign covariate drift, leading to false alarms or missed degradation signals.

Recent advances have integrated machine learning with statistical testing. Hinder et al. [16] combined JS-Divergence with feature importance analysis, while Webb et al. [37] introduced techniques for early drift detection by analyzing changes in low-density regions. Despite these improvements, these methods remain fundamentally reactive rather than proactive when confronted with delayed labels.

2.2 Model Monitoring Systems

Production model monitoring systems have evolved beyond simple performance tracking. Pozzolo et al. [30] developed adaptive learning frameworks for credit card fraud detection, though computational costs limit practical adoption [32]. Modern approaches employ multi-faceted monitoring stacks. Breck et al. [29] introduced a comprehensive validation framework examining data quality, model staleness, and prediction drift simultaneously.

These sophisticated systems remain largely reactive—they either observe performance degradation (requiring delayed labels) or detect statistical data drift (an imperfect proxy for performance degradation). They do not predict future model errors before ground truth labels become available.

2.3 Anomaly and Out of Distribution Detection

Anomaly detection and Out-of-Distribution (OOD) detection approaches identify irregular patterns and data points that deviate from expected distributions. Statistical anomaly detection methods like Isolation Forest [23] and One-Class SVM [36] establish decision boundaries around normal data. Deep learning approaches have expanded these capabilities, with methods such as Variational Autoencoders demonstrating particular effectiveness in practical applications like credit card fraud detection [33].

For OOD detection, Hendrycks and Gimpel [14] proposed Maximum Softmax Probability (MSP) for detecting OOD samples. Lee et al. [21] improved this approach with Mahalanobis distance-based confidence scores, while Liu et al. [24] demonstrated even better performance using energy-based models that leverage energy scores derived from logit outputs.

While these methods can signal model degradation through emerging anomaly clusters or distribution shifts, they have limitations for proactive monitoring. They primarily focus on identifying individual anomalous or out of distribution instances rather than systematic degradation patterns, and don't directly assess whether model predictions will be incorrect.

2.4 Meta-modeling for Error Prediction and Anomaly Detection

Our approach in PRODEM employs meta-modeling for error prediction, where auxiliary models predict the errors of primary fraud detection models. Several foundational works have explored this paradigm: Platanios et al. [28] developed a framework for estimating machine learning model accuracy without ground truth labels, while Raghu et al. [31] used meta-models to predict when deep learning models would fail in medical imaging classification tasks. Xiao et al. [39] proposed a meta-modeling framework for model error prediction in computer vision tasks, though their approach relies on dense feature representations specific to image data that do not transfer well to financial transaction data. Han et al. [12] propose SuperMentor, an oracle framework for predicting model correctness across in-domain, out-of-domain, and adversarial inputs with cross-model generalization capabilities, but their approach operates on static image datasets with readily available ground truth labels, making it unsuitable for delayed-feedback scenarios typical of fraud detection.

Another relevant paradigm comes from anomaly detection methods using reverse distillation [5,18,25,27]. In this approach, a "student" model is trained to reproduce the feature representations of a "teacher" model exposed only to normal data. When encountering anomalous samples, the student's inability to accurately reconstruct the teacher's output generates high reconstruction error, serving as an anomaly score. This principle of identifying deviations from learned norms aligns conceptually with our goal of predicting model errors when encountering evolving fraud patterns.

Building on these foundational ideas, PRODEM addresses the specific challenge of delayed labels in financial fraud detection through a novel meta-modeling approach with reverse distillation. Unlike traditional reactive methods that wait for confirmed fraud labels, our framework proactively identifies potential model failures before significant financial losses accumulate, enabling timely intervention in the face of evolving fraud patterns.

3 Methodology

3.1 Problem Formulation

Let $\mathcal{D}_{\text{train}} = \{(x_i, y_i)\}_{i=1}^{N}$ represent the training dataset used to develop a fraud detection model, where each sample consists of tabular features $x_i \in \mathbb{R}^d$ and a corresponding binary fraud label $y_i \in \{0, 1\}$. The deployed fraud detection model $f_{\text{deploy}} : \mathbb{R}^d \to [0, 1]$ maps input features to fraud probability estimations, with a decision threshold θ determining the binary prediction: $\hat{y}_i = \mathbf{1}[f_{\text{deploy}}(x_i) > \theta]$.

In operational environments, financial institutions continuously receive new data $\mathcal{D}_{\text{recent}}$ requiring immediate predictions. However, the corresponding ground truth labels only become available after a significant delay period τ (typically

1–6 months), creating a blind spot during which model degradation may occur undetected. This delay can be formalized as: y_t becomes available only at time $t + \tau$ where t represents the timestamp of an observation.

The objective of PRODEM is to develop a meta-model $f_{\text{meta}} : \mathbb{R}^d \to [0, 1]$ that estimates the probability that the deployed model will make an error on a given input x:

$$f_{\text{meta}}(x) = P(\hat{y} \neq y | x) = \begin{cases} 1, & \text{if } f_{\text{deploy}}(x) \text{ incorrectly predicts } y \\ 0, & \text{otherwise} \end{cases} \quad (1)$$

By accurately estimating the deployed model's error probability distribution on recent data, the meta-model enables early detection of model degradation during the label lag period, allowing for timely interventions before significant financial losses materialize.

3.2 PRODEM Framework Overview

Our PRODEM framework, illustrated in Fig. 1, addresses the challenge of detecting model degradation during the label lag period through a two-tier architecture:

Deployed Model. The deployed model f_{deploy} represents the production fraud detection system in operation. In financial fraud detection domains, these models are predominantly tree-based ensemble algorithms (e.g., Gradient Boosted Trees [4,19], Random Forests [3]) due to their effectiveness with tabular data, interpretability requirements, and operational efficiency constraints. The deployed model remains fixed throughout the monitoring process, as it represents the actual production system under surveillance.

Meta-model. The meta-model f_{meta} serves as a specialized error predictor designed to anticipate the deployed model's misclassifications. Unlike the deployed model, the meta-model is not subject to the same operational constraints, enabling the utilization of more sophisticated architectures to capture nuanced patterns of model degradation. We implement the meta-model as a neural network with residual connections and attention mechanisms. This design allows f_{meta} to flexibly model complex error patterns that emerge from shifting data distributions, including evolving fraud strategies and gradual feature drift.

The meta-model processes the same input features as the deployed model but produces two outputs: (1) an approximation of the deployed model's prediction and (2) a probability estimate of the deployed model making an error.

This design enables PRODEM to provide actionable early warnings about reliability decay in the absence of fresh ground-truth labels, helping institutions mitigate risk before degradation materially impacts business performance. This dual output architecture is essential for the reverse distillation process described below.

3.3 Reverse Distillation Approach

Traditional knowledge distillation [11,17] transfers knowledge from a complex teacher model to a simpler student model. PRODEM inverts this paradigm through "reverse distillation", where a more sophisticated meta-model learns to model the behavior of a simpler deployed model with the specific objective of predicting its errors.

This approach is motivated by the operational reality in financial fraud detection, where production models must prioritize inference speed and interpretability over complexity. By allowing the meta-model to develop an internal representation of the deployed model's decision boundaries, we enable it to identify regions of uncertainty, blind spots, and failure modes that emerge as data distributions evolve over time.

3.4 Model Architecture

Deployed Model Architecture. The deployed model typically utilizes tree-based ensemble methods such as XGBoost [4] or LightGBM [19], which are industry standards for fraud detection tasks. The specific architecture of the deployed model is not altered by PRODEM—instead, PRODEM treats it as a black box system that produces fraud probability scores.

Meta-model Architecture. The meta-model employs a neural network architecture with the following key components:

$$h_1 = \text{ReLU}(W_1 x + b_1) \tag{2}$$

$$h_i = h_{i-1} + \text{ReLU}(W_i h_{i-1} + b_i) \quad \text{for } i \in \{2, \ldots, L-1\} \tag{3}$$

$$z_{\text{meta}} = W_L h_{L-1} + b_L \tag{4}$$

$$p_{\text{meta}} = \sigma(W_{\text{err}} h_{L-1} + b_{\text{err}}) \tag{5}$$

where h_i represents the hidden layer activations, z_{meta} represents the logits mimicking the deployed model, and p_{meta} represents the probability of the deployed model making an error. The residual connections ($h_i = h_{i-1} + \ldots$) [13] facilitate gradient flow through deep networks, allowing the meta-model to learn complex representations that capture both the deployed model's behavior and its failure modes.

Additionally, we incorporate a self-attention mechanism [34] to enable the model to focus on feature interactions that are particularly relevant for error prediction:

$$Q = W_Q h_j, \quad K = W_K h_j, \quad V = W_V h_j \tag{6}$$

$$\text{Attention}(Q, K, V) = \text{softmax}\left(\frac{QK^T}{\sqrt{d_k}}\right) V \tag{7}$$

$$h_j^{\text{attn}} = \text{Attention}(Q, K, V) + h_j \tag{8}$$

This enables the meta-model to dynamically weight feature importance based on context, aiding detection of subtle patterns that precede model failures.

3.5 Training Methodology

Composite Loss Function. The meta-model is trained using a composite loss function that balances two objectives:

$$\mathcal{L}_{\text{total}} = \alpha \mathcal{L}_{\text{logit}} + (1-\alpha)\mathcal{L}_{\text{error}} \tag{9}$$

where $\alpha \in [0,1]$ is a hyperparameter controlling the trade-off between the two components.

The logit matching loss $\mathcal{L}_{\text{logit}}$ facilitates the meta-model's understanding of the deployed model's decision-making process:

$$\mathcal{L}_{\text{logit}} = \text{MSE}(z_{\text{deploy}}, z_{\text{meta}}) + \beta \cdot \text{KL}\left(\sigma\left(\frac{z_{\text{deploy}}}{T}\right) \middle\| \sigma\left(\frac{z_{\text{meta}}}{T}\right)\right) \tag{10}$$

where $\text{MSE}(\cdot,\cdot)$ is mean squared error, $\text{KL}(\cdot\|\cdot)$ is Kullback-Leibler divergence, $\sigma(\cdot)$ is the softmax function, z_{deploy} and z_{meta} are the logits from the deployed and meta-models respectively, T is a temperature parameter controlling distribution softness, and β is a balancing hyperparameter.

The error prediction loss $\mathcal{L}_{\text{error}}$ employs focal loss [22], an enhanced version of binary cross-entropy that addresses class imbalance by down-weighting easy-to-classify examples:

$$\mathcal{L}_{\text{error}} = -\gamma \cdot [c_{\text{true}} \cdot (1-p_{\text{meta}})^\gamma \cdot \log(p_{\text{meta}}) + (1-c_{\text{true}}) \cdot p_{\text{meta}}^\gamma \cdot \log(1-p_{\text{meta}})] \tag{11}$$

where c_{true} is the ground truth correctness indicator, p_{meta} is the meta-model's predicted probability of error, and $\gamma \geq 0$ is the focusing parameter that reduces the loss contribution from easy examples.

Temporal Training Protocol. To effectively address model degradation in out-of-time scenarios, we implement a rigorous temporal training protocol with structured chronological data partitioning. The complete dataset $\mathcal{D}$ is partitioned into three segments:

$$\mathcal{D} = \mathcal{D}_{\text{train}} \cup \mathcal{D}_{\text{meta}} \cup \mathcal{D}_{\text{test}} \quad \text{where} \quad t_{\text{train}} < t_{\text{meta}} < t_{\text{test}} \tag{12}$$

where t represents the timestamps associated with each partition.

- $\mathcal{D}_{\text{train}}$ (first N months): Used exclusively to train the deployed model
- $\mathcal{D}_{\text{meta}}$ (subsequent M months, typically $M < N$): Used to train the meta-model
- $\mathcal{D}_{\text{test}}$ (remaining available data): Used for evaluation

This temporal separation ensures that the deployed model f_{deploy} is trained on past data, reflecting a realistic production scenario, while the meta-model f_{meta} learns to identify errors arising from temporal distribution shifts. This setup allows for an accurate evaluation of the meta-model's ability to anticipate model degradation before it affects business metrics.

3.6 Degradation Detection Mechanism

Operational Metrics Estimation. To operationalize model degradation detection, we construct a monitoring system based on meta-model error predictions. The meta-model enables estimation of critical performance metrics without requiring ground truth labels, providing early signals of degradation during the label lag period. We first estimate the confusion matrix components using meta-model predictions with a threshold ϵ:

$$\widehat{\text{FP}} = \sum_{i=1}^{|\mathcal{D}_{\text{recent}}|} \hat{y}_i \cdot \mathbb{I}[p_{\text{meta}}(x_i) > \epsilon] \tag{13}$$

$$\widehat{\text{FN}} = \sum_{i=1}^{|\mathcal{D}_{\text{recent}}|} (1 - \hat{y}_i) \cdot \mathbb{I}[p_{\text{meta}}(x_i) > \epsilon] \tag{14}$$

$$\widehat{\text{TP}} = \sum_{i=1}^{|\mathcal{D}_{\text{recent}}|} \hat{y}_i \cdot \mathbb{I}[p_{\text{meta}}(x_i) \leq \epsilon] \tag{15}$$

$$\widehat{\text{TN}} = \sum_{i=1}^{|\mathcal{D}_{\text{recent}}|} (1 - \hat{y}_i) \cdot \mathbb{I}[p_{\text{meta}}(x_i) \leq \epsilon] \tag{16}$$

Here, $\hat{y}_i$ is the deployed model's binary prediction, $p_{\text{meta}}(x_i)$ is the meta-model's predicted probability of error for input x_i, and $\mathbb{I}[\cdot]$ is the indicator function that returns 1 if the condition is true and 0 otherwise. Using these estimated confusion matrix components, we calculate key performance metrics that financial institutions prioritize:

$$\widehat{\text{VDR}} = \frac{\sum_{i:\hat{y}_i=1} \text{Amount}_i \cdot \mathbb{I}[p_{\text{meta}}(x_i) \leq \epsilon]}{\sum_i \text{Amount}_i \cdot y_i} \tag{17}$$

$$\widehat{\text{FAR}} = \frac{\widehat{\text{FP}}}{\widehat{\text{TP}}} \tag{18}$$

where VDR (Value Detection Rate) measures the proportion of total fraud value correctly identified by the model, and FAR (False Alarm Rate) quantifies the ratio of false positives to true positives. In fraud detection, due to significant class imbalance, we monitor estimated False Positives ($\widehat{\text{FP}}$) directly as a degradation signal. Since true negatives (TN) vastly outnumber other components and remain relatively stable, an increase in false positives serves as an effective proxy for model degradation without requiring the full FPR calculation. The threshold ϵ is typically calibrated using historical data to optimize the trade-off between detection sensitivity and specificity.

Degradation Detection Heuristics. We establish degradation detection heuristics based on these estimated metrics by comparing them against baseline performance values:

$$\text{Degradation Alert} = \begin{cases} 1, & \frac{\widehat{\text{VDR}}_t}{\text{VDR}_{\text{baseline}}} < \delta_{\text{VDR}} \quad \text{or} \\ & \frac{\widehat{\text{FAR}}_t}{\text{FAR}_{\text{baseline}}} > \delta_{\text{FAR}} \quad \text{or} \\ & \frac{\widehat{\text{FP}}_t}{\text{FP}_{\text{baseline}}} > \delta_{\text{FP}} \\ 0, & \text{otherwise} \end{cases} \quad (19)$$

where δ_{VDR}, δ_{FAR}, and δ_{FP} are configurable thresholds (typically set to 0.75, 1.25, and 1.25 respectively) that trigger alerts when VDR decreases significantly or when FAR or FP increases significantly compared to the baseline.

4 Experiments

In this section, we present a thorough evaluation of the PRODEM framework on two financial fraud detection datasets, showcasing its ability to identify model degradation early—before ground truth labels become available.

4.1 Experimental Setup

Datasets. We evaluate PRODEM on two proprietary datasets from a payment network company.

- **Transaction Fraud Dataset (TF-Dataset):** This dataset contains card transaction data from a large issuer spanning 9 months with over 3 million transactions per month. Approximately 50% of transactions are declined by the issuer bank through their risk management systems. The feature set includes diverse risk scores, merchant identifiers, transaction type indicators, velocity features, and historical transaction patterns. The fraud rate among approved transactions is 0.42%. The dataset exhibits significant temporal patterns in both feature distributions and fraud tactics.
- **Account Fraud Dataset (AF-Dataset):** This dataset focuses on account-level (card-level) fraud detection for a large issuer spanning 9 months. It contains approximately 5 million active accounts per month with a positive class rate of 0.91%. Features include account profile characteristics, aggregated transaction patterns, risk scores, spending behavior statistics, and historical dispute information. This dataset exhibits pronounced seasonal effects and regional fraud pattern evolution.

Temporal Data Partitioning. Following the temporal protocol described in Sect. 3, we partition each dataset as follows. For both the TF and AF-Datasets, we use months 1–2 for $\mathcal{D}_{\text{train}}$ (deploy model training), month 3 for $\mathcal{D}_{\text{meta}}$ (meta-model training), and months 4–9 for $\mathcal{D}_{\text{test}}$ (evaluation).

The months 4–9 for $\mathcal{D}_{\text{test}}$ have been referred to as months 1–6 in the results section for better readability and ease of explanation.

4.2 Baselines

We compare PRODEM against established approaches for model monitoring and drift detection:

Statistical Distribution Monitoring

- **Kolmogorov-Smirnov (KS) Test**: Applied to top 20 features by importance to detect univariate distribution shifts.
- **Kullback-Leibler (KL) Divergence**: Measures distribution shifts in continuous features.

Output Distribution Monitoring

- **Maximum Class Probability (MCP)** [15]: Monitors the maximum prediction probability of the deployed model. Predictions with MCP below a threshold are flagged as potential errors.
- **Class Probability Entropy (CPE)** [26]: Calculates the entropy of the prediction probability distribution. Higher entropy indicates greater uncertainty in the model's prediction, potentially signaling an error.

Implementation Details

- **Fraud Detection Model** (f_{deploy}): XGBoost trained on $\mathcal{D}_{\text{train}}$ with 150 trees (max depth=10, learning rate=0.05) and subsampling (row=0.8, column=0.8). Hyperparameters optimized via optuna [1] using 5-fold cross-validation and weighted log-loss to address class imbalance (1:99 for TF-Dataset, 1:55 for AF-Dataset).
- **Meta-Model**: FT-Transformer [10] with tokenized tabular inputs and a Transformer encoder with multi-head self-attention. Architecture: 4 transformer blocks (hidden sizes: 256, 128, 64, 32), residual connections, layer normalization, SeLU activations, dropout (0.2), and L2 regularization (0.001). Optimized using Adam (lr=0.001) with cosine annealing, composite loss from Sect. 3 ($\alpha = 0.3$, $T = 2.0$), batch size 4096, trained for 100 epochs with early stopping, implemented in PyTorch and trained on NVIDIA A100 GPUs (80GB).
- **Baselines**: Baselines include Kolmogorov-Smirnov (KS) Test ($p < 0.01$), Kullback-Leibler (KL) Divergence ($KL > 0.5$), Maximum Class Probability (MCP) ($MCP < 0.7$), and Class Probability Entropy (CPE) ($CPE > 0.8$).

5 Results and Analysis

5.1 Error Prediction Performance

We first evaluate its ability to accurately predict when the deployed model will make errors. This error prediction capability forms the foundation of our proactive degradation detection framework. Table 1 presents the meta-model's performance in predicting deployed model errors across the two datasets, compared against baseline approaches.

Table 1. Error prediction performance comparison across datasets (best results in bold)

Dataset	Method	EDP	EDR
TF-Dataset	MCP	0.43	0.37
	CPE	0.51	0.48
	PRODEM	**0.66**	**0.64**
AF-Dataset	MCP	0.42	0.41
	CPE	0.45	0.49
	PRODEM	**0.68**	**0.65**

It's important to note that traditional statistical techniques (KS Test and KL Divergence) are not included in this comparison as they detect feature or score distribution drift rather than predicting specific model errors at the instance level. Their detection mechanisms operate at a distributional level, which is fundamentally different from the error prediction task evaluated here.

The results demonstrate that PRODEM achieves significant improvements in both precision (EDP) and recall (EDR) of error detection compared to uncertainty-based methods (MCP and CPE). For the TF-Dataset, PRODEM achieves an error detection precision of 0.66 and recall of 0.64, representing improvements of 29.4% and 33.3% respectively over the best baseline method. Similar improvements are observed for the AF-Dataset, with PRODEM achieving 51.1% higher precision and 32.7% higher recall compared to the best baseline.

This superior error prediction capability stems from the meta-model's ability to learn specific error patterns of the deployed model through our reverse distillation approach, enabling more accurate identification of potential misclassifications in the complex financial fraud domains represented by our proprietary datasets.

5.2 Model Degradation Detection

We next analyze how PRODEM's error prediction capability translates into early detection of model degradation compared to baseline approaches. Table 2

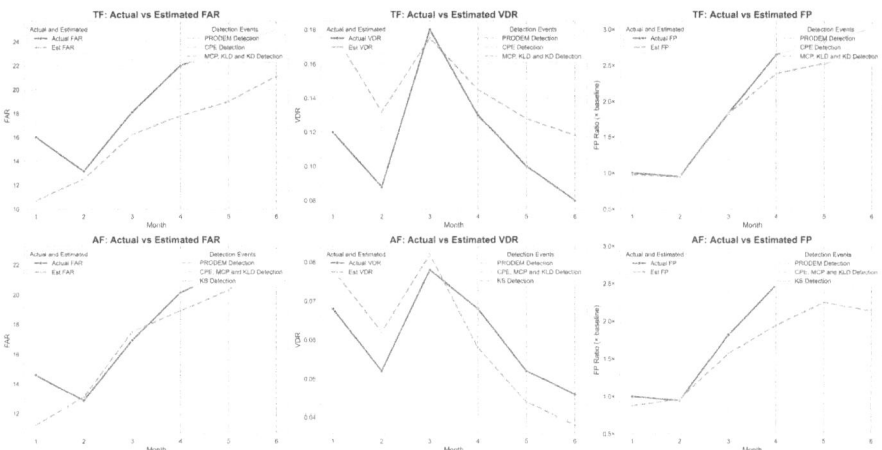

Fig. 2. Temporal comparison of estimated (PRODEM) versus actual performance metrics (VDR, FAR, and false positives) for TF-Dataset and AF-Dataset over the six-month testing period. Vertical markers indicate the month of degradation detection for different methods, with PRODEM demonstrating earlier detection (month 4) compared to baseline approaches. (To preserve data confidentiality, the Y-axis values for False Positives are presented as ratios normalized to the baseline month (Month 1).)

Table 2. Model degradation detection timing across datasets (lower month number indicates earlier detection)

Method	TF-Dataset (Month)	AF-Dataset (Month)
KS Test	6	6
KL Divergence	6	5
MCP	6	5
CPE	5	5
PRODEM	4	4

summarizes the performance of PRODEM and baseline approaches, showing the month in which each method first identified significant performance deterioration.

The results demonstrate that PRODEM provides significantly earlier detection of model degradation compared to baseline methods. For the TF-Dataset, PRODEM detected degradation in Month 4, while the best baseline methods only identified issues in Month 5. For the AF-Dataset, PRODEM detected degradation in Month 4, a full month before any baseline approach.

5.3 Temporal Performance Monitoring

Finally, we analyze how PRODEM monitors model performance over time compared to the actual performance metrics derived from ground truth labels. This analysis is crucial for understanding how accurately PRODEM can track degradation patterns in deployed models throughout the label delay period. Figure 2 shows the estimated versus actual performance metrics for both datasets over the testing period.

For the TF-Dataset, our analysis reveals significant changes in key metrics over the six-month monitoring period. The value detection rate (VDR) showed substantial fluctuations, with a 55.6% decrease from Month 1 to Month 6. PRODEM effectively tracked these changes, with estimated VDR following a similar pattern, showing a 34.1% decline over the same period. Most critically, false positives increased dramatically by 201% from Month 1 to Month 6. PRODEM successfully estimated this trend, projecting a 170% increase in false positives over the same timeframe. The false acceptance rate (FAR) estimates by PRODEM showed a consistent upward trend, increasing by 56% from Month 1 to Month 6.

For the AF-Dataset, we also observed notable variations in key metrics. The VDR decreased by 32.4% from Month 1 to Month 6. PRODEM accurately tracked this degradation, with estimated VDR decreasing by 51.3%. False positives increased dramatically by 173% over the monitoring period. PRODEM's estimates closely followed this trend, projecting a 144% increase in false positives. The FAR estimates showed a steady increase of 48% from Month 1 to Month 6.

For both datasets, PRODEM demonstrated remarkable accuracy in tracking critical metric changes during periods of significant degradation. The average deviation between PRODEM's estimated metrics and actual metrics was approximately 14.5% for VDR and 7.2% for false positives throughout the testing period. This confirms PRODEM's effectiveness in providing advance warning of model degradation, with particularly strong performance in tracking false positive rate increases, a critical concern in fraud detection systems where the cost of false positives directly impacts customer experience and operational efficiency.

6 Conclusion

We introduced PRODEM, a proactive framework for detecting model degradation in financial fraud detection systems under label delay constraints. Leveraging a meta-modeling approach with reverse distillation, PRODEM identifies performance deterioration without requiring immediate ground truth. Evaluations on two proprietary datasets show PRODEM provides a 1–2 month advance warning over traditional monitoring, enabling timely intervention. Key contributions include a meta-modeling approach for proactive error prediction of fraud models, a reverse distillation-based loss, and a temporal training protocol for out-of-time degradation. PRODEM significantly improves error detection precision and recall over baselines.

Future work includes incorporating explainability, and developing adaptive monitoring thresholds based on the severity and type of detected degradation patterns.

7 Ethics Statement

Our proposed framework does not raise any ethical concerns. However, it is essential to acknowledge that ethical applications of financial fraud detection can greatly benefit from the improved early warning capabilities and performance enhancements provided by PRODEM. To ensure responsible and socially beneficial deployment of machine learning in financial systems, it is crucial to exercise caution, transparency, and fairness in model monitoring and adaptation. This involves not only maintaining accountability in how alerts are generated and acted upon, but also ensuring that model updates do not reinforce existing biases or disproportionately impact specific customer segments over time or across different demographics.

References

1. Akiba, T., Sano, S., et al.: Optuna: a next-generation hyperparameter optimization framework. In: Proceedings of the 25th ACM SIGKDD International Conference on Knowledge Discovery & Data Mining, pp. 2623–2631 (2019)
2. Berger, V.W., Zhou, Y.: Kolmogorov-smirnov test: Overview. Statistics reference online, Wiley statsref (2014)
3. Breiman, L.: Random forests. Machine learning (2001)
4. Chen, T., Guestrin, C.: XGBoost: a scalable tree boosting system. In: Proceedings of the 22nd ACM SIGKDD International Conference on Knowledge Discovery and Data Mining, pp. 785–794 (2016)
5. Deng, H., Li, X.: Anomaly detection via reverse distillation from one-class embedding. In: Proceedings of the IEEE/CVF Conference on Computer Vision and Pattern Recognition, pp. 9737–9746 (2022)
6. Dries, A., Rückert, U.: Adaptive concept drift detection. The ASA Data Science Journal, Statistical Analysis and Data Mining (2009)
7. Friedman, A.: Global financial report, 2024. NASDAQ (2024)
8. Gama, J.a., Žliobaitundefined, I., et al.: A survey on concept drift adaptation. ACM Comput. Surv. (2014)
9. Garg, N.: Feature engineering for fraud detection. Fennel (2022)
10. Gorishniy, Y., Rubachev, I., et al.: Revisiting deep learning models for tabular data. Advances in Neural Information Processing Systems (2021)
11. Gou, J., Yu, B., et al.: Knowledge distillation: A survey. International Journal of Computer Vision (2021)
12. Han, S., et al.: An oracle for in-domain, out-of-domain, and adversarial errors. arXiv preprint (2024)
13. He, K., Zhang, X., et al.: Deep residual learning for image recognition. In: Proceedings of the IEEE Conference on Computer Vision and Pattern Recognition (2016)
14. Hendrycks, D., Basart, S., et al.: Scaling out-of-distribution detection for real-world settings. arXiv preprint (2019)
15. Hendrycks, D., Gimpel, K.: A baseline for detecting misclassified and out-of-distribution examples in neural networks. arXiv preprint (2016)
16. Hinder, F., Vaquet, V., Hammer, B.: Feature-based analyses of concept drift. Neurocomputing (2024)

17. Hinton, G., Vinyals, O., Dean, J.: Distilling the knowledge in a neural network. arXiv preprint (2015)
18. Jiang, Y., Cao, Y., Shen, W.: A masked reverse knowledge distillation method incorporating global and local information for image anomaly detection. Knowledge-Based Systems (2023)
19. Ke, G., Meng, Q., et al.: LightGBM: a highly efficient gradient boosting decision tree. Advances in Neural Information Processing Systems (2017)
20. Kulatilleke, G.K.: Challenges and complexities in machine learning based credit card fraud detection. arXiv preprint (2022)
21. Lee, K., Lee, K., et al.: A simple unified framework for detecting out-of-distribution samples and adversarial attacks. Advances in Neural Information Processing Systems (2018)
22. Lin, T.Y., Goyal, P., et al.: Focal loss for dense object detection. In: Proceedings of the IEEE International Conference on Computer Vision, pp. 2980–2988 (2017)
23. Liu, F.T., Ting, K.M., Zhou, Z.H.: Isolation forest. In: 8th IEEE International Conference on Data Mining, pp. 413–422 (2008)
24. Liu, W., Wang, X., et al.: Energy-based out-of-distribution detection. Advances in Neural Information Processing Systems (2020)
25. Liu, X., Wang, J., et al.: Unlocking the potential of reverse distillation for anomaly detection. In: Proceedings of the AAAI Conference on Artificial Intelligence, pp. 5640–5648 (2025)
26. Macêdo, D., Ren, T.I., et al.: Entropic out-of-distribution detection. IEEE Transactions on Neural Networks and Learning Systems (2021)
27. Nasser, S.A., Gupte, N., Sethi, A.: Reverse knowledge distillation: training a large model using a small one for retinal image matching on limited data. In: Proceedings of the IEEE/CVF Winter Conference on Applications of Computer Vision, pp. 7778–7787 (2024)
28. Platanios, E., et al.: Estimating accuracy from unlabeled data: a probabilistic logic approach. Advances in Neural Information Processing Systems (2017)
29. Polyzotis, N., Zinkevich, M., et al.: Data validation for machine learning. Proceedings of Machine Learning and Systems (2019)
30. Pozzolo, A.D., Bontempi, G.: Adaptive machine learning for credit card fraud detection (2015)
31. Raghu, M., Blumer, K., et al.: The algorithmic automation problem: Prediction, triage, and human effort. arXiv preprint (2019)
32. Sethi, T.S., Kantardzic, M., Arabmakki, E.: Monitoring classification blindspots to detect drifts from unlabeled data. In: 2016 IEEE 17th International Conference on Information Reuse and Integration (IRI), pp. 142–151 (2016)
33. Tingfei, H., Guangquan, C., Kuihua, H.: Using variational auto encoding in credit card fraud detection. IEEE Access (2020)
34. Vaswani, A., Shazeer, N., et al.: Attention is all you need. Advances in Neural Information Processing Systems (2017)
35. Veit, A., Wilber, M.J., et al.: Residual networks behave like ensembles of relatively shallow networks. Advances in Neural Information Processing Systems (2016)
36. Vert, R., Vert, J.P., Schölkopf, B.: Consistency and convergence rates of one-class SVMs and related algorithms. Journal of Machine Learning Research (2006)
37. Webb, G.I., Hyde, R., Cao, H., Nguyen, H.L., Petitjean, F.: Characterizing concept drift. Data Min. Knowl. Disc. **30**(4), 964–994 (2016). https://doi.org/10.1007/s10618-015-0448-4
38. Wiki: Wirecard scandal. Fennel (2020)

39. Xiao, T., Xia, T., et al.: Learning from massive noisy labeled data for image classification. In: IEEE Conference on Computer Vision and Pattern Recognition (2015)
40. Yurdakul, B.: Statistical properties of population stability index. Western Michigan University (2018)

Health, Biology, Bioinformatics or Chemistry

WoundAmbit: Bridging State-of-the-Art Semantic Segmentation and Real-World Wound Care

Vanessa Borst[1(✉)], Timo Dittus[1], Tassilo Dege[2], Astrid Schmieder[2], and Samuel Kounev[1]

[1] University of Würzburg, 97070 Würzburg, Germany
{vanessa.borst,timo.dittus,samuel.kounev}@uni-wuerzburg.de
[2] University Hospital of Würzburg, 97070 Würzburg, Germany
{Dege_T,Schmieder_A}@ukw.de

Abstract. Chronic wounds affect a large population, particularly the elderly and diabetic patients, who often exhibit limited mobility and co-existing health conditions. Automated wound monitoring via mobile image capture can reduce in-person physician visits by enabling remote tracking of wound size. Semantic segmentation is key to this process, yet wound segmentation remains underrepresented in medical imaging research. To address this, we benchmark state-of-the-art deep learning models from general-purpose vision, medical imaging, and top methods from public wound challenges. For a fair comparison, we standardize training, data augmentation, and evaluation, conducting cross-validation to minimize partitioning bias. We also assess real-world deployment aspects, including generalization to an out-of-distribution wound dataset, computational efficiency, and interpretability. Additionally, we propose a reference object-based approach to convert AI-generated masks into clinically relevant wound size estimates and evaluate this, along with mask quality, for the five best architectures based on physician assessments. Overall, the transformer-based TransNeXt showed the highest levels of generalizability. Despite variations in inference times, all models processed at least one image per second on the CPU, which is deemed adequate for the intended application. Interpretability analysis typically revealed prominent activations in wound regions, emphasizing focus on clinically relevant features. Expert evaluation showed high mask approval for all analyzed models, with VWFormer and ConvNeXtS backbone performing the best. Size retrieval accuracy was similar across models, and predictions closely matched expert annotations. Finally, we demonstrate how our AI-driven wound size estimation framework, *WoundAmbit*, is integrated into a custom telehealth system. Our code and supplementary material are available on GitHub and Zenodo, respectively.

Supplementary Information The online version contains supplementary material available at https://doi.org/10.1007/978-3-032-06118-8_17.

Keywords: Semantic Segmentation · Benchmarking · Deep Learning · CNN · Transformer · Clinical Application · Tele-Medicine · Wound Care

1 Introduction

Wound care is a critical aspect of healthcare, particularly for chronic wounds that require ongoing monitoring and treatment. Current clinical practice often relies on manual wound measurements, such as estimating wound area by multiplying its longest length by its largest perpendicular width using a ruler or metric tape—although this often leads to overestimation due to irregular wound shapes [26]. Langemo et al. further reported differing interpretations among clinicians regarding how to define and measure wound length and width [16]. This lack of standardization contributes to measurement subjectivity and may limit comparability between assessments. An alternative approach involves tracing the wound on a transparent film and estimating the area using a metric grid, which may offer improved measurement reliability but still suffers from subjectivity in boundary delineation and partial cell interpretation [16,26]. Beyond potential inconsistencies, manual assessments are often invasive, relying on either proximity to or direct physical contact with the wound. This may cause patient discomfort and requires in-person visits with healthcare professionals (HCPs), posing logistical challenges for both patients and providers. Automated wound segmentation offers a promising alternative, as AI-driven wound size estimation from RGB images can be integrated into various systems, particularly mobile phones with cameras. This enhances accessibility, enabling remote wound monitoring from home without requiring specialized hardware. Unlike tracing methods, AI-based approaches are non-invasive, eliminating direct wound contact.

This shift toward automation aligns with broader advancements in AI-driven semantic segmentation, which have mainly been shaped by the evolution of convolutional neural networks (CNNs) and the emergence of vision transformers (ViTs). Thisanke et al. [29] review modern transformer-based approaches, whereas Minaee et al. [20] focus on deep learning (DL) for image segmentation excluding ViTs. Recently, (multi-modal) vision foundation models, such as Segment Anything [15], have gained attention due to their large-scale pretraining and versatility across different downstream tasks [1]. Medical image segmentation has also transitioned towards DL. Azad et al. present a comprehensive review of recent advances using ViTs [2], while Rayed et al. [23] review DL approaches more broadly. Additionally, foundation models like Segment Anything have been adapted for medical imaging, as demonstrated by MedSAM [19].

In contrast, wound segmentation remains relatively underexplored, partly due to the scarcity of relevant datasets. Notable exceptions with more than 1,000 wound images include FUSeg [31] and DFUC [14], both of which provide annotated images of diabetic foot ulcer (DFU) for public challenges. Additionally, Oota et al. [21] provide a dataset with 2,686 images of eight wound types, where annotations extend beyond the wound to include peri-wound skin areas.

Regarding existing wound segmentation techniques, early methods focused primarily on traditional feature engineering-based machine learning [32]. Over time, DL approaches such as WSNet [21], FUSegNet [6] and other CNN-based techniques [5,8,17,18,30] have emerged, alongside a few approaches for interactive wound segmentation [37]. However, certain limitations remain:

1. Limited Adoption of SotA Vision Models for Wound Analysis: Despite advancements in computer vision, investigations into the suitability of state-of-the-art (SotA) models, particularly ViTs, for wound segmentation remain limited. A 2022 survey on DL for wound analysis [38] did not mention any transformer-based segmentation methods, and recent breakthroughs in general-purpose (GP) vision models have yet to be applied to wound analysis.

2. Lack of Consideration for Practical Deployment: Few studies evaluate efficiency metrics such as GMACs/FLOPs alongside segmentation performance [21,30], and few report inference times or latency [21,37]. However, computational complexity is a critical factor for resource-constrained settings such as the medical sector, where GPU availability is limited. With few exceptions, such as the visualization of feature maps from different layers [37], explainable AI techniques are rarely applied despite their potential to improve trust among clinicians. Lastly, model generalizability to out-of-distribution (OOD) data is often overlooked, even though assessing robustness is crucial due to variability in wound types, skin tones, and uncontrolled home-based monitoring conditions such as lighting, background, and hardware.

3. Gap Between Segmentation and Clinically Relevant Wound Size: Existing public challenges (FUSeg, DFUC) and most wound segmentation approaches [6,8,17,18,30] do not address the conversion of segmentation masks into real-world wound size. Exceptions include Wang et al. [32], who rely on a specialized imaging box, and Chairat et al. [4], who use a custom calibration chart with a U-Net-based model incorporating EfficientNet/MobileNetv2 encoders for wound segmentation—but do not assess size retrieval accuracy. Chino et al. [5] incorporate measurement ruler and tape detection as a third class in a U-Net-based model and combine it with pixel density estimation to determine wound area. Similarly, Foltynski and Ladyzynski [7] train a CNN to detect both wounds and dual calibration markers that need to be placed below and above the wound. Proprietary solutions like Swift Skin & Wound [22] and imitoWound [12] exist but provide little insight into their calibration methods and algorithms.

To address these limitations, we introduce *WoundAmbit*, an end-to-end solution for automated wound size estimation from RGB images that bridges the gap between modern DL and practical wound care. To the best of our knowledge, this study is the first to systematically transfer a diverse set of SotA GP vision models to the wound domain and benchmark them against both medical and wound-specific segmentation methods within a unified evaluation framework. As summarized in Fig. 1, our key contributions are two-fold:

1. Comprehensive DL Benchmark: We conduct a rigorous benchmarking study by systematically selecting 12 SotA DL architectures from wound-specific, medical, and GP vision models, covering a diverse range of design paradigms, including CNNs, ViTs, and hybrid models. To ensure comparability, all models are trained under standardized conditions on publicly available data and evaluated using 5-fold cross-validation (CV). In addition, our evaluation framework emphasizes clinically relevant properties by assessing generalizability on a dedicated OOD dataset. Specifically created for this work, the dataset comprises 343 wound images taken at various body sites. Moreover, we analyze computational efficiency, including trainable parameters, Giga Multiply-Accumulate Operations (GMACs), and inference times on both GPU and CPU. Lastly, we investigate model interpretability using Gradient-weighted Class Activation Mapping (Grad-CAM) visualizations to assess clinically relevant decision-making.

2. Real-World Deployment: To translate AI-generated wound masks into clinically meaningful size estimates, we develop and validate a reference object (RO)-based approach for precise wound surface measurement. Unlike existing methods that require neural networks to segment calibration stickers [5,7], our approach leverages ArUco marker detection, making it independent of the AI algorithm used for segmentation. To evaluate reliability, we construct a dataset of 20 diverse wound images and obtain expert assessments of AI-generated mask quality from three dermatologists. Additionally, we compare AI-derived wound size estimates with physician annotations to quantify measurement accuracy. Finally, we propose a practical integration strategy for embedding AI-driven wound size estimation into a custom telemedicine framework for remote monitoring.

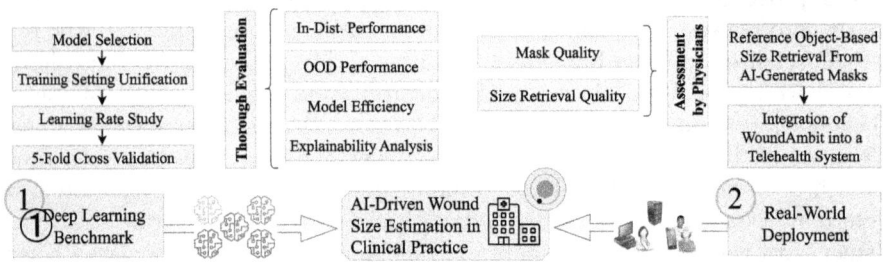

Fig. 1. Schematic visualization of our *WoundAmbit* approach.

The paper is structured as follows: Sect. 2 describes the DL benchmark (Fig. 1, left), covering model selection, methodology, datasets, and results. Section 3 details the size retrieval process and its evaluation, along with the integration of *WoundAmbit* into a specially designed telehealth system (Fig. 1, right). Finally, Sect. 4 discusses key findings, and Sect. 5 concludes the study.

2 Deep Learning Benchmark

2.1 Model Selection

Given the large number of novel methods introduced in recent years, it is impractical to include all current SotA models in this study. To ensure a benchmarking process that is as representative and balanced as possible, we devise four categories, selecting several representatives from each of them as follows:

(I) *DFU segmentation*: To specifically address the challenges of wound segmentation (WS), we include the best-performing models from two publicly available DFU segmentation challenges, as they are directly tailored to the domain of interest (HarDNet-DFUS [17], FUSegNet [6]). (II) *Medical segmentation*: Medical segmentation (MS) architectures, such as U-Net and its variants, have demonstrated broad applicability across diverse medical imaging tasks [28]. To assess the potential of recent architectures that have shown effectiveness beyond wound care, we select three models with strong performance in medical image segmentation outside the wound domain (FCBFormer [25], HiFormer-B [10], MISSFormer [11]). (III) *GP SS models*: To incorporate cutting-edge developments, we include two widely recognized GP semantic segmentation (SS) models (SegFormer-B3 [35] and SegNeXt-L [9]), along with a recent multi-scale decoder (VWFormer [36]) for SS. The VWFormer model is integrated with two different backbones, MiT-B3 and ConvNeXt-S, denoted as VW-MiT and VW-Conv, respectively. (IV) *GP vision models*: To account for advanced (multi-task) vision models (VM), we select two promising approaches from this category (InternImage-T [33], TransNeXt-Tiny [27]). As common in literature, we adapt them for segmentation by integrating a UPerHead [34] decoder. (V) *Baseline*: Apart from these categories, we include U-Net [24], a proven and widely used model in biomedical segmentation, as a baseline.

Table 1 summarizes our final selection, striking a balance between domain specificity, cross-domain variety, and methodological diversity. The key ideas of all architectures are briefly summarized in Sect. A.1, with further details available in the corresponding publications. Overall, our selection process is guided by the following criteria: (I) *Architectural diversity*: To ensure a comprehensive representation of various design paradigms, we aim for a balance between CNN-based, ViT-based, and hybrid methods. (II) *Computational efficiency*: Given the limited resources in healthcare settings, we prioritize models that offer a good trade-off between performance and computational feasibility. For GP models, we select architectures with approximately 50–60M parameters, while wound-specific and medical models range from 30–70M parameters, mainly due to the limited availability of varied model sizes in these domains. (III) *Scientific impact and recognition*: We select models with significant visibility in their respective fields, prioritizing those published in high-impact conferences and journals. (IV) *Code availability*: To minimize the risk of implementation errors, we limit our selection to models with publicly available code.

Table 1. Overview of the selected methods besides our baseline U-Net [24].

	Healthcare-Related					General-Purpose		
Cat.	Model	Type	Size	Y.	Cat.	Model	Type	Size Y.
MS	FCBFormer [25]	Hybrid	53M	'22	SS	SegFormer-B3 [35]	Transf.	48M '21
	HiFormer-B [10]	Hybrid	30M	'23		SegNeXt-L [9]	CNN	49M '22
	MISSFormer [11]	Transf.	43M	'23		2× VWFormer [36]	-Depends-[1]	'24
WS	HarDNet-DFUS [17]	CNN	52M	'22	VM	InternImage-T [33][2]	CNN	58M '23
	FUSegNet [6]	CNN	71M	'24		TransNeXt-Tiny [27][2]	Transf.	58M '24

[1] 51M with MiT-B3/ 57M with ConvNext-S   [2] Parameter count includes UPerHead decoder

2.2 Unified Training Procedure: Methodological Details

We establish a unified benchmarking environment by standardizing the training process as follows: To ensure an unbiased comparison while enabling the use of pre-trained weights, the deep learning methods were implemented with their architecture-specific settings, as recommended in their respective official publications and code repositories. Specifically, we use ImageNet-pretrained backbones for all methods. While maintaining key architectural parameters (e.g., layer configurations and activation functions), we standardize other training settings across all models. These include input tensor dimensions, the number of training epochs, early stopping criteria, optimizer type, loss function, and the data augmentation pipeline. Further details on preprocessing, data augmentation, and exact training configurations are provided in Sect. A.2. To minimize biases associated with fixed learning rates, we conduct a preliminary hyperparameter tuning step for each architecture, optimizing the learning rate within a predefined search range ($10^{-4}, 5 \times 10^{-5}, 10^{-5}$). The best-performing learning rate for each method (see Sect. A.2) is then used for subsequent five-fold CV, while all other training settings remain unified. Overall, this ensures that performance differences arise from the intrinsic capabilities of the architectures rather than variations in training configurations, particularly data augmentation.

2.3 Standardized Evaluation Procedure

Our assessment strategy employs a unified evaluation framework, incorporating both traditional segmentation metrics and practical aspects essential for clinical applications. For *segmentation performance*, we use metrics such as mean Intersection over Union (mIoU), Dice Similarity Coefficient (mDSC), precision (mPrc), and recall (mRec). These metrics evaluate performance on both our main dataset and unseen OOD data, with the latter specifically assessing the *generalization capability* across diverse wound types. In terms of *model efficiency*, we report the number of trainable parameters and GMACs, along with mean inference time for GPU and CPU execution and throughput in images per second (IPS). Finally, we assess *explainability* using *Grad-CAM*-based visualizations. Further information and implementation details are available in Sect. A.3.

2.4 Datasets

Our experiments mainly rely on two datasets, detailed in Sect. A.4. The first, *CFU*, is used for model training, including learning rate studies and final CV. It consists of a custom combination of the publicly available DFUC'22 dataset [14], which contains 2,000 annotated images, and the FUSeg'21 challenge dataset [31], with 1,010 labeled images. After removing duplicates and highly similar images, 2,887 unique images remain for our experiments. Additionally, we use the DFUC'22 test set for external validation of our models via the challenge's live leaderboard. The second dataset, denoted as *out-of-distribution (OOD)*, was collected at the University Hospital of Würzburg with approval from the local ethics committee. It comprises 343 expert-annotated wound images from various anatomical sites, extending beyond foot ulcers. To better reflect real-world clinical conditions, where patient-acquired images often lack standardized imaging protocols, certain wounds were intentionally captured multiple times from varying distances, angles, and perspectives. Notably, *OOD* is used exclusively for evaluation, not for training. Due to privacy regulations, it remains confidential; however, selected examples are shared at GitHub with written consent.

2.5 Performance on CFU Dataset and DFUC'22 Live Leaderboard

Table 2 presents the 5-fold CV results on CFU alongside each model's performance on the DFUC'22 live leaderboard. For the latter, instead of selecting the best checkpoint from individual folds, segmentation masks are generated using pixel-wise majority votes (PMVs) across all five instances of each architecture. This approach mitigates overfitting to individual training folds while leveraging the collective strengths of multiple trained instances.

On CFU, TransNeXt demonstrated the highest performance, achieving a mIoU of 79.8 and an mDSC of 88.7. SegNeXt followed closely with a mIoU of 79.5 and an mDSC of 88.6, exhibiting strong consistency across the CV folds. With similarly low inter-fold variability, SegFormer ranked third, achieving a mIoU of 78.9 and an mDSC of 88.2. On the DFUC'22 leaderboard, TransNeXt also achieved the highest performance among our models, with a mIoU of 62.8 and an mDSC of 73.0, slightly surpassing SegNeXt and VW-Conv—the latter ranking third despite its moderate performance on CFU. Notably, TransNeXt ranked 6th out of 60 (top 10%) based on the best submission per participant despite no dataset-specific optimization, which highlights its strong out-of-the-box performance. In contrast, U-Net and most medical approaches, except FCB-Former, showed lower segmentation performance and ranked further down on both CFU and DFUC'22.

Table 2. 5-fold CV (mean±SD, %) and ensemble DFUC'22 leaderboard scores.

Type	Avg. CFU				DFUC'22	
	mIoU↓	mDSC	mPrc	mRec	mIoU	mDSC
TransNeXt	**79.8 ± 1.4**	**88.7 ± 0.8**	**90.9 ± 0.4**	**86.7 ± 1.8**	**62.8**	**73.0**
SegNeXt	79.5 ± 0.7	88.6 ± 0.4	90.7 ± 0.6	86.6 ± 0.6	62.1	72.3
SegFormer	78.9 ± 0.8	88.2 ± 0.5	90.4 ± 0.7	86.1 ± 1.4	61.8	72.1
FCBFormer	78.6 ± 1.5	88.0 ± 0.9	90.6 ± 0.6	85.6 ± 1.9	62.0	72.2
InternImage	78.5 ± 0.9	88.0 ± 0.5	89.8 ± 1.5	86.2 ± 0.6	61.7	72.0
VW-MiT	78.5 ± 1.7	87.9 ± 1.0	90.2 ± 1.1	85.8 ± 2.2	61.7	72.0
VW-Conv	78.4 ± 0.5	87.9 ± 0.3	90.1 ± 1.9	85.9 ± 2.0	62.0	72.3
FUSegNet	78.0 ± 1.3	87.6 ± 0.8	90.6 ± 0.7	84.9 ± 1.3	61.3	71.6
HarDNet	76.9 ± 1.4	86.9 ± 0.9	88.3 ± 2.4	85.8 ± 2.5	60.4	70.8
U-Net	74.1 ± 0.9	85.1 ± 0.6	88.1 ± 1.1	82.5 ± 1.5	57.6	68.0

2.6 Performance on Out-of-Distribution (OOD) Data

Table 3 presents the segmentation performance on the unseen OOD dataset, which includes previously unobserved anatomical regions, such as the head and breast, thereby assessing model generalization to domain shifts. In addition to reporting the average and standard deviation (SD) across the five CV models per architecture, we again provide PMV results to ensure a more stable and unbiased evaluation. Notably, for all models, the PMV performance surpasses the average performance of the best models from individual folds in both mIoU and mDSC, further confirming its robustness. TransNeXt demonstrated the strongest generalization, achieving the highest mIoU (79.4) and mDSC (88.5) in the PMV setting, followed closely by InternImage (mIoU 78.8, mDSC 88.1) and VW-MiT (mIoU 78.0, mDSC 87.6). The performance drop relative to the in-distribution CFU data was minimal (≤0.5pp mIoU, ≤0.3pp mDSC) for the top three models. InternImage even showed a 0.3pp improvement in mIoU, indicating strong adaptability to novel wound types. SegFormer, VW-Conv, and HarDNet also maintained competitive performance relative to CFU (~1pp mIoU drop). FCB-Former achieved the highest absolute PMV scores among the medical architectures (mIoU 76.5, mDSC 86.7). In contrast, the remaining medical models, except for HarDNet, exhibited substantial performance declines (4–7.9pp mIoU), with HiFormer dropping below 68% mIoU. Notably, SegNeXt, despite its strong in-distribution and DFUC'22 performance, saw a sharp decline of 3.7pp in mIoU.

Table 3. Segmentation performance (mean ± SD, %) on the OOD dataset using the five trained CV models, with CFU mean IoU and DSC for reference.

Type	Avg. CFU		Avg. OOD				Maj. vote OOD			
	mIoU	mDSC	mIoU	mDSC	mPrc	mRec	mIoU↓	mDSC	mPrc	mRec
TransNeXt	**79.8**	**88.7**	**78.3 ± 1.7**	**87.8 ± 1.1**	93.6 ± 0.2	**82.7 ± 1.9**	**79.4**	**88.5**	94.3	**83.4**
InternImage	78.5	88.0	76.0 ± 3.2	86.3 ± 2.1	92.4 ± 0.6	81.1 ± 3.6	78.8	88.1	93.7	83.2
VW-MiT	78.5	87.9	75.7 ± 1.6	86.2 ± 1.0	92.8 ± 0.5	80.5 ± 2.0	78.0	87.6	93.7	82.3
SegFormer	78.9	88.2	76.3 ± 1.2	86.5 ± 0.7	93.1 ± 0.6	80.8 ± 1.4	77.7	87.5	94.1	81.7
VW-Conv	78.4	87.9	74.9 ± 2.7	85.7 ± 1.8	93.1 ± 0.8	79.4 ± 3.5	77.2	87.1	94.4	80.9
FCBFormer	78.6	88.0	74.0 ± 1.9	85.1 ± 1.3	93.2 ± 1.0	78.3 ± 2.7	76.5	86.7	94.5	80.0
HarDNet	76.9	86.9	73.0 ± 2.6	84.4 ± 1.7	91.1 ± 2.1	78.7 ± 4.1	75.9	86.3	93.1	80.4
SegNeXt	79.5	88.6	74.5 ± 1.7	85.4 ± 1.1	93.4 ± 0.3	78.6 ± 2.0	75.8	86.2	94.4	79.4
FUSegNet	78.0	87.6	71.5 ± 3.2	83.4 ± 2.2	**94.2 ± 0.8**	74.9 ± 3.9	74.0	85.1	**95.7**	76.5
U-Net	74.1	85.1	65.6 ± 2.7	79.2 ± 2.0	91.9 ± 0.6	69.7 ± 3.3	67.5	80.6	93.3	70.9
MISSFormer	70.0	82.3	64.3 ± 2.6	78.2 ± 2.0	88.7 ± 1.6	70.1 ± 3.5	66.0	79.5	90.2	71.1
HiFormer	73.8	84.9	63.1 ± 5.1	77.3 ± 3.9	90.8 ± 2.0	67.7 ± 6.3	65.9	79.4	92.4	69.6

2.7 Model Efficiency Analysis

We report key computational metrics in Table 4. Among all architectures, FUSeg-Net has the highest number of trainable parameters (71M), while HiFormer and U-Net are the smallest. In terms of GMACs, MISSFormer is the most efficient, whereas U-Net, and, especially, TransNeXt and InternImage exhibit higher computational complexity. Interestingly, parameter count and GMACs do not always directly correspond to inference time and throughput (TP). For instance, despite having similar parameter counts to most models (50–60M), TransNeXt and FCB-Former exhibit considerably higher inference times and lower TP, making them the slowest on both GPU and CPU. In contrast, U-Net, despite having the third-highest GMAC count, achieves the fastest GPU inference time, highlighting the influence of architectural design and optimizations on computational efficiency. The results reveal a trade-off between efficiency and segmentation performance. While models such as U-Net, MISSFormer, and HiFormer excel in inference speed on both GPU and CPU, advanced vision models like TransNeXt and InternImage offer superior segmentation performance at a moderate computational cost. Notably, even TransNeXt, the slowest model, maintains a throughput of approximately one IPS on the CPU and up to 24 IPS on the GPU.

Table 4. Evaluation of model efficiency, with OOD maj. vote mIoU for reference.

Type	OOD mIoU↓	Params (in M)	GMACs	∅ Inference Time ± SD (in ms) GPU	∅ Inference Time ± SD (in ms) CPU	TP (in IPS) GPU	TP (in IPS) CPU
TransNeXt	**79.4**	57.74	238.41	41.58 ± 0.10	1012.75 ± 243.11	24.05	0.99
InternImage	78.8	58.37	234.23	28.71 ± 0.29	692.35 ± 42.90	34.83	1.44
VW-MiT	78.0	51.42	62.79	25.65 ± 0.11	439.98 ± 55.75	38.98	2.27
SegFormer	77.7	47.22	71.18	23.54 ± 0.08	429.89 ± 17.95	42.48	2.33
VW-Conv	77.2	57.00	77.43	25.55 ± 0.03	339.08 ± 38.59	39.13	2.95
FCBFormer	76.5	52.96	149.93	51.27 ± 0.09	875.13 ± 41.01	19.51	1.14
HarDNet	75.9	51.06	138.92	38.01 ± 0.16	669.29 ± 17.98	26.31	1.49
SegNeXt	75.8	48.77	64.18	29.50 ± 0.42	616.49 ± 59.53	33.90	1.62
FUSegNet	74.0	70.97	35.51	32.99 ± 0.13	526.02 ± 69.17	30.31	1.90
U-Net	67.5	31.03	192.67	**13.79 ± 0.02**	307.96 ± 15.82	**72.50**	3.25
MISSFormer	66.0	42.46	**7.16**	17.78 ± 0.15	**203.07 ± 19.05**	56.24	**4.92**
HiFormer	65.9	**25.51**	11.51	14.09 ± 0.13	251.57 ± 19.80	70.96	3.98

2.8 Explainability Insights

To assess the decision-making of our models, we applied *Grad-CAM* to generate visual explanations of predictions. Figure 2 presents visualizations for the top three and two lowest-performing models from Table 3, along with the predicted segmentation masks (red) for selected OOD images. Additional comparisons across architectures and further examples of different body localization, wound size, and color variations are provided in Sect. A.5.

By comparing heatmaps with ground truth (GT) masks (green), we qualitatively assess model reliability, focusing on whether activations align with clinically relevant wound features rather than artifacts. Across all models, strong activations were frequently observed in wound regions, aligning well with GT masks. Additionally, non-wound regions often exhibited minimal to no activation, suggesting effective prioritization of pathological features. Qualitative comparisons indicate that higher-performing models from Table 3 tend to generate sharper heatmap boundaries and achieve more precise wound localization, whereas lower-performing models exhibit weaker or more diffuse activations (3, 7). In some cases, non-wound objects (e.g., shoes, 5) were misidentified as wounds, while certain wound regions (6, 7, 8), including those near image edges (9), were not fully captured, especially by lower-performing models. Additionally, weaker models occasionally generated pixelated or irregular mask predictions, as indicated by frayed or poorly defined red contours (7, 11, 12). While not necessarily generalizable, these qualitative insights align with quantitative performance metrics and enhance interpretability for clinicians, allowing for a deeper understanding of model behavior and fostering greater trust in AI systems.

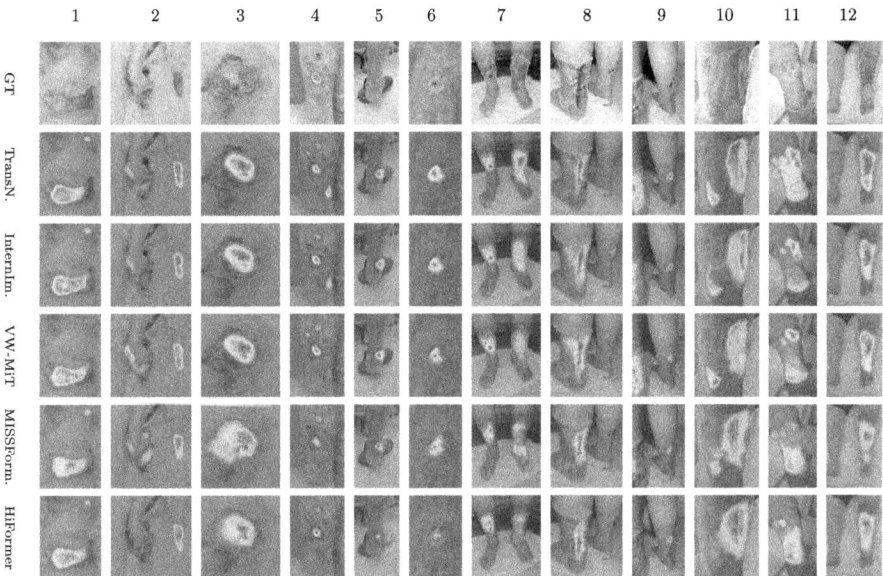

Fig. 2. *Grad-CAM* for exemplary OOD images, alongside their GT annotation.

3 Real-World Deployment

3.1 Automated Size Retrieval from AI-Generated Masks

Reference Object (RO) Design. Based on Chairat et al. [4], we developed a custom RO with slight adjustments to size and layout (see Fig. 3a). Our RO is placed next to the wound and features four ArUco markers, each with a 12 mm side length and a 4 mm margin of white space to facilitate accurate detection. To enhance functionality, we included a Macbeth color chart with 24 color patches between the markers, aligned such that the top and bottom edges of the patch groups align with the marker corners to simplify automated extraction.

Benefits. Unlike existing methods [5,7], our ArUco-based RO, with its known dimensions, enables precise object size estimation independent of AI algorithms. Notably, this approach eliminates the need for including RO detection as an additional class in model training. For future applications, the Macbeth color chart enables color calibration and wound color assessment. In environments with few natural reference points (e.g., human skin), the fixed design helps estimate camera position and rotation, which could be used for real-time patient guidance during image capture (e.g., adjusting distance or angle).

Size Retrieval Process. We detect the ArUco markers using OpenCV's `ArucoDetector`. To estimate the pixel-to-millimeter (px/mm) ratio, we design a robust approach that utilizes multiple ArUco markers whenever possible, computing the ratio using predefined real-world distances between specific marker pairs. By calculating the mean px/mm ratio across all available pairs, we reduce the impact of perspective distortion and measurement noise. Moreover, this approach enables more stable estimation, even in cases where some markers are partially occluded or missing. If only one marker is detected, we estimate the px/mm ratio by averaging its width and height. Afterward, we convert segmented wound areas into square millimeters using this ratio. In addition, we determine the wound's height and width following standard clinical measurement practices [16]. We identify the longest diagonal of each mask contour (with at least seven points). Then, a perpendicular vector is computed and moved incrementally along the diagonal. At each step, we measure the distance between intersections of the perpendicular line and the contour, selecting the two points with the greatest separation to define the second diagonal, representing wound width. Figure 3 demonstrates the size retrieval process for three representative patients. Green contours indicate detected markers and wound regions, while pink lines represent the diagonals approximating wound height and width. Red numbers show the retrieved marker IDs. Notably, accurate wound size estimation requires the RO to be placed as close as possible to the wound and, crucially, within the same plane to minimize distortion. In contrast, Subfig. 3c shows a failure case where the wound is identified correctly, but its size is underestimated due to the markers being positioned closer to the camera than the wound.

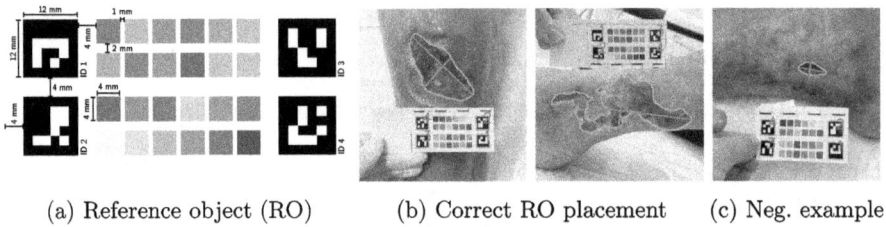

(a) Reference object (RO)   (b) Correct RO placement   (c) Neg. example

Fig. 3. Visualization of the size retrieval process for exemplar real-world patients.

Evaluation. To evaluate performance, we collect $N = 20$ diverse wound images using our RO and an iPhone 11. The top five methods, selected based on PMV mIoU scores from the OOD dataset, are assessed on these images using PMVs per architecture. Additionally, an ensemble of all $5 \times 5 = 25$ models is constructed. For qualitative evaluation, $|D| = 3$ dermatologists independently review AI-generated masks. A total of 120 image-mask pairs ($N \times 6$ AI variants) are presented in random order, with each mask rated as either "good" or "bad". Physicians also estimate wound sizes and select the best mask per image. Figure B.1 provides screenshots of the annotation tool. We define the following for evaluation: The *Clinical Mask Approval (CMA)* measures how often physicians rate the masks as "good" across all images and evaluators. The *Expert Choice Rate (ECR)* quantifies the proportion, averaged across all images and dermatologists, where a model's mask is selected as the best of six for a given image.

$$\mathbf{CMA} = \frac{\#\ \text{Good}}{|D| \times N} \times 100 \quad \mathbf{ECR} = \frac{\#\ \text{Times selected as best}}{|D| \times N} \times 100\%$$
(1) (2)

Since physicians provide separate height and width estimates instead of direct area measurements, we use these as proxies for size estimation accuracy. The GT height and width for image i are defined as the **mean** of all $|D|$ physician estimates, denoted as $H_{GT}^{(i)}$ and $W_{GT}^{(i)}$. To assess size retrieval quality, we employ the Mean Absolute Error (MAE) and Mean Absolute Percentage Error (MAPE). For each dimension $X \in \{H, W\}$, these metrics quantify the deviation between model predictions $X_{pred}^{(i)}$ and the expert-derived GT $X_{GT}^{(i)}$:

$$\mathbf{MAE} = \frac{1}{N}\sum_{i=1}^{N}|X_{pred}^{(i)} - X_{GT}^{(i)}| \quad \mathbf{MAPE} = \frac{1}{N}\sum_{i=1}^{N}\frac{|X_{pred}^{(i)} - X_{GT}^{(i)}|}{X_{GT}^{(i)}} \times 100\%$$
(3) (4)

However, size estimation in medical imaging is inherently subjective, leading to significant variability among physicians [13]. To ensure a meaningful evaluation, we quantify inter-rater variability using a relative deviation metric. We exclude any image i where the following deviation exceeds a threshold of 0.5 in either height or width annotations, with $X \in H, W$ representing the dimension, and $X_{d_j}^{(i)}$ denoting the size annotation provided by physician d_j for image i:

$$\mathbf{Relative\ Deviation} = \frac{\max(X_{d_1}^{(i)}, X_{d_2}^{(i)}, X_{d_3}^{(i)}) - \min(X_{d_1}^{(i)}, X_{d_2}^{(i)}, X_{d_3}^{(i)})}{\mathrm{median}(X_{d_1}^{(i)}, X_{d_2}^{(i)}, X_{d_3}^{(i)})}$$
(5)

After removing inconsistently annotated images, we use the remaining seven for error calculations (see Table 5). Figure 4 confirms their variability in wound shape, size, and skin tone, ensuring a representative subset for size retrieval evaluation. We also report the mean predicted height and width (MPH, MPW) with SD across the $N = 7$ images, alongside the average wound dimensions estimated by the $|D|$ physicians. This analyzes model consistency across wound types and retrieval capabilities relative to expert estimates. For completeness, Table B.1 includes the masks, raw size predictions (including area), and expert estimates for all 20 images, which are also shared at GitHub with written consent.

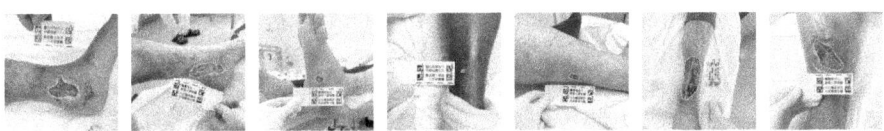

Fig. 4. Overview of the seven wounds with consistent expert size estimates.

The CMA ranged from 83.3% to 86.7% across models, reflecting high mask quality and strong physician approval. ECR varied notably, with VW-Conv achieving the highest approval rate (35.0%) and TransNeXt and the Ensemble the lowest (8.3%). For size retrieval, all models performed similarly, with MPH and MPW closely aligning with the GT. On average, height estimates were slightly overestimated, while width was slightly underestimated. Nevertheless, consistently low MAE (≤ 4.4 mm height, ≤ 3.2 mm width) and MAPE ($\leq 14.1\%$ height, $\leq 16.2\%$ width) indicate robust size retrieval across wound sizes.

Table 5. Expert-based mask and size retrieval assessment.

Model	Mask Quality ($N = 20$)		Size Retrieval Quality ($N = 7$)					
			Height			Width		
	CMA[1]	ECR[1]	MPH [2,3]	MAE[2]	MAPE[1]	MPW [2,4]	MAE[2]	MAPE[1]
TransNeXt	85.0	8.3	**54.6 ± 41.0**	4.4	12.3	27.2 ± 15.6	3.2	15.8
InternImage	**86.7**	15.0	54.9 ± 40.9	3.9	12.2	**26.6 ± 15.0**	3.2	16.2
VW-MiT	**86.7**	13.3	55.4 ± 41.5	4.3	14.1	27.7 ± 16.0	**2.3**	13.3
SegFormer	83.3	13.3	54.8 ± 41.2	**3.8**	12.0	27.1 ± 15.8	2.6	**13.2**
VW-Conv	85.0	**35.0**	54.8 ± 41.6	4.0	**9.9**	**26.6 ± 15.8**	3.2	14.4
Ensemble	**86.7**	8.3	55.0 ± 41.3	4.1	12.2	27.0 ± 15.7	2.9	15.1

[1] In %
[2] In mm
[3] Mean H_{GT}: 54.3 ± 41.6
[4] Mean W_{GT}: 29.2 ± 16.3

3.2 Seamless Integration into a Custom Telehealth System

We integrated the AI module, which demonstrated superior performance in terms of ECR, VW-Conv, and wound size retrieval, into a custom-developed telehealth platform to enable future evaluation of its impact on patient outcomes. The system architecture (see Fig. 5) consists of three core components: (1) the *WoundAIssist* mobile application [3], (2) a web interface for physicians, and (3) a backend with a dedicated microservice for AI processing. Among other features, patients use our purpose-built app, *WoundAIssist*, to capture and upload wound images at regular intervals, accompanied by self-reported data on wound-specific factors (e.g., pain, itching, oozing) and overall well-being (e.g., mood, activity impact, quality of life) [3]. HCP use a web-based dashboard for remote patient monitoring, providing a concise summary of essential patient information. The dashboard also includes a detailed wound view (Fig. 5, right, translated), which displays the selected wound images alongside the AI-predicted wound area (①). Additionally, the dashboard features trajectory curves for all patient-reported wound scores and AI-derived wound size progression (②). To support continuous model refinement, the system incorporates a feedback mechanism, allowing clinicians to assess the segmentation masks by a simple approval process (③).

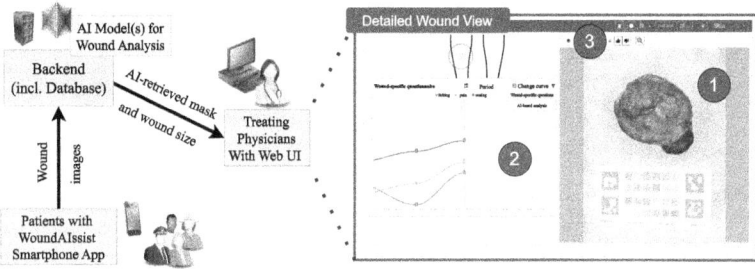

Fig. 5. Simplified visualization of the overall telehealth system.

The system is currently deployed on a secure, GDPR-compliant cloud server and is actively used as part of an ongoing longitudinal clinical study. Approximately 30 patients are expected to participate, each using the *WoundAIssist* app on their personal smartphones over six months. This long-term clinical trial aims to empirically assess the effectiveness of the overall telehealth solution, with a focus on patient adherence and wound care outcomes. It also enables the collection of real-world images captured by patients, which provide a valuable basis for both validating the performance of the proposed AI-based wound size estimation and informing future improvements to enhance its robustness.

4 Discussion and Outlook

This study provides a comprehensive benchmark of various DL models for wound segmentation, addressing real-world challenges in clinical deployment and telehealth applications. Interestingly, many of the top-performing models achieved comparable performance on the evaluated datasets, suggesting that binary wound segmentation may be a relatively straightforward task for advanced deep learning methods. This phenomenon may be attributed to the distinctive visual characteristics exhibited by wounds in conventional samples, which enable modern architectures to extract relevant features effectively.

Although no clear trend emerged between CNN- and ViT-based models, the results on both the in-distribution CFU and the DFUC'22 live leaderboard indicate the superior performance of modern GP architectures, such as TransNeXt, over specialized medical models. Similarly, the top five models on the OOD dataset were GP architectures, further emphasizing the superiority of contemporary SS and vision models over specialized medical techniques in handling OOD data. This enhanced performance is further supported by visual analysis of Grad-CAM heatmaps. Despite the higher computational demands of the top-performing models, inference times remained within practical limits. With a minimum throughput of at least one image per second on the CPU, all models are considered suitable for clinical use and remote wound size monitoring, given the manageable data volumes. Expert evaluations of mask quality and automated size estimates from the top five models yielded promising results, with high mask approval rates and size estimates closely aligning with dermatologist annotations. While no architecture clearly outperformed the others in size retrieval, VW-Conv was most favored by experts for best mask selection.

While our wound size estimation framework, *WoundAmbit*, holds great potential, it also presents limitations and highlights directions for future research:

RO Placement and Robustness Analysis Using Real-World Data. The evaluation primarily used publicly available and OOD images captured in controlled hospital settings. To improve model robustness and assess size estimation in telemedicine contexts, it is essential to include images from home environments, particularly those taken by patients using smartphones. These images exhibit greater variability in lighting, background, and image quality, which may introduce practical challenges, such as suboptimal RO placement or partial occlusion of ArUco markers. Accurate size estimation requires the RO to be approximately coplanar with the wound surface; however, the current system lacks a mechanism to guide patients in placing the RO correctly. Incorrect positioning can cause perspective distortion and reduced measurement accuracy. Future versions could incorporate real-time user guidance, such as augmented reality feedback, to assist patients during image capture. Moreover, our evaluation included only a single image with partially occluded ArUco markers, limiting our ability to quantify the impact of incomplete or failed marker detection. Future work should involve systematic stress testing to assess how partial occlusions, non-coplanar RO placement, or complete detection failure affect size estimation accuracy. To improve robustness in such scenarios, alternative strategies should be explored to maintain functionality. The patient-captured images from our ongoing longitudinal clinical study can provide a diverse and realistic dataset to evaluate and improve model robustness under suboptimal, real-world conditions.

Model Selection. While efforts were made to select a representative set of models, the evaluation is constrained by the chosen architectures. The three lowest-performing models – U-Net, MISSFormer, and HiFormer – are notably smaller in terms of parameters, which may introduce a slight bias. However, the general trend favoring the GP SS and GP vision models remains consistent, even regarding the larger medical networks.

Over-Reliance on Technology. From a clinical perspective, *WoundAmbit* serves as a decision support system, not a replacement for physicians. While it provides automated wound size tracking, clinicians continue to review both the original wound image and the AI-generated output, ensuring that clinical decisions are not based solely on AI predictions. Nevertheless, the potential risk of over-reliance on technology should be further explored in future studies.

Clinical Validation. Ultimately, clinical validation of *WoundAmbit* is crucial to confirm its effectiveness in practice beyond the scope of technical evaluation. The ongoing longitudinal study will provide critical insight, and follow-up analyses should explore patient adherence over extended periods as well as the system's overall impact on wound management outcomes and patient well-being.

5 Conclusion

This work advances automated wound segmentation by benchmarking 12 SotA DL methods from GP vision, medical segmentation, and wound care. We address challenges such as domain variability, computational constraints, and model interpretability. Our evaluation on both in-distribution and OOD datasets demonstrates that modern GP models, especially TransNeXt and VWFormer, exhibit strong generalization and remain computationally feasible for clinical use. While our AI-driven wound size estimation framework, *WoundAmbit*, shows strong clinical promise, future work will focus on expanding the dataset with smartphone images from diverse patient demographics and conditions for model finetuning. Additionally, integrating *WoundAmbit* with existing clinical systems and assessing patient reported outcomes in clinical trials will be crucial for evaluating its real-world impact. Lastly, incorporating the OOD dataset and prospectively collected smartphone images into the training is expected to improve model performance further. Overall, this work represents an important step toward bridging recent advances in computer vision with real-world wound care, offering the potential to improve remote wound size monitoring and enhance patient care.

Supplementary Materials. The trained k-fold models can be accessed via Zenodo at 10.5281/zenodo.15123640. The complete source code is archived on Zenodo at 10.5281/zenodo.15682317 and actively maintained on GitHub. Additional materials are provided in the supplementary document available at 10.5281/zenodo.15673941.

Acknowledgments. We thank Luisa Deutzmann for her support in creating the 20-image dataset for size retrieval evaluation and Caroline Glatzel for her contributions to manual size annotation and assessment of AI-generated masks.

Ethics. The authors declare no conflicts of interest. Ethical approval for this study was waived by the Ethics Committee of the Medical Faculty of the University of Würzburg. All patients provided informed consent for the publication of their photographs.

References

1. Awais, M., et al.: Foundation models defining a new era in vision: a survey and outlook. IEEE Trans. Pattern Anal. Mach. Intell. **47**(4) (2025)
2. Azad, R., et al.: Advances in medical image analysis with vision transformers: a comprehensive review. Med. Image Anal. **91** (2024)
3. Borst, V., et al.: WoundAIssist: a patient-centered mobile app for AI-assisted wound care with physicians in the loop. arXiv (2025). https://arxiv.org/abs/2506.06104
4. Chairat, S., Chaichulee, S., Dissaneewate, T., Wangkulangkul, P., Kongpanichakul, L.: AI-assisted assessment of wound tissue with automatic color and measurement calibration on images taken with a smartphone. Healthcare **11**(2) (2023)

5. Chino, D.Y., Scabora, L.C., Cazzolato, M.T., Jorge, A.E., Traina-Jr, C., Traina, A.J.: Segmenting skin ulcers and measuring the wound area using deep convolutional networks. Comput. Methods Programs Biomed. **191** (2020)
6. Dhar, M.K., Zhang, T., Patel, Y., Gopalakrishnan, S., Yu, Z.: FUSegNet: a deep convolutional neural network for foot ulcer segmentation. Biomed. Sig. Process. Control **92** (2024)
7. Foltynski, P., Ladyzynski, P.: Internet service for wound area measurement using digital planimetry with adaptive calibration and image segmentation with deep convolutional neural networks. Biocybernetics Biomed. Eng. **43**(1) (2023)
8. Goyal, M., Yap, M.H., Reeves, N.D., Rajbhandari, S., Spragg, J.: Fully convolutional networks for diabetic foot ulcer segmentation. In: IEEE International Conference on Systems, Man, and Cybernetics (2017)
9. Guo, M.H., Lu, C.Z., Hou, Q., Liu, Z.N., Cheng, M.M., Hu, S.M.: SegNeXt: rethinking convolutional attention design for semantic segmentation. In: NeurIPS (2022)
10. Heidari, M., et al.: HiFormer: hierarchical multi-scale representations using transformers for medical image segmentation. In: WACV (2023)
11. Huang, X., Deng, Z., Li, D., Yuan, X., Fu, Y.: MISSFormer: an effective transformer for 2D medical image segmentation. IEEE Trans. Med. Imaging **42**(5) (2022)
12. imito AG: imitoWound (2025). https://imito.io/en/imitowound
13. Jørgensen, L.B., Sørensen, J.A., Jemec, G.B., Yderstræde, K.B.: Methods to assess area and volume of wounds – a systematic review. Int. Wound J. **13**(4) (2016)
14. Kendrick, C., et al.: Translating clinical delineation of diabetic foot ulcers into machine interpretable segmentation. In: Diabetic Foot Ulcers Grand Challenge (2025)
15. Kirillov, A., et al.: Segment anything. In: ICCV (2023)
16. Langemo, D., Anderson, J., Hanson, D., Hunter, S., Thompson, P.: Measuring wound length, width, and area: which technique? Adv. Skin Wound Care **21**(1) (2008)
17. Liao, T.Y., Yang, C.H., Lo, Y.W., Lai, K.Y., Shen, P.H., Lin, Y.L.: HarDNet-DFUS: enhancing backbone and decoder of HarDNet-MSEG for diabetic foot ulcer image segmentation. In: Diabetic Foot Ulcers Grand Challenge (2023)
18. Liu, X., Wang, C., Li, F., Zhao, X., Zhu, E., Peng, Y.: A framework of wound segmentation based on deep convolutional networks. In: International Congress on Image and Signal Processing, Biomedical Engineering and Informatics (2017)
19. Ma, J., He, Y., Li, F., Han, L., You, C., Wang, B.: Segment anything in medical images. Nat. Commun. **15**(1) (2024)
20. Minaee, S., Boykov, Y., Porikli, F., Plaza, A., Kehtarnavaz, N., Terzopoulos, D.: Image segmentation using deep learning: a survey. IEEE Trans. Pattern Anal. Mach. Intell. **44**(7) (2022)
21. Oota, S.R., Rowtula, V., Mohammed, S., Liu, M., Gupta, M.: WSNet: towards an effective method for wound image segmentation. In: WACV (2023)
22. Ramachandram, D., et al.: Fully automated wound tissue segmentation using deep learning on mobile devices: cohort study. JMIR mHealth and uHealth **10**(4) (2022)
23. Rayed, M.E., Islam, S.S., Niha, S.I., Jim, J.R., Kabir, M.M., Mridha, M.: Deep learning for medical image segmentation: state-of-the-art advancements and challenges. Inf. Med. Unlocked (2024)
24. Ronneberger, O., Fischer, P., Brox, T.: U-Net: convolutional networks for biomedical image segmentation. In: Navab, N., Hornegger, J., Wells, W.M., Frangi, A.F. (eds.) MICCAI 2015. LNCS, vol. 9351, pp. 234–241. Springer, Cham (2015). https://doi.org/10.1007/978-3-319-24574-4_28

25. Sanderson, E., Matuszewski, B.J.: FCN-transformer feature fusion for polyp segmentation. In: Medical Image Understanding and Analysis (2022)
26. Shaw, J., Bell, P.M.: Wound measurement in diabetic foot ulceration. In: Global Perspective on Diabetic Foot Ulcerations, chap. 5. IntechOpen (2011)
27. Shi, D.: TransNeXt: robust foveal visual perception for vision transformers. In: CVPR (2024)
28. Siddique, N., Paheding, S., Elkin, C.P., Devabhaktuni, V.: U-Net and its variants for medical image segmentation: a review of theory and applications. IEEE Access **9** (2021)
29. Thisanke, H., Deshan, C., Chamith, K., Seneviratne, S., Vidanaarachchi, R., Herath, D.: Semantic segmentation using vision transformers: a survey. Eng. Appl. Artif. Intell. **126** (2023)
30. Wang, C., et al.: Fully automatic wound segmentation with deep convolutional neural networks. Sci. Rep. **10**(1) (2020)
31. Wang, C., et al.: FUSeg: the foot ulcer segmentation challenge. Information **15**(3) (2024)
32. Wang, L., Pedersen, P.C., Agu, E., Strong, D.M., Tulu, B.: Area determination of diabetic foot ulcer images using a cascaded two-stage SVM-based classification. IEEE Trans. Biomed. Eng. **64**(9) (2017)
33. Wang, W., et al.: InternImage: exploring large-scale vision foundation models with deformable convolutions. In: CVPR (2023)
34. Xiao, T., Liu, Y., Zhou, B., Jiang, Y., Sun, J.: Unified perceptual parsing for scene understanding. In: Ferrari, V., Hebert, M., Sminchisescu, C., Weiss, Y. (eds.) ECCV 2018. LNCS, vol. 11209, pp. 432–448. Springer, Cham (2018). https://doi.org/10.1007/978-3-030-01228-1_26
35. Xie, E., Wang, W., Yu, Z., Anandkumar, A., Alvarez, J.M., Luo, P.: SegFormer: simple and efficient design for semantic segmentation with transformers. In: NeurIPS (2021)
36. Yan, H., Wu, M., Zhang, C.: Multi-scale representations by varying window attention for semantic segmentation. In: ICLR (2024)
37. Zhang, P., et al.: Interactive skin wound segmentation based on feature augment networks. IEEE J. Biomed. Health Inf. **27**(7) (2023)
38. Zhang, R., Tian, D., Xu, D., Qian, W., Yao, Y.: A survey of wound image analysis using deep learning: classification, detection, and segmentation. IEEE Access **10** (2022)

Offline Reinforcement Learning for Community-Acquired Pneumonia Management: A Feasibility Study

Alex Beeson[1,2(✉)], Keith Couper[2,3], and Giovanni Montana[1,4,5]

[1] Warwick Manufacturing Group, University of Warwick, Coventry, UK
{alex.beeson,g.montana}@warwick.ac.uk
[2] Warwick Medical School, University of Warwick, Coventry, UK
k.couper@warwick.ac.uk
[3] Critical Care Unit, University Hospitals Birmingham NHS Foundation Trust, Birmingham, UK
[4] Department of Statistics, University of Warwick, Coventry, UK
[5] Alan Turing Institute, London, UK

Abstract. Community-acquired pneumonia (CAP) remains a leading cause of hospital admission and mortality requiring dynamic clinical decision making as patients' conditions evolve. In this work, we formulate the management of CAP as a sequential decision-making problem and utilise reinforcement learning (RL) as a framework for discovering improved treatment strategies. We leverage a large-scale repository of routinely collected hospital data from the PIONEER hub and conduct an offline RL investigation under real-world complexities such as irregular sampling, missingness and variable treatment patterns. Through an extensive data transformation pipeline, we construct state-action trajectories suitable for RL and then train and evaluate policies via conservative Q-learning and fitted Q-evaluation, achieving initial—though modest—improvements in reducing 30-day mortality. In addition to these preliminary outcomes, our findings underscore the need for refined offline RL methods and rigorous validation to fully realize the potential of using large routine healthcare databases like PIONEER for clinical decision support.

Keywords: offline reinforcement learning · community-acquired pneumonia

1 Introduction

Pneumonia is an infection of the lungs that inhibits oxygen intake [13]. Although most cases are mild-to-moderate and patients respond well to standard treatments, serious complications can arise in vulnerable populations such as children,

---

Supplementary Information The online version contains supplementary material available at https://doi.org/10.1007/978-3-032-06118-8_18.

older adults and those with comorbidities. Pneumonia is typically classified by its site of initial infection—community-acquired pneumonia (CAP) versus hospital-acquired pneumonia (HAP). In the UK, CAP incidence rises sharply with age, from 7.99 per 1,000 among those aged 65+ to 41.94 per 1,000 among those aged 90+ [25]. Pneumonia causes roughly 29,000 deaths per year, making it the third leading cause of lung-disease mortality. In hospitalized patients, 5–15% of patients die within 30 days, increasing to 30% for those admitted to intensive care units [5].

Dynamic treatment regimes (DTRs) provide individualized, time-adaptive strategies to manage patients as their clinical status evolves [4]. Conventional optimization often relies on sequential multiple assignment randomized trials (SMARTs), in which treatments are re-randomized at defined decision points [27]. However, these trials can be costly and typically require simplified intervention timings and treatment options that limit their applicability in practice [3]. Reinforcement learning (RL) has emerged as a powerful framework for discovering more flexible DTRs, showing promise in areas such as drug dosing, intervention timing, laboratory test scheduling and targeting, and more [41]. CAP presents a compelling case study for RL since it is both prevalent and clinically complex, requiring repeated, individualised treatment decisions that incorporate factors such as infection severity, comorbidities and changing clinical characteristics [31].

One advantage of modelling the management of CAP as a sequential decision-making problem is the existence of large repositories of retrospective data, which RL can exploit *offline*—i.e. purely from existing patient trajectories—rather than through prospective experimentation. Offline RL is particularly appealing in healthcare because ethical, logistical, and safety constraints typically preclude trial-and-error interactions or additional randomization [22]. By using historical data, the RL agent can learn policies that might improve health outcomes without placing patients at risk.

In this paper, we investigate whether offline RL applied to retrospective CAP patient data can yield improved policies for reducing 30-day mortality. By framing CAP management as a sequential decision-making task, we report initial, though modest, performance gains using RL-based approaches, highlighting how conservative RL strategies help mitigate extrapolation errors arising when real-world data only partially cover the space of possible actions. Our main contribution is an in-depth exploration of the challenges involved in applying RL to large-scale, routinely collected clinical data that exhibits features such as irregular sampling, extensive missingness and highly variable treatment patterns. Taken together, these findings underscore the promise of RL-based DTRs for pneumonia management and the substantial methodological effort required to transform retrospective health records into effective decision support tools.

2 Related Work

Several studies have already investigated the use of RL to optimize distinct aspects of clinical care, demonstrating RL's potential in guiding medical decisions such as drug dosing and treatment timing. Examples include optimal intravenous fluid and vasopressor dosing for sepsis [14], morphine titration for pain relief [23], heparin anticoagulation regimens [21], chemotherapy scheduling in cancer [40] and radiotherapy scheduling [33]. Researchers have also applied RL to weaning patients from mechanical ventilation [28], scheduling laboratory tests [6] and targeting specific laboratory test values [36]. While these works showcase the promise of RL in a variety of clinical contexts, they often either assume some degree of ongoing interaction with an environment (e.g. simulations) or depend on data-collection protocols not readily available in routine care.

Offline RL aims to learn optimal policies solely from retrospective data, addressing ethical, logistical and safety barriers that preclude further data gathering in many settings such as healthcare. However, directly applying established approaches such as Q-learning to fixed datasets can lead to severe overestimation bias, particularly when the learned policy evaluates actions outside the data distribution [9,19]. Many offline RL methods have thus been developed to mitigate this bias. For continuous action spaces, solutions often involve policy constraints [8], conservative value estimation [16], uncertainty estimation [1], in-distribution learning [15] or hybrid approaches [2]. Several have been successfully adapted to discrete settings. For example, discrete BCQ [7] limits actions for target Q-values to those with high probability under a learned behaviour policy. In CQL [16], Q-values for actions within the dataset are "pushed up" while out-of-distribution actions are "pushed down." Finally, discrete IQL [24] applies in-distribution learning via expectile regression and infers policies using advantage weighted behavioural cloning. These methods, while still emerging, offer promising tools to address the unique challenges of working with static hospital databases where patient safety and limited interaction make active data collection infeasible.

3 PIONEER Data Hub

PIONEER is a health data research hub for acute care within University Hospitals Birmingham (UHB) NHS Foundation Trust. The hub provide secure access to routinely collected healthcare records that undergo a rigorous curation procedure to ensure high quality, including removing malformed fields, de-duplicating records, mapping items to standard ontologies and other cleansing processes.

For our study, we requested records of adults (18+ years) diagnosed with pneumonia based on administrative coding of diagnoses (ICD-10 and SNOMED codes) or searches of key terms in medical records (i.e. CURB-65), who received antibiotics within 48 h of admission. CURB-65 is a diagnostic metric used to determine the severity of CAP upon presenting in hospital [20] while ICD-10 and SNOMED are medical classification systems used by the NHS. A full list of codes is provided in the Appendix[1]. This initial extraction yielded 47,972 care spells for 36,885 patients for the time period April 2018 and September 2022.

---

[1] Appendix available here - https://github.com/AlexBeesonWarwick/OfflineRLCAP/tree/main.

Structure wise, each admission-to-discharge episode is identified by a *care spell id*, allowing multiple spells per patient. Data is split into tables that include both time-dependent data (e.g. observations, interventions) and time-independent data (e.g. demographics). Further details and an example of the relational structure are provided in the Appendix.

As part of a cohort refinement procedure, we first excluded COVID-19 diagnoses to avoid data inconsistencies arising as a result of the global pandemic and the potential overlap with CAP. Next, to distinguish community- from hospital-acquired pneumonia, we required that both a pneumonia diagnosis and a CAP-specific antibiotic appeared within 24 h of admission. These antibiotics were taken from the CAP section of the Trust's Adult Guidelines for Antimicrobial Prescribing [32], namely: Amoxicillin, Co-amoxiclav, Clarithromycin, Doxycycline and Levofloxacin. This refinement procedure resulted in a final cohort of 10,707 care spells for 9,147 patients. Of these, 88% had just one care spell, 9% had two, 2% had three, and fewer than 1% had four or more.

4 Methodology

4.1 Offline Reinforcement Learning

We start by defining a Markov Decision Process (MDP) $M = <S, A, T, R, \gamma>$ where S is the state space, A the action space, $T(s' \mid s, a)$ the environment dynamics, $R(s, a)$ the reward function and $\gamma \in [0, 1]$ the discount factor [29]. An autonomous agent interacts with this MDP by following a state-dependent policy $\pi(s)$, with the objective of discovering an optimal policy $\pi^*(s)$ that maximises the expected discounted sum of rewards, $\mathbb{E}_\pi \left[\sum_{t=0}^{\infty} \gamma^t r(s_t, a_t) \right]$.

In discrete action spaces this objective can be achieved through Q-learning. The Q-function $Q^\pi(s, a)$ defines the value of taking action a in state s following policy π thereafter and optimal Q-values can be obtained by repeated application of the Bellman optimality equation:

$$Q^*(s, a) = r(s, a) + \gamma \, \mathbb{E}_{s' \sim T} \left[\max_{a'} Q^*(s', a') \right] .$$

The optimal policy can then be extracted by taking the action that maximises the optimal Q-value at each state, i.e. $\pi(s) = \arg\max_a Q(s, a)$. Alternatively, actions can be chosen stochastically based on Q-values, for example using a softmax. The probability of action a at state s is denoted $\pi(a \mid s)$.

The scale and complexity of real-world tasks often necessitates the use of function approximation methods. To this effect, Q-functions are parameterised with learnable parameters θ, which are updated to minimise the following loss:

$$L(\theta) = \frac{1}{|B|} \sum_{(s,a,r,s') \sim \mathcal{B}} (Q_\theta(s, a) - y(r, s'))^2 ,$$

where $y(r, s') = r + \gamma \max_{a'} Q_\theta(s', a')$ is the target value and $\mathcal{B}$ is a replay buffer of transitions which is uniformly sampled during training [26].

In offline scenarios, an agent can no longer interact with the environment itself and must instead learn from a pre-existing set of interactions $\mathcal{B}$ collected from some (potentially unknown) behaviour policy or set of policies π_β [17]. With environment interaction prohibited, errors in Q-values estimates are free to compound and propagate during training. Specifically, Q-value estimates for out-of-distribution (OOD) actions (i.e. those not present in $\mathcal{B}$) are prone to overestimation bias as a consequence of the maximisation carried out when determining target values [30]. The end result is spurious Q-value estimates and by extension highly sub-optimal policies. In order to mitigate the detrimental effects of overestimation bias, Q-values must be regularised by staying "close" to actions within the existing set.

In conservative Q-learning (CQL) [16] Q-value estimates are regularised by "pushing down" on estimates for out-of-distribution actions and "pushing up" on estimates for in-distribution actions. Such an adjustment is effectively "gap-expanding" in Q-values between in-distribution and out-of-distribution actions, leading the agent to favour actions more like those in the data when updating the Q-function.

The manner in which Q-values are pushed down can be varied. For each state we can for example use the average Q-value for the all actions, but in practice a more effective approach is to use a type of softmax, leading to the following modified loss:

$$L(\theta) = \frac{1}{|\mathcal{B}|} \sum_{(s,a,r,s') \sim \mathcal{B}} (Q_\theta(s,a) - y(r,s'))^2$$
$$+ \beta \sum_{(s,a) \sim \mathcal{B}} \Big[\log \sum_{a_i \in A} \exp(Q_\theta(s,a_i)) - Q_\theta(s,a) \Big],$$

where β is a hyperparameter that controls the level of conservatism.

4.2 Off-Policy Evaluation

The most accurate and straightforward way to evaluate a policy is to deploy it in the environment and record its return $G(t) = \sum_{t=0}^{T} \gamma^t r_t$. However, in settings involving DTRs rolling out policies without prior assurances on their quality would be considered unacceptable, not least because of the concerns regarding patient safety. Instead, the policy must also be evaluated, not just learnt, in the offline setting. This is the motivation behind off-policy evaluation (OPE), which seeks to estimate the value of one policy using transitions collected from another. In the context of offline RL, this equates to estimating the value of an offline trained policy π_e using transitions from the data set $\mathcal{B}$, originally collected by behaviour policy π_β.

Off-policy evaluation is an important and active research area in its own right and there have been many approaches put forward seeking to provide accurate estimators with desirable properties [34]. For the purpose of this study we make use of fitted Q-evaluation (FQE) [18], in which a Q-function is trained using the

Bellman expectation equation and the property $V(s) = \sum_{a \in A} \pi(a \mid s) Q(s, a)$ used as the basis for a policy value estimate.

Specifically, a parameterised Q-function $Q_\phi(s, a)$ is learnt using the following loss:

$$L(\phi) = \frac{1}{|B|} \sum_{(s,a,r,s') \sim \mathcal{B}} \Big(Q_\phi(s, a) - r - \gamma V(s') \Big)^2,$$

where $V(s') = \sum_{a' \in A} \pi(a' \mid s') Q_\phi(s', a')$.

The estimate of the policy value is then:

$$\hat{V}(\pi_e) = \frac{1}{N} \sum_{i=1}^{N} \sum_{a \in A} \pi_e(a \mid s_0^i) Q_\phi(s_0^i, a),$$

where s_0 is the initial state.

Although this is a biased estimator of $V(\pi_e)$, in general it has low variance since it only requires a one-step estimate during training. This contrasts to other OPE methods such as importance sampling and its per-decision/weighted variants [29] which suffer from high variance due to importance weights becoming either vanishingly small or exponentially large in cases where the evaluation and behaviour policy are significantly different and/or trajectories are long. Furthermore, using FQE allows us to establish a relationship between Q-values and mortality rate, which we can utilise as part of an evaluation protocol.

In order to apply RL methods to the PIONEER data, we must define states, actions and rewards in an MDP framework. This necessitates a range of data pre-processing tasks, including the aforementioned cohort refinement, as well as variable selection and the derivation of clinically relevant features. We also need to align each patient record with appropriate action labels (e.g. administered medications) and design a reward function that captures 30-day mortality. Below, we provide an abridged explanation of these steps, and direct the reader to the Appendix for a full detailed description.

4.3 Variable Selection and Derivation

A crucial first step was to identify variables suitable for modelling patient states, actions and rewards. To this effect, we conducted a table-by-table review guided by four criteria:

1. **Clinical relevance:** Variables had to reflect a patient's health (e.g. vital signs, laboratory results) or administered treatments (e.g. antibiotics) relevant to managing CAP.
2. **Usability:** We required data amenable to deep learning, excluding unstructured free text without consistent numerical or categorical encoding.
3. **Coverage:** Items needed sufficient coverage across the final cohort to enable robust learning. Variables recorded in only a small fraction of care spells were generally discarded.

4. **Imputability:** For potentially informative items with lower coverage, we assessed whether missing data could be addressed with nominal values, derived values or other proxies.

Applying these criteria yielded 41 variables spanning observations, laboratory tests, radiography, comorbidities, demographics and drug administration. Where helpful, we derived additional features (e.g. mapping Troponin or D-dimer to "normal/high/not-recorded"). This process established a broad foundation for representing patient health and relevant clinical parameters.

4.4 Constructing the MDP

Once the pertinent variables were selected, we defined a MDP for offline RL. Unlike simulated settings, *real-world clinical data do not arrive in neatly spaced intervals*, nor does a reward event happen immediately after each clinical decision. Hence, reconciling real-world complexity with the structure of MDPs required several design decisions.

States. For each decision point, we aggregated the chosen variables into a single state representation of the patient. However, since hospitals record different measurements at different times, many entries appeared "missing" when pivoted and joined into a uniform table. To handle this, we adopted a *sample-and-hold* strategy [14], carrying the most recent observed value forward until a new measurement arrived. Where no prior value existed (e.g. early in a care spell) or the data were inherently sparse, we used nominal or median-based imputation.

Actions. We focused on antibiotic administration, concatenating a drug with its route (enteral or parenteral) into a single *drug-route* action. In reality, patients could receive multiple antibiotics simultaneously or switch among them at varying frequencies, which the data did not always capture explicitly. As a compromise, we either (a) limited actions to single antibiotic-route pairs in variable-length windows or (b) allowed up to two antibiotic–route pairs in fixed windows (Sect. 4.5). If no antibiotics were administered for an extended period (e.g. 36 h), or no antibiotic was given in the first interval, we labeled the action "no treatment." These simplifications approximate real care patterns, although they inevitably lose detail about multi-drug regimens.

Reward and Terminal State. We used a sparse reward keyed to 30-day mortality, a standard outcome metric for pneumonia [37]. If the patient was alive at 30 days, we assigned a reward of $+1$, if not, -1. The terminal state was the patient's final recorded state on or before day 30.

4.5 Time-Step Definitions

Discretizing the data into steps for an MDP presents further challenges because antibiotic schedules and patient evolution rarely conform to uniform intervals. In light of this, we explored two main approaches:

Fixed Time Step. We partitioned each patient's timeline into windows of 8, 12, or 24 h. Within each window:

1. **State:** Continuous variables were aggregated by median, categorical variables by mode, and missing values imputed via sample-and-hold or nominal/median substitution.
2. **Action:** Up to two *drug-route* pairs were concatenated. If no antibiotics were administered for >36 h or none appeared in the first window, the action was "no treatment."

This approach maintains a regular MDP structure but may misrepresent real antibiotic timing and overlooks finer nuances like overlapping regimens.

Variable Time Step. We subdivided each patient's timeline at actual antibiotic events, creating a new window whenever a drug was administered. If 36 h elapsed without any antibiotic, a "no treatment" window was inserted. States reflected the most recent measurement values at each event. This strategy captures real scheduling more accurately yet violates the fixed-step MDP assumption and does not easily allow antibiotic combinations in a single step.

4.6 Processed Data Sets

Having defined states, actions and rewards, we applied the above imputation and time-step procedures to yield four final data sets: **Fixed 8 h**, **Fixed 12 h**, **Fixed 24 h** and **Variable** windows (based on antibiotic events). They differ primarily in how time is discretized and how multi-antibiotic use is handled. In each, the terminal state is day 30 or earlier if the patient died or was discharged, and the reward is set by 30-day mortality. Table 1 outlines key cohort characteristics, with lists of ethnicity, comorbidities and antibiotic-routes provided in the Appendix. While these transformations approximate real patient trajectories for offline RL, they inevitably sacrifice some detail due to irregular sampling, missing data and partially documented regimens.

5 Experimental Results

5.1 Set-Up and Implementation

We evaluate four offline policies for CAP management: a **random policy** that selects actions uniformly from the entire action space; a **behaviour policy** that replicates the empirical distribution of observed actions; a **DQN** policy trained via standard Q-learning; a **CQL** policy trained using conservative Q-learning as outlined Sect. 4.1. We use FQE as detailed in Sect. 4.2 to estimate each policy's expected return using the processed dataset.

For DQN, CQL and FQE each Q-function comprised a 2-layer MLP with ReLU activation functions and 256 nodes, taking as input a state and outputting a Q-value for each action. We set the discount factor $\gamma = 1$ and used the Huber

Table 1. Overview of the patient cohort. FiO$_2$ (OT): derived values for patients receiving oxygen therapy. D-dimer, Troponin-I, Troponin-T: N = Normal, H = High, NR = Not Recorded. See Table O in the Appendix for additional details on ethnicity groups, comorbidity definitions and antibiotics (ABX).

Category	Feature	Mean (SD)	Feature	Mean (SD)
Demographics	Age	73.9 (15.7)	Male (N, %)	5390 (50.3)
	Non-survivors (N, %)	1727 (16.1)	Ethnicity	7 types
	Comorbidity	22 types		
Observations	AVPU scale	3.96 (0.25)	Respiratory rate	18.6 (3.3)
	Diastolic BP	70.7 (12.9)	Systolic BP	125.1 (22.6)
	Heart rate	85.2 (17.4)	Temperature	36.4 (0.7)
	NEWS2	3.17 (2.6)	O$_2$ sats (%)	94.8 (3.3)
Lab Analysis	Base excess	0.15 (5.1)	Blood K	4.21 (0.74)
	Blood Na	138 (6.1)	pCO$_2$	6.01 (1.82)
	pO$_2$	8.04 (5.46)	Basophils	0.05 (0.06)
	Eosinophils	0.17 (0.38)	Haematocrit	0.34 (0.07)
	Haemoglobin	113 (22.5)	Lymphocytes	1.72 (8.9)
	Mean cell Hb	29.4 (3.0)	Mean cell volume	89.6 (7.7)
	Monocytes	0.87 (1.44)	Neutrophils	9.01 (7.9)
	Platelets	290 (143)	Red cell count	3.83 (0.75)
	White cell count	11.4 (11.2)	Albumin	29.1 (6.8)
	Alkaline phosphatase	134 (144)	Calcium	2.2 (0.2)
	Total protein	62.0 (8.8)	C-reactive protein	101 (91.7)
	Alanine transferase	35.7 (97.3)	Urea	9.12 (6.94)
Imaging	Chest X-ray (N, %)	8334 (77.9)		
Derived	FiO$_2$ (OT)	0.28 (0.23)	D-dimer	N, H, NR
	Trop-T	N, H, NR	Trop-I	N, H, NR
Treatment	ABX+Route	9 types		

loss to update network parameters. We used a dual critic approach, taking the mean across two Q-value estimates for target Q-values. We made use of separate target networks for estimating target Q-values, updating these networks according to Polyak averaging with update rate 0.005. Networks were trained via stochastic gradient descent using the Adam optimizer with learning rate $3e^{-4}$ and batch size 256. For CQL we trained networks for 500k gradient steps and for FQE we trained networks for 1M gradient steps. For the conservative hyperparameter in CQL we used $\beta \in \{1, 2, 5\}$.

We split the processed data into training and validation sets at a ratio of 80/20. Data was split based on trajectories as opposed to individual transitions as the goal is to generalise treatment policies to new care spells. For each of the processed data sets, we created five different training and validation splits and

Table 2. Policy value estimates (mean ± standard error) computed by fitted Q-evaluation across 5 training/validation splits. The β in CQL is a hyperparameter controlling the level of conservatism (higher values equate to more conservatism).

Data set	Behaviour	Random	DQN	CQL $\beta=1$	CQL $\beta=2$	CQL $\beta=5$
Fixed 8 h	0.75 ± 0.00	0.42 ± 0.01	0.12 ± 0.21	0.76 ± 0.00	0.78 ± 0.00	0.79 ± 0.00
Fixed 12 h	0.76 ± 0.00	0.22 ± 0.02	0.17 ± 0.19	0.79 ± 0.00	0.79 ± 0.00	0.78 ± 0.00
Fixed 24 h	0.73 ± 0.00	0.21 ± 0.01	0.59 ± 0.17	0.76 ± 0.00	0.75 ± 0.00	0.76 ± 0.00
Variable	0.76 ± 0.01	0.41 ± 0.01	0.72 ± 0.04	0.79 ± 0.00	0.80 ± 0.00	0.81 ± 0.00

we report policy value estimates using means ± one standard error. Numerical state features were normalised to compensate for differences in scales between measurement types.

5.2 Policy Evaluation and Mortality Prediction

In Table 2 we report the policy value estimates for each of our chosen policies. Overall, we see CQL marginally outperforms the behaviour policy in most scenarios, whereas DQN often matches or falls below the random policy, especially for shorter fixed length windows (i.e. 8 h and 12 h windows). This underscores the importance of conservative regularization in alleviating overestimation when data coverage is incomplete.

In order to interpret policy values estimates in the context of mortality, we first have to establish a relationship between the two entities and then use this relationship to make predictions. To establish a relationship, similar to previous work [39] we create a set of bins for behaviour policy value estimates and within each bin calculate the mortality rate (number of deaths divided by number of care spells). In Fig. 1 we visualise the results, which indicate an inverse relationship between value estimates and mortality rates for each data set. To quantify this relationship, we fit a logistic regression model and use it to predict the mortality rate for each of our policies. We superimpose the models onto Fig. 1 and summarise predictions in Table 3 alongside the results of statistical significance testing between CQL and the behaviour policy using a two-sided paired t-test.

Table 3. Mortality rates (mean ± standard error) across 5 data splits. For CQL, the best-performing β value is shown. P-values obtained from two-sided paired t-test.

Data set	Behaviour	Random	DQN	CQL	p-value
Fixed 8 h	16.4 ± 0.3	21.2 ± 0.4	28.6 ± 4.0	15.6 ± 0.4	0.009
Fixed 12 h	16.4 ± 0.3	25.2 ± 0.6	28.2 ± 3.8	15.6 ± 0.3	<0.001
Fixed 24 h	16.5 ± 0.3	24.4 ± 0.6	19.1 ± 3.0	15.8 ± 0.4	0.004
Variable	16.6 ± 0.3	21.7 ± 0.8	17.3 ± 0.6	15.8 ± 0.4	0.003

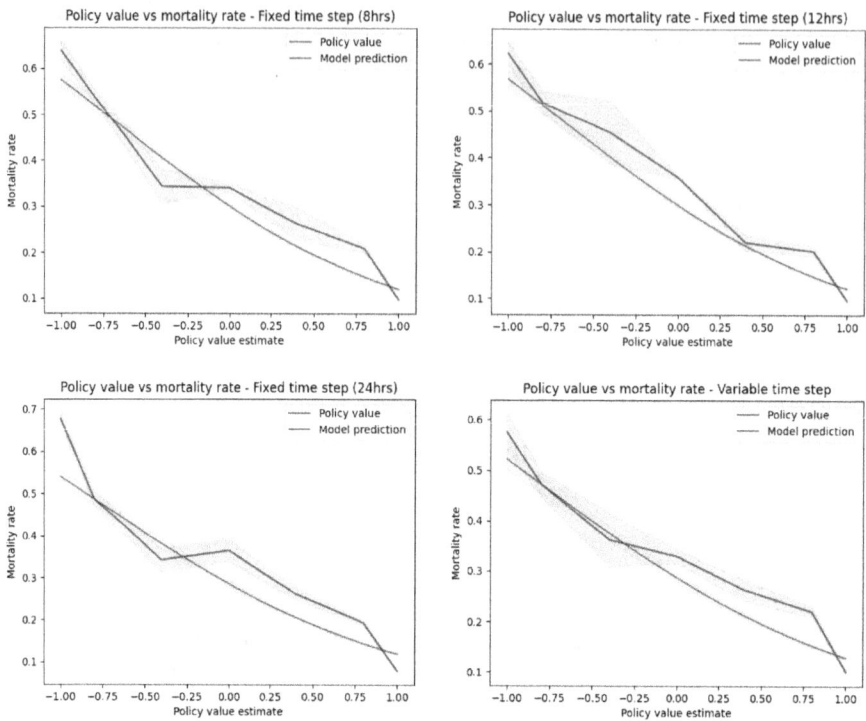

Fig. 1. Policy value estimate vs. mortality rate. For each data set there appears to be an inverse relationship between policy value estimates and mortality rate (blue). For predictive purposes we model this relationship using logistic regression (green). (Color figure online)

Although the resulting estimated mortality reductions are statistically significant at the 5% significance level, they are relatively modest, consistently favouring CQL over the observed (behaviour) policy. A breakdown by patient age in Table 4 further suggests that older patients (those at higher risk) might benefit more, with slightly larger reductions in predicted mortality. However, it should be pointed out these reductions are not always statistically significant at the 5% level when accounting for multiple testing using a Bonferroni correction in which the significance level is (conservatively) adjusted to 1%, reflecting the intrinsic complexities in real-world data and the offline setting's constraints.

Table 4. Mortality rates (mean ± standard error) across 5 splits. For each data set, we list Behaviour vs. CQL (best β), the absolute reduction and associated p-values.

Data set	Age group	Behaviour	CQL	Reduction	p-value
Fixed 8 h	<65	13.5 ± 0.4	13.3 ± 0.5	0.2	0.362
	65–79	15.8 ± 0.4	15.1 ± 0.5	0.7	0.006
	80–84	17.2 ± 0.3	16.2 ± 0.3	1.0	0.007
	85–89	18.8 ± 0.4	17.4 ± 0.5	1.4	0.011
	90+	19.1 ± 0.3	17.9 ± 0.5	1.2	0.068
Fixed 12 h	<65	13.9 ± 0.4	13.4 ± 0.4	0.5	0.005
	65–79	15.7 ± 0.4	15.1 ± 0.3	0.6	0.004
	80–84	17.3 ± 0.1	16.1 ± 0.2	1.2	0.011
	85–89	18.4 ± 0.4	17.3 ± 0.3	1.1	0.007
	90+	18.7 ± 0.5	17.8 ± 0.1	0.9	0.170
Fixed 24 h	<65	13.6 ± 0.3	13.5 ± 0.3	0.1	0.413
	65–79	15.5 ± 0.4	15.4 ± 0.4	0.1	0.266
	80–84	17.2 ± 0.2	16.9 ± 0.3	0.3	0.226
	85–89	18.9 ± 0.5	17.3 ± 0.4	1.6	0.002
	90+	19.4 ± 0.3	17.6 ± 0.4	1.8	0.004
Variable	<65	14.2 ± 0.3	14.0 ± 0.4	0.2	0.300
	65–79	16.1 ± 0.3	15.4 ± 0.4	0.7	0.005
	80–84	17.4 ± 0.3	16.7 ± 0.3	0.7	0.034
	85–89	18.4 ± 0.4	17.1 ± 0.4	1.3	0.018
	90+	19.1 ± 0.3	17.7 ± 0.4	1.4	0.017

6 Discussion and Conclusions

In this work we have conducted a feasibility study looking at whether offline RL can be used to reduce 30-mortality for patients with CAP. We have undertaken an extensive set of data pre-processing procedures to convert source data into states, actions and rewards then used this processed data to train and evaluate policies offline. Our initial results indicate that agents trained offline using CQL are able to learn treatment policies that marginally improve overall mortality compared to the behaviour policy, as evaluated using FQE and a logistic regression model. Agents trained using DQN with no offline modifications fail to improve over the behaviour policy and in some cases perform no better than a random policy.

Future Work. Our study has generated several lines of enquiry for future work, one of which is to investigate alternative approaches for aggregating state variables. In particular, including dispersion metrics (e.g. interquartile ranges, variances) or explicitly encoding temporal structure (e.g. concatenating previous states or tracking state changes across timesteps) might yield a more expressive representation of a patient's evolving health status. Additionally, architectures beyond a simple MLP, such as LSTMs [10] or transformers [35], could better capture the time-series nature of clinical data.

We also see scope for more nuanced action spaces. Our current setup merges an antibiotic with its route of administration, but escalation/de-escalation steps, dose variations, oxygen therapy, or ICU admission could be treated as distinct actions, possibly leading to more complete policies. Another direction lies in rethinking the reward structure. We used a sparse reward tied to 30-day mortality, but additional outcomes (e.g. hospital length-of-stay, ICU admissions) or intermediate measures (e.g. improving FiO_2) could create a denser, more informative signal for the agent.

Data Preprocessing Challenges. A key aspect of this work was the substantial and iterative data-processing effort required to align routine hospital records with the assumptions of RL. Although Sect. 4 points to an ordered sequence of steps, in practice we repeatedly revisited earlier decisions. For example, our initial patient selection excluded only COVID-19 cases, but this required modification upon discovering diagnosis codes did not clearly distinguish between CAP and HAP. Similarly, deriving variables like FiO_2 required cross-referencing multiple tables (Observations, Ventilation) that occasionally contradicted each other. Each iteration demanded thorough testing to ensure consistency and avoid introducing new errors.

Time-Step Definitions and Antibiotic Regimens. Defining the temporal granularity for state-action pairs proved especially challenging. We explored two main strategies: fixed-length windows (8, 12, or 24 h) to preserve an approximate Markov property, and variable-length windows that aligned with recorded antibiotic administrations to reflect real-world treatment intervals. Each approach had drawbacks. Fixed windows often failed to capture the actual frequency or timing of drug administration, while variable windows lost regular time steps. Neither method could fully capture multi-drug regimens because the data only recorded drug administration at the singular level. Hence, our policy comparisons inevitably compare approximations rather than an exact record of patient care.

Imputation Strategies. Although a sample-and-hold approach populated most state variables when new observations were temporarily absent, many transitions still lacked any recent value. We chose a median-based imputation in these scenarios, on the premise that clinicians might initially assume typical or population-level values before test results are available. Alternative approaches (e.g. regression or k-nearest neighbours) might yield more tailored estimates but would greatly increase the pipeline's complexity, requiring separate predictive models for each of the numerous clinical variables. In addition, sample-and-hold itself is subject to limitations since it assumes values remain constant in between time points, which may not necessarily be the case.

Comorbidities and Cause of Death. Including some comorbidity flags (i.e. past diagnoses) in the state space enhanced our representation of patient risk. Yet it remained difficult to fully represent the broader clinical ramifications of these comorbidities, such as additional medications or whether a patient's death was unrelated to CAP. Designing a more expansive action space, or refining the reward to account for other causes of death, would require careful modelling and extensive data given the multifactorial nature of hospital mortality.

Policy Evaluation and Mortality Prediction. To evaluate our learned policies, we relied on FQE to estimate Q-values offline. We also modelled the relationship between Q-values and 30-day mortality using logistic regression, observing an inverse correlation that suggests our Q-function captures meaningful clinical signals. However, a more comprehensive validation could involve qualitative assessments of suggested actions by domain experts or prospective trials in controlled settings. The former would be a vital step in gaining assurances to facilitate the latter, assessing not just the safety of proposed actions but also the plausibility, both as a single treatment option and as part of a regimen. We did not have the resources available to conduct a formal qualitative assessment of actions for this particularly study, however it is something we would seek to include as part of future work.

Implications and Next Steps. Despite the inherent complexity and partial success of our approach, this study highlights the promise of offline RL for the management of CAP. Building upon these findings might involve more advanced RL formulations, such as semi-Markov decision processes (SMDPs), partially observable Markov decision processes (POMDPs) and/or hierarchical reinforcement learning (HRL). In a SMDP [11] the time between actions can vary, which may better align with how treatment are administered in cases such as CAP. In a POMDP [38] the agent cannot directly observe the underlying state, which may better reflect the observational nature of healthcare data. In HRL [12] tasks are split into high-level and low-level sub-tasks, which are governed by different policies that operate together to achieve an overall objective. In a healthcare setting this could equate to having a high-level policy that determines when to treat a patient and a low-level policy that selects the specific treatment. Efforts could also be directed toward curating data sets specifically with RL needs in mind to avoid many of the pitfalls we encountered.

Concluding Remarks. Overall, our feasibility study provides initial evidence that offline RL can yield marginally better outcomes than historical practice for CAP management, but it also illustrates the formidable challenges of adapting real-world healthcare data to the structure demanded by RL algorithms. Addressing these challenges—through richer state spaces, refined action definitions, improved reward signals, and more robust ways to handle missing data—will be essential for unlocking the full potential of RL in clinical settings. By continuing to refine data acquisition procedures and incorporate innovative RL techniques, we can move toward safer, more effective data-driven decision support for pneumonia and other complex conditions.

Acknowledgments. This work was supported by PIONEER, the Health Data Research Hub in Acute Care, which is affiliated with Health Data Research UK. PIONEER: Data curation and licensed access for this study through PIONEER has been approved by the East Midlands (Derby) REC (20/EM/0158) and is supported by the Confidentiality Advisory Group (Reference 20/CAG/0084). This study is also granted ethical approval by the University of Warwick's Biomedical and Scientific Research Ethics Committee (BSREC 82/21-22). AB acknowledges support from University of Warwick and University Hospitals Birmingham NHS Foundation Trust. GM acknowledges support from a UKRI AI Turing Acceleration Fellowship (EPSRC EP/V024868/1). The authors also acknowledge the support and guidance of Prof. Gavin Perkins from the University of Warwick.

Disclosure of Interests. The authors have no competing interests to declare that are relevant to the content of this article.

References

1. An, G., Moon, S., Kim, J.H., Song, H.O.: Uncertainty-based offline reinforcement learning with diversified Q-ensemble. In: Advances in Neural Information Processing Systems, vol. 34, pp. 7436–7447 (2021)
2. Beeson, A., Montana, G.: Balancing policy constraint and ensemble size in uncertainty-based offline reinforcement learning. Mach. Learn. **113**(1), 443–488 (2024)
3. Bigirumurame, T., Uwimpuhwe, G., Wason, J.: Sequential multiple assignment randomized trial studies should report all key components: a systematic review. J. Clin. Epidemiol. **142**, 152–160 (2022)
4. Chakraborty, B., Murphy, S.A.: Dynamic treatment regimes. Ann. Rev. Stat. Appl. **1**(1), 447–464 (2014)
5. Chalmers, J., Campling, J., Ellsbury, G., Hawkey, P.M., Madhava, H., Slack, M.: Community-acquired pneumonia in the United Kingdom: a call to action. Pneumonia **9**, 1–6 (2017)
6. Cheng, L.F., Prasad, N., Engelhardt, B.E.: An optimal policy for patient laboratory tests in intensive care units. In: BIOCOMPUTING 2019: Proceedings of the Pacific Symposium, pp. 320–331. World Scientific (2018)
7. Fujimoto, S., Conti, E., Ghavamzadeh, M., Pineau, J.: Benchmarking batch deep reinforcement learning algorithms. arXiv preprint arXiv:1910.01708 (2019)
8. Fujimoto, S., Gu, S.S.: A minimalist approach to offline reinforcement learning. In: Advances in Neural Information Processing Systems, vol. 34, pp. 20132–20145 (2021)
9. Fujimoto, S., Meger, D., Precup, D.: Off-policy deep reinforcement learning without exploration. In: International Conference on Machine Learning, pp. 2052–2062. PMLR (2019)
10. Hochreiter, S.: Long Short-Term Memory. Neural Computation. MIT-Press (1997)
11. Hu, Q., Yue, W.: Markov Decision Processes with Their Applications, vol. 14. Springer, New York (2007). https://doi.org/10.1007/978-0-387-36951-8

12. Hutsebaut-Buysse, M., Mets, K., Latré, S.: Hierarchical reinforcement learning: a survey and open research challenges. Mach. Learn. Knowl. Extr. **4**(1), 172–221 (2022)
13. Kaplan, W., Wirtz, V., Mantel-Teeuwisse, A., Stolk, P., Duthey, B.: Priority medicines for Europe and the world 2013 update. Technical report, World Health Organisation (2013)
14. Komorowski, M., Celi, L.A., Badawi, O., Gordon, A.C., Faisal, A.A.: The artificial intelligence clinician learns optimal treatment strategies for sepsis in intensive care. Nat. Med. **24**(11), 1716–1720 (2018)
15. Kostrikov, I., Nair, A., Levine, S.: Offline reinforcement learning with implicit Q-learning. In: International Conference on Learning Representations (2021)
16. Kumar, A., Zhou, A., Tucker, G., Levine, S.: Conservative Q-learning for offline reinforcement learning. In: Advances in Neural Information Processing Systems, vol. 33, pp. 1179–1191 (2020)
17. Lange, S., Gabel, T., Riedmiller, M.: Batch Reinforcement Learning, vol. 12, pp. 45–73. Springer, Heidelberg (2012). https://doi.org/10.1007/978-3-642-27645-3_2
18. Le, H., Voloshin, C., Yue, Y.: Batch policy learning under constraints. In: International Conference on Machine Learning, pp. 3703–3712. PMLR (2019)
19. Levine, S., Kumar, A., Tucker, G., Fu, J.: Offline reinforcement learning: tutorial, review, and perspectives on open problems. arXiv preprint arXiv:2005.01643 (2020)
20. Lim, W.S., et al.: Defining community acquired pneumonia severity on presentation to hospital: an international derivation and validation study. Thorax **58**(5), 377–382 (2003)
21. Liu, J., et al.: Value function assessment to different RL algorithms for heparin treatment policy of patients with sepsis in ICU. Artif. Intell. Med. **147**, 102726 (2024)
22. Liu, S., See, K.C., Ngiam, K.Y., Celi, L.A., Sun, X., Feng, M.: Reinforcement learning for clinical decision support in critical care: comprehensive review. J. Med. Internet Res. **22**(7), e18477 (2020)
23. Lopez-Martinez, D., Eschenfeldt, P., Ostvar, S., Ingram, M., Hur, C., Picard, R.: Deep reinforcement learning for optimal critical care pain management with morphine using dueling double-deep Q networks. In: 2019 41st Annual International Conference of the IEEE Engineering in Medicine and Biology Society (EMBC), pp. 3960–3963. IEEE (2019)
24. Luo, J., Dong, P., Wu, J., Kumar, A., Geng, X., Levine, S.: Action-quantized offline reinforcement learning for robotic skill learning. In: 7th Annual Conference on Robot Learning (2023)
25. Millett, E.R., Quint, J.K., Smeeth, L., Daniel, R.M., Thomas, S.L.: Incidence of community-acquired lower respiratory tract infections and pneumonia among older adults in the united kingdom: a population-based study. PLoS ONE **8**(9), e75131 (2013)
26. Mnih, V., et al.: Playing atari with deep reinforcement learning. arXiv preprint arXiv:1312.5602 (2013)
27. Murphy, S.A.: An experimental design for the development of adaptive treatment strategies. Stat. Med. **24**(10), 1455–1481 (2005)
28. Prasad, N., Cheng, L.F., Chivers, C., Draugelis, M., Engelhardt, B.E.: A reinforcement learning approach to weaning of mechanical ventilation in intensive care units. arXiv preprint arXiv:1704.06300 (2017)
29. Sutton, R.S., Barto, A.G.: Reinforcement Learning: An Introduction. MIT Press (2018)

30. Thrun, S., Schwartz, A.: Issues in using function approximation for reinforcement learning. In: Proceedings of the Fourth Connectionist Models Summer School, Hillsdale, NJ, vol. 255, p. 263 (1993)
31. Torres, A., et al.: Challenges in severe community-acquired pneumonia: a point-of-view review. Intensive Care Med. **45**(2), 159–171 (2019). https://doi.org/10.1007/s00134-019-05519-y
32. University Hospital Birmingham NHS Foundation Trust: Adult guidelines for antimicrobial prescribing. https://www.uhb.nhs.uk/Downloads/pdf/controlled-documents/AntimicrobialPrescribingGuidelines.pdf. Accessed 1 Sept 2023
33. Tseng, H.H., Luo, Y., Cui, S., Chien, J.T., Ten Haken, R.K., Naqa, I.E.: Deep reinforcement learning for automated radiation adaptation in lung cancer. Med. Phys. **44**(12), 6690–6705 (2017)
34. Uehara, M., Shi, C., Kallus, N.: A review of off-policy evaluation in reinforcement learning. arXiv preprint arXiv:2212.06355 (2022)
35. Vaswani, A.: Attention is all you need. In: Advances in Neural Information Processing Systems (2017)
36. Weng, W.H., Gao, M., He, Z., Yan, S., Szolovits, P.: Representation and reinforcement learning for personalized glycemic control in septic patients. arXiv preprint arXiv:1712.00654 (2017)
37. Wiemken, T.L., et al.: Predicting 30-day mortality in hospitalized patients with community-acquired pneumonia using statistical and machine learning approaches. Univ. Louisville J. Respir. Infect. **1**(3), 10 (2017)
38. Wiering, M.A., Van Otterlo, M.: Reinforcement learning. Adapt. Learn. Optim. **12**(3), 729 (2012)
39. Wu, X., Li, R., He, Z., Yu, T., Cheng, C.: A value-based deep reinforcement learning model with human expertise in optimal treatment of sepsis. NPJ Digit. Med. **6**(1), 15 (2023)
40. Yang, C.Y., Shiranthika, C., Wang, C.Y., Chen, K.W., Sumathipala, S.: Reinforcement learning strategies in cancer chemotherapy treatments: a review. Comput. Methods Programs Biomed. **229**, 107280 (2023)
41. Yu, C., Liu, J., Nemati, S., Yin, G.: Reinforcement learning in healthcare: a survey. ACM Comput. Surv. (CSUR) **55**(1), 1–36 (2021)

TempEHR: A Temporal Dependency-Based Approach for Synthesizing Electronic Health Records

Emmanuella Budu[✉], Amira Soliman, Farzaneh Etminani, and Thorsteinn Rögnvaldsson

Halmstad University, Halmstad 301 18, Sweden
{emmanuella.budu,amira.soliman,farzaneh.etminani,
thorsteinn.rognvaldsson}@hh.se

Abstract. Synthetic Electronic Health Records (EHRs) provide a viable means of accessing EHR data while addressing the privacy concerns related to the use of EHRs. A key characteristic of EHRs is the irregular timing of clinical events, admissions, and associated temporal trends. Many existing models for generating synthetic EHRs overlook these temporal irregularities, often assuming uniform intervals between clinical events for each patient and neglecting the time component, which hinders the representation of true temporal dynamics. To address these limitations, we propose TempEHR, a framework designed to synthesise EHRs, emphasising temporal awareness. We employ a time-aware Variational Autoencoder (VAE), specifically a Maximum Mean Discrepancy VAE (MMD-VAE), leveraging Time-aware Long Short-Term Memory (T-LSTM) layers to generate temporal synthetic EHRs along with time information. Simultaneously, we enhance the temporal awareness of our proposed model with a novel network we refer to as a TrendFinder. TrendFinder leverages a moving average to extract the temporal patterns inherent in irregular longitudinal EHR data. This approach seeks to enhance the fidelity and usefulness of synthetic EHRs for research and clinical applications. We assess the effectiveness of TempEHR using EHRs from the Medical Information Mart for Intensive Care (MIMIC-IV) repository. Our results demonstrate the potential of the proposed method in capturing the temporal patterns present in EHRs in utility, fidelity and privacy evaluations.

Keywords: synthetic data · Electronic Health Records (EHRs) · temporal data · time-series analysis

1 Introduction

Recent advancements in artificial intelligence (AI) have accelerated research in studies on data-driven medicine, where electronic health records (EHRs) serve as the primary data source for these studies. EHRs are a valuable source of

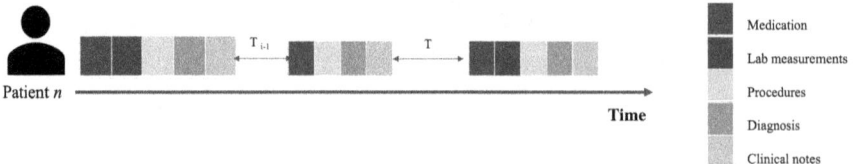

Fig. 1. An illustration of the irregularities in patient records. Time intervals are not regular, i.e., $T_{i-1} \neq T$, and different actions and measurements can be done at each visit.

information to facilitate such research studies and enhance patient care outcomes [1] as they encompass time-sequenced records of various clinical events and interactions between patients and healthcare providers over time [2].

One promising area in the work on EHRs is the generation of synthetic EHRs using deep generative models such as Generative Adversarial Networks (GANs), Variational Autoencoders (VAEs), Diffusion Models, and most recently, Large Language Models. This is being investigated as a viable means of obtaining EHRs that do not compromise the privacy regulations surrounding real EHRs [1]. Significant efforts have been made in recent years in several studies [3–8] to generate diverse and temporal synthetic EHRs. Although viable, these existing approaches ignore one fundamental characteristic of EHRs and assume regularity between clinical events in patient records, which is an unrealistic perception.

EHRs are inherently irregular due to varied patient visits, admissions and interactions, as illustrated in Fig. 1. In healthcare, we encounter multivariate EHRs with irregularities attributed to missing recordings, irregular patient visits, and varying lab measurements. This irregularity can also be attributed to economic and social factors [5], such as accessibility to healthcare facilities in underprivileged societies.

Existing EHR generation methods proposed in several studies [1,4,6] employ recurrence methods such as Recurrent Neural Networks (RNNs) and Long Short-Term Memory networks (LSTMs) [9,10] that assume regular intervals between successive elements. This is a significant limitation because it compromises the validity of the generated EHRs, as the temporal dependency is inaccurately modelled. Several studies [9–11] have shown that using vanilla recurrence models such as LSTMs to model irregular data leads to subpar and inconsistent performance in modelling progression patterns in EHRs. In addition, some studies [12] have demonstrated that traditional recurrence architectures also struggle with representing or learning the trends present in temporal data.

More recent studies in synthetic EHR generation have begun addressing the challenges posed by the inherent temporal irregularities in EHRs. For example, Yoon et al. [1] explored incorporating irregular time information as an additional feature in observed patient data before synthesising the data. While this method attempts to model temporal irregularity, it treats the irregularities associated with clinical events as just another feature in the observed EHR data. As a result, the approach limits the generative model's ability to fully capture and leverage the temporal dependencies between events, as the model does not fully account for the time irregularities in the data.

Other research efforts [13,14] have sought to address the challenge of modelling temporal irregularity in synthetic EHRs by transforming time information into embedding vectors that are concatenated with the latent space representation during training. However, modelling the complexities of temporal irregularity in synthetic EHR generation remains an underexplored area. Moreover, several studies have emphasised the critical role of modelling irregular time intervals when synthesising EHRs [5,6,14], highlighting the importance of advancing research in this domain.

Building on these efforts, we present TempEHR, which explores a time-aware approach that leverages time information to enhance the generative model's ability to capture temporal dependencies within EHRs. Our approach employs an information-maximising variational autoencoder (MMD-VAE) [15] with time-aware long short-term memory networks (T-LSTMs) [9], transforming time intervals between clinical events into weights. These weights are used to adjust the memory in the recurrence layers, emphasising close events. Inspired by the work of Lin et al. [16], we supplement this with a novel module, which we call TrendFinder, which learns the underlying temporal trends in the real data to enhance the quality of the synthetic EHRs.

To the best of our knowledge, this is the first work to combine time-aware models, such as T-LSTMs, with trend-extracting methods within a generative framework for synthetic EHRs. To this end, the contributions of this work are as follows:

– We propose TempEHR, a generative framework for synthesising temporal EHRs that accounts for the irregular patterns and associated temporal trends inherent in EHRs.
– We leverage the time intervals between clinical events as weights to prioritise recent data and capture the temporal patterns in irregular EHRs.
– We introduce a novel TrendFinder module that leverages a time exponential moving average to learn the underlying trends in irregularly timed EHRs.
– We evaluate the effectiveness of TempEHR on a real-world publicly available EHR dataset on fidelity, utility and privacy measures.

2 Related Work

2.1 Modelling Irregular Data in Deep Learning

Irregularity in sequenced or temporal data refers to temporal data characterised by non-uniform intervals between successive time points. This may arise from irregular sampling, variable observations, and misaligned time points [10]. Irregular data is particularly common in healthcare, where data is often recorded at inconsistent intervals due to varying processes, patient behaviours, and conditions. This paper specifically addresses the challenge of modelling irregularity related to varying intervals between successive time points in EHRs.

In deep learning for temporal data, recurrent models such as RNNs and LSTMs are among the most widely used architectures. Despite their success across various tasks, these models face challenges when dealing with irregular data as they typically assume fixed or relatively small intervals between successive data points [9,10]. As a result, they are often inefficient in handling data with irregular intervals, struggling to capture the evolving patterns in temporal data [11]. Common approaches to handling this include incorporating additional information about irregularities, such as indicators or time intervals, before using a recurrence model [17]. In contrast, some studies have examined methods that modify the underlying LSTM model by adding time-gating mechanisms [10] or transforming the time intervals between consecutive observations into weights, which adjust the contents of the hidden state accordingly [9]. Moreover, attention models have been employed to help the model focus on recent parts of the input by using positional encodings [10].

2.2 Synthesising Temporal EHRs

Existing methods for generating temporal EHRs often utilise recurrent architectures within deep generative models, such as GANs and VAEs. Recurrence-based GAN models, including TimeGAN [3], TAP-GAN [4], DAAE [7], and EHR-Safe [1], initially employ an autoencoder to learn the underlying representations of real EHRs that are used in combination with a GAN to generate synthetic EHRs.

Similarly, Biswal and Ghosh [5] utilise a VAE with convolutions, while Nikolentzos et al. [8] introduced an approach that employs a Variational Graph Autoencoder (VGA) to model patient trajectories. Other research efforts, such as EHR-M-GAN [6], combine a VAE and a GAN with Coupled Recurrent Networks (CRN) to generate mixed-type longitudinal EHRs.

Additionally, some studies have explored the use of diffusion models [14] to generate synthetic temporal EHRs. However, most assume a fixed interval for clinical events for the EHRs.

An emerging focus in recent studies is the generation of synthetic EHRs that handle the time irregularity inherent in EHRs. For instance, EHR-Safe [1] employs an autoencoder-based framework that models the irregular timing of events as a feature. However, it does not use these time intervals to guide the overall generation process.

IGAMT [13] and EHRPD [14] also address irregularities by learning the relationships between features across different time steps. IGAMT utilises a transformer-based encoder-decoder framework, while EHRPD employs a diffusion-based autoencoder structure. Both models calculate time intervals between events, converting these increments into embedding vectors concatenated with the latent space representation of the EHR data.

EHR-Safe [1], IGAMT [13], and EHRPD [14] all explore different approaches for addressing temporal irregularity in EHR generation. However, the field is still under-explored and presents opportunities for further research.

2.3 Moving Averages

Moving averages (MA) are key concepts in temporal data analysis, defined as a time series generated by averaging consecutive values from the original data [18]. For a given time series $x_i, x_{i+1}, \ldots, x_k$, the moving average over k time steps can be expressed as:

$$\text{MA}_t = \frac{1}{k} \sum_{i=t-k+1}^{t} x_i \quad (1)$$

In time series analysis, moving averages serve two main purposes: they help to track the behaviour of a time series by smoothing out fluctuations and revealing underlying trends, and they are also used to forecast future values [18,19].

Different variations of moving average methods exist, with the most common being the simple moving average, which computes the arithmetic mean of a set of observations. The cumulative moving average calculates an average by including all previous data points, while exponential moving averages apply a smoothing factor to prioritise recent observations.

Moving averages can also be adapted for irregular temporal data. In such cases, the moving averages are adjusted to account for the time intervals between observations. Menth and Hauser [19] proposed various techniques for incorporating these time intervals into the moving average calculations for irregular temporal data.

3 TempEHR

3.1 Problem Definition

Let $D = \{(x_i, a_i)\}_{i=1}^{N}$ represent the multivariate EHR dataset, where N is the total number of patient records. Each record x_i is a sequence of events for different variables, and a_i is the corresponding sequence of inter-admission intervals, representing the time between consecutive events. Specifically, $x_i = \{x_i^1, x_i^2, \ldots, x_i^T\}$, where x_i^t denotes the event at time step t for the i-th patient, and $a_i = \{a_i^1, a_i^2, \ldots, a_i^{T-1}\}$, where a_i^t denotes the associated time interval at time step t for the i-th patient. The goal is to learn an approximate distribution $\hat{p}(D)$, from which we can sample data points to create a synthetic dataset, $\hat{D}$.

3.2 TempEHR

TempEHR[1] comprises a time-aware VAE combined with an additional moving average-based neural network, which we call the TrendFinder, to handle the irregularity inherent in EHRs as illustrated in Fig. 2. TempEHR simultaneously learns a latent representation of the irregular EHRs and the underlying trend across time. This yields an enriched latent space that can be used to synthesise temporal EHRs and the associated time intervals.

---
[1] Code repository for TempEHR: https://github.com/EmmanuellaBudu/TempEHR.

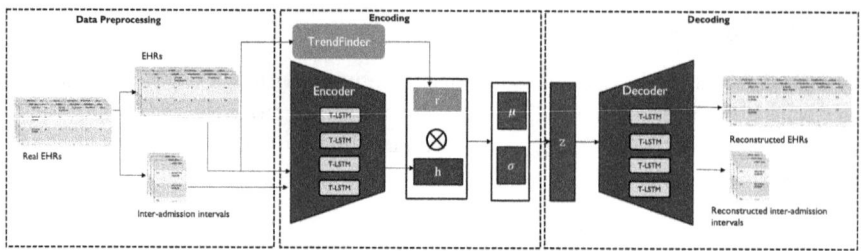

Fig. 2. Overview of TempEHR. TempEHR leverages a T-LSTM-based VAE to generate synthetic EHRs and associated time intervals.

3.3 Learning Temporal Dependencies

TempEHR utilises T-LSTM layers [9] within the encoder and decoder modules of a VAE framework. The Encoder takes as input the multivariate EHRs containing clinical events along with the associated time intervals, Δt, between visits/admissions. The time intervals Δt are transformed into weights using a time decay function in the Encoder. These weights are then used to adjust the cell state contents, subsequently influencing the learned hidden representation h, from the T-LSTM-based Encoder.

Additionally, we incorporate a TrendFinder network inspired by the work of Lin et al. [16] that employs a time exponential moving average (TEMA) to identify trends, r. The motivation for using TrendFinder is to learn the temporal dependencies in irregularly-timed data better. By enhancing the latent representation, we aim to improve overall model performance in generating high-fidelity synthetic EHRs. TEMA is described in Eq. 2:

$$\text{TEMA}_t = e^{-\Delta t/\tau} \cdot x_t + \left(1 - e^{-\Delta t/\tau}\right) \cdot \text{TEMA}_{(t-1)} \qquad (2)$$

where: x_t is the value at time t, τ is the time constant, Δt is the time difference between t and $t-1$. We employ TEMA after evaluating various moving average methods to identify the most effective one. Additionally, it aligns with the inherent mechanisms of T-LSTMs, emphasising recent values. This approach enables us to capture the underlying trend despite the irregularities effectively.

Next, the representations r and h are concatenated and passed through linear layers to generate μ and σ vectors, which parameterise the latent space z. The latent space z is regularised with Maximum Mean Discrepancy (MMD) to obtain a more informative prior [15] as compared to the traditional Kullback-Leibler (KL) divergence. Next, the Decoder uses samples from z to reconstruct the input EHRs and the associated time intervals.

Table 1. Description of datasets.

	MIMIC-CHF	MIMIC
Total Admissions	8835	21380
Total Patients	1767	2138
Total Features	24	23
Max Seq. Length	5	10

3.4 TempEHR Loss

TempEHR employs three loss functions during training to generate synthetic EHRs. First, we utilise a VAE loss, which is composed of a reconstruction loss and an MMD loss on the latent space, where $p(z)$ is the prior distribution and $q(z)$ is the posterior distribution over the EHRs:

$$\mathcal{L}_{\text{VAE}} = \mathcal{L}_{\text{Reconstruction}} + \lambda_1 \mathcal{MMD}\left[p(z), q(z)\right] \quad (3)$$

Second, we incorporate a mean squared error (MSE) loss to model the time intervals explicitly. This loss penalises the difference between the real-time and generated time intervals. This explicit focus on time intervals provides finer control over time, which is critical in this context:

$$\mathcal{L}_{\text{Time}} = \lambda_2 \text{MSE}(a_{\text{real}}, a_{\text{syn}}) \quad (4)$$

The total loss is a weighted sum of the reconstruction loss, MMD loss, and time loss, where the weights, λ_1 and λ_2 are empirically determined to balance the contributions of each term:

$$\mathcal{L}_{\text{total}} = \mathcal{L}_{\text{Reconstruction}} + \lambda_1 \mathcal{MMD}\left[p(z), q(z)\right] + \lambda_2 \mathcal{L}_{\text{Time}} \quad (5)$$

4 Experiments

4.1 Datasets

We utilise real-world EHRs from the Medical Information Mart for Intensive Care (MIMIC-IV) data repository. This publicly accessible database contains de-identified patient records from the Beth Israel Deaconess Medical Centre, covering the years from 2001 to 2012 [20].

For this study, we extracted two separate sets of EHRs from the hospital module, which includes records from general hospital stays. We target a cohort of heart failure patients (MIMIC-CHF) alongside a general group of patients without specific disease diagnoses (MIMIC) as done in previous studies [1]. We extract demographics, vital signs, lab measurements, and co-morbidity flags. The characteristics of the datasets are described in Table 1.

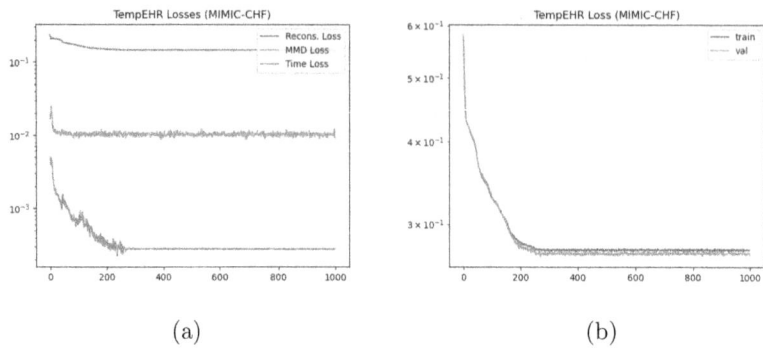

Fig. 3. TempEHR training and validation losses on MIMIC-CHF dataset.

The dataset is organised so that each patient is represented by a time-ordered sequence of admissions containing data recorded during that admission, often known as a patient trajectory. The dataset includes both discrete and continuous values. During preprocessing, discrete values are transformed into continuous values by mapping them to the range [0,1], following the approach described in [21]. The interval [0,1] is divided into sections based on the cumulative probability of each unique discrete value. Each discrete value is then mapped to a point within its corresponding section. Additionally, all continuous values are normalised to the range [0,1].

4.2 Baselines

We consider two baseline temporal generative models: (i) EHR-M-GAN [6], a dual-VAE model with a Coupled Recurrent Network (CRN) generator for generating heterogeneous temporal EHRs, and (ii) TimeGAN [3], a state-of-the-art GAN-based time-series data generator that employs LSTMs or Gated Recurrent Units (GRUs). For these baselines, we model the irregular timing of events as a feature [1]. Due to some code unavailability, technical challenges, and time constraints with the implementations of some other related works [1,13,14], we were unable to directly include the models as baselines. Despite these limitations, the selected baselines are useful benchmarks for evaluating our proposed method.

4.3 Training Details

TempEHR is implemented in PyTorch and trained with the Adam optimiser and a learning rate of 0.001. We employ a reduce-on-plateau learning rate scheduler to adapt the learning rate during training. Furthermore, we partition the datasets using a 70:30 split; the loss from training on the MIMIC-CHF is illustrated in Fig. 3, showing the combined losses and individual losses. The rest of the model parameters are as follows: hidden size:128, latent size:64, encoder and decoder layers:3, λ_1: 4.97, λ_2:0.39.

4.4 Evaluation

This study employs a comprehensive evaluation framework to assess the synthetic EHRs generated by TempEHR and the baseline models, focusing on *fidelity*, *utility* and *privacy* [22] evaluations. Fidelity refers to the faithfulness of the synthetic data to the real data. We employ fidelity measures to assess whether the structural and temporal relationships in the real EHRs have been replicated in synthetic EHRs. Specifically, we assess structural similarity in low dimensions using Uniform Manifold Approximation and Projection (UMAP), discriminative accuracy [3,6], and temporal dynamics [23] using Dynamic Time Warping (DTW) and trend similarity. In contrast, utility focuses on assessing the usefulness of synthetic data compared to real data. Specifically, we assess the performance of a predictive model trained on the synthetic EHRs and tested on the real EHRs. Lastly, privacy measures evaluate whether real patient information has been leaked into the synthetic data. We employ the membership inference attack to determine whether real patient records used to train the generative model can be inferred based on the synthetic data. We report results averaged over three independently generated synthetic datasets.

5 Results and Discussions

5.1 Structural Similarity with Dimensionality Reduction

We first assess the structural similarity between real and synthetic EHRs by visualising a low-dimensional representation of the data with UMAP, presented in Fig. 4. The blue points indicate real patient admissions, while the red points represent synthetic patient admissions. To ensure comparable visualisations, we combine the real and synthetic EHR datasets, add an indicator variable, and transform them into a lower-dimensional space.

From the visualisation, we observe that the coverage of the synthetic EHRs generated by TempEHR overlaps the real EHRs better than the synthetic EHRs generated by TimeGAN and EHR-M-GAN for the MIMIC-CHF and MIMIC datasets. TempEHR captures most of the significant and minor clusters present in the real data. This demonstrates that the TempEHR is better at replicating the underlying distribution of the real EHR data, which is important given the complexity of healthcare datasets such as EHRs. A synthetic EHR dataset should effectively replicate the global structural properties of real EHRs.

5.2 Discriminative Accuracy

To assess how distinguishable the synthetic patient trajectories are from the real patient trajectories, we compute the discriminative accuracy [6] of a T-LSTM-based classifier evaluated on data generated by TimeGAN, EHR-M-GAN, and TempEHR. A classifier that cannot distinguish between real and synthetic EHRs would achieve an accuracy of 0.5.

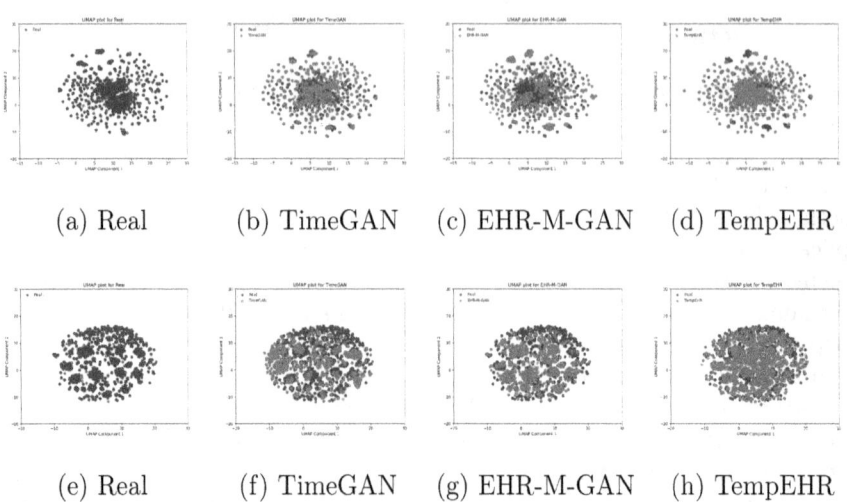

(a) Real (b) TimeGAN (c) EHR-M-GAN (d) TempEHR

(e) Real (f) TimeGAN (g) EHR-M-GAN (h) TempEHR

Fig. 4. UMAP visualisation for real and synthetic admission data from MIMIC-CHF (top row) and MIMIC (bottom row) patients.

As shown in Table 2, TempEHR achieves a lower discriminative accuracy of 0.751 (±0.042) in the MIMIC-CHF dataset compared to TimeGAN (0.778 ±0.011) and EHR-M-GAN (0.757 ±0.028). The classifier struggles more to distinguish TempEHR-generated trajectories from real EHRs, indicating that TempEHR better preserves the sequential structure of real EHRs, making them appear more realistic.

For the MIMIC dataset, the discriminative accuracies for all models are close to 0.5, with TempEHR achieving an accuracy of 0.534 (±0.032). This indicates that the classifier has difficulty differentiating between real and synthetic trajectories across the models. All models generate synthetic EHRs that are nearly indistinguishable from the real EHRs.

Table 2. Discriminative scores and predictive errors. In both cases, lower values indicate better performance.

Metric	Model	MIMIC-CHF	MIMIC
Discriminative Accuracy	TimeGAN	0.778 ± 0.011	**0.525 ± 0.030**
	EHR-M-GAN	0.757 ± 0.028	0.540 ± 0.011
	TempEHR	**0.751 ± 0.042**	0.534 ± 0.032
Predictive Error (MAE)	Real	**0.243 ± 0.000**	**0.230 ± 0.000**
	TimeGAN	0.268 ± 0.014	0.243 ± 0.010
	EHR-M-GAN	0.266 ± 0.007	**0.238 ± 0.004**
	TempEHR	**0.262 ± 0.002**	0.242 ± 0.009

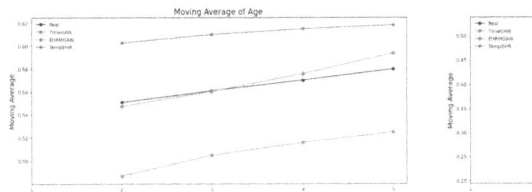 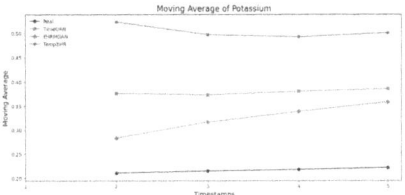

Fig. 5. Moving average across time for the features, Age and Potassium in real and synthetic data. Moving average starts at timestep 2.

5.3 Trend Similarity

Trends describe the overall change in data across time. We compute feature-level trend similarity scores, focusing on continuous variables such as patient age, lab values and vital signs.

First, we classify trends by assessing the probability of variables increasing, decreasing, fluctuating or remaining constant over time within a predefined normal range according to the MIMIC repository [20] (except for age). We then compare these distributions between the real and synthetic EHRs. As an example, we illustrate the moving average over time along with the probability distribution of possible trends for Age and Potassium from the MIMIC-CHF dataset, as shown in Figs. 5 and 6.

We employ Jensen-Shannon Divergence (JSD) between the distributions, shown in Table 3, to quantify the similarity. Scores range from 0 (identical distributions) to 1(dissimilar distributions).

As shown in Table 3, TempEHR shows more consistent trend similarity scores compared to EHR-M-GAN and TimeGAN, indicating better trend replication. For patients' ages with clear trends over time, TempEHR consistently outperforms both models due to its TrendFinder Network, which models the temporal dependency.

However, some inconsistencies are observed in Fig. 6, such as deviations in age trends among a small subset of the synthetic EHRs. This originates from the limitations of modelling temporal relationships in the generative process [24]. While these can be addressed through further processing of the generated EHRs, our analysis focuses on the raw generated EHRs to evaluate the trends in the data.

In reality, EHRs often contain complex, nonlinear temporal patterns that generative models struggle to fully capture [24]. TimeGAN and EHR-M-GAN exhibit variabilities across the different variables, while TempEHR demonstrates a more consistent performance. This reflects TempEHR's potential to model temporal trends and maintain the global structure of the real EHRs.

5.4 Temporal Dynamics

We employ a multivariate DTW-based assessment [23] to evaluate the similarity in overall temporal dynamics between patient trajectories in the real and

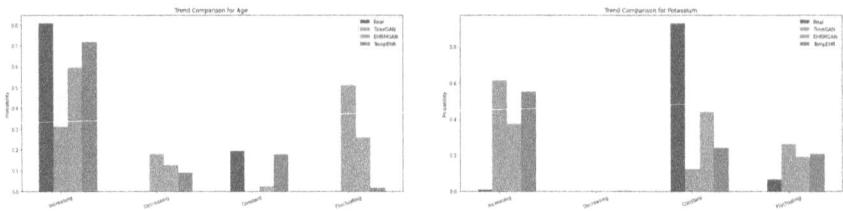

Fig. 6. Histogram showing the probability of belonging to different trends over time for the features Age and Potassium.

synthetic EHRs. DTW is a time-series similarity measure that quantifies the similarity between time series that may have different local shifts and speeds [25]. We first compute pairwise DTW similarity scores [26] in a real-vs-synthetic setting to assess the similarity, comparing real patient trajectories with synthetic trajectories. We then report the average DTW similarity score of the most similar synthetic patient trajectories in Table 4. This measures how well the synthetic data captures the temporal dynamics in the real patient trajectories. The similarity score ranges from 0 to 1, where 0 indicates dissimilarity and 1 indicates similarity.

The table shows that TempEHR consistently achieves high DTW scores across the MIMIC-CHF and MIMIC cohorts, with scores of 0.649 ($\pm$0.002) and 0.633 ($\pm$0.001), respectively. TimeGAN also demonstrates strong capabilities in modelling the temporal dynamics of patient trajectories. On the other hand, EHR-M-GAN has the lowest scores among the models, which suggests it has challenges in accurately replicating the underlying temporal movements and shifts in the real patient trajectories.

A crucial aspect of EHR synthesis is modelling the temporal nature of real EHRs. In real EHRs, the order and timing of events are crucial as they influence clinical decisions. As such, the time between clinical events plays an important role in modelling. Most studies on EHR modelling tend to ignore this. Thus producing outputs that may not fully capture the temporal patterns present in real patient trajectories [9]. TempEHR attempts to address this by incorporating time information between patient visits in the generative model, enabling it to better replicate shifts in values better over time.

5.5 Predictive Errors

We evaluate the utility of the generated data on a downstream sequence prediction task using the TSTR framework. Specifically, we train a T-LSTM-based model to predict different patient outcomes. For the MIMIC-CHF cohort, we predict whether a patient visit was planned or not. In contrast, for the MIMIC cohort, we predict the hospital expire flag, which indicates whether a patient died during hospitalisation or survived.

We compare the Mean Absolute Error (MAE) of the predictions from the synthetic data with the predictions from the real data as a baseline. Table 2

Table 3. Trend similarity on continuous variables in the MIMIC-CHF and MIMIC-RSP cohorts. Lower scores (bolded) are optimal. SBP: Systolic Blood Pressure, DBP: Dystolic Blood Pressure, O2sat: Oxygen Saturation, Resprate: Respiration Rate.

Dataset	Variable	TimeGAN	EHR-M-GAN	TempEHR
MIMIC-CHF	Age	0.661 ± 0.132	0.415 ± 0.019	**0.199 ± 0.009**
	Potassium	0.711 ± 0.167	**0.387 ± 0.080**	0.513 ± 0.056
	Urea Nitrogen	0.129 ± 0.072	**0.067 ± 0.009**	0.143 ± 0.016
	Sodium	0.424 ± 0.006	0.465 ± 0.027	**0.377 ± 0.134**
	Creatinine	0.324 ± 0.057	0.173 ± 0.165	**0.140 ± 0.060**
	Chloride	0.368 ± 0.067	0.412 ± 0.058	**0.267 ± 0.022**
	Hematocrit	0.144 ± 0.115	**0.076 ± 0.021**	0.143 ± 0.021
	Hemoglobin	0.105 ± 0.085	**0.028 ± 0.010**	0.147 ± 0.034
MIMIC	Age	0.831 ± 0.001	0.832 ± 0.001	**0.545 ± 0.100**
	Heartrate	**0.069 ± 0.001**	0.125 ± 0.052	0.124 ± 0.099
	Resprate	0.189 ± 0.001	0.194 ± 0.044	**0.116 ± 0.019**
	O2sat	0.206 ± 0.001	**0.072 ± 0.036**	0.262 ± 0.109
	SBP	**0.102 ± 0.001**	0.152 ± 0.016	0.103 ± 0.052
	DBP	0.289 ± 0.001	**0.175 ± 0.016**	0.260 ± 0.063
	Hemoglobin	0.118 ± 0.066	**0.057 ± 0.003**	0.135 ± 0.106
	Glucose	0.138 ± 0.001	0.175 ± 0.010	**0.127 ± 0.022**
	Temperature	0.439 ± 0.001	**0.396 ± 0.005**	0.468 ± 0.069

shows the MAE for the CHF and MIMIC datasets. The table shows that the TempEHR-generated data performs comparably to the real data for predictive purposes, obtaining an MAE of 0.262 (±0.002) in the MIMIC-CHF dataset and 0.242 (±0.009) in the MIMIC dataset. This demonstrates that machine learning models trained on TempEHR-generated data can generalise well to real-world scenarios, maintaining low prediction errors. Notably, TimeGAN and EHR-M-GAN yield relatively low predictive errors as well.

Evaluating the utility of EHR generation models allows us to determine whether these generated EHRs can be utilised for medical or clinical purposes, such as analysing healthcare policies and planning resources [23].

5.6 Privacy Evaluation

We assess the privacy preservation of the generated data using membership inference attack as in previous studies [1,6], and report the accuracy of these attacks. An optimal attack accuracy is approximately 0.5, indicating that the attacker's performance is no better than random guessing.

As illustrated in Fig. 7, TempEHR achieves a relatively lower attack accuracy of 0.612 (±0.038) for the MIMIC-CHF cohort and 0.616 (±0.072) for the MIMIC cohort. Likewise, TimeGAN and EHR-M-GAN obtain attack accuracies of 0.624

Table 4. Average pairwise DTW similarity scores between patient trajectories from the real and synthetic data. Higher scores (bolded) indicate the closest match to real data.

	MIMIC-CHF	MIMIC
TimeGAN	0.535 ± 0.001	**0.669 ± 0.001**
EHR-M-GAN	0.546 ± 0.002	0.304 ± 0.002
TempEHR	**0.649 ± 0.002**	0.633 ± 0.001

(± 0.072) and 0.632 (± 0.112) for the MIMIC-CHF cohort, respectively. For the MIMIC cohort, TimeGAN and EHR-M-GAN report accuracies of 0.609 (± 0.181) and 0.628 (± 0.093), respectively.

Notably, all models yield attack accuracies close to 0.6, with TempEHR yielding consistently low accuracies across both the MIMIC-CHF and MIMIC datasets. This indicates similar levels of privacy preservation and limited leakage of patient identities. The near-random attack accuracy for TempEHR, TimeGAN, and EHR-M-GAN demonstrates their effectiveness in maintaining patient identities while generating plausible synthetic EHRs.

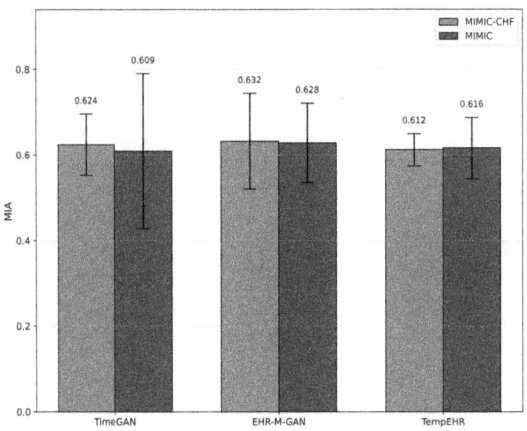

Fig. 7. Accuracy on MIA

5.7 Ablation Studies

To evaluate the effectiveness of the components of TempEHR, we conduct an ablation study to assess the contribution of each component. We report the discriminative scores and predictive errors from these in Table 5. The experiments are described as follows: S-1: TempEHR without the TrendFinder, S-2: TempEHR without T-LSTM layers, and S-3: TempEHR without time loss.

Table 5. Discriminative scores and predictive errors from ablation studies. S-1:TempEHR without the TrendFinder, S-2: TempEHR without T-LSTM layers, S-3: TempEHR without time loss.

	Model	MIMIC-CHF	MIMIC
Discriminative Accuracy	S-1	0.806 ± 0.032	0.537 ± 0.019
	S-2	0.793 ± 0.018	0.574 ± 0.080
	S-3	0.791 ± 0.039	0.573 ± 0.043
Predictive Score	S-1	0.291 ± 0.012	0.258 ± 0.004
	S-2	0.267 ± 0.017	0.277 ± 0.013
	S-3	0.289 ± 0.018	0.254 ± 0.009

From Table 5, we observe that T-LSTM layers, TrendFinder, and time loss components all contribute to the overall performance of TempEHR in learning an enriched representation of the data and generating synthetic EHRs.

6 Conclusions

In this work, we proposed TempEHR, a generative framework for synthesising irregularly-timed EHRs. TempEHR enhances the generation of synthetic EHRs by incorporating an enriched latent state representation that captures temporal dynamics, enabling more consistent replication of temporal dependencies in real EHRs than previous generators. In modelling healthcare data, capturing the order and timing of clinical events is essential for evaluating a patient's health status at any point in time. Our results demonstrate that TempEHR can preserve the global and temporal relationships of real EHRs, achieving low predictive errors and a more consistent performance across most evaluation measures. These findings highlight its potential for improving synthetic EHRs for healthcare research and innovation.

Although TempEHR performs well on most temporal patterns, some remain challenging, as seen in the trend similarity scores. In future work, we aim to refine the architecture to better replicate complex clinical patterns, enhancing the quality of synthetic EHRs for healthcare applications.

References

1. Yoon, J., et al.: EHR-Safe: generating high-fidelity and privacy-preserving synthetic electronic health records. NPJ Digit. Med. **6**(1), 1–11 (2023). https://www.nature.com/articles/s41746-023-00888-7
2. Lee, J.M., Hauskrecht, M.: Personalized event prediction for electronic health records. Artif. Intell. Med. **143**, 102620 (2023). http://arxiv.org/abs/2308.11013, arXiv:2308.11013

3. Yoon, J., Jarrett, D., van der Schaar, M.: Time-series generative adversarial networks. In: Wallach, H., Larochelle, H., Beygelzimer, A., Alché-Buc, F.d., Fox, E., Garnett, R. (eds.) Advances in Neural Information Processing Systems, vol. 32. Curran Associates, Inc. (2021). https://proceedings.neurips.cc/paper/2019/file/c9efe5f26cd17ba6216bbe2a7d26d490-Paper.pdf
4. Hashemi, A.S., Etminani, K., Soliman, A., Hamed, O., Lundström, J.: Time-series anonymization of tabular health data using generative adversarial network. In: 2023 International Joint Conference on Neural Networks (IJCNN), pp. 1–8 (2023). https://ieeexplore.ieee.org/document/10191367, iSSN: 2161-4407
5. Biswal, S., Ghosh, S.: EVA: Generating longitudinal electronic health records using conditional variational autoencoders. In: Proceedings of Machine Learning Research, vol. 149, p. 22 (2021)
6. Li, J., Cairns, B.J., Li, J., Zhu, T.: Generating synthetic mixed-type longitudinal electronic health records for artificial intelligent applications. NPJ Digit. Med. **6**(1), 1–18 (2023). https://www.nature.com/articles/s41746-023-00834-7, number: 1 Publisher: Nature Publishing Group
7. Lee, D., Yu, H., Jiang, X., Rogith, D., Gudala, M., Tejani, M., Zhang, Q., Xiong, L.: Generating sequential electronic health records using dual adversarial autoencoder. J. Am. Med. Inf. Assoc. **27**(9), 1411–1419 (2020). https://academic.oup.com/jamia/article/27/9/1411/5912632
8. Nikolentzos, G., Vazirgiannis, M., Xypolopoulos, C., Lingman, M., Brandt, E.G.: Synthetic electronic health records generated with variational graph autoencoders. NPJ Digit. Med. **6**(1), 1–12 (2023). https://www.nature.com/articles/s41746-023-00822-x, number: 1 Publisher: Nature Publishing Group
9. Baytas, I.M., Xiao, C., Zhang, X., Wang, F., Jain, A.K., Zhou, J.: Patient subtyping via time-aware LSTM networks. In: Proceedings of the 23rd ACM SIGKDD International Conference on Knowledge Discovery and Data Mining, pp. 65–74. KDD 2017, Association for Computing Machinery, New York, NY, USA (2017). https://dl.acm.org/doi/10.1145/3097983.3097997
10. Shukla, S.N., Marlin, B.M.: A survey on principles, models and methods for learning from irregularly sampled time series (2021). http://arxiv.org/abs/2012.00168, arXiv:2012.00168
11. Zhang, Y., Yang, X., Ivy, J., Chi, M.: ATTAIN: attention-based time-aware LSTM networks for disease progression modeling, pp. 4369–4375 (2019). https://www.ijcai.org/proceedings/2019/607
12. Wu, Y., et al.: Effective LSTMs with seasonal-trend decomposition and adaptive learning and niching-based backtracking search algorithm for time series forecasting. Expert Syst. Appl. **236**, 121202 (2024). https://www.sciencedirect.com/science/article/pii/S0957417423017049
13. Wang, W., Tang, P., Lou, J., Shao, Y., Waller, L., Ko, Y.a., Xiong, L.: IGAMT: privacy-preserving electronic health record synthesization with heterogeneity and irregularity. In: Proceedings of the AAAI Conference on Artificial Intelligence, vol. 38, no. 14, pp. 15634–15643 (2024). https://ojs.aaai.org/index.php/AAAI/article/view/29491
14. Zhong, Y., et al.: Synthesizing multimodal electronic health records via predictive diffusion models (2024). http://arxiv.org/abs/2406.13942, arXiv:2406.13942
15. Zhao, S., Song, J., Ermon, S.: InfoVAE: balancing learning and inference in variational autoencoders. In: Proceedings of the AAAI Conference on Artificial Intelligence, vol. 33, pp. 5885–5892 (2019)

16. Lin, T., Guo, T., Aberer, K.: Hybrid neural networks for learning the trend in time series. In: Proceedings of the 26th International Joint Conference on Artificial Intelligence, pp. 2273–2279. IJCAI 2017, AAAI Press, Melbourne, Australia (2017)
17. Choi, E., Bahadori, M.T., Schuetz, A., Stewart, W.F., Sun, J.: Doctor AI: predicting clinical events via recurrent neural networks. In: JMLR Workshop Conference Proceedings, vol. 56, pp. 301–318 (2016). https://www.ncbi.nlm.nih.gov/pmc/articles/PMC5341604/
18. Hyndman, R.J.: Moving averages, pp. 866–869. Springer, Heidelberg (2011). https://doi.org/10.1007/978-3-642-04898-2_380
19. Menth, M., Hauser, F.: On moving averages, histograms and time-DependentRates for online measurement. In: Proceedings of the 8th ACM/SPEC on International Conference on Performance Engineering, pp. 103–114. ICPE 2017, Association for Computing Machinery, New York, NY, USA (2017). https://dl.acm.org/doi/10.1145/3030207.3030212
20. Johnson, A.E.W., et al.: MIMIC-III, a freely accessible critical care database. Sci. Data **3**(1), 160035 (2016). https://www.nature.com/articles/sdata201635
21. Patki, N., Wedge, R., Veeramachaneni, K.: The synthetic data vault. In: 2016 IEEE International Conference on Data Science and Advanced Analytics (DSAA), pp. 399–410. IEEE, Montreal, QC, Canada (2016). http://ieeexplore.ieee.org/document/7796926/
22. Budu, E., Etminani, K., Soliman, A., Rögnvaldsson, T.: Evaluation of synthetic electronic health records: a systematic review and experimental assessment. Neurocomputing **603**, 128253 (2024). https://www.sciencedirect.com/science/article/pii/S0925231224010245
23. Budu, E., Soliman, A., Rögnvaldsson, T., Etminani, F.: Evaluating temporal fidelity in synthetic time-series electronic health records. In: 2024 IEEE Conference on Artificial Intelligence (CAI), pp. 541–548 (2024). https://ieeexplore.ieee.org/abstract/document/10605528
24. Liu, Y., Wijewickrema, S., Li, A., Bester, C., O'Leary, S., Bailey, J.: Timetransformer: integrating local and global features for better time series generation (2024). http://arxiv.org/abs/2312.11714, arXiv:2312.11714
25. Berndt, D.J., Clifford, J.: Using dynamic time warping to find patterns in time series. In: Proceedings of the 3rd International Conference on Knowledge Discovery and Data Mining, pp. 359–370. AAAIWS 1994, AAAI Press (1994)
26. Wang, N., et al.: Sequential data-based patient similarity framework for patient outcome prediction: algorithm development. J. Med. Internet. Res. **24**(1), e30720 (2022). http://www.ncbi.nlm.nih.gov/pubmed/34989682

Federated Learning Towards the Unknown: A Deep Dive Into Diabetic Retinopathy Prediction from Real-World EHR Structured Data on Unseen Diabetic Centers

Alessandro Cacciatore[1(✉)], Mariachiara Di Cosmo[2], Emanuele Frontoni[3], and Michele Bernardini[4]

[1] Department of Humanities, University of Macerata, Macerata, Italy
a.cacciatore1@unimc.it
[2] The BioRobotics Institute, Sant'Anna School of Advanced Studies, Pisa, Italy
mariachiara.dicosmo@santannapisa.it
[3] Department of Political Sciences, Communication and International Relations, University of Macerata, Macerata, Italy
emanuele.frontoni@unimc.it
[4] Department of Theoretical and Applied Sciences, eCampus University, Novedrate, Italy
michele.bernardini@uniecampus.it

Abstract. The compatibility of Federated Learning (FL) models with unseen Out-Of-Federation (OOF) centers remains a critical yet underexplored challenge, particularly when dealing with heterogeneous data. To address this gap, this study proposes a data-driven approach to assess the feasibility of applying an FL model to OOF centers. The case study explored is the prediction of diabetic retinopathy from multiple real-world, highly heterogeneous electronic health records. An FL XGBoost model (FL-XGB) is trained across five in-federation (IF) centers, showing an average test Area Under the ROC Curve (AUC) of 75.27%. A novel metric, the OOF Applicability (OFA) predictor, is introduced to estimate whether FL-XGB could be safely applied to the 15 OOF centers. OFA combines statistical and learnable features from both IF and OOF centers and is used as a predictor for a regression model, employed to estimate the performance of FL-XGB (in terms of AUC) on OOF datasets. The regression model achieved a confidence of 76% in predicting AUC values, with a statistically significant p-value ($\ll 0.001$). The average discrepancy between the predicted and observed AUC values was 6%. Overall, FL-XGB shows robust performance on IF centers and the OFA predictor plays a crucial role in assessing its applicability to infer on unseen OOF centers. By providing statistically significant estimations, OFA effectively identifies OOF centers whose characteristics are too divergent from what the FL model can effectively manage. Our codes are available at https://github.com/geronimaw/OFA4FL.

Keywords: Federated Learning · Out-of-Federation · Electronic Health Records · Predictive Modeling · Diabetic Retinopathy

1 Introduction

Diabetic Retinopathy (DR) is a leading complication of diabetes and a major cause of vision impairment and blindness worldwide. It currently affects approximately 103 million diabetic patients, a number expected to rise to 161 million by 2045 [1]. Despite its severity, DR often goes undetected in its early stages, resulting in reactive rather than preventive treatments. Early detection is essential, as timely intervention can significantly lower the risk of severe vision loss and enhance the quality of life for those affected.

Machine Learning (ML) and Deep Learning (DL) techniques have shown great promise in DR diagnosis, particularly when applied to retinal fundus images and optical coherence tomography scans [2]. While these imaging modalities are widely adopted to identify disease markers and grade disease severity [3,4], Electronic Health Records (EHRs) remain underutilized in DR research, despite providing continuous and comprehensive insight into a patient's health journey. EHRs contain invaluable longitudinal data, such as demographics, clinical history, comorbidities, and routine laboratory results, which makes them suitable for early detection of DR risk and monitoring its progression [5]. Several studies have investigated ML models for predicting DR onset in diabetic patients using EHR data, and eXtreme Gradient Boosting (XGBoost) has consistently outperformed other classical ML models, such as logistic regression, support vector machines, artificial neural networks and random forests, in diabetic DR risk prediction [6–10]. Despite the promising results, these studies rely on the aggregation of data from multiple centers into a single repository, an approach that simplifies model training and is impractical in real-life scenarios due to privacy concerns and regulatory restrictions surrounding patient data. Moreover, centralizing data leads to less generalizable models, as they fail to capture the variability of data collected across diverse healthcare institutions, ultimately limiting their applicability.

Federated Learning (FL) [11] is a decentralized approach that offers the possibility to tackle these challenges by enabling multiple centers to collaboratively train a shared predictive model without exchanging data, thereby preserving patient privacy and adhering to data governance policies [12,13]. Despite these advantages, FL models face significant hurdles in real-world applications, particularly when dealing with Out-of-Federation (OOF) centers, whose data characteristics differ from those of the In-Federation (IF) centers and often exhibit high variability and heterogeneity in real-world scenarios. Therefore, this study is guided by the following research question:

Is it possible to determine whether an FL model can be reliably applied to OOF centers? How can we assess its compatibility with unseen data?

To address this question, we propose the novel Out-of-Federation Applicability (OFA) predictor, which evaluates whether an FL XGBoost model (FL-XGB)

can be effectively used on data from an OOF center. OFA is a data-driven predictor that leverages a combination of statistical features (e.g., class imbalance, missing values) and latent features extracted via unsupervised DL techniques to quantitatively assess the FL model reliability to infer on OOF centers. Figure 1 shows the proposed framework, where FL-XGB is trained on IF centers and OFA assesses its compatibility with OOF centers.

The main contributions of this work are as follows:

- Introduction of the OFA predictor, a novel methodology integrating statistical and learnable features to determine the applicability of FL models to unseen centers.
- Introduction of the Out-of-Federation Suitability Score (OSS), a quantitative metric derived from the OFA outcomes, providing an interpretable measure of FL model applicability to OOF centers.
- Development of an FL framework based on XGBoost, called FL-XGB, designed and trained to predict DR risk from real-world EHR data collected from multiple diabetic centers.

To the best of our knowledge, this study is the first to introduce an approach to evaluate the compatibility of FL models with OOF centers, providing a data-driven framework to address privacy concerns, regulatory restrictions, and generalizability challenges in DR risk prediction from EHR data.

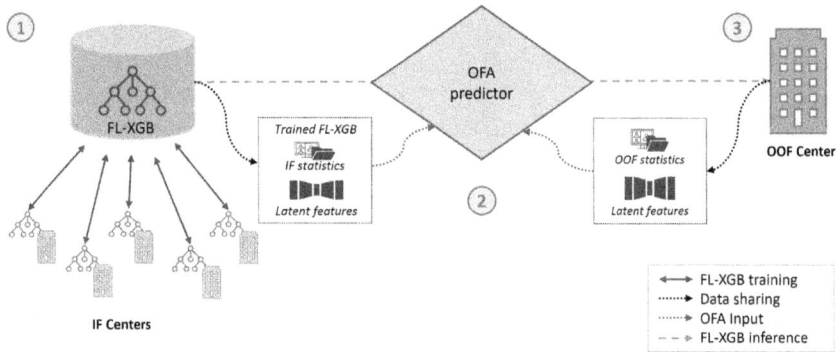

Fig. 1. Overview of the proposed framework for Diabetic Retinopathy (DR) risk prediction using a global XGBoost model (FL-XGB). (1) The process begins with the FL-XGB model being trained across five In-Federation (IF) centers, with blue arrows showing the flow of model updates. (2) The trained FL-XGB model and statistical features from IF and Out-Of-Federation (OOF) centers are fed to the novel Out-of-Federation Applicability (OFA) predictor to assess compatibility. (3) If the evaluation from the OFA predictor indicates sufficient compatibility, the FL-XGB model is applied to the OOF center for inference. (Color figure online)

1.1 Related Works

Although EHR data are essential for early-stage DR onset prediction and preventive care, their integration into predictive models remains largely unexplored. While recent studies [6–10] demonstrated the potential of EHRs for DR risk prediction, they rely on centralized approaches, overlooking privacy concerns as well as the distributed nature of EHRs. The advent of FL has created new opportunities for collaborative learning with EHRs across multiple healthcare institutions, enabling predictive modeling for various clinical tasks while preserving patient privacy [14,15]. However, to the best of our knowledge, FL for EHR-based DR prediction has been explored in only one study [16], which optimizes a logistic regression model in an FL fashion on 22 centers. While this work achieved a sensitivity of 72% on real-world EHRs, it relied on dataset undersampling to balance classes, a strategy that likely oversimplified the task.

Outside of the DR and diabetes research domain, most studies involving FL in clinical tasks artificially create homogeneity in the federation by splitting a single dataset to simulate multiple FL clients. This approach facilitates experimentation but fails to reflect the complexity of real-world EHR collections [17]. To better handle heterogeneous data within the federation, strategies such as client selection [17] or client similarity metrics [18,19] have been introduced. However, these strategies often require preventive feature space transformation, which may reduce the interpretability and applicability of the models to real-world EHR data. Similarly, in the broader field of FL, literature primarily addresses data heterogeneity inside the federation [20,21] or between federations [22]. However, the challenge of FL model generalizability to OOF centers has been recently tackled by studies such as [23–25], in which the FL model is explicitly trained to generalize well across both seen and unseen environments.

In light of these considerations, our work addresses a key gap in the field of FL in healthcare by effectively training an FL model on real-world EHR data despite their imbalance and heterogeneity across classes and centers. Furthermore, while previous studies focused on ways to train an FL model to increase its generalizability towards OOF data, our work investigates ways to predict whether a pre-trained FL model can be effectively applied to OOF data based on information such as class imbalance, dataset size, missing values, and latent features extracted in an unsupervised manner. This shifts the focus from generalization to compatibility estimation between a trained FL model and a new center.

2 Methods

2.1 Data and Predictive Task Definition

The study leverages EHR datasets from 20 diabetic centers across Italy, containing patient records organized into three fields: i) demographic information (e.g., gender, age, diabetes duration), ii) pathology data (comorbidities), and iii) laboratory test results. Patients are classified into two groups—DR and control—based on specific observational temporal windows, following established preprocessing criteria [6,8]. The objective, framed as a binary classification task, is to predict the likelihood of DR development in diabetic patients. The classification is based on 62 predictors, including laboratory test results averaged over the observational period, demographic information such as gender and age, and potential comorbidities. Missing data were handled using an extra-value imputation strategy.

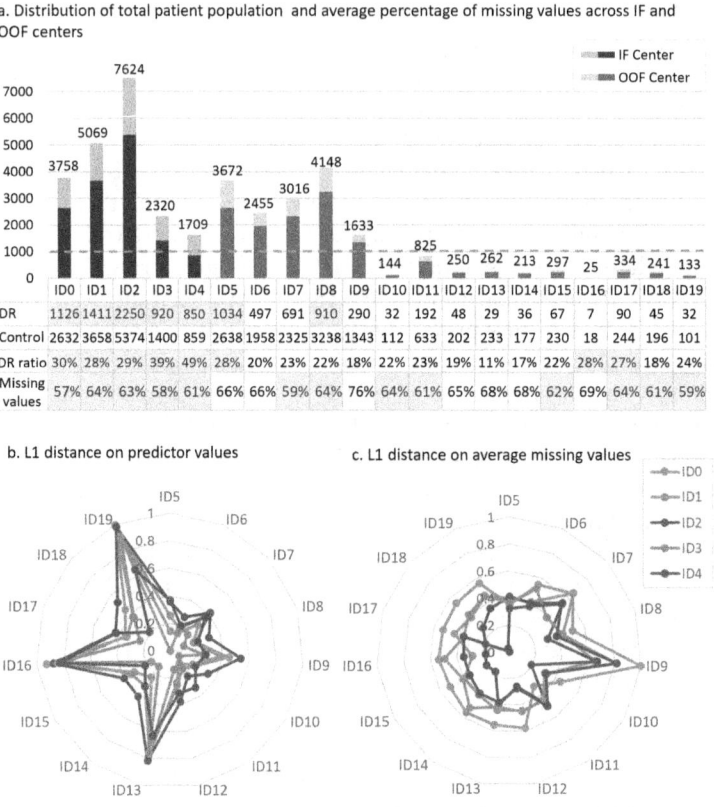

Fig. 2. Statistical summary of the involved datasets. (a) Patient distribution across IF (blue) and OOF (green) centers, with total counts above the bars. The table details DR/control counts (also visually differentiated within the bars by hues, with lighter shades for DR), the DR ratio, and the percentage of missing data. IF selection criteria are marked: a 1000-patient threshold (dotted line), and DR counts ≥ 800, DR ratio $\geq 25\%$, and missing values $<65\%$ (red in the table). (b-c) Radar charts representing the L1 distances of each OOF center from the federation based on predictor values (b) and missing data percentages (c), with scales normalized from 0 to 1. (Color figure online)

The diabetic centers are categorized into two groups, as shown in Fig. 2:

- *IF centers:* 5 centers (ID0-ID4) involved in the FL-XGB training and validation, selected based on data quality, volume, and diversity criteria: >1000 total patients, ≥800 DR patients, ≥25% DR patients, and <65% missing values.
- *OOF centers:* 15 centers (ID5-ID19), used for external validation, exhibiting high variability in patient numbers, predictor distributions, and missing data.

The inclusion criteria ensure that IF centers have sufficient data volume, diversity, and quality to support robust model training. As shown in Fig. 2a, the federation includes 20480 patients, while OOF centers collect data about 17648 patients. OOF centers exhibit a wide range of data characteristics, including extremely small numbers of patients and significantly high percentages of missing values. Preliminary analyses were carried out to assess the similarity between IF and OOF centers, focusing on the mean, median, 75th percentile, and range (minimum and maximum values) of predictors and percentages of missing values. In Fig. 2b–c, the normalized L1 distance between IF and OOF centers is depicted in terms of the 75th percentile of predictors and missing values, respectively. This variability reflects real-world heterogeneity, with notable differences from the federation in OOF centers such as ID13, ID16, and ID19, characterized by greater data sparsity and distribution discrepancies compared to IF centers.

2.2 Federated Framework

To predict DR onset in diabetic patients, the FL framework uses XGBoost [26], a tree-based boosting algorithm known for its effectiveness in handling sparse, imbalanced and complex datasets, making it well-suited for EHR data [27]. This choice is further supported by multiple studies that demonstrate superior XGBoost performance over other ML models in EHR-based DR prediction task [6–10]. These strengths, combined with FL, allow FL-XGB to leverage heterogeneous datasets to train a generalized, privacy-preserving model applicable to diverse patient populations. Five IF centers collaboratively train the global model by sharing model updates (gradients) with a central server that aggregates them via Federated Averaging [11]. This ensures compliance with data governance policies and patient privacy regulations.

2.3 Out-of-Federation Applicability (OFA) Predictor

In a real-world scenario, a trained FL model can be made publicly available, enabling other centers to use it for testing purposes on the same task. However, factors such as data distribution, class imbalance, and missing values—which can vary significantly across real-world EHR datasets—can affect model performance on OOF data [28]. Taking these factors into account, we introduce the OFA predictor. Given a model trained on a federation of centers and an OOF center C_{OF}, OFA predicts the model's performance on C_{OF} in terms of the Area Under the ROC Curve (AUC). This prediction is based on a combination of properties of C_{OF} and metadata about the IF centers, grouped as follows:

- Statistical characteristics (S_c) of C_{OF}: Cardinality, class imbalance, and distributions of missing values and average predictors. The last two characteristics are compared with the corresponding distributions from each IF center, which are released as metadata.
- Prediction confidence (p_{pred}): The FL-XGB model's output on C_{OF}, serving as a measure of the alignment between C_{OF} and all IF centers.
- Latent representations (L_{AE}) of C_{OF}: The predictors in C_{OF} are projected into a low-dimensional latent space via an autoencoder and compared with the latent representations of each IF center, also released as metadata.

The metadata required from the federation can be shared while ensuring OFA's compliance with regulatory restrictions.

Formulation. OFA is based on the hypothesis that there is a (linear) correlation between the FL-XGB model's AUC performance on C_{OF} and a combination of the above-mentioned properties, X_{OFA}, defined as follows:

$$X_{OFA} = S_c \times L_{AE} \times p_{pred} = \left(\frac{\eta}{n} \times D_{L1,miss} \times D_{L1,feat}\right) \times D_{AE,feat} \times p_{pred} \tag{1}$$

where i) η is the imbalance ratio (negative/positive samples) in C_{OF}; ii) n is the cardinality of C_{OF}; iii) $D_{L1,feat}$ is the average L1 distance between C_{OF} and all the IF centers, calculated for the 75th percentile of their predictors (see Fig. 2b); iv) $D_{AE,feat}$ is same metric but calculated for centroids in a 6-dimensional latent space generated by an autoencoder (details in Sect. 2.4); v) $D_{L1,miss}$ measures the same distance in terms of missingness (see Fig. 2c); vi) p_{pred} is the average probability predicted by FL-XGB over all samples in C_{OF}. The variables composing X_{OFA} are selected for their relevance in capturing differences between the OOF center and the federation. The relationship between these variables and model performance was empirically validated through experimentation.

Finally, linear regression is used to estimate the relationship between X_{OFA} and AUC obtained from the FL-XGB model on C_{OF}:

$$AUC_{OFA} = m \times X_{OFA} + q \tag{2}$$

where the parameters m and q need to be regressed from a set of OOF centers to fit the distribution at hand.

Scoring. To further refine decision-making, we define an OOF Suitability Score (OSS) based on the OFA-predicted AUC values (AUC_{OFA}). This score assesses whether applying the FL-XGB model to a specific OOF center C_{OF} is advisable, and it is computed by comparing AUC_{OFA} on C_{OF} against the average performance across IF centers ($\overline{AUC_{IF}}$), while also incorporating the predictive strength of OFA's linear regression, quantified by $r^2[\%]$. $OSS \in [0, 100]$ is defined by the formula:

$$OSS\% = r^2 \times \frac{100 - |AUC_{OFA} - \overline{AUC}_{IF}|}{100} \qquad (3)$$

Higher values indicate greater confidence in the model's ability to generalize to the OOF center, and $OSS \geq 50\%$ indicates that the FL-XGB model can be safely applied to the OOF center. The average OSS, if computed on a significant number of OOF centers, is particularly meaningful for new centers that do not have annotations or the possibility to train their own model.

2.4 Implementation Details

Table 1. Range of XGBoost hyperparameters used for training the DR prediction model. Regarding the scale for positive weight hyperparameter, η is defined as the number of negative samples over the number of positive samples. The objective function was also tuned among three different loss functions: Binary Cross Entropy (BCE), Weighted BCE (w-BCE) and Focal BCE (f-BCE). The hyperparameters α and γ marked with an asterisk (*) were only applied to f-BCE and w-BCE, respectively.

Hyperparameter	Range
Number of estimators	$\{3, 5, \mathbf{7}, 9, 12, 15, 25\}$
Maximum tree depth	$\{15, 25, \mathbf{50}, 75, 100\}$
Learning rate	$\{0.01, \mathbf{0.05}, 0.1, 1\}$
Subsample ratio	$\{0.3, \mathbf{0.5}, 0.7, 0.9, 1\}$
Column sample ratio	$\{0.3, 0.5, 0.7, 0.9, \mathbf{1}\}$
L2 regularization term (λ)	$\{1, 3, 5, 7, \mathbf{10}, 15\}$
Scale for positive class weight	$\eta \times \{0.5, \mathbf{1}, 3, 5, 10\}$
Imbalance parameter (α^*)	$\{1, \mathbf{2}, 3, 4, 5\}$
Focusing parameter (γ^*)	$\{1, 1.5, \mathbf{2}, 2.5, 3\}$
Objective function	$\{\mathbf{BCE}, \text{w-BCE}, \text{f-BCE}\}$

FL-XGB. Following a thorough experimental evaluation, the optimal training configuration for DR prediction using FL-XGB is established after a 10-fold cross-validation and an extensive grid search to maximize $\overline{AUC}_{IF}$. A list of the optimal hyperparameters can be found in Table 1. Regardless of AUC value maximization, the column sample ratio, i.e., the number of randomly sampled columns among the 62 predictors, is set to 1. This choice is driven by the high inhomogeneity among centers and aimed to prevent weak learners in XGBoost from relying on unimportant predictors during training.

To address class imbalance, a weight for positive samples (*scale_pos_weight*) is applied, and Binary Cross Entropy (BCE) is selected as the objective function. Additionally, two other objective functions were tested in this study—namely, Weighted BCE (w-BCE) and Focal BCE (f-BCE), as they are designed to handle imbalanced datasets. The FL framework, implemented using the Flower platform [29], involves training each model locally for five rounds before sending them to the central server for aggregation using Federated Averaging [11]. Feature importance is analyzed using the 'weight' strategy, emphasizing the frequency of predictors used to split nodes across the model's trees.

OFA. The optimal OFA predictor is determined by varying the variables involved in the computation of X_{OFA} and the relationship between them, as explained in the next Section. A critical aspect pertains to the design of the autoencoder architecture, which consists of two layers (16 and 32 neurons) in the encoder and specular layers for the decoder, with a latent space dimension of 6, determined from a grid search from the set [3, 6, 9, 12]. Hidden layers are activated by Leaky ReLU, while sigmoid is used for the output layer. The autoencoder is trained for 100 epochs using a batch size of 64, a learning rate of 0.001, and the Adam optimizer, with mean squared error as the loss function.

To evaluate the predictive relationship of OFA between X_{OFA} and AUC_{OFA}, all OOF centers are utilized except for ID11 and ID16, which are left out to test the model due to their unique characteristics in terms of sample size (25 for ID16) and missingness rate (76% in ID9), as shown in Fig. 2.

2.5 Ablation Studies

To assess the robustness and generalizability of FL-XGB, we conducted numerous experiments. While performing a wide hyperparameters grid search as in Table 1, as Ablation Study 1 (AS1), we explored different loss functions (BCE, w-BCE, and f-BCE) to handle class imbalance and evaluated which of these loss functions was the most suitable for the task. Moreover, we evaluated different sets of IF centers in order to obtain the optimal federation in Ablation Study 2 (AS2). In particular, we tested federations with a varying number of centers (from 3 to 7 centers), including those that strictly adhere to the inclusion criteria (see Sect. 2.1) and those that marginally met these criteria (i.e., ID5 and ID8) to evaluate the impact of center diversity and data heterogeneity on model performance.

To evaluate the effectiveness of the OFA predictor, two ablation studies were carried out to provide insights into the obtained results and enhance the correlation between the designed X_{OFA} and the AUC predictions from the FL-XGB model. Ablation Study 3 (AS3) investigates whether non-learnable statistical features are more or less significant than deep representations extracted by an autoencoder in assessing the compatibility of a C_{OF} with the FL-XGB model. Specifically, we compared the OFA predictor with two alternative variants: OFA_{L1}, which excludes $D_{AE,feat}$ from Eq. 1, and OFA_{AE}, which excludes $D_{L1,feat}$ and only uses learnable latent representations of the predictors. Finally, Ablation Study 4 (AS4) aims to assess the impact of each variable on the relationship between X_{OFA} and FL-XGB's performance on C_{OF}, as well as the impact of other variables that were not included in the final X_{OFA} definition, such as the alignment between the feature importance vectors obtained from the FL-XGB model and those from a locally-trained XGBoost.

It is important to note the absence of comparisons with similar state-of-the-art approaches, due to the lack of directly comparable work in the literature. Instead, our focus has been on exploring and validating this novel approach within the context of our datasets and operational constraints.

2.6 Evaluation Metrics

To evaluate the performance of the FL-XGB model and the OFA predictor, AUC is selected as the main performance metric due to its effectiveness in providing a balanced evaluation of model discrimination. Additionally, Sensitivity ($Sens$) and Specificity ($Spec$) are used to gauge the accuracy in identifying DR and control patients, respectively.

To assess whether X_{OFA} correlates significantly with AUC predicted by FL-XGB, statistical measures such as p-value and r^2 are employed. If the regressed linear model (Eq. 2) shows $p > 0.05$ and/or $r^2 < 0.6$, it is discarded as statistically insignificant. Additionally, the effectiveness of the OFA prediction is measured via the difference, referred to as ΔAUC, between the predicted AUC_{OFA} and the actual AUC obtained by the FL-XGB model.

3 Results

Table 2 summarizes the performance of FL-XGB compared to locally-trained XGBoost models on IF centers. FL-XGB achieves an average $\overline{AUC}_{IF}$ of 75.27%, closely matching the 75.21% average AUC of the local models. Notably, FL-XGB improves $Sens$ to 69.51%, up from 66.46% in local models, enhancing the ability to correctly identify positive cases. However, this improvement in $Sens$ comes at the expense of $Spec$, which decreases to 68.43% compared to 86.24% in local models. Center ID3 demonstrates the most substantial improvement from the federation with respect to the locally-trained model, with a 4.57% increase in AUC and a 5.23% increase in $Sens$. The last two columns of Table 2 include results from AS1, which was meant to analyze which objective function yielded best results among BCE, w-BCE, and f-BCE. While the last two functions are specifically tailored for imbalanced datasets, BCE achieves the best performance, with an average AUC of 75.27%. FL-XGB trained with f-BCE achieves the highest $Sens$ score (84.45% against 69.51% from BCE), but this comes at the expense of $Spec$, which decreases to 40.79% (against 68.43% with BCE). Given the crucial importance of $Spec$, especially in healthcare, BCE is considered the optimal loss function.

Table 3 shows results from AS2, i.e., how different federation compositions impact FL-XGB performance across diverse clinical scenarios. $Conf_{IF3}$ includes centers ID0, ID1, and ID2; $Conf_{IF4}$ includes centers ID0, ID1, ID2, and ID4; $Conf_{IF5}$ is the federation introduced in Fig. 2 (ID0, ID1, ID2, ID3, and ID4); additionally, ID5 was included in $Conf_{IF6}$, and ID5 and ID8 were included in

Table 2. Performance comparison of local XGBoost models and Federated Learning (FL) with XGBoost model (FL-XGB) using different objective functions (BCE, w-BCE, and f-BCE, as per Ablation Study 1) is reported in terms of Area Under the Curve (AUC), Specificity ($Spec$) and Sensitivity ($Sens$). All metrics are expressed as a percentage (%).

IF Center	Local XGBoost			FL-XGB (BCE)			FL-XGB (w-BCE)			FL-XGB (f-BCE)		
	AUC	Spec	Sens	AUC	Spec	Sens	AUC	Spec	Sens	AUC	Spec	Sens
ID0	74.09	85.99	66.23	74.68	67.67	67.49	72.35	67.67	67.49	70.71	30.97	89.13
ID1	75.51	88.98	65.59	76.10	65.69	69.39	72.82	65.69	69.39	72.16	49.93	80.88
ID2	78.68	86.18	69.83	74.13	64.84	66.29	67.53	64.84	66.29	68.86	44.44	80.41
ID3	72.15	79.17	66.76	76.72	76.87	71.99	76.15	76.87	71.99	76.90	27.18	96.71
ID4	75.61	90.89	63.90	74.75	67.12	72.38	69.27	67.12	72.38	70.59	51.43	75.12
Average	75.21	86.24	66.46	**75.27**	**68.43**	**69.51**	71.62	68.42	69.50	71.85	40.79	**84.45**

Table 3. Results from Ablation Study 2 (AS2), in which different configurations with varying numbers of In-Federation (IF) centers are tested. Average test performance are reported in terms of Area Under the Curve (AUC), Specificity (Spec), and Sensitivity (Sens) for each configuration. Metrics are expressed as a percentage (%).

Configuration	ID0	ID1	ID2	ID3	ID4	ID5	ID8	AUC	Spec	Sens
$Conf_{IF3}$ (3 centers)	✓	✓	✓	✗	✗	✗	✗	71.19	38.78	79.81
$Conf_{IF4}$ (4 centers)	✓	✓	✓	✗	✓	✗	✗	71.63	30.27	84.67
$Conf_{IF5}$ (5 centers)	✓	✓	✓	✓	✓	✗	✗	**75.27**	**68.43**	**69.51**
$Conf_{IF6}$ (6 centers)	✓	✓	✓	✓	✓	✓	✗	72.61	44.16	77.39
$Conf_{IF7}$ (7 centers)	✓	✓	✓	✓	✓	✓	✓	71.79	40.22	80.23

$Conf_{IF7}$. Both ID5 and ID8 meet three out of four inclusion criteria outlined in Sect. 2.1. The optimal federation results to be $Conf_{IF5}$.

Extending our analysis from the federation to the unseen OOF centers, we assess how FL-XGB performs beyond the training environment. Table 4 presents the performance of the FL-XGB in terms of AUC for all OOF centers, across which the FL model scores an average AUC of 58.16%, lower than $\overline{AUC}_{IF}$ (75.27%) reported for IF centers. Particularly poor predictions are obtained for ID13 and ID19 (AUC of 22.22% and 33.33%, respectively), while FL performance on ID7 ($AUC = 76.08\%$) is stronger than $\overline{AUC}_{IF}$.

Table 4 also shows the results of the OFA predictor, which assesses the applicability of FL-XGB to OOF. The upper part of the table includes the centers involved in the OFA regression process, whereas the lower part shows the two centers (ID9 and ID16) used to test the regressed predictor's accuracy. For each OOF center, FL-XGB results are compared to those obtained from the OFA predictor and its variants, OFA$_{L1}$ and OFA$_{AE}$. The OFA predictor demonstrates an average prediction error (i.e., ΔAUC) of 6.13% and an average OSS of 63.70%. Centers ID5, ID6, ID7, and ID8 exhibit the highest OSS values, around 72%:

Table 4. Performance comparison between FL-XGB and OFA predictor in its variants: OFA as fully defined in Eq. 1, OFA_{L1} using only statistical information, and OFA_{AE} based on autoencoder latent space features only (Ablation Study 3). The regression prediction error (ΔAUC) represents the average absolute difference between the AUC_{OFA} values and the AUC values scored by FL-XGB. Similarly, the OSS score is reported for each OFA variant. The bottom part of the table reports the performance calculated over the two OOF centers (ID9 and ID16) excluded from the OFA regression process. All metrics are expressed as a percentage (%).

OOF Center	FL-XGB AUC	OFA ΔAUC	OFA OSS	OFA_{L1} ΔAUC	OFA_{L1} OSS	OFA_{AE} ΔAUC	OFA_{AE} OSS
ID5	69.26	−0.59	71.64	−0.30	68.77	+1.53	59.60
ID6	51.14	+17.15	71.35	+17.21	68.32	+18.81	59.08
ID7	76.08	−7.63	71.47	−7.79	68.28	−5.50	59.47
ID8	61.07	+7.50	71.56	+7.75	68.67	+9.50	59.47
ID10	48.72	+5.58	60.62	+8.21	59.94	−7.51	41.15
ID11	64.06	+2.74	70.20	+2.95	67.34	+2.71	57.10
ID12	57.00	+2.73	64.78	+1.91	61.39	−2.38	49.51
ID13	22.22	+4.16	39.20	+3.02	36.68	+12.01	36.79
ID14	56.94	−0.57	62.20	−1.27	59.01	−7.38	46.36
ID15	73.91	−10.51	67.60	−11.37	64.06	−12.21	53.93
ID17	73.33	−7.47	69.48	−9.78	64.80	−6.59	57.08
ID18	69.00	−10.36	63.94	−10.01	61.45	−12.38	50.76
ID19	33.33	−2.72	42.45	−0.54	42.22	+9.40	42.10
Average	58.16	**6.13**	**63.70**	6.32	60.84	8.30	51.72
ID9	68.37	−3.60	68.65	-	-	-	-
ID16	56.35	−2.61	60.19	-	-	-	-

ID5 is correctly predicted by OFA ($\Delta AUC = -0.59\%$); ID7 and ID8 are slightly under and overestimated by OFA ($\Delta AUC = -7.63\%$ and $\Delta AUC = +7.50\%$, respectively); while ID6 is largely overestimated by OFA ($\Delta AUC = +17.15\%$). ID13 and D19 obtain the lowest OSS values (39.20% and 42.45%), which is due to the fact that, although FL-XGB performance on both OOF centers is correctly predicted by OFA ($\Delta AUC = +4.16\%$ and $\Delta AUC = -2.72\%$), these two centers are the ones on which FL-XGB performs the worst ($AUC = 22.22\%$ and $AUC = 33.33\%$). For the remaining OOF centers, OSS values range between 60.62% and 70.20%, while ΔAUC values vary from -10.51% to +5.58%. The last columns of Table 4 report the results from AS3, i.e., the comparison between OFA and its variants, OFA_{L1} and OFA_{AE}. From this comparison, the complete OFA model demonstrates superior accuracy. It achieves a lower average ΔAUC of 6.13%, compared to 6.32% for OFA_{L1} and 8.30% for OFA_{AE}, indicating that the integration of both statistics and latent representations provides a more comprehensive assessment of the applicability of FL-XGB to C_{OF}. On ID9 and

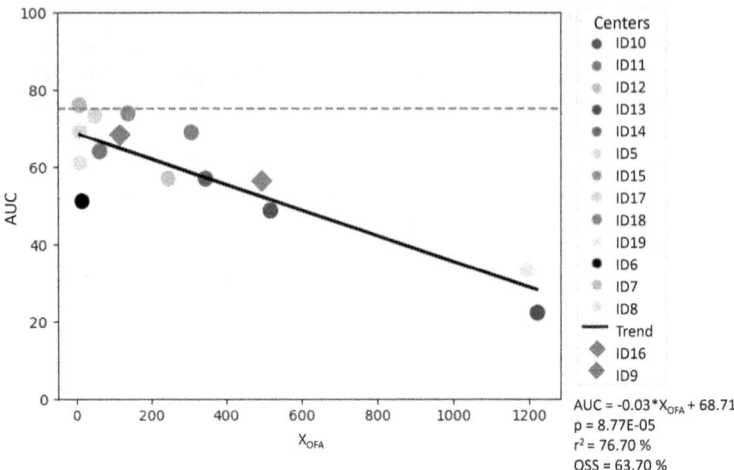

Fig. 3. Scatter plot illustrating the relationship between OFA predictions and actual AUC test values for OOF centers. The black line represents the linear regression between X_{OFA} and AUC predicted by FL-XGB. The regressed linear equation, r^2, $p-value$, and average OOF Suitability Score (OSS) are also reported. The dashed red line indicates the average performance of the FL-XGB model on IF centers ($\overline{AUC}_{IF}$ = 75.27%). All OOF centers are represented with a colored circle, except for ID9 and ID16 shown as diamonds, as they were excluded from the linear regression and used to evaluate the regressed OFA model.

ID16, FL-XGB scores AUC values of 68.37% and 56.35%, while the OFA predictor proves quite accurate, with ΔAUC of -3.60% and -2.61%. The resultant OSS values are 68.65% for ID9 and 60.19% for ID16.

The performance of the OFA predictor across the OOF centers is also represented in Fig. 3, which illustrates the relationship between the designed X_{OFA} comprehensive variable and the actual AUC values scored by FL-XGB on OOF centers. The linear regression $f : X_{AUC} \rightarrow AUC$, shown as a black line, explains 76.70% of the variance (as indicated by r^2), with a statistically significant p-value ($\ll$ 0.001), underscoring OFA's effectiveness in capturing the correlation between AUC performance from a pre-trained FL-XGB and the information about C_{OF} summarized in X_{OFA}. The effectiveness of the OFA predictor is further underscored in Table 5, which outlines the results from AS4, i.e., the impact of each variable in explaining the correlation between performance from FL-XGB on C_{OF} and X_{OFA}. The final row shows that X_{OFA}, as defined in Eq. 1, can explain up to 76.7% of the variance of the distribution shown in Fig. 3.

Table 5. Results from Ablation Study 4 (AS4): impact of the variables involved in X_{OFA} in predicting the performance from FL-XGB on a given C_{OF}. The variables are: imbalance (η), cardinality (n), distances between features distributions ($D_{L1,feat}$ and $D_{AE,feat}$), distance between missing values distributions ($D_{L1,miss}$), and predicted probability (or confidence, p_{pred}). Each row is associated with the final r^2, i.e., the explained variance in the relationship between X_{OFA} and AUC values scored by FL-XGB on OOF centers. The last row corresponds to the definition of X_{OFA} in Eq. 1.

OFA variables	r^2 (%)
$\eta \,/\, n$	52.9
$\eta \times D_{AE,feat}/n$	54.0
$\eta \times D_{L1,feat} \,/\, n$	70.6
$\eta \times D_{L1,feat} \times D_{AE,feat} \,/\, n$	72.1
$\eta \times D_{L1,feat} \times D_{AE,feat} \times D_{L1,miss}/n$	75.7
$\eta \times D_{L1,feat} \times D_{AE,feat} \times D_{L1,miss} \times p_{pred}/n$	76.7

4 Discussion

Deploying FL models in real-world scenarios is challenging due to not only data variability across centers, but also internal variability [30]. Differences in demographics, healthcare standards, and acquisition protocols further increase heterogeneity, which impacts both training and deployment. While FL enables privacy-compliant collaborative learning, it does not automatically guarantee the same level of generalization to every center, whether within or outside the federation. Hence, rather than focusing on building a universally generalizable model, this study aims to explore the feasibility of deploying an existing FL model on data from unseen OOF centers. This perspective shifts the focus from generalization to compatibility estimation between a trained FL model and a new center.

To investigate this, FL-XGB has been trained and tested on five IF centers. As shown in Table 2, its average performance across the federation ($\overline{AUC}_{IF} = 75.27\%$) closely matches that of locally trained models (75.21%). However, FL-XGB demonstrates greater consistency across centers, with a lower standard deviation in AUC (1.08 vs. 2.39 for local XGBoost). This stability is likely due to FL mitigating overfitting to center-specific data characteristics. Notably, FL-XGB also improves $Sens$ by +8.48%, a crucial advantage for DR early detection, where accurately identifying at-risk patients is essential.

Beyond the training phase, applying FL models to OOF centers introduces further complexity, as their data distributions may significantly differ from IF data. Notably, our goal is not to demonstrate that FL-XGB performs well on all OOF centers, but to provide a tool (the OFA predictor) that can predict whether an FL model is suitable for a given OOF dataset before deployment. FL-XGB's performance on OOF centers is, in many cases, comparable to that observed on the IF centers. Centers ID5, ID7, ID15, ID17, ID18, and ID9 share similar data characteristics with the IF centers (see Fig. 2), which results in strong performance from FL-XGB ($AUC > 69\%$) despite limitations such as the high volume of missing data or small and strongly unbalanced datasets. This suggests that FL-XGB itself has strong potential for real-world application, particularly valuable for centers that, due to limited data resources, could not train their own models. To estimate the performance of an FL model on OOF data, the OFA predictor has been developed and applied to the case study of DR risk prediction using real-world EHRs from 20 diabetic centers. OFA uses 13 OOF centers to regress a linear relationship between AUC from FL-XGB and X_{OFA}, a special variable designed to represent key features of an OOF center and its differences from the IF centers. As shown in Table 4, OFA effectively detects OOF centers that are incompatible with FL-XGB. For example, the poor performance of FL-XGB on ID13 and ID19 (AUC of 22.22% and 33.33%) is accurately identified by X_{OFA} (see Fig. 3), which can be seen as a function that maps OOF centers based on their compatibility with FL-XGB. Additionally, OSS values discourage the use of FL-XGB on these unsuitable centers (39.20% for ID13 and 42.45% for ID19). On the other hand, for centers where $OSS \geq 60\%$, OFA maintains prediction errors ΔAUC within an 8-point margin and only a few cases reaching higher error rates, with a maximum ΔAUC of +17.15 points. Also, when tested on ID9 and ID16, centers left out of the regression process, OFA displays prediction errors ΔAUC within a tolerable range ($< 4\%$), proving its consistency on OOF data.

Table 5 shows the impact of each variable in explaining the correlation between performance from FL-XGB on C_{OF} and X_{OFA}. The basic variables η and n accounted for 52.9% of the AUC-X_{OFA} variance. The integration of the $D_{L1,feat}$ considerably improved the regression model, elevating r^2 to 70.6%, which is further refined by the introduction of $D_{L1,feat}$ and $D_{AE,feat}$ ($r^2 = 72.1\%$). This suggests that feature distribution statistics have a crucial role in explaining the difference between OOF and IF centers, as well as that latent features capture additional nuances not evident through direct statistical measures alone. Final X_{OFA} also includes $D_{L1,miss}$ and p_{pred}, reaching r^2 of 76.7%. This importance is further confirmed by comparing the performance of the two main OFA variants, OFA_{L1} (using only statistical information) and OFA_{AE} (leveraging only distances on latent space features), as reported in Table 4. Although the overall behaviors of the OFA variants are similar, both OFA_{L1} and OFA_{AE} tend to exhibit larger errors, especially for centers with moderate compatibility. Figure 3 illustrates the regression accuracy for the relationship between X_{OFA} and AUC scores from FL-XGB on the OOF datasets. The OFA predictor seems to capture the information needed to separate the datasets, aligning reasonably well with actual AUC scores. However, centers ID5, ID6, ID7 and ID8 present a challenge: they have similar X_{OFA} but exhibit substantial variation in FL-XGB performance, ranging from approximately 50% to 76% in AUC. This suggests that the variables included in X_{OFA} may not fully explain the relationship between X_{OFA} and FL-XGB's AUC.

It is worth mentioning that OFA's performance can be heavily influenced by FL-XGB's training parameters. In particular, XGBoost is often trained with a feature subsampling approach, in which only some predictors are randomly selected during model training. While this method reduces the risk of overfitting and enhances model reliability, it can lead to inconsistent outputs and sub-optimal feature selection, particularly in datasets with extensive missing data or imbalanced features [31]. In datasets characterized by high sparsity, random feature selection can skew model reproducibility and reliability, depending on the predictors selected during training. To address this issue, we trained the FL-XGB model using all available features, avoiding random column subsampling for weak learners. This approach balances the trade-off between maximizing accuracy and ensuring robustness and reproducibility across diverse healthcare settings. Another important aspect concerns model interpretability and clinical validity. Future work will explore strategies to ensure that the estimated feature importance aligns with its actual clinical relevance.

We also plan to assess the generalizability of the OFA predictor on other medical use cases and multi-centric datasets. For instance, we will test it on EHRs from general practitioners [32] to evaluate its robustness in a different clinical context. In parallel, we will investigate alternative base models and FL strategies to verify the OFA stability under different ML configurations. While XGBoost was selected for its well-established effectiveness with tabular data, class imbalance, and missing values [6–10], exploring other models and learning paradigms may reveal complementary strengths or uncover limitations in the current implementation. Further directions include validating OFA in vertical FL settings and through multi-view analyses [33], as well as integrating differential privacy techniques [34] to enhance data protection and ensure privacy compliance in real-world deployments.

5 Conclusion

This study proposed an innovative OFA predictor which, by combining statistical and latent features of OOF data, demonstrated statistical significance in determining whether an FL model can be effectively applied to OOF centers, thus answering the research question in Sect. 1. Many clinical centers, due to their data characteristics or limited resources, cannot develop their own model, but could substantially benefit from accessing a robust FL model. The flexibility and privacy focus of the FL-XGB framework, combined with the OFA predictor's ability to evaluate its compatibility with OOF data, offer a valuable solution for DR screening across diverse clinical settings, potentially making a significant impact on diabetic preventive care. The experimental findings suggest how the OFA predictor may play a key role in ensuring the safe and effective deployment of FL models in OOF settings, offering a new paradigm for the adaptability and scalability of AI in clinical practice.

Disclosure of Interests. The authors did not receive support from any funding organization in the public, commercial, or not-for-profit sectors for the present work.

References

1. Tan, T.E., Wong, T.Y.: Diabetic retinopathy: looking forward to 2030. Front. Endocrinol. **13**, 1077669 (2023)
2. Sebastian, A., Elharrouss, O., Al-Maadeed, S., Almaadeed, N.: A survey on deep-learning-based diabetic retinopathy classification. Diagnostics **13**(3), 345 (2023)
3. Skouta, A., Elmoufidi, A., Jai-Andaloussi, S., Ouchetto, O.: Deep learning for diabetic retinopathy assessments: a literature review. Multimedia Tools Appl. **82**(27), 41701–41766 (2023)
4. Tajudin, N.M.A., et al.: Deep learning in the grading of diabetic retinopathy: a review. IET Comput. Vis. **16**(8), 667–682 (2022)
5. Tapuria, A., Porat, T., Kalra, D., Dsouza, G., Xiaohui, S., Curcin, V.: Impact of patient access to their electronic health record: systematic review. Inform. Health Soc. Care **46**(2), 194–206 (2021)
6. Bernardini, M., Romeo, L., Mancini, A., Frontoni, E.: A clinical decision support system to stratify the temporal risk of diabetic retinopathy. IEEE Access **9**, 151864–151872 (2021)
7. Yang, C., et al.: Usefulness of machine learning for identification of referable diabetic retinopathy in a large-scale population-based study. Front. Med. **8**, 773881 (2021)
8. Nicolucci, A., et al.: Prediction of complications of type 2 diabetes: a machine learning approach. Diab. Res. Clin. Pract. **190**, 110013 (2022)
9. Piersanti, A., et al.: Diabetic retinopathy detection: a machine-learning approach based on continuous glucose monitoring metrics. In: Costin, H.N., Magjarević, R., Petroiu, G.G. (eds.) EHB 2023. IFMBE Proceedings, vol. 109, pp. 763–773. Springer, Cham (2023). https://doi.org/10.1007/978-3-031-62502-2_86
10. Wan, X., et al.: Predicting diabetic retinopathy based on routine laboratory tests by machine learning algorithms. Eur. J. Med. Res. **30**(1), 1–19 (2025)
11. McMahan, B., Moore, E., Ramage, D., Hampson, S., y Arcas, B.A.: Communication-efficient learning of deep networks from decentralized data. In: Artificial Intelligence and Statistics, pp. 1273–1282. PMLR (2017)
12. Dang, T.K., Lan, X., Weng, J., Feng, M.: Federated learning for electronic health records. ACM Trans. Intell. Syst. Technol. **13**(5), 1–17 (2022)
13. Brisimi, T.S., Chen, R., Mela, T., Olshevsky, A., Paschalidis, I.C., Shi, W.: Federated learning of predictive models from federated electronic health records. Int. J. Med. Inform. **112**, 59–67 (2018)
14. Oh, W., Nadkarni, G.N.: Federated learning in health care using structured medical data. Adv. Kidney Dis. Health **30**(1), 4–16 (2023)
15. Moshawrab, M., Adda, M., Bouzouane, A., Ibrahim, H., Raad, A.: Reviewing federated machine learning and its use in diseases prediction. Sensors **23**(4), 2112 (2023)
16. Islam, H., Mosa, A., et al.: A federated mining approach on predicting diabetes-related complications: demonstration using real-world clinical data. In: AMIA Annual Symposium Proceedings, vol. 2021, p. 556 (2022)
17. Kim, J., Kim, J., Hur, K., Choi, E.: EHRFL: federated learning framework for heterogeneous EHRs and precision-guided selection of participating clients. arXiv preprint arXiv:2404.13318 (2024)
18. Ghosh, A., Chung, J., Yin, D., Ramchandran, K.: An efficient framework for clustered federated learning. IEEE Trans. Inf. Theory **68**(12), 8076–8091 (2022)

19. Elhussein, A., Gürsoy, G.: Privacy-preserving patient clustering for personalized federated learnings. In: Machine Learning for Healthcare Conference, pp. 150–166. PMLR (2023)
20. Li, T., Sahu, A.K., Zaheer, M., Sanjabi, M., Talwalkar, A., Smith, V.: Federated optimization in heterogeneous networks. In: Proceedings of Machine Learning and Systems, vol. 2, pp. 429–450 (2020)
21. Deng, Y., Kamani, M.M., Mahdavi, M.: Distributionally robust federated averaging. In: Advances in Neural Information Processing Systems, vol. 33, pp. 15111–15122 (2020)
22. Chen, Y., Lu, W., Qin, X., Wang, J., Xie, X.: Metafed: federated learning among federations with cyclic knowledge distillation for personalized healthcare. IEEE Trans. Neural Netw. Learn. Syst. (2023)
23. Zhang, L., Lei, X., Shi, Y., Huang, H., Chen, C.: Federated learning with domain generalization. arXiv preprint arXiv:2111.10487 (2021)
24. Nguyen, A.T., Torr, P., Lim, S.N.: Fedsr: a simple and effective domain generalization method for federated learning. In: Advances in Neural Information Processing Systems, vol. 35, pp. 38831–38843 (2022)
25. Ma, M., Li, T., Peng, X.: Beyond the federation: topology-aware federated learning for generalization to unseen clients. In: Forty-first International Conference on Machine Learning (2024)
26. Chen, T., Guestrin, C.: XGBoost: a scalable tree boosting system. In: Proceedings of the 22nd ACM SIGKDD International Conference on Knowledge Discovery and Data Mining, pp. 785–794 (2016)
27. Zhang, P., Jia, Y., Shang, Y.: Research and application of XGBoost in imbalanced data. Int. J. Distrib. Sens. Netw. **18**(6), 15501329221106936 (2022)
28. Kruse, C.S., Stein, A., Thomas, H., Kaur, H.: The use of electronic health records to support population health: a systematic review of the literature. J. Med. Syst. **42**(11), 214 (2018)
29. Beutel, D.J., et al.: Flower: a friendly federated learning research framework. arXiv preprint arXiv:2007.14390 (2020)
30. Rauniyar, A., et al.: Federated learning for medical applications: a taxonomy, current trends, challenges, and future research directions. IEEE Internet Things J. (2023)
31. Dunn, J., Mingardi, L., Zhuo, Y.D.: Comparing interpretability and explainability for feature selection. arXiv preprint arXiv:2105.05328 (2021)
32. Bernardini, M., Romeo, L., Frontoni, E., Amini, M.-R.: A semi-supervised multi-task learning approach for predicting short-term kidney disease evolution. IEEE J. Biomed. Health Inform. **25**(10), 3983–3994 (2021)
33. Ma, C., Qiu, X., Beutel, D., Lane, N.: Gradient-less federated gradient boosting tree with learnable learning rates. In: Proceedings of the 3rd Workshop on Machine Learning and Systems, pp. 56–63 (2023)
34. Dolo, B., Loukil, F., Boukadi, K.: Early detection of diabetes mellitus using differentially private SGD in federated learning. In: 2022 IEEE/ACS 19th International Conference on Computer Systems and Applications, pp. 1–8 (2022)

HAGAPS: Hierarchical Attentive Graph Neural Networks for Predicting Alternative Polyadenylation Site Quantification

Eleni Giovanoudi[✉] and Dimitrios Rafailidis

University of Thessaly, Volos, Greece
{egiovanoudi,draf}@uth.gr

Abstract. Alternative polyadenylation (APA) is a critical process that enables genes to generate mRNA transcripts with different $3'$ untranslated regions. Notably, during a transcription event, only one polyadenylation (poly(A)) site is used. Thus, estimating the relative usage of alternative poly(A) sites within a gene, known as the poly(A) site quantification problem, is crucial for unraveling the regulatory mechanisms of APA. However, existing approaches either frame the problem as a non-quantitative binary classification task or ignore the RNA structural information. To address these limitations, we propose a novel Hierarchical Attentive Graph Neural Network model for alternative poly(A) site quantification prediction, namely HAGAPS. To the best of our knowledge, we are the first to leverage Graph Neural Networks and RNA secondary structures to quantitatively predict the usage of multiple alternative poly(A) sites. In particular, our model employs a poly(A) site-level message passing network, incorporating RNA secondary structure information. In addition, to account for the competing interactions among poly(A) sites, HAGAPS integrates a gene-level message passing network combined with a nucleotide attention mechanism. Our experimental evaluation on publicly available datasets demonstrates that the proposed HAGAPS model significantly outperforms several state-of-the-art methods. Finally, for reproduction purposes, we make the implementation of HAGAPS publicly available at https://github.com/egiovanoudi/HAGAPS.

Keywords: Hierarchical graph neural networks · Attention mechanism · Polyadenylation site quantification · Alternative polyadenylation · RNA secondary structure

1 Introduction

The central dogma of molecular biology describes the fundamental flow of genetic information in an eukaryotic gene through transcription, post-transcriptional modification, and translation processes [9]. In particular, genetic information is

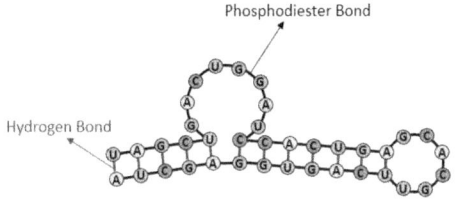

Fig. 1. Example of a RNA secondary structure.

first transcribed into pre-mRNA, which undergoes post-transcriptional modifications to become mature mRNA, and is then translated into the corresponding protein. One critical post-transcriptional process is polyadenylation, responsible for creating the mature 3' ends of nearly all eukaryotic mRNAs by adding a polyadenylation (poly(A)) tail at the 3' end of the premRNA [34]. It is a two-step reaction that involves an endonucleolytic cleavage near the 3' end of the pre-mRNA and synthesis of the poly(A) tail at the cleavage site, commonly referred to as the poly(A) site. Importantly, studies have shown that polyadenylation influences multiple aspects of mRNA metabolism, including stability, translation efficiency, transcription termination, and localization [2,8,20,30,35].

A key regulatory feature of polyadenylation is the presence of multiple poly(A) sites within a gene. Alternative poly(A) sites generate different mRNA transcripts with distinct 3' untranslated regions (3' UTRs), a process known as alternative polyadenylation (APA) [32]. APA is controlled by interactions between cis-regulatory elements located in the vicinity of poly(A) sites and the associated trans factors [13]. Among these cis-elements, the most well-known is the hexamer AAUAAA and its variants. In mammalian genes, APA is highly prevalent, with more than half of human genes undergoing this process, playing a crucial role in modulating gene regulation dynamics [12,31]. Furthermore, various human diseases, including cancer, alpha-thalassemia, and IPEX syndrome, have been linked to dysregulation of APA [10]. Hence, comprehensive understanding of poly(A) sites and the regulatory mechanisms governing APA are essential for unraveling its role in normal physiology and disease pathology.

Research has indicated that RNA secondary structures near poly(A) sites also impact APA by determining the accessibility of cis-elements to the polyadenylation machinery [1,7]. The primary structure of RNA refers to its linear sequence of nucleotides, connected by phosphodiester bonds along the RNA backbone. The secondary structure arises when complementary bases within the RNA strand form hydrogen bonds, creating structural motifs such as hairpins, bulges, stems, and internal loops. Base-pairing hydrogen bonds occur between A-U and C-G pairs, as well as less stable G-U pairs [16]. An example of a RNA structure illustrating these two types of bonds is shown in Fig. 1. Meanwhile, Graph Neural Networks (GNNs) have been developed to analyze graph-structured data by leveraging the relationships and topological information among nodes. In RNA secondary structure analysis, GNN-based methods have been employed to address various biological problems, including mRNA subcellular localization, RNA-protein binding, and gene silencing [22,25,26,39]. However, these studies are not incorporated into APA analysis.

There has been a long-standing interest in identifying poly(A) sites within genomic sequences. Various models have been developed to distinguish sequences that contain a poly(A) site from those that do not, defining the poly(A) site recognition problem [5,18,19,27,37]. Beyond recognition, a key aspect of APA is that during each transcription event, only a single poly(A) site within the gene is utilized. Consequently, the selection of alternative poly(A) sites within a gene is intrinsically competitive, where usage of one poly(A) site over another is often attributed to its relative strength. This challenging task of estimating the relative usage of alternative poly(A) sites within the same gene is referred to as the poly(A) site quantification problem [21]. Several computational approaches have emerged to address this problem using RNA-seq data [6,14,15,36,40]. Significant progress has also been made in inferring the relative strength of poly(A) sites based on genomic sequences. Early methods focus on predicting the stronger poly(A) site from a pair, framing the poly(A) site quantification problem as a binary classification problem [1,21]. However, this approach has notable limitations, as it fails to account for the competition between multiple poly(A) sites within a gene and does not provide quantitative predictions of usage. Subsequently, regression-based methods were developed to address the challenge of multiple competing poly(A) sites [23,24]. Despite their advantages, these methods do not take advantage of the RNA secondary structure information.

In summary, the current challenges in poly(A) site quantification prediction from genomic sequences are i) the lack of consideration for the competition among multiple poly(A) sites within a gene, and ii) the omission of the RNA secondary structure information. To address the shortcomings of existing approaches, we propose the HAGAPS model, making the following contributions:

- We present a novel architecture of Hierarchical GNNs to improve alternative poly(A) site quantification prediction. In particular, we introduce a hierarchical design of custom Message Passing Networks (MPNs), that is the Site and the Gene MPN, to predict the usage of all poly(A) sites within a gene, regardless of the number of competing sites.
- We design the Site MPN, leveraging the RNA secondary structure information. In doing so, the proposed model learns a more representative depiction of the poly(A) sites, capturing both sequential and structural patterns, thereby enabling communication between nucleotides within a site.
- We facilitate communication between poly(A) sites within a gene through the Gene MPN in combination with a nucleotide attention mechanism. This approach ensures that the model accounts for the competing interactions among alternative poly(A) sites.

The rest of the paper is organized as follows, in Sect. 2 we provide an overview of related work, and Sect. 3 details the architecture of the proposed HAGAPS model. In Sect. 4, we present the experimental evaluation of our model against baseline methods, and Sect. 5 concludes our work.

2 Related Work

Initially, computational methods were proposed to address the poly(A) site recognition problem based on genomic sequences. For instance, Kalkatawi et al. [19] present an artificial neural network and a random forest model that leverage human genomic sequence properties. These properties include thermodynamic, physico-chemical, and statistical features. Magana-Mora et al. [27] introduce a new set of hand-crafted features combined with a recognition model. Their approach employs multiple classifiers in a tree-like decision structure, optimized using genetic algorithms. Xia et al. [37] design a deep learning model based on Convolutional Neural Networks (CNNs) with group normalization. Additionally, they employ transfer learning to adapt the model for a different species. Kalkatawi et al. [18] propose a CNN-based method for recognizing various genomic signals and regions, including poly(A) signals and translation initiation sites. The model relies on genomic neighborhoods and spatial correlations. However, these methods cannot predict the relative strength of poly(A) sites.

The first study to tackle the poly(A) site quantification problem based on genomic sequences was conducted by Leung et al. [21]. Their approach employs a CNN-based model to predict the stronger poly(A) site from a given pair of competing sites. Arefeen et al. [1] also cast poly(A) site quantification as a pairwise comparison task, incorporating RNA secondary structure features in the DeepPASTA model. Nevertheless, both methods define quantification as a binary classification problem, failing to provide quantitative usage predictions. Restricting competition to only two poly(A) sites is a significant limitation, as studies indicate that a substantial proportion of mammalian genes have more than two alternative poly(A) sites [11,38]. Moreover, DeepPASTA does not utilize GNNs, and its one-hot encoding representation of secondary structures loses valuable structural information [25]. Subsequently, Li et al. [23] formulate poly(A) site quantification as a regression task, considering all competing sites within a gene. Their approach employs CNNs, followed by a Bidirectional Long Short Term Memory (BiLSTM) network to capture interactions between competing poly(A) sites. In addition, Linder et al. [24] present a sequence-based residual neural network with dilated convolutions. Nonetheless, these models do not take into account any RNA secondary structure information.

GNN-based models incorporating RNA secondary structures have been proposed to address various biological problems. For example, Li et al. [22] integrate RNA sequences and secondary structures to predict mRNA subcellular localization. Four parallel feature extractors are constructed using Multi-Layer Perceptrons (MLPs), multi-head attention mechanisms, and GNNs. Yan et al. [39] design a GNN-based approach that learns the RNA sequence and secondary structure information using a recurrent GNN and a BiLSTM for RNA-protein binding prediction. Long et al. [26] present a GNN framework for siRNA efficacy prediction. A variety of siRNA and mRNA features are extracted, including sequence encodings and base-pairing probabilities. However, since these methods are not designed for APA analysis, they do not consider the relationships among alternative poly(A) sites.

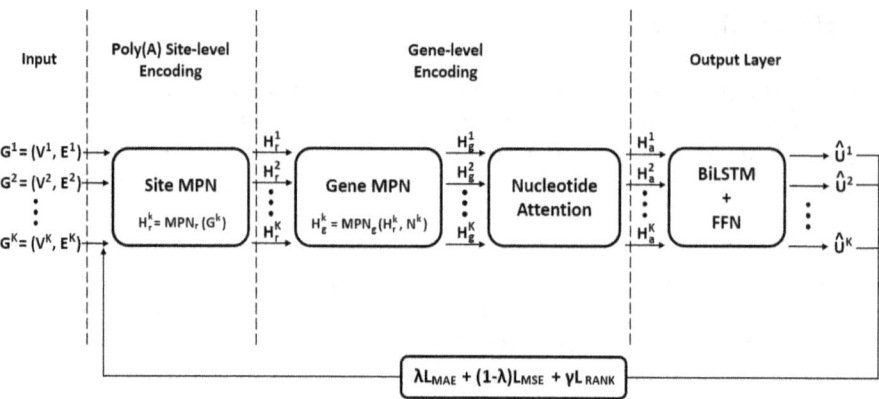

Fig. 2. Overview of the proposed HAGAPS model.

3 The Proposed HAGAPS Model

The HAGAPS model is designed to predict the usage values of the different poly(A) sites within a gene. The input is a graph $\mathcal{G}^k = (\mathcal{V}^k, \mathcal{E}^k)$ for each poly(A) site $k \in [1, K]$, where the node set $\mathcal{V}^k$ is derived from the encoded RNA sequence and the edge set $\mathcal{E}^k$ is determined by the RNA secondary structure. Notably, genes do not have a uniform number of poly(A) sites, that is K is not a constant. To accommodate this variability, HAGAPS is designed to handle inputs of different sizes, ensuring flexibility across genes. As illustrated in Fig. 2, the model adopts a two-level hierarchical encoding structure, poly(A) site-level and gene-level encoding, leveraging hierarchical GNNs with two custom MPNs. Specifically, the poly(A) site level consists of the Site MPN and the gene level consists of the Gene MPN and a nucleotide attention mechanism. Firstly, each $\mathcal{G}^k$ is processed by the Site MPN, which encodes information at the poly(A) site level, that is each site is independently encoded based on its sequence and structure. Nodes are updated via message passing with their neighborhoods, defined from both sequential and structural relationships. This process results in the node embedding $\mathbf{H}_r^k \in \mathbb{R}^{l \times h}$, where l is the length of the RNA sequence and h is the hidden embedding size. To capture interactions between alternative poly(A) sites within the same gene, the model then performs gene-level encoding. More specifically, the Gene MPN first updates eack poly(A) site's embedding $\mathbf{H}_r^k$ based on messages from its neighborhood, that is the rest $K - 1$ poly(A) sites, producing $\mathbf{H}_g^k \in \mathbb{R}^{l \times h}$. Then, the nucleotide attention integrates both $\mathbf{H}_r^k$ and $\mathbf{H}_g^k$ to enhance poly(A) site representation. These interactions ensure that the prediction for each poly(A) site is influenced by the entire gene context, yielding the embedding $\mathbf{H}_a^k$. Finally, $\mathbf{H}_a^k$ is passed through an output layer to generate the predicted usage value $\hat{\mathbf{U}}^k \in [0, 1]$. During the training process, HAGAPS minimizes the error between predicted and true usage values using the $\mathcal{L}_{MAE}$ and $\mathcal{L}_{MSE}$ losses, while also optimizing poly(A) site ranking via the $\mathcal{L}_{RANK}$ loss.

3.1 Sequence and Structure Representation

Each poly(A) site k is represented as a graph $\mathcal{G}^k = (\mathcal{V}^k, \mathcal{E}^k)$, where $\mathcal{V}^k$ is the set of node features derived from the RNA sequence and $\mathcal{E}^k$ is the set of weighted edges determined by the RNA secondary structure. Given an initial RNA sequence $S = \{s_i | i = 1, 2, \ldots, l\}$, we encode S using a mapping function:

$$m(s_i) = \begin{cases} 1, & \text{if } s_i = A \\ 2, & \text{if } s_i = T \text{ or } U \\ 3, & \text{if } s_i = C \\ 4, & \text{if } s_i = G \end{cases}. \tag{1}$$

Thus, we obtain the node set $\mathcal{V} = \{v_i | i = 1, 2, \ldots, l\}$, where $v_i = m(s_i)$.

The structure of a poly(A) site is defined by two types of bonds between nucleotides: i) phosphodiester bonds between consecutive nucleotides and ii) hydrogen bonds between complementary bases. The edge set regarding phosphodiester bonds is defined as:

$$\mathcal{E}_{cov} = \{(i, i+1, w_{cov}(i, i+1)) | 0 \leq i \leq l-1\}, \tag{2}$$

where $w_{cov}(i, i+1)$ is the edge weight, set to a constant value of 1, as these bonds always do exist. To obtain hydrogen bonds, we use the RNAplfold package [3], which, given an RNA sequence, outputs probable RNA secondary structures based on thermodynamic principles. Rather than relying solely on the minimum free energy structure, we retain an ensemble of probable structures to capture the inherent uncertainty and dynamics of RNA folding. The probability of a given structure X for sequence S is defined as:

$$p(X|S) = \frac{1}{Z} e^{-\beta E(X,S)}, \tag{3}$$

where Z is a partition function and $E(X, S)$ represents the free energy of S under X [28,39]. Considering all possible secondary structures in a thermodynamic equilibrium, the base-pairing probability for nucleotides i and j is then computed as:

$$p([i,j]|S) = \sum_{[i,j] \in X} p(X|S). \tag{4}$$

Based on these probabilities, we define the edge set for hydrogen bonds as:

$$\mathcal{E}_{base} = \{(i, j, w_{base}(i, j)) | p([i,j]|S) > 0\}, \tag{5}$$

where $w_{base}(i, j) = p([i,j]|S)$ is the edge weight, reflecting the likelihood of base pairing. Finally, the overall weighted edge set is the union of the phosphodiester and hydrogen bond edge sets:

$$\mathcal{E} = \mathcal{E}_{cov} \cup \mathcal{E}_{base}, \tag{6}$$

ensuring a comprehensive structural representation of the poly(A) site.

3.2 Site MPN

Firstly, each poly(A) site is encoded independently to ensure that the model learns a representation based on its sequence and structure. The encoding process begins by passing $\mathcal{V}^k$ through an embedding layer that maps each distinct nucleotide to a dense vector representation in a h-dimensional space, resulting in $\mathcal{G}'^k = (\mathcal{V}'^k, \mathcal{E}^k)$. Next, $\mathcal{G}'^k$ is passed to a custom MPN, namely the Site MPN, as shown in Fig. 2, consisting of a GNN and a CNN. This way, we obtain the node embedding $\mathbf{H}_r^k \in \mathbb{R}^{l \times h}$ from MPN_r for the kth poly(A) site:

$$\mathbf{H}_r^k = \mathrm{MPN}_r(\mathcal{G}'^k) = \mathrm{CNN}(\mathrm{GNN}(\mathcal{G}'^k)). \tag{7}$$

This approach allows the model to effectively integrate both structural and sequential information. Our GNN employs auto-regressive moving average graph convolutional (ARMAConv) layers [4], as follows:

$$\mathbf{H}^k = \frac{1}{C} \sum_{c=1}^{C} \mathbf{H}_c^{k(T)} \tag{8}$$

with $\mathbf{H}_c^{k(T)}$ being recursively defined by:

$$\mathbf{H}_c^{k(t+1)} = \sigma(\mathbf{D}^{-\frac{1}{2}} \mathbf{A} \mathbf{D}^{-\frac{1}{2}} \mathbf{H}_c^{k(t)} \mathbf{W}_1 + \mathbf{H}^{k(0)} \mathbf{W}_2), \quad 1 \leq t \leq T, \ 1 \leq c \leq C. \tag{9}$$

Here, $\mathbf{A} \in \mathbb{R}^{l \times l}$ is the weighted adjacency matrix, $\mathbf{D}$ is the degree matrix, $\mathbf{W}_1, \mathbf{W}_2 \in \mathbb{R}^{h \times h}$ are trainable parameters, T is the number of ARMAConv layers, C is the number of parallel stacks of layers, and $\sigma(\cdot)$ is the non-linear activation function ReLU. Then, the node embedding $\mathbf{H}^k \in \mathbb{R}^{l \times h}$ is further refined by the CNN, which is a two-layer convolutional network with batch normalization, max-pooling, and the non-linear activation function LeakyReLU:

$$\mathbf{H}_r^k = \mathrm{CNN}(\mathbf{H}^k). \tag{10}$$

This design allows MPN_r to effectively capture both local and long-range dependencies in the RNA sequence. Regarding local interactions, each nucleotide embedding is updated using hydrogen and phosphodiester bond information using Eq. (8) and (9). As for long-range dependencies, messages from more distant nucleotides along the RNA backbone are aggregated via Eq. (10).

3.3 Gene MPN and Nucleotide Attention

The gene-level network facilitates communication between each poly(A) site k and its neighborhood within the gene, that is the rest of the poly(A) sites of the gene. This interaction ensures that the predicted usage value of a given poly(A) site is influenced by the alternative sites, effectively capturing poly(A) site competition within the gene. To achieve this, we construct the neighborhood of poly(A) site k as:

$$\mathbf{N}^k = \sum_{\substack{d=1 \\ d \neq k}}^{K} \mathbf{H}_r^d. \tag{11}$$

This formulation allows the model to handle the variable number of poly(A) sites across genes. Then, we feed the poly(A) site-level representation $\mathbf{H}_r^k$, along with its neighborhood $\mathbf{N}^k$, into the Gene MPN (Fig. 2):

$$\mathbf{H}_g^k = \mathrm{MPN}_g(\mathbf{H}_r^k, \mathbf{N}^k) = \mathrm{LSTM}(\mathbf{H}_r^k, \mathbf{N}^k), \tag{12}$$

where MPN_g is composed of a one-layer LSTM network with ReLU activation. The output $\mathbf{H}_g^k \in \mathbb{R}^{l \times h}$ provides an updated representation of the poly(A) site, determined by messages from the other sites in the gene. To further refine the representation, we employ a nucleotide attention mechanism, as illustrated in Fig. 2, with the following architecture:

$$\mathbf{a}^k = \mathbf{H}_r^{k\top} \mathbf{H}_g^k \tag{13a}$$

$$\mathbf{w}_i^k = \frac{\exp(\mathbf{a}_i^k)}{\sum_{j=1}^{l} \exp(\mathbf{a}_j^k)} \tag{13b}$$

$$\mathbf{b}^k = \sum_{i=1}^{l} \mathbf{w}_i^k \mathbf{H}_{i,r}^k \tag{13c}$$

$$\mathbf{H}_a^k = [\mathbf{H}_g^k; \mathbf{b}^k]. \tag{13d}$$

Thus, we obtain the attended context embedding $\mathbf{H}_a^k \in \mathbb{R}^{l \times 2h}$, which incorporates sequence-dependent interactions along the spatial axis of the RNA [33].

In summary, each poly(A) site k is initially influenced by the remaining $K-1$ competing sites using Eq. (12). Then, the attention mechanism utilizes both the individual poly(A) site-level embedding and the gene-level updated embedding to enhance the representation through Eq. (13a)–(13d).

Finally, $\mathbf{H}_a^k$ is passed to a BiLSTM layer with LeakyReLU to learn a more global nucleotide embedding, and a two-layer Feed-Forward Network (FFN) with LeakyReLU and Softmax respectively, to obtain the final predicted usage value $\hat{\mathbf{U}}^k$.

3.4 Model Optimization

The loss function of the model consists of three parts:

- $\mathcal{L}_{MAE}$ is the Mean Absolute Error (MAE) loss between the predicted $\hat{\mathbf{U}}$ and true $\mathbf{U}$ usage values:

$$\mathcal{L}_{MAE} = \frac{1}{K} \sum_{k=1}^{K} |\hat{\mathbf{U}}^k - \mathbf{U}^k| \tag{14}$$

- $\mathcal{L}_{MSE}$ is the Mean Squared Error (MSE) loss between the predicted $\hat{\mathbf{U}}$ and true $\mathbf{U}$ usage values:

$$\mathcal{L}_{MSE} = \frac{1}{K} \sum_{k=1}^{K} (\hat{\mathbf{U}}^k - \mathbf{U}^k)^2 \tag{15}$$

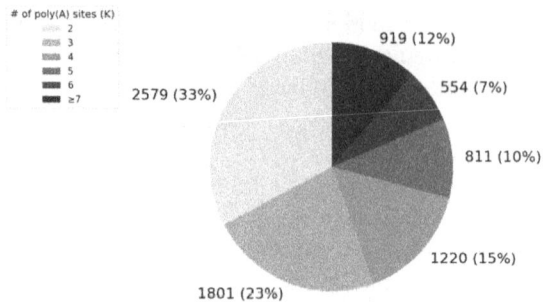

Fig. 3. Distribution of genes based on the number of alternative poly(A) sites K in the BL and SP datasets.

- $\mathcal{L}_{RANK}$ penalizes deviations from the expected ranking of poly(A) sites within a gene. It is computed as:

$$\mathcal{L}_{RANK} = 1 - corr(\hat{r}, r), \tag{16}$$

where $corr$ denotes the Spearman correlation coefficient, and $\hat{r}$, r are the predicted and true rankings, respectively. Both rankings are determined by placing the poly(A) sites in descending order based on their predicted and true usage values.

Thus, we formulate the joint loss function:

$$\mathcal{L} = \lambda \mathcal{L}_{MAE} + (1-\lambda)\mathcal{L}_{MSE} + \gamma \mathcal{L}_{RANK}, \tag{17}$$

where γ and λ are regularization parameters that control the influence of the $\mathcal{L}_{RANK}$ and $\mathcal{L}_{MAE}$, $\mathcal{L}_{MSE}$ losses, respectively. More specifically, λ governs the balance between $\mathcal{L}_{MAE}$ and $\mathcal{L}_{MSE}$.

Optimization. Our proposed HAGAPS model was developed in PyTorch. Since HAGAPS is designed to process all alternative poly(A) sites within a gene simultaneously, we group poly(A) sites by their corresponding gene before passing them to the model. This means that the batch size refers to the number of gene groups rather than individual poly(A) sites. During training, in each epoch, the model learns a low-dimensional representation of the initial poly(A) sites via the joint loss function $\mathcal{L}$ of Eq. (17). By minimizing the $\mathcal{L}_{MAE}$ and $\mathcal{L}_{MSE}$ losses of Eq. (14) and (15), HAGAPS outputs usage values that are closer to the ground truths. Furthermore, optimizing the $\mathcal{L}_{RANK}$ loss of Eq. (16) improves the model's ability to correctly capture the relative strength of poly(A) sites. Optimization is achieved through backpropagation using the Adam optimizer.

4 Experiments

4.1 Datasets

For the model evaluation, we use two publicly available poly(A) site quantification datasets[1]. The data were derived from the fibroblast cell lines of the C57BL/6J (BL) and SPRET/EiJ (SP) mouse strains [23,38]. To build a poly(A) site reference for the two strains, the total RNA was extracted from their fibroblasts, and then subjected to 3′ region extraction and deep sequencing [17]. Subsequently, 3′ mRNA sequencing was performed to quantify poly(A) site usage, with usage values computed based on sequencing read counts. The sequence surrounding each cleavage site was extracted. While both datasets contain the same poly(A) sites associated with the same genes, they differ in their sequences, due to single nucleotide polymorphisms and indels, as well as in their poly(A) site usage values.

In the preprocessing phase, following the evaluation protocol of [23], we excluded poly(A) sites with missing usage values, thus retaining 30,940 poly(A) sites belonging to 7,884 genes for each dataset. As mentioned in Sect. 3, the number of alternative poly(A) sites K varies across genes. Figure 3 illustrates the distribution of genes according to the number of associated poly(A) sites in the two datasets. Next, we randomly split the genes into training, validation and testing sets with a 6:2:2 ratio, yielding 4,730 genes for training, 1,577 for validation, and 1,577 for testing. The dataset was split at the gene level rather than at the poly(A) site level to ensure that all poly(A) sites within the same gene remained in the same set, preserving their competing interactions. This splitting process was repeated five times for each dataset, and we report the average experimental results with the standard deviation.

4.2 Evaluation Protocol

To evaluate the models' ability to predict poly(A) site quantification, we report the following evaluation metrics:

- *Mean Absolute Error (MAE)* between the predicted $\hat{\mathbf{U}}$ and ground truth $\mathbf{U}$ usage values:

$$\text{MAE} = \frac{1}{F} \sum_{f=1}^{F} |\hat{\mathbf{U}}^f - \mathbf{U}^f|, \tag{18}$$

  where F is the total number of poly(A) sites across all genes in the testing set.
- *Root Mean Squared Error (RMSE)* between the predicted $\hat{\mathbf{U}}$ and ground truth $\mathbf{U}$ usage values:

$$\text{RMSE} = \sqrt{\frac{1}{F} \sum_{f=1}^{F} (\hat{\mathbf{U}}^f - \mathbf{U}^f)^2}. \tag{19}$$

---
[1] Datasets.

- *Highest Usage Prediction Accuracy (HUPA)* evaluates the ability of predicting the poly(A) site with the highest usage within a gene. It is defined as the percentage of genes whose strongest poly(A) site is correctly predicted:

$$\text{HUPA} = \frac{M_{ch}}{M}, \qquad (20)$$

where M is the total number of genes in the testing set, and M_{ch} is the number of genes with correctly identified highest-usage poly(A) sites [23].

In doing so, we assess the models on the direct regression task of poly(A) site usage prediction (MAE and RMSE), as well as the important task of identifying the strongest poly(A) site within a gene (HUPA).

4.3 Compared Methods

- **Allocator**[2] consists of four parallel feature extractors, two for RNA sequences and two for RNA secondary structures. The model utilizes MLPs, multi-head attention mechanisms and GNNs [22].
- **RNASSR-Net**[3] utilizes a CNN to extract RNA sequence features and a GCN to capture RNA secondary structure features. In addition, the spatial importance learned by the CNN guides the GCN training process [25].
- **RPI-Net**[4] learns the RNA sequence and secondary structure information with a recurrent GNN and a BiLSTM. Moreover, a Set2Set model is employed to pool the node embeddings along the spatial axis of the RNA [39].
- **APARENT2**[5] employs a sequence-based residual neural network incorporating dilated convolutions [24].
- **DeeReCT-APA**[6] utilizes a CNN-BiLSTM architecture. The CNN extracts RNA sequence features and the BiLSTM models the competing interactions between poly(A) sites [23].
- **HAGAPS-Seq** is a variant of the proposed model, omitting the GNN in the Site MPN and the RNA secondary structure information.
- **HAGAPS-Site** is a variant of the proposed model, without the Gene MPN.
- **HAGAPS** is the proposed model.

The parameters of the examined models have been determined via cross-validation and we report the best results in our experiments. For the proposed method, the learning rate is set to 1e-3 with a batch size of 32 across both datasets. The parameter analysis of HAGAPS is further investigated in Sect. 4.5.

---

[2] Allocator code.
[3] RNASSR-Net code.
[4] RPI-Net code.
[5] APARENT2 code.
[6] DeeReCT-APA code.

Table 1. Average MAE, RMSE, and HUPA of the proposed HAGAPS method, when compared with its variants and the baselines on the BL and SP datasets. Bold values indicate the best method.

Datasets	Methods	MAE	RMSE	HUPA
BL	Allocator	0.2387 ± 0.0021	0.3851 ± 0.0054	0.4159 ± 0.0105
	RNASSR-Net	0.2350 ± 0.0032	0.3778 ± 0.0062	0.4814 ± 0.0077
	RPI-Net	0.2118 ± 0.0044	0.3369 ± 0.0085	0.5978 ± 0.0144
	APARENT2	0.2290 ± 0.0043	0.3231 ± 0.0105	0.4685 ± 0.0147
	DeeReCT-APA	0.2081 ± 0.0272	0.2755 ± 0.0215	0.5646 ± 0.0590
	HAGAPS-Seq	0.1824 ± 0.0035	0.2717 ± 0.0039	0.5910 ± 0.0070
	HAGAPS-Site	0.1751 ± 0.0047	0.2648 ± 0.0025	0.6086 ± 0.0058
	HAGAPS	**0.1696 ± 0.0050**	**0.2599 ± 0.0043**	**0.6257 ± 0.0059**
SP	Allocator	0.2456 ± 0.0193	0.3762 ± 0.0170	0.4183 ± 0.0295
	RNASSR-Net	0.2328 ± 0.0021	0.3770 ± 0.0073	0.4888 ± 0.0200
	RPI-Net	0.2157 ± 0.0023	0.3403 ± 0.0048	0.5698 ± 0.0232
	APARENT2	0.2313 ± 0.0044	0.3325 ± 0.0104	0.4632 ± 0.0124
	DeeReCT-APA	0.2133 ± 0.0267	0.2839 ± 0.0196	0.5362 ± 0.0674
	HAGAPS-Seq	0.1811 ± 0.0052	0.2767 ± 0.0044	0.5990 ± 0.0086
	HAGAPS-Site	0.1808 ± 0.0026	0.2740 ± 0.0043	0.5905 ± 0.0072
	HAGAPS	**0.1770 ± 0.0026**	**0.2688 ± 0.0036**	**0.6159 ± 0.0067**

4.4 Performance Evaluation

In Table 1, we show the experimental results of the examined models on the BL and SP datasets, in terms of average MAE, RMSE, and HUPA. The results indicate that the proposed HAGAPS model and its variants outperform the baseline models across all metrics in both datasets. In particular, the GNN-based models, that is Allocator, RNASSR-Net, and RPI-Net, overlook the relationships between competing poly(A) sites. Ignoring the co-existence of multiple poly(A) sites within a gene, which determines how the total usage is distributed among them, results in lower prediction accuracy. Meanwhile, DeeReCT-APA and APARENT2 do not incorporate RNA secondary structure information, relying solely on RNA sequences. Therefore, these methods do not take advantage of the poly(A) site structural data, lacking a more meaningful representation. Regarding the variants of the HAGAPS model, that is HAGAPS-Seq and HAGAPS-Site, they outperform the other baselines, highlighting the valuable contributions of the Gene and Site MPNs, respectively. Nevertheless, the HAGAPS-Seq variant underperforms compared to HAGAPS-Site and HAGAPS, emphasizing the significance of RNA secondary structures and GNNs in the analysis of poly(A) sites. Likewise, HAGAPS-Site performs worse than HAGAPS, underscoring the importance of the custom attention-based modeling of poly(A) site interactions. Overall, the proposed HAGAPS model consistently achieves the

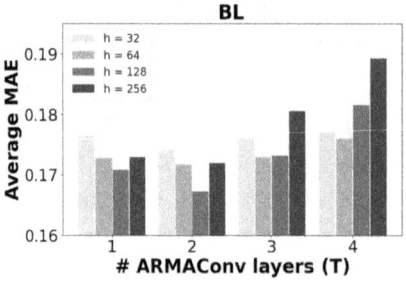
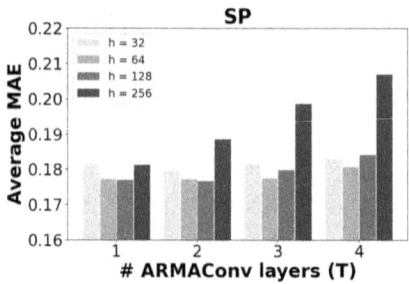

Fig. 4. Average MAE of HAGAPS on the BL and SP datasets when varying the number of ARMAConv layers T and the hidden embedding size h.

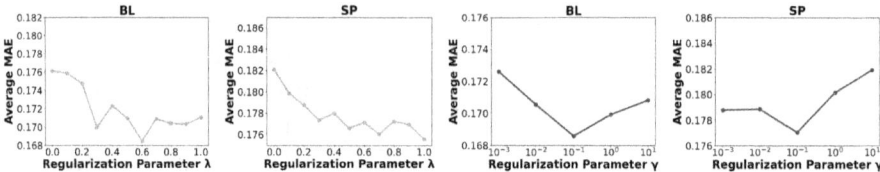

Fig. 5. Average MAE of HAGAPS on the BL and SP datasets when varying the regularization parameters λ and γ.

best performance across all metrics on the two datasets. By leveraging hierarchical GNNs through two levels of MPNs, poly(A) site and gene level, HAGAPS delivers the most accurate predictions for both poly(A) site usage, expressed by the lowest MAE and RMSE, and the identification of the strongest poly(A) site in a gene, corresponding to the highest HUPA values.

4.5 Parameter Tuning

The most important parameters in our model are i) the hidden embedding size h, ii) the number of ARMAConv layers T in the Site MPN, iii) the regularization parameter λ for the $\mathcal{L}_{MAE}$ and $\mathcal{L}_{MSE}$ losses, and iv) the regularization parameter γ for the $\mathcal{L}_{RANK}$ loss. For $h = \{32, 64, 128, 256\}$ we vary $T \in [1, 4]$ by a step of 1. In Fig. 4, we demonstrate the impact of h and T, reporting the average MAE on the BL and SP datasets. We observe that the best architecture is obtained with $h = 128$ and $T = 2$ for both datasets. Notably, selecting significantly higher or lower values for h and T leads to overfitting or underfitting, preventing the model from effectively capturing poly(A) site representations. Figure 5 illustrates the effect of the regularization parameters λ and γ in Eq. (17), on the performance of our model in terms of MAE across the two datasets. In particular, we vary $\lambda \in [0, 1]$ by a step of 0.1, where lower values emphasize the $\mathcal{L}_{MSE}$ loss and higher values prioritize the $\mathcal{L}_{MAE}$ loss. Aiming for a balance between the two loss functions, we fix λ to 0.3 for both datasets. Moreover, we vary γ in $\{10^{-3}, 10^{-2}, 10^{-1}, 10^0, 10^1\}$ and observe that the best performance is achieved

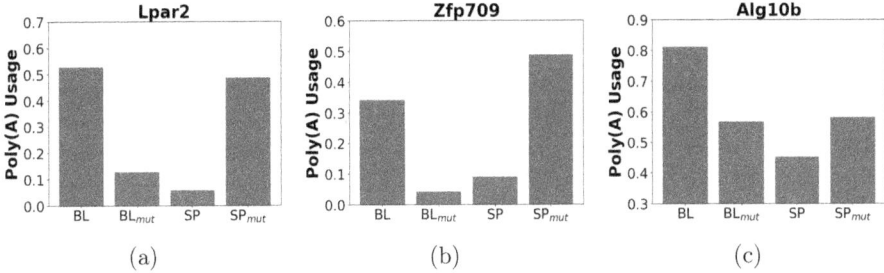

Fig. 6. Predicted usage values of the original BL, SP and the mutated BL_{mut}, SP_{mut} poly(A) sites. BL_{mut} and SP_{mut} denote the respective BL and SP sequences with a variation. (a) BL_{mut} has the G substitution and SP_{mut} has the canonical A instead of G for the *Lpar2* gene. (b) BL_{mut} has the T substitution and SP_{mut} has the canonical A instead of T for the *Zfp709* gene. (c) BL_{mut} has the UUUU insertion and SP_{mut} lacks the insertion for the *Alg10b* gene.

when setting $\gamma = 10^{-1}$ for both datasets. Lower values of γ result in decreased performance, highlighting the importance of the $\mathcal{L}_{RANK}$ loss in capturing the relative strength of competing poly(A) sites. However, excessively high γ values also degrade performance, as they place disproportionate emphasis on the $\mathcal{L}_{RANK}$ loss, diminishing the contributions of $\mathcal{L}_{MAE}$ and $\mathcal{L}_{MSE}$.

4.6 Case Study: Impact of Sequence Variations on APA

To further investigate the ability of HAGAPS in understanding APA regulation, we leverage experimental findings from [38]. The study demonstrates that specific sequence variations in the SP strain relative to the BL strain (Sect. 4.1) in the distal poly(A) site of three genes, that is *Lpar2*, *Zfp709*, and *Alg10b* (Ensembl Gene IDs: ENSMUSG00000031861, ENSMUSG00000056019, ENSMUSG00000075470), result in reduced poly(A) site usage in the SP strain compared to BL. Specifically, these variations include a substitution from A to G in *Lpar2*, a substitution from A to T in *Zfp709*, and an insertion of UUUU in *Alg10b*. To assess whether HAGAPS can predict the impact of these sequence alterations on poly(A) site usage, we generate two additional mutated sequences for each gene, along with their respective structures, by swapping the sequence differences between BL and SP [23,38]. Our analysis in Fig. 6 showcases the ability of the proposed model to capture the effects of the variations on poly(A) site usage. In all three genes, the SP strain exhibits lower predicted usage than BL. Moreover, consistent with experimental observations, the mutated BL_{mut} shows reduced usage relative to BL, whereas the mutated SP_{mut} exhibits higher usage compared to SP. Consequently, these results highlight the potential of HAGAPS to contribute to the study of APA, offering valuable insights that may advance gene regulation research.

5 Conclusion

In this study, we presented HAGAPS, a hierarchical GNN-based approach for alternative poly(A) site quantification prediction. The two key factors of the proposed model are i) the poly(A) site-level MPN that integrates RNA secondary structure information, and ii) the gene-level MPN coupled with a nucleotide attention mechanism to capture the competing interactions between multiple alternative poly(A) sites. Our experimental evaluation demonstrates the superiority of HAGAPS compared to several state-of-the-art methods. In addition, we conducted a case study, showcasing the model's ability in uncovering the underlying mechanisms of APA. An interesting future direction is the incorporation of a parameter-evolving strategy between alternative poly(A) sites, enhancing communication within the gene [29].

Disclosure of Interests. The authors have no competing interests to declare that are relevant to the content of this article.

References

1. Arefeen, A., Xiao, X., Jiang, T.: DeepPASTA: deep neural network based polyadenylation site analysis. Bioinformatics **35**(22), 4577–4585 (2019)
2. Barreau, C., Paillard, L., Osborne, H.B.: AU-rich elements and associated factors: are there unifying principles? Nucleic Acids Res. **33**(22), 7138–7150 (2005)
3. Bernhart, S.H., Hofacker, I.L., Stadler, P.F.: Local RNA base pairing probabilities in large sequences. Bioinformatics **22**(5), 614–615 (2006)
4. Bianchi, F.M., Grattarola, D., Livi, L., Alippi, C.: Graph neural networks with convolutional ARMA filters. IEEE Trans. Pattern Anal. Mach. Intell. **44**(7), 3496–3507 (2021)
5. Bogard, N., Linder, J., Rosenberg, A.B., Seelig, G.: A deep neural network for predicting and engineering alternative polyadenylation. Cell **178**(1), 91–106 (2019)
6. Bonfert, T., Friedel, C.C.: Prediction of Poly(A) sites by Poly(A) read mapping. PLoS ONE **12**(1), e0170914 (2017)
7. Brown, P.H., Tiley, L.S., Cullen, B.R.: Effect of RNA secondary structure on polyadenylation site selection. Genes Dev. **5**(7), 1277–1284 (1991)
8. Colgan, D.F., Manley, J.L.: Mechanism and regulation of mRNA polyadenylation. Genes Dev. **11**(21), 2755–2766 (1997)
9. Crick, F.: Central dogma of molecular biology. Nature **227**(5258), 561–563 (1970)
10. Danckwardt, S., Hentze, M.W., Kulozik, A.E.: 3′ end mRNA processing: molecular mechanisms and implications for health and disease. EMBO J. **27**(3), 482–498 (2008)
11. Derti, A., et al.: A quantitative atlas of polyadenylation in five mammals. Genome Res. **22**(6), 1173–1183 (2012)
12. Di Giammartino, D.C., Nishida, K., Manley, J.L.: Mechanisms and consequences of alternative polyadenylation. Mol. Cell **43**(6), 853–866 (2011)
13. Elkon, R., Ugalde, A.P., Agami, R.: Alternative cleavage and polyadenylation: extent, regulation and function. Nat. Rev. Genet. **14**(7), 496–506 (2013)
14. Gruber, A.J., et al.: Discovery of physiological and cancer-related regulators of 3′ UTR processing with KAPAC. Genome Biol. **19**, 1–17 (2018)

15. Ha, K.C., Blencowe, B.J., Morris, Q.: QAPA: a new method for the systematic analysis of alternative polyadenylation from RNA-SEQ data. Genome Biol. **19**, 1–18 (2018)
16. Higgs, P.G.: RNA secondary structure: physical and computational aspects. Q. Rev. Biophys. **33**(3), 199–253 (2000)
17. Hoque, M., et al.: Analysis of alternative cleavage and polyadenylation by 3′ region extraction and deep sequencing. Nat. Methods **10**(2), 133–139 (2013)
18. Kalkatawi, M., Magana-Mora, A., Jankovic, B., Bajic, V.B.: DeepGSR: an optimized deep-learning structure for the recognition of genomic signals and regions. Bioinformatics **35**(7), 1125–1132 (2019)
19. Kalkatawi, M., et al.: Dragon polyA spotter: predictor of poly (A) motifs within human genomic DNA sequences. Bioinformatics **28**(1), 127–129 (2012)
20. Lau, A.G., et al.: Distinct 3′ UTRs differentially regulate activity-dependent translation of brain-derived neurotrophic factor (BDNF). Proc. Natl. Acad. Sci. **107**(36), 15945–15950 (2010)
21. Leung, M.K., Delong, A., Frey, B.J.: Inference of the human polyadenylation code. Bioinformatics **34**(17), 2889–2898 (2018)
22. Li, F., Bi, Y., Guo, X., Tan, X., Wang, C., Pan, S.: Advancing MRNA subcellular localization prediction with graph neural network and RNA structure. Bioinformatics **40**(8), btae504 (2024)
23. Li, Z., et al.: DeeReCT-APA: prediction of alternative polyadenylation site usage through deep learning. Genomics Proteomics Bioinformatics **20**(3), 483–495 (2022)
24. Linder, J., Koplik, S.E., Kundaje, A., Seelig, G.: Deciphering the impact of genetic variation on human polyadenylation using APARENT2. Genome Biol. **23**(1), 232 (2022)
25. Liu, Z., Luo, F., Du, B.: RNA secondary structure representation network for RNA-proteins binding prediction. In: Proceedings of the AAAI Conference on Artificial Intelligence, vol. 35, pp. 362–370 (2021)
26. Long, R., et al.: siRNADiscovery: a graph neural network for siRNA efficacy prediction via deep RNA sequence analysis. Briefings Bioinf. **25**(6), bbae563 (2024)
27. Magana-Mora, A., Kalkatawi, M., Bajic, V.B.: Omni-PolyA: a method and tool for accurate recognition of Poly(A) signals in human genomic DNA. BMC Genomics **18**, 1–13 (2017)
28. McCaskill, J.S.: The equilibrium partition function and base pair binding probabilities for RNA secondary structure. Biopolymers Original Res. Biomolecules **29**(6-7), 1105–1119 (1990)
29. Pareja, A., et al.: EvolveGCN: evolving graph convolutional networks for dynamic graphs. In: Proceedings of the AAAI Conference on Artificial Intelligence, vol. 34, pp. 5363–5370 (2020)
30. Richard, P., Manley, J.L.: Transcription termination by nuclear RNA polymerases. Genes Dev. **23**(11), 1247–1269 (2009)
31. Tian, B., Hu, J., Zhang, H., Lutz, C.S.: A large-scale analysis of mRNA polyadenylation of human and mouse genes. Nucleic Acids Res. **33**(1), 201–212 (2005)
32. Tian, B., Manley, J.L.: Alternative polyadenylation of mRNA precursors. Nat. Rev. Mol. Cell Biol. **18**(1), 18–30 (2017)
33. Vinyals, O., Bengio, S., Kudlur, M.: Order matters: sequence to sequence for sets. In: Proceedings of the International Conference on Learning Representations (2016)
34. Wahle, E., Kühn, U.: The mechanism of 3′ cleavage and polyadenylation of eukaryotic pre-mRNA. Prog. Nucleic Acid Res. Mol. Biol. **57**, 41 (1997)
35. Wickens, M., Anderson, P., Jackson, R.J.: Life and death in the cytoplasm: messages from the 3′ end. Current Opin. Genet. Dev. **7**(2), 220–232 (1997)

36. Xia, Z., et al.: Dynamic analyses of alternative polyadenylation from RNA-SEQ reveal a $3'$-UTR landscape across seven tumour types. Nat. Commun. **5**(1), 5274 (2014)
37. Xia, Z., et al.: DeeReCT-PolyA: a robust and generic deep learning method for PAS identification. Bioinformatics **35**(14), 2371–2379 (2019)
38. Xiao, M.S., Zhang, B., Li, Y.S., Gao, Q., Sun, W., Chen, W.: Global analysis of regulatory divergence in the evolution of mouse alternative polyadenylation. Mol. Syst. Biol. **12**(12), 890 (2016)
39. Yan, Z., Hamilton, W.L., Blanchette, M.: Graph neural representational learning of RNA secondary structures for predicting RNA-protein interactions. Bioinformatics **36**(Supplement_1), i276–i284 (2020)
40. Ye, C., Long, Y., Ji, G., Li, Q.Q., Wu, X.: APAtrap: identification and quantification of alternative polyadenylation sites from RNA-seq data. Bioinformatics **34**(11), 1841–1849 (2018)

Do Protein Transformers Have Biological Intelligence?

Fudong Lin[1], Wanrou Du[2], Jinchan Liu[3], Tarikul Milon[4], Shelby Meche[4], Wu Xu[4], Xiaoqi Qin[2], and Xu Yuan[1(✉)]

[1] University of Delaware, Newark, DE 19716, USA
{fudong,xyuan}@udel.edu
[2] Beijing University of Posts and Telecommunications, Haidian, Beijing 100876, China
{wanroudu,xiaoqiqin}@bupt.edu.cn
[3] Yale University, New Haven, CT 06520, USA
jinchan.liu@yale.edu
[4] University of Louisiana at Lafayette, Lafayette, LA 70504, USA
{tarikul-islam.milon1,wu.xu}@louisiana.edu

Abstract. Deep neural networks, particularly Transformers, have been widely adopted for predicting the functional properties of proteins. In this work, we focus on exploring whether Protein Transformers can capture biological intelligence among protein sequences. To achieve our goal, we first introduce a protein function dataset, namely *Protein-FN*, providing over 9000 protein data with meaningful labels. Second, we devise a new Transformer architecture, namely *Sequence Protein Transformers (SPT)*, for computationally efficient protein function predictions. Third, we develop a novel Explainable Artificial Intelligence (XAI) technique called *Sequence Score*, which can efficiently interpret the decision-making processes of protein models, thereby overcoming the difficulty of deciphering biological intelligence bided in Protein Transformers. Remarkably, even our smallest SPT-Tiny model, which contains only 5.4M parameters, demonstrates impressive predictive accuracy, achieving 94.3% on the Antibiotic Resistance (AR) dataset and 99.6% on the Protein-FN dataset, all accomplished by training from scratch. Besides, our Sequence Score technique helps reveal that our SPT models can discover several meaningful patterns underlying the sequence structures of protein data, with these patterns aligning closely with the domain knowledge in the biology community. We have officially released our Protein-FN dataset on Hugging Face Datasets https://huggingface.co/datasets/Protein-FN/Protein-FN. Our code is available at https://github.com/fudong03/BioIntelligence.

Keywords: Protein Transformers · Explainable AI · AI for Science

---

Supplementary Information The online version contains supplementary material available at https://doi.org/10.1007/978-3-032-06118-8_22.

1 Introduction

Proteins serve as the architects of life, orchestrating an extraordinary range of functions that bring vitality and complexity to the biological world. Their roles encompass everything from catalyzing critical biochemical reactions to facilitating precise cellular communication. Decoding the intricate relationship between a protein's sequence, structure, and functional properties holds the key to unraveling these life-sustaining mysteries. This endeavor is more than a scientific pursuit; it is a profound exploration of the fundamental processes that define life itself.

Since the intricate patterns of protein sequences are analogous to the syntactic and semantic structures found in human languages, existing state-of-the-art Protein Language Models (PLMs) [6,24,32,34,38,49,52,55,56,59] harness the advanced language models [20,67] to decipher how the intricate structures of protein sequences dictate their functional properties. However, these methods require pre-training on millions or even billions of protein sequences for satisfactory performance. The excessive computational demands of self-supervised pre-training render PLMs unattainable for resource-constrained research groups.

In this work, we develop a computationally efficient Transformer architecture, namely Sequence Protein Transformer (SPT), for unraveling the complex interplay between a protein's sequence and its functional property, by leveraging the Transformer architectures in the vision domain [21,30,45,66]. Specifically, our work focuses on answering the following research question: *Can our Protein Transformers learn biological intelligence underlined in protein sequences?*

To help answer this question, we first introduce a new protein function dataset called *Protein-FN*, offering over 9000 protein data, with each containing the protein's 1D amino acid sequences, 3D structures, as well as its functional properties annotated by biological experts of our team. Second, different from PLMs, where the protein sequence is naturally encoded by the letter abbreviation of amino acids (*e.g.*, with letter "A" for representing the amino acid "Alanine"), how to encode the protein data for new Transformer architecture remains unexplored, making the applications of existing Vision Transformers (ViT) variants [4,7,9,16,21,25,30,41–45,66,70] for protein function predictions technically infeasible. We develop the Sequence Protein Transformer (SPT) model to address this issue. Featuring an innovative embedding mechanism tailored for protein data, our SPT model excels in predicting the functional properties of proteins. Remarkably, it can achieve a superior prediction performance without relying on computationally extensive self-supervised pre-training. Third, Explainable Artificial Intelligence (XAI) techniques [8,23,27,28,36,61,63], especially those Transformer-specific solutions [1,9,11,12,68,71], can offer insightful perspectives into the decision-making mechanisms of deep neural networks (DNNs), making them suitable for deciphering biological intelligence resided in Protein Transformers. However, current XAI approaches face significant challenges when handling protein sequences that vary in the number of amino acids. They either fail to accommodate these variances or incur substantial computational burdens, *e.g.*, $\mathcal{O}(L^2 \cdot P^4)$ for Attention Flow [1], where L and P represent the model depth and the protein sequence length, respectively. Consequently, these methods prove impractical for analyzing the biological insight within protein sequences. In this study, we introduce the Sequence Score, a novel gradient-based

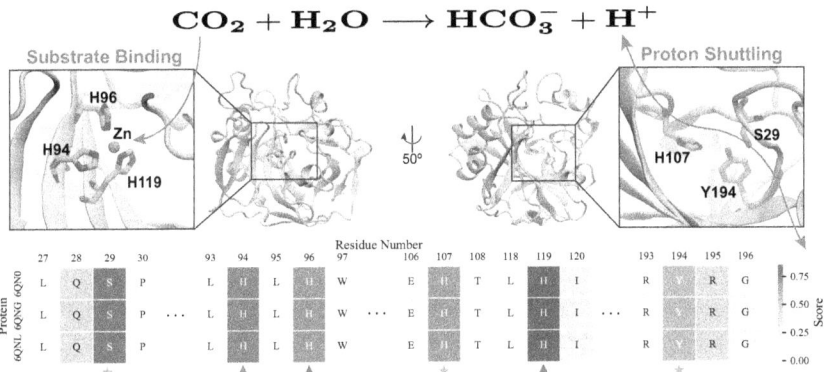

Fig. 1. Illustration of two key conserved motifs, *i.e.*, "His94-His96-His119" and "Ser29-His107-Tyr194", for the Carbonic Anhydrases, a vital enzyme class. Here, "His" (Histidine), "Ser" (Serine), and "Tyr" (Tyrosine) are the amino acids forming these motifs, abbreviated as "H", "S", and "Y", respectively. The residual numbers signify the positions of amino acids within the protein sequence. In the upper section, two figures, along with a corresponding equation, utilize the protein "6QN0" as an example to visualize the three-dimensional structures of the motifs and elucidate their roles in catalyzing the reaction. A heatmap in the lower section displays the importance scores generated by our approach, with the motifs "His94-His96-His119" and the "Ser29-His107-Tyr194" distinctly marked with red triangles and orange stars, respectively. (Color figure online)

XAI approach, tailored specifically to manage protein sequences of varying amino acid lengths. It advances existing Transformer-specific XAI solutions through its computational efficiency, which *scales linearly* with protein sequence length. This advancement facilitates a more efficient and effective interpretation of the biological intelligence bided in Protein Transformers.

Our Sequence Score technique has successfully identified several meaningful biological patterns, showcasing its prowess in revealing the biological intelligence ingrained in Protein Transformers. For example, Carbonic Anhydrases (CAs) are a class of enzymes vital to many biological processes, such as respiration and acid-base balance in organisms. Central to the functionality of these enzymes are two highly conserved motifs: "His94-His96-His119" and "Ser29-His107-Tyr194". The "His94-His96-His119" pattern, known as the zinc-binding motif, plays a critical role in the catalytic activity of CAs. These histidine residues coordinate with a zinc ion, which is essential for the hydration of carbon dioxide, to realize a primary reaction catalyzed by CAs. This interaction is fundamental to maintain the enzyme's active site structure and its catalytic efficiency. On the other hand, the "Ser29-His107-Tyr194" motif is crucial for substrate specificity and the orientation of water molecules in the active site. This motif contributes to the positioning and polarization of water molecules, facilitating the transfer of protons and hence supporting the enzyme's catalytic mechanism. By applying our Sequence Score technique to interpret the prediction results of our SPT models, we discover that our models can capture the importance of the "His94-His96-His119" and the "Ser29-His107-Tyr194" motifs for the functional properties of CAs. Figure 1 (see its heatmap) shows the importance scores for the three proteins of the CA class, where our Sequence Score technique assigns very high scores on both the "His94-His96-His119" (marked by red triangles) and the "Ser29-His107-Tyr194" (marked by orange stars) patterns. This exhibits that our SPT models have captured biological intelligence underlined in the protein sequence for predicting the functional properties of proteins.

2 Related Work

Protein Language Models. Protein Language Models (PLMs) have demonstrated remarkable performance across a spectrum of biological tasks. AlphaFold [38] is a well-known study in PLMs, and it uses multiple sequence alignment to predict the 3D structure of proteins. Recently, PLMs are also developed for predicting the functional properties of proteins, including single sequence-based methods, *i.e.*, TAPE [55], ESM-1b [59], and ESM-1v [52], multiple sequence alignment-based approaches, *i.e.*, MSA Transformer [56], and others [2,6,22,24,26,32,34,49,57,58]. Despite their effectiveness, PLMs require extensive pre-training on millions of protein data for satisfactory performance, making them computationally inaccessible for resource-limited groups. Different from prior studies, our SPT model can achieve superb performance in protein function predictions by training from scratch. Therefore, it advances previous PLMs by significantly reducing the computational overhead. We hope that the exceptionally computational efficiency of our SPT model can shed light on future work in adopting its model architecture for protein-relevant tasks.

XAI Techniques. Explainable Artificial Intelligence (XAI) methods provide valuable insights into the decision-making processes of deep neural networks (DNNs), making them well-suited for interpreting biological intelligence underlined in Protein Transformers. The mainstream XAI techniques targeting DNNs can be roughly grouped into two categories, *i.e.*, XAI for CNNs and XAI for Transformers. The former category is popularized by Grad-CAM [61], which weights the activation maps by global-average-pooled gradients flowing into the last convolutional layer. Subsequently, saliency-based [18,50,62], activation-based [39,73], perturbation-based [27,28,48,54,72], and gradient-based [8,10,15,19,23,29,36,37,63,64,69] XAI techniques are developed for deciphering the decision-making processes of CNNs. Despite their popularity, these methods face challenges when applied to Protein Transformers due to the structural differences between Transformers [67] and CNNs. Recently, Attention Rollout and Attention Flow [1], which map information flow using a Directed Acyclic Graph, has been proposed to interpret the decision-making processes in Transformer architectures, with its success inspiring a volume of Transformer-specific XAI techniques [9,11–14,68,71]. However, existing XAI solutions for Protein Transformers typically involve substantial computational demands, *e.g.*, $\mathcal{O}(L^2 \cdot P^4)$ for Attention Flow, with L and P respectively representing the depth of the model and the length of the protein sequence, making them infeasible to decipher the biological insight underlined in long protein sequences. This stems from their requirement to aggregate information from attention weights throughout every layer of the Transformer Encoders. In sharp contrast, our Sequence Score technique, while classified in the second category, revolutionizes the interpretation of decision-making processes in Transformers. This achievement stems

Table 1. Overview of our Protein-FN dataset

Datasets	Samples	Classes					
		Protease	Kinase	Receptor	Carbonic Anhydrase	Phosphatase	Isomerase
Training	7211	2439	2003	1172	972	343	282
Test	1803	628	499	265	234	89	88
Total	9014	3067	2502	1437	1206	431	371

from its linear complexity with respect to the protein sequence length. Therefore, our solution significantly advances previous Transformer-specific XAI techniques in computational efficiency, making it well-suited for interpreting the biological intelligence resided in Protein Transformers.

3 The Protein-FN Dataset

We introduce our curated protein function dataset, namely *Protein-FN*, designed specifically for such biological tasks as protein function prediction [52,59], motif identification and discovery [40], *etc*.. Table 1 presents the details of our ProFunc-9K dataset. This dataset, sourced from the Protein Data Bank (PDB) [53], provides diverse 1D amino acid sequences, 3D protein structures, functional properties of 9014 proteins (7211 and 1803 samples for the training and the test datasets, respectively). These proteins, after carefully examined by biological experts in our team, fall into six categories, *i.e.*, protease, kinase, receptor, carbonic anhydrase, phosphatase, and isomerase. Notably, kinases, phosphatases, proteases, and receptors play essential roles in signal transduction. Most drugs act on proteins involved in signal transduction. Isomerases and carbonic anhydrases are two enzymes that are not directly involved in signal transduction pathways, but they catalyze critical reactions.

4 Our Approaches

To unveil the biological intelligence embedded within Protein Transformers, we have developed two key innovations: i) the Sequence Protein Transformer (SPT), designed for the efficient and effective prediction of protein functions, and ii) the Sequence Score, aimed at efficiently interpreting the decision-making processes of Protein Transformers.

4.1 Problem Statement

Given a protein dataset consisting of N samples, denoted as $\mathbb{X} = \{(x_i, y_i) \mid i \in 1, 2, \cdots, N\}$, each sample $x \in \mathbb{R}^{P \times 1}$ represents the primary structure (*i.e.*, the sequence of amino acids) of the protein. Here, P denotes the sequence length, and $y \in [C]$ indicates the specific function of the protein, *e.g.*, protease, kinase, receptor, *etc*.. Notably, the length of the primary structure of proteins, *i.e.*, the number of amino acids in a polypeptide chain, can vary widely in the real scenario. In this work,

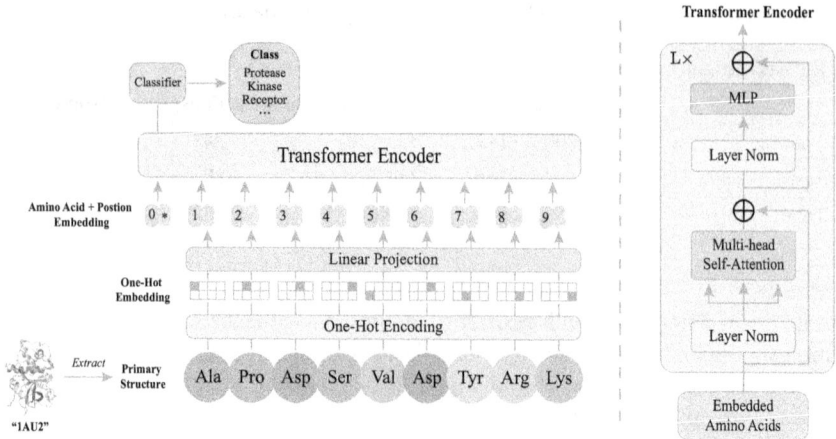

Fig. 2. The architecture of our Sequence Protein Transformers (SPT) model.

our goals are twofold. First, we aim to develop a simple, computation-efficient Protein Transformer (PT) $f_\theta : \mathbb{R}^{P \times 1} \rightarrow [C]$ for accurate protein function predictions, where θ denotes the PT's hyperparameters. Second, we plan to propose a novel Explainable Artificial Intelligence (XAI) technique, which can efficiently interpret long protein sequences. As such, given a well-trained PT model f_θ, the proposed XAI technique $g : \mathbb{R}^{P \times 1} \rightarrow \mathbb{R}^{P \times 1}$ can decode its biological intelligence by deciphering its decision-making process.

4.2 Our Sequence Protein Transformer

To achieve our goal, we propose a simple, computation-efficient Transformer architecture, namely Sequence Protein Transformer (SPT), for predicting the functional properties of proteins. It can achieve superb prediction performance without relying on computation-intensive self-supervised pre-training.

Figure 2 shows an overview of our model architecture. We start by extracting the primary structure $x \in \mathbb{R}^{P \times 1}$, *i.e.*, a sequence of amino acids, from a protein (*e.g.*, "1AU2"). Then, the one-hot encoding is utilized to encode the sequence of amino acids. As such, each amino acid is represented by a binary vector of length d. Note that we set $d = 20$ in this study as there are 20 types of amino acids. Next, a linear projection layer Proj: $\mathbb{R}^{P \times d} \rightarrow \mathbb{R}^{P \times D}$ is used to project the low dimensional one-hot embedding $E_{\text{oh}} \in \mathbb{R}^{P \times d}$ to the high dimensional amino acid embedding $E_{\text{ami}} \in \mathbb{R}^{P \times D}$, *i.e.*,

$$E_{\text{ami}} = \text{Proj}\left(\text{OH}(x)\right). \tag{1}$$

Here, D is the hidden size of the Transformer Encoder, and OH represents one-hot encoding. Similar to prior Transformer variants [21,45,66], our model prepends a learnable classification token $E_{\text{cls}} \in \mathbb{R}^{1 \times D}$ to the embedding sequence. As such, the input sequence of the Transformer Encoder can be obtained by summing up the amino acid embedding and the positional embedding $E_{\text{pos}} \in \mathbb{R}^{(P+1) \times D}$. Finally, the head of the output sequence $z \in \mathbb{R}^{1 \times D}$, encoded by a stack of Transformer blocks, is fed to a linear classifier for protein function predictions, i.e., $\hat{y} = W^T z + b$, with W and b respectively representing the weights and the bias of the classifier, and $\hat{y} \in [C]$ indicating the predicted protein function.

The rightmost chart of Fig. 2 depicts the architecture of the Transformer Encoder, where each Transformer block consists of a Multi-head Self-Attention (MSA) block [67] and an MLP block. Each of the two blocks includes a Layer Normalization [5] before the block and the residual connection [31] after the block. Similar to previous studies [21,45,66,70], the MLP block is a two-layer neural network with a GELU non-linearity. Mathematically, our Transformer Encoder can be expressed as below,

$$\begin{aligned} E_0 &= [E_{\text{cls}}; E_{\text{ami}}^1; E_{\text{ami}}^2; \cdots ; E_{\text{ami}}^P] + E_{\text{pos}}, \\ E'_\ell &= \text{MSA}(\text{Norm}(E_{\ell-1})) + E_{\ell-1}, \\ E_\ell &= \text{MLP}(\text{Norm}(E'_\ell)) + E'_\ell, \\ z &= \text{Norm}(E_L^0). \end{aligned} \quad (2)$$

Here, $\ell = 1, 2, \cdots, L$ indicates the ℓ-th block of Transformer Encoder. Different from prior Transformer variants, our Transformer Encoder has a flexible number of positional embeddings, enabling the SPT to address the primary structure of proteins, whose sequence lengths vary significantly. Inspired by the Multi-head Self-Attention (MSA) mechanism [67], our MSA block here is devised to capture the global protein representation by learning the dependency among a sequence of amino acids, i.e.,

$$\begin{aligned} \text{MSA}(Q, K, V) &= \text{Concat}(\text{head}_1, \cdots, \text{head}_h) W^O, \\ \text{head}_i &= \text{Softmax}(Q_i K_i^T / \sqrt{d_k}) V_i, \\ \text{where } Q_i &= Q W_i^Q, \ K_i = K W_i^K, \ V_i = V W_i^V. \end{aligned} \quad (3)$$

Here, Concat indicates the operation of feature concatenation, h is the number of attention heads, and $d_k = D/h$ represents the dimension for queries, keys, and values of the Attention mechanism. Like those in prior studies [21,41,60,67], $W_i^Q \in \mathbb{R}^{D \times d_k}$, $W_i^K \in \mathbb{R}^{D \times d_k}$, $W_i^V \in \mathbb{R}^{D \times d_k}$, and $W^O \in \mathbb{R}^{D \times D}$ are four learnable projection matrices.

4.3 Our Sequence Score

Interpreting the biological intelligence encoded in Protein Transformers (PT) demands an XAI technique capable of handling long protein sequences composed of a substantial number of amino acids. Previous Transformer-specific XAI methods [1,11,12,68,71] have proven effective in elucidating the decision-making processes of various Transformer models [21,45]. However, their use is predominantly limited to analyzing shorter token sequences, due to their substantial computational overhead involved in aggregating attention weights across all layers of Transformer Encoders. This limitation is particularly problematic for interpreting Protein Transformers (PTs), which analyze amino acid sequences that often feature extensive lengths, thus obstructing their potential to unlock the decision-making processes within PTs. To address this challenge, we introduce the Sequence Score, an innovative XAI method characterized by its time complexity *growing linearly* with the protein sequence. This feature renders it exceptionally suitable for decoding the biological intelligence usually embedded within protein sequences.

Given a decision of interest (*e.g.*, the protease class), our Sequence Score, with respect to the gradients of a well-trained PT model, can generate a sequence of important scores, based on the primary structure of proteins. Next, we introduce the details of our Sequence Score technique. Consider a decision interest of class $c \in [C]$, our Sequence Score technique first calculates the gradient of the logit for the class c, with respect to feature maps $\boldsymbol{A} \in \mathbb{R}^{P \times D}$ of any Transformer block (*e.g.*, the last block of Transformer Encoders), *i.e.*, $\frac{\partial y^c}{\partial \boldsymbol{A}}$. Here, the term "logit" refers to the classification score before being passed through a sigmoid (or softmax) function to produce a probability distribution over the classes. Then, the neuron importance weight $\boldsymbol{w}^c \in \mathbb{R}^D$, is obtained by performing global average pooling over the sequence length (indexed by j), *i.e.*,

$$w^c = \frac{1}{P} \sum_{j=1}^{P} \frac{\partial y^c}{\partial \boldsymbol{A}_j}. \tag{4}$$

Next, we arrive at the importance score for the j-th amino acid S_j^c by summing up a weighted combination of the feature map activations $\boldsymbol{A}$, *i.e.*,

$$S_j^c = \sum_{k=1}^{D} w_k^c \boldsymbol{A}^k, \quad j = 1, 2, \cdots, P. \tag{5}$$

Similar to prior XAI techniques [10,61], attention is paid solely to features that positively affect the prediction of interest. In other words, the negative importance scores should be dropped. Meanwhile, our preliminary experimental results indicate that if the primary structure of proteins is too long, the importance score for each amino acid will be small (*i.e.*, < 0.001). We develop a novel trick to address the two issues simultaneously, expressed as follows,

$$S_j^c = \frac{\max(0, S_j^c)}{\max(\boldsymbol{S}^c)}, \quad j = 1, 2, \cdots, P. \tag{6}$$

Here, the numerator and the denominator of (6) serve for dropping the negative scores and normalizing the positive scores, respectively. As such, our Sequence Score technique can interpret biological intelligence underlined in PT models by revealing their decision-making processes when predicting the functional properties of proteins. It is noteworthy that the computation of our Sequence Score technique achieves linear time complexity, denoted as $\mathcal{O}(D \cdot P)$, where D represents the hidden dimension of the Transformer Encoders and P denotes the length of the protein sequences. This efficiency underscores its suitability for analyzing the intricate biological intelligence embedded in protein structures.

Table 2. Model variants of our Sequence Protein Transformers (SPT), with their model details listed below

Model	Layers	Hidden Size D	Head	MLP Size	Parameters
SPT-Tiny	12	192	4	768	5.4M
SPT-Small	12	384	6	1536	21.5M
SPT-Base	12	768	12	3072	85.5M

5 Experiments and Results

5.1 Experimental Settings

Datasets. We conduct experiments across three benchmarks: i) **Protein-FN**, having 9,014 protein data with their 1D amino acid sequences, 3D protein structures, and functional properties; ii) **Antibiotic Resistance (AR)** [51], containing 3,416 protein samples, each associated with its antibiotic type; and iii) **Metal Ion Binding (MIB)** [33], offering 7,332 single protein sequences, collected from PDB with annotation as metal ion binding.

Model Variants. We set our Sequence Protein Transformers (SPT) configurations based on the Transformer settings reported in previous studies [21,66]. Three model variants, *i.e.*, SPT-Tiny, SPT-Small, and SPT-Base, are developed, tailored for protein function predictions across different scales of data. Table 2 presents the model details of those SPT variants. Specifically, all SPT variants are composed of 12 layers of Transformer blocks, with their hidden sizes set to 192, 384, and 768, and their numbers of heads set to 4, 6, and 12, respectively for the SPT-Tiny, the SPT-Small, and the SPT-Base models. The MLP sizes are fixed to four times of their corresponding hidden sizes.

Compared Approaches. As our SPT models belong to the single sequence-based Protein Transformers, we consider three prominent single sequence-based Protein Language Models (PLMs), *i.e.*, **TAPE** [55], **ESM-1b** [59], and **ESM-1v** [52], for baseline comparison. The hyperparameters for PLM counterparts, if not specified, are set as reported in their original literature.

Hyperparamters. In sharp contrast to prior PLMs [52,55,59], our SPT models do not require computationally extensive self-supervised pre-training. Instead, they are all trained from scratch by employing the AdamW [47] optimizer with $\beta_1 = 0.9$, $\beta_2 = 0.999$, and a weight decay of 0.05. The training epochs for SPT variants are set to 100, including 5 warmup epochs. We utilize the cosine decay learning rate schedule [46], with a base learning rate of $1e-3$ and a layer-wise learning rate decay [17] of 0.75. Following [30], we also apply the label smoothing [65] and the path dropping [35], with their values both set to 0.1. As such, our SPT models are superb computation-efficient. All experiments were conducted on a lab computer with an RTX 4090 GPU, having its memory usage consistently <9.6%.

Table 3. Comparisons to state-of-the-art PLM counterparts on the Protein-FN dataset, where the last two columns respectively report the error rates on the training and the test sets, with the best results shown in bold

Methods	Parameters	GFLOPs	Training Error (%)	Test Error (%)
TAPE (scratch)	92.4M	21.4	2.39	11.59
TAPE (pre-trained)			0.34	0.55
ESM-1b (scratch)	650M	160	1.11	11.73
ESM-1b (pre-trained)			1.33	1.86
ESM-1v (pre-trained)	650M	160	0.55	0.58
SPT-Tiny	**5.4M**	**1.4**	0.39	0.41
SPT-Small	21.5M	5.1	0.22	0.38
SPT-Base	85.5M	19.4	**0.11**	**0.31**

5.2 Comparisons to Protein Language Models

Experiments on the Protein-FN Dataset. We conducted experiments on the *Protein-FN* dataset to evaluate the performance of our SPT models. Three state-of-the-art PLMs mentioned in Sect. 5.1 are taken into account as baselines for comparison. Table 3 presents experimental results, where two notations, *i.e.*, "pre-trained" and "scratch", respectively indicate the counterparts with and without the self-supervised pre-training[1]. Here, we consider both computational complexity and model performance. The former is measured by the number of parameters and GFLOPs[2] calculated under a sequence of amino acids, while the latter is characterized by the top-1 error rates on the training and the test sets.

We have three observations. First, our SPT-Tiny model (containing only 5.4M parameters) achieves an exceptionally low test set error rate of 0.41%, outperforming all competitors, in terms of both computational efficiency and prediction accuracy. Moreover, its impressive capabilities in protein function predictions are achieved with the GFLOPs value of just 1.4. This represents a computational demand at least 15.2× lower than that of its competitors, underscoring the model's remarkable balance between efficiency and accuracy. Second, our SPT-Base model achieves the best error rate of 0.11% and 0.31% respectively on the training and the test sets. This notable performance underscores a key finding: scaling up our model's size corresponds to a marked enhancement in its capabilities. Third, training PLMs from scratch may lead to substantial overfitting. This issue is evident in the significant discrepancies observed between training and test set performance outcomes, *e.g.*, the error rate of 2.39% *v.s.* 11.59% for the TAPE (scratch) model and of 1.11% *v.s.* 11.73% for the ESM-1b (scratch) model. In sharp contrast, our SPT models, despite trained from scratch, show excellent generaliza-

---
[1] ESM-1v (scratch) is the same as ESM-1b (scratch) as they use the same structure but are pre-trained on different datasets.
[2] GFLOPs, or Giga Floating Point Operations, is a metric that quantifies a model's computational complexity. It indicates the number of billion floating-point operations needed by a model per second.

Table 4. Overall comparisons to PLMs on the AR and MIB datasets, with best results shown in bold

Methods	AR		MIB	
	GFLOPs	Test Error (%)	GFLOPs	Test Error (%)
TAPE (scratch)	106.3	11.8	65.7	39.8
TAPE (pre-trained)		7.3		34.2
ESM-1b (scratch)	172.1	11.1	79.1	40.1
ESM-1b (pre-trained)		8.6		35.9
ESM-1v (pre-trained)	172.1	9.8	79.1	33.3
SPT-Tiny	**19.2**	5.7	**5.6**	37.1
SPT-Small	31.2	4.5	18.5	32.7
SPT-Base	105.6	**4.3**	65.7	**32.1**

tion abilities. This can be attributed to our SPT's design in the amino acid embedding, which lifts the requirement of self-supervised pre-training to learn meaningful protein representations.

Experiments on the AR and MIB Datasets. Here, we conducted experiments on the two widely-used benchmarks, *i.e.*, Antibiotic Resistance (AR) and Metal Ion Binding (MIB), for further exhibiting the effectiveness of our SPT models for protein function predictions. Table 4 presents experimental results. It is observed that our SPT-Base model beats all PLM counterparts on both datasets, with the best test error rates of 4.3% and 32.1% on the AR and MIB datasets. In addition, our SPT models stand out for their computational efficiency. Taking the AR dataset for instance, our SPT-Tiny model not only achieves a low test error rate of 5.7% but did so with just 19.2 GFLOPs of computational demand. This efficiency makes it at least 5.5 times faster than previous PLMs, marking a significant advancement in processing speed and energy consumption. Finally, without self-supervised pre-training, previous PLMs suffer from a significant performance degradation (See 3rd *v.s.* 4th rows and 5th *v.s.* 6th rows). On the contrary, our SPT models, though trained from scratch, achieves superb prediction performance outcomes. This can be attributed to the effectiveness of our novel protein embedding mechanism.

We've further evaluated our SPT models, comparing them with traditional bioinformatics approaches and conducting detailed ablation studies, with corresponding experimental results deferred to Appendices A.1 and A.2, respectively.

5.3 Evaluation on Our Sequence Score Technique

We consider two metrics proposed in the prior study [3], *i.e.*, **Faithfulness** and **Stability**, to evaluate the efficacy of our Sequence Score technique for explaining Protein Transformers. In this section, we present the experimental results regarding the *faithfulness* metric. The evaluation of the *stability* of our Sequence Score technique is detailed in Appendix B.1 of the supplementary materials for conserving space. In

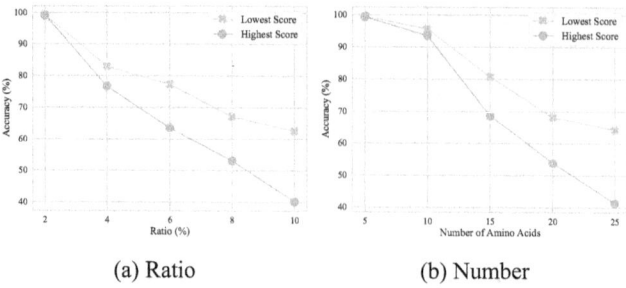

(a) Ratio   (b) Number

Fig. 3. Comparisons of prediction performance by masking amino acids with the highest and the lowest importance scores under (a) masking a certain ratio of amino acids and (b) masking a specific number of amino acids. (Color figure online)

particular, *faithfulness* measures the degree to which the importance values which are attributed to amino acids, are aligned with their actual impact on the final prediction, expecting that amino acids with substantial effects will receive correspondingly high importance scores.

Here, we adopt the *deletion* method [54] to evaluate the *faithfulness* of our Sequence Score technique. Its key idea is to observe accuracy degradation incurred by masking a certain ratio (or number) of amino acids, with masked amino acids chosen based on their importance scores, *i.e.*, those with the highest scores *v.s.* those with the lowest scores. A larger drop in prediction accuracy, resulted from masking amino acids with high importance scores than with low scores, indicates that the assigned scores are well aligned with amino acids' actual significance to the final predictions.

Figure 3a illustrates the results of our experiments that involve selectively masking amino acids at various ratios. Our findings reveal a consistent pattern: masking amino acids identified as highly important invariably leads to a larger decline in prediction performance, versus masking amino acids with lower importance scores. For example, when the masking ratio is set to 10%, masking amino acids that have the highest importance scores results in performance degradation to be 22.41% greater than that resulted from masking those with the lowest importance scores. Additionally, lifting the masking ratio from 2% to 10% yields a noticeably faster decline in prediction performance when masking amino acids with the highest scores (see the blue line) than with the lowest scores (see the green line). This demonstrates a direct relationship between the importance scores assigned to the amino acids and their actual influence levels on the predictive accuracy of the model.

Complementing these findings, Fig. 3b illustrates similar trends under a different experimental setting, where various numbers of amino acids are masked. As the number of masked amino acids increases from 5 to 25, prediction performance is observed to degrade significantly faster when masking amino acids with the highest scores than with the lowest scores. Specifically, a masking number of 25 leads to a substantial larger performance decline, *i.e.*, by 58.16%, when masking amino acids with the highest importance scores than with the lowest scores, *i.e.*, only by 35.41%. These statistical

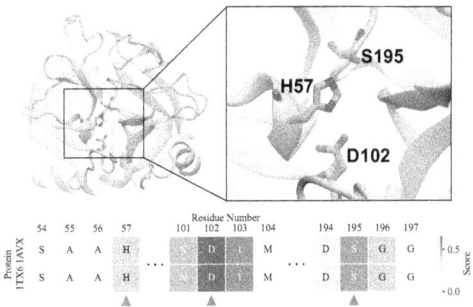

Fig. 4. Illustration of the catalytic triad, *i.e.*, "His57-Asp102-Ser195", in the two proteins of serine proteases. Here, "His", "Asp", and "Ser" are abbreviated as "H", "D" and "S", respectively. The figure in the upper section utilizes the protein "1TX6" as an example to show the 3D structure of the catalytic triad, while the heatmap in the lower section visualizes the importance scores generated by our Sequence Score technique, with amino acids corresponding to the catalytic triad distinctly marked by red triangles. (Color figure online)

observations confirm that our Sequence Score technique adheres to the principle of *faithfulness* when interpreting Protein Transformers.

We have also conducted experiments to assess the *faithfulness* of our Sequence Score technique by simulating protein mutations, with their results deferred to Appendix B.2 of supplementary materials.

5.4 Discovery of Catalytic Triad in Serine Proteases

This section further interprets biological intelligence resided in Protein Transformers by unveiling its discovery of the catalytic triad in serine proteases. Serine proteases, a group of proteases, are crucial enzymes involved in a myriad of biological functions, including digestion, immune response, and blood coagulation. At the heart of their catalytic mechanism lies the catalytic triad, a set of three coordinated amino acids, usually following the pattern of "His57-Asp102-Ser195". This triad forms a potent synergistic unit essential for the enzyme's function. Figure 4 depicts importance scores for the two proteins of serine proteases. It is obvious that our SPT models can identify the significance of the catalytic triad (marked by red triangles) for serine proteases. These results further confirm that our Protein Transformers can capture biological intelligence inherent within protein sequences.

It is worth noticing that the catalytic triad's importance extends beyond its biochemical role; its evolutionary conservation across various serine proteases underscores a fundamental mechanism critical to many physiological processes. Moreover, the detailed understanding of this triad, including the specific residue numbers, has been instrumental in the design of targeted pharmaceutical inhibitors to modulate serine protease activity in treating various diseases, such as cancer, inflammatory disorders, and coagulopathies. Hopefully, the capability of our SPT models to discover the catalytic triad of serine proteases can shed light on future studies, aided by the Protein Transformers for understanding the biochemical, physiological, and pharmaceutical processes.

6 Conclusion

This work has explored the capabilities of Protein Transformers in capturing biological intelligence resided in protein sequences. To achieve our goal, we first introduced the *Protein-FN* dataset, offering over 9000 protein sequence data as well as their functional properties created laboriously by biological experts. Then, we developed the Sequence Protein Transformers (SPT), a computationally efficient Transformer architecture, able to precisely predict the functional properties of proteins by leveraging their primary structures. Thanks to its novel protein embedding mechanism, our SPT models can achieve superb prediction performance without the requirement of self-supervised pretraining. Finally, we have developed the Sequence Score, a novel Explainable Artificial Intelligence (XAI) technique that advances beyond current Transformer-specific XAI solutions in terms of computational efficiency. This efficiency increases linearly with the length of protein sequences, making it well-suited for analyzing the complex biological intelligence encoded within Protein Transformers. Extensive experimental results exhibited that our SPT models are efficient and effective in predicting the functional properties of proteins. Moreover, the devised Sequence Score technique helps reveal that our SPT models can capture important patterns underlying protein sequences, with these patterns aligning closely with the domain knowledge in the biology community. This demonstrates the capabilities of our Protein Transformers in capturing biological intelligence resided in protein sequences.

Acknowledgments. This work was supported in part by NSF under Grants 2019511 and 2425812. Any opinions and findings expressed in the paper are those of the authors and do not necessarily reflect the views of funding agencies.

References

1. Abnar, S., Zuidema, W.H.: Quantifying attention flow in transformers. In: Annual Meeting of the Association for Computational Linguistics (ACL) (2020)
2. Alley, E.C., Khimulya, G., Biswas, S., AlQuraishi, M., Church, G.M.: Unified rational protein engineering with sequence-based deep representation learning. Nat. Methods (2019)
3. Alvarez-Melis, D., Jaakkola, T.S.: Towards robust interpretability with self-explaining neural networks. In: Bengio, S., Wallach, H.M., Larochelle, H., Grauman, K., Cesa-Bianchi, N., Garnett, R. (eds.) Neural Information Processing Systems 2018 (NeurIPS) (2018)
4. Arnab, A., Dehghani, M., Heigold, G., Sun, C., Lucic, M., Schmid, C.: ViViT: a video vision transformer. In: International Conference on Computer Vision (ICCV) (2021)
5. Ba, J.L., Kiros, J.R., Hinton, G.E.: Layer normalization. arXiv preprint arXiv:1607.06450 (2016)
6. Baek, M., et al.: Accurate prediction of protein structures and interactions using a three-track neural network. Science (2021)
7. Bao, H., Dong, L., Piao, S., Wei, F.: BEiT: BERT pre-training of image transformers. In: International Conference on Learning Representations (ICLR) (2022)
8. Barkan, O., et al.: GAM: explainable visual similarity and classification via gradient activation maps. In: International Conference on Information and Knowledge Management (CIKM) (2021)

9. Caron, M., et al.: Emerging properties in self-supervised vision transformers. In: International Conference on Computer Vision (ICCV) (2021)
10. Chattopadhyay, A., Sarkar, A., Howlader, P., Balasubramanian, V.N.: Grad-CAM++: generalized gradient-based visual explanations for deep convolutional networks. In: Winter Conference on Applications of Computer Vision (WACV) (2018)
11. Chefer, H., Gur, S., Wolf, L.: Generic attention-model explainability for interpreting bimodal and encoder-decoder transformers. In: International Conference on Computer Vision (ICCV) (2021)
12. Chefer, H., Gur, S., Wolf, L.: Transformer interpretability beyond attention visualization. In: Conference on Computer Vision and Pattern Recognition (CVPR) (2021)
13. Chen, Z., Silvestri, F., Tolomei, G., Wang, J., Zhu, H., Ahn, H.: Explain the explainer: interpreting model-agnostic counterfactual explanations of a deep reinforcement learning agent. IEEE Trans. Artif. Intell. **5**(4), 1443–1457 (2022)
14. Chen, Z., et al.: GREASE: generate factual and counterfactual explanations for GNN-based recommendations. arXiv preprint arXiv:2208.04222 (2022)
15. Chen, Z., Silvestri, F., Wang, J., Zhang, Y., Tolomei, G.: The dark side of explanations: poisoning recommender systems with counterfactual examples. In: Proceedings of the 46th International ACM SIGIR conference on Research and Development in Information Retrieval, pp. 2426–2430 (2023)
16. Chu, T., et al.: BoneMet: an open large-scale multi-modal murine dataset for breast cancer bone metastasis diagnosis and prognosis. In: The Thirteenth International Conference on Learning Representations (ICLR) (2025)
17. Clark, K., Luong, M.-T., Le, Q.V., Manning, C.D.: ELECTRA: pre-training text encoders as discriminators rather than generators. In: International Conference on Learning Representations (2019)
18. Dabkowski, P., Gal, Y.: Real time image saliency for black box classifiers. In: Neural Information Processing Systems (NeurIPS) (2017)
19. Desai, S., Ramaswamy, H.G.: Ablation-CAM: visual explanations for deep convolutional network via gradient-free localization. In: Winter Conference on Applications of Computer Vision (WACV) (2020)
20. Devlin, J., Chang, M.-W., Lee, K., Toutanova, K.: BERT: pre-training of deep bidirectional transformers for language understanding. In: North American Chapter of the Association for Computational Linguistics: Human Language Technologies (NAACL-HLT) (2019)
21. Dosovitskiy, A., et al.: An image is worth 16x16 words: transformers for image recognition at scale. In: ICLR (2021)
22. Elnaggar, A., et al.: ProtTrans: toward understanding the language of life through self-supervised learning. IEEE Trans. Pattern Anal. Mach. Intell. **44**(10), 7112–7127 (2021)
23. Englebert, A., Cornu, O., De Vleeschouwer, C.: Backward recursive class activation map refinement for high resolution saliency map. In: International Conference on Pattern Recognition (ICPR) (2022)
24. Evans, R., et al.: Protein complex prediction with AlphaFold-Multimer. biorxiv (2021)
25. Fan, H., et al.: Multiscale vision transformers. In: International Conference on Computer Vision (ICCV) (2021)
26. Finn, R.D., et al.: Pfam: the protein families database. Nucleic Acids Res. (2014)
27. Fong, R., Patrick, M., Vedaldi, A.: Understanding deep networks via extremal perturbations and smooth masks. In: International Conference on Computer Vision (ICCV) (2019)
28. Fong, R.C., Vedaldi, A.: Interpretable explanations of black boxes by meaningful perturbation. In: International Conference on Computer Vision (ICCV) (2017)
29. Fu, R., Hu, Q., Dong, X., Guo, Y., Gao, Y., Li, B.: Axiom-based Grad-CAM: towards accurate visualization and explanation of CNNs. In: British Machine Vision Conference (BMVC) (2020)

30. He, K., Chen, X., Xie, S., Li, Y., Dollár, P., Girshick, R.B.: Masked autoencoders are scalable vision learners. In: Conference on Computer Vision and Pattern Recognition (CVPR) (2022)
31. He, K., Zhang, X., Ren, S., Sun, J.: Deep residual learning for image recognition. In: Computer Vision and Pattern Recognition (CVPR) (2016)
32. Hsu, C., et al.: Learning inverse folding from millions of predicted structures. In: International Conference on Machine Learning (ICML) (2022)
33. Hu, M., et al.: Exploring evolution-aware & -free protein language models as protein function predictors. In: Neural Information Processing Systems (NeurIPS) (2022)
34. Hu, M., et al.: Exploring evolution-aware &-free protein language models as protein function predictors (2022)
35. Huang, G., Sun, Yu., Liu, Z., Sedra, D., Weinberger, K.Q.: Deep networks with stochastic depth. In: Leibe, B., Matas, J., Sebe, N., Welling, M. (eds.) ECCV 2016. LNCS, vol. 9908, pp. 646–661. Springer, Cham (2016). https://doi.org/10.1007/978-3-319-46493-0_39
36. Jalwana, M.A.A.K., Akhtar, N., Bennamoun, M., Mian, A.: CAMERAS: enhanced resolution and sanity preserving class activation mapping for image saliency. In: Conference on Computer Vision and Pattern Recognition (CVPR) (2021)
37. Jiang, P.-T., Zhang, C.-B., Hou, Q., Cheng, M.-M., Wei, Y.: LayerCAM: exploring hierarchical class activation maps for localization. IEEE Trans. Image Process. **30**, 5875–5888 (2021)
38. Jumper, J., et al.: Highly accurate protein structure prediction with AlphaFold. Nature **596**(7873), 583–589 (2021)
39. Kim, B., et al.: Interpretability beyond feature attribution: quantitative testing with concept activation vectors (TCAV). In: International Conference on Machine Learning (ICML) (2018)
40. Kondra, S., Sarkar, T., Raghavan, V., Wu, X.: Development of a TSR-based method for protein 3-D structural comparison with its applications to protein classification and motif discovery. Front. Chem. **8**, 602291 (2021)
41. Lin, F., et al.: MMST-ViT: climate change-aware crop yield prediction via multi-modal spatial-temporal vision transformer. In: International Conference on Computer Vision (ICCV) (2023)
42. Lin, F., Guillot, K., Crawford, S., Zhang, Y., Yuan, X., Tzeng, N.-F.: An open and large-scale dataset for multi-modal climate change-aware crop yield predictions. In: Proceedings of the 30th ACM SIGKDD Conference on Knowledge Discovery and Data Mining (KDD), pp. 5375–5386 (2024)
43. Lin, F., Lou, J., Yuan, X., Tzeng, N.-F.: Towards robust vision transformer via masked adaptive ensemble. In: Proceedings of the 33rd ACM International Conference on Information and Knowledge Management (CIKM), pp. 1389–1399 (2024)
44. Lin, F., et al.: Comprehensive transformer-based model architecture for real-world storm prediction. In: Joint European Conference on Machine Learning and Knowledge Discovery in Databases (ECML-PKDD), pp. 54–71 (2023)
45. Liu, Z., et al.: Swin transformer: hierarchical vision transformer using shifted windows. In: International Conference on Computer Vision (ICCV) (2021)
46. Loshchilov, I., Hutter, F.: SGDR: stochastic gradient descent with warm restarts. In: International Conference on Learning Representations (ICLR) (2016)
47. Loshchilov, I., Hutter, F.: Decoupled weight decay regularization. In: International Conference on Learning Representations (ICLR) (2019)
48. Lundberg, S.M. Lee, S.-I.: A unified approach to interpreting model predictions. In: Neural Information Processing Systems (NeurIPS) (2017)
49. Luo, S., Su, Y., Peng, X., Wang, S., Peng, J., Ma, J.: Antigen-specific antibody design and optimization with diffusion-based generative models for protein structures (2022)

50. Mahendran, A., Vedaldi, A.: Visualizing deep convolutional neural networks using natural pre-images. Int. J. Comput. Vis. (IJCV) **120**(3), 233–255 (2016)
51. McArthur, A.G., et al.: The comprehensive antibiotic resistance database. Antimicrob. Agents Chemother. **57**(7), 3348–3357 (2013)
52. Meier, J., Rao, R., Verkuil, R., Liu, J., Sercu, T., Rives, A.: Language models enable zero-shot prediction of the effects of mutations on protein function (2021)
53. PDB: Protein data bank (PDB) (2023)
54. Petsiuk, V., Das, A., Saenko, K.: RISE: randomized input sampling for explanation of black-box models. In: British Machine Vision Conference (BMVC), p. 151 (2018)
55. Rao, R., et al.: Evaluating protein transfer learning with tape. In: Neural Information Processing Systems (NeurIPS) (2019)
56. Rao, R., et al.: MSA transformer. In: International Conference on Machine Learning (ICML) (2021)
57. Rao, R., Meier, J., Sercu, T., Ovchinnikov, S., Rives, A.: Transformer protein language models are unsupervised structure learners. In: International Conference on Learning Representations (ICLR) (2021)
58. Riesselman, A.J., Ingraham, J.B., Marks, D.S.: Deep generative models of genetic variation capture the effects of mutations. Nat. Methods (2018)
59. Rives, A., et al.: Biological structure and function emerge from scaling unsupervised learning to 250 million protein sequences. Proc. Nat. Acad. Sci. **118**(15) (2021)
60. Rombach, R., Blattmann, A., Lorenz, D., Esser, P., Ommer, B.: High-resolution image synthesis with latent diffusion models. In: Computer Vision and Pattern Recognition (CVPR) (2022)
61. Selvaraju, R.R., Cogswell, M., Das, A., Vedantam, R., Parikh, D., Batra, D.: Grad-CAM: visual explanations from deep networks via gradient-based localization. In: International Conference on Computer Vision (ICCV) (2017)
62. Simonyan, K., Vedaldi, A., Zisserman, A.: Deep inside convolutional networks: visualising image classification models and saliency maps. In: International Conference on Learning Representations Workshop (ICLRW) (2014)
63. Srinivas, S., Fleuret, F.: Full-gradient representation for neural network visualization. In: Neural Information Processing Systems (NeurIPS) (2019)
64. Sundararajan, M., Taly, A., Yan, Q.: Axiomatic attribution for deep networks. In: International Conference on Machine Learning (ICML) (2017)
65. Szegedy, C., Vanhoucke, V., Ioffe, S., Shlens, J., Wojna, Z.: Rethinking the inception architecture for computer vision. In: Computer Vision and Pattern Recognition (CVPR) (2016)
66. Touvron, H., Cord, M., Douze, M., Massa, F., Sablayrolles, A., Jégou, H.: Training data-efficient image transformers & distillation through attention. In: Meila, M., Zhang, T. (eds.) International Conference on Machine Learning (ICML) (2021)
67. Vaswani, A., et al.: Attention is all you need. In: Neural Information Processing Systems (NeurIPS) (2017)
68. Voita, E., Talbot, D., Moiseev, F., Sennrich, R., Titov, I.: Analyzing multi-head self-attention: specialized heads do the heavy lifting, the rest can be pruned. In: Annual Meeting of the Association for Computational Linguistics (ACL) (2019)
69. Wang, H., et al.: Score-CAM: score-weighted visual explanations for convolutional neural networks. In: Conference on Computer Vision and Pattern Recognition Workshop (CVPRW) (2020)
70. Wang, W., et al.: Pyramid vision transformer: a versatile backbone for dense prediction without convolutions. In: International Conference on Computer Vision (ICCV) (2021)
71. Xie, W., Li, X.-H., Cao, C.C., Zhang, N.L.: ViT-CX: causal explanation of vision transformers. In: International Joint Conference on Artificial Intelligence (IJCAI) (2023)

72. Zeiler, M.D., Fergus, R.: Visualizing and understanding convolutional networks. In: Fleet, D., Pajdla, T., Schiele, B., Tuytelaars, T. (eds.) ECCV 2014. LNCS, vol. 8689, pp. 818–833. Springer, Cham (2014). https://doi.org/10.1007/978-3-319-10590-1_53
73. Zhou, B., Khosla, A., Lapedriza, À., Oliva, A., Torralba, A.: Learning deep features for discriminative localization. In: Conference on Computer Vision and Pattern Recognition (CVPR) (2016)

SigBERT: Combining Narrative Medical Reports and Rough Path Signature Theory for Survival Prediction in Oncology

Paul Minchella[1,2,3]($\boxtimes$), Loic Verlingue[2], Stéphane Chrétien[3], Rémi Vaucher[3], and Guillaume Metzler[3]

[1] Université Claude Bernard Lyon 1, 69100 Villeurbanne, France
paul.minchella@lyon.unicancer.fr
[2] Léon Bérard Center, 69008 Lyon, France
loic.verlingue@lyon.unicancer.fr
[3] Laboratoire ERIC, 69500 Bron, France
{stephane.chretien,r.vaucher,guillaume.metzler}@univ-lyon2.fr

Abstract. Electronic medical reports (EHR) contain a vast amount of information that can be leveraged for machine learning applications in healthcare. However, existing survival analysis methods often struggle to effectively handle the complexity of textual data, particularly in its sequential form. Here, we propose SigBERT, an innovative temporal survival analysis framework designed to efficiently process a large number of clinical reports per patient. SigBERT processes timestamped medical reports by extracting and averaging word embeddings into sentence embeddings. To capture temporal dynamics from the time series of sentence embedding coordinates, we apply signature extraction from rough path theory to derive geometric features for each patient, which significantly enhance survival model performance by capturing complex temporal dynamics. These features are then integrated into a LASSO-penalized Cox model to estimate patient-specific risk scores. The model was trained and evaluated on a real-world oncology dataset from the Léon Bérard Center corpus, with a C-index score of 0.75 (sd 0.014) on the independent test cohort. SigBERT integrates sequential medical data to enhance risk estimation, advancing narrative-based survival analysis.

Keywords: NLP · Signature Transform · Survival Analysis · Oncology

1 Introduction

1.1 Background

Survival analysis plays a fundamental role in medicine (oncology, cardiology, nephrology, critical care, etc.) where predicting the prognosis of the patient is crucial to guide clinical decision-making. They help determine treatment strategies, assess the efficacy of therapeutic interventions, refine clinical trial eligibility criteria, aid in risk stratification and early intervention planning. The

Cox Proportional Hazards [7] model has long been the gold standard since it was published in survival analysis due to its interpretability and effectiveness in identifying prognostic factors. One of its key advantages is its ability to effectively account for censoring, which arises when the event of interest (*e.g.*, death, relapse, or disease progression) has not yet occurred for certain patients by the end of the study period. Even without an observed event, censored patients provide valuable information by contributing to likelihood, as their recorded survival time improves risk estimation despite incomplete event data. This feature makes the model particularly robust in real-world clinical settings, where missing or censored data are very common. Over the past decade, more recent advances in survival analysis have explored neural network-based models, which offer a powerful alternative by capturing complex, non-linear relationships within patient data [15,18].

However, a key limitation of many survival models is their reliance on static patient snapshots rather than dynamic, time-dependent data. Integrating structured (*e.g.*, biomarkers, lab tests) and unstructured data (*e.g.*, clinical narratives) is crucial but intricate. Addressing these challenges requires advanced NLP methods for processing unstructured clinical narratives, along with statistical techniques to enhance predictive accuracy and clinical applicability.

1.2 Related Works

Recent advancements in survival analysis have introduced dynamic models capable of integrating time-dependent patient data. Dynamic-DeepHit [17] employs RNNs with attention mechanisms to process sequential biomarkers and treatments. Transformer-based approaches like BERTSurv [30] leverage pretrained language models to extract survival-relevant features from unstructured clinical notes, enhancing survival prediction. Meanwhile, CoxSig [3] incorporates signature transforms and controlled differential equations to model time-dependent features.

Table 1 provides a survey and summarizes the performance of several recent survival models across different medical domains and datasets, highlighting their architectural choices and whether they incorporate sequential information. Our model SigBERT compares favorably with these methods. Specifically, it achieves a C-index of 0.75, a mean td-AUC of 0.794, and an IBS below 0.25 over 10 years-values that align well with or exceed several state-of-the-art models, such as CoxSig or Penalized Regression Calibration. While some deep learning approaches like Dynamic-DeepHit or Survival Seq2Seq achieve higher td-AUC, these results are often obtained on synthetic or ICU-based datasets with structured biomarker sequences, which differ substantially from our real-world oncology setting involving complex, unstructured textual data. It is also important to note that strict comparison remains challenging due to differing data modalities and availability, as most datasets used in these works are not publicly accessible or shareable due to clinical data protection policies. In contrast, our study demonstrates strong results on a large-scale real oncology dataset, highlighting the practical relevance and robustness of our method in operational conditions.

Table 1. Overview of state-of-the-art survival models across domains. All reported metrics are taken from the original publications; no external re-evaluation was performed on our dataset.

Model Paper	Field & Datasets	Model Architecture	Sequential Features	C-index	td-AUC	BS
SigBERT (Ours)	Oncology, narrative reports (Léon Bérard)	OncoBERT + Signature + Cox LASSO	Yes, NLP with path signatures	0.75	0.80	≪0.25
MSK-CHORD [13]	Oncology, Real-world (MSK-CHORD)	Random Survival Forest (RSF)	No, features at fixed time point	[0.58, 0.83]	–	–
CoxSig [3]	Maintenance, synthetic + real (NASA, Califrais)	Cox model + Signature transforms	Yes, time-series encoded with Signature	–	[0.74, 0.87]	[0.09, 0.15]
BERTSurv [30]	ICU (MIMIC-III, not oncology)	Transformer (BERT)	Yes, from sequential clinical notes (NLP)	0.7	–	–
DySurv [21]	ICU (MIMIC-III, eICU)	CVAE + LSTM	Yes, sequential EHR (structured)	≈0.60	–	included
Survival Seq2Seq [24]	General (MIMIC-IV + synthetic)	Seq2Seq (GRU-D + Attention)	Yes, hospital time series	–	[0.84, 0.91]	–
Dynamic-DeepHit [17]	Cystic Fibrosis (UK Registry)	Deep RNN + Temporal Attention	Yes, repeated biomarker vectors	[0.94, 0.96]	td-AUC	–
DeepSurv [15]	General + oncology (e.g., METABRIC)	DNN with Cox PH loss	No, static baseline covariates	[0.61, 0.86]	–	–
Landmark Endpoint [10]	Liver disease (PBC), Aging (PAQUID)	Landmark (Cox, RSF, penalized)	Yes, repeated biomarker measures	–	[0.73, 0.87]	[0.076, 0.089]
Penalized Reg. Calib. [27]	Neuromuscular (DMD, MARK-MD)	Penalized Cox + Mixed Effects	Yes, blood biomarker sequences	[0.7, 0.8]	[0.73, 0.87]	–

1.3 Our Contributions

Our approach contributes to survival analysis by leveraging rich representations from NLP-based embeddings, combined with signature transforms to capture the temporal dynamics of patients' follow-up, thus demonstrating the impact of unstructured clinical narratives in oncology risk estimation.

Additionally, our pipeline supports multi-data integration, enabling future incorporation of structured patient data, such as tumor stage, demographic factors, and tumor topography. Moreover, the use of signature transforms allows us to process a very large number of clinical reports per patient without incurring a prohibitive computational cost. Unlike traditional models that struggle with long sequences due to high memory and time complexity, our method efficiently encodes all available follow-up data for each patient. Please refer to our GitHub repository at https://github.com/MINCHELLA-Paul/SigBERT for access to the code. The notebook `SigBERT_study.ipynb` provides numerous complementary results.

2 Method

Our dataset consists of the following information: Each patient is associated with a set of medical reports, each recorded at a specific timestamp, providing a longitudinal sequence of textual data. In addition, we have access to each patient's time in the study and event status, indicating whether the patient experienced the event of interest (*e.g.*, death) or was censored. This forms the foundation for our survival analysis pipeline. One can refer to Fig. 1 at any time for an overview of our global pipeline.

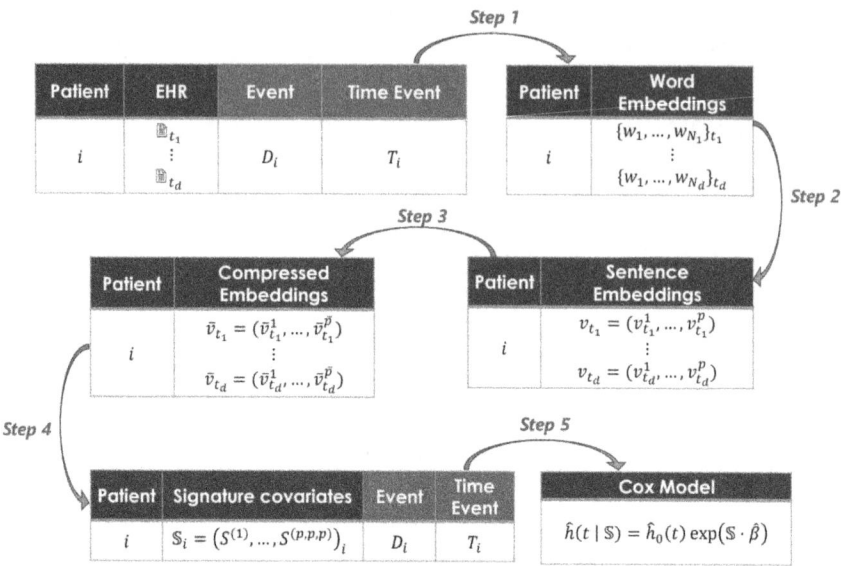

Fig. 1. Global Pipeline: A five-step approach for SigBERT. **Step 1:** Extract word embeddings from medical reports using OncoBERT. **Step 2:** Compute sentence embeddings by averaging word embeddings for each report. **Step 3:** Compress the sentence embeddings through a dimensionality reduction mapping. **Step 4:** Apply the signature transform to extract coefficients capturing temporal dynamics as covariates. **Step 5:** Use a Cox model with LASSO regularization to estimate risk scores.

Before computing embeddings, raw clinical reports are preprocessed to clean and standardize the textual data. The reports are loaded from structured files, with unnecessary columns removed. The text field (constituting the report at time t) is cleaned by stripping redundant metadata, such as the report source when it appears at the beginning. Duplicate reports are dropped to avoid repetition. In parallel, all date-related columns are converted to a consistent datetime format. This preprocessing step helps ensure the text input is clean and coherent, while preserving the temporal structure needed for downstream analysis.

To process long clinical texts, we kept the entire content of each medical report without truncation. Note that OncoBERT [29], being a fine-tuned version of CamemBERT [20], inherits a maximum input length of 512 tokens due to its RoBERTa-based architecture. We will describe it in more detail in the following section. We did not apply any length filtering or summarization at this stage.

Furthermore, to better simulate real-world clinical scenarios, we deliberately mask the last (at least) 100 observed days from each patient's record. This ensures that predictions rely on earlier medical data rather than immediate pre-mortem indicators, improving generalization for prospective survival analysis.

2.1 Embeddings Computation

The first step of our pipeline involves transforming unstructured medical reports into numerical representations using OncoBERT [29]. It is a CamemBERT-based language model fine-tuned on a large corpus of oncology-related clinical notes from Léon Bérard Center, making it particularly suited for extracting meaningful representations from oncology-specific narratives. This approach enables us to numerically encode the semantic information embedded in the textual data while preserving the rich clinical context contained within patient histories. We obtain a dictionary mapping each word (token) to its corresponding embedding vector within the learned (fine-tuned) vector space of dimension $p = 768$. It can be formally expressed as follows for a given patient i:

$$\{\text{word}_1 : v_{w_1}, \ldots, \text{word}_{N_t} : v_{w_{N_t}}\}_i,$$

where N_t is the number of unique tokens in the medical report at time t.

It is worth emphasizing that the superior performance of OncoBERT is consistent with expectations for a risk estimation task in oncology based on French clinical narratives. OncoBERT is a domain-specific language model fine-tuned on cancer-related French medical reports, and thus better captures the linguistic and clinical nuances of the data (including specialized oncology vocabulary and domain-specific phrasing). As such, it is not surprising that this specialized NLP model outperforms more generic approaches: for instance, Word2Vec-based embeddings [22], even with carefully tuned parameters, reach at most a concordance index of 0.6, while CamemBERT-based embeddings reach at most 0.7.

We aim to aggregate these representations into a single vector per report, so that each patient's medical record at time t is captured as a meaningful numerical representation. Thus, we employ the Smooth Inverse Frequency (SIF) method proposed by [1], a robust unsupervised approach for computing sentence embeddings. For a arbitrary report s, its representation is given by:

$$v_s = \frac{1}{|s|} \sum_{w \in s} \frac{a}{f(w) + a} \; v_w \;\; \in \mathbb{R}^p,$$

where $f(w)$ represents the frequency of a given word in the corpus, and a is a smoothing parameter (typically set to 10^{-3}).

While it is common practice to use the CLS token output from BERT-based models to represent entire input sequences, we explored an alternative approach for encoding clinical reports. Although the CLS token was initially considered in our pipeline, we ultimately adopted the SIF method based on retrospective evaluation results and its strong theoretical foundations. Specifically, SIF-based sentence embeddings yielded consistently better predictive performance, including a higher C-index (0.75 vs. 0.70), improved time-dependent AUC, and lower Brier Scores. We attribute these gains to the robustness of the SIF method, which re-weights and averages token-level embeddings to form a more stable and generalizable sentence-level representation. Moreover, SIF offers a practical advantage when handling long clinical texts: by aggregating token embeddings across the entire report - possibly by processing it in overlapping chunks - it allows us to capture information beyond the 512-token input limit inherent to BERT models. In contrast, the CLS token is extracted from a truncated version of the input (limited to 512 tokens) and its representation is tightly dependent on the pretraining and fine-tuning stages of the language model - whereas our OncoBERT model was not specifically optimized for the downstream use of CLS embeddings in survival prediction tasks.

At this point, a patient i with N_i clinical reports can be formally represented by a collection of p-dimensional time-indexed vectors as follows:

$$\left(v_{t_1}, \ldots, v_{t_{N_i}}\right)_i^\top \in \mathbb{R}^{N_i \times p}.$$

We will define the signature transform in the following section, which is the mathematical framework used to extract features from time series for our survival model. For now, it is sufficient to note that for p time series and a given truncation level L, the number of signature coefficients to compute is given by $\frac{p^{L+1}-1}{p-1} = O(p^L)$. This quantity grows exponentially with respect to the number of channels (i.e., time series dimensions) involved. For instance, with $p = 768$ and $L = 3$, this results in approximately 4.5×10^8 coefficients, which is computationally intractable.

We are thus compelled to reduce the dimensionality of the sentence embeddings. This requirement also brings significant advantages. The first is computational: reducing p greatly improves the numerical feasibility of downstream processing. The second is theoretical: the original embedding space of dimension p may be projected into a lower-dimensional space of size $\bar{p}$ while retaining most of the information relevant to our prediction task, namely risk estimation. By applying a linear transformation, we can map the embeddings into this compressed space and carry out computations much more efficiently.

A straightforward approach is to apply Principal Component Analysis (PCA) on all sentence embeddings in the training set to obtain a compression matrix R_{comp}. From a linear algebra perspective, $R_{\text{comp}} \in \mathbb{R}^{\bar{p} \times p}$ is a projection matrix whose rows correspond to the top $\bar{p}$ principal components, i.e., the orthonormal directions that capture the highest variance in the original p-dimensional embedding space. Applying R_{comp} to each sentence embedding results in a lower-dimensional representation in $\mathbb{R}^{\bar{p}}$ that retains as much relevant information as possible in terms of variance. This baseline method is simple to implement, computationally efficient, and often yields satisfactory results in practice.

We define the compressed vector as $\bar{v}_s := R_{\text{comp}} \cdot v_s$. This transformation preserves most of the semantic information while reducing the dimensionality of the paths from $p = 768$ to, for instance, $\bar{p} = 25$. Then, a patient with N_i reports can be formally represented by a family of $\bar{p}$ time series as follows:

$$\left(\bar{v}_{t_1}, \ldots, \bar{v}_{t_{N_i}}\right)_i^\top \in \mathbb{R}^{N_i \times \bar{p}}.$$

The choice of this compression value is based on a retrospective study evaluating the trade-off between computational cost and the C-index achieved on the test set. By progressively increasing the compressed dimension ($\bar{p} = 10, 15, 20, 25, 30, \ldots$), we observed convergence of the C-index on the test set starting from $\bar{p} = 25$. This value was identified as the optimal candidate, as it provides satisfactory performance while guaranteeing computational efficiency.

2.2 Signature Features Extraction

The signature of a path [5], adapted for rough path theory by Terry Lyons [19], provides a systematic method for encoding sequential data into geometric features, using iterated integrals. Consider a p-dimensional path (which means each coordinates form a path), denoted as $v = (v^1, \ldots, v^p)$, defined over the interval $[0, T]$. For any integer $k \geq 1$, any sequence of indices $i_1, \ldots, i_k \in \{1, \ldots, p\}$, any $0 \leq t_1 < \cdots < t_k \leq T$, the iterated integral signature of v up to time $t \in [0, T]$ is defined as:

$$S(v)_{0,t}^{(i_1,\ldots,i_k)} = \int_{0<t_k<t} \cdots \int_{0<t_1<t_2} dv_{t_1}^{i_1} \ldots dv_{t_k}^{i_k}.$$

The collection of these features is organized in tensor form which uniquely encodes the path and is defined as:

$$S^k(v) = \left(S(v)_{0,T}^{(i_1,\ldots,i_k)}\right)_{(i_1,\ldots,i_k)\in\{1,\ldots,p\}^k} \in (\mathbb{R}^p)^{\otimes k}.$$

Thus, the truncated signature up to order L naturally belongs to the truncated tensor algebra $\mathcal{T}^{\leq L}(\mathbb{R}^p) = \bigoplus_{k=0}^{L}(\mathbb{R}^p)^{\otimes k}$ of order L over $\mathbb{R}^p$:

$$S^{\leq L}(v) = \left(S^k(v)\right)_{k=0}^{L} \in \mathcal{T}^{\leq L}(\mathbb{R}^p).$$

In addition to encoding temporal dynamics, this approach handles sequences of varying lengths and is invariant to translation and temporal reparameterization (see [6]), making it well-suited for patients with different study entry points and durations. Moreover, one of the most fundamental and computationally advantageous properties of the signature transform is Chen's identity, which provides a recursive structure for computing signatures efficiently. Given two continuous paths $X : [a, b] \to \mathbb{R}^d$ and $Y : [b, c] \to \mathbb{R}^d$, their concatenation is defined as the path $X * Y : [a, c] \to \mathbb{R}^d$ such that:

$$(X * Y)_t = \begin{cases} X_t, & t \in [a, b], \\ X_b + (Y_t - Y_b), & t \in [b, c]. \end{cases}$$

Chen's identity states that the signature of a concatenated path can be factorized as the tensor product of the signatures of its subpaths:

$$S(X * Y) = S(X) \otimes S(Y).$$

This property is particularly useful in computational applications, as it allows for the efficient computation of path signatures by processing segments separately and combining their signatures multiplicatively, rather than computing the full iterated integral from scratch.

Finally, for a given patient i, the set of extracted covariates over their follow-up period, is denoted as:

$$\mathbb{S}_i = \left(S^{(1)}, \ldots, S^{(1,1)}, \ldots, S^{(1,1,1)}, \ldots, S^{(\bar{p},\bar{p},\bar{p})} \right)_i.$$

In order to ensure unicity of signature, the usual framework incorporates a monotonic component, especially time component. Thus, each patient's time series has been transformed into a set of covariates, providing a structured approach to handling sequential data. This transformation enables the extraction of meaningful temporal features, paving the way for their integration into a regression-based survival model, such as the Cox Proportional Hazards model, to assess patient-specific risk factors.

2.3 Survival Analysis Modelling

Our choice to illustrate the impact of textual data focused on the model of [7], which accounts for censored patients, *i.e.*, those for whom the event of interest T (e.g., death, relapse) has not yet occurred. These observations still contribute to the likelihood estimation, helping to reduce bias and improve the robustness of predictions. The goal is to estimate the probability of a patient surviving beyond time t, noted as $\mathcal{S}(t \mid \mathbb{S}) := \mathbb{P}(T \geq t \mid \mathbb{S})$ when knowing their covariates $\mathbb{S}$. This estimation relies on the key concept of instantaneous hazard rate h, which quantifies the infinitesimal probability of the event occurring at t and is related to survival through the following equation:

$$\mathcal{S}(t \mid \mathbb{S}) = \exp\left(-\int^t h(s \mid \mathbb{S})\,\mathrm{d}s \right).$$

Cox [7] proposed the generalized linear model:

$$h(t \mid \mathbb{S}) = h_0(t) \cdot \exp\left(\mathbb{S} \cdot \boldsymbol{\beta} \right),$$

where $\boldsymbol{\beta} \in \mathbb{R}^{\bar{p}}$ is the vector of parameters to be estimated, and h_0 is the baseline hazard, common to all patients, as estimated by [4]. We define $\eta := \mathbb{S} \cdot \boldsymbol{\beta}$, referred to as the risk score. Estimating $\boldsymbol{\beta}$ involves managing a substantial number of covariates. As mentioned earlier, this is due to the signature transform, which generates a high-dimensional feature space: for p input channels and a truncation level L, the number of resulting signature coefficients scales as $\mathcal{O}(p^L)$. Even after dimensionality reduction, the resulting covariate space remains large. To reduce the risk of overfitting and improve model stability, we apply the LASSO (*Least Absolute Shrinkage and Selection Operator*) regularization to the Cox model, as originally introduced in [28]:

$$\widehat{\boldsymbol{\beta}}^{\ell_1} \in \underset{\boldsymbol{\beta}}{\mathrm{argmax}} \; \log \mathrm{PL}(\boldsymbol{\beta}) - \lambda \|\boldsymbol{\beta}\|_1, \tag{1}$$

where $\mathrm{PL}(\boldsymbol{\beta})$ is the partial likelihood defined in [8], and $\lambda > 0$ the regularization parameter. $\|\boldsymbol{\beta}\|_1$ is the ℓ_1-norm of the parameters $\boldsymbol{\beta}$. The impact of LASSO regularization is twofold: it shrinks some coefficients towards zero, effectively removing less relevant covariates, and it selects only the most important predictors for survival, enhancing model stability. The objective function from (1) to be minimized, with log applied, is explicitly formulated as:

$$\ell(\boldsymbol{\beta}) = \sum_{i:\delta_i=1} \left[\mathbb{S}_i \boldsymbol{\beta} - \log \sum_{j \in \mathcal{R}_i} \exp\left(\mathbb{S}_j \boldsymbol{\beta}\right) \right] - \lambda \sum_{k=1}^{\bar{p}} \beta_k.$$

This formulation provides an explicit likelihood function to be maximized algorithmically, with $\delta_i \in \{0, 1\}$ determining whether an event (e.g., death) has been observed for patient i, associated with study duration T_i, and $\mathcal{R}_i$ represents the risk set *i.e.*, set of individuals still at risk at time of T_i, that is $\mathcal{R}_i = \{j : T_j \geq T_i\}$. Moreover, by enforcing sparsity, the LASSO-regularized Cox model significantly reduces the number of active covariates, leading to faster computational performance. This suggests that the model achieves a favorable balance between overfitting and underfitting, leveraging a compact and efficient representation of the risk factors while maintaining strong predictive power. Finally, the estimated risk score under LASSO regularization is obtained simply as the dot product:

$$\widehat{\eta} = \mathbb{S} \cdot \widehat{\boldsymbol{\beta}}^{\ell_1}.$$

Consequently, our methodology assigns each patient - characterized by a series of medical reports - an estimated risk score $\widehat{\eta}$, effectively capturing the temporal evolution of their clinical trajectory. This structured approach enables a comprehensive integration of narrative data into survival analysis.

3 Experiments

3.1 Cohort

This study complies with the General Data Protection Regulation (GDPR) and falls within the scope of scientific research conducted in the legitimate interest of cancer research, in accordance with Articles 6.1.f and 9.2.j of Regulation (EU) No. 2016/679. This project has been officially registered under the MR004 declaration (V3.2, 23/08/2021) at the Léon Bérard Center, ensuring compliance with legal and ethical standards for processing health data. The data have been carefully anonymized and can only be used within the framework of this study. No patient were opposed to this study. To ensure the reliability of our data, we selected a study cohort consisting of patients hospitalized - at least once - at the Léon Bérard Center from 2000 to 2024, with comprehensive follow-up throughout their medical care to ensure data completeness and accuracy.

The dataset consists of a clean and structured text corpus containing 274,420 medical reports from 7,121 patients, among whom 4,983 are deceased and 2,138 are censored. Reports mainly include consultation reports (63%) and hospital stay reports (32%). Each patient has an average of 39 medical reports (sd 25), reflecting the longitudinal nature of the dataset. The dataset covers all types of cancer, allowing for broad applicability of the survival analysis. The most prevalent cancer types include breast cancer (25%), gynecological cancers (9.7%), gastrointestinal cancers (8.6%), lung cancer (5.5%), prostate cancer (7%), endocrine tumors (4.6%), among others. The median survival time in the cohort is 1,024 days (approximately 2 years and 10 months) and the study period spans from 1997 to 2020, covering the 5th to 95th percentile of diagnosis dates.

3.2 Hyperparameter Search

Our experimental setup is designed to ensure reproducibility, robustness, and realistic evaluation in a complex real-world clinical context. We emphasize that our NLP model, OncoBERT - fine-tuned on oncology-specific clinical notes - is used as is throughout the study without further task-specific adaptation, thereby reflecting practical deployment scenarios. The survival model was trained on a cohort of 3,560 patients (136,748 reports) and evaluated on a separate test set of 3,561 patients (137,672 reports), using a structured and stratified train-test split to preserve temporal and distributional consistency. To calibrate the model, we conducted a grid search for the LASSO regularization parameter λ within the range [0.001, 10], using a fixed step size of 0.001. We selected the value that maximized the cross-validation concordance index (C-index) averaged over five independent validation folds, within the training dataset. Our careful hyperparameter tuning, combined with a large dataset and relevant baseline comparisons, supports the reliability of our results and confirms the model's ability to handle high-dimensional sequential text data.

At this step, the longitudinal data were transformed using the signature method, effectively eliminating any temporal constraints that could arise when subdividing the dataset for cross-validation. The selection criterion aimed to maximize the C-index through five-fold cross-validation. Specifically, for each candidate value of λ, the model was trained on a partition of the training cohort and evaluated on held-out subsets - within the training set -, maintaining equal proportions across folds.

The optimal value was then chosen as the one yielding the highest mean C-index, promoting robust generalization and avoiding overfitting. This tuning process was crucial for balancing model sparsity and predictive accuracy.

3.3 Performance Metrics

The validation process involved random splitting, where the test set was divided into ten disjoint subsets. Model evaluation was then repeated independently on each of these subsets, allowing us to compute mean performance metrics along with their standard deviations. To ensure a comprehensive evaluation, we rely on well-established metrics: the concordance index (C-index), the time-dependent AUC and the Brier Score. These metrics collectively provide a robust assessment of the model's predictive performance by capturing complementary aspects of survival prediction accuracy. The C-index, a fundamental metric in survival analysis introduced by [12], measures the proportion of concordant pairs among all possible pairs. Specifically, if patient j experiences the event before patient i, then the model should assign a higher risk score to j. It is expressed as followed:

$$\text{C-index} = \frac{\sum_{i,j} \mathbb{1}_{\{T_j < T_i\}} \cdot \mathbb{1}_{\{\hat{\eta}_j > \hat{\eta}_i\}} \cdot \delta_j}{\sum_{i,j} \mathbb{1}_{\{T_j < T_i\}} \cdot \delta_j},$$

where T_i and T_j represent the observed survival times of patients i and j, respectively. The estimated risk scores assigned by the model to these patients are denoted as $\hat{\eta}_i$ and $\hat{\eta}_j$. The indicator variable δ_j equals 1 if patient j experienced the event, and 0 otherwise. A C-index of 1 characterizes a perfect model, while a C-index of 0.5 corresponds to random performance. A C-index above 0.7 is generally considered satisfactory.

Its time-dependent counterpart, the td-AUC, is defined and then integrated over the relevant time interval (see [16,25]). It evaluates the model's ability to discriminate between patients who experience an event at time t and those who survive beyond t. This allows for a more precise assessment of the model's predictive power at different time points. By incorporating dynamic survival probabilities, the td-AUC provides a temporal perspective on model performance and is particularly valuable in contexts where the ability to predict risk evolves over time. It is defined as:

$$\widehat{\text{AUC}}(t) = \frac{\sum_{i,j} \mathbb{1}_{\{T_i > t\}} \mathbb{1}_{\{T_j \leq t\}} \cdot \mathbb{1}_{\{\hat{\eta}_j > \hat{\eta}_i\}} \cdot \delta_j(t)}{\sum_{i,j} \mathbb{1}_{\{T_i > t\}} \mathbb{1}_{\{T_j \leq t\}} \cdot \delta_j(t)}.$$

Finally, the function also provides a single summary measure that refers to the mean of the AUC(t) over the time range $[\tau_1, \tau_2]$:

$$\overline{\text{AUC}}(\tau_1, \tau_2) = \frac{1}{\widehat{G}(\tau_1) - \widehat{G}(\tau_2)} \int_{\tau_1}^{\tau_2} \widehat{\text{AUC}}(t) \, d\widehat{G}(t),$$

where $\widehat{G}(t)$ is the Kaplan-Meier estimator [14] of the survival function. This accounts for censoring and provides a single summary measure of model performance across the specified time interval.

In recent years, growing attention has been paid to the calibration of survival models, not just their discriminative ability. While metrics such as the C-index remain central for assessing a model's ability to rank individuals by risk, they do not capture whether predicted survival probabilities are well-aligned with observed outcomes. As a result, proper evaluation now typically includes both discrimination and calibration metrics, to ensure that models are not only capable of ranking patients but also of assigning realistic survival probabilities. Calibration error is quantified by the Brier Score (BS) that evaluates the accuracy of survival predictions by assessing how close the estimated survival probability is to the actual survival status of each individual (also see [16,25]). With previous notations, and denoting $\mathcal{V}$ the set of individuals, the Brier Score can be expressed, at time t, as:

$$\mathrm{BS}(t) = \frac{1}{|\mathcal{V}|} \sum_{i \in \mathcal{V}} \left[\mathbb{1}_{\{T_i \leq t\}} \frac{\left(0 - \widehat{\mathcal{S}}(t \mid \mathbb{X}_i)\right)^2}{\widehat{G}(T_i)} \delta_i + \mathbb{1}_{\{T_i > t\}} \frac{\left(1 - \widehat{\mathcal{S}}(t \mid \mathbb{X}_i)\right)^2}{\widehat{G}(t)} \right].$$

Similar to the td-AUC, the Integrated Brier Score (IBS) provides a global average measure of calibration over a predefined time range $[\tau_1, \tau_2]$, defined as:

$$\mathrm{IBS}(\tau_1, \tau_2) = \frac{1}{\tau_2 - \tau_1} \int_{\tau_1}^{\tau_2} \mathrm{BS}(t) \, \mathrm{d}t.$$

A useful reference point for evaluating the BS (or the IBS) is the naive baseline, where the survival probability $\mathcal{S}(t)$ is set to a constant value of 0.5 for all individuals. In this case, the Brier Score simplifies to $\mathrm{BS}(t) = 0.25$. Thus, a BS (or an IBS) below 0.25 is considered a good indicator of calibration.

3.4 Experimental Results

All our results are summarized in Table 2. Our model achieves a mean C-index of 0.75 (sd 0.014) with a 95% confidence interval [0.7419, 0.7596] (calculated by Jackknife method [11]), indicating good discriminative ability and suggesting the viability of our temporal approach.

Table 2. Evaluation results for our pipeline.

Metric	Test Set
Patients	3,561
Reports	137 672
C-index (mean)	0.75 (sd 0.014)
$\mathrm{CI}_{0.95}$ for C-index	[0.7419, 0.7596]
Correlation log(Time) $\sim$ Risk	Pearson: -0.533 (sd 0.0359)
	Spearman: -0.530 (sd 0.0459)
Mean td-AUC over 10 years	0.794 (sd 0.029)
Integrated Brier Score	3 years: 0.0532 (sd 0.0029)
	5 years: 0.1055 (sd 0.0062)
	10 years: 0.2183 (sd 0.0153)

Figure 2 (a) illustrates the evolution of the C-index on the test set as a function of the number of known reports per patient. The evaluation starts with only two reports per patient, progressively incorporating one additional report at a time until the maximum available number is reached for each patient. The resulting monotonic increase in performance highlights the ability of the signature transform to effectively leverage sequential information, demonstrating its impact on improving the model's predictive accuracy as more medical history is incorporated. This demonstrates that as the number of known time points

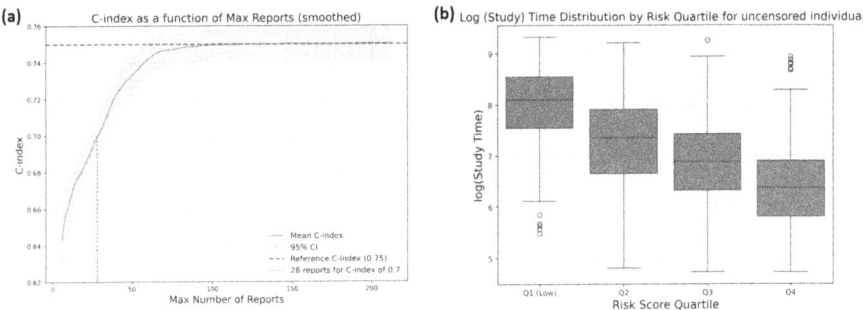

Fig. 2. (a) Test C-index progression as a function of the maximum number of known reports per patient; (b) Log-transformed study time distribution across risk quartiles. (a) The C-index starts at 0.63 with only two reports per patient and increases steadily, reaching 0.70 at 28 reports and converging to 0.75 beyond 100 reports. This highlights how access to a richer medical history improves prediction, especially with reports closer to the event. (b) Boxplots illustrate the distribution of log-transformed survival times across predicted risk quartiles. Despite some natural overlap due to the complexity of survival data, a clear decreasing trend is observed: higher predicted risk scores align with shorter observed survival times. Both ANOVA and Kruskal-Wallis tests yield p-values below 10^{-5}, confirming the statistical significance of this separation.

increases, more information can be extracted, leading to a more accurate estimation of overall survival.

The mean td-AUC over 10 years is 0.794 (sd 0.029), and the IBS remains below 0.25 up to 10 years, reaching 0.0532 (sd 0.0029) at 3 years, suggesting that the model maintains good predictive accuracy while ensuring proper calibration. These results align with state-of-the-art model performance while being obtained in a complex real-world clinical setting, reinforcing the credibility of our approach.

The correlation between the logarithm of the time event for uncensored $\log(T)$ and the estimated risk score $\widehat{\eta}$ is significantly negative (Pearson: -0.533, Spearman: -0.530, both with p-value $<10^{-5}$), demonstrating that higher estimated risk scores are associated with shorter survival times. This reinforces the model's ability to capture meaningful risk stratification.

Figure 2 (b) further illustrates this relationship by displaying the distribution of log-transformed study durations across predicted risk quartiles. Despite some natural overlap due to the complexity of survival prediction, a clear trend emerges: Patients with shorter survival times tend to be classified into higher risk quartiles.

Additionally, the model effectively handles a large number of clinical reports, leveraging more than 100,000 medical documents for training and evaluation. The extensive dataset ensures robust performance assessment over numerous time points, highlighting the scalability and real-world applicability of our approach.

To assess its added value, we compared it to several naive baseline methods. First, we considered using only the last available clinical report for each patient, extracting its sentence embedding and feeding it directly into a Cox model; this resulted in a low C-index of 0.55. We then tested a simple average of all sentence embeddings per patient as input to the same model, which led to a slightly improved yet still unsatisfactory C-index of 0.57. Lastly, we evaluated the Cox-Time model [16], which incorporates temporal features directly as covariates; it achieved a C-index of 0.63. These results demonstrate that simplistic representations or direct time encodings are insufficient to accurately capture the temporal complexity of patient trajectories. In contrast, our method, grounded in rigorous mathematical feature extraction, substantially improves performance, emphasizing the importance of modeling temporal dynamics with structured and principled approaches.

Our project relies on several specialized packages to ensure efficiency and accuracy throughout the pipeline. `SIF` [1] implements the smooth inverse frequency method for computing sentence embeddings. The extraction of path signatures, a core component of our feature representation, is performed using `iisignature` [26], which exploits Chen's identity for efficient computation of iterated-integral signatures. For the survival model, we employ `skglm` [2], a high-performance package designed for generalized linear models, allowing efficient LASSO-penalized Cox regression. The estimation of survival functions, risk scores, and baseline hazards is handled through `lifelines` [9], which provides a comprehensive framework for survival analysis. Finally, we use `sksurv` [23] to compute key evaluation metrics, such as the concordance index, time-dependent AUC, and Brier Score, supporting rigorous model assessment.

Furthermore, the use of compression, LASSO regularization, and Chen's identity for signatures enables efficient training and inference, requiring only a few minutes once word embeddings are extracted, highlighting another unique advantage of our model.

4 Conclusion

Our model SigBERT highlights the potential of leveraging sequential textual data for survival analysis in oncology by introducing a structured and reproducible pipeline. Indeed, the judicious combination of a fine-tuned NLP model, signature transforms to capture the temporal progression of patient follow-ups, and a Cox model with LASSO regularization leads to consistent and promising results. These findings pave the way for extending the model to the entire patient database, enabling broader generalization of the approach.

Among the limitations of our study, one key constraint lies in the necessity of compressing the original high-dimensional embeddings before applying the signature transform. Without this step, the number of coefficients to compute becomes prohibitively large, rendering the approach computationally intractable. While this compression might initially seem restrictive, it opens an interesting avenue of research into the sparsity and intrinsic geometry of the embedding space.

It suggests that only a carefully selected subset or combination of embedding dimensions may be sufficient for effective risk estimation and survival prediction.

Another important consideration is the dependency on OncoBERT, which, although specifically fine-tuned for our oncology dataset, can in principle be replaced with other natural language models. Furthermore, our model is currently best suited to data collected at the Léon Bérard Center, where follow-up medical reports are systematically available. A more thorough assessment of the model's generalizability will require applying it to sequential textual data from patients in other institutions and clinical settings. To date, we have not benchmarked alternative language models on this specific survival task, which is partly due to the novelty of our approach (combining NLP embeddings with signature transforms and Cox survival modeling). As such, our pipeline represents a first step toward this direction, and future work will be needed to assess the impact of alternative embedding strategies within this framework.

A key avenue for improvement lies in integrating tabular and sequential data alongside textual embeddings. In future work, we plan to systematically compare different survival models to assess their relative performance. While we employed the Cox LASSO model due to its strong empirical results in our experiments, a broader benchmarking study is required. This will involve evaluating alternative approaches such as Random Survival Forests, Cox Neural Networks, and Cox Elastic Net, among others. Establishing a standardized comparison framework will allow us to identify the most robust and interpretable survival models for oncology risk estimation. Finally, by combining narrative and structured data - such as patient characteristics, disease features, and biological markers -, we aim to develop a multimodal survival model capable of providing more personalized and accurate oncology care.

Acknowledgments. This study was funded by SHAPE-Med@Lyon.

Disclosure of Interests. The other authors declare no potential conflicts of interest.

References

1. Arora, S., Liang, Y., Ma, T.: A simple but tough-to-beat baseline for sentence embeddings. In: International Conference on Learning Representations (ICLR) (2017). Published as a Conference Paper at ICLR 2017
2. Bertrand, Q., Klopfenstein, Q., Bannier, P.-A., Gidel, G., Massias, M.: Beyond L1: faster and better sparse models with skglm. In: NeurIPS (2022)
3. Bleistein, L., Nguyen, V.T., Fermanian, A., Guilloux, A.: Dynamical survival analysis with controlled latent states (2024). arXiv:2401.17077 [stat.ML]. https://arxiv.org/abs/2401.17077
4. Breslow, N.E.: Contribution to the discussion of the paper by D. R. Cox. J. Roy. Stat. Soc. Ser. B (Methodol.) **34**(2), 216–217 (1972)
5. Chen, K.T.: Iterated integrals and exponential homomorphisms. Proc. Lond. Math. Soc. **3**(4), 502–512 (1954)
6. Chevyrev, I., Kormilitzin, A.: A primer on the signature method in machine learning (2025). arXiv:1603.03788 [stat.ML]. https://arxiv.org/abs/1603.03788

7. Cox, D.R.: Regression models and life-tables. J. Roy. Stat. Soc. Ser. B (Methodol.) **34**(2), 187–202 (1972). https://doi.org/10.1111/j.2517-6161.1972.tb00899.x
8. Cox, D.R.: Partial likelihood. Biometrika **62**(2), 269–276 (1975). https://doi.org/10.1093/biomet/62.2.269
9. Davidson-Pilon, C.: lifelines: survival analysis in Python. J. Open Source Softw. **4**(40), 1317 (2019). https://doi.org/10.21105/joss.01317
10. Devaux, A., Genuer, R., Peres, K., Proust-Lima, C.: Individual dynamic prediction of clinical endpoint from large dimensional longitudinal biomarker history: a landmark approach. BMC Med. Res. Methodol. **22**(1), 188 (2022). https://doi.org/10.1186/s12874-022-01660-3
11. Efron, B.: The Jackknife, the Bootstrap and Other Resampling Plans. CBMS-NSF Regional Conference Series in Applied Mathematics, vol. 38. SIAM (1982). https://doi.org/10.1137/1.9781611970319
12. Harrell, F.E., Califf, R.M., Pryor, D.B., Lee, K.L., Rosati, R.A.: Evaluating the yield of medical tests. J. Am. Med. Assoc. **247**(18), 2543–2546 (1982)
13. Jee, J., Fong, C., Pichotta, K., et al.: Automated real-world data integration improves cancer outcome prediction. Nature **636**, 728–736 (2024). https://doi.org/10.1038/s41586-024-08167-5
14. Kaplan, E.L., Meier, P.: Nonparametric estimation from incomplete observations. J. Am. Stat. Assoc. **53**(282), 457–481 (1958). https://doi.org/10.2307/2281868
15. Katzman, J.L., Shaham, U., Cloninger, A., Bates, J., Jiang, T., Kluger, Y.: DeepSurv: personalized treatment recommender system using a Cox proportional hazards deep neural network. BMC Med. Res. Methodol. **18**(1) (2018). https://doi.org/10.1186/s12874-018-0482-1
16. Kvamme, H., Borgan, Ø., Scheel, I.: Time-to-event prediction with neural networks and Cox regression. J. Mach. Learn. Res. **20**(116), 1–30 (2019). http://jmlr.org/papers/v20/18-424.html
17. Lee, C., Yoon, J., van der Schaar, M.: Dynamic-DeepHit: a deep learning approach for dynamic survival analysis with competing risks based on longitudinal data. IEEE Trans. Biomed. Eng. (2019). https://par.nsf.gov/servlets/purl/10099761
18. Lee, C., Zame, W.R., Yoon, J., van der Schaar, M.: DeepHit: a deep learning approach to survival analysis with competing risks. In: Proceedings of the Thirty-Second AAAI Conference on Artificial Intelligence (AAAI-18), pp. 2314–2321. AAAI Press (2018), Section: Discriminative Performance
19. Lyons, T.J.: Differential equations driven by rough signals. Revista Matemática Iberoamericana **14**(2), 215–310 (1998)
20. Martin, L., et al.: CamemBERT: a tasty French language model. In: Proceedings of the 58th Annual Meeting of the Association for Computational Linguistics. Association for Computational Linguistics (2020). https://doi.org/10.18653/v1/2020.acl-main.645
21. Mesinovic, M., Watkinson, P., Zhu, T.: DySurv: dynamic deep learning model for survival analysis with conditional variational inference (2024). arXiv:2310.18681 [cs.LG]. https://arxiv.org/abs/2310.18681
22. Mikolov, T., Chen, K., Corrado, G., Dean, J.: Efficient estimation of word representations in vector space (2013). arXiv:1301.3781 [cs.CL]. https://arxiv.org/abs/1301.3781
23. Pölsterl, S.: scikit-survival: a library for time-to-event analysis built on top of scikit-learn. J. Mach. Learn. Res. **21**(212), 1–6 (2020). http://jmlr.org/papers/v21/20-729.html

24. Pourjafari, E., et al.: Survival Seq2Seq: a survival model based on sequence to sequence architecture (2022). arXiv:2204.04542 [cs.LG]. https://arxiv.org/abs/2204.04542
25. Pölsterl, S.: Evaluating survival models (2019). https://k-d-w.org/blog/2019/05/evaluating-survival-models/
26. Reizenstein, J., Graham, B.: The iisignature library: efficient calculation of iterated-integral signatures and log signatures (2018). arXiv:1802.08252 [cs.DS]. https://arxiv.org/abs/1802.08252
27. Signorelli, M., Spitali, P., Szigyarto, C.A., Tsonaka, R.: Penalized regression calibration: a method for the prediction of survival outcomes using complex longitudinal and high-dimensional data. Stat. Med. **40**(27), 6178–6196 (2021). https://doi.org/10.1002/sim.9178
28. Tibshirani, R.: The Lasso method for variable selection in the Cox model. Stat. Med **16**(4), 385–395 (1997). https://doi.org/10.1002/(SICI)1097-0258(19970228)16:4<385::AID-SIM380>3.0.CO;2-3
29. Vienne, R., Filori, Q., Susplugas, V., Crochet, H., Verlingue, L.: Abstract 3475: prediction of nausea or vomiting, and fatigue or malaise in cancer care. Cancer Res. **84**, 3475 (2024). https://doi.org/10.1158/1538-7445.AM2024-3475
30. Zhao, Y., Hong, Q., Zhang, X., Deng, Y., Wang, Y., Petzold, L.: BERTSurv: BERT-based survival models for predicting outcomes of trauma patients (2021). arXiv:2103.10928 [cs.AI]. https://arxiv.org/abs/2103.10928

TIDS: A Thermal Imaging Dataset for Subclinical Mastitis in Dairy Sheep

Georgios Botsoglou[1], Marios Lysitsas[2], Dimitris Dimitriadis[1](✉), Constantina Tsokana[1], George Valiakos[2], and Grigorios Tsoumakas[1]

[1] Aristotle University of Thessaloniki, Thessaloniki, Greece
{gbotso,dndimitri,greg}@csd.auth.gr, ctsokana@vet.auth.gr
[2] University of Thessaly, Volos, Greece
{mlysitsas,georgevaliakos}@uth.gr

Abstract. Subclinical mastitis (SCM) in dairy sheep is a significant challenge in the agricultural and veterinary sectors, leading to substantial financial losses for farmers and negatively impacting overall dairy sheep productivity. It often goes unnoticed due to the absence of clinical signs, making early diagnosis particularly difficult. However, early identification of SCM is critical, as it allows for timely intervention that can prevent disease progression, reduce economic losses, and minimize the need for costly treatments. This work focuses on detecting SCM in dairy sheep using a non-invasive thermal imaging approach. A major limitation in this field is the lack of available datasets, as acquiring such data presents several challenges. Capturing clear thermal images of dairy sheep udders is hindered by factors such as animal movement, environmental conditions, and variability in breed, health, and udder size. Furthermore, large, diverse sample sizes are required, making data acquisition resource-intensive. Ethical concerns regarding animal welfare and the high cost of thermal imaging equipment add to the complexity. These challenges hinder the use of data-driven techniques, such as deep learning models, which require large datasets. In this paper, our contributions are two-fold: first, we introduce a novel dataset, TIDS, along with an explanatory analysis supported by domain expertise. Second, we apply deep learning models to detect SCM in dairy sheep and provide a comprehensive methodology, marking a novel approach in this area.

Keywords: Subclinical Mastitis · Thermal Images · Convolutional Neural Networks · Deep Learning

1 Introduction

Mastitis is defined as inflammation of varying degrees of severity of the mammary gland, and constitutes a crucial pathological condition for dairy ruminants, including lactating ewes [1–3]. The two primary types of mastitis encountered are clinical and subclinical. Clinical mastitis has symptoms that can be perceived macroscopically during clinical examination of the animal and/or is associated with alteration, visible with the naked eye, in the characteristics of the milk. It is severe and requires treatment. However, the majority of cases encountered in sheep belong to the subclinical type of the disease, where there are no visible symptoms or observable changes in the macroscopic characteristics of the obtained milk [1,4]. However, inflammation and histological lesions are present [5]. Therefore, in animals with SCM, a decrease in the milk production, milk yield, and cheese-making properties is documented.

Moreover, the prevalence of the disease in dairy flocks is estimated at 5–30%, or even more [4,6]. Through this considerable reduction in productivity and quality, significant economic losses are caused in sheep farms worldwide [7–9], while animal welfare concerns are also considerable [3,10]. Finally, public health and food safety concerns regarding SCM are not negligible, since pathogens with zoonotic potential are regularly implicated in SCM cases and the production of enterotoxins in milk is possible [4,11].

Identification of SCM is challenging, due to the total absence of any detectable clinical changes and requires specific tests in milk. As a result, it is regularly underdiagnosed. The tool currently utilized most for screening is the estimation of somatic cell count in milk using the California Mastitis Test (CMT). However, the gold standard for identification of the etiologic agents of SCM, which are usually bacteria, is aerobic culture. This approach has certain limitations and requirements, mostly regarding cost and time. Therefore, evaluation and establishment of new fast and non-invasive diagnostic tools is considered beneficial [1,2].

Infrared thermography (IRT) is a technology with numerous potential applications in both human and veterinary medicine, since it provides real-time and non-invasive measurements of body temperature through converting infrared radiation emitted by the heat source into respective pixel intensity [12,13]. Promising implementations have been described in literature and adopted in various medical fields, that mainly concern its evaluation as a diagnostic tool through the detection of increased temperature values, as a result of pyrexia or localized inflammation in variable pathological conditions [14]. Similarly, in veterinary medicine, infrared thermography has been investigated for the detection of body temperature variations of the examined animals, with promising results in various fields, like bovine mastitis [12]. Besides, in mastitis, inflammatory processes occurring in the mammary gland increase the udder's inner and surface temperatures [13,15]. This allows for the employment of IRT for the detection of these variations, even in cases of SCM [15–17]. In that regard, it has also been examined in ovine mastitis with promising results [18–21], but current data are rather limited yet.

Deep learning has been applied to predictive tasks using IRT [22]. Specifically, computer vision-based learning models analyze patterns in thermal images to classify them accordingly. However, in our study of thermal imaging for SCM detection in dairy sheep, several challenges arise. To the best of our knowledge, no publicly available datasets exist for training and testing deep learning models in this domain. Consequently, there is also a lack of related research leveraging deep learning for SCM prediction in dairy sheep. This leads to our central research question: "Can we develop a high-quality thermal image dataset with input from domain experts to enable the creation of effective deep learning models?".

To address this question, we collected thermal images from 16 dairy sheep farms and carried out extensive manual work to classify the images as healthy or affected by SCM, using somatic cell count (SCC) measurements conducted in laboratories. The dataset was carefully curated, and various preprocessing steps were performed to ensure compatibility with our deep learning models. Since this dataset is newly introduced, we also conducted an exploratory analysis with domain experts to extract relevant features. This analysis highlighted the challenges of addressing the classification problem using statistical or traditional machine learning approaches. Finally, several deep learning models were applied as baselines for evaluation. Our results are promising, while the dataset also presents several challenges that the research community can further explore.

Figure 1 provides an overview of the workflow presented in this paper. Specifically, we first collected thermal images and milk samples from sheep farms to construct the TIDS dataset. This dataset was then used both for in-depth analysis and for training and evaluating classification models using machine learning and deep learning techniques.

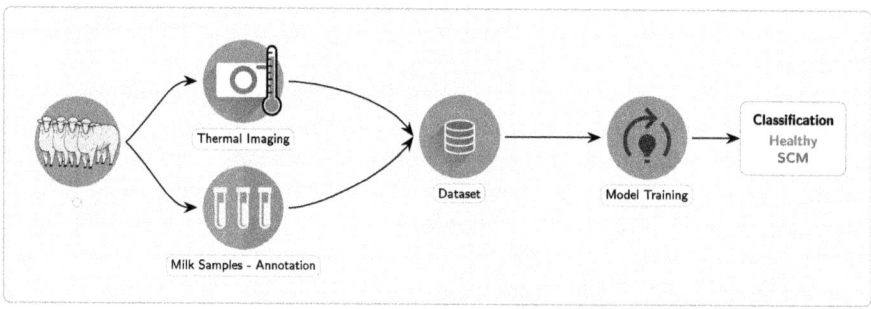

Fig. 1. Schematic overview of the creation of TIDS, combining thermal images and annotated milk samples to support the classification of healthy and SCM cases.

The remainder of this paper is organized as follows. Section 2 provides a detailed description of the dataset, including the acquisition process conducted by domain experts, the preprocessing steps required for data preparation, and the exploratory analysis. Section 3 outlines the baseline models used and the learning process and presents the results along with a discussion of key findings. Section 4 reviews related work, Sect. 5 discusses the results in detail, and Sect. 6 concludes the paper with suggestions for future research.

2 The Dataset

In this section, we introduce the TIDS (Thermal Imaging Dataset for Subclinical Mastitis in Dairy Sheep)[1]. We first outline the dataset acquisition process, detailing the camera used, its settings, the selected farms, and the criteria for image collection. Next, we describe the preprocessing steps applied to prepare the images for classification. Given that this dataset is newly introduced, we also conducted an exploratory analysis to examine key statistical insights related to SCM. With guidance from domain experts, we defined relevant features and trained various machine learning classifiers on the features produced.

2.1 Acquisition

Farms and Animals Included in this Study. A total of 16 dairy sheep farms located in central Greece were selected for this study according to the following criteria: breeding Lacaune sheep (crossbred or purebred), having an automatic milking system, documentation and availability of detailed history of every previous pathological condition and treatment of the selected animals, and vaccination for contagious agalactia. All ewes were examined prior to the sampling by the same experienced personnel, to ensure that they are phenotypically healthy, free of clinical mastitis and other systemic diseases. Moreover, to achieve uniformity regarding the lactation stage and reduce its effect in the obtained results, each selected animal was between the 2nd and the 4th month of its lactation period at the moment of the sampling. The number of animals included from each farm ranged from 25 to 66.

Collection of Milk Samples. A single visit was carried out to each farm and milk samples were collected during routine morning milking. All the relevant procedures were carried out according to the guidelines provided by the National Mastitis Council. In particular, pledgets and 70% ethyl alcohol solution were used to thoroughly scrub both teats of each udder. Initially, CMT was performed. The first three streams were discarded, and then the necessary quantity of milk was added to the paddle disc for the test. Subsequently, two sterile vials with preservative (0.1 g sodium azide, Merck KGaA, Darmstadt, Germany) were aseptically filled with approximately 40 mL of milk for the SCC test with Lactoscan SCC counter. Each vial was labeled with the date, animal code, and side of the udder half and milk samples were transported to the laboratory within two hours. All the procedures mentioned above were performed by the same experienced personnel to reduce the subjectivity of CMT assessment and ensure similar sampling conditions.

Thermal Imaging. Thermal images were received from each animal, just before obtaining milk samples, using a FLIR E96 24° camera (Teledyne FLIR

---

[1] The dataset can be accessed at https://doi.org/10.5281/zenodo.15619247.

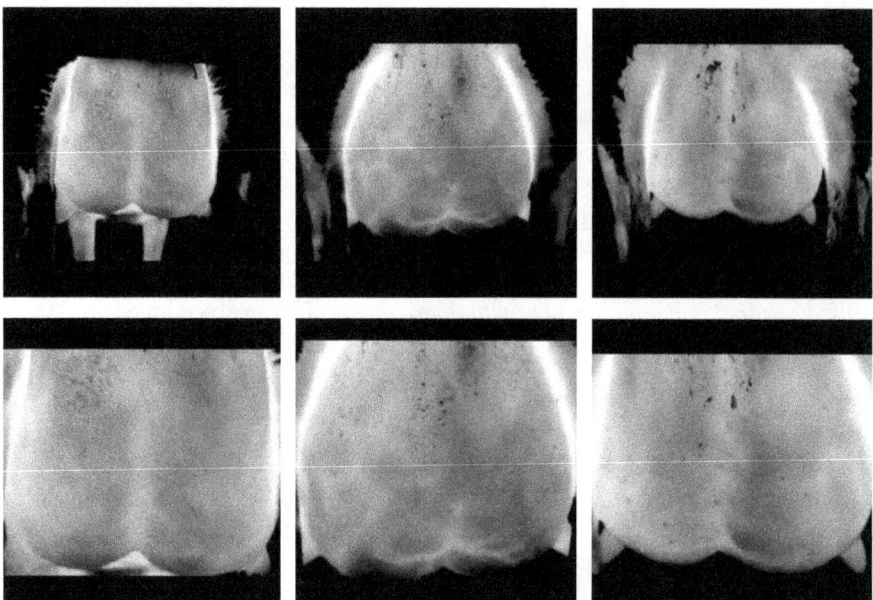

Fig. 2. Thermal imaging examples showing paired full and cropped ROI images. Samples 1–2 (columns 1–2) are healthy, while Sample 3 (column 3) is affected by SCM. Top row shows full thermal images, bottom row shows corresponding cropped regions of interest. Thermal intensity is displayed with white indicating higher temperatures and black indicating lower temperatures.

LLC., Wilsonville, OR, USA). Initially, environmental conditions (temperature and humidity) were recorded using a COMET U3120 Datalogger (COMET SYSTEM s.r.o., Roznov pod Radhostem, Czech Republic) and the obtained measurements were evaluated in the corresponding camera settings fields. Emissivity was set to 0.98. Then, images were taken at a distance of 70 cm from the posterior surface of the udder. All procedures were carried out before milking and in the milking parlor to avoid the effects of climatic conditions (wind, rain, etc.). Examples of thermal images are shown in Fig. 2.

Somatic Cell Count. [2] A direct fluorescent image low-magnification microscopic recognition method was utilized for the SCC, using a LACTOSCAN SCC counter and the compatible kit, according to the guidelines provided by the manufacturer (Milkotronic Ltd., Nova Zagora, Bulgaria). This technique enables the detection and quantification of somatic cells in milk by fluorescent staining of cellular DNA, followed by low-magnification microscopic recognition, providing a rapid and reliable assessment of udder inflammation, while it has been previously employed in dairy sheep [23], demonstrating reliability for SCM detection.

---

[2] the number of somatic cells found in a millilitre of milk.

Before the test, milk samples were heated to 40°C using a water bath, cooled to 20°C and vortexed for 15–20 s to distribute fat uniformly. Then each milk sample was diluted with water at a ratio of 1:1 ratio immediately before testing, as recommended by the manufacturer, since ovine milk typically contains >5% fat. A quantity of 100µl of the diluted samples was inoculated in microtubes containing SOFIA GREEN lyophilized dye and they were vortexed for approximately 10 sec. Subsequently, 8µl were received from the microtubes and added in a predefined chamber of a four-chamber disposable chip that was inserted in the analyzer. All udder halves were classified in five categories according to the number of somatic cells per ml of the respective milk sample (1: <250,000; 2: 250,000–500,000; 3: 500,000–1,500,000; 4: 1,500,000–5,000,000; 5: >5,000,000), based on the results obtained from the Lactoscan SCC counter. Thresholds suggested in literature for discrimination of subclinical mastitis from healthy udder halves [1,4,24] and the empirical SCC ranges corresponding to positive CMT results were used in this categorization, to further classify SCM cases according to the severity of the inflammation process. All samples of the categories 3, 4 and 5 were defined as SCM-positive, while samples of the categories 1 and 2, as healthy. The classification was performed at the udder half level; however, for the purposes of model development and evaluation, the health status was assigned at the animal level. Specifically, animals with at least one udder half classified as category 3, 4, or 5 were labeled as SCM, while animals with both udder halves in categories 1 or 2 were considered healthy. All animals included in the analysis had high-quality thermal images with clear visibility of the udder surface, ensuring consistent input quality across cases.

2.2 Preprocessing

The dataset consists of 418 thermal images, each corresponding to a different dairy sheep - 207 images from sheep affected by SCM and 211 from healthy sheep. The dataset was further preprocessed, as this is a crucial step in training deep learning models to enhance their generalization ability and robustness. A number of preprocessing steps taken are explained, alongside various transformations meant to help the model given the limited amount of samples.

The udder region was manually cropped from each thermal image to remove irrelevant areas outside the region of interest. The cropped images were then resized to 224 × 224 pixels to standardize input dimensions for further processing. Resizing was performed by adjusting the largest dimension to 224 pixels while maintaining the original aspect ratio. In experiments involving deep learning, padding was then applied as necessary to achieve the final square dimensions. Figure 2 shows some examples before and after cropping.

2.3 Exploratory Analysis

Thermal imaging analysis for SCM detection has received limited attention in the literature. Exploratory data analysis was performed to examine the patterns and characteristics in the thermal data, which can support the later development of predictive models.

Feature Extraction. Key features for thermal image classification were identified through a comprehensive review of relevant literature. A set of features was extracted, encompassing statistical measures such as average (mean) temperature, maximum (hottest) temperature, and temperature variation (standard deviation) within the thermal image. To better understand how temperatures are spread out in the thermal image, percentiles (25th, 50th, and 75th) were used, along with the interquartile range (IQR), which shows the range where most temperatures fall. The difference between the highest and lowest temperatures (maximum and minimum intensity) was also measured to show the full range of temperature variation in the area. Shape characteristics were described using skewness and kurtosis, which provide insight into the asymmetry and peakedness of the temperature distribution, respectively. Information entropy was calculated to assess the complexity and variability of the pixel intensity patterns, with higher values indicating more diverse temperature distributions. Morphological features were derived by applying image erosion, and the mean pixel value of the eroded images was used to capture the structural characteristics and spatial distribution of high-temperature regions.

Although it might appear self-evident that feature distributions differ between healthy and affected udders, Mann-Whitney U tests were employed to rigorously quantify these differences. Significant differences ($p < 0.05$) were observed in mean and percentile intensities, IQR, skewness, kurtosis, and eroded mean, indicating that these features capture meaningful physiological variations and serve as effective discriminators. In contrast, standard deviation, temperature range difference, and entropy did not show significant differences, suggesting limited discriminatory power when considered individually.

Figure 3[3] illustrates the distributions of several image-derived features across healthy and mastitis-affected groups. The mean intensity for healthy samples shows a bimodal distribution, suggesting possible subgroups within the class, while the mastitis group is more unimodal and shifted toward lower values. The percentile features (25th, 50th, and 75th) consistently exhibit leftward shifts in the mastitis group, reflecting reduced thermal intensity. All percentile histograms show sharply peaked central bins, likely due to value rounding or discrete measurement effects. The IQR distribution is narrower and more concentrated in healthy samples, whereas mastitis samples show higher variability and a long tail. In terms of shape, skewness is more negative in healthy samples, while kurtosis is slightly higher, indicating heavier tails. Both features again show pro-

---

[3] The histograms generated using Seaborn's [25] histplot function with the default binning strategy (bins='auto'). This method automatically determines the number and width of bins based on the data distribution, optimizing the balance between resolution and smoothness. This adaptive binning allows each feature's histogram to best represent the underlying data characteristics without manual bin width specification.

nounced central peaks, indicating non-Gaussian behavior. The eroded mean is higher in healthy cases and displays more symmetry, while mastitis samples show a slight leftward skew. Temperature range difference is heavily right-skewed with a dominating spike near 1.0 for both groups, suggesting a ceiling effect. Entropy is tightly distributed around 6.5–7.0 with little variation, but mastitis samples trend slightly lower.

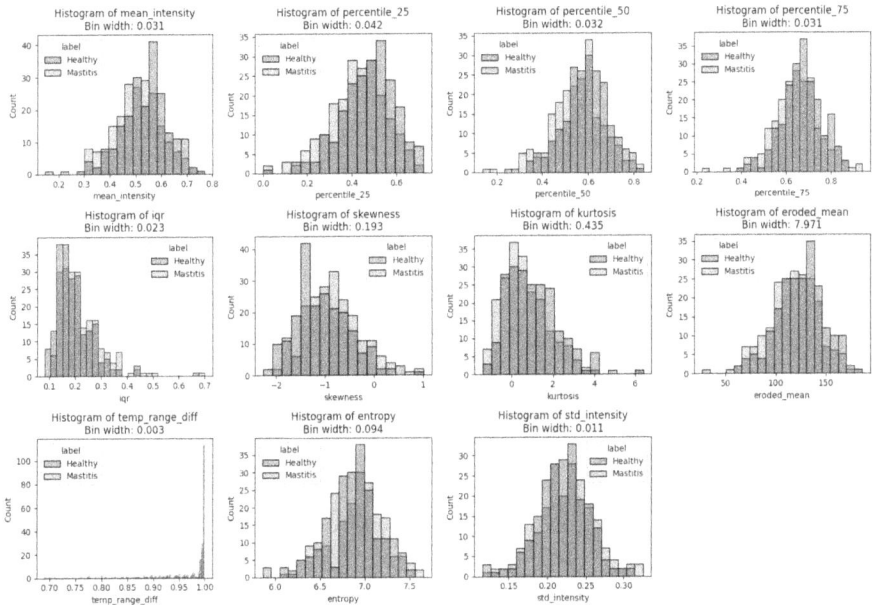

Fig. 3. Distribution of the Features for Healthy and SCM-Affected Udders. Histograms show the count distribution for each feature, with separate distributions for healthy and mastitis cases

Finally, the standard deviation of intensity is among the most normally distributed features, with healthy samples slightly more peaked and centered. These patterns highlight not only differences between the two classes but also the non-normal and often discretized nature of several features, which has implications for statistical modeling and classifier choice.

Classification. Various machine learning models were trained and optimized. The dataset (418 thermal images) is split into training and testing sets using an 80-20 split. We excluded temperature range difference feature from the set of features, since we observed extremely low variance across both healthy and mastitis samples. Feature scaling is applied using z-score normalization to standardize the features, which is critical for models sensitive to input scale, such as SVM and K-Nearest Neighbors (KNN).

Table 1. Best Parameters for Different Models

Model	Best Parameters
SVM	C: 1, Gamma: 0.01, Kernel: RBF
XGBoost	Learning Rate: 0.1, Max Depth: 4, Estimators: 300
Logistic Regression	C: 0.01, Penalty: L2
Random Forest	Max Depth: 5, Min Split: 5, Estimators: 200
KNN	Neighbors: 9, Weights: Uniform
Gradient Boosting	Learning Rate: 0.2, Max Depth: 5, Estimators: 300
AdaBoost	Learning Rate: 0.01, Estimators: 200

Hyperparameter tuning is performed for each model with a grid search in a 5-fold cross-validation manner in the training set. The models evaluated include SVM, XGBoost, Logistic Regression, Random Forest, KNN, Gradient Boosting, AdaBoost, Naive Bayes and Linear Discriminant Analysis (LDA). Most of these models were implemented using the scikit-learn library[4], a widely used Python toolkit for machine learning that provides efficient and user-friendly tools for model training, evaluation, and validation. The XGBoost model was integrated separately using its dedicated Python package due to its specialized implementation for gradient boosting[5]. For each model, a predefined grid of hyperparameters is explored to identify the optimal configuration. The best hyperparameters are used to train the final models, and predictions are made on the test set.

For the models where parameter tuning was conducted the best performing parameters found are presented in Table 1.

The resulting classification performance metrics for each model are presented in Table 2. Accuracy is defined as

$$\text{Accuracy} = \frac{TP + TN}{TP + TN + FP + FN}.$$

The F1 score is the harmonic mean of precision and recall:

$$F1 = 2 \times \frac{\text{Precision} \times \text{Recall}}{\text{Precision} + \text{Recall}},$$

where precision and recall are given by

$$\text{Precision} = \frac{TP}{TP + FP}, \quad \text{Recall} = \frac{TP}{TP + FN}.$$

Here, TP, TN, FP, and FN denote true positives, true negatives, false positives, and false negatives, respectively. All metrics were calculated using the default classification threshold of 0.5 on predicted probabilities. Feature importance analysis revealed that entropy, skewness, 25th percentile and Kurtosis were the most significant features for the model's predictive performance.

---

[4] https://scikit-learn.org/.
[5] https://pypi.org/project/xgboost/.

Table 2. Performance metrics for different models. The highest F1-score is shown in bold.

Model	F1 Score	Precision	Recall	Accuracy
SVM	0.5823	0.6571	0.5227	0.6071
XGBoost	**0.7010**	0.6415	0.7727	0.6548
Logistic Regression	0.5526	0.6562	0.4773	0.5952
Random Forest	0.6667	0.6744	0.6591	0.6548
KNN	0.5600	0.6774	0.4773	0.6071
Gradient Boosting	0.6875	0.6346	0.7500	0.6429
AdaBoost	0.6990	0.6102	0.8182	0.6310
Naive Bayes	0.5789	0.6875	0.5000	0.6190
LDA	0.5385	0.6176	0.4773	0.5714

The feature importance of models which support their identification are shown in Table 3. The feature importance analysis reveals that skewness and entropy are consistently among the top three most important features across all models, highlighting their strong predictive power for SCM detection. Notably, AdaBoost places an exceptionally high importance on skewness (0.5129), making it the most dominant feature in any model. Feature importance analysis indicates that statistical properties such as skewness and entropy tend to have higher importance scores compared to other features, suggesting a relatively greater influence on the models' predictions.

Table 3. Top 3 Most Important Features for Each Model with Importance Scores

Model	Feature	Importance Score
XGBoost	Skewness	0.1111
	Entropy	0.1072
	25th Percentile	0.1040
Random Forest	Skewness	0.1324
	Entropy	0.1205
	Kurtosis	0.1060
Gradient Boosting	Entropy	0.2168
	Skewness	0.1509
	Kurtosis	0.1272
AdaBoost	Skewness	0.5129
	Entropy	0.2965
	25th Percentile	0.1907

3 Experimental Design and Results

3.1 Baseline Models

As baselines to this dataset we used the ResNet-18 [26], DenseNet-121 [27] and EfficientNet B0 [28]. These models are widely used and have demonstrated strong generalization across a variety of vision tasks [29–31]. They present an excellent balance between computational efficiency, accuracy, and implementation simplicity. They have extensive pretrained weights and stable implementations available in libraries like PyTorch [32] and TensorFlow [33], which is especially useful in small-data regimes. The models, pretrained on ImageNet, were used with their original classification heads replaced by a binary classification head. Due to the small sample size only the final layers were finetuned. The dataset was split into training, validation, and test sets in a 60-20-20 ratio. The training set was used for model optimization, the validation set for hyperparameter tuning and model selection, and the test set for final performance evaluation.

To augment the dataset and improve the model's generalization ability, a series of transformations were applied. First, a random horizontal flip was used with a probability of 50%, enabling the model to become invariant to horizontal orientations. A small random rotation, within a range of $\pm 10°$, was applied to help the model handle minor variations in object orientation without excessive distortion. Additionally, a random affine transformation was performed, translating the image by up to 10% of its width and height in both directions. This introduced slight shifts in object position, enhancing the model's robustness to positional changes. A random resized crop was also employed, where the image was cropped to between 80% and 100% of its original size, ensuring that the model could adapt to different object scales. Finally, a mild Gaussian blur with a kernel size of 5 and a random sigma value between 0.1 and 3.0 was applied to simulate varying focus levels, while maintaining sufficient image clarity. These transformations collectively increased the diversity of the dataset, aiding in the development of a more robust model capable of handling variations in orientation, position, scale, and focus.

The hyperparameter search space for the optimization process was tuned using Optuna [34]. Each model was trained with the Tree-structured Parzen Estimator (TPE) search algorithm executed for 50 trials. The optimization target set is the maximization of validation F1-score. To accommodate the specific challenges of training on a small dataset, we carefully defined the search space to include both core training parameters and regularization strategies. The learning rate, a parameter controlling update magnitude during training, was logarithmically sampled between 1e-5 and 1e-2. This wide range was chosen to allow exploration from cautious to aggressive updates, particularly important when fine-tuning on small datasets where large updates can easily lead to overfitting or instability. For batch size, we explored discrete values (16, 32, 64) to balance between training stability (smaller batches) and computational efficiency (larger batches). We tested both Adam and SGD optimizers. Adam offers adaptive learning rates and typically converges faster, while SGD provides a useful

Table 4. Optimal training parameters for each model

Model	Optimizer	Learning Rate	Weight Decay	Batch Size	Dropout
ResNet-18	SGD	2.60e-4 (FC), 7.79e-4 (Conv.)	1.30e-3	32	0.06
DenseNet-121	Adam	8.5e-4	2.9e-4	16	0.13
EfficientNet B0	SGD	8.98e-4 (FC), 2.15e-5 (Conv.)	4.68e-3	16	0.40

contrast in update dynamics and is known for strong generalization in some contexts. Weight decay—a form of L2 regularization—was sampled from a log scale between 1e-5 and 1e-2. It helps prevent overfitting by penalizing large weights, which is useful in settings with limited data. We also varied the number of unfrozen layers (1 or 3) to control the degree of fine-tuning. Unfreezing more layers allows the model to adapt more to the new data, but increases overfitting risk—especially in data-scarce scenarios. Finally, dropout rates between 0.0 and 0.5 were explored as a regularization method to improve generalization. For each run, binary cross-entropy loss was the optimization target and F1-score was monitored per epoch for train and validation sets. Experiments were set to run for 100 epochs with early stopping set, having a patience of 20 epochs.

The best-performing configuration for each architecture involved different fine-tuning strategies. For ResNet-18, unfreezing the final convolutional layer along with the fully connected layer resulted in the highest validation performance. For DenseNet-121, optimal results were achieved by training only the fully connected layer. In the case of EfficientNet B0, unfreezing just the last convolutional layer led to the best generalization. Table 4 presents the optimal parameters for each model.

3.2 Results

The hyperparameter optimization (Table 4) revealed architecture-specific preferences: DenseNet-121 favored the adaptive learning of Adam, while ResNet-18 and EfficientNet-B0 benefited from SGD's fine-grained control. Notably, EfficientNet-B0 required a markedly lower learning rate for its convolutional layers (2.15e-5) compared to its FC layer (8.98e-4), highlighting the importance of preserving pretrained feature extractors while adapting task-specific heads.

The experimental results offer a baseline for the novel dataset provided. DenseNet-121 achieved the highest overall performance, with an F1-score of 0.6575 and accuracy of 63.77%. Its precision was 63.16%, and recall was 68.57%. EfficientNet-B0 exhibited the highest recall 74.29%, indicating superior sensitivity to positive cases, but suffered from lower precision 56.52%, reflecting a higher rate of false positives. ResNet-18 delivered intermediate results, with moderate precision 56.82% and the lowest accuracy 57.97% among the models (Table 5).

The moderate performance ceiling (best F1 < 0.66) likely reflects fundamental challenges in SCM detection.

Table 5. Comparison of Model Performance Metrics

Model	F1 Score	Precision	Recall	Accuracy
ResNet-18	0.6329	0.5682	0.7143	0.5797
DenseNet-121	0.6575	0.6316	0.6857	0.6377
EfficientNet B0	0.6420	0.5652	0.7429	0.5797

4 Related Work

Subclinical mastitis detection is crucial in livestock management. IRT offers a non-invasive method by detecting udder temperature changes indicative of inflammation [35,36].

Early studies showed strong correlations between udder skin surface temperature (SST) and CMT scores in cows [16]. Subsequent research validated the use of IRT for mastitis diagnosis in sheep [18], Girolando and Jersey cows [37], and Holstein Friesian cows [38], demonstrating its diagnostic capabilities comparable to traditional methods like CMT and SCC. Studies also explored IRT's use in detecting E.coli-induced mastitis [39] and in various environmental conditions [40,41].

Various algorithms have been designed and implemented for the automated analysis of thermal images [42–44], and IRT's utility has been extended to dairy goats [45] and buffaloes [46]. These studies consistently highlight IRT's potential for early subclinical mastitis detection across species, showing strong correlations with CMT and SCC.

A similar approach utilizing SVMs and stochastic neighbor embedding was recently published [19]. While the results are promising, achieving 84% accuracy, the dataset is not publicly available, and the test set is highly imbalanced.

This paper contributes a novel sheep udder thermal image dataset and a perspective of using deep learning models for detecting SCM, establishing a baseline for future research.

5 Discussion

The feature analysis revealed distinct thermal patterns between healthy and SCM-affected udders. Statistically significant differences were observed in features describing overall temperature (mean intensity) and distribution shape (skewness, kurtosis). Features related to central tendency, such as mean intensity and percentiles (25th, 50th, 75th), exhibited statistically significant differences. Standard deviation, and entropy, showed limited univariate discriminative power though entropy's inclusion in machine learning models training hinted at complementary roles in combination with other features.

Among traditional machine learning models, ensemble methods such as AdaBoost, XGBoost, and Random Forest demonstrated a relatively balanced performance. XGboost achieved the highest F1-score (0.701) while the AdaBoost achieved the highest recall (0.8182) indicating stronger sensitivity to SCM cases, though at the cost of precision (0.6102). Random Forest exhibited comparable F1-scores (0.6667), with feature importance rankings highlighting skewness, entropy, and percentile values as key contributors. Skewness, in particular, emerged as a prominent feature across models, potentially reflecting its ability to encode asymmetric thermal patterns linked to inflammation. Linear models, such as logistic regression, lacked in performance, likely due to their limited capacity to model non-linear relationships in the data.

Experiments with neural networks, involving DenseNet-121, ResNet-18 and EfficientNet-B0, resulted in lower performance compared to traditional models. DenseNet-121 achieved the highest F1-score (0.6575) and accuracy (63.77%) among the evaluated architectures, though its performance remained slightly lower than XGBoost. Notably, traditional machine learning models achieved moderately higher performance compared to neural networks in this study. This observation may reflect the advantages of handcrafted features, which incorporate domain-specific knowledge and reduce reliance on large-scale data. Neural networks, faced limitations due to the small number of samples, which was prohibitive for the effective learning of discriminative feature extraction from the images.

The overall performance ceiling observed across all models highlights the inherent challenges involved in detecting SCM through thermal imaging. One of the key difficulties stems from the complex nature of the dataset itself, which presents several factors that complicate the classification of udders as either healthy or affected by mastitis.

Firstly, the thermal images contain various sources of noise, such as the presence of sheep hair, which can interfere with accurate temperature measurements. These irregularities can introduce distortions in the image data, making it harder to reliably differentiate between healthy and SCM-affected udders. Additionally, thermal images often suffer from occlusions, where parts of the udder may be obscured by the animal's body or other factors, reducing the amount of visible data available for analysis.

Furthermore, environmental conditions significantly influence the temperature of the udders, adding another layer of complexity to the task. Factors such as ambient temperature, humidity, and sunlight can cause variations in the thermal readings, making it difficult to distinguish between healthy udders and those affected by SCM. This environmental variability introduces a degree of uncertainty, as the temperature difference between a healthy and an SCM-affected udder may be subtle and heavily influenced by external conditions.

6 Conclusions and Future Work

Detecting SCM using thermal imaging and artificial intelligence is a challenging task due to the absence of visible clinical symptoms and the need for high sensitivity and specificity in detection algorithms. Nevertheless, overcoming these challenges is crucial, as early and accurate detection of SCM can significantly improve animal welfare, reduce economic losses in the dairy industry, and enhance milk quality and herd health management.

This paper tackles these challenges by introducing a new, expert-validated dataset to the research community, which, to the best of our knowledge, is the first of its kind for dairy sheep. This makes it a significant contribution to the field. Additionally, the paper presents initial baseline results on this dataset. To our knowledge, no other researchers have applied deep learning for SCM detection using thermal imaging in dairy sheep, emphasizing the novelty and importance of this work.

In future work, we should focus on expanding the dataset by collecting more thermal images from diverse environments and improving annotation methods based on confirmed inflammation. Closer-range imaging could enhance resolution and detection accuracy. Exploring advanced models like Vision Transformers and leveraging transfer learning could further improve performance, if a larger dataset is available. Enhancing model interpretability through better visualization techniques is also crucial. Additionally, long-term studies tracking individual sheep could help develop predictive models, improving early detection and disease management in real-world farm settings.

Acknowledgments. This research was co-funded by Greece and the European Union in the framework: Sub-Measure 16.1–16.2–Establishment and operation of Operational Team (O.T.) of the European Innovation Partnership (EIP) for agricultural productivity and sustainability–Establishment and operation of Operational Team (O.T.) of the European Innovation Partnership (EIP) for agricultural productivity and sustainability under grant number M16SYN2-00202 THERMASHEEP-Application of Infrared Thermography (IRT) Technology as a Subclinical Mastitis Diagnostic Tool: Improving Welfare and Productivity Indicators in Sheep and Goat Farms.

Disclosure of Interests. The authors have no competing interests to declare that are relevant to the content of this article.

References

1. Fragkou, I., Boscos, C., Fthenakis, G.: Diagnosis of clinical or subclinical mastitis in ewes. Small Rumin. Res. **118**, 86–92 (2014)
2. Libera, K., et al.: Potential novel biomarkers for mastitis diagnosis in sheep. Animals **11**, 2783 (2021)
3. Gelasakis, A., Mavrogianni, V., Petridis, I., Vasileiou, N., Fthenakis, G.: Mastitis in sheep-the last 10 years and the future of research. Vet. Microbiol. **181**, 136–146 (2015)
4. Contreras, A., et al.: Mastitis in small ruminants. Small Rumin. Res. **68**, 145–153 (2007)
5. Arteche-Villasol, N., Fernández, M., Gutiérrez-Expósito, D., Pérez, V.: Pathology of the mammary gland in sheep and goats. J. Comp. Pathol. **193**, 37–49 (2022)
6. Giadinis, N., et al.: "Milk-drop syndrome of ewes": investigation of the causes in dairy sheep in Greece. Small Rumin. Res. **106**, 33–35 (2012)

7. Leitner, G., et al.: Changes in milk composition as affected by subclinical mastitis in sheep. J. Dairy Sci. **87**, 46–52 (2004)
8. De Olives, A., Díaz, J., Molina, M., Peris, C.: Quantification of milk yield and composition changes as affected by subclinical mastitis during the current lactation in sheep. J. Dairy Sci. **96**, 7698–7708 (2013)
9. Martí-De Olives, A., Peris, C., Molina, M.: Effect of subclinical mastitis on the yield and cheese-making properties of ewe's milk. Small Rumin. Res. **184**, 106044 (2020)
10. Gougoulis, D., Kyriazakis, I., Papaioannou, N., Papadopoulos, E., Taitzoglou, I., Fthenakis, G.: Subclinical mastitis changes the patterns of maternal-offspring behaviour in dairy sheep. Vet. J. **176**, 378–384 (2008)
11. Benkerroum, N.: Staphylococcal enterotoxins and enterotoxin-like toxins with special reference to dairy products: an overview. Crit. Rev. Food Sci. Nutr. **58**, 1943–1970 (2018)
12. Rekant, S., Lyons, M., Pacheco, J., Arzt, J., Rodriguez, L.: Veterinary applications of infrared thermography. Am. J. Vet. Res. **77**, 98–107 (2016)
13. Machado, N., et al.: Using infrared thermography to detect subclinical mastitis in dairy cows in compost barn systems. J. Therm. Biol **97**, 102881 (2021)
14. Lahiri, B., Bagavathiappan, S., Jayakumar, T., Philip, J.: Medical applications of infrared thermography: a review. Infrared Phys. Technol. **55**, 221–235 (2012)
15. Tommasoni, C., Fiore, E., Lisuzzo, A., Gianesella, M.: Mastitis in dairy cattle: on-farm diagnostics and future perspectives. Animals **13**, 2538 (2023)
16. Çolak, A., Polat, B., Okumus, Z., Kaya, M., Yanmaz, L., Hayirli, A.: Early detection of mastitis using infrared thermography in dairy cows. J. Dairy Sci. **91**, 4244–4248 (2008)
17. Sinha, R., et al.: Infrared thermography as non-invasive technique for early detection of mastitis in dairy animals-a review. Asian J. Dairy Food Res. **37**, 1–6 (2018)
18. Martins, R., et al. Mastitis detection in sheep by infrared thermography. Res. Veter. Sci. **94**, 722–724 (2013)
19. Tselios, C., Alexandropoulos, D., Pantopoulos, C., Athanasiou, G.: Thermal imaging and dimensionality reduction techniques for subclinical mastitis detection in dairy sheep. Animals **14**, 1797 (2024)
20. Lysitsas, M., Spyrou, V., Billinis, C., Valiakos, G.: Coagulase-negative staphylococci as an etiologic agent of ovine mastitis, with a focus on subclinical forms. Antibiotics. **12**, 1661 (2023)
21. Korelidou, V., Simitzis, P., Massouras, T., Gelasakis, A.: Infrared thermography as a diagnostic tool for the assessment of mastitis in dairy ruminants. Animals **14**, 2691 (2024)
22. Ramesh, V.: A review on application of deep learning in thermography. Int. J. Eng. Manag. Res. **7**, 489–493 (2017)
23. Michael, C., Lianou, D., Vasileiou, N., Mavrogianni, V., Petinaki, E., Fthenakis, G.: Longitudinal study of subclinical mastitis in sheep in Greece: an investigation into incidence risk, associations with milk quality and risk factors of the infection. Animals **13**, 3295 (2023)
24. Vasileiou, N., et al.: Role of staphylococci in mastitis in sheep. J. Dairy Res. **86**, 254–266 (2019)
25. Waskom, M.: Seaborn: statistical data visualization. J. Open Source Softw. **6**, 3021 (2021)
26. He, K., Zhang, X., Ren, S., Sun, J.: Deep residual learning for image recognition. In: Proceedings of the IEEE Conference on Computer Vision and Pattern Recognition, pp. 770–778 (2016)

27. Huang, G., Liu, Z., Van Der Maaten, L., Weinberger, K.: Densely connected convolutional networks. In: Proceedings of the IEEE Conference on Computer Vision and Pattern Recognition, pp. 4700–4708 (2017)
28. Tan, M., Le, Q.: Efficientnet: rethinking model scaling for convolutional neural networks. In: International Conference On Machine Learning, pp. 6105–6114 (2019)
29. Chauhan, T., Palivela, H., Tiwari, S.: Optimization and fine-tuning of DenseNet model for classification of COVID-19 cases in medical imaging. Int. J. Inf. Manag. Data Insights **1**, 100020 (2021)
30. Majumder, R.: Efficient classification of pulmonary pneumonia and tuberculosis alongside normal and non-X-ray images with minimal resources and maximum accuracy. MedRxiv, pp. 2024-12 (2025)
31. UÇan, M., Kaya, B., Kaya, M.: Multi-class gastrointestinal images classification using EfficientNet-B0 CNN model. In: 2022 International Conference On Data Analytics For Business And Industry (ICDABI), pp. 1–5 (2022)
32. Ketkar, N., Moolayil, J., Ketkar, N., Moolayil, J.: Introduction to pytorch. In: Deep Learning With Python: Learn Best Practices Of Deep Learning Models With PyTorch, pp. 27–91 (2021)
33. Singh, P., Manure, A., Singh, P., Manure, A.: Introduction to tensorflow 2.0. In: Learn TensorFlow 2.0: Implement Machine Learning And Deep Learning Models With Python, pp. 1–24 (2020)
34. Akiba, T., Sano, S., Yanase, T., Ohta, T., Koyama, M.: Optuna: a next-generation hyperparameter optimization framework. In: Proceedings Of The 25th ACM SIGKDD International Conference On Knowledge Discovery & Data Mining, pp. 2623–2631 (2019)
35. Sharun, K., et al.: Advances in therapeutic and managerial approaches of bovine mastitis: a comprehensive review. Vet. Q. **41**, 107–136 (2021)
36. Sathiyabarathi, M., et al.: Infrared thermography: a potential noninvasive tool to monitor udder health status in dairy cows. Vet. World **9**, 1075 (2016)
37. Ribeiro, I., et al.: Infrared thermography for detection of clinical and subclinical mastitis in dairy cattle: comparison between Girolando and Jersey breeds. Ciência Animal Brasileira **24**, e-76726 (2023)
38. Sathiyabarathi, M., et al.: Investigation of body and udder skin surface temperature differentials as an early indicator of mastitis in Holstein Friesian crossbred cows using digital infrared thermography technique. Vet. World **9**, 1386 (2016)
39. Metzner, M., Sauter-Louis, C., Seemueller, A., Petzl, W., Zerbe, H.: Infrared thermography of the udder after experimentally induced Escherichia coli mastitis in cows. Vet. J. **204**, 360–362 (2015)
40. Pamparienė, I., et al.: Thermography based inflammation monitoring of udder state in dairy cows: sensitivity and diagnostic priorities comparing with routine California mastitis test. J. Vibroeng. **18**, 511–521 (2016)
41. Velasco-Bolaños, J., et al.: Application of udder surface temperature by infrared thermography for diagnosis of subclinical mastitis in Holstein cows located in tropical highlands. J. Dairy Sci. **104**, 10310–10323 (2021)
42. Lima, M., Pandorfi, H.: Thermal image thresholding for automatic detection of bovine mastitis. Int. J. Comput. Appl. **975**, 8887 (2021)
43. Bradski, G., Kaehler, A., et al.: OpenCV. Dr. Dobb's J. Softw. Tools **3** (2000)
44. Khakimov, A., Pavkin, D., Yurochka, S., Astashev, M., Dovlatov, I.: Development of an algorithm for rapid herd evaluation and predicting milk yield of mastitis cows based on infrared thermography. Appl. Sci. **12**, 6621 (2022)

45. FA, P., BP, P., RG, S., et al.: Application of infrared thermography as a determinant of sub-clinical mastitis in sapera dairy goats. Indon. J. Anim. Vet. Sci./Jurnal Ilmu Ternak Dan Veteriner **27** (2022)
46. Kittur, P., et al.: Correlation of udder thermogram and somatic cell counts as a tool for detection of subclinical mastitis in buffaloes. Vet. Res. Commun. 1–9 (2024)

Mitigating Data Scarcity in Polymer Property Prediction via Multi-task Auxiliary Learning

Gabriel A. Pinheiro[1,3], Marcos G. Quiles[1], Juarez L. F. Da Silva[2], and Xiaoli Z. Fern[3(✉)]

[1] Institute of Science and Technology, Federal University of São Paulo, São Paulo, Brazil
{gabriel.pinheiro,quiles}@unifesp.br
[2] Institute of Chemistry, University of São Paulo, São Paulo, Brazil
juarez_dasilva@iqsc.usp.br
[3] School of Electrical Engineering and Computer Science, Oregon State University, Corvallis, USA
xiaoli.fern@oregonstate.edu

Abstract. Polymers are fundamental materials with numerous applications in everyday life, making their synthesis, characterization, and property measurement critically important. Machine learning (ML) algorithms offer promising opportunities to accelerate polymer screening with high accuracy, yet significant challenges persist. Unlike small molecules with fixed structures, polymers, especially copolymers formed by polymerizing two or more distinct monomers, can be modeled at multiple scales (atomic, monomer, or repeat-unit level) and exhibit inherent variability due to the stochastic polymerization process, which affects connectivity, chain length, conformations, and compositional complexity. Additionally, the scarcity of labeled polymer data with high-fidelity, experimentally measured properties poses a challenge for ML training. In this work, we tackle these challenges by (1) proposing CoPolyGNN (CoPolymer Graph Neural Network), a multi-scale model that employs a GNN encoder to learn representations of polymer repeating units or individual monomers, combined with an attention-based readout function that aggregates these representations with explicit monomer proportion information; (2) compiling a large dataset of polymers annotated with both simulated and experimentally measured properties; and (3) introducing a supervised auxiliary training framework to mitigate data scarcity in polymer property prediction. We empirically validate CoPolyGNN on datasets of polymer properties measured under real experimental conditions. Our findings demonstrate that augmenting the main task with auxiliary tasks leads to beneficial performance gains. Consequently, our work provides a neural architecture and training framework enabling practitioners to predict polymer properties from simple text notations of repeat units or monomers and their proportions, achieving strong performance even with limited training data. (Code available at https://github.com/CIDAG/CoPolyGNN).

Supplementary Information The online version contains supplementary material available at https://doi.org/10.1007/978-3-032-06118-8_25.

© The Author(s), under exclusive license to Springer Nature Switzerland AG 2026
I. Dutra et al. (Eds.): ECML PKDD 2025, LNAI 16021, pp. 426–442, 2026.
https://doi.org/10.1007/978-3-032-06118-8_25

Keywords: Multitask Learning · Polymers · Property Prediction

1 Introduction

Polymers are macromolecules composed of repeating chemical units covalently bonded to form long chains or networks [21], with versatile properties that make them essential in everyday products from packaging, synthetic clothing to advanced biomedical devices [10]. As technology progresses, it is essential to design polymers with properties that meet the evolving needs of society, such as high-energy-density capacitors [13], molecular imprinting [20], gas separation [27], and biocompatible or (bio)degradable materials [28]. However, designing polymers involves navigating a vast space of possible polymeric materials, where few structure-property relationships are known, and the screening of potential polymers through wet-lab experiments remains expensive and time-consuming, while simulations, such as those relying on force fields, often struggle to reproduce experimental properties [4, 37].

Polymer informatics has emerged to accelerate polymer discovery by leveraging machine learning (ML) for property prediction [37]. However, polymers differ significantly from small molecules, whose fixed and well-defined structures have enabled substantial success using ML models such as graph neural networks (GNNs). The exact structure of a polymer is complex and challenging to characterize precisely due to the stochastic nature of polymerization processes, resulting in inherent variations in chain length, sequence, and network architecture [36]. This poses challenges in adapting ML models originally designed for small and well-defined molecular structures to polymers. As a result, polymers are typically modeled based on their fundamental building blocks, which are small molecules such as monomers or repeating units. In the literature, several studies have focused on polymer property prediction, either using molecular fingerprints or one-hot encoding (OHE) applied to these building blocks [4, 34]. An alternative approach has involved using GNNs to learn fingerprints in an end-to-end fashion, typically based on the graph structure of the monomers [9, 23].

Additionally, polymer informatics also suffers from the challenge of data scarcity, which limits the accuracy and generalizability of predictive models. Existing work has considered multi-task learning (MTL) to mitigate the data scarcity issue through shared learning across related multiple related tasks [25]. In this context, both molecular fingerprints and GNNs have been explored using data from simulations, experiments, or their combination. For example, [28] demonstrated that training an MTL model with both simulated and experimental data improved the accuracy of predicting experimental ring-opening polymerization enthalpy. MTL aims to solve multiple tasks simultaneously, but in practical applications, there is often a primary focus on a specific polymer property. In such scenarios, others tasks can serve as auxiliary tasks, facilitating knowledge transfer and improving generalizability of the learned model. This strategy, known as multi-task auxiliary learning (MTAL), helps the model prioritize the main task while leveraging auxiliary tasks for knowledge transfer.

MTAL could provide a promising solution to the challenges in polymer informatics, however, the effectiveness of this approach depends on careful task selection, as inappropriate auxiliary tasks can introduce negative transfer.

This work presents a three hold effort to address the above mentioned challenges.

- First, we propose CoPolyGNN (CoPolymer Graph Neural Network), a neural polymer encoder that integrates a GNN-based monomer encoder with an attention-based readout function to learn copolymer representations at multiple scales while also handling simpler cases like homopolymers (polymer comprised of a single monomer or repeating unit). Unlike prior polymer representation models, CoPolyGNN explicitly incorporates monomer structural information and their proportions through an attention mechanism, leading to more expressive polymer representations.
- Second, we curate a comprehensive polymer property dataset from existing literature, comprising over 70.000 polymers and their experimental and simulated properties across 35 unique properties (e.g., chemical reactivity, electronic, thermal, and other polymer-relevant characteristics) obtained through simulations and/or experiments. This large-scale dataset serves as a valuable resource for training robust polymer property prediction models, particularly in data-limited scenarios.
- Third, we explore multiple MTAL strategies to effectively address data scarcity. Specifically, we investigate two distinct classes of MTAL approaches: (1) treating all tasks distinct from the main task as predefined auxiliary tasks and integrating them into a unified loss function using weighting heuristics such as Gradient Cosine Similarity (GCS) [6] and Online Learning for Auxiliary Losses (OL-AUX) [18]; and (2) assuming that auxiliary tasks are unknown and dynamically learning an optimal set of auxiliary tasks, as in Task Affinity Grouping (TAG) [8]. By systematically evaluating these strategies, we show that MTAL achieves superior performance in most tasks compared to the single-task learning (STL) version of CoPolyGNN, as well as traditional methods such as fingerprint-based descriptors. Furthermore, our top result improves upon the strongest baseline by approximately 50%. These findings underscore the potential of MTAL in leveraging auxiliary tasks to enhance learning and generalization, offering a promising approach to mitigating data scarcity in polymer informatics.

Together, these contributions provide a self-contained pipeline that allows practitioners to build polymer property prediction models with limited experimental data while leveraging a rich set of auxiliary tasks and a large-scale polymer dataset. Our MTAL framework offers a scalable and generalizable solution for enhancing polymer informatics through data-efficient learning.

2 Background

This section first introduces key aspects of polymers and then guides the reader to the application of ML in polymer science for property prediction.

2.1 Basic Concepts of Polymers

Polymers have always been with us, yet the scientific understanding of their nature became clear in the mid-20th century with the rise of plastics. The term originates from the Greek words *poly*, meaning many, and *mer*, meaning unit. This etymology reflects their fundamental structure, as they are macromolecules generated through polymerization, in which small molecules called monomers join together to form long chains. After being incorporated into the polymer, monomers serve as structural units, establishing stable covalent bonds with adjacent units. If a polymer is composed of a single type of monomer, it is classified as a homopolymer. If it is composed of two or more distinct monomers, it is called a copolymer. Additionally, the arrangement of each monomer in the polymer chain influences the classification of copolymers into random, alternating, block, and graft types [7].

One fundamental concept in polymer science is the repeating unit, which is the smallest structural segment of the polymer that recurs along the chain. The repeating and structural units of a polymer may differ. For instance, in a homopolymer, both units are identical, whereas in copolymers, the arrangement of multiple monomeric units causes the repeating and structural units to differ. Moreover, such arrangements lead to diversity in architecture, composition, and patterning, making copolymers some of the most commercially important polymers, such as those utilized in plastics, rubbers, and coatings. For most synthetic polymers, structural characteristics (e.g., chain length, architecture) can also be influenced by stochastic factors during polymerization, regardless of the method. This results in polymers being polydisperse in molecular weight, meaning that the molecular weights of the polymers follow a distribution. Therefore, we typically refer to their average molecular weight, and experimental measurements reflect this average [7,21]

In short, polymers pose challenges in structural representation, as their precise connectivity beyond polymerization points remains uncertain. While some polymerization methods reduce variations and yield more uniform structures, a perfectly predictable structure is not guaranteed. For standard ML, which usually relies on well-defined input representations, this structural variability requires a careful choice of representation strategies that capture both structural information and uncertainty. This has resulted in polymers typically being described by their building blocks, such as their monomers or repeating units.

2.2 Machine Learning for Polymer Property Prediction

Given the complexity of polymers and the vast design space, computational approaches, such as physical molecular modeling and data-driven methods, have become attractive for predicting their properties by offering a lower-cost, faster alternative to experimental characterization. In this realm, polymer informatics leverages ML to predict diverse polymer properties, such as thermodynamic and mechanical properties, among others [2]. Such strategies often utilize molecular descriptors, GNNs, or language model-based methods to extract representations from the monomers or repeating units that describe the polymer. Fingerprints are a traditional type of molecular descriptor, and they rely on domain expertise to capture the presence or absence of chemical substructures. Popular options include the hierarchical editing language for macromolecules, which is widely used in pharmaceutical and industrial applications, the extended-connectivity fingerprint, Molecular ACCess System (MACCS) keys, and others [13,31,39]. Furthermore, OHE and topological descriptors, such as those available in RDKit, are also commonly applied in these processes [3,24].

For example, [39] proposed a hierarchical fingerprinting scheme with four levels to capture physical and chemical interactions that contribute to predicting gas permeation properties. This hierarchical approach starts at the atomic scale by counting the occurrence of atomic triples. The second level involves counting building blocks from a predefined list, the third incorporates quantitative structure-property relationship descriptors, and the fourth accounts for morphological descriptors. Instead of focusing on hierarchical fingerprinting, [19] proposed a data augmentation method based on the iterative rearrangement of polymer fragments. Specifically, it follows a process similar to window slicing, in which the repeating unit is disassembled into smaller fragments and recombined in a way that preserves the polymer backbone. The recombined structure is then processed into molecular fingerprints.

In contrast, there are studies that extract polymer representations without relying on handcrafted features. One such direction is GNN-based methods, in which a graph is used to describe the molecular connectivity of the building block (i.e., monomers or repeating units), where vertices represent atoms and edges represent bonds. In cases involving copolymers, the polymer representation is typically a weighted sum of monomer representations, with weights based on their ratios [9,35]. This approach is also a common practice in fingerprint methods and OHE [24,25]. [2] introduced a GNN that uses a graph with parameterized stochastic edges to capture the average structure of the repeating unit. Following up on this, [9] extended such a framework under self-supervised learning, considering node-, edge-, and graph-level pre-training tasks to improve representation learning as a way to reduce the impact of limited data on supervised tasks.

Another approach to representation learning involves textual token-based models, particularly transformer-based methods like TransPolymer [33], PolyBERT [15], and PolyCL [38]. In addition, MTL has been explored to exploit correlations between properties, improving generalizability and mitigating data scarcity [14,16]. It is typically implemented as a hard parameter model, relying on either GNN- [23,26,32] or transformer-based [22,22,30] encoders. For example, [23] introduced PolymerGNN, an MTL framework that concatenates the embeddings from a GNN along with resin properties to predict the glass transition temperature and inherent viscosity of homopolymers and copolymers. A different approach uses a fingerprint-based representation in a multilayer perceptron to predict polymer properties from in-house simulation datasets and experimental measurements reported in the literature [14].

Nevertheless, most existing methods still rely on either monomer-based or repeating-unit-based representations separately. For this reason, we propose an ML model that captures polymer structure with a multi-scale approach within a unified architecture and replaces a simple weighted sum of monomer embeddings with an attention-based readout mechanism that dynamically learns the contribution of each polymer component. This flexible design extends its applicability to a broader range of polymer architectures, from homopolymers to copolymers. Furthermore, we explore our model within an MTAL framework, which, to the best of our knowledge, has not been previously applied to polymer data to mitigate data scarcity.

3 Methodology

In this section, we introduce the core workings of CoPolyGNN and the techniques for training it in the MTAL setting, as illustrated in Fig. 1.

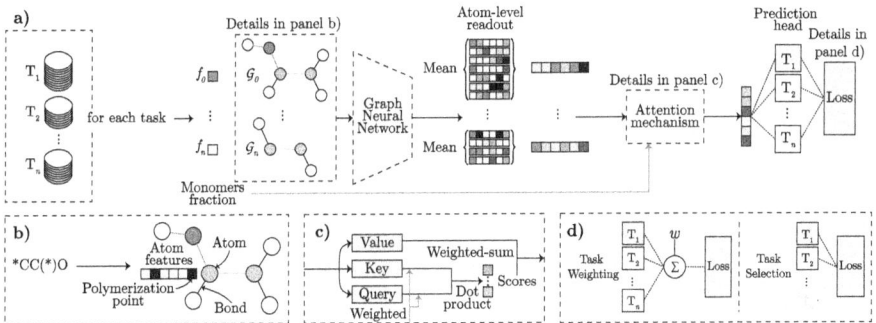

Fig. 1. Overview of the proposed CoPolyGNN in an MTAL setting. (a) For each task in the pool of polymer datasets, we first build the graph representation of the monomers, which are fed to the first component of CoPolyGNN, a GNN encoder that produces monomer-level embeddings. These monomer-level embeddings are passed through a readout function to generate a polymer-level embedding for the predictive tasks. After this, an MTAL scheme is used to assign importance to each auxiliary predictive task according to the main task. (b) Illustrates the encoding process of p-SMILES into a graph and highlights the polymerization atom feature to indicate the connectivity between monomers. (c) Shows the attention-based readout function that weights the importance of monomers for the predictive task. (d) Depicts the two types of MTAL strategies used to train CoPolyGNN.

3.1 Polymer Representation

We express a polymer as a set of monomer graphs $\{\mathcal{G}_0, \mathcal{G}_1, \ldots, \mathcal{G}_n\}$, where each $\mathcal{G}_i$ is built on the p-SMILES (Simplified Molecular-Input Line-Entry System) notation[1] and is assigned a monomer fraction f_i such that $\sum_{i=0}^{n} f_i = 1$. p-SMILES extends SMILES strings by incorporating the '*' character to represent polymerization points in monomers. We convert p-SMILES into a graph following the natural molecular encoding, where atoms are represented as nodes and chemical bonds are treated as edges of the graph. Each atom is represented by a feature vector, which includes the atom type (with OHE), atomic number, aromaticity, hybridization states (sp, sp^2, and sp^3), and the number of explicitly attached hydrogen atoms, with the addition of a binary feature, where 1 indicates a polymerization point and 0 indicates the absence of one. Figure 1(b) shows this process of reading the p-SMILES string and extracting atomic descriptors using the RDKit Python package (version 2024.03.6) [17].

3.2 CoPolyGNN

The representation of a polymer requires more than a conventional molecular graph, as their structure emerges from many factors, such as the combination of multiple monomers and how often each appears. CoPolyGNN was designed to handle such complexity by combining two processing blocks to learn a polymer embedding. The first block is a Graph Isomorphism Network (GIN), which operates on each monomer graph in $\{\mathcal{G}_0, \mathcal{G}_1, \ldots, \mathcal{G}_n\}$ for the given polymer. GIN was chosen for its theoretical equivalence to the Weisfeiler-Lehman graph isomorphism test and its strong performance across diverse chemical tasks [12]. It initiates encoding with a message-passing operation that updates each atom's representation over k iterations by aggregating information from its neighbors and itself, as defined in Eq. 1.

$$m_v^{(k)} = \left(1 + \epsilon^{(k)}\right) \cdot h_v^{(k-1)} + \sum_{u \in \mathcal{N}(v)} h_u^{(k-1)},$$
$$h_v^{(k)} = \text{MLP}^{(k)}\left(m_v^{(k)}\right),$$
(1)

where $h_v^{(k-1)}$ denotes the representation of atom v at iteration $k-1$ (note that h_v^0 is the initial feature vector of the atom, defined when constructing the graph), $\mathcal{N}(v)$ represents the neighboring atoms of v, $\epsilon^{(k)}$ is either a learnable parameter or a fixed scalar, and $\text{MLP}^{(k)}$ represents the multilayer perceptron associated with the k-th iteration. After k iterations, each atom's representation encodes the structural information from its k-hop neighborhood, and monomer-level representations are then obtained via average pooling.

The second block employs a readout function that aggregates monomer-level representations into a polymer-level representation using attention mechanism, as depicted in Fig. 1(c). The attention mechanism dynamically learns the context-dependent contributions of individual monomer units to the overall polymer behavior. This design captures the fact that interactions between monomers

---

[1] The repeating unit can be interpreted as a simplified form of the monomer-based representation, where a single graph is used and $f_0 = 1$.

in a polymer are neither strictly linear nor merely additive. Monomer-level representations are projected through three linear layers to compute the query (Q), key (K), and value (V) matrices. A dot product is then calculated between the transformed Q and the sum of K across monomers to capture interactions between monomers and the global representation. The result is normalized by the square root of the key dimensionality (d_k), followed by a softmax operation, softmax $\left(\frac{(FQ)(\sum_i F_i K_i)^\top}{\sqrt{d_k}} \right) V$, where F is a diagonal matrix with f_i on the diagonal, i.e., $F = diag(f_1, f_2, ..., f_n)$. This scales the query and key vectors of the i-th monomer by its proportion f_i before computing the dot product, ensuring that the monomer contribution to the attention scores are weighted according to their fractions in the polymer.

3.3 CoPolyGNN Multi-task Auxiliary Learning

In this section, we discuss the MTAL training strategy for CoPolyGNN. Our MTL data contains polymer data on 35 different tasks, each with varying number of examples. During training, we adopt a sampling approach wherein each task contributes an equally sized batch in each iteration. This ensures balanced representation across tasks, irrespective of the data size of individual tasks. After each batch is processed, the auxiliary task selection strategy determines how to update the parameters based on the relevance of different tasks, as shown in Fig. 1(d). Specifically, we examine three strategies for MTAL: GSC [6], OL-AUX [18], and TAG [8].

The first two methods, GCS and OL-AUX, integrate auxiliary tasks into a unified loss function $\mathcal{L}$ by assigning heuristic-based weights w_i to each auxiliary task i:

$$\mathcal{L} = \frac{1}{N_{\text{main}}} \sum_{k=1}^{N_{\text{main}}} \left(y_{\text{main}}^{(k)} - \hat{y}_{\text{main}}^{(k)} \right)^2 + \sum_{i=1}^{T} \frac{w_i}{N_i} \sum_{k=1}^{N_i} \left(y_i^{(k)} - \hat{y}_i^{(k)} \right)^2, \quad (2)$$

where N_i represents the number of data points for task i.

Specifically, the key idea of GCS is to include an auxiliary task in the total loss only if its gradient exhibits non-negative cosine similarity with the main task gradient on shared parameters. Therefore, GCS assigns $w_i = 1$ when the cosine similarity between the gradients is non-negative and $w_i = 0$ otherwise [6].

OL-AUX follows a similar idea, but it treats w_i as model parameters with its own loss function. This loss function measures the negative dot product between gradients of the main task, $\nabla_{\theta_t} \mathcal{L}_{\text{main}}(\theta_t)$, and each auxiliary task, $\nabla_{\theta_t} L_i(\theta_t)$, at iteration t. The gradient update for w_i is given by $\frac{\partial \mathcal{L}_{\text{weights}}}{\partial w_i} = -\alpha \nabla_{\theta_t} \mathcal{L}_{\text{main}}(\theta_t)^T \nabla_{\theta_t} L_i(\theta_t)$, where θ_t represents the model parameters and α is the learning rate [18].

In contrast, TAG selects an optimal set of auxiliary tasks without using a unified weighted loss function. To achieve this, it maximizes inter-task affinity scores, denoted by $Z_{i \to j}^t$, a metric that quantifies the influence of auxiliary task

i on the main task j [8]. In this context, i represents a set of auxiliary tasks, and j corresponds to the main task, with $Z^t_{i \to j}$ formally defined in Eq. 3.

$$Z^t_{i \to j} = 1 - \frac{L_j(x^t, \theta^{t+1}_{s|i}, \theta^t_j)}{L_j(x^t, \theta^t_s, \theta^t_j)} . \qquad (3)$$

To compute this quantity, the model relies on the parameters of the shared encoder ($\theta^{t+1}_{s|i}$ or θ^t_s) and the parameters of the prediction head for task j, denoted as θ^t_j. Note that in $Z^t_{i \to j}$, the numerator utilizes the shared encoder parameters after being updated for the auxiliary task i ($\theta^{t+1}_{s|i}$), while the denominator employs the shared encoder parameters trained to predict the main task j (θ^t_s). Consequently, a positive value of $Z^t_{i \to j}$ signifies that updating the shared parameters reduces the loss of the main task compared to the values of the original parameters. At each training iteration, a batch of data is sampled for each task, and the model computes the mean squared error. The gradients are then backpropagated only through the parameters associated with the corresponding tasks. TAG selects the subset of auxiliary tasks that maximizes $Z^t_{i \to j}$ as the optimal support set for the main task. We then use this selected auxiliary tasks to fine-tune the weights of the model.

4 Dataset

We curated a dataset of 70 827 polymers by compiling data from recent publications on polymers published between 2020 and 2024, where SMILES strings are used to describe the building blocks of the polymers [1,2,5,11,13,14,23,24,27–29]. This dataset encompasses several chemical species, H, C, N, O, F, Na, Si, P, S, Cl, Ge, Br, and I, as well as homopolymers and copolymers with structures such as linear, branched, and cyclic, which is an indicator of the diversity within it. Moreover, it spans 35 distinct properties, some of which have experimental and simulated data, while others are available only from simulations or experiments. Figure 2 illustrates the distribution of diverse properties in the dataset, which can include chemical reactivity, electronic-nuclear properties, thermal properties, and others. We also indicate whether the data come from experiments (in blue) or simulations (in black). As can be seen, 3280 polymers (about 5 %) correspond to experimental data, which points to the limited size of the experimental dataset and the challenges associated with gathering such data.

We applied a series of preprocessing steps to prepare the datasets. First, we ensured consistency by reading p-SMILES with RDKit. Some datasets represented polymerization points using special characters such as '[Th]' and '[Ce]', which we replaced with '*', the standard notation for polymerization points. Next, we canonized p-SMILES to standardize their representation and removed duplicate entries within each task by averaging target values and merging identical strings. Overall, polymers were described using two common formats: (1) monomers with their respective fractions and (2) repeating units. Of the total

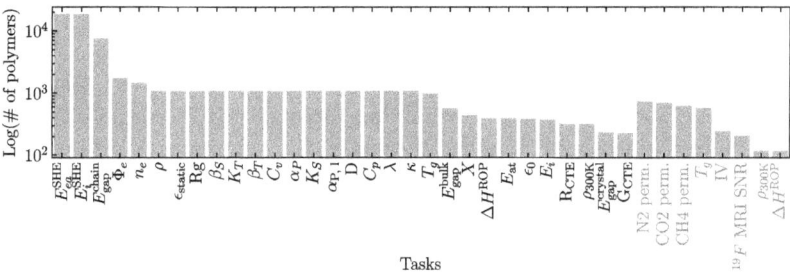

Fig. 2. Distribution of the number of polymers per task: Electron affinity with respect to the standard hydrogen potential - SHE (E_{ea}^{SHE}), Ionization potential with respect to the SHE (E_i^{SHE}), Bandgap - Chain (E_{gap}^{chain}), Electron injection barrier (Φ_e), Refractive index (n_e), Density (ρ), Static dielectric constant (ϵ_{static}), Radius of gyration (Rg), Isentropic compressibility (β_S), Bulk modulus (K_T), Compressibility (β_T), Constant volume (C_v), Volume expansion coefficient (α_P), Isentropic bulk modulus (K_S), Linear expansion coefficient ($\alpha_{P,l}$), Self-diffusion coefficient (D), Constant pressure (C_p), Thermal conductivity (λ), Thermal diffusivity (κ), Glass transition temperature (T_g), Bandgap - Bulk (E_{gap}^{bulk}), Crystallization tendency (X), Ring-opening polymerization enthalpy (ΔH^{ROP}), Atomization energy (E_{at}), Dielectric constant (ϵ_0), Ionization energy (E_i), Rubber coefficient of thermal expansion (R_{CTE}), Density at 300K (ρ_{300K}), Bandgap - Crystal ($E_{gap}^{crystal}$), Glass coefficient of thermal expansion (G_{CTE}), N2 permeability (N2 perm.), CO2 permeability (CO2 perm.), CH4 permeability (CH4 perm.), Inherent viscosity (IV), and ^{19}F magnetic resonance imaging signal-to-noise ratio (^{19}F MRI SNR). Experimentally measured properties are shwon with blue labels, and simulated properties are shown with black labels. Three properties include both experimental and simulated data.

polymers in our dataset, 33 342 are described using repeating units, while the remainder are characterized by monomers. Among these, 36 994 polymers are composed of two monomers, with the maximum number of monomers in a polymer reaching 7. Additionally, we standardized property units across datasets for consistency. We did not merge polymers with identical p-SMILES when properties were derived from different simulation methodologies, as a way to enhance diversity and incorporate additional data into our MTAL framework.

Moreover, our final dataset contains polymers relevant for a variety of applications, such as gas separation membranes, high-voltage insulation, and controlled drug release. Yet, property co-occurrence exists. The mean number of polymers that overlap in property pairs is 252 and the median is 49. This is due to the relatively small size of most datasets, typically under 1000 samples, and the broad diversity of polymer applications. Among the 703 possible task pairs, 454 have fewer than 100 co-occurring polymers, while three tasks exhibit minimal co-occurrence across nearly all task pairs. This diversity and overlap create a possible scenario for MTAL.

5 Experiment Configuration

First, we perform hyperparameter optimization by modifying the batch size to 16, 32 and 64, the latent representation dimensionality to 32 and 64, dropout to 1×10^{-1}, 2×10^{-1} and 4×10^{-1}, and the Adam optimizer learning rate to 1×10^{-2} and 1×10^{-3}. Optimization was conducted using MTL without auxiliary task selection to ensure unbiased hyperparameter tuning. We performed a grid search where, for each hyperparameter combination, training involved sequentially sampling a batch per task, computing the mean squared error, and backpropagating gradients only through the corresponding task parameters. The best hyperparameter combination was selected based on the performance of the model across the majority of tasks. Subsequently, we evaluated the impact of incorporating the attention mechanism compared to that of weighting the monomer embeddings according to their respective fractions. We again selected the optimal model as the one that consistently achieved superior performance in the majority of property prediction tasks.

For MTAL, all models were trained for 10 epochs, each epoch containing a number of iterations proportional to the batch count of the largest dataset. A k-fold-like approach ($k = 10$) was adopted for the experimental datasets (i.e., main task), where $k-2$ folds were used for training, 1 fold for validation, and the remaining fold for testing. In contrast, the simulated datasets were exclusively used for training, as they were designed for auxiliary tasks. Furthermore, we saw that OL-AUX and TAG have update rules (see Sect. 3.3) that involve additional parameter updates. This introduces computational overhead, so updates for MTAL here were performed every T steps. For OL-AUX, we initialized the weights of all auxiliary tasks to 1 and updated them every 10 epochs. For TAG, we set the step interval to 10 as well, and fine-tuning was performed over 10 epochs using the optimal auxiliary task group.

As a reference for evaluating the MTAL framework, we trained a random forest model on individual tasks. Specifically, we conducted experiments using three different descriptors commonly used for polymers: (1) a set of molecular features available in RDKit, (2) the MACCS fingerprint, and (3) the OHE representation of the monomers. For polymers composed of multiple monomers, we computed a weighted sum of the descriptors of individual monomers to construct a single feature vector representing the entire polymer. This setup allows us to explore whether models based on handcrafted features and classical learners provide a viable alternative. For additional comparison, we also included an STL version of our model to evaluate the added benefit of MTAL compared to the core architecture.

6 Results and Discussion

This section presents results obtained from our experiments. We began by optimizing the hyperparameters of the proposed model, followed by an investigation of the attention mechanism for the readout function, and finally evaluating the performance of our MTAL model in predicting 9 experimental properties.

6.1 Optimizing Hyperparameters

Hyperparameter choices are essential in guiding a model to its optimal performance. To determine the ideal model configuration, we started our investigation with a grid search using the hyperparameter space defined in Sect. 5. The optimal settings identified were a learning rate of 1×10^{-3}, a batch size of 16, a dropout rate of 0.1 and a latent representation dimensionality of 64. Among the hyperparameters, we observed that the learning rate had the most significant impact on reducing error across most properties, while the others introduced only marginal improvements.

Moreover, we determined the number of iterations per epoch by considering the batch count of the largest dataset. Given that the optimal batch size was 16, each training epoch consisted of 1036 iterations. For the experimental datasets, which are the tasks we carry out and aim to improve, this number of iterations proved sufficient to achieve convergence, as a full training cycle is equivalent to 1726 (280) passes through the smallest (largest) experimental datasets. Throughout the training iterations, we observed that the losses initially decreased steadily but tended to stabilize toward the end, with no significant improvement after a certain point. However, there are instances where the training loss decreases rapidly, but the validation loss does not follow the same trend, creating a noticeable gap between them. Such behavior is evident in tasks associated with the smallest datasets, containing 116, 117, and 204 polymers, respectively.

6.2 Impact of the Attention Mechanism

This study examines the impact of using an attention mechanism as part of the readout function, as detailed in Sect. 3.2. Table 1 shows the results and compares them with a readout function that weights the monomer embeddings according to their respective fractions. We report the performance in terms of the MAE of the validation set over 10 folds. As can be seen, the attention-based readout function generally tends to minimize both the mean and the standard deviation of the error across the properties, showing a subtle, but consistent improvement in performance. In particular, the readout function that uses monomer fractions was shown as a competitive alternative and outperformed the attention-based approach in the ^{19}F MRI SNR prediction task.

We believe that the proposed readout function allowed the model to capture more complex monomer interactions and prioritized their contributions to polymer properties by dynamically adjusting their weights. Moreover, its generalization capability is likely to benefit significantly from the use of larger datasets, as it is naturally a data-hungry method. At the same time, we highlight that the simplicity of the fraction-based method promotes interpretability while still delivering strong performance.

6.3 Multi-task Auxiliary Learning

Here, we assessed the performance of CoPolyGNN under MTAL setting in predicting experimental polymer properties using the hyperparameter configura-

Table 1. Comparison of the performance of our model using an attention-based readout (w/ attn) and a fraction-weighting readout (w/o attn) for predicting experimental properties: ΔH^{ROP} (kJ mol^{-1}), ρ_{300K} (g cm^{-3}), ^{19}F MRI SNR (1), T_g (K), IV (dL g^{-1}), and CH_4, CO_2, and N_2 permeability (Barrer).

	w/ attn	w/o attn
ΔH^{ROP}	6.33 ± 2.67	6.51 ± 2.30
ρ_{300K}	0.07 ± 0.03	0.08 ± 0.03
^{19}F MRI SNR	6.42 ± 1.15	6.18 ± 1.15
T_g	4.12 ± 2.01	4.20 ± 1.42

	w/ attn	w/o attn
IV	0.04 ± 0.02	0.05 ± 0.02
T_g	17.75 ± 2.00	19.00 ± 4.44
CH_4 perm.	0.31 ± 0.02	0.33 ± 0.04
CO_2 perm.	0.26 ± 0.02	0.29 ± 0.03
N_2 perm.	0.28 ± 0.02	0.30 ± 0.02

tion that yielded the best results. These results were compared against three descriptors commonly employed for polymer property prediction as a way to provide a contrast and evaluate whether traditional feature-engineering approaches could offer a viable alternative to our design. For the molecular descriptors, we constructed polymer-level representations by computing a weighted sum of the monomer-level features. Table 2 summarizes the test set errors across the 10 folds, where the same k-fold split was consistently applied to all models.

Table 2. Test Error for Predicting Experimental Polymer Properties. The best result for each task is shown in bold and ties occur where rounding masks marginal differences. See Table 1 for property units.

	STL (Random Forest)			MTAL (Ours)		
	RDKit	MACCS	OHE	GCS	OL-AUX	TAG
ΔH^{ROP}	**8.26 ± 2.79**	10.73 ± 3.69	-	9.75 ± 3.53	9.20 ± 2.65	9.05 ± 2.77
ρ_{300K}	0.12 ± 0.03	0.13 ± 0.04	-	**0.12 ± 0.05**	0.12 ± 0.04	0.12 ± 0.05
^{19}F MRI SNR	8.48 ± 2.23	7.65 ± 1.66	**6.97 ± 1.20**	8.21 ± 1.96	8.94 ± 1.53	8.06 ± 1.47
T_g	6.84 ± 2.40	6.53 ± 2.30	12.28 ± 4.09	6.20 ± 1.93	6.45 ± 2.11	**5.61 ± 1.78**
IV	0.06 ± 0.02	0.06 ± 0.02	0.06 ± 0.02	0.06 ± 0.02	0.06 ± 0.02	**0.05 ± 0.02**
T_g	26.49 ± 4.50	27.24 ± 4.92	-	28.01 ± 4.27	26.48 ± 4.47	**24.02 ± 4.79**
CH_4 perm.	0.45 ± 0.05	0.52 ± 0.05	-	0.45 ± 0.04	0.44 ± 0.04	**0.23 ± 0.04**
CO_2 perm.	0.40 ± 0.05	0.45 ± 0.07	-	0.37 ± 0.05	0.36 ± 0.05	**0.20 ± 0.04**
N_2 perm.	0.41 ± 0.04	0.48 ± 0.05	-	0.38 ± 0.05	0.38 ± 0.05	**0.32 ± 0.03**

The first important point to highlight is that we aimed to train a model capable of leveraging the maximum amount of information available about the polymers. To achieve this, the T_g experimental datasets were divided into two subsets because some polymers with this property included additional features beyond the p-SMILES notation, for instance, the molecular weight. This feature was reported by [23]. In these cases, we concatenated the additional features with the representation learned by the CoPolyGNN and used this combined input for the prediction head. Secondly, our MTAL model outperformed the baseline predictors in 7 out of 9 tasks, as shown in Table 2. While the overall performance gains were modest, the last three properties in Table 2 showed significant improvements, with approximately 48 %, 50 %, and 22 % gains over the best baseline results for CH_4, CO_2, and N_2 permeability, respectively.

Among MTAL strategies, TAG showed consistent prominence by outperforming the others with a significant margin and achieving the best performance on 6 tasks. However, during task selection for this method, no single auxiliary task appeared consistently across all folds, which may be influenced by the variability present in small datasets and the sensitivity of the model to data splits. In comparison, heuristic-based task weighting approaches showed marginal improvements over the baseline, with more favorable results observed in nearly half of the cases. Moreover, the experimental properties presented in Table 2 are organized by dataset size, with the smallest datasets positioned at the top and the largest at the bottom. We observed that, overall, the models struggled more with datasets containing fewer samples, even when the best results were achieved. This highlights the challenges posed by limited data availability.

We also investigated whether the improvement shown in Table 2 stemmed from the inclusion of auxiliary tasks or from the predictive power of the model itself. To address this question, Table 3 compares the results of our MTAL with a version of our model trained on the main task without auxiliary tasks, i.e., STL. We report the results obtained on the test set averaged over 10 folds. As a result, the MTL model outperformed STL across all tasks, which demonstrates the contribution of auxiliary tasks to improved performance on the main task.

Table 3. Comparison of the performance of STL and MTAL for predicting experimental properties. See Table 1 for property units.

	STL	MTAL
ΔH^{ROP}	9.43 ± 3.34	9.05 ± 2.77
ρ_{300K}	0.13 ± 0.05	0.12 ± 0.05
^{19}F MRI SNR	8.67 ± 1.37	8.06 ± 1.47
T_g	6.61 ± 2.20	5.61 ± 1.78

	STL	MTAL
IV	0.06 ± 0.02	0.05 ± 0.02
T_g	28.14 ± 4.99	24.02 ± 4.79
CH_4 perm.	0.41 ± 0.03	0.23 ± 0.04
CO_2 perm.	0.38 ± 0.05	0.20 ± 0.04
N_2 perm.	0.41 ± 0.05	0.32 ± 0.03

7 Conclusion

In this work, we addressed key challenges in polymer informatics to predict polymer properties by proposing CoPolyGNN, a GNN-based representation model for copolymers, curating a large-scale polymer dataset, and exploring MTAL strategies to tackle data scarcity. We conducted several experiments to optimize hyperparameters and investigated 3 techniques for MTAL, namely, GSC, OL-AUX, and TAG. Our results demonstrate that CoPolyGNN, when combined with MTAL, consistently outperforms STL and baseline models, achieving up to 50 % improvement in prediction accuracy for gas permeability and notable gains in other polymer properties. This validates the practical applicability of our approach across diverse experimental tasks, from glass transition temperature to gas separation performance. Moreover, our findings highlight how data-efficient learning and a flexible, multi-scale model can improve ML performance despite data scarcity. This is particularly relevant for polymer science, where data availability remains a bottleneck for computational design, and a model capable of handling the inherent structural variability of polymers is essential. Future work will investigate how the proposed framework generalizes across different polymer datasets and tasks, with a focus on identifying factors that influence task transferability.

Acknowledgments. The authors gratefully acknowledge support from FAPESP (São Paulo Research Foundation) and Shell, projects No. 2017/11631 − 2, 2021/08852 − 2, 2022/13536−5, and 2022/09285−7. This study was financed in part by the Coordenação de Aperfeiçoamento de Pessoal de Nível Superior - Brasil (CAPES) – Finance Code 001. The authors also thank for the infrastructure provided to our computer cluster by the Institute of Science and Technology – Campus São José dos Campos. Special thanks to Professor Cory M. Simon from Oregon State University for his valuable contributions and mentorship, which played a crucial role in the completion of this work.

Disclosure of Interests. The authors have no competing interests to declare that are relevant to the content of this article.

References

1. Afzal, M.A.F., et al.: High-throughput molecular dynamics simulations and validation of thermophysical properties of polymers for various applications. ACS Appl. Polymer Mater. **3**(2), 620–630 (2020)
2. Aldeghi, M., Coley, C.W.: A graph representation of molecular ensembles for polymer property prediction. Chem. Sci. **13**(35), 10486–10498 (2022)
3. Arora, A., Lin, T.S., Rebello, N.J., Av-Ron, S.H., Mochigase, H., Olsen, B.D.: Random forest predictor for diblock copolymer phase behavior. ACS Macro Lett. **10**(11), 1339–1345 (2021)
4. Cencer, M.M., Moore, J.S., Assary, R.S.: Machine learning for polymeric materials: an introduction. Polym. Int. **71**(5), 537–542 (2022)
5. Choi, S., et al.: Automated bigsmiles conversion workflow and dataset for homopolymeric macromolecules. Sci. Data **11**(1), 371 (2024)
6. Du, Y., Czarnecki, W.M., Jayakumar, S.M., Farajtabar, M., Pascanu, R., Lakshminarayanan, B.: Adapting auxiliary losses using gradient similarity. arXiv preprint arXiv:1812.02224 (2018)
7. Ebewele, R.: Polymer Science and Technology. CRC Press (2000)
8. Fifty, C., Amid, E., Zhao, Z., Yu, T., Anil, R., Finn, C.: Efficiently identifying task groupings for multi-task learning. Adv. Neural. Inf. Process. Syst. **34**, 27503–27516 (2021)
9. Gao, Q., Dukker, T., Schweidtmann, A.M., Weber, J.M.: Self-supervised graph neural networks for polymer property prediction. Mol. Syst. Des. Eng. **9**(11), 1130–1143 (2024)

10. Geyer, R., Jambeck, J.R., Law, K.L.: Production, use, and fate of all plastics ever made. Sci. Adv. **3**(7), e1700782 (2017)
11. Hayashi, Y., Shiomi, J., Morikawa, J., Yoshida, R.: Radonpy: automated physical property calculation using all-atom classical molecular dynamics simulations for polymer informatics. npj Comput. Mater. **8**(1), 222 (2022)
12. Jiang, S., Dieng, A.B., Webb, M.A.: Property-guided generation of complex polymer topologies using variational autoencoders. npj Comput. Mater. **10**(1), 139 (2024). https://doi.org/10.1038/s41524-024-01328-0
13. Kamal, D., et al.: Novel high voltage polymer insulators using computational and data-driven techniques. J. Chem. Phys. **154**(17) (2021)
14. Kuenneth, C., Rajan, A.C., Tran, H., Chen, L., Kim, C., Ramprasad, R.: Polymer informatics with multi-task learning. Patterns **2**(4) (2021)
15. Kuenneth, C., Ramprasad, R.: polybert: a chemical language model to enable fully machine-driven ultrafast polymer informatics. Nat. Commun. **14**(1), 4099 (2023)
16. Kuenneth, C., Schertzer, W., Ramprasad, R.: Copolymer informatics with multi-task deep neural networks. Macromolecules **54**(13), 5957–5961 (2021)
17. Landrum, G.: Rdkit: Open-source cheminformatics (2012), http://www.rdkit.org
18. Lin, X., Baweja, H., Kantor, G., Held, D.: Adaptive auxiliary task weighting for reinforcement learning. In: Advances in Neural Information Processing Systems, vol. 32 (2019)
19. Lo, S., Seifrid, M., Gaudin, T., Aspuru-Guzik, A.: Augmenting polymer datasets by iterative rearrangement. J. Chem. Inf. Model. **63**(14), 4266–4276 (2023)
20. Neres, L.C.S., Feliciano, G.T., Dutra, R.F., Sotomayor, M.D.P.T.: Development of a selective molecularly imprinted polymer for troponin t detection: a theoretical-experimental approach. Mater. Today Commun. **30**, 102996 (2022)
21. Odian, G.: Principles of Polymerization. Wiley India Pvt, Limited (2004)
22. Qiu, H., Liu, L., Qiu, X., Dai, X., Ji, X., Sun, Z.Y.: Polync: a natural and chemical language model for the prediction of unified polymer properties. Chem. Sci. **15**(2), 534–544 (2024)
23. Queen, O., et al.: Polymer graph neural networks for multitask property learning. npj Comput. Mater. **9**(1), 90 (2023)
24. Reis, M., et al.: Machine-learning-guided discovery of 19f mri agents enabled by automated copolymer synthesis. J. Am. Chem. Soc. **143**(42), 17677–17689 (2021)
25. Shukla, S.S., Kuenneth, C., Ramprasad, R.: Polymer informatics beyond homopolymers. MRS Bull. **49**(1), 17–24 (2024)
26. St John, P.C., et al.: Message-passing neural networks for high-throughput polymer screening. J. Chem. Phys. **150**(23) (2019)
27. Tiwari, S.P., et al.: Creation of polymer datasets with targeted backbones for screening of high-performance membranes for gas separation. J. Chem. Inf. Model. **64**(3), 638–652 (2024)
28. Toland, A., et al.: Accelerated scheme to predict ring-opening polymerization enthalpy: simulation-experimental data fusion and multitask machine learning. J. Phys. Chem. A **127**(50), 10709–10716 (2023)
29. Tran, H., Toland, A., Stellmach, K., Paul, M.K., Gutekunst, W., Ramprasad, R.: Toward recyclable polymers: ring-opening polymerization enthalpy from first-principles. J. Phys. Chem. Lett. **13**(21), 4778–4785 (2022)
30. Wang, F., Guo, W., Cheng, M., Yuan, S., Xu, H., Gao, Z.: Mmpolymer: A multimodal multitask pretraining framework for polymer property prediction. In: Proceedings of the 33rd ACM International Conference on Information and Knowledge Management, CIKM 2024, pp. 2336–2346. ACM, New York, NY, USA (2024). https://doi.org/10.1145/3627673.3679684

31. Wilbraham, L., Sprick, R., Jelfs, K., Zwijnenburg, M.: Mapping binary copolymer property space with neural networks, chem (2019)
32. Xie, T., et al.: Accelerating amorphous polymer electrolyte screening by learning to reduce errors in molecular dynamics simulated properties. Nat. Commun. **13**(1), 3415 (2022)
33. Xu, C., Wang, Y., Barati Farimani, A.: Transpolymer: a transformer-based language model for polymer property predictions. npj Comput. Mater. **9**(1), 64 (2023)
34. Xu, P., Chen, H., Li, M., Lu, W.: New opportunity: machine learning for polymer materials design and discovery. Adv. Theor. Simul. **5**(5), 2100565 (2022)
35. Yan, C., Feng, X., Li, G.: From drug molecules to thermoset shape memory polymers: a machine learning approach. ACS Appl. Mater. Interfaces **13**(50), 60508–60521 (2021). https://doi.org/10.1021/acsami.1c20947
36. Yan, C., Li, G.: The rise of machine learning in polymer discovery. Adv. Intell. Syst. **5**(4), 2200243 (2023)
37. Zhao, Y., Mulder, R.J., Houshyar, S., Le, T.C.: A review on the application of molecular descriptors and machine learning in polymer design. Polym. Chem. **14**(29), 3325–3346 (2023)
38. Zhou, J., Yang, Y., Mroz, A.M., Jelfs, K.E.: Polycl: contrastive learning for polymer representation learning via explicit and implicit augmentations. Digit. Disc. (2025)
39. Zhu, G., Kim, C., Chandrasekarn, A., Everett, J.D., Ramprasad, R., Lively, R.P.: Polymer genome-based prediction of gas permeabilities in polymers. J. Polym. Eng. **40**(6), 451–457 (2020)

Enhancing Detection of *Leishmania* spp. Amastigotes in Canine Lymph Node Smear Images: Evaluating the Effectiveness of Synthetic Data in Augmenting Existing Datasets

Dimitrios Tsikos[1], Irene Chatzipanagiotidou[2], Dimitris Dimitriadis[1(✉)], Constantina N Tsokana[1], George Valiakos[2], Labrini V Athanasiou[1,2], and Grigorios Tsoumakas[1]

[1] Aristotle University of Thessaloniki, Thessaloniki, Greece
{dndimitri,greg}@csd.auth.gr, ctsokana@vet.auth.gr, lathan@vet.uth.gr
[2] University of Thessaly, Volos, Greece
georgevaliakos@uth.gr

Abstract. Leishmaniosis is a parasitic mammalian disease that severely affects humans and dogs. Early diagnosis is crucial and associated with improved prognosis and treatment outcomes. A key diagnostic component is the detection of *Leishmania* amastigotes, the etiological agent of the disease, in cytologic preparations via microscopy. However, reliance on operator expertise limits its accesibility in veterinary clinics. Deep learning offers a promising approach for automating *Leishmania* amastigote detection, yet data limitations and the time-consuming, error-prone nature of real data annotation process remain significant challenges. This study explores the use of synthetic data to address these challenges and improve deep learning performance in detecting *Leishmania* amastigotes in microscopic images from canine lymph node aspirates. We propose an automated, two-stage synthetic data generation approach. First, structured representations of healthy and infected cells are created based on real microscopy data, incorporating randomized morphological features and material properties to mimic optical characteristics. Then, these elements are assembled into composite images with controlled variations in spatial arrangement, lighting, and perspective to enhance dataset diversity. The final output is annotated images designed for training object detection models. By supplementing real datasets with synthetic images, we address data scarcity and imbalance issues, improving model accuracy and generalization. Our results show that incorporating synthetic data significantly enhances deep learning models' ability to detect *Leishmania* amastigotes, offering a promising solution for veterinary diagnostics. Additionally, we introduce a new dataset that combines both original and synthetic data, contributing to further research into this important zoonotic disease.

Supplementary Information The online version contains supplementary material available at https://doi.org/10.1007/978-3-032-06118-8_26.

Keywords: *Leishmania* · canine lymph node smears · synthetic data · object detection · deep learning · artificial intelligence

1 Introduction

Leishmaniosis is a vector-borne disease caused by protozoan parasites of the genus *Leishmania*. Among the 30 identified species [1], *Leishmania infantum* is the most widespread [2] and is responsible for Visceral Leishmaniasis (VL) in humans and Canine Leishmaniosis (CanL) in dogs, both of which can be fatal if left untreated[1]. The World Health Organization (WHO) reports that human Leishmaniasis occurs in over 90 countries, with an estimated 50,000 to 90,000 new VL cases annually, though only 25–45% are officially reported[2].

Transmission occurs through the bite of infected female sandflies during blood feeding from their hosts [4]. Following the sandfly bite, metacyclic promastigotes are phagocytized by the host's immune cells, where they transform into amastigotes and rapidly multiply, leading to cell lysis. Once released, *Leishmania* amastigotes can invade new cells [5]. The outcome of the infection depends on both host factors and the virulence of the parasite [5–7].

Early and accurate diagnosis is crucial for improving prognosis and preventing further parasite dissemination within the host and its environment [8]. In dogs, treatment efficacy varies depending on symptom severity, parasitic load, and the host's immune response. While treatment aims to control clinical signs and improve the dog's quality of life, complete elimination of the parasite is rare, and the risk of relapse remains substantial [3,5–7]. Therefore, continuous monitoring of dogs affected by CanL is essential.

Diagnosing CanL is challenging and involves a combination of clinical examination, clinicopathological testing, cytology, serology, and molecular diagnostic techniques [9]. Parasitological diagnosis provides a conclusive identification of infection by directly observing amastigotes in cytologic preparations [10] from lymphoid organs (like bone marrow, lymph nodes, and spleen), liver, and skin, which typically harbor a high parasitic load [11,12].

Cytologic examination of stained lymph node smears is commonly used in routine laboratory settings due to the less invasive nature of lymph node aspiration compared to bone marrow and spleen biopsies [11]. However, the specificity of lymph node smear microscopy heavily relies on the operator's expertise, with high sensitivity achieved when a minimum of 100, ideally 1,000, oil immersion fields of high-quality smears are examined [12]. Moreover, the repeatability and reproducibility of this method remain uncertain [10]. Therefore, this method is infrequently performed in veterinary clinics due to a lack of experience among general practitioners in identifying *Leishmania* amastigotes via microscopy and the time constraints associated with examining the required number of fields.

To address these challenges, automating the detection of *Leishmania* amastigotes in microscopic images without the need for specialized equipment or extensive expertise is crucial. Diagnostic tools that enable accurate and efficient analysis of lymph node aspirate images would provide general practitioners with a

---

[1] https://www.cdc.gov/parasites/leishmaniasis/epi.html.
[2] https://www.who.int/news-room/fact-sheets/detail/leishmaniasis.

useful tool for diagnosing *Leishmania* infection in dogs, ultimately saving time and enhancing diagnostic capabilities for more effective monitoring of treatment outcomes and disease progression.

Deep learning models have the potential to enhance the diagnosis of *Leishmania*. Several studies have demonstrated promising results in both humans and animals using deep learning techniques [14,17]. However, a major challenge remains: the limited availability of data and the time-consuming process of acquiring it. In this paper, we address this issue by introducing a synthetic data generation technique that has not been previously applied to *Leishmania* diagnosis. Our results, obtained using a state-of-the-art deep learning model for object detection to identify *Leishmania* amastigotes, show that incorporating synthetic data improves performance compared to using only real images.

The remainder of this paper is structured as follows. Section 2, provides an overview of related work. Section 3 describes our dataset, detailing the image acquisition process and preprocessing steps. Section 4 presents the methodology for generating synthetic data. In Sect. 5, we outline the experimental setup, while Sect. 6 discusses the results. Finally, Sect. 7 concludes the paper.

2 Related Work

Early methods relied on classical image processing techniques, such as Difference of Gaussians (DoG) filtering for segmentation [18], which provided automation but lacked robustness due to variations in staining and imaging conditions [19]. As research progressed, ML emerged as a viable alternative.

In 2018, a U-Net model was introduced to segment *Leishmania* parasites in microscopy images [20]. The dataset, containing 45 images of *Leishmania* infected macrophages, faced class imbalance, which was mitigated through augmentation strategies. However, model generalization was constrained by the dataset's limited size. By 2022, the Viola-Jones algorithm was implemented for binary classification of infected and non-infected cells [21]. The dataset comprised 300 images from 50 slides prepared from skin scrapings obtained from human patients suspected for Leishmaniasis. Although, their approach offered computational efficiency, precision and recall remained suboptimal compared to state-of-the-art deep learning models. Similarly, ML classifiers was employed, including K-Nearest Neighbors, Naïve Bayes, Support Vector Machines, and Logistic Regression, to diagnose CanL [22]. Using tabular data from 340 canine cases, which included physical examination records and serological test results, their best model—logistic regression—achieved an accuracy of 75%.

Deep learning has emerged as a more effective approach for *Leishmania* parasites detection in comparison with traditional ML methods. In bibliography the two main tasks applied in *Leishmanias* parasites detection problem is classification, which determines whether an image contains infected cells, and object detection, which identifies and localizes parasites within an image. While classification is computationally simpler and widely used, object detection presents a more challenging problem, requiring accurate spatial localization alongside classification.

Classification-based approaches have demonstrated strong results. CNN-based feature extraction and color space transformations were applied to detect visceral *Leishmania* amastigotes, using a dataset of 150 images obtained from bone marrow slides from human patients [23]. The model improved detection accuracy but struggled with false positives. Similarly, pre-trained CNNs such as ResNet and InceptionV3 were used to classify microscopic images from bone marrow smears of human patients as positive or negative for the presence of *Leishmania* amastigotes using a dataset consisting of 150 microscopic images [24]. In order to overcome the obstacle of limited data, data augmentation techniques -like contrast adjustments and flipping- were applied. The techniques led to a significant improvement in classification accuracy. In 2024, the LeishFuNet was introduced, a deep learning model that achieved the impressive 98.95% accuracy and 98,92% F1-score in detecting *Leishmania* amastigotes using a dataset of 239 Giemsa-stained microscopic images [25]. In this case transfer learning was used to address data scarcity issues, making it a scalable solution for leishmaniosis diagnostics.

Object detection methods, while more complex, provide additional information for parasite localization. [26] focused on automating parasite detection and counting by applying segmentation techniques such as the Otsu method and morphological operations, using a dataset of manually labeled Giemsa-stained microscopy images. Their method excelled in recall, effectively identifying intracellular parasites, although precision remained a challenge due to false positives in heavily stained regions. YOLOv5 and Faster R-CNN were fine-tuned on a dataset of 1858 manually labeled images, including 244 Cutaneous Leishmaniasis cases, 68 Visceral Leishmaniasis cases, and 1420 monocyte samples [14]. The model achieved a mean average precision (mAP) of 73%, with a precision of 68% and recall of 69%, marking a significant improvement over traditional segmentation methods. Augmentation strategies were crucial in enhancing model robustness and performance, especially for detecting parasites in low-contrast images.

The limited availability of labeled datasets is a critical challenge in Leishmaniosis research. The main causes behind that are the difficulties in obtaining well-annotated microscopy images, interlaboratory staining variations, and ethical concerns surrounding data sharing. In order to overcome this data scarcity, many data augmentation techniques are employed.

Basic augmentation pipelines, which contain rotation flips, zoom transformations and contrast modifications, have proven effective in increasing dataset diversity. [14] used a combination of rotation, flipping, scaling, translation, and shearing to create diverse representations of *Leishmania* parasites in Giemsa-stained images, ensuring that their YOLOv5-based detection model could perform well under different staining conditions. [26] applied contrast modifications and color space transformations by converting images to the hue, saturation, and intensity (HSI) model, improving the distinction between parasites and background noise. These augmentation strategies played a crucial role in mitigating the risks of overfitting and ensuring that models could effectively handle real-world variations in microscopic imaging.

Lack of data is a regular challenge across all sectors that tend to adapt machine learning solutions. However, in recent years, there has been a growing shift toward synthetic data to further bridge the gap. Techniques like generative adversarial networks and real-world simulations are now being leveraged to create diverse, high-quality training data, improving model performance in scenarios where acquiring real data is costly or impractical. [27] explored the use of synthetic datasets in deep learning for computer-vision-assisted manufacturing tasks, demonstrating how artificially generated data can improve model accuracy and robustness. Similarly, [28] conducted a comprehensive survey on the creation and use of synthetic data in computer vision and medical imaging. They highlighted that synthetic data could address challenges related to limited patient populations, inconsistent data quality, and imbalanced disease stage distributions. By incorporating synthetic data, the models achieved improved accuracy and generalizability, effectively mitigating biases introduced during data collection and improving the objectivity and consistency of medical imaging applications.

In line with these directions and current trends, we integrate deep learning and synthetic data generation to detect *Leishmania* amastigotes, an approach that has not been previously explored. The promising results of the newly generated images, combined with the high accuracy of deep learning techniques, offer fresh insights to address this challenge and similar issues within the research community. Furthermore, the annotated dataset accompanying this work, along with the open-source synthetic data generation code, serves as a valuable resource for further study.

3 The Dataset

In this section, we present the dataset used in our study. Specifically, we detail the acquisition phase, during which we captured microscopic images of lymph node samples from dogs with canine leishmaniosis suspected of leishmaniosis in laboratory settings. We then describe the pre-processing phase, where the dataset was prepared for the object detection task. In addition, we introduce a utility dataset that we explored to enhance the performance of our models.

3.1 Acquisition

The lymph node smears used in this study were archived materials from previous studies conducted in the Diagnostic Laboratory, Clinic of Medicine, Faculty of Veterinary Medicine, School of Health Sciences, University of Thessaly. The preparation of the lymph node smears followed a specific protocol. A non-aspiration fine-needle biopsy technique was performed using a 21-gauge needle attached to a 10-mL syringe, targeting either the prescapular or popliteal lymph nodes of dogs. After collection, the material was placed on 76 x 26 mm glass slides for microscopy and the overlapping content was smeared using the squash method.

The lymph node smears were air-dried, fixed in methyl alcohol, and stained with Giemsa. We conducted a light microscopy examination of the lymph node smears using an optical microscope (OLYMPUS model BX4, Olympus, Germany) with a 1000× magnification lens. Microscopic examination included 10 to 1,000 oil immersion fields (OIFs, ×1000), depending on the detection and density of amastigotes. A lymph node smear was considered positive when *Leishmania* amastigotes were identified as round to oval organisms, measuring 2–5 μμ m in diameter, with an eccentric nucleus, a kinetoplast exhibiting more intense basophilic staining compared to the nucleus, and a visible cellular membrane. Smears that tested positive were stored for later image acquisition using an OLYMPUS model BX4 microscope (Olympus, Germany) coupled with a ZEISS Axiocam ERc 5 s 5-megapixel all-in-one microscope camera (ZEISS, Germany) and a BioBlue.Lab microscope (Euromex, Holland) coupled with a CMEX 5 digital camera (Euromex, Holland).

3.2 Preprocessing

The 201 microscopic images[3] collected during the acquisition phase underwent further processing to prepare them for the object detection task. First, we annotated the dataset using the Computer Vision Annotation Tool (CVAT)[4], a recommended tool for such tasks [29]. Each image was labeled to identify instances of *Leishmania* amastigotes, ensuring high-quality ground truth data. We reviewed and annotated the images, marking regions containing parasites. The annotated dataset was then exported in the YOLO (You Only Look Once) [30] object detection format. To enhance diversity and improve model generalization, we supplemented the dataset with an additional 128 publicly available images from infected human patients [17].

The dataset consists of images with varying resolutions, which posed a challenge for uniform processing. Since the model selected for training requires input images of a fixed rectangfular shape, we applied padding to standardize all images before resizing them to 1280×1280 pixels. This preprocessing step ensures consistency across the dataset and optimizes compatibility with the training framework.

4 Synthetic Data Generation

The process of generating synthetic data involved two primary pipelines[5]. Both pipelines were developed using Blender's python API [31]. The first pipeline

---

[3] The dataset can be accessed at https://doi.org/10.5281/zenodo.15700017.
[4] https://www.cvat.ai/.
[5] The source code for generating the synthetic data can be accessed at https://github.com/tsikinio/Synthetic-data-for-Leishmania-spp.-amastigotes-detection.git.

was responsible for generating individual images of cells, either infected with parasites or not.

This step aimed to create a diverse set of cell images (Fig. 1) that could later be used to construct synthetic microscopic samples. To achieve this, various procedural generation techniques were implemented to introduce natural variability in the shape, size, and texture of the cells. These characteristics were randomized within predefined limits to ensure that the dataset encompassed a broad spectrum of biological diversity. To characterize the cells and infected cells, we examined the key features of *Leishmania* amastigotes as detailed in previous studies [12,13]. These features include the size and shape of the amastigotes, their relative dimensions, internal staining patterns, properties of the kinetoplast and nucleus, and the characteristics of the host cell. In addition to these biological traits, it is also important to consider parameters related to synthetic data generation—such as the number of images, cells per image, and parasites per image—which are not directly tied to the biological characterization but are essential for the image synthesis process.[6]

Additionally, custom materials were created and applied to each cell and parasite to replicate the visual characteristics of real biological samples, such as texture, staining patterns, and structural details. This approach enhances the perceived authenticity of the synthetic dataset, ensuring it visually aligns with what practitioners typically observe in real microscopic images.

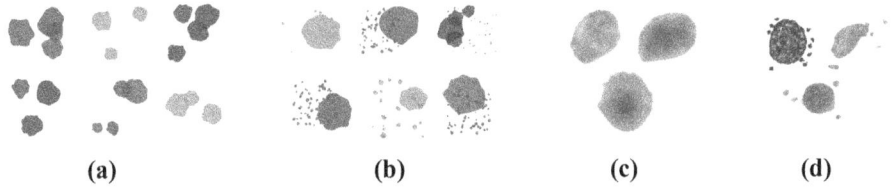

Fig. 1. (a) Synthetic images of healthy cells, (b) synthetic images of infected cells, (c) healthy cells extracted from real images, and (d) infected cells extracted from real images.

To further enrich the collection of the infected and healthy cells generated by the initial pipeline, we extracted samples of both infected and healthy cells from some real images Fig. 1). These manually cropped samples were used along with the synthetic cells images for synthetic image generation.

Once a large and diverse repository of individual cell images was created, the second pipeline was used to generate full synthetic images.

This stage involved placing the previously generated cell images onto background textures. Background selection was performed to ensure visual consistency with real microscopy slides. The infected and non infected cells were

---

[6] The Appendix A.1 provides additional details on the parameters involved in synthetic data generation, specifying which are related to biological traits and which pertain solely to the image synthesis process.

positioned randomly but under controlled constraints to prevent significant overlaps, ensuring a natural spatial distribution within each image. The cells were also subjected to transformations such as random scaling, rotation, and lighting variations to enhance realism. A key aspect of this pipeline was the structured randomization, which ensured that each synthetic image remained unique while adhering to biological plausibility. The parameters for this process can be found in Appendix A.2.

The output of this pipeline consisted of synthetic images accompanied by their corresponding annotations. The annotation process was automated, using the known placements of infected cells within each image. Using camera projection methods, precise bounding boxes were generated and saved in the YOLO object detection format, ensuring compatibility with the real dataset.

The entire process involved extensive parametrization, allowing for controlled variation in cell shapes, parasite distributions, lighting conditions, and other critical factors. This high degree of parameterization was essential in creating a dataset capable of improving the generalization performance of the machine learning model, and it is one of the greatest advantages of synthetic data.

To further enhance the realism of our synthetic dataset, we incorporated advanced image processing techniques aimed at bridging the gap between synthetic and real microscopic images. Specifically, we applied Gaussian noise and blur, both of which are commonly observed in real microscopy because of sensor imperfections and other environmental factors. By simulating these characteristics, we aim to make our synthetic images more photorealistic, thus improving the ability of the model to generalize to real-world data (Fig. 2).

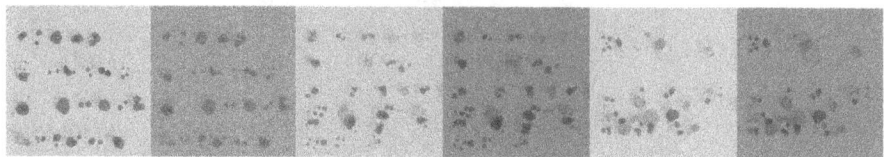

Fig. 2. Synthetic images before noise augmentation (left) and after noise augmentation (right).

The generation of one annotated synthetic images in our approach took in average 1.25 ± 0.083 seconds, whereas the image processing step, which involved applying Gaussian noise and blur to 130 images, required negligible time.

5 Experimental Setup

This section outlines the chosen configurations and environment for our experiments. First, we describe the datasets used for the experiments. Then, we detail the deep learning model selected for the object detection task and justify our choice. We then describe the training process and conclude with the post-processing phase, which played a key role in enhancing models' performance. All experiments were conducted on a machine equipped with an AMD Ryzen 9 5900X 12-core CPU, 16 GB of RAM, and an NVIDIA GeForce RTX 4090 GPU.

5.1 Datasets

As mentioned earlier, in Sect. 3, our dataset consists of 201 microscopic images of canine lymph node smears supplemented with 128 publicly available images -as detailed in Sect. 3 -resulting in a total of 329 instances. This dataset was used to perform 5-fold cross-validation, where each fold involved a different split of the full dataset into training, validation, and test sets with a 70-15-15 % ratio. Using this approach, we trained five models exclusively on real microscopic images (RMI).

Next, we expanded these datasets by generating 330 synthetic images (SI) through our proposed method (Sect. 4), increasing the total number of instances to 639. The number of synthetic images was chosen to maintain a 1:1 ratio with the real data, as introducing a bias toward synthetic data could lead the trained model to generalize better on synthetic images rather than real-world samples. The synthetic data was split using a 70-15-15% distribution and integrated into the RMI datasets, resulting in five augmented sets. Using these expanded datasets, we trained five models incorporating real microscopic images and synthetic images (RMI+SI).

5.2 Model Selection

Leishmania amastigotes detection is a quite complex task that requires high accuracy. At the same time inference speed is a critical factor considering that the proposed approach can be used in real-time applications in laboratories or veterinary clinics. To identify the most suitable model for our case, we conducted multiple training runs using different architectures. Specifically, we evaluated three state-of-the-art models [14]: YOLO v11, Faster R-CNN ResNet152 V1 (1024×1024) [15], and SSD ResNet101 V1 FPN (1024 × 1024) [16]. All models were trained on one of the folds of the combined RMI+SI dataset, using the same hyperparameters. Specifically learning rate was set to 0.005, batch size to 8 while all other parameters were kept at their default values as defined by the Ultralytics library[7]. Their performance was evaluated on the validation set containing both real and synthetic images. Based on the results of this experiment (as presented in Table 1), YOLOv11 emerged as the most effective model among those evaluated.

The architecture of YOLOv11 builds upon previous versions with key improvements, such as a more efficient backbone network for feature extraction, advanced neck components that refine spatial relationships, and an optimized

---

[7] https://docs.ultralytics.com/.

Table 1. Performance comparison of the three models

Models	mAP50	Recall
YOLO v11	0.692	0.652
Faster R-CNN Resnet152 V1 1024 × 1024	0.564	0.467
SSD ResNet101 V1 FPN 1024 × 1024	0.569	0.523

detection head for accurate bounding box regression and classification. The inclusion of transformer-based attention mechanisms enhances the model's capability to focus on relevant regions, making it particularly effective for detecting small objects, like *Leishmania* amastigotes. Additionally, the redesigned anchor-free detection mechanism reduces computational overhead while maintaining high detection precision. These architectural advancements make YOLOv11 the optimal choice for our use case. In our experiments, we used also the YOLOv11 pre-trained weights since our dataset is too small for training from scratch.

5.3 Model Training

We followed three different training processes for evaluating the impact of synthetic data for detecting *Leishmania* amastigotes. In the first approach, the model was trained exclusively on real data. In the second, training was performed using a combination of real and synthetic data. Finally, in the third approach, the model was initially trained on both real and synthetic data, followed by a fine-tuning phase using only real data.

The training processes were monitored using real-time logging, with key performance metrics computed after each iteration. The model's performance was evaluated based on mAP, Precision, Recall, and F1-score. The training process was also tracked using box loss and focal loss metrics, along with evaluation metrics on the validation set, to ensure efficient learning and prevent overfitting. Once the training was over, the best model was saved and ready for further evaluation.

Training on Real Data. We trained and validate five different models on the five folds arised from the RMI dataset. The objective was to evaluate the models' performance when trained purely on real data. The hyperparameters were selected to maximize model's performance. Specifically, all models were trained with an early stopping mechanism, using a patience threshold of 50 epochs - meaning training would terminate if no significant improvement was observed over 50 consecutive epochs. As a result, the five models were trained for varying durations, ranging from 101 to 131 epochs depending on convergence behavior. Leveraging the hyperparameter tuning feature provided by Ultralytics, the initial learning rate was set to 0.0063, while the final learning rate was adjusted to 0.00951. All other parameters were kept at their default values as defined by the Ultralytics library. Additionally, computational limitations necessitated the utilization of a batch size of 8. Finally, the data augmentation features offered by Ultralytics were enabled using their default settings. These included random color transformations such as hue, saturation and brightness adjustments, along with random translations, scaling and horizontal flipping. These enhancements aimed to increase the variability of the datasets.

Utilizing Synthetic Data. Two processes were followed for evaluating the impact of synthetic data. In the first process, the models were trained on the folds derived from the RMI+SI dataset. In the second, the best-performing models from this initial process were further fine-tuned on the RMI dataset (RMI+SI+RMI) for a few epochs to further enhance their performance.

During the first process, the five models were trained for varying durations, ranging from 133 to 150 epochs, due to the early stopping mechanism with a patience threshold of 50 epochs. Following hyperparameter tuning the initial learning rate was set to 0.00503 and the final learning rate to 0.0085. Additionally a batch size of 8 was selected balancing efficiency and process' computational cost. All the other parameters, including data augmentation, were set to the default values provided by Ultralytics library.

Once the initial training process was completed, the best-performing model from each fold was saved for further refinement. To enhance its ability to generalize to real-world data, the models' weights were fine-tuned using the RMI dataset consisting exclusively of real microscopic images. In order to avoid catastrophic forgetting- the models' disposition to forget the previously learned knowledge- a selective fine-tuning approach was adopted. Specifically, the backbone layers were frozen, preserving the feature extraction capabilities developed during pretraining. This allowed the training process to focus solely on adjusting the external layers, which are responsible for higher-level decision-making, ensuring that the models would adapt effectively to the real data without compromising its foundational learned features.

To ensure stable convergence and effective adaptation to real data during fine-tuning, specific adjustments were made to the training configuration. A lower batch size of 2 was chosen to allow more precise weight updates, given the smaller dataset and the need for refinement without drastic parameter shifts. Additionally, after hyperparameter tuning the initial learning rate was set to 0.00918 and the final learning rate to 0.0098. Finally the patience value was set to 5 epochs, since the model had already been exposed to the real images and it was more prone to overfitting. All other parameters, including data augmentation, were retained as initially configured.

After 12 to 14 epochs, the best-performing models were saved and ready for further evaluation.

5.4 Post-processing and Validation

Once the training process was over, we applied tiling inference to enhance detection accuracy using the open source framework Slicing Aided Hyper Inference (SAHI) [32]. This approach is particularly useful when detecting small objects, such as *Leishmania* infected regions, where every detail matters [33]. By analyzing smaller regions of the image, the model can focus on fine-grained features, leading to improved detection performance compared to processing the entire image at once. In our approach, the tiles have a slight overlap to ensure that no cell is partially cropped. Inference is performed on each tile with a confidence threshold of 0.3 as an optimal threshold effectively balances precision and recall.

After processing image tiles, we used Non-Maximum Suppression (NMS) [34] to remove duplicate bounding box detections. Because overlapping tiles can lead to multiple detections of the same object, NMS selects the highest-confidence prediction and eliminates others based on their overlap. We used Intersection over Union (IoU) as the overlap metric, with a threshold of 0.2. If the IoU between two boxes exceeds 0.2, the box with the lower confidence score is discarded. This ensures only the most accurate detections are retained. We also managed the overlapping region between adjacent tiles to be 0.2 and tile size to be 640 × 640.

6 Results

To assess the impact of synthetic data on the training process, a comparative study was conducted using three distinct training strategies. The first approach involved training exclusively on the RMI dataset. The second used a combined dataset of RMI and SI (RMI+SI) for training. The third built upon the second by applying an additional fine-tuning phase using only the RMI dataset (RMI+SI+RMI). Evaluation was carried out on the test sets of each fold of the RMI dataset. Each fold included a different subset of images in the test set to ensure an objective evaluation and minimize the risk of biased performance results. No data augmentations were applied to any test set. Table 2 presents the evaluation metrics of the trained models. For each training approach, the table reports the mean values and standard deviations computed across the five cross-validation folds.

Table 2. Performance comparison of the three models

Datasets	Recall	F1-score	mAP50
RMI	0.4954±0.0721	0.3853±0.0436	0.3854±0.0462
RMI+SI	0.6174±0.1226	0.5447±0.0645	0.5593±0.1254
RMI+SI+RMI	0.7220±0.0715	0.4678±0.0355	0.6019±0.0462

The models initially trained solely on real microscopic images (RMI) exhibited several critical limitations in their detection performance. They often failed in low-contrast regions, where infected cells blended into the background, and in densely populated areas, where overlapping structures led to frequent misdetections or omissions. Additionally, the models struggled to generalize across the morphological variability of infected cells, an essential aspect in the detection of *Leishmania*, resulting in a high false-negative rate and occasional false positives, where background elements or healthy cells were incorrectly classified as infected.

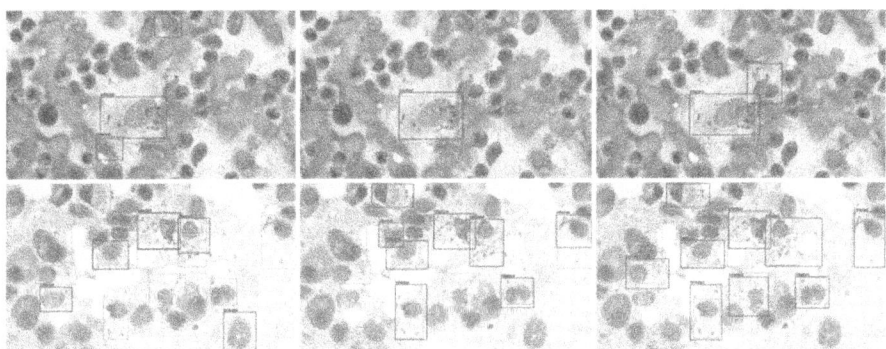

Fig. 3. Performance comparison results for two examples. The predicted bounding boxes are shown in red, while the ground truth annotations are displayed in green. The images on the left display the predictions from RMI, those in the center correspond to RMI+SI, and the ones on the right to RMI+SI+RMI. (Color figure online)

Introducing synthetic data in the first fine-tuning stage (RMI+SI) led to a substantial improvement in detection capability, with mAP50 increasing by approximately 0.17 compared to training solely on real data. This stage also resulted in noticeable gains in recall and F1-score, indicating enhanced sensitivity and overall detection balance. However, these improvements were accompanied by increased variability across cross-validation folds, particularly in recall, suggesting a trade-off between performance and stability. The second fine-tuning phase on real data (RMI+SI+RMI) further improved mAP50 to its highest value and reduced standard deviations across metrics, indicating the models' more consistent generalization ability.

A performance comparison example of the three models is presented in Fig. 3, using two images from one of the five test sets that were used for model evaluation.

7 Conclusions and Future Work

This paper presents a novel approach for detecting *Leishmania* amastigotes in canine lymph node smears through synthetic data generation. Specifically, we utilized a small dataset of microscopic images of canine lymph node smears to create synthetic data, aligning with current advancements in the field. The performance of this approach was evaluated using a state-of-the-art deep learning model for object detection. By adopting this technique, we address key challenges in medical imaging for deep learning, such as limited dataset availability, labor-intensive manual annotation, and class imbalance.

Using five-fold cross-validation, our model achieved an average mAP50 of 60.19%, an average Recall of 72.20%, and an average F1-score of 46.78% demonstrating competitive performance in comparison to existing methods. Notably, [14] explored various object detection frameworks for *Leishmania* amastigotes detection in human samples, with YOLOv5 achieving a mAP of 73%, Precision of 68%, and Recall of 69%. The proposed solution approaches these results while utilizing only one-fifth of the real data used in the referenced study, demonstrating the effectiveness of the synthetic data. Additionally, the results suggest that synthetic data augmentation not only compensates for small dataset sizes but also enhances detection reliability by contributing to the creation of a more diverse and robust dataset.

Moreover, with minor modifications, particularly in annotation format, the proposed pipeline can be adapted for other tasks such as segmentation and classification. For instance, in the case of [20], it could effectively address class imbalance, providing a more balanced dataset for training without relying solely on traditional oversampling techniques.

Future research will focus on enhancing the realism of synthetic data to further improve model efficiency and generalization. A key objective is to explore whether an ML model trained exclusively on synthetic data can achieve competitive performance, potentially reducing the reliance on real-world annotated datasets. Additionally, further improvements in accuracy and confidence levels will be pursued by refining model architectures, optimizing training strategies, and incorporating more diverse synthetic variations. Furthermore, future efforts will focus on real-world deployment to ensure the model's robustness and practicality in veterinary diagnostics and field applications. Lastly, given that the synthetic data generation pipeline is highly task-specific, it is important to evaluate its performance on other tasks and datasets to enhance its generalization ability and applicability.

References

1. Akhoundi, M., et al.: Molecular targets and diagnosis: Mol. Aspects Med. **57**, 1–29 (2017)
2. Azami-Conesa, I., Gómez-Muñoz, M., Martínez-Díaz, R.: A systematic review (1990–2021) of wild animals infected with zoonotic *leishmania*. Microorganisms **9**, 1101 (2021)
3. Solano-Gallego, L., et al.: Leishvet guidelines for the practical management of canine leishmaniosis. Parasites Vectors **4**, 1–16 (2011)
4. Maroli, M., Feliciangeli, M., Bichaud, L., Charrel, R., Gradoni, L.: Phlebotomine sandflies and the spreading of leishmaniases and other diseases of public health concern. Med. Vet. Entomology. **27**, 123–147 (2013)
5. Morales-Yuste, M., Martín-Sánchez, J., Corpas-López, V.: Canine leishmaniasis: update on epidemiology, diagnosis, treatment, and prevention. Vet. Sci. **9**, 387 (2022)
6. Ribeiro, R., Michalick, M., Silva, M., Dos Santos, C., Frézard, F., Silva, S.: Canine leishmaniasis: an overview of the current status and strategies for control. Biomed. Res. Int. **2018**, 3296893 (2018)

7. Saridomichelakis, M.: Advances in the pathogenesis of canine leishmaniosis: epidemiologic and diagnostic implications. Vet. Dermatol. **20**, 471–489 (2009)
8. Capistrano Costa, N., et al.: Exploring bioinformatics solutions for improved leishmaniasis diagnostic tools: a review. Molecules **29**, 5259 (2024)
9. Paltrinieri, S., et al.: Guidelines for diagnosis and clinical classification of leishmaniasis in dogs. J. Am. Vet. Med. Assoc. **236**, 1184–1191 (2010)
10. Guerra, J., et al.: Evaluation of cytopathological techniques for the diagnosis of canine visceral leishmaniosis with lymph node samples. J. Comp. Pathol. **172** 62–71 (2019)
11. Noli, C., Saridomichelakis, M.: An update on the diagnosis and treatment of canine leishmaniosis caused by Leishmania infantum (syn. L. chagasi). Vet. J. **202**, 425–435 (2014)
12. Saridomichelakis, M., Mylonakis, M., Leontides, L., Koutinas, A., Billinis, C., Kontos, V.: Evaluation of lymph node and bone marrow cytology in the diagnosis of canine leishmaniasis (leishmania infantum) in symptomatic and asymptomatic dogs. Am. J. Tropical Med. Hygiene **73**, 82–86 (2005)
13. Knottenbelt, C.: RE Raskin, DJ Meyer, Canine and feline cytology: a color atlas and interpretation guide, Elsevier Saunders, 2016, ISBN 9781455740833, 544 p. and 1200 colour illustrations; £97.99 (hard) (2016)
14. Tekle, E., Dese, K., Girma, S., Adissu, W., Krishnamoorthy, J., Kwa, T.: Deepleish: a deep learning based support system for the detection of leishmaniasis parasite from giemsa-stained microscope images. BMC Med. Imaging **24**, 152 (2024)
15. Ren, S., He, K., Girshick, R., Sun, J.: Faster R-CNN: towards real-time object detection with region proposal networks. In: Advances in Neural Information Processing Systems (NeurIPS), vol. 28, 2015
16. Liu, W., et al.: SSD: single shot multibox detector. In: Leibe, B., Matas, J., Sebe, N., Welling, M. (eds.) Computer Vision – ECCV 2016, LNCS, vol. 9905, Springer, pp. 21–37 (2016)
17. Sadeghi, A., Sadeghi, M., Fakhar, M., Zakariaei, Z., Sadeghi, M., Bastani, R.: A deep learning-based model for detecting leishmania amastigotes in microscopic slides: a new approach to telemedicine. BMC Infect. Dis. **24**, 551 (2024)
18. Leal, P., et al.: Automatic assessment of leishmania infection indexes on in vitro macrophage cell cultures. In: Image Analysis And Recognition: 9th International Conference, ICIAR 2012, Aveiro, Portugal, 25–27 June 2012. Proceedings, Part II 9, pp. 432–439 (2012)
19. Nogueira, P.: Determining leishmania infection levels by automatic analysis of microscopy images. ArXiv Preprint ArXiv:1311.2621 (2013)
20. Górriz, M., et al.: Leishmaniasis parasite segmentation and classification using deep learning. In: Articulated Motion And Deformable Objects: 10th International Conference, AMDO 2018, Palma De Mallorca, Spain, 12–13 July 2018, Proceedings 10, pp. 53–62 (2018)
21. Zare, M., et al.: A machine learning-based system for detecting leishmaniasis in microscopic images. BMC Inf. Dis. **22**, 48 (2022)
22. Ferreira, T., et al.: Diagnostic classification of cases of canine leishmaniasis using machine learning. Sensors. **22**, 3128 (2022)
23. Borges, A., Gonçalves, C., Dias, V., Sousa, E., Costa, C., Silva, R.: Visceral leishmaniasis detection using deep learning techniques and multiple color space bands. In: International Conference On Intelligent Systems Design And Applications, pp. 492–502 (2022)
24. Gonçalves, C., et al.: Automatic detection of visceral leishmaniasis in humans using deep learning. Signal, Image Video Process. **17**, 3595–3601 (2023)

25. Sadeghi, A., et al.: Potential diagnostic application of a novel deep learning-based approach for covid-19. Sci. Rep. **14**, 280 (2024)
26. Portuondo-Mallet, L., Mollineda-Diogo, N., Orozco-Morales, R., Lorenzo-Ginori, J.: Detection and counting of leishmania intracellular parasites in microscopy images. Front. Med. Technol. **6**, 1360280 (2024)
27. Manettas, C., Nikolakis, N., Alexopoulos, K.: Synthetic datasets for deep learning in computer-vision assisted tasks in manufacturing. Procedia CIRP. **103**, 9th (2021)
28. Paproki, A., Salvado, O., Fookes, C.: Synthetic data for deep learning in computer vision & medical imaging: a means to reduce data bias. ACM Comput. Surv. **56**, 1–37 (2024)
29. Pangal, D., Kugener, G., Shahrestani, S., Attenello, F., Zada, G., Donoho, D.: A guide to annotation of neurosurgical intraoperative video for machine learning analysis and computer vision. World Neurosurgery. **150**, 26–30 (2021)
30. Redmon, J., Divvala, S., Girshick, R., Farhadi, A.: You only look once: unified, real-time object detection. In: Proceedings Of The IEEE Conference On Computer Vision And Pattern Recognition, pp. 779–788 (2016)
31. Conlan, C. The blender python API. In: Precision 3D Modeling And Add (2017)
32. Akyon, F., Altinuc, S., Temizel, A.: Slicing aided hyper inference and fine-tuning for small object detection. In: 2022 IEEE International Conference On Image Processing (ICIP), pp. 966–970 (2022)
33. Shewajo, F., Fante, K.: Tile-based microscopic image processing for malaria screening using a deep learning approach. BMC Med. Imaging **23**, 39 (2023)
34. Neubeck, A., Van Gool, L.: Efficient non-maximum suppression. In: 18th International Conference On Pattern Recognition (ICPR 2006), vol. 3 pp. 850–855 (2006)

ActiveVisium: Leveraging Active Learning to Enhance Manual Pathologist Annotation in 10x Visium Spatial Transcriptomics Experiments

Jelica Vasiljević(✉), Ines Berenguer Veiga, Kerstin Hahn, Petra Schwalie, and Alberto Valdeolivas

Roche Pharma Research and Early Development, Roche Innovation Center Basel, Basel, Switzerland
{jelica.vasiljevic,ines.berenguer_veiga,kerstin.hahn,petra.schwalie, alberto.valdeolivas}@roche.com

Abstract. Spatial transcriptomics (ST) technologies offer valuable insights into tissue organisation by capturing gene expression within its spatial context. Among these, 10x Visium stands out for its capacity to integrate gene expression profiles with histological images, facilitating multi-modal tissue analysis. However, comprehensive analysis requires manual pathologist's annotations at the capture spot level, a labour-intensive and time-consuming process that demands a significant amount of pathologists' time. Given the scale of studies involving multiple ST samples, manual annotation becomes impractical, and no automated solutions currently exist. To address this, we introduce ActiveVisium, an active learning framework designed to enhance spot-level annotation in 10x Visium datasets. To the best of our knowledge, ActiveVisium is the first framework to leverage tissue morphology and, optionally, gene expression data to automate large-scale spot annotation while selecting the most informative ones for manual labelling. Furthermore, this approach enables transfer learning across similar samples, thereby reducing annotation time for entire studies. Evaluations across breast cancer, colorectal cancer, and healthy kidney samples demonstrate that ActiveVisium has the potential to significantly improve annotation efficiency and consistency. All code and data are publicly available.

Keywords: Spatial transcriptomics · Active learning · Digital Pathology · Deep Learning · 10x Visium

1 Introduction

Recent advancements in high-throughput technologies and imaging methods have enabled the development of ST, allowing for the capture of gene expres-

---

Supplementary Information The online version contains supplementary material available at https://doi.org/10.1007/978-3-032-06118-8_27.

© The Author(s), under exclusive license to Springer Nature Switzerland AG 2026
I. Dutra et al. (Eds.): ECML PKDD 2025, LNAI 16021, pp. 459–475, 2026.
https://doi.org/10.1007/978-3-032-06118-8_27

sion profiles within their native tissue context and opening new opportunities for investigating tissue organisation and function [17]. Various ST technologies are available [6], where some, such as 10x Visium [21], integrate gene expression data with histological images, facilitating simultaneous analysis of molecular and morphological features of a tissue sample. With both modalities available—gene expression data and histological images—molecular analyses are often cross-referenced with pathologist annotations on the corresponding whole slide images (WSIs) [1,24]. Such a multi-perspective view of tissue is especially important for gaining a comprehensive understanding of tissue organisation, as some differences may only be visible at the molecular level. For example, in a Colorectal Cancer (CRC) study [24], spots with similar morphological features that were uniformly annotated as tumours by a pathologist exhibited distinct gene expression profiles.

The 10X Visium [21] platform is one of the most widely utilised ST technologies [30], compatible with both fresh-frozen (FF) and formalin-fixed, paraffin-embedded (FFPE) tissue sections. It allows for the capture of near-whole transcriptome readouts in specially designed barcoded spots, which can be mapped to a histological image of the tissue, as illustrated in Fig. 1. The standard Visium platform employs capture slides containing approximately 5,000 spatially barcoded spots, each with a diameter of 55 μm. Additionally, slides with 11,000 spots are available. For a comprehensive analysis, annotations by pathologists should ideally correspond to individual capture spots, as illustrated in Fig. 1.

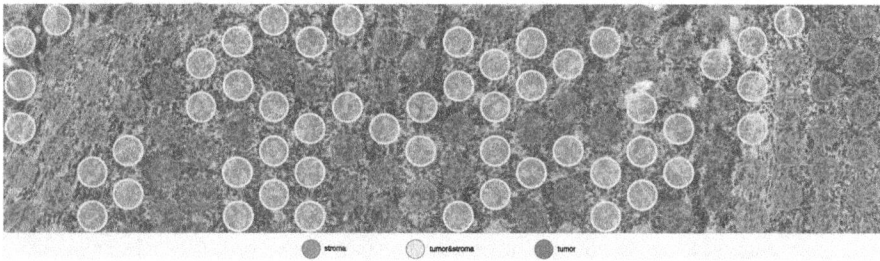

Fig. 1. Spot-level annotations in a FF colorectal cancer sample. Each spot, 55 μm in diameter, is labelled based on the tissue composition it covers. Standard 10x Visium slides have 5000 barcoded spots.

To obtain relevant biological information, a typical experimental study design requires multiple samples under different conditions. This usually involves biological and, occasionally, technical replicates to draw statistically significant conclusions. Furthermore, each sample is processed in a separate Visium capture area, each requiring its own annotations for comprehensive analysis. In these conditions, the annotation task becomes highly repetitive, time-consuming, and error-prone. As a result, the annotation process can often take hours or even days, depending on factors such as the number of samples, tissue heterogeneity, the number of spots covered by the tissue, and the level of detail required in the annotations. Annotations can be broad—such as distinguishing between tumour and non-tumour areas—or more detailed, such as identifying heterogeneous spots with mixed content, referred to as mixed spots (e.g. tumor&stroma spots in Fig. 1). In particular, mixed spots can help delineate region boundaries, which are important for understanding key biological processes. For instance, cell communication at the tumour-stroma interface plays a vital role in tumour growth and progression [32]. Therefore, identifying and annotating those spots is crucial yet highly time-consuming, as it requires examining the composition of the tissue within each spot in the anatomical boundary region. This manual and labour-intensive process of spot-level annotation significantly limits the number of samples that can be thoroughly correlated with the pathologist's input. Furthermore, the variability in annotation complexity among samples and experiments poses a major challenge for developing universal automated solutions. Currently, there are no existing solutions that fully address this issue.

To tackle these challenges, we present ActiveVisium—the first active learning-based framework, to our knowledge, that offers case- and pathologist-specific support for manual annotations in ST datasets. ActiveVisium identifies the most informative spots for pathologist manual labelling by utilizing morphological and, optionally, molecular features from tissue samples while automatically annotating the remaining spots. This framework significantly reduces the annotation workload for pathologists, resulting in a more efficient, scalable, and consistent annotation process.

2 Related Work

A standard procedure in ST data analysis involves grouping spots based on shared transcriptomic profiles, morphological features, or spatial proximity. This grouping helps identify functional regions within the tissue and uncovers the *biological identity* of each spot [33], linking them to specific spatial domains or cellular niches [23,33]. Nevertheless, the biological interpretation of these groups remains a downstream step, often relying on marker genes or differential gene expression analysis, usually cross-referenced with manual pathologist annotations [23,33]. However, the time-consuming nature and complexity of manual annotation tasks pose a significant challenge to the number of samples that can be thoroughly analysed. While regional annotations (e.g., assigning a single label to a large tissue area covering several dozen spots) offer a seemingly straightforward way to reduce such manual effort, this approach often fails to account for critical spatial heterogeneity. This is particularly true for small, low-represented, or transitional regions, such as mixed or boundary spots common in technologies like 10x Visium. Therefore, despite its time commitment, individual, spot-by-spot expert annotation remains the most reliable approach for precise characterisation.

Similar bottlenecks in obtaining high-quality manual annotations also arise in the digital pathology (DP) field. Despite significant progress in Artificial Intelligence (AI)-based solutions [20], these methods still heavily depend on (manual)

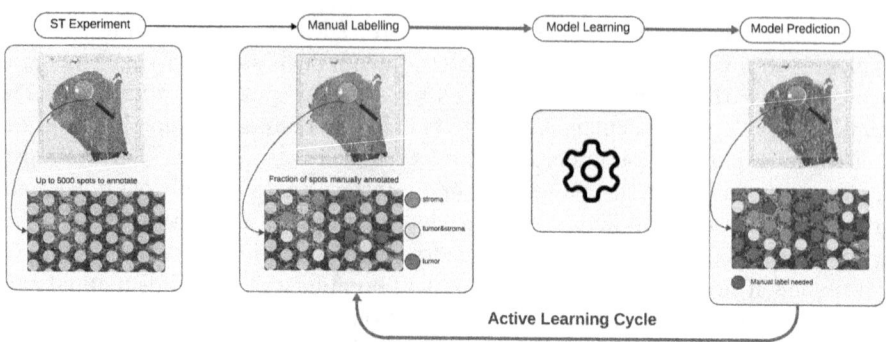

Fig. 2. The ActiveVisium framework leverages active learning to streamline spot-level annotations in ST experiments. Pathologists begin by annotating an initial subset of spots, which is used to train a model for predicting annotations on the remaining spots. Subsequently, additional spots are selected for annotation, enabling pathologists to review and refine the model's predictions. Once these new annotations are incorporated, the model is retrained with the updated dataset. This process continues until the expert is satisfied with the model's predictions or until correcting the model's potential errors requires less effort than annotating a new set of suggested spots.

expert annotations, which are both resource-intensive and time-consuming to produce [28]. Consequently, numerous workflows have been developed to alleviate annotation demands, including methods to accelerate manual labelling [7,14,26].

Active learning, a paradigm aimed at maximising performance with minimal labelled data, is widely adopted in DP to minimize annotation effort. These approaches, used for tasks like cell classification [25] and whole-slide image annotation [16], iteratively select the most informative data points for labelling. To improve learning efficiency, many active learning techniques leverage pre-trained models, frequently initialized with ImageNet weights [9,12]. The recent emergence of foundation models in DP [2,29] is further enhancing these approaches through the development of integrated active learning frameworks [5].

The existence of a wide range of methods designed to automate the labelling process in DP underscores a crucial point: for large datasets requiring expert annotation, it is often more practical and efficient for experts to review and validate model predictions rather than manually label every individual data point [11,25]. However, such strategies have yet to be effectively translated to ST, in part due to the novelty of the field and the unique challenges posed by spot-level annotations. This motivated the development of the ActiveVisium framework, which leverages foundational models and active learning strategies to minimize the number of spots requiring manual annotation. This approach significantly reduces the workload for experts, addressing a challenge that, to the best of our knowledge, has been largely unexplored in the literature.

3 Methods

ActiveVisium is a framework that leverages active learning to optimize and accelerate manual spot-level annotations in 10x Visium ST experiments. It starts with a small set of manually annotated spots and iteratively selects additional spots for annotation, progressively improving predictions for the remaining spots. Figure 2 presents an overview of the workflow.

In ST technologies such as 10x Visium, WSI is co-registered with the capture area containing gene expression capture spots. Let I_{WSI} represent a WSI obtained as part of such ST experiment, where the positions of gene expression capture spots are mapped onto the image. We define S_{all} as the set of tuples:

$$S_{\text{all}} = \{(x_i, g_i) \mid x_i \in \mathbb{R}^{H \times W \times 3}, g_i \in \mathbb{R}^n, i \in \{1, \ldots, N\}\}$$

where: $x_i \in \mathbb{R}^{H \times W \times 3}$ represents an image patch extracted from I_{WSI} corresponding to a capture spot i, and $g_i \in \mathbb{R}^n$ is the gene expression vector for the same spot, with n denoting the number of detected genes and N the total number of capture spots covered by tissue. The spatial dimensions $H \times W$ correspond to the pixel area covered by a capture spot (in standard 10x Visium experiments, this corresponds to a circle with a diameter of 55 μm).

Furthermore, let $S_{\text{ann}} \subset S_{\text{all}}$ represent the subset consisting of manually annotated spots provided by the pathologist ($|S_{\text{ann}}| \ll |S_{\text{all}}|$). Starting from the initial set of annotated spots $S_{\text{ann\_init}}$, the active learning pipeline is established to accelerate the process of obtaining annotations for the remaining spots in the following way:

1. **Model Learning:** The model is trained using the available annotations S_{ann} (initially $S_{\text{ann}} = S_{\text{ann\_init}}$) to predict labels for all remaining spots (see 3.1 for details).
2. **Data Acquisition Strategy:** Predictions are generated for all spots in $S_{\text{all}} \setminus S_{\text{ann}}$. Using a predefined active learning strategy, an additional set $S_{\text{to\_ann}} \subseteq S_{\text{all}} \setminus S_{\text{ann}}$ of M spots is selected for expert annotation.
3. **Expert Annotation:** The pathologist reviews the model's predictions for spots in $S_{\text{all}} \setminus (S_{\text{ann}} \cup S_{\text{to\_ann}})$ and assigns labels to the newly selected spots in $S_{\text{to\_ann}}$. The set of annotated spots is then updated as $S_{\text{ann}} = S_{\text{ann}} \cup S_{\text{to\_ann}}$.
4. **Iteration:** Steps 1–3 are repeated iteratively until the model achieves accurate predictions across S_{all}, or until correcting misclassified samples requires more effort than annotating a new set $S_{\text{to\_ann}}$, as determined by an expert.

3.1 Model Training

Let $f_{\text{morph}} : \mathbb{R}^{H \times W \times 3} \to \mathbb{R}^{d_m}$ and $f_{\text{ge}} : \mathbb{R}^n \to \mathbb{R}^{d_g}$ be feature extractors mapping image patches and gene expression profiles to d_m- and d_g-dimensional embeddings, respectively. A classifier $\phi \cdot \mathbb{R}^d \to \mathbb{R}^K$ projects embeddings into K classes, where K is specified by a pathologist.

We consider two settings - an unimodal setting where $d = d_m$ and only morphological features are used and, a multimodal setting where a fusion layer

$h : \mathbb{R}^{d_m+d_g} \to \mathbb{R}^d$ combines outputs from f_{morph} and f_{ge}, providing the fused representation $h(f_{\text{morph}}(x), f_{\text{ge}}(x))$ as input to ϕ.

Morphological features are extracted using pre-trained DP foundational models. Each spot $x \in S_{\text{all}}$ is mapped to the feature representation of the foundational model, which is stored to accelerate training. This representation is then processed through a Multi-Layer Perceptron (MLP) to obtain the morphological feature representation $f_{\text{morph}}(x)$. Similarly, gene expression features are processed by the gene expression feature extractor f_{ge}, which maps them into a latent space using an MLP. To ensure consistent feature representation across all capture spots within the sample, we identify the top 1,000 highly variable genes (HVGs) across the sample. The normalized and log-transformed expression levels of these HVGs are used as features for each spot and subsequently mapped into the latent space via an MLP. Nevertheless, given that the field of foundational models in DP and ST is actively evolving [18,27], ActiveVisium is designed to support the seamless integration of state-of-the-art and emerging models. This flexibility extends to the classifier ϕ, which is implemented as a configurable stack of MLPs, allowing for adaptability to various classification tasks.

Our model leverages the UNI framework [2] for morphological feature extraction. The classifier includes a single hidden layer with 128 neurons. Both gene expression and morphology branches use projection heads with 128 neurons and LeakyReLU activation. The fusion layer integrates these features via a normalization layer, an MLP with 256 neurons, LeakyReLU activation, and a dropout layer.

During each active learning iteration, the model is trained for 50 epochs, selecting the best-performing model based on validation loss, following standard practice in active learning literature [10]. The initial set $S_{\text{ann\_init}}$ is determined using k-means clustering in the morphological representation space of all spots, where $n_{clusters} = |S_{init}|$. In our experiments, we set the size of the initial annotation set $|S_{init}| = 55$. To ensure comprehensive class representation, in cases where the initial k-means clustering fails to encompass all classes (a scenario often encountered in datasets with highly imbalanced class distributions, such as the kidney tissue samples used in this study), the initial dataset S_{init} is augmented by randomly selecting and incorporating one spot from the annotation pool for each unrepresented class.

In real-world applications of ActiveVisium, using a predefined validation set is impractical, as annotating data solely for validation during active learning is not feasible. Consequently, this setting is used only to report experimental results. In practical applications, the training strategy adapts based on the size of S_{ann}, assuming no available validation set. For small S_{ann}, the model is trained for 50 epochs (configurable), after which the final model is retained for evaluation. With larger S_{ann}, the annotated data is split into training and validation sets during each model training, saving the model based on validation performance.

In the initial iteration, the model is initialized with random weights. Subsequent iterations reuse the model from the previous iteration as the starting point.

Weighted categorical cross-entropy loss is employed to address data imbalance. The class weights are dynamically recalculated in each active learning cycle as the inverse of class frequencies.

3.2 Data Acquisition Strategy

To select M spots for manual annotation, a hybrid least-confidence and diversity-based sampling approach is implemented. At iteration i, the model predicts labels for non-annotated spots $S_i = S_{\text{all}} \setminus S_{\text{ann}}$, and each spot $x_j \in S_i$ is assigned an uncertainty score:

$$\text{score}(x_j) = \left[1 - P_{\Theta_i}(y_j^* \mid x_j)\right] \times \frac{K}{K-1}$$

where y_j^* is the highest softmax output, Θ_i are model parameters at iteration i, and K is the number of classes. This score reflects the model's uncertainty about its most confident prediction for each spot, with higher scores indicating greater uncertainty.

While active learning methods vary widely [22], least-confidence uncertainty sampling is chosen as the default due to its simplicity and effectiveness across datasets [5,28]. Nevertheless, the framework remains flexible regarding its active learning strategy. Recent evaluations confirm that incorporating diversity into uncertainty-based selection enhances performance and can outperform more complex strategies [3,5]. Therefore, diversity is incorporated using a k-means clustering approach: the top 5% most uncertain spots are grouped into M clusters within a feature space defined by morphological representations (or a combined feature space in a multimodal setting). From each cluster, the spot closest to the centroid is selected for annotation. As a baseline, we also include random sampling, in which M spots are chosen randomly from $S_{\text{all}} \setminus S_{\text{ann}}$, with each spot having an equal probability of selection, irrespective of uncertainty score.

3.3 Expert Annotation

Expert annotations are conducted using Loupe Browser, the standard software for exploring outputs from 10x Visium experiments. Loupe provides an intuitive graphical interface that enables pathologists to interact with ST data easily. Given that pathologists are already familiar with using Loupe for manual spot annotation, we opted to integrate ActiveVisium with it to maintain this workflow. Pathologists annotate selected spots in Loupe and export the results as CSV files. Likewise, ActiveVisium generates predictions and selects spots for annotation also in CSV format, ensuring seamless import into Loupe for further review and refinement.

3.4 Datassets

ActiveVisium framework was evaluated on a diverse set of 10x Visium ST datasets, encompassing human and mouse samples from various tissues and

Table 1. Dataset Summary

Specimen	Tissue	Pres.	Reference	Spots	Classes	Ann. Time
Human	Colorectal (Cancer)	FF	SN048_A121573_Rep1	2,750	8	~8 h
			SN048_A121573_Rep2	2,906	7	~8 h
			SN123_A595688_Rep1	1,394	11	~8 h
	Breast (Cancer)	FFPE	–	4,992	11	~12 h
	Kidney (Healthy)	FFPE	–	5,928	11	~12 h
Mouse	Kidney (Healthy)	FFPE	–	3,124	14	~3 h

pathological conditions, including breast and colorectal cancer (CRC) (human), as well as healthy kidney tissue (human and mouse). Breast cancer and kidney samples were FFPE-preserved samples, while CRC samples were FF-preserved. Experienced pathologists manually annotated each dataset at the spot level, determining the number of classes based on tissue morphology. Table 1 presents a concise overview of the datasets used, while the Appendix provides detailed dataset descriptions, including references for each dataset.

The annotation process was highly time-intensive, with complexity varying across samples. Individual samples required between 3 to 12 h of continuous annotation time, with a typical case taking 8 h of continuous work per sample. This substantial time investment translates to multiple days needed to complete annotations across all datasets. These annotations serve as the ground truth for evaluation purposes in this study. Each dataset is divided into a training set (annotation pool), comprising 90% of the total spots covered by a tissue, and a test set, containing the remaining 10%. Additionally, 10% of the training set is set aside as a validation set to monitor training progress. The split is performed to maintain the class distribution, ensuring a proportional representation of all classes across the data splits.

4 Results

In this section, we showcase the effectiveness of the ActiveVisium framework across various tasks: simulated annotation experiments in both unimodal and multimodal contexts (Sect. 4.1), cross-sample annotation transfer illustrated through a CRC case study (Sect. 4.2), enhancement of annotation consistency (Sect. 4.3), and significant time savings in the annotation process (Sect. 4.4). Furthermore, we provide practical guidelines for the optimal utilization of ActiveVisium (Sect. 4.5).

4.1 Evaluating ActiveVisium: Simulated Annotation Experiments

All datasets used in this study are entirely manually annotated by a trained pathologist. To simulate the active learning process, we initially considered all spots in each fully annotated dataset as unlabeled. In each active learning iteration, ActiveVisium selects a subset of spots for annotation, which are then incorporated into the training data for the next iteration.

Experiments are conducted in both unimodal (morphology only) and multimodal (morphology and gene expression) settings, with three independent runs of ActiveVisium performed for each dataset within each setting. In each active learning iteration, we fixed $M = 55$ spots to be chosen for annotation, selected based on the given experimental strategy, and this process is repeated for 10 rounds. The evaluation metrics include the average weighted F-score and the percentage of misclassified spots (along with standard deviations), compared to manual annotations that are treated as the ground truth.

Following the evaluation protocol outlined in Zhang et al. (2023) [31], Fig. 3 presents active learning performance on the annotation pool, which aligns closely with the purpose of ActiveVisium—annotating a whole sample using a limited amount of provided data. To ensure a comprehensive evaluation, results on held-out test sets are included in the Appendix. Additionally, fully supervised model performances (both unimodal and multimodal) are reported to estimate the upper-bound performance.

The results obtained across various datasets suggest that using AI-based assistance for annotations is beneficial. In the early stages of training, both active learning and random sampling show promising trends in reducing misclassified samples and increasing the weighted F-score. However, active learning strategies consistently outperform random sampling, demonstrating the advantages of guided annotation over random approaches. The most significant changes are observed in the initial iterations, emphasizing the importance of following the model's suggestions for annotation in the early steps. Nonetheless, the quantitative results should be interpreted with caution, taking into account the limitations and variability associated with manual annotations (see more in Sect. 4.3).

The impact of multimodal approaches varies among samples and does not uniformly improve performance (see Fig. 3). For instance, while the breast cancer sample shows substantial improvement, the human kidney sample exhibits only minimal benefit. This inconsistency likely arises from the degree of alignment between gene expression profiles and pathologist annotations, as morphology and gene expression can capture different biological aspects of tissue. To quantify this alignment, we first performed Louvain clustering at multiple resolutions- a hyperparameter that determines the total number of clusters- on the highly variable genes in the gene expression space. We then assessed the correspondence between the resulting clusters and the manual pathologist annotations using the Adjusted Rand Index (ARI)[1]. The breast cancer sample achieved the best ARI

---

[1] An ARI of 1 indicates a perfect match, while an ARI close to 0 suggests the agreement is no better than random.

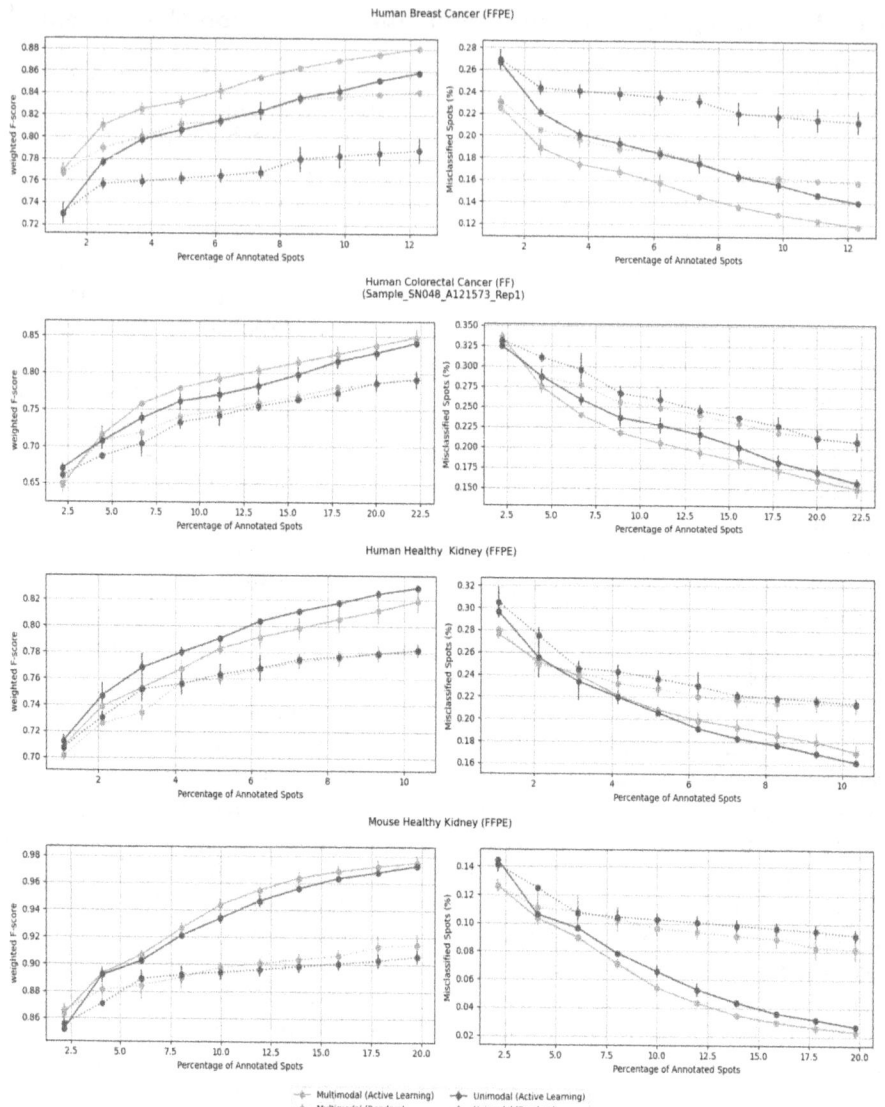

Fig. 3. Performance comparison of ActiveVisium across all evaluated datasets, including multimodal and unimodal settings. Each approach is assessed against its random sampling.

of 0.49 (resolution 0.7), notably higher compared to the human kidney sample had the best ARI of 0.17 (resolution 0.3). Therefore, it is not surprising that the incorporation of gene expression data led to significant performance gains in the breast cancer dataset, whereas the multimodal approach offered only marginal benefits in the human kidney sample. Additional ARI results across different Louvain clustering resolutions and samples are provided in the Appendix.

4.2 Cross-Sample Annotation Transfer: A Colorectal Cancer Case Study

To ensure statistically robust biological conclusions, ST studies typically comprise multiple samples from a certain tissue or disease type. Some experiments also include replicate samples from the same subject, obtained from consecutive tissue sections. In this context, our goal is to evaluate the generalizability of a model trained on a single sample by assessing its performance in two scenarios: (i) a replicate from a consecutive section of the same patient and (ii) a morphologically and pathologically similar sample from a different patient.

We evaluated the transfer learning ability of ActiveVisium on human FF resection samples from a CRC study [24]. Specifically, we trained a model in an active learning setting on Sample_SN048_A121573_Rep1 and subsequently applied it to its replicate, Sample_SN048_A121573_Rep2 and the sample from a different patient, Sample_SN123_A595688_Rep1. Manual annotations, obtained from the original study [24] served as ground truth. Since annotations were independently performed per sample, some classes present in the original sample were not available in the others. To ensure consistency in evaluation, we standardized the labels by merging similar classes and excluding non-corresponding ones (see Appendix).

In a zero-shot setting, we evaluated inter-observer variability by comparing the annotations provided by ActiveVisium— which has no annotated spots in this sample— to those manually annotated by a pathologist. In the unimodal setting, the average inter-observer agreement for the replicate sample was 0.59(0.01), while for the sample coming from a different patient, it was 0.52(0.02), indicating moderate agreement [13]. This level of concordance translates to a substantial proportion of correctly classified spots. For instance, on average, 89% and 82% of tumour spots are correctly classified in the replicate and in the sample from a different patient, respectively.

For multimodal annotation transfer, we first integrated and batch-corrected gene expression among samples with Harmony [8]. Then, highly variably genes were identified in the integrated set, and the active learning multimodal model is trained using the sample Sample_SN048_A121573_Rep1. Then, we applied it to the replicate and the sample from another patient. This approach yields inter-observer agreements of 0.061(0.00) for the replicate and 0.53(0.05) for the other sample, indicating substantial and moderate agreement, respectively. The multimodal approach is particularly beneficial for enhancing the detection rate of spots with mixed composition. For instance, when transferring to another sample, the percentage of correctly classified spots covering both tumour and stroma increased from 41,91% in an unimodal setting to 66.5% in a multimodal setting. These results are not surprising, as transcriptomic heterogeneity is more evident in mixed spots, where genes specific to various anatomical regions come together in different proportions based on their composition. In contrast, it is more challenging to identify them based on morphological features only.

The ActiveVisium approach has the potential to greatly reduce annotation time by transferring labels from samples with similar morphological features. This is especially advantageous for studies involving multiple samples with similar features. However, pathologists still need to review and correct annotations, which can include leveraging initial predictions from transfer learning to initiate the active learning process.

4.3 ActiveVisium Improves Annotation Consistency

Consistency in annotations is crucial for the accuracy and reliability of ST data analysis. To assess whether ActiveVisium enhances this consistency, we evaluated its performance on an FFPE human kidney sample, where discrepancies between its predictions and expert annotations were most pronounced. Given the subjectivity of manual annotations, we investigated whether these misclassifications resulted from noisy manual labels rather than from model errors.

The human kidney sample consists of 5,928 annotated spots categorized into 11 classes. The initial manual annotation process took approximately 12 h over several days, making it difficult to establish consistent labelling criteria, particularly in heterogeneous regions. Three independent ActiveVisium runs are conducted, each comprising 10 active learning cycles. The model's predictions were then compared to the original manual labels. We found 606 instances where all three models, after completing the 10th iteration of active learning, consistently classified these instances differently from the original manual annotations. A detailed breakdown of the misclassified instances by category is included in the Appendix. The pathologist who performed the initial manual annotations reviewed these spot annotations 20 weeks later, comparing the model predictions with the original annotations.

Upon investigation, the pathologist changed the annotations for 330 spots (54.46%) - 307 accepted the model prediction, while 23 received new annotations (disagreement between model prediction, but also with the original annotation). This highlights inconsistencies in the original annotations and the challenge of maintaining uniform criteria over time. As expected, most of the changes occurred in heterogeneous areas (e.g., tubule vs. tubule-interstitium regions). While these findings confirm spot-level annotation inconsistencies, this experimental setting may be subject to confirmation bias [4] - experts might question their original annotations when faced with conflicting model predictions. Nevertheless, these results suggest that ActiveVisium enhances annotation consistency by promoting uniform criteria throughout the process. This is particularly evident in certain classes, such as glomeruli, where the model successfully identified and corrected annotations that were clearly overlooked or misclassified in the original manual process (see Appendix).

4.4 Accelerating Annotation: Time Savings with ActiveVisium

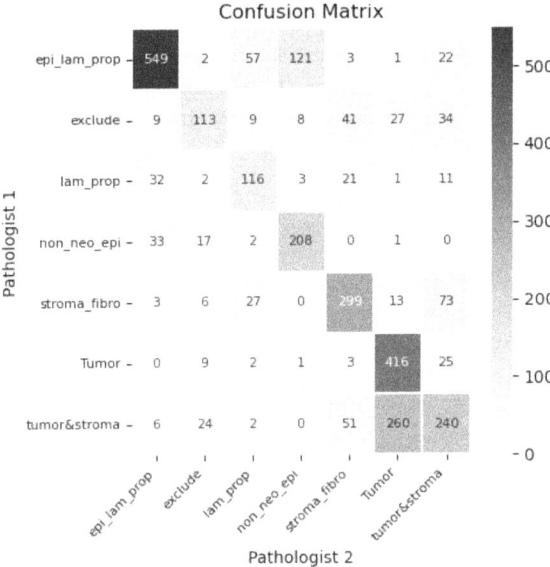

Fig. 4. Confusion matrix comparing spot-level annotations between Pathologist 1 (manual annotation) and Pathologist 2 (ActiveVisium-assisted annotation) for Sample_SN048_A121573_Rep2.

This section quantifies the time savings achieved by ActiveVisium compared to fully manual annotation using Sample_SN048_A121573_Rep2 (2906 spots, 7 classes). Two pathologists were asked to annotate the sample—one did it entirely by hand, while the other used ActiveVisium. Pathologist 1, who performed the manual annotation at the spot level, estimated that the task took approximately 8 h of uninterrupted work. In contrast, Pathologist 2, after a brief orientation and practice with ActiveVisium, annotated the same sample in just 1 h and 15 min, achieving a moderate inter-observer agreement of 0.6 with Pathologist 1. The ActiveVisium workflow involved an initial annotation of 102 spots in 17 min. This was followed by two active learning iterations, each annotating 55 spots in an average of 10 min, resulting in 211 annotated spots (7% of all spots). After each active learning iteration, Pathologist 2 spent approximately 7 min inspecting model predictions. Following the second iteration, Pathologist 2 assessed that the model's predictions were sufficiently accurate for the task at hand (with minor corrections needed) and that further active learning iterations were unnecessary. This correction process, applied to 42 spots, took 13 min and 17 s, ultimately resulting in 253 pathologist-provided annotations.

Final annotations occasionally differed from Pathologist 1's. These divergences were most pronounced in heterogeneous regions—like at the transition between the tumour and the stroma—where annotation criteria are inherently subjective and vary between experts. This is illustrated in the confusion matrix in Fig. 4. Despite these discrepancies, Pathologist 2 verified that this final set accurately represents their annotation style and provides a representative annotation of the sample. These differences are consistent with the inter-observer variability commonly encountered in pathology [19], further demonstrating ActiveVisium's potential as a valuable, personalised assistant that adapts to individual pathologist workflows.

4.5 Guidelines for Effective Use of ActiveVisium

Given the human-in-the-loop nature of ActiveVisium, it is reasonable to anticipate that expert interactions may deviate from theoretical expectations, and that is what we observe in practical application. For example, experts might prioritize annotating spots they find more relevant over algorithm-selected ones, particularly in early iterations when classification criteria are not yet fully established. Additionally, they may focus on correcting model errors rather than annotating new spots, which can shift model performance closer to random sampling approaches—shown in this study to be inferior to active learning strategies. To improve ActiveVisium's efficiency, we recommend establishing clear classification criteria and annotating representative spots in the first iteration. At least two active learning iterations should be completed before prioritizing error correction, as early predictions tend to be less reliable due to limited data. Once the model stabilizes, reviewing and correcting predictions is beneficial.

5 Limitations and Conclusion

This study introduces ActiveVisium, an active learning-based framework designed to streamline manual spot annotation in 10x Visium ST experiments. It demonstrates significant potential for reducing annotation workload and improving consistency across diverse tissue types. However, we acknowledge several key limitations.

A primary challenge in evaluating active learning frameworks, such as ActiveVisium, lies in the inherent trade-off between minimizing annotation effort and the need for comprehensive performance assessment. This *validation paradox* [10] is further amplified by the relatively small dataset sizes (in terms of the number of samples available) and the difficulty in establishing a reliable ground truth due to inherent noise and inter- and intra-observer variability in pathologists' annotations. Consequently, while a traditional train-test-validation split was performed for consistency with the literature, we focus on performance within the annotation pool as a more relevant indicator of the model's utility.

The choice of the annotation tool presents another limitation. While we utilized the Loupe Browser for its familiarity and accessibility, its design is not optimal for active learning annotation tasks. Therefore, more specialized applications should be developed. This aspect was not explored at this stage of our research, as we focused on a proof-of-concept study using an established tool which pathologists were already familiar with. Developing a dedicated tool was beyond the scope of this study. However, we envision integrating ActiveVisium into a broader workflow in the future.

Beyond the limitations discussed above, several possibilities exist for future enhancement of ActiveVisium. Given the dynamic shifts in data distribution inherent to active learning, adaptive hyperparameter tuning [15] and more sophisticated regularization techniques are expected to improve learning efficiency and robustness. Furthermore, integrating multi-scale learning and leveraging the spatial context of spots are promising strategies. Finally, given the increasing adoption of Visium HD with its significantly higher resolution ($2\mu m$ bins compared to 55μ m spots in standard Visium), future work should prioritize adapting ActiveVisium to this platform, as the manual annotation of these high-resolution datasets is anticipated to present a substantial bottleneck.

Looking ahead to the future applications of ActiveVisium, it is important to clarify its role in relation to pathologists. ActiveVisium is designed to complement, not replace, their expertise. By automating repetitive and time-intensive annotation tasks, it allows pathologists to focus on higher-level analysis and interpretation.

Acknowledgments. This work was supported by the Roche Postdoctoral Fellowship (RPF) programme. We sincerely thank Andrew Janowczyk and Julio Saez-Rodriguez for productive scientific discussions around the topics covered in this manuscript.

Data and Code Availability. All code and data used in this study—including manual pathologist annotations, configuration files, model checkpoints, and intermediate results—are available at 10.5281/zenodo.15625539 and github.com/jelica-vasiljevic/ActiveVisium.

Disclosure of Interests. All the authors are currently employed by F. Hoffmann-La Roche Ltd.

References

1. Arora, R., et al.: Spatial transcriptomics reveals distinct and conserved tumor core and edge architectures that predict survival and targeted therapy response. Nat. Commun. **14**(1), 5029 (2023)
2. Chen, R.J., et al.: Towards a general-purpose foundation model for computational pathology. Nat. Med. **30**(3), 850–862 (2024)
3. Doucet, P., Estermann, B., Aczel, T., Wattenhofer, R.: Bridging diversity and uncertainty in active learning with self-supervised pre-training. In: ICLR 2024 Workshop on Practical Machine Learning for Low Resource Settings, arXiv preprint arXiv:2403.03728 (2024)
4. Evans, T., et al.: The explainability paradox: challenges for xai in digital pathology. Futur. Gener. Comput. Syst. **133**, 281–296 (2022)
5. Gupte, S.R., Aklilu, J., Nirschl, J.J., Yeung-Levy, S.: Revisiting active learning in the era of vision foundation models. Trans. Mach. Learn. Res. (TMLR) (2024)
6. Hahn, K., et al.: Points to consider from the estp pathology 2.0 working group: overview on spatial omics technologies supporting drug discovery and development. Toxicol. Pathol. 01926233241311258 (2025)

7. Koohbanani, N.A., Jahanifar, M., Tajadin, N.Z., Rajpoot, N.: Nuclick: a deep learning framework for interactive segmentation of microscopic images. Med. Image Anal. **65**, 101771 (2020)
8. Korsunsky, I., et al.: Fast, sensitive and accurate integration of single-cell data with harmony. Nat. Methods **16**(12), 1289–1296 (2019)
9. Lee, S., et al.: Interactive classification of whole-slide imaging data for cancer researchers. Can. Res. **81**(4), 1171–1177 (2021)
10. Lüth, C., Bungert, T., Klein, L., Jaeger, P.F.: Navigating the pitfalls of active learning evaluation: a systematic framework for meaningful performance assessment. In: NeurIPS 2023 (2023)
11. Lutnick, B., et al.: A user-friendly tool for cloud-based whole slide image segmentation with examples from renal histopathology. Commun. Med. **2**(1), 105 (2022)
12. Ma, S., Du, H., Curran, K.M., Lawlor, A., Dong, R.: Adaptive curriculum query strategy for active learning in medical image classification. In: International Conference on Medical Image Computing and Computer-Assisted Intervention, pp. 48–57. Springer (2024)
13. McHugh, M.L.: Interrater reliability: the kappa statistic. Biochemia medica **22**(3), 276–282 (2012)
14. Miao, R., Toth, R., Zhou, Y., Madabhushi, A., Janowczyk, A.: Quick annotator: an open-source digital pathology based rapid image annotation tool. J. Pathol. Clin. Res. **7**(6), 542–547 (2021)
15. Munjal, P., Hayat, N., Hayat, M., Sourati, J., Khan, S.: Towards robust and reproducible active learning using neural networks. In: Proceedings of the IEEE/CVF Conference on Computer Vision and Pattern Recognition, pp. 223–232 (2022)
16. Qiu, J., et al.: Adaptive region selection for active learning in whole slide image semantic segmentation. In: International Conference on Medical Image Computing and Computer-Assisted Intervention, pp. 90–100. Springer (2023)
17. Rao, A., Barkley, D., França, G.S., Yanai, I.: Exploring tissue architecture using spatial transcriptomics. Nature **596**(7871), 211–220 (2021)
18. Schaar, A.C., et al.: Nicheformer: a foundation model for single-cell and spatial omics. bioRxiv, pp. 2024–04 (2024)
19. Smits, L.J., et al.: Diagnostic variability in the histopathological assessment of advanced colorectal adenomas and early colorectal cancer in a screening population. Histopathology **80**(5), 790–798 (2022)
20. Song, A.H., et al.: Artificial intelligence for digital and computational pathology. Nat. Rev. Bioeng. **1**(12), 930–949 (2023)
21. Ståhl, P.L., et al.: Visualization and analysis of gene expression in tissue sections by spatial transcriptomics. Science **353**(6294), 78–82 (2016)
22. Tharwat, A., Schenck, W.: A survey on active learning: state-of-the-art, practical challenges and research directions. Mathematics **11**(4), 820 (2023)
23. Túrós, D., Vasiljevic, J., Hahn, K., Rottenberg, S., Valdeolivas, A.: Chrysalis: decoding tissue compartments in spatial transcriptomics with archetypal analysis. Commun. Biol. **7**(1), 1520 (2024)
24. Valdeolivas, A., et al.: Profiling the heterogeneity of colorectal cancer consensus molecular subtypes using spatial transcriptomics. NPJ Precis. Oncol. **8**(1), 10 (2024)
25. Wal, D., et al.: Biological data annotation via a human-augmenting ai-based labeling system. NPJ Digit. Med. **4**(1), 145 (2021)
26. Walker, C., et al.: Patchsorter: a high throughput deep learning digital pathology tool for object labeling. npj Digit. Med. **7**(1), 164 (2024)

27. Wang, C.X., Cui, H., Zhang, A.H., Xie, R., Goodarzi, H., Wang, B.: scgpt-spatial: continual pretraining of single-cell foundation model for spatial transcriptomics. bioRxiv, pp. 2025–02 (2025)
28. Wang, H., Jin, Q., Li, S., Liu, S., Wang, M., Song, Z.: A comprehensive survey on deep active learning in medical image analysis. Med. Image Anal. 103201 (2024)
29. Xu, H., et al.: A whole-slide foundation model for digital pathology from real-world data. Nature 1–8 (2024)
30. Xu, Z., et al.: Stomicsdb: a comprehensive database for spatial transcriptomics data sharing, analysis and visualization. Nucleic Acids Res. **52**(D1), D1053–D1061 (2024)
31. Zhang, J., et al.: Labelbench: a comprehensive framework for benchmarking adaptive label-efficient learning. J. Data-centric Mach. Learn. Res. (2023)
32. Zhang, W., Huang, P.: Cancer-stromal interactions: role in cell survival, metabolism and drug sensitivity. Can. Biol. Ther. **11**(2), 150–156 (2011)
33. Zhou, Y., He, W., Hou, W., Zhu, Y.: Pianno: a probabilistic framework automating semantic annotation for spatial transcriptomics. Nat. Commun. **15**(1), 2848 (2024)

TempoBiGen: A Curated Generative Model for Healthcare Mobility Logs with Visit Duration

Hieu Vu, Alberto M. Segre, and Bijaya Adhikari[✉]

University of Iowa, Iowa City, IA 52242, USA
{hieu-vu,alberto-segre,bijaya-adhikari}@uiowa.edu

Abstract. Healthcare facilities, which serve vulnerable populations such as patients and the elderly, are also hotspots where pathogens drive nosocomial infections. Accurately modeling pathogen transmission within these settings is essential for understanding their dynamics and enhancing preparedness and intervention strategies. A key barrier to achieving high-fidelity models of pathogen transmission within healthcare facilities is the scarcity of fine-grained, high-quality mobility logs that capture real-world interactions. Data synthesis offers a promising solution by generating realistic mobility datasets. Existing methods can generate synthetic mobility logs while preserving the temporal evolution of the original data's structural properties. However, these approaches are limited in two key ways: (1) they typically overlook the bipartite structure inherent in mobility logs (e.g., interactions between healthcare workers and rooms), and (2) they fail to account for the duration of interactions, a critical factor in transmission dynamics. Building on top of existing work, we introduce TempoBiGen, a curated generative model designed to address these shortcomings. TempoBiGen explicitly models bipartite temporal networks and incorporates visit duration in a post-processing step, producing high-fidelity, ready-to-use synthetic mobility logs. We evaluated TempoBiGen using real-world mobility logs gathered from healthcare facilities, assessing its performance in preserving snapshot-based graph properties (e.g., degree distribution and connected components size) and replicating temporal dynamics through disease spread simulations. Our results demonstrate that the proposed approach leads to a robust and effective tool for generating synthetic mobility data, offering additional resources to enhance modeling and analyzing hospital mobility patterns.

Keywords: Deep Temporal Graph Generative Model · Hospital Bipartite Graph · Interaction duration modeling

1 Introduction

Contact patterns between healthcare providers (HCPs) and patients observed during patient-care delivery within healthcare facilities also serve as potential pathways for *Healthcare Associated Infections* (HAIs) and *Antimicrobial Resistance Organisms* (AMROs) transmissions [2,10,22]. Moreover, these interactions also facilitate the spread of respiratory infections such as influenza and COVID-19 [3,17]. Since healthcare facilities such as inpatient units and long-term care facilities house vulnerable populations, it is imperative to *i)* model accurate dynamics of both fomite-mediated (for HAIs and AMROs) [12] and person-person infection (for respiratory diseases) spread and *ii)* infer latent infections [13], and *iii)* design effective intervention strategies to mitigate further harm [16].

A major obstacle to this is the lack of fine-grained high-resolution mobility data collected from healthcare facilities. Such data is challenging to obtain as there are numerous technical and administrative hurdles [4]. A number of prior work circumvent the lack of data by leveraging randomized (random mixing [11] or random graphs [15]) and/or statistical (stochastic block models, Watts-Strogratz models [1,27]) contact pattern models for disease spread simulation. A different line of prior work employs wearable sensors (such as Radio-frequency identification devices, RFID) in healthcare facilities to capture the mobility patterns [5]. However, these studies are often limited to small facilities or to a unit/ward within a larger facility, as large-scale deployment still remains a challenge.

Even when fine-grained healthcare mobility data is available, sharing the data with public health experts and epidemiological modelers is challenging, as these data typically have numerous policy restrictions [8]. These administrative restrictions are primarily designed to protect patients' privacy. To enable high-fidelity epidemiological modeling within healthcare facilities while respecting these restrictions, here we ask the following question: Given a large corpus of fine-grained healthcare mobility data, is it possible to generate a *novel* yet *representative* synthetic data? Here, by novel, we mean that the generated data is only allowed a non-significant overlap with the original data, and by representative, we mean that the generated data has similar statistical properties as the original one.

An obvious solution to the question above is to represent the mobility log as a temporally dynamic network and use an existing off-the-shelf graph generative model [9,29] to generate synthetic data. However, most existing approaches blindly train a generative model (such as adversarial generative model, diffusion model, or probabilistic model) over graphs with the hope of capturing statistical properties such as degree distribution, clustering coefficients, and diameter. These approaches fail to capture the intricate relationship between the HCWs and patients, the domain constraints posed by HCWs shifts and care patterns, and other HCW behaviors such as the time between visits. To overcome the shortcomings mentioned above, we start with an existing temporal graph generative model and extend it to include bipartite constraints in our model. We then further extend to generate realistic visit duration (which prior works ignore).

Our contributions are as follows:

- We propose an extension to an existing temporal graph generation model to account for the bipartite nature of the hospital mobility data and to explicitly model visit duration for fine-grained data generation.

– We conduct extensive experiments with mobility data collected from large-scale healthcare facilities and contrast the generated data against the original data via a diverse set of metrics, including snapshot-based graph properties, HCWs shift properties, and disease spread simulations. We showed that our model is able to generate realistic mobility logs for a variety of units within healthcare facilities, each exhibiting unique care patterns.

2 Related Work

Mobility Logs Collection in Healthcare Facilities. Numerous efforts have been made to collect fine-grained, high-quality hospital mobility logs to improve the understanding of care patterns and facilitate early predictions of healthcare-associated infections (HAIs). Several studies have explored the use of wearable devices to track interactions among healthcare workers (HCWs) and between HCWs and specific locations [6,21,26]. While these approaches provide detailed mobility data, they are often constrained by small participant pools, short data collection periods, and the high cost of wearable devices, limiting their scalability and generalizability.

Data Synthesis for Temporal Interaction Graphs. Synthetic data generation for temporal interaction graphs focuses on preserving both structural and temporal patterns. Prior approaches fall into two categories: *motif-based methods* and *deep generative models*. *Motif-based methods* use recurring substructures to guide generation. Early work modeled the evolution of motifs over time, albeit in discretized snapshots that loses detailed timestamp information. For example, STM [24] and DyMOND [28] either utilize a frequency-based method or model the arrival rates of a fixed set of atomic static motifs (edge, wedge, triangle) over active node sequences. The MTM model [19] extended this by dynamically learning transitions among arbitrary motifs. These approaches are efficient and interpretable but limited in capturing global dynamics and rich node/edge features. *Deep generative models* offer greater expressiveness. TAGGEN [30], TG-GAN [29] and STGEN [18] utilize the GAN framework to improve fidelity by modeling edge timestamps in continuous time. However, they over rely on deep architecture to capture the temporal dynamics, which may limit interpretability and scalability. TIGGER [9] advanced this approach with a scalable recurrent model based on Temporal Point Processes, enhancing fine-grained temporal accuracy and scalability. Collectively, these methods highlight an ongoing shift towards integrating scalability and more expressive temporal modeling in generative frameworks.

In summary, existing approaches for temporal interaction graph generation range from motif-based methods emphasizing the benefit of capturing local structures to deep generative models that capture intricate temporal dependencies. However, to the best of our knowledge, no prior work has addressed the generation task specifically for bipartite temporal networks jointly with visit duration. To address this gap, we introduce TEMPOBIGEN, which explicitly models bipartite temporal networks and incorporates visit duration in a post-processing step, producing high-fidelity, ready-to-use synthetic mobility logs for downstream tasks such as disease simulation.

3 Our Approach

HCW mobility within healthcare facilities is best represented as a *Temporal Bipartite Graph*, $\mathcal{G}(\mathcal{H}, \mathcal{R}, \mathcal{E}, \mathcal{C})$ where the first partition $\mathcal{H}$ represents HCWs and the second component $\mathcal{R}$ represents the rooms occupied by patients. A temporal bipartite edge $e(h, r, t, d) \in \mathcal{E}_c$ describes an interaction - a visit of a HCW $h \in \mathcal{H}$ to a room $r \in \mathcal{R}$ starting at time t for a total duration of d within a class $c \in \mathcal{C}$. In our application, a class is a healthcare unit within a hospital where the logs are collected.

Problem Description. We pose the problem of generating synthetic healthcare mobility logs as a one-shot generative problem, where only one instance of temporal graph $\mathcal{G}$ is revealed to the learning algorithm with the goal of learning a generative model $P(\mathcal{G})$ that maximizes the likelihood of generating $\mathcal{G}$ by leveraging its structural and temporal properties. Once trained, one can sample a new mobility log $\mathcal{G}'$ from $P(\mathcal{G})$. Ideally, $\mathcal{G}'$ should have similar structural/temporal properties as $\mathcal{G}$ and lead to a similar dynamics of HAI spread while having as few overlap with $\mathcal{G}$ as possible.

Approach Overview. We propose a two-stage solution to our problem. In *Stage 1*, we learn and sample $\tilde{\mathcal{G}}' \sim P(\tilde{\mathcal{G}}')$ using our proposed conditional bipartite recurrent generative model, where $\tilde{\mathcal{G}}'$ is a modified version of $\mathcal{G}$ without duration information. In *Stage 2*, after estimating the probability distribution of visit durations from the training data, we sample durations for each generated visit in $\tilde{\mathcal{G}}'$ to construct the final sampled graph $\mathcal{G}'$. An overview of our proposed method is illustrated in Fig. 1.

3.1 Stage 1: Learn $P(\tilde{\mathcal{G}}')$

Recall that $\tilde{\mathcal{G}}'$ does not have duration and is a simple streaming temporal bipartite graph. To learn $P(\tilde{\mathcal{G}}')$, we extend an existing temporal graph generation approach, TIGGER [9], to handle bipartite edges.

Background on TIGGER and Temporal Random Walk Modeling. To model temporal interaction graphs, TIGGER first extracts temporal random walks from the graph and models their distribution using Temporal Point Processes (TPPs) [7] combined with autoregressive modeling. This approach provides flexibility in capturing temporal dynamics. Formally, given a temporal graph $\mathcal{G}$, TIGGER first samples a set of random walks $\mathcal{S}$ to define $P(\mathcal{G}) := \prod_{S \in \mathcal{S}} P_\theta(S)$, where $P_\theta(S)$ is parameterized by a recurrent generative model with a TPP-based event time modeling head. By operating on random walks, TIGGER effectively leverages the sparsity of real-world graphs, making it scalable to large networks. Additionally, its simple model design allows for

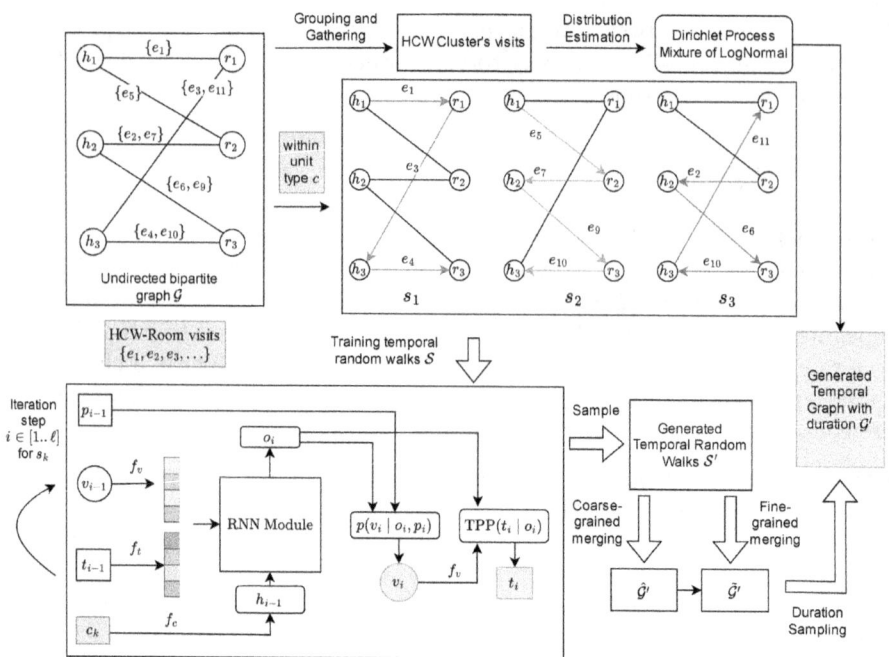

Fig. 1. Overview of proposed method.

extension to inductive settings by incorporating a multi-node decoder. Instead of learning a distribution over node IDs, this decoder jointly learns a mixture model of node embeddings. In this work, to mitigate the data scarcity problem in modeling a single continuous-time temporal graph, we adopt the same assumption of transferring the learning task from modeling the distribution of a temporal graph to modeling the distribution of conditional temporal random walks and only focus on the transductive generative task.

Conditional Temporal Random Walks on Bipartite Graphs. We first extract random walks in the temporal bipartite network $\mathcal{G}$. Formally, a conditional random walk on a bipartite temporal graph is defined as follows:

Definition 1. *Given a class c, we define a conditional temporal random walk (CDTR) S on a bipartite interaction graph $\mathcal{G}$ of length ℓ, starting from a node v at time t, as a sequence $S = \{s_1, s_2, \ldots, s_\ell\}$, where each tuple $s_i \in S$ is a (node, time) pair. The walk starts with $s_1 = (v,t)$, and for all $i \in [2..\ell]$, we require that $(s_{i-1}.v, s_i.v, s_i.t) \in \mathcal{E}_c$, and $s_{i-1}.v$ and $s_i.v$ belong to different node partitions.*

Conditional Bipartite Recurrent Generative Model (BiTIGGER). Note that, while TIGGER can be trained on temporal bipartite random walks, it does not explicitly model the bipartite nature of the graph, which can lead to the generation of non-bipartite walks (and eventually non-bipartite graphs). Hence, for our application, it is critical to modify TIGGER to handle the bipartite nature of our mobility logs. We start by defining the probability of a conditional bipartite temporal graph for a given class c, $P(\mathcal{G}|c) := P(\mathcal{S}|c)$, with $\mathcal{S}$ being the set of CTRWs extracted from $\mathcal{G}$ (Definition 1). Assuming the independence of random walks, it can be expressed as the product of the probabilities of individual random walks, i.e., $P(\mathcal{S}|c) = \prod_{S \in \mathcal{S}} p(S|c)$. As we only generate conditional RWs, to ease our notation, we will omit c in the condition and recall it when necessary. In a manner similar to [9], each individual $p(S)$ can be defined as the product of the time and the node probabilities as follows:

$$p(S) = p(s_1) \prod_{i=2}^{\ell} p(s_i.v \mid (s_1, \ldots, s_{i-1})) \times p(s_i.t \mid (s_i.v, (s_1, \ldots, s_{i-1}))) \quad (1)$$

Each of the conditional probabilities for node and time can now be modeled using a Recurrent Neural Network (RNN) [20]. The hidden state and output state of a RNN cell is updated as $\mathbf{h}_i = \text{rnn}_\theta^{\text{hidden}}(\mathbf{h}_{i-1}, s_{i-1})$ and $\mathbf{o}_i = \text{rnn}_\theta^{\text{output}}(\mathbf{h}_{i-1}, s_{i-1})$ respectively. We further incorporate the class condition into the initial hidden state $\mathbf{h}_0 = \mathbf{f}_c(c)$, where $\mathbf{f}_c(\cdot)$ is a learnable embedding function. We can simplify the conditional probabilities as follows:

$$p(S) = p(s_1) \prod_{i=2}^{\ell} p(s_i.v \mid \mathbf{o}_i) \times p(s_i.t \mid s_i.v, \mathbf{o}_i) \quad (2)$$

To explicitly model the bipartite nature of our random walks, we introduce three key modifications. First, we define a partition indicator p_i for each node v_i in the walk, which alternates between the two node partitions—$\mathcal{H}$ and $\mathcal{R}$. This ensures that consecutive nodes in a bipartite random walk always belong to different partitions.

Second, we employ dedicated prediction heads for each partition indicated by p_i. By doing so, we restrict the prediction at each step to only the appropriate partition, thereby guaranteeing that generated edges always connect nodes from different partitions. This partition-specific prediction also reduces the prediction space at each step, simplifying the learning process and improving model efficiency.

Finally, to determine when a random walk should terminate, we introduce a special end-of-walk token, denoted by $\bot$, which does not belong to either partition. At each step, the model first predicts the probability of ending the walk with $\bot$, and if not, proceeds to predict the next node from the appropriate partition as indicated by p_i. This approach ensures that the generated random walks are both valid and consistent with the bipartite structure of the underlying graph.

The overall conditional probability of generating a node $s_i.v$ at step i is thus computed as follows:

$$p(s_i.v = v \mid \mathbf{o}_i) = p(\bot|\mathbf{o}_i) \times \mathbb{I}[s_i.v = \bot]$$
$$+ (1 - p(\bot|\mathbf{o}_i)) \times \mathbb{I}[p_i = \mathcal{H}] \times p(s_i.v = v|\mathbf{o}_i, p_i = \mathcal{H})$$
$$+ (1 - p(\bot|\mathbf{o}_i)) \times \mathbb{I}[p_i = \mathcal{R}] \times p(s_i.v = v|\mathbf{o}_i, p_i = \mathcal{R}) \quad (3)$$

with the probabilities $p(s_i.v = v|\mathbf{o}_i, p_i)$ and $p(\bot|\mathbf{o}_i)$ expanded as follows:

$$\begin{aligned}p(s_i.v = v|\mathbf{o}_i, p_i) &= \theta_v^{(p_i)}(\mathbf{o}_i) \\ &= \theta_v^{(p_i)}(\text{rnn}_\theta^{\text{output}}(\mathbf{h}_{i-1}, (s_{i-1}.v, s_{i-1}.t))) \\ &= \theta_v^{(p_i)}(\text{rnn}_\theta^{\text{output}}(\mathbf{h}_{i-1}, (\mathbf{f}_v(s_{i-1}.v) \parallel \mathbf{f}_t(s_{i-1}.t)))) \\ &= \frac{\exp(\mathbf{W}_v^{O(p_i)}\mathbf{o}_i)}{\sum_{\forall u \in \mathcal{V}} \exp(\mathbf{W}_u^{O(p_i)}\mathbf{o}_i)}\end{aligned} \quad (4)$$

where $\mathbf{W}_v^{O(p_i)}$ is in $\mathbb{R}^{|\mathcal{H}| \times d_O}$ if $v \in \mathcal{H}$ and $\mathbb{R}^{|\mathcal{R}| \times d_O}$ if $v \in \mathcal{R}$, $\theta_v^{(p_i)}$ is parameters for the prediction head for partition p_i, and d_O is the dimension of vector $\mathbf{o}_i$. Similar to [9], $\mathbf{f}_v(\cdot)$ and $\mathbf{f}_t(\cdot)$ are embedding functions for the node and time, respectively, and $\parallel$ denotes concatenation. We also have $p(\bot|\mathbf{o}_i) = \text{Sigmoid}(\mathbf{W}_\bot^O \mathbf{o}_i)$ with $\mathbf{W}_\bot^O \in \mathbb{R}^{1 \times d_O}$.

Proposed by [25] and employed by [9], TPPs under the form of a mixture of log-normal distribution showcases strong performance in modeling inter-event time within a sequence of events. We also utilize it here and provide its formulation for the sake of completeness:

$$p(s_i.t \mid s_i.v, \mathbf{o}_i) = p(s_i.t - s_{i-1}.t \mid s_i.v, \mathbf{o}_i) = \theta_t(\Delta t \mid s_i.v, \mathbf{o}_i)$$
$$= \sum_{k=1}^{K} \phi_k^K \frac{1}{\Delta t \sigma_k^K \sqrt{2\pi}} \exp\left(-\frac{(\log \Delta t - \mu_k^K)^2}{2(\sigma_k^K)^2}\right) \quad (5)$$

where Δt is time difference between $s_i.t$ and $s_{i-1}.t$, $p(t)$ is parameterized by θ_t and $\mu_k^K, \sigma_k^K, \phi_k^K$ are parameters of θ_t.

$$\mu_k^K = \mathbf{W}_k^{\mu K}(\mathbf{f}_v(s_i.v) \parallel \mathbf{o}_i), \quad \sigma_k^K = \exp(\mathbf{W}_k^{\sigma K}(\mathbf{f}_v(s_i.v) \parallel \mathbf{o}_i))$$

$$\phi_k^K = \frac{\exp(\mathbf{W}_k^{\phi K}(\mathbf{f}_v(s_i.v) \parallel \mathbf{o}_i))}{\sum_{j=1}^{K} \exp(\mathbf{W}_j^{\phi K}(\mathbf{f}_v(s_i.v) \parallel \mathbf{o}_i))}$$

with K is number of components in the Log-Normal Mixture distribution and $\mathbf{W}_k^{\mu K}, \mathbf{W}_k^{\sigma K}, \mathbf{W}_k^{\phi K} \in \mathcal{R}^{(d_v + d_O)}, \forall k$. Note that every component's learnable weights are shared across each time stamp in the sequence.

Similar to TIGGER, we train our proposed model to minimize the negative log-likelihood:

$$\mathcal{L}(\mathcal{S}) = \sum_{c \in \mathcal{C}} -\log p(\mathcal{S}|c) = -\sum_{c \in \mathcal{C}} \sum_{S \in \mathcal{S}} \log p(S|c) \qquad (6)$$

with $\log p(S|c)$ is given in Eq. 1. Once trained, we can follow Algorithm 1 in [9] to sample synthetic bipartite CTRWs for each class $c \in \mathcal{C}$.

Visits Construction via Coarse-Grained and Fine-Grained Random Walks Merging. After sampling a set $\hat{\mathcal{S}}$ of CTRWs, we need to construct the final temporal graph $\tilde{\mathcal{G}}'$, representing the synthetic collection of HCW-Room visits. For scalability, we employ the independent random walk sampling, which has a downside of generating redundant sets of CTRWs. By redundancy, we mean that the same HCW-Room pair appears in multiple random walks. Due to the redundancy in the sampled CTRWs, simply taking the union of the generated events from samples can lead to a noisy graph with multiple visits of the same HCW to different rooms at the same (or very close) time, which is not realistic. Previous works such as TG-GAN [29] and STGEN [18] circumvent this by using a non-parallel generation process, trading off the efficiency for event consistency. TIGGER [9] instead proposed a merging process that retains top frequent edges proportional to their occurrence in the sampled CTRWs based on the true graph statistics. However, this approach requires maintaining a distribution for each unique timestamp in the generated data, which is problematic for fine-grained temporal resolution as: 1) the number of unique timestamps becomes very large and mostly noisy due to the stochasticity of the model, and 2) the distribution of events at each timestamp is extremely sparse and insufficient to give a reliable estimation. Thus, when aggregating sampled CTRWs, we aim to achieve the following two goals: 1) reduce noise in the generated events, and 2) preserve the continuity of events up to a constant gap δ. To this end, we employ a three-step merging process: coarse-grained merging, fine-grained merging, and a final refinement step.

Step 1: Coarse-grained merging - Obtain $\hat{\mathcal{G}}^{(d)}$. Recall that the number of unique timestamps in our sampled CTRWs is larger than that in the original data. Hence, the number of events taking place in each unique time-stamp is relatively low and therefore it is unlikely that a unique HCW-Room pair appears more than once in each timestamp. Hence, frequency based filtering cannot be done at each timestamp. To address this, we first extract a collection of the most frequent HCW-Room pairs for each day from the sampled CTRWs and filter out the rest, reducing the noise in the generated events. Additionally, note that daily-snapshot graphs are also standard in evaluating graph-based properties [9, 18, 29].

Formally, we first obtain a distribution of the occurrence of HCW-Room pairs for each day of the synthetic data:

$$\hat{p}^d(\{h_i, r_i\}) = \frac{\alpha(h_i, r_i, d)}{\sum_{\{h_j, r_j\} \in \hat{P}^d} \alpha(h_j, r_j, d)}$$

where $\alpha(h_i, r_i, d)$ is the number of times the edge (h_i, r_i) appears in day d and $\hat{P}^d = \{(h,r) | (h,r,t) \in \hat{S}_d, t \in d\}$. Then, we keep sampling from this distribution until we get the required number of pairs for that day, which is extracted from the training data of the corresponding day.

Step 2: Fine-grained merging - Obtain $\tilde{\mathcal{G}}^{(d)}$. Coarse-grained merging is effective in preserving the sparsity of the graph. However, it cannot maintain the continuity of events. Specifically, coarse-grained merging corresponds to the case where the minimum time gap δ between consecutive visits of an HCW to a room is set to one day (86,400 seconds), which is not realistic. To address this issue, we perform fine-grained merging to merge the visits that are within δ of each other.

We employ two strategies to ensure this: 1) Snapshot-based merging strategy, where we divide the examined period into grids of length δ and fuse edges within the same grid cell; 2) Adaptive merging strategy, where starting from the first visit, looping in sorted order of start time, we fuse the visits that are within δ period of each other. In both cases, we maintain the average start time $\bar{t}$ and the number of events that were merged together, denoted by $\beta(h_i, r_i, \bar{t})$, for each fused edge. Note that the tuples $(h_i, r_i, \bar{t})$ are unique and, at this point, the edges are not necessarily δ apart (due to averaging of the start time) and we need a refining step to ensure this.

Step 3: Refining $\tilde{\mathcal{G}}^{(d)}$.
Subsample Daily Visits: The fine-grained merging step may retain more than one visit for each HCW-Room pair each day, and we denote this number as $\hat{\alpha}(h_i, r_i, d)$ (note that $\hat{\alpha}(h_i, r_i, d) \leq \alpha(h_i, r_i, d)$). However, it usually results in the total number of visits being significantly higher than the actual number in the training data. Thus, to preserve the sparsity of the original data, we subsample the set of daily visits obtained from Step 2 proportionally to $\hat{\alpha}(h_i, r_i, d)$. The number of visits to be sampled for each pair $\tilde{n}^d(\{h_i, r_i\})$ is defined as follows:

$$\tilde{n}^d(\{h_i, r_i\}) = \frac{\hat{\alpha}(h_i, r_i, d)}{\sum_{(h_j, r_j) \in \tilde{P}_d} \hat{\alpha}(h_j, r_j, d)} \times n_v^d$$

where $\tilde{P}$ is the set of $(\{h_i, r_i\})$ pair that remain after Step 2 and n_v^d is the number of required visits for each day, which is extracted from the training data. Among all possible visits $(h_i, r_i, \bar{t})$ for each (h_i, r_i) pair, we sample $\tilde{n}^d(\{h_i, r_i\})$ visits proportional to $\beta(h_i, r_i, t)$ with the following distribution:

$$\tilde{p}_{h_i, r_i}(\bar{t}) = \frac{\beta(h_i, r_i, \bar{t})}{\sum_{t \in \tau_{h_i, r_i}} \beta(h_j, r_j, t)}$$

with $\tau_{h_i, r_i} = \{\bar{t} | (h, r, \bar{t}) \in \tilde{E}_d, h = h_i, r = r_i\}$.

Resolve conflicts for each HCW: An HCW usually has many visits in a single day, and those visits must be at least δ time apart. As mentioned above, this constraint may not be satisfied after the merging steps. We define a conflict as a pair of consecutive visits that violate this temporal separation requirement. To resolve such conflicts, we retain the visit associated with the higher fused-edge count, $\beta(h_i, r_i, \bar{t})$, and discard the other. Specifically, for each HCW, we iterate through their visits in chronological order and accumulate only the valid ones. The first visit is always included. For each subsequent visit, we check whether it conflicts with the last accepted visit: if no conflict occurs, it is added to the valid set; otherwise, the visit with the higher fused-edge count is retained.

3.2 Stage 2: Duration Sampling

Given a set of visits for each HCW, our goal is to sample realistic durations for each visit. Examining the visit duration in our data, we noticed that the distribution of visit durations is strongly right-skewed, with multiple peaks. A straightforward baseline is to uniformly sample durations between a lower bound (the minimum observed duration) and an upper bound (the gap to the next visit). While this approach does not capture the right-skewed nature of real visit durations, it serves as a reasonable baseline, especially since our evaluation focuses on truncated snapshot graphs that depend more on aggregate duration distributions and are less sensitive to individual visit details. Below, we describe our approach for estimating and sampling from the duration distribution, which aims to better preserve the duration patterns observed in the training data.

Estimating Duration Distribution. The most natural way of sampling visit duration is to sample from the set of observed durations based on their frequencies. However, this simple approach ignores the continuous nature of the data and may inadvertently reveal individual care patterns, thus raising privacy concerns. Additionally, some HCWs have very few visits during the examined period. Repeatedly sampling observed duration for these HCWs introduces bias towards the observed values. To address this, we aggregate data from multiple HCWs and estimate a duration distribution for each group.

However, since we are generating data conditioned on unit type, clustering HCWs within each unit separately can lead to inconsistencies. For example, we may encounter cases where an HCW absent from the training data for a unit appears in the generated samples for that unit, making it unclear which estimated distribution to use for sampling durations. To address this, we cluster HCWs across all units based on their embeddings, and then sample durations conditioned on these global clusters. This ensures consistency and applicability of the duration distributions to all generated visits. Below, we outline our step-by-step process for learning the probability distribution of visit durations.

Transform Duration Data into Log-Space: As noted, our duration distribution is right-skewed, and a straightforward way to model the duration data X is to use a mixture of log-normal distributions. Furthermore, we know that $Y = \ln(X)$ follows a mixture of Normal distributions, which is easier to model and well-supported by many off-the-shelf libraries. So the first step is to transform the duration data X into log-space $Y = \ln(X)$.

Fit a Gaussian Mixture Model to the Log-Transformed Data: Once we transform the data into the log-space, we can fit a Gaussian Mixture Model (GMM) to capture the complex mixing patterns in the data. A GMM assumes that Y is generated from K components, each with mean μ_k, standard deviation σ_k, and mixing probability π_k, where $\sum_{k=1}^{K} \pi_k = 1$. Since the optimal number of components K is unknown and the data exhibits a diverse range of mixing patterns, we employ a Dirichlet Process Mixture of Normals, which allows for automatic determination of K. Specifically, we use the BayesianGaussianMixture class from sklearn package [23] to fit a GMM with Dirichlet Process prior to obtain the parameters π_k, μ_k, and σ_k for each remaining active component $k = 1, 2, \ldots, K$.

Sampling from the Mixture of Normal Distributions. When sampling the duration for each visit, we know both the start time of the current visit and the next visit for the HCW. Therefore, the sampled duration must be bounded above by the gap to the next visit, and below by the minimum duration observed in the data to capture realistic visit patterns.

Let the bounds for a sequence of visits be $[a_1, b_1], [a_2, b_2], \ldots, [a_m, b_m]$, where a_i is the minimum allowed duration and b_i is the gap to the next visit (minus a slack, if desired). Since we model durations in log-space, $X = \exp(Y)$, a sample $X \in [a_i, b_i]$ corresponds to $Y \in [c_i, d_i]$ with $c_i = \ln(a_i)$ and $d_i = \ln(b_i)$. Note that the mixture probability density function (pdf) for variable Y is as follows:

$$f_Y(y) = \sum_{k=1}^{K} \pi_k \cdot \mathcal{N}\left(y \mid \mu_k, \sigma_k^2\right),$$

Thus, the pdf for Y truncated to $[c_i, d_i]$ is given by:

$$f_{Y|\text{trunc}}(y) = \frac{f_Y(y)}{P(c_i \leq Y \leq d_i)} \text{ for } y \in [c_i, d_i],$$

where the normalization constant is:

$$P(c_i \leq Y \leq d_i) = \int_{c_i}^{d_i} f_Y(y)\, dy = \sum_{k=1}^{K} \pi_k \cdot P(c_i \leq Y \leq d_i | \text{component } k).$$

and for each component k, we have:

$$P_k = P(c_i \leq Y \leq d_i | \text{component } k) = \Phi\left(\frac{d_i - \mu_k}{\sigma_k}\right) - \Phi\left(\frac{c_i - \mu_k}{\sigma_k}\right)$$

where Φ is the standard normal CDF. The adjusted mixing probability for component k within $[c_i, d_i]$ is then:

$$\pi_k' = \frac{\pi_k P_k}{\sum_{j=1}^{K} \pi_j P_j}$$

Now, we can generate a sample by the following steps:

- Choose a component k with probability π'_k.
- Sample Y from the normal distribution $N(\mu_k, \sigma_k^2)$ truncated to $[c_i, d_i]$.
- Transform back to $X = \exp(Y)$.

This approach ensures that sampled durations are both realistic and consistent with the temporal constraints of the generated visits.

Generating Duration for Each Visit. Applying the above sampling technique, we generate duration information for each synthetic visit. For each HCW, we first compute the gap between consecutive visits to serve as the upper bound for the sampled duration. To ensure realistic transitions between rooms, we subtract a *slack gap* (e.g., 30 s) from this upper bound, preventing the duration from occupying the entire interval. The lower bound is set as the minimum observed duration from the training data. We then sample durations from the truncated mixture distribution within these bounds. The final output is a set of temporal edges (h, r, t, d), forming the synthetic temporal graph $\mathcal{G}'$.

4 Experiments

In this section, we present the performance of our proposed approach in capturing the daily-snapshot graph properties, disease spread characteristics, and HCW care patterns. All of our experiments were conducted on an AMD EPYC 7763 machine with 2TB memory and 8 NVIDIA A30 GPUs each with 24GB memory. Our code is available at https://github.com/hieuvt29/TempoBiGen.

Our experiments are designed to answer the following questions: 1) Does the generated graph capture the statistical properties of the daily snapshots of the original data? 2) Is the disease spread the same in the generated graph compared to the original network? 3) Does our model generate realistic mobility logs that capture HCW shift patterns?

Datasets: Here we use a collection of proprietary datasets obtained via a data use agreement. The data consists of more than 44 million HCP-room visits collected from 25 different healthcare facilities in the US, ranging in size from small rural facilities to large-scale tertiary-care facilities. We use a subsampled two weeks of data for the experiments below with 1939 HCWs (33 job types), 263 rooms, and a total of 118,209 visits across 10 unit types.

Testing Models: In the following experiments, we set $\delta = 120$ (2 minutes) - heuristically chosen based on the training data. We use the suffix "_CG" to denote methods that only use the coarse-grained merging, where edges are merged for the whole day. Note that this approach cannot retain the visit start time within a day. The suffix "_FG" denotes the methods that only use fine-grained merging, where edges are merged only based on δ. The suffix "_unif" refers to the uniform visit duration sampling method. The reported results are averaged over all unit types and averaged over 3 generated graphs for each method, with standard deviation in parentheses. For a concise plot, we use "TBG" to denote our proposed TEMPOBIGEN method. The best values are in bold.

Table 1. Performance based on mean absolute error (standard deviation in parentheses) between sampled and true daily-snapshot graphs.

Method	% Edge Overlap	Mean Degree	Wedge Count	PLE	Edge Entropy	LCC	NC	Mean BC	Mean CC	Has Duration?
Actual_Median	N/A	5.6269	2502.15	1.7960	0.9274	86.35	1.2	0.0246	0.3411	No
TIGGER_CG	76.1927	0.3878	75.50	0.0740	**0.0068**	6.75	0.1	0.0019	0.0162	No
	(0.1889)	(0.0023)	(2.2287)	(0.0037)	(0.0001)	(0.13)	(0.0)	(0.0001)	(0.0007)	
BiTIGGER_CG	75.7778	**0.3690**	**63.30**	0.0755	0.0069	**6.60**	0.1	**0.0014**	**0.0157**	No
	(0.2401)	(0.0020)	(1.25)	(0.0032)	(0.0004)	(0.09)	(0.0)	(0.0001)	(0.0001)	
BiTIGGER_FG	**23.4438**	2.5149	2024.02	0.4916	0.0292	44.10	1.0	0.0300	0.1201	Yes
	(0.2904)	(0.0184)	(6.64)	(0.0303)	(0.0004)	(0.23)	(0.1)	(0.0018)	(0.0024)	
BiTIGGER_FG_unif	**23.4438**	2.5149	2024.02	0.4916	0.0292	44.10	1.0	0.0300	0.1201	Yes
	(0.2904)	(0.0184)	(6.64)	(0.0303)	(0.0004)	(0.23)	(0.1)	(0.0018)	(0.0024)	
TBG_adapt	64.2953	0.6650	692.40	0.0761	0.0087	9.60	0.1	0.0034	0.0189	Yes
	(0.3571)	(0.0096)	(13.31)	(0.0019)	(0.0001)	(0.09)	(0.0)	(0.0003)	(0.0002)	
TBG_snap	68.2677	0.4688	464.70	0.0707	0.0080	7.65	0.1	0.0026	0.0159	Yes
	(0.0652)	(0.0092)	(4.66)	(0.0003)	(0.0004)	(0.09)	(0.0)	(0.0001)	(0.0004)	
TBG_unif_adapt	64.4092	0.6859	667.25	0.0831	0.0091	9.00	0.1	0.0035	0.0191	Yes
	(0.2257)	(0.0043)	(11.96)	(0.0025)	(0.0003)	(0.22)	(0.0)	(0.0001)	(0.0005)	
TBG_unif_snap	68.3447	0.4610	484.45	**0.0657**	0.0079	7.90	0.1	0.0026	0.0158	Yes
	(0.0995)	(0.0072)	(5.21)	(0.0029)	(0.0003)	(0.29)	(0.0)	(0.0001)	(0.0001)	

4.1 Snapshot Graph Properties

In this experiment, we evaluate daily-graph properties. Similar to [9], we report the median absolute error for 9 different graph properties. The results are summarized in Table 1.

From the table, we observe that methods using only coarse-grained merging perform better across most metrics. This is expected, as evaluating based on daily graphs means that merging at the day level retains the most frequently occurring HCW-Room pairs while filtering out noisy signals. However, these methods fail to preserve the precise start times of events, making them unsuitable for our downstream tasks. On the other hand, relying solely on fine-grained merging introduces excessive noise, leading to unrealistic graphs where an HCW appears to have an unreasonably high number of visits per day. Our approach, which combines both coarse-grained and fine-grained merging, strikes a balance between preserving daily graph properties and maintaining event-level details, resulting in a middle-ground performance. Notice that, due to the low number of active HCWs each day for each unit type, we are expected to see a high percentage of overlapping edges for daily-snapshots.

4.2 Disease Simulation

The core motivation of this work is to enable accurate disease modeling, which requires a generative approach that preserves disease spread patterns in the original contact network. To evaluate how well our method preserves these patterns, we start by constructing a weighted temporal graph of HCWs based on their visits. Visits are divided into 12-hour snapshot graphs, aligning with typical hospital shifts. Edges are formed between HCWs who visit the same room within a snapshot. Edge-weight for edge (h_1, h_2) is computed as $w(h_1, h_2) =$

$\sigma(d_1 + d_2 + 10 \times d_{12})$, with $\sigma(x) = 1/(1 + e^{-x})$, where d_1 and d_2 are the duration visit for h_1 and h_2 respectively, d_{12} is the overlap duration. We use a factor of 10 to account for the increased likelihood of disease transmission when HCWs share a room simultaneously.

For disease simulation, we use the well-known SIR compartmental model with an edge-weight-adjusted transmission rate [14]. We run 50 simulations for each unit type with base transmission rate $\beta = 0.35$, recovery rate $\gamma = 0.2$, and number of initially infected HCWs in the first snapshot of 10. We then compare attack rates between real data and different approaches using box plots.

Figure 2 highlights the difference between considering and ignoring duration information. It clearly shows that, given the same assumption of base transmission rate, ignoring the duration information (unweighted) consistently leads to higher attack rates compared to the weighted version. This suggests that the duration information is crucial for capturing more realistic transmission scenarios.

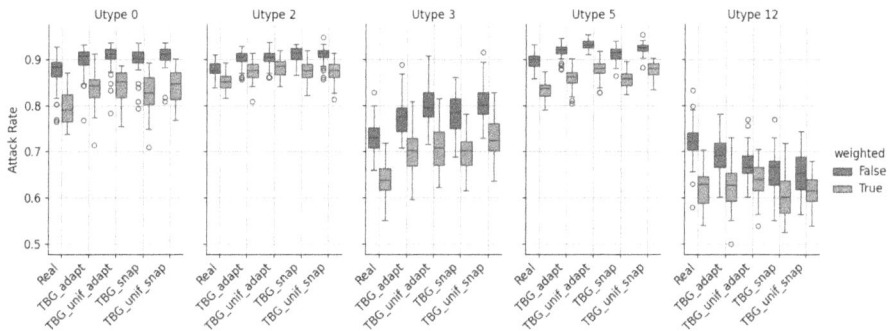

Fig. 2. Comparison with and without edge weights.

We further compare the attack rates across all unit types with weighted data. The absolute difference between attack rates of each method against that of true data averaged over all unit types is shown in legend Fig. 3. The results show that TEMPOBIGEN with the adaptive strategy performs the best, achieving the lowest average difference, followed by the snapshot-based approach, and both clearly outperform the uniform sampling methods. Additionally, having different attack rates for different unit types demonstrates that our generative model effectively captures the unique characteristics of each unit type.

4.3 Shift Efficiency and Uniformity

To assess how well the generated data follows care patterns for each unit type, we compute shift efficiency and uniformity across different methods. *Shift efficiency* is defined as the ratio of total shift visit duration to the full shift duration (a value between 0 and 1), while *shift uniformity* is the number of unique rooms

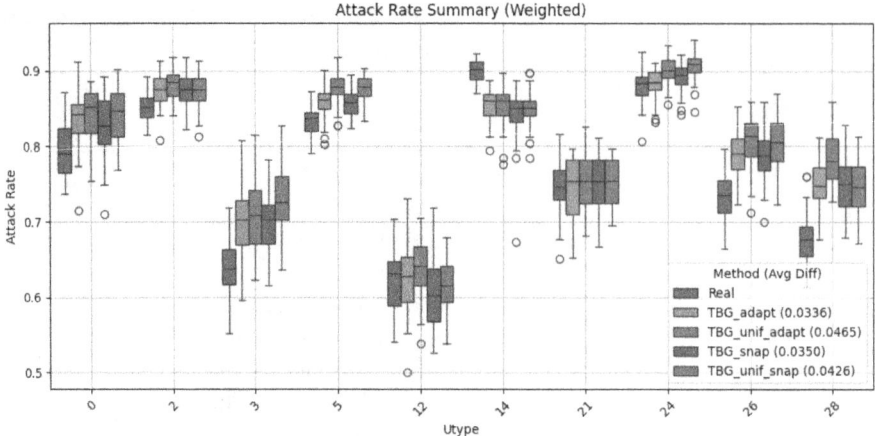

Fig. 3. Attack rates for different methods.

serviced per shift divided by the total number of shift visits (also between 0 and 1, small numbers mean more attention on fewer rooms). Table 2 shows the average absolute differences between the two values of our methods and baselines against those of the original data. The results indicate that non-trivial sampling methods significantly improve shift uniformity but are less effective in maintaining shift efficiency.

Table 2. Average Efficiency and Uniformity Differences.

Method	Avg. Efficiency Difference	Avg. Uniformity Difference
TBG_adapt	0.37098	0.29616
TBG_unif_adapt	**0.30222**	0.45497
TBG_snap	0.34981	**0.28193**
TBG_unif_snap	0.32082	0.31203

5   Conclusion

In this paper, we presented a generative model to produce realistic mobility graphs within healthcare facilities. Following the state-of-the-art temporal graph generation literature, we formulated a one-shot learning problem and extended existing methods to address conditional bipartite graph generation problem with temporal edge duration sampling. Specifically, we proposed a two-stage approach. First, we extended TIGGER to handle bipartite graphs and combine coarse-grained and fine-grained merging into our sampling procedure to construct a bipartite temporal graph. Second, given the generated HCW-Room visits, we added a post-processing module to generate realistic visit durations. Our results demonstrate that the proposed approach effectively captures visit duration patterns, preserves the statistical properties of daily-snapshot graphs, and enables realistic disease simulations. Extending our work for the inductive setting (where new nodes arrive over time) and formally incorporating privacy (for example, via differentiable privacy) are promising future directions.

Acknowledgments. The authors acknowledge feedback from members of the Computational Epidemiology research group at the University of Iowa and the CDC MInD-Healthcare group. This work was supported by the CDC under cooperative agreement U01-CK000594. Its contents are solely the responsibility of the authors and do not necessarily represent the official views of CDC.

References

1. Abbe, E.: Community detection and stochastic block models: recent developments. J. Mach. Learn. Res. **18**(177), 1–86 (2018)
2. Adhikari, B., Lewis, B., Vullikanti, A., Jiménez, J.M., Prakash, B.A.: Fast and near-optimal monitoring for healthcare acquired infection outbreaks. PLoS Comput. Biol. **15**(9), e1007284 (2019)
3. Capolongo, S., Gola, M., Brambilla, A., Morganti, A., Mosca, E.I., Barach, P.: Covid-19 and healthcare facilities: a decalogue of design strategies for resilient hospitals. Acta Bio Medica: Atenei Parmensis **91**(9-S), 50 (2020)
4. Casey, D.: Challenges of collecting data in the clinical setting. NT Res. **9**(2), 131–141 (2004)
5. Coletti, P., et al.: A data-driven metapopulation model for the Belgian covid-19 epidemic: assessing the impact of lockdown and exit strategies. BMC Infect. Dis. **21**, 1–12 (2021)
6. Fournet, J., Barrat, A.: Contact patterns among high school students. PLoS ONE **9**(9), e107878 (2014)
7. Goldschmidt, U.: An introduction to the theory of point processes (2016). https://api.semanticscholar.org/CorpusID:63985456
8. Gostin, L.O., Levit, L.A., Nass, S.J.: Beyond the hipaa privacy rule: enhancing privacy, improving health through research (2009)
9. Gupta, S., Manchanda, S., Bedathur, S., Ranu, S.: Tigger: scalable generative modelling for temporal interaction graphs. In: Proceedings of the AAAI Conference on Artificial Intelligence, vol. 36, pp. 6819–6828 (2022)
10. Haque, M., Sartelli, M., McKimm, J., Bakar, M.A.: Health care-associated infections–an overview. Infection Drug Resistance 2321–2333 (2018)
11. Hethcote, H.W.: The mathematics of infectious diseases. SIAM Rev. **42**(4), 599–653 (2000)
12. Jang, H., et al.: Detecting sources of healthcare associated infections. In: Proceedings of the AAAI Conference on Artificial Intelligence, vol. 37, pp. 4347–4355 (2023)

13. Jang, H., Pai, S., Adhikari, B., Pemmaraju, S.V.: Risk-aware temporal cascade reconstruction to detect asymptomatic cases. Knowl. Inf. Syst. **64**(12), 3373–3399 (2022)
14. Kamp, C., Moslonka-Lefebvre, M., Alizon, S.: Epidemic spread on weighted networks. PLOS Comput. Biol. **9**(12), 1–10 (2013). https://doi.org/10.1371/journal.pcbi.1003352
15. Keeling, M.J., Eames, K.T.: Networks and epidemic models. J. R. Soc. Interface **2**(4), 295–307 (2005)
16. Kiji, M., Hasan, D.H., Segre, A.M., Pemmaraju, S.V., Adhikari, B.: Near-optimal spectral disease mitigation in healthcare facilities. In: 2022 IEEE International Conference on Data Mining (ICDM), pp. 999–1004. IEEE (2022)
17. Lansbury, L.E., Brown, C.S., Nguyen-Van-Tam, J.S.: Influenza in long-term care facilities. Influenza Other Respir. Viruses **11**(5), 356–366 (2017)
18. Ling, C., Cao, H., Zhao, L.: Stgen: deep continuous-time spatiotemporal graph generation. In: Machine Learning and Knowledge Discovery in Databases: European Conference, ECML PKDD 2022, Grenoble, France, 19–23 September 2022, Proceedings, Part III, pp. 340–356. Springer, Heidelberg (2022). https://doi.org/10.1007/978-3-031-26409-2_21
19. Liu, P., Sariyüce, A.E.: Using motif transitions for temporal graph generation. In: Proceedings of the 29th ACM SIGKDD Conference on Knowledge Discovery and Data Mining, pp. 1501–1511 (2023)
20. Medsker, L.R., Jain, L., et al.: Recurrent neural networks. Des. Appl. **5**(64–67), 2 (2001)
21. Monsalve, M.N., Pemmaraju, S.V., Thomas, G.W., Herman, T., Segre, A.M., Polgreen, P.M.: Do peer effects improve hand hygiene adherence among healthcare workers? Infection Control Hosp. Epidemiol. **35**(10), 1277–1285 (2014)
22. Morrison, L., Zembower, T.R.: Antimicrobial resistance. Gastrointest. Endoscopy Clinics **30**(4), 619–635 (2020)
23. Pedregosa, F., et al.: Scikit-learn: machine learning in python. J. Mach. Learn. Res. **12**, 2825–2830 (2011)
24. Purohit, S., Holder, L.B., Chin, G.: Temporal graph generation based on a distribution of temporal motifs. In: Proceedings of the 14th International Workshop on Mining and Learning with Graphs, vol. 7 (2018)
25. Shchur, O., Biloš, M., Günnemann, S.: Intensity-free learning of temporal point processes. arXiv preprint arXiv:1909.12127 (2019)
26. Vanhems, P., et al.: Estimating potential infection transmission routes in hospital wards using wearable proximity sensors. PloS One **8**(9), e73970 (2013)
27. Watts, D.J., Strogatz, S.H.: Collective dynamics of 'small-world' networks. Nature **393**(6684), 440–442 (1998)
28. Zeno, G., La Fond, T., Neville, J.: Dymond: dynamic motif-nodes network generative model. In: Proceedings of the Web Conference 2021, pp. 718–729 (2021)
29. Zhang, L., Zhao, L., Qin, S., Pfoser, D., Ling, C.: TG-GAN: continuous-time temporal graph deep generative models with time-validity constraints. In: Proceedings of the Web Conference 2021, pp. 2104–2116 (2021)
30. Zhou, D., Zheng, L., Han, J., He, J.: A data-driven graph generative model for temporal interaction networks. In: Proceedings of the 26th ACM SIGKDD International Conference on Knowledge Discovery & Data Mining, pp. 401–411 (2020)

Industry (4.0, 5.0, Manufacturing, ...)

Near-Infrared Spectroscopy and Image Classification of Refuse Derived Fuels to Increase Cement Production Quality

Jonas Fischer[1()], Luca Fehler[2], Kevin Treiber[2], and Viktor Scherer[1]

[1] Chair of Energy Plant Technology, Ruhr University Bochum, 44791 Bochum, Germany
{fischer,scherer}@leat.rub.de
[2] VDZ Technology gGmbH, 40476 Düsseldorf, Germany
{luca.fehler,kevin.treiber}@vdz-online.de

Abstract. Refuse derived fuels (RDF), produced from municipal and industrial waste, provide an alternative to fossil fuels like coal or lignite in the cement production, thereby reducing the significant CO_2 emissions typically associated with cement production. The composition of RDF is often unknown, which limits the substitution rate, since otherwise the risk of impacting cement quality would increase. In this contribution, both near-infrared spectroscopy (NIRS) and RGB images were used to analyze RDF in an at-line measurement on a conveyor belt setup. The goal was to classify individual RDF particles in one of six fractions (paper, foils, 3D plastic, rubber, foams, textiles), since the fractions differ in combustion and flight behavior and therefore influence cement quality. For this, training, validation, and test data were obtained from 11,526 manually sorted RDF particles, sampled from various German cement plants and processed using an at-line conveyor belt setup. The NIRS data were processed using a small convolutional neural network (CNN) to provide the respective fraction, yielding an accuracy of 99.5%. The images were processed with different CNNs with transfer learning, yielding an accuracy of 96.7%. In a second phase, both NIRS and image predictions were combined by soft voting, yielding an accuracy of 99.7%. This validates the method under lab conditions and lays the groundwork for an application in a cement plant.

Keywords: Classification · Refuse derived fuel · Cement production · Near-infrared · CNN · Transfer learning

1 Introduction

1.1 Cement Production and Refuse Derived Fuels

Cement is the most used building material worldwide [5]. Its main component, cement clinker, is produced from limestone, $CaCO_3$. Clinker consists of a mixture of CaO minerals, which give cement its characteristic properties. From the chemical formulas of clinker formation it is obvious that producing clinker requires the removal of carbon dioxide from the limestone. This happens in the calcination reaction, shown in Eq. (1).

$$\text{CaCO}_3(s) \rightarrow \text{CaO}(s) + \text{CO}_2(g), \Delta h_r = +1780 \text{kJ/kg} \qquad (1)$$

The reaction enthalpy of +1780 kJ/kg indicates that the reaction is highly endothermic. Consequently, the calcination reaction occurs at 900 °C [2]. Combined with other necessary reactions and heat losses, the mean specific thermal energy demand in the German cement production is 2807 MJ per 1 ton of cement [28]. The required heat is provided by direct combustion in a horizontal rotary kiln (diameter 3–6 m, length up to 100 m). The raw limestone (ground into a fine meal) is conveyed by gravity due to a kiln incline of approx. 5% and a kiln rotation of ca. 1–4 rpm [14]. The fuels are injected together with the combustion air into the kiln at the main burner in counter flow to the raw limestone. The combustion of the fuels provides temperatures of 1450 °C near the flame [14].

The main emission of the cement production is CO_2, both from the fuels and the calcination reaction. An average German cement plant emits 586 kg of CO_2 per ton of cement [27]. While the emissions of the calcination are inevitable, the emissions of the fuel are directly influenced by the type of fuel used. Traditionally, fossil fuels like lignite and pulverized coal are combusted. This comes with several disadvantages: First, the fuels are expensive, finite and not locally available. Second, fossil fuels increase the carbon dioxide emissions of the cement production, which also, in countries with CO_2 certificates or tax further increase the fuel price. Third, the higher CO_2 emissions result in the acceleration of anthropogenic climate change. It is estimated that cement production is responsible for around 8% of worldwide CO_2 emissions [13]. 60% of these emission originate from the calcination reaction itself, but the remaining 40% originate from the energy supply, mainly from the fuels [28].

Alternative fuels can help to mitigate these disadvantages. These fuels can be used tires, sewage sludge or animal bone meal, but the biggest proportion are refuse derived fuels (RDF), made from industrial and municipal waste. RDF are produced from waste in several steps, mainly involving shredding to sizes of few centimeters and removal of metals. RDF are not only cheap, in some cases they have a negative price (considered as waste incineration), which helps stabilizing production prices. In terms of CO_2 emissions certificates, RDF are also cheaper, since they 1) have a better carbon to hydrogen ratio and 2) contain a certain amount of biodegradable waste, which is considered CO_2 neutral. In total, RDF produces only around 50 g CO_2 per provided MJ energy [18] (lignite: $111 \, gCO_2/MJ$ [11], coal: $94 \, gCO_2/MJ$ [11]). Since industrial and municipal waste are generated at all urban and industrial areas, RDF do not need long and expensive routes of transport. The substitution ratios of alternative fuels in cement production differ worldwide: Austria (79% [22]) and Germany (73% [28]) are in pole position, the EU average is 46%, while the United States only use 15% and Asian countries like China, South Korea and Japan use 11% [22]. In India, the substitution ratio is minimal, with a percentage of only 3% [22]. Since the waste input streams differ over time and location, so does the RDF composition. The composition can be divided in six fractions: Paper and cardboard, foils, three-dimensional plastics, foams, textiles, and rubber. These fractions differ both in flight and combustion behavior and are therefore not equally suitable for the combustion in a cement plant. 3D plastics, for example, often hit the clinker bed not completely combusted, which produces reducing conditions in the clinker bed and therefore lower cement quality [1].

1.2 Near-Infrared Spectroscopy

Near-infrared spectroscopy (NIRS) is a method to determine the structure of molecules. It is a type of vibrational spectroscopy in which molecules are exposed to electromagnetic radiation. Depending on their structure, different vibrational modes (e.g., stretching, bending, or twisting) are possible. For energy in the near-infrared (NIR) wavelength range to be absorbed, a molecule must exhibit a dipole moment [16,23]. This makes NIRS particularly useful for detecting molecular bonds such as C=O, O-H, and C-H.

A typical NIRS setup consists of two main components. First, a light source emitting radiation in the NIRd wavelength range of 800–2500 nm, such as halogen lamps, LEDs, or lasers. The light interacts with a sample and is reflected from the sample. Second, the reflected light is detected by an NIRS detector, such as a silicon photodiode, photomultiplier tube, or an indium gallium arsenide (InGaAs) sensor, which differ in their detection wavelength ranges. The change in light intensity due to light absorption in the sample (measured as dimensionless absorbance) is then plotted as a function of wavelength, resulting in a characteristic spectrum [16,23].

Unlike mid-infrared (MIR) spectroscopy, where fundamental molecular vibrations are dominant, NIRS spectra primarily consist of overtones and combination bands. Overtones are harmonic vibrations that occur at integer multiples of the fundamental vibrational frequency [16]. In NIRS, the most prominent overtones originate from C-H, O-H, and N-H bonds, making the technique particularly sensitive to organic compounds and water.

For molecules with more than two atoms ($N > 2$), the number of vibrational degrees of freedom is given by $3N - 6$ [16]. As a result, NIR spectra can be complex, with overlapping absorption bands. While characteristic peaks can be associated with specific molecular bonds, manual classification based solely on NIR spectra is challenging. Therefore, statistical and machine learning methods are essential for the automated classification and analysis of NIRS data.

1.3 Main Contributions

The literature on classification and evaluation of RDF in the cement process is limited. The approach of fuel classification through proximate analysis and hierarchical learning [7] still relies on slow and labor-intensive laboratory analyses. Several methods for RDF classification using NIRS exist, but they lack proper validation: In [29], a classifier applied to pure substances (e.g., PET) was used to predict RDF heating values. Since the fuel was not manually sorted, true labels were unavailable, meaning the accuracy and effectiveness of the classifier in predicting RDF fractions could not be verified. In Sevcik [21], FT-NIRS was combined with a Support Vector Machine, but only a small number of artificial model fuel samples were used (2–8 per fraction). Krämer and Flamme [12] report a commercial product for real-time RDF heating value analysis, but neither its accuracy nor the underlying algorithms are specified. For RDF classification using RGB images, an initial approach is proposed in Peddireddy et al. [17], but it still depends on manual sorting, essentially shifting the sorting process from a conveyor belt to a desk-based workstation. Additionally, a study from Tahir et al. [24] presents a method to detect and classify waste based on video recordings taken after processing municipal solid waste (MSW) through a mechanical sorting line. The method demonstrates an accuracy of 0.70. In Fischer et al. [9], a similar approach for RDF classification based on images showed an accuracy of 0.71. A combination of image and NIRS classification for RDF classification is not yet known.

2 Experiments

2.1 Experimental Setup

The experimental setup is designed as either an offline or at-line method to classify individual RDF particles and hence determine the composition of a fuel. The setup is constructed around a conveyor belt. An image is shown in Fig. 1. A camera, Basler a2A1920-160ucPRO with 2.3 MP and 168 fps, is mounted on top of the conveyor belt, such that the recorded images are not distorted by an angle. Laterally, both an infrared light source, a tungsten halogen lamp, and an near-infrared detector, Viavi 1700 ES, are mounted at an angle to the conveyor belt. The NIRS detector is an indium gallium arsenide detector with measurable wavelength in the range of 908 - 1676 nm. The measurement time is 9.2 ms and the wavelength resolution is 6.19 nm. To provide rich meta data, an environment sensor 2JCIE-BU01 from OMRON is used. It can be connected by USB 3.0 and measures temperature, humidity, illuminance, barometric pressure, sound noise, 3-axis acceleration, and TVOC (Total volatile organic compounds). Accuracies are given in [15].

The particles are fed by vibration over a 8 mm sieve to the conveyor belt. This ensures both no fines and dust on the conveyor belt, and separation of individual particles, such that they do not overlap and can clearly be distinguished from another. A measurement is triggered by a color change of central pixels against an average background of the black conveyor belt. For each measurement, one image, one NIR spectrum and one set of meta-data are stored into a SQL database. Each particle is assigned an unique ID (UUID4) and each experiment is grouped into a batch of particles. For the database creation, RDF mixtures from different cement plants were beforehand manually sorted into batches of the six fractions. The manual sorting was executed due to a pre-determined sorting

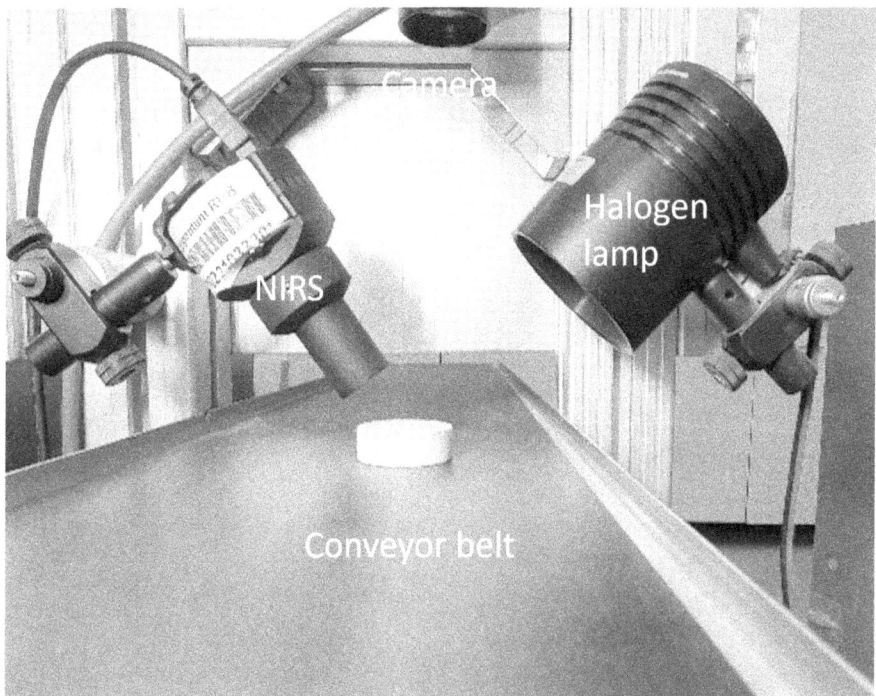

Fig. 1. Experimental setup consisting of camera (middle up) over a conveyor belt (middle) and a NIRS (left) with a halogen lamp (right).

catalog which defines optic, material and haptic of the particles. The presorted RDF particles were then fed to the experimental setup, hence, the batch labels could later be used as labels for classification.

2.2 Experimental Dataset

In Table 1, the numbers of particles per fraction in the database are listed, resulting in a total number of 11,526. Since the fractions in RDF mixtures do not occur equally, it follows that the numbers per fraction in the database are not evenly distributed either. Rubber for example is rarer than other fractions, resulting only in 1066 samples, while textiles with 2580 samples are slightly oversampled. In Fig. 2, example images for each fraction are shown. Here, some problematic characteristics of RDF for quality control can be seen: RDF particles differ in size, tend to stick together and sometimes are black or transparent. Also, the particles are not always perfectly centered in the image. In Fig. 3, example NIR spectra for each fraction are depicted, showing typical behavior: While both plastic fractions, 3D plastics and foils, have distinct peaks around 1200 nm and 1450 nm, the fractions paper and cardboard (PC) and textiles show one broad peak from 1450 nm to 1650 nm. Rubber and foams show only smaller peaks.

Table 1. Number of samples per fraction.

Fraction	Number
Foils	2188
3D plastics	1321
Paper and Cardboard	2442
Rubber	1066
Foams	1929
Textiles	2580
Total	11526

Especially for rubber, this is the case due to the dominant black color of the particles, which leads to an higher NIRS absorbance regardless of the material.

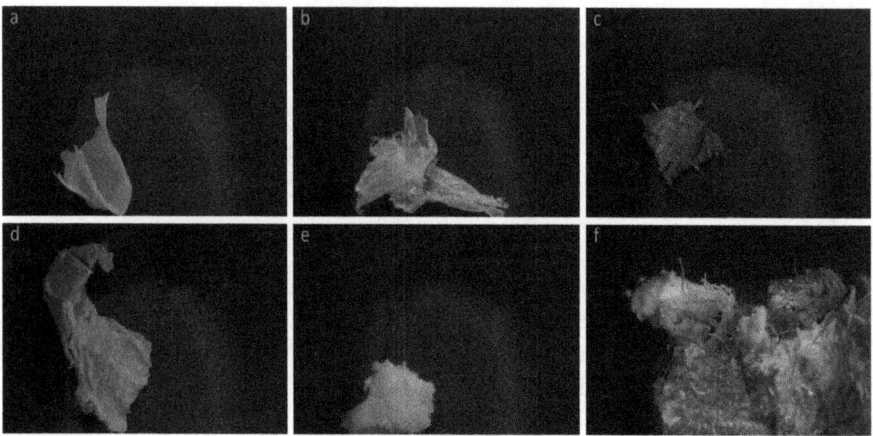

Fig. 2. Examples of RDF images per fraction: a 3D plastic, b foils, c rubber, d paper and cardboard, e foams, f textiles.

The dataset is published at https://doi.org/10.5281/zenodo.14859683 [8]. For all following classification tasks, 10% of each fraction were used as each validation and test data, leaving 80% for the training data. In a first step, image and NIRS classification were executed separately, while in a second step, the results were combined. The implementation of neural networks was realized with TensorFlow [26]. The training was executed on a NVIDIA GeForce RTX 4070 Ti Super GPU (VRAM = 16 GB).

2.3 Image Classification

The images of the training data set were used together with the labels, inherited from the batch identities, to classify the samples in one of the six different frac-

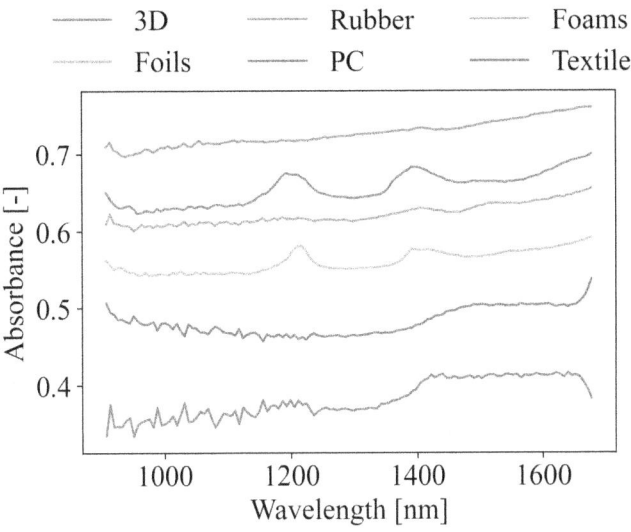

Fig. 3. Examples of NIR spectra per fraction.

tions. For this, different convolutional neural networks (CNNs) were compared, namely Xception [4], ResNet-50 [10] and EfficientNets B0-B5 [25]. An overview is given in Table 2.

Table 2. Used CNN based models with trainable parameters (including upstream and downstream), input size, ImageNet Top1 and Top3 accuracies.

Base model	Trainable Parameters	Input size	ImageNet Acc. Top1	ImageNet Acc. Top3	Source
B0	4,219,433	$224 \times 224 \times 3$	0.771	0.933	[25]
B1	6,745,101	$240 \times 240 \times 3$	0.791	0.944	[25]
B2	7,955,327	$260 \times 260 \times 3$	0.801	0.949	[25]
B3	10,987,189	$300 \times 300 \times 3$	0.816	0.957	[25]
B4	17,911,269	$380 \times 380 \times 3$	0.829	0.964	[25]
B5	28,784,765	$456 \times 456 \times 3$	0.836	0.967	[25]
ResNet50	23,858,950	$224 \times 224 \times 3$	0.7715	0.933	[10]
Xception	21,132,718	$229 \times 229 \times 3$	0.79	0.945	[4]

Additionally to this CNNs, from here on called "base models", some other layers were added, such that the data flow is as follows:

1. Input layer with size according to base model between $224 \times 2244 \times 3$ and $4564 \times 4564 \times 3$ pixel.

2. Data augmentation layer with random flip, random translation, random rotation, random zoom, random contrast and random brightness.
3. Normalization layer.
4. Base model CNN.
5. Global average pooling layer.
6. Dropout Layer (0.5).
7. Batch normalization layer.
8. Dense connected layer with 128 nodes.
9. Output layer with softmax activation.

To increase training speed, all CNNs were trained with transfer learning, using the weights from the ImageNet dataset [19]. In transfer learning, the training is split into two training phases. The first phase is used to only train the dense connected layer at the end of the network with a high learning rate ($\alpha = 1e^{-3}$). In the second step, the whole network is trained, but with a smaller learning rate ($\alpha = 1e^{-5}$). In this publication, both phases lasted 50 epochs. The optimizer used is Adam with categorical crossentropy as loss function. The batch size was selected as 16, except for EfficientNetB5 as base model, where the batch size needed to be reduced to 8 due to a lack of more VRAM. Bigger EfficientNets therefore were not tested.

2.4 NIRS Classification

For the classification based on NIRS measurement, the feature is the absorbance over the wavelength after some preprocessing (125 data points per sample), which is described in the following. After being loaded from the data base, a Savitzky-Golay filter [20] is applied to each spectrum. This is a common practice in chemometrics and it serves two purposes: First, smoothing of the data, reducing the measurement noise and second, a robust way to find a smooth derivative. Derivatives can help increase classification results since mostly peaks of absorbance are used to determine the identity of a sample. The filter is a finite filter with kernel length K_{len}, applied to the spectrum values x at position a by multiplying with kernel values K_r, as shown in Eq. (2).

$$\bar{x}_a = \sum_{r=1}^{K_{len}} K_r x_{r-a} \qquad (2)$$

K_r depend on both K_{len} and the derivative d. Also, $d = 0$ is possible, which only applies a smoothing function to the measurement values. In Fig. 4(a), the example spectra from Fig. 3 are shown after the application of the Savitzky-Golay filter ($K_{len} = 15$, $d = 0$). Since spectral data are heavily dependent on the lighting situation, the default mean value is not equal, such that a normalization is necessary to make NIRS measurements comparable and useful for classification. In this contribution, normalization is done with the standard normal variate (SNV). With SNV, the spectrum is normalized as shown in Eq. (3). First, the mean value of the spectrum $\bar{x}$ is subtracted. This leads to a new mean of 0. Second, the difference is divided by the standard deviation s. In this way, the variance σ is equal 1.

$$x_{SNV} = \frac{x - \bar{x}}{s} \qquad (3)$$

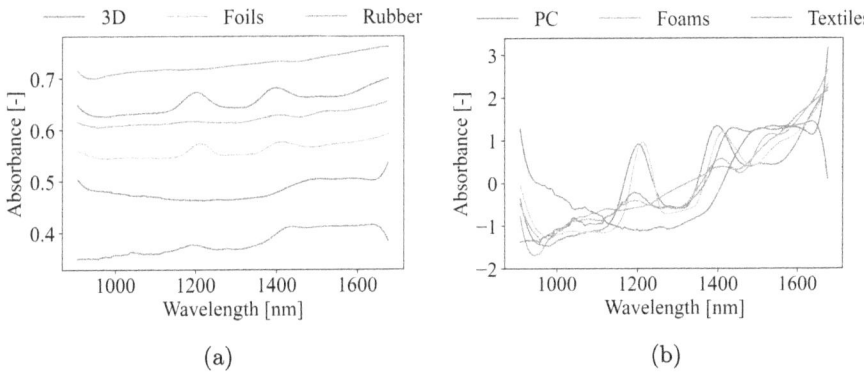

Fig. 4. Data preprocessing of NIRS data example from Fig. 3. Left: Savitzky-Golay filter with $K_{len} = 15$ and $d = 0$ applied to example spectra. Right: Standard normal variate applied to results from left.

The result is the feature used for the NIRS classification with mean of 0 and variance equal 1. In Fig. 4(b), the spectra from Fig. 3 with SNV normalization are shown. The labels are, analogous to the image classification, derived from the batch identities. In Fig. 5, the structure of the used neural network for NIRS classification is shown. In the upper half, two blocks of 1D convolutional layers combined with batch normalization and maximum pooling process the spectrum, similar to [3]. An 1D convolution is, like the Savitzky-Golay filter, a finite filter, but with learned kernel values K_r. In this neural network, the 1D convolutional layers apply 64 filters each with a kernel size of 5. The second half consists of three dense connected layers with 128, 32 and 6 nodes. The last node activates with the softmax function, while all other layers activate with ReLu. In between of the blocks, Gaussian noise is added as data augmentation to increase robustness against measurement noise. Additionally, a dropout of 0.5 is used during training to prevent overfitting. The structure adds up to 255270 trainable parameters.

2.5 Combined Image and NIRS Classification

Combining predictions from different classifiers can benefit the accuracy of the prediction. For combining the predictions c_i^j of sample i and classifier j, different options are possible. In hard voting, the class with most predictions votes c_i^j is voted. When using only two classifiers, this would either result in an unanimous

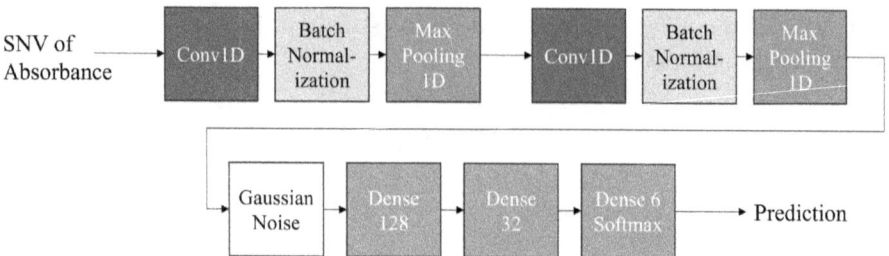

Fig. 5. Neural network structure for NIRS classification. The first half consists of two time, 1D convolutional layer, batch normalization and maximum pooling. The second half consist of dense connected layers. During training, Gaussian noise added in between.

vote or a tie, which cannot increase the accuracy. Another form of voting is soft voting [31], where the prediction probabilities p_i^j are used as shown in Eq. (4).

$$p_i = \sum_{j=1}^{C} w_j p_i^j \qquad (4)$$

C is the number of classifiers and w_j are weights. In this contribution, both the unweighted case ($w_{j=1,2} = 1$) as well as the weighted case are tested. For the weighted case, the weight of the classifiers are their accuracy on the test data. In majority voting, the prediction with the highest probability is used, as shown in Eq. (5).

$$c_i = argmax(p_i^1, ..., p_i^j) \qquad (5)$$

3 Results and Discussion

3.1 Image Classification

In Fig. 6(a), the accuracies of the image classification with different base models are shown over the number of trainable parameters of the whole network with all upstream and downstream layers. First, it can easily be seen that both Xception and ResNet, although having a high number of trainable parameters, do not perform better than some smaller base models tested (EfficientNet B0-B3). For the EfficientNet base models, a linear correlation between trainable parameters and accuracy can be stated. In Fig. 6 (b), the accuracies are plotted over the corresponding training time. Surprisingly here, ResNet is the base model with the lowest training time, but differences to Xception an EfficientNets B0-B3 are small. For the EfficientNets models, there is again a quasi linear correlation between accuracy and training time as seen between training parameters and training time. Highest accuracies can be observed with base models EfficientNet B4 (accuracy=0.967) and B5 (accuracy=0.979). Although B5 provides the highest accuracy, training time is nearly double (7.1 h instead of 4.8 h) of B4, and can only barely be executed on the employed hardware. Hence, EfficientNet B4 is selected as base model for the image classification part. In Table 3, the confusion matrix for the image classification is listed. Foils and 3D plastics are often confused due to their optical similarity. Paper/cardboard has the lowest precision of 93.85%, which results in mispredicted samples for all fractions except rubber. This fraction has a recall of 100%, meaning only rubber samples were predicted as rubber. To measure the effect of transfer learning, the training with EfficientNet B4 was again executed with random initial weights. The training plan remained the same (50 epochs $\alpha = 1e^{-3}$, 50 epochs $\alpha = 1e^{-5}$), except that in the first phase also the whole model was trained. The training took 7.3 h, which is 1.5 times the required training time for the EfficientNet B4 using transfer learning. Although the accuracy on training and test data was high after the training, the accuracy on the test data was just 0.27, only slightly better than random. This shows the benefits of the transfer learning technique.

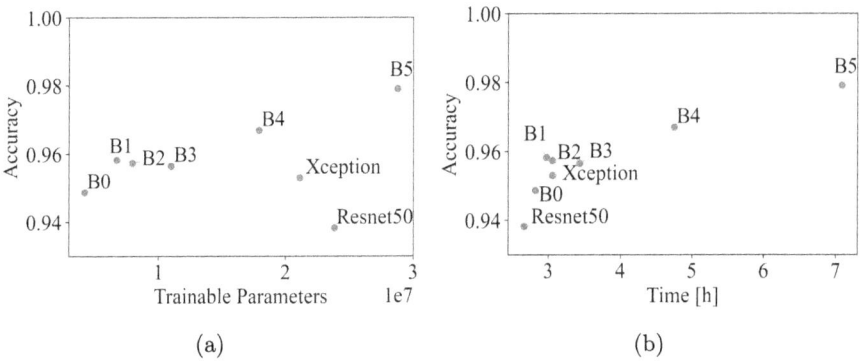

Fig. 6. Accuracies on the test data set of Xception, ResNet 50 and Efficientnet B0-B5 over (a) the number of trainable parameters (left) and (b) over the required training time in hours.

Table 3. Confusion Matrix for image classification.

		Predictions					
		3D Plastics	Foils	Rubber	Paper	Foams	Textiles
Identity	3D Plastics	0.9621	0.0303	0.0	0.0076	0.0	0.0
	Foils	0.0138	0.9725	0.0	0.0092	0.0	0.0046
	Rubber	0.0094	0.0	0.9623	0.0	0.0189	0.0094
	Paper	0.0164	0.0164	0.0	0.9385	0.0205	0.0082
	Foams	0.0	0.0052	0.0	0.0052	0.9896	0.0
	Textiles	0.0	0.0	0.0	0.0	0.0233	0.9767

3.2 NIRS Classification

The accuracies for NIRS classification with derivatives $d = 0, 1, 2$ are 0.995, 0.724 and 0.763, respectively. Surprisingly, the results for $d = 0$ with an accuracy of 0.995 are the highest. This might be due to the convolutional layers in the used neural network, which, in combination with the smoothing Savitzky-Golay filter and SNV normalization, extract the required information to distinguish the different fractions. When using $d = 0$, not only peaks in the spectra are used for the prediction, but the whole shape and absolute values of the curve. Both differ drastically between two groups: While the 3D plastics and foil fractions show narrow, sharp peaks, the other fractions show broad peaks over many wavelengths (see Fig. 3). In Table 4, the confusion matrix for the NIRS classification is shown. For the fractions foils, 3D plastic and textiles the precisions are 100% and for textiles also the recall is 100%. Between 3D plastic and foils no mix-up occurred.

In Fig. 7, the feature importance by permutation is shown. For this, the feature was permuted 100 times for each wavelength with a kernel size of 5 (equal to the 1D Conv. layer kernel). This means, for each wavelength, the two adjacent values above and below were also permuted. The highest feature importance is observed at wavelength 1650 nm, which represents the rising absorbance at the upper end of the spectra. This is likely due to an olefinic C-H overtone at 1680 nm or an aromatic C-H overtone at 1685 nm [23]. Another region of high feature importance is the region around 1500 nm, which is probably due to the broad peaks of the textile and paper/cardboard fractions corresponding to O-H overtones [23] from cellulose [6]. The peaks at 1400 nm and 1200 nm correspond to the peaks of foils and 3D plastics (see Fig. 3), and their C-H (1200 nm) and O-H groups (1400 nm) [23]. The peak at 1130 nm may be the third overtone of C-H groups [30], for example seen in a small absorbance peak of textile particles.

Table 4. Confusion Matrix for NIRS classification.

		Predictions					
		3D Plastics	Foils	Rubber	Paper	Foams	Textiles
Identity	3D Plastics	1.00	0.0	0.0	0.0	0.0	0.0
	Foils	0.0	1.00	0.0	0.0	0.0	0.0
	Rubber	0.0189	0.0189	0.9623	0.0	0.0	0.0
	Paper	0.0041	0.0	0.0	0.9959	0.0	0.0
	Foams	0.0	0.0	0.0	0.0052	0.9948	0.0
	Textiles	0.0	0.0	0.0	0.0	0.0	1.00

3.3 Combined Image and NIRS Classification

The accuracies for unweighted soft voting, weighted soft voting and majority voting are listed were 0.997, 0.996 and 0.997. The differences between these methods

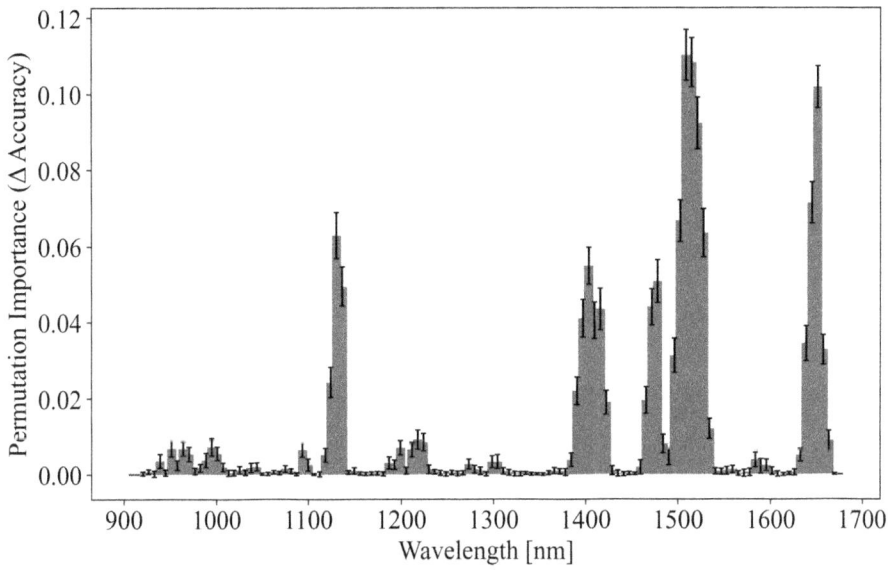

Fig. 7. Feature importance by permutation.

are only small, but the unweighted soft voting combination and majority voting provided both the best results with an accuracy of 0.997.

In Table 5, the confusion matrix for the combined classification with unweighted soft voting is shown. Only the predictions for some rubber samples are incorrectly predicted as 3D plastic or foils, but all other predictions are correct. Majority voting showed the same results with the same samples being predicted incorrectly. The remaining incorrectly predicted samples are three rubber particles, one black particle and two off-centered particles, shown in Fig. 8. All three samples were also falsely predicted with NIRS, while being predicted correctly with images. All of the falsely predicted samples of the image classification were predicted correctly with NIRS and vice versa. Each sample was therefore at least once predicted correctly.

Another approach, which can increase the robustness of the method is the application of a threshold t: Only predictions with a $p_i^j > t$ are admitted for the final prediction, otherwise the prediction is either only based on the other method or the sample has to be rejected in order not to compromise the statement about the composition. For $t = 0.9$, 96.2% of all predictions from the EfficientNet B4 and 99.9% of all predictions from the NIRS CNN were above the threshold.

In comparison to reported accuracies in literature (around 0.7, see Sect. 1.3), the accuracies for both image and NIRS classification separate and combined are higher. In comparison to these approaches, this contribution uses a bigger and manual labeled data set.

Table 5. Confusion Matrix for combined classification.

		Predictions					
		3D Plastics	Foils	Rubber	Paper	Foams	Textiles
Identity	3D Plastics	1.0000	0.0	0.0	0.0	0.0	0.0
	Foils	0.0	1.0000	0.0	0.0	0.0	0.0
	Rubber	0.0094	0.0189	0.9717	0.0	0.0	0.0
	Paper	0.0	0.0	0.0	1.0000	0.0	0.0
	Foams	0.0	0.0	0.0	0.0	1.0000	0.0
	Textiles	0.0	0.0	0.0	0.0	0.0	1.0000

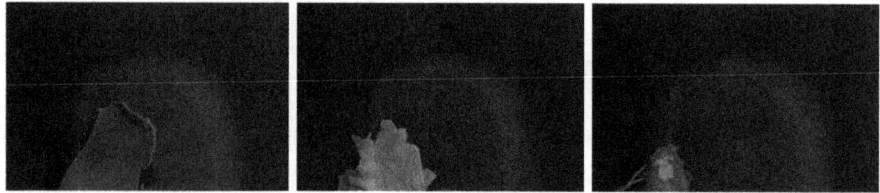

Fig. 8. Samples incorrectly predicted with unweighted soft voting.

4 Conclusion

Two different measurement techniques were used to characterize refuse derived fuels (RDF), RGB images and near-infrared spectroscopy (NIRS). A dataset with 11526 samples was created with samples from different cement plants on an lab set-up. The dataset was then used to classify RDF in one of six fractions: paper, foils, 3D plastic, rubber, foams, textiles. In a first step, image and NIRS classification were considered separately. For image classification, transfer learning for different CNNs with pre-trained ImageNet weights was tested. The highest accuracy in proportions to training effort and trainable parameters was achieved with EfficientNets. For use in the combined predictor, EfficientNet B4, which showed an accuracy of 0.967 on the test data, was selected. For the NIRS classification, a self-designed CNN with 1D convolutional layers was used. Surprisingly, the CNN showed better results when using the spectrum directly instead of a derivative of the spectrum. This predictor showed an accuracy of 0.995 on test data. To combine both methods in a second step, soft voting and majority voting were tested, which increased the accuracy to 0.997. With this, the combined technique is lab validated. Nevertheless, a validation in a cement plant is the next required step. For example, influences of the harsh environment in a cement plant (vibration, dust, humidity) need to be examined.

Acknowledgments. The IGF Project (01IF22676N) is supported within the programme for promoting the Industrial Collective Research (IGF) of the German Ministry of Economic Affairs and Energy.

Disclosure of Interests. The authors have no competing interests to declare that are relevant to the content of this article.

References

1. Bodendiek, N., van Thriel, H., Schäfer, S., Hoenig, V., Wirtz, S., Scherer, V.: Untersuchung der Wechselwirkung von Brennstoffpartikeln und Zementklinker zur Erhöhung des Ersatzbrennstoff-Einsatzes: 30. Deutscher Flammentag (2021)
2. Chatterjee, A.K.: Cement Production Technology: Principles and Practice. Chapman and Hall/CRC, Milton (2018). https://ebookcentral.proquest.com/lib/kxp/detail.action?docID=5372003
3. Chen, X., et al.: Probing 1D convolutional neural network adapted to near-infrared spectroscopy for efficient classification of mixed fish. Spectrochimica Acta. Part A Mol. Biomol. Spectroscopy **279**, 121350 (2022). https://doi.org/10.1016/j.saa.2022.121350
4. Chollet, F.: Xception: deep learning with depthwise separable convolutions. In: Proceedings of the IEEE Conference on Computer Vision and Pattern Recognition (2017). https://doi.org/10.1109/CVPR.2017.195
5. Crow, J.M.: The concrete conundrum. Chemistry World (2008). https://www.rsc.org/images/Construction_tcm18-114530.pdf
6. dos Santos, E.O., Silva, A.M.S., Fragoso, W.D., Pasquini, C., Pimentel, M.F.: Determination of degree of polymerization of insulating paper using near infrared spectroscopy and multivariate calibration. Vib. Spectrosc. **52**(2), 154–157 (2010). https://doi.org/10.1016/j.vibspec.2009.12.004
7. Elmaz, F., Büyükçakır, B., Yücel, Ö., Mutlu, A.Y.: Classification of solid fuels with machine learning. Fuel **266**, 117066 (2020). https://doi.org/10.1016/j.fuel.2020.117066
8. Fischer, J., Fehler, L., Treiber, K., Scherer, V.: Near-Infrared Spectroscopy and Image Classification of Refuse-Derived Fuels for Cement Production. https://doi.org/10.5281/zenodo.14859682
9. Fischer, J., Wirtz, S., Scherer, V.: Random forest classifier and neural network for fraction identification of refuse-derived fuel images. Fuel **341**, 127712 (2023). https://doi.org/10.1016/j.fuel.2023.127712
10. He, K., Zhang, X., Ren, S., Sun, J.: Deep Residual Learning for Image Recognition. http://arxiv.org/pdf/1512.03385
11. Juhrich, K.: CO_2-Emissionsfaktoren für fossile Brennstoffe: Climate Change 27/2016
12. Krämer, P., Flamme, S.: Real-time analysis of solid recovered fuels using sensor technology. In: Thomé-Kozmiensky, K.J., Thiel, S. (eds.) Waste Management, pp. 339–348. Thomé-Kozmiensky Verlag GmbH, Nietwerder (2015)
13. Lehne, J., Preston, F.: Making Concrete Change: Innovation in Low-carbon Cement and Concrete. https://www.chathamhouse.org/sites/default/files/publications/research/2018-06-13-making-concrete-change-cement-lehne-preston.pdf
14. Locher, F.W.: Zement: Grundlagen der Herstellung und Verwendung. Verlag Bau+Technik, Düsseldorf (2000). https://ebookcentral.proquest.com/lib/kxp/detail.action?docID=2029875

15. OMRON Corporation: Environment Sensor (USB Type) Environment Sensor (USB Type) 2JCIE-BU01: User's Manual. https://components.omron.com/eu-en/sites/components.omron.com.eu/files/ds_related_pdf/A279-E1.pdf#page=125.09
16. Ozaki, Y., Huck, C., Tsuchikawa, S., Engelsen, S.B. (eds.): Near-Infrared Spectroscopy. Springer, Singapore (2021). https://doi.org/10.1007/978-981-15-8648-4
17. Peddireddy, S., Longhurst, P.J., Wagland, S.T.: Characterising the composition of waste-derived fuels using a novel image analysis tool. Waste Manag. (New York, N.Y.) **40**, 9–13 (2015). https://doi.org/10.1016/j.wasman.2015.03.015
18. Pohl, M., Becker, G., Heller, N., Birnstengel, B., Zotz, F.: Auswirkungen des nationalen Brennstoffemissionshandels auf die Abfallwirtschaft
19. Russakovsky, O., et al.: ImageNet large scale visual recognition challenge. Int. J. Comput. Vis. (IJCV) **115**(3), 211–252 (2015). https://doi.org/10.1007/s11263-015-0816-y
20. Savitzky, A., Golay, M.J.E.: Smoothing and differentiation of data by simplified least squares procedures. Anal. Chem. **36**(8), 1627–1639 (1964). https://doi.org/10.1021/ac60214a047
21. Ševčík, M.: Near-infrared spectroscopy for refuse derived fuel feasibility study of inorganic chlorine content quantification: classification of waste material components using hyperspectral imaging. https://www.diva-portal.org/smash/record.jsf?pid=diva2:1281468
22. Sharma, P., Sheth, P.N., Mohapatra, B.N.: Recent progress in refuse derived fuel (RDF) co-processing in cement production: direct firing in kiln/calciner vs process integration of RDF gasification. Waste Biomass Valorization **13**(11), 4347–4374 (2022). https://doi.org/10.1007/s12649-022-01840-8
23. Siesler, H.W. (ed.): Near-infrared spectroscopy: Principles, instruments, applications. Wiley-VCH, Weinheim, 2. reprint edn. (2005)
24. Tahir, J., Ahmad, R., Tian, Z.: Calorific value prediction models of processed refuse derived fuel 3 using ultimate analysis. Biofuels **14**(1), 69–78 (2023). https://doi.org/10.1080/17597269.2022.2116771
25. Tan, M., Le, Q.V.: EfficientNet: Rethinking Model Scaling for Convolutional Neural Networks (2019). https://doi.org/10.48550/arXiv.1905.11946
26. TensorFlow Developers: TensorFlow (2024). https://doi.org/10.5281/ZENODO.4724125
27. Verein Deutscher Zementwerke e.V.: Umweltdaten der deutschen Zementindustrie (2022). https://www.vdz-online.de/wissensportal/publikationen/umweltdaten-der-deutschen-zementindustrie-2022
28. Verein Deutscher Zementwerke e.V.: Umweltdaten der deutschen Zementindustrie (2023). https://www.vdz-online.de/wissensportal/publikationen/umweltdaten-der-deutschen-zementindustrie-2023
29. Verga, S., et al.: Estimation of the lower heating value of solid recovered fuel based on swir hyper-spectral images and machine learning. In: 2022 12th Workshop on Hyperspectral Imaging and Signal Processing: Evolution in Remote Sensing (WHISPERS), pp. 1–5. IEEE (2022). https://doi.org/10.1109/WHISPERS56178.2022.9955135
30. Weyer, L.G., Lo, S.C.: Spectra–structure correlations in the near–infrared. In: Griffiths, P.R., Chalmers, J.M. (eds.) Handbook of Vibrational Spectroscopy. Wiley (2001). https://doi.org/10.1002/0470027320.s4102
31. Zhou, Z.H. (ed.): Machine learning. Springer eBook Collection, Springer, Singapore (2021). https://doi.org/10.1007/978-981-15-1967-3

From Lab to Factory: Pitfalls and Guidelines for Self-/Unsupervised Defect Detection on Low-Quality Industrial Images

Sebastian Hönel(✉) and Jonas Nordqvist

Linnæus University, Växjö, Sweden
{sebastian.honel,jonas.nordqvist}@lnu.se

Abstract. The detection and localization of quality-related problems in industrially mass-produced products has historically relied on manual inspection, which is costly and error-prone. Machine learning has the potential to replace manual handling. As such, the desire is to facilitate an unsupervised (or self-supervised) approach, as it is often impossible to specify all conceivable defects ahead of time. A plethora of prior works have demonstrated the aptitude of common reconstruction-, embedding-, and synthesis-based methods in laboratory settings. However, in practice, we observe that most methods do not handle low data quality well or exude low robustness in unfavorable, but typical real-world settings. For practitioners it may be very difficult to identify the actual underlying problem when such methods underperform. Worse, often-reported metrics (e.g., AUROC) are rarely suitable in practice and may give misleading results. In our setting, we attempt to identify subtle anomalies on the surface of blasted forged metal parts, using rather low-quality RGB imagery only, which is a common industrial setting. We specifically evaluate two types of state-of-the-art models that allow us to identify and improve quality issues in production data, without having to obtain new data. Our contribution is to provide guardrails for practitioners that allow them to identify problems related to, e.g., (lack of) robustness or invariance, in either the chosen model or the data reliably in similar scenarios. Furthermore, we exemplify common pitfalls in and shortcomings of likelihood-based approaches and outline a framework for proper empirical risk estimation that is more suitable for real-world scenarios.

Keywords: Unsupervised Anomaly Detection · Anomaly Localization · Normalizing Flows · Industrial Visual Inspection · Low-Quality Imagery · Robust Evaluation · Out-of-Distribution Detection · Computer Vision in Manufacturing

1 Introduction

Industrial manufacturing requires quality assurance. A common approach to quality evaluation is through manual visual inspection, which is expensive, repetitive, and error-prone [10]. Recent advances in deep learning and computer vision have boosted interest in automated self- or unsupervised anomaly detection methods [5]. In such approaches, acquiring nominal (defect-free) data is affordable, but exhaustively defining abnormal defect variants often proves difficult or impossible. Thus, anomaly detection (AD) is framed as an out-of-distribution challenge, distinguishing nominal samples from those outside the known distribution [24]. A related task, anomaly localization (AL), further identifies where anomalies occur, benefiting interpretability by providing visual cues and enabling human-in-the-loop systems [30].

AD/AL methods in visual inspection generally fall into three categories: embedding-, reconstruction-, and synthesis-based approaches [6]. Embedding-based approaches use pretrained feature extractors. Reconstruction approaches exploit differences between input and reconstructed images, or encodings and decodings thereof, to detect anomalies [32]. Synthesis methods train classifiers by generating artificial defects to differentiate them from nominal samples, effectively combining unsupervised and semi-supervised approaches [33]. Semi-supervised approaches are now generally preferred. Unsupervised methods often lack reliability in precisely detecting out-of-distribution cases, whereas fully-supervised methods require costly data labeling, suffer limited data availability, and cannot easily handle unknown defect types or label noise [30].

Visual-inspection AD methods are commonly evaluated on standard datasets such as MVTec AD [1] or Magnetic Tile Defects (MTD) [13]. However, these benchmark datasets largely come from controlled laboratory environments. Hence, most images feature simple setups, single centered objects with uniform backgrounds, static orientations and camera distances, and lack realistic disturbances such as reflections, shadows, or blur. Recently, Jezek et al. [16] introduced the Metal Parts Defect Detection (MPDD) dataset, a more challenging real-world scenario encompassing some typical practical issues. Their evaluation demonstrates a significant deterioration of state-of-the-art performance, especially for image-level AD, highlighting the gap between lab-based benchmarks and real production environments.

In view of this gap, this paper explores practical problems related to data quality, modeling choices, and proper evaluation. Important data-related challenges include excessively subtle anomalies relative to natural variance, unwanted background disturbances, reflections, and other unfavorable image-capturing conditions. Additionally, certain conditions can impact models differently. While introducing rotations or varying viewpoints can broaden data diversity and generalization, the effectiveness of these augmentations strongly depends on the model chosen. Some models handle image variations like object scale or position robustly, while others decline significantly in performance if these transformations occur among the objects themselves.

Regarding performance evaluation, anomaly detection results frequently use area under the receiver operating characteristic curve (AUROC). Although AUROC is valuable when comparing methods within identical datasets, interpreting reported AUROC values across different publications or scenarios should be done with caution. Its interpretation strongly depends on the underlying data and evaluation strategies. Often only maximum or average AUROC scores are reported, lacking uncompromising replication. Importantly, classifiers built from selected thresholds for anomaly scores are rarely evaluated rigorously using proper repeated cross-validation or bootstrapping methods that provide reliable estimates of empirical risk and realistic performance in deployment scenarios. Our contributions are summarized as follows:

1. We overview critical data-acquisition and data-quality issues encountered in practice, and suggest directions for improvement.
2. We investigate how core architectural components in current AD/AL methods respond differently to specific real-world issues, offering practical recommendations for properly pairing datasets with models.
3. We propose an evaluation framework based on adequate outer resampling to accurately estimate empirical model risk and derive confidence intervals, better predicting factory-floor model performance.

The remainder of this paper is structured as follows. In Sect. 2, we present the relevant background, related work, and describe the concrete dataset and problem we attempt solving. In Sect. 3, we elucidate limitations of flow-based architectures. Section 4 is dedicated to outlining and validating a robust estimation framework. Lastly, Sect. 5 offers a discussion and an outlook on future work.

2 Background and Related Work

Anomaly detection in imagery is a critical task in various domains, including industrial inspection, medical imaging, and security, where identifying irregularities is essential. Due to the rarity and diversity of anomalies, unsupervised and semi-supervised learning approaches are commonly employed, as they enable detection without the need for extensively labeled (complementary) datasets.

Unsupervised methods typically identify anomalies by modeling the distribution of normal samples. One widely used approach involves reconstruction-based techniques, such as autoencoders [12], where the model is trained to reconstruct normal data, and anomalies are inferred from high reconstruction errors [28]. Another method leverages generative adversarial networks (GANs) [8], assessing deviations from the learned distribution to detect anomalies [19]. A third strategy involves normalizing flows, which estimate the likelihood of feature maps and classify low-likelihood regions as anomalous [25,26], where the latter case is further discussed in Sect. 3.1. Additionally, clustering techniques such as k-means and DBSCAN can be utilized, where data points identified as outliers are considered anomalies.

In the context of self-supervised learning, techniques such as synthetic anomaly generation or auxiliary tasks have been explored to enhance feature representation learning, thereby improving anomaly detection performance (e.g., [11]). The current state-of-the-art in the realm of AD is a method which utilizes several techniques in AD. This method is further described in Sect. 3.2.

2.1 Normalizing Flows

Let $d \geq 1$ be an integer, and consider a vector $\mathbf{x} \in \mathbb{R}^d$. A normalizing flow models the distribution of $\mathbf{x}$ using a diffeomorphic transformation T, which is bijective and smooth along with its inverse. The transformation is applied to a latent variable $\mathbf{z}$ drawn from a base distribution $p_\mathbf{z}(\mathbf{z})$. Given $\mathbf{x} = T(\mathbf{z})$, the density of $\mathbf{x}$ follows from the change-of-variables formula

$$p_\mathbf{x}(\mathbf{x}) = p_\mathbf{z}(\mathbf{z}) \left| \det J_T(\mathbf{z}) \right|^{-1}, \quad \text{where } \mathbf{z} = T^{-1}(\mathbf{x})$$

and $J_T(\mathbf{z})$ is the Jacobian of T. In practice, T is parameterized, and in the context of normalizing flows, the set of parameters θ for a transformation T is learned by a so-called *conditioner*, typically implemented by some fully-connected neural network. Training a normalizing flow involves minimizing the forward Kullback–Leibler divergence between the data distribution $p_\mathbf{x}(\mathbf{x})$ and the transformed base distribution $\widehat{p}_\mathbf{x}(\mathbf{x}; \theta)$. The loss function is:

$$\begin{aligned}\mathcal{L}(\theta) &= D_{\mathrm{KL}}\left(p_\mathbf{x}(\mathbf{x}) \,\|\, \widehat{p}_\mathbf{x}(\mathbf{x}; \theta)\right) = -\mathbb{E}_{p_\mathbf{x}(\mathbf{x})}\left[\log\left(\widehat{p}_\mathbf{x}(\mathbf{x};\theta)\right)\right] + C \\ &= -\mathbb{E}_{p_\mathbf{x}(\mathbf{x})}\left[\log\left(p_\mathbf{z}\left(T^{-1}(\mathbf{x};\theta)\right)\right) + \log\left|\det J_{T^{-1}}(\mathbf{x})\right|\right] + C,\end{aligned}$$

where C is a constant. This may be estimated via Monte Carlo sampling. For further details, see, e.g., [18].

2.2 Some Problems of Purely Likelihood-Based Approaches of AD

Likelihood-based deep generative models have been widely used in anomaly detection. However, there are a number of critical limitations which makes these prone to failure. One of these problems is that the model may assign higher likelihood to data which may be semantically different although still normal in some sense. For instance, models trained on Cifar-10 have been shown to assign higher likelihoods to images from SVHN. One explanation to this problem has been proposed in [4], where the argument is that there is a dependence on the entropy of the dataset, which gives rise to unwanted behavior. Another problem is that likelihood-based models struggle in high-dimensional spaces where background statistics dominate the likelihood estimation. However, to circumvent these issues it is suggested in [21] to use likelihood ratios instead of crude likelihoods to handle the background statistics.

2.3 Our Problem and Dataset

The dataset consists of medium-resolution images of blasted forged steel coupling links ("G-links") captured using an area-scan camera as the coupling link was translated and rotated by an industrial robot [14]. This means that each individual piece is captured by roughly 120 images over different angles. Damaged pieces were collected using the regular manual inspection process in the production environment over an extended time frame. In the training set, there are 3,424 images of non-defect coupling links for training. The validation set is comprised of 568 images, 165 of which contain a defect. Figure 1 shows four defective samples with surface dents, deeper deformations, and scratches. These kind of anomalies arise naturally in production. Defects can be comparatively subtle and typically exhibit less variance then the embossing on the items. Furthermore, the links and the background both reflect the camera's flash.

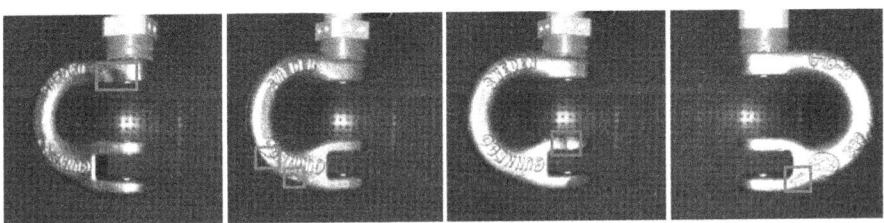

Fig. 1. Four defective examples from the G-link dataset. Anomalies are coarsely marked using a red bounding box (zoom for more details). (Color figure online)

3 Discovery of Limitations Through Normalizing Flows

When our project started in early 2023, one of the state of the art methods in unsupervised anomaly detection and -localization was a method called *"Fully Convolutional Cross-Scale-Flows for Image-based Defect Detection"*, here and after called "CS-Flow" [26]. Over the course of approx. 1.5 years, we would attempt to facilitate it to solve our own problem (see Sect. 2.3). In mid-2024, CS-Flow was superseded by a new state of the art method called *"A Unified Anomaly Synthesis Strategy with Gradient Ascent for Industrial Anomaly Detection and Localization"*, or, as its authors abbreviate it, "GLASS" [6]. As of writing this, GLASS is still undefeated.

In this section, we outline our journey of attempting to facilitate CS-Flow and adapting it to our problem. This journey is characterized by an iterative and hypothesis-/evidence-based approach. Our endeavors allowed us to unveil the intricate and inconspicuous issues related to data quality, choice of model, and evaluation approach. For full disclosure, comprehensibility, and reproducibility, each step is associated with a notebook in the replication package [15]. The remainder of this section is dedicated to the larger steps in this process. All experiments were run on an NVIDIA 8xH100/80GB machine.

3.1 Previous SotA: Convolutional Cross-Scale Normalizing Flow

CS-Flow [26] is a technique that processes image embeddings through a specialized normalizing flow to compute likelihoods of feature maps, which are then used to distinguish anomalies from normal samples.

The method begins by resizing each image into three different scales and passing them through a frozen feature extractor, EfficientNet-B5 [29], to generate three corresponding feature maps representing the image at multiple resolutions. A key component of CS-Flow is a unique coupling block that captures interactions between feature maps at different scales. These coupling blocks are stacked to form a normalizing flow, whose output is evaluated against a multivariate standard normal distribution with diagonal covariance matrix. The resulting likelihood determines whether an image is anomalous, based on a threshold τ.

In the paper, CS-Flow is evaluated on the MVTec AD dataset, achieving an average AUROC of 98.7. It reports state-of-the-art performance in eleven out of 15 categories. Furthermore, their approach processes feature maps in a fully convolutional (equivariant) manner, thus retaining positional information, enabling the identification of specific regions of anomalies. To achieve this, an anomaly score is assigned to each local position (i, j) of the feature map by aggregating values along the channel dimension using the L_2-norm. Regions with high norm values in the output feature tensors indicate potential anomalies.

3.2 Current SotA: Global and Local Anomaly Co-synthesis Strategy

GLASS is a three-way discriminator (*i.e.*, not a probabilistic model) that draws from all three branches of AD: embedding, reconstruction, and especially synthesis [6]. It uses a frozen feature extractor, as well as a feature adaptor, which is a fully-connected network that learns a useful representation of those features. It requires foreground masks of the objects of interest in order to synthesize so-called local anomalies. For a local anomaly, GLASS blends the foreground mask with a randomly generated mask first. Then, using a texture from the Describable Textures Dataset [7], the resulting patches are overlayed, thereby simulating an anomaly. This results in pixel-accurate augmentations, making the entire method self-supervised. Another type of synthetic anomaly that is generated are so-called global anomalies. For each batch, GLASS takes the derivative of itself with respect to the nominal sample. Then, Gaussian noise is added, and the sample is changed using truncated projection of the gradient (*i.e.*, the sample is changed such that its loss under the current model increases). Finally, the loss is computed along three branches: The discriminator shall predict all zeros for nominal samples, all ones for global anomalies (*i.e.*, anomalous everywhere), and all zeros except in the augmented regions for local anomalies.

Note that GLASS operates optionally under one of two distribution hypotheses: the hypersphere and manifold hypotheses. Under the first hypothesis, it is assumed that all nominal samples can be encompassed by a compact hypersphere and that all out-of-distribution samples have a distance from the center that is greater than that of any in-distribution sample [9]. Under the second hypothesis, it is assumed that all nominal samples lie within a lower-dimensional, locally linear manifold distribution. The local linearity and the fact that the manifold is homeomorphic to Euclidean space allows GLASS to define a distance under which a sample is considered to lie outside the in-distribution manifold [27]. By synthesizing global anomalies, a nominal sample is gradually worsened until it is considered to be located outside the in-distribution manifold. Interestingly, our dataset of coupling links conforms to a *cyclic manifold*, because the objects themselves repeatedly assume previously-assumed angles [20]. This might also explain why we generally achieve better results by operating GLASS under the manifold hypothesis.

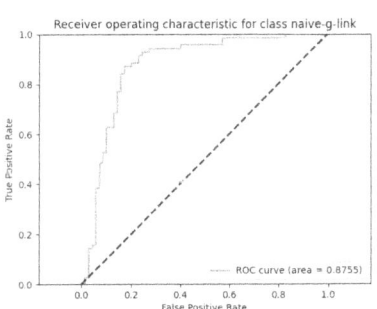
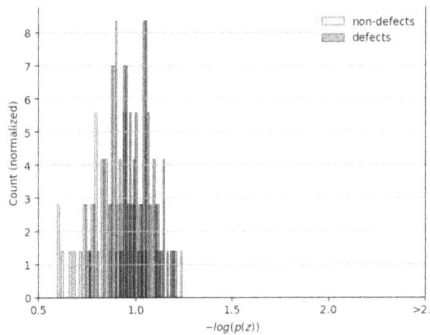

Fig. 2. ROC-curve (left) and anomaly scores (right) for the naive G-Link application under CS-Flow. Scores of nominal and anomalous samples overlap significantly.

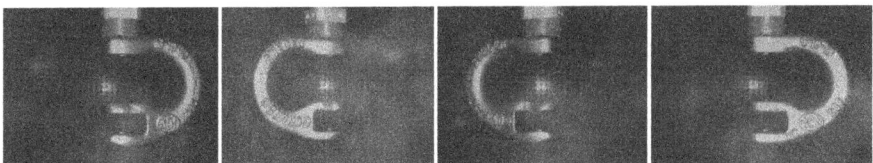

Fig. 3. Two defective samples (left) and two nominal samples (right). Anomaly scores of nominal samples sometimes greatly exceed those of actual defective samples (increased gamma and contrast). Often, high scores are assigned to the background.

3.3 Naïve Application to Raw Dataset

The first step was to attempt to use CS-Flow as an off-the-shelf solution and apply it to raw imagery of our dataset of forged coupling links. We have not made changes to the default configuration, which was used to achieve state-of-the-art results on the MVTec AD dataset. By default, images are resized to 768 × 768 pixels. Two smaller versions of the same image are used, one in 384 × 384 and one in 192 × 192, as CS-Flow facilitates a multi-scale approach that extracts and combines features from all three images per sample. The default architecture comprises four coupling blocks, applies gradient-clipping, and uses 1,024 units in the fully-connected networks that are the conditioners to each coupling block. The training runs for 240 epochs by default, with an intermediate evaluation step every 60 epochs.

Table 1. Summary of AUROC scores across models and datasets. Note that the AUROC of the MVTec AD datasets are based on a rotated dataset as described in Sect. 3.5.

Model	Trained On	AUROC
CS-Flow	MVTec AD	0.631
	MVTec AD (rot.)	0.939
	Naïve G-Link	0.871
	Masked G-Link	0.802
	CE G-Link	0.867
GLASS	CE G-Link	**0.941**

The evaluation of the obtained results from this step promised a skillful model. Typically, the reported AUROC on the test set would be ≥ 0.87 and the plot of the anomaly scores (which are derived from the negative log-likelihood an image produces) would indicate a somewhat good separability of scores. An example histogram and ROC-curve are shown in Fig. 2 and results in Table 1.

The next evaluation step was to inspect the anomalous regions. Four typical examples are shown in Fig. 3. It becomes apparent that most of the low-likelihood pixels are assigned to the background. The highlighted anomalous regions are not concordant with the actual location of the defect. Even worse, it would appear that the residual anomaly maps roughly cover the area where the coupling link is *usually* spatially present. What we mean by that is that most images in our dataset show the coupling link rotated (to a varying degree) along the fixture's axis to one or the other side. One could argue that if we were to interpolate all images of our dataset, the result would perhaps show the silhouette of a somewhat "double-link", which represents the average of it. Since a normalizing flow learns a complex probability distribution, it would approximate this average image, which is in disparity with any single image. This in turn allows us to conclude and hypothesize three things:

1. We hypothesize that strong object-variance can have detrimental effects when the underlying model is a deep density estimator.
2. The background should be blacked out in order to prohibit the model from assigning high (or any positive) anomaly score to it.
3. We have a Husky–Snow problem, likely caused by too-large spatial object variance.

The "Husky–Snow" problem, sometimes also referred to as "Clever-Hans" problem, is used to demonstrate how a model may learn unintended background features—in this case, a model distinguishing between wolves and huskies using background snow presence—rather than the animal itself (or discriminative features thereof) as the distinguishing factor. More formally, these so-called local interpretable model-agnostic explanations were introduced by Ribeiro et al. [23]. What this means for us is that the model has not learned any useful representation of the underlying problem. It might have memorized specialized patterns or shortcuts from the training set without extracting broader features to achieve the relatively high AUROC. One may also consider the average image (silhouette) as intrinsic noise in the training set: Without sufficient capacity for generalization (or compensating invariances) in the model, it appears we are posing a contradictory problem in the first place. Recall that in a standard normalizing flow architecture, the available learning capacity is restricted to the conditioners, which learn the parameters θ, required by the transformation $T(\mathbf{x}; \theta)$. In other words, between the (frozen) feature extractor and the flow itself, CS-Flow does not currently offer some form of learnable embedding.

3.4 Segmentation and Background Removal

The primary consequence from our naïve application to the coupling links dataset is to remove (or to black out) the background from each image, including removal of the sometimes visible fixture atop. However, since we find ourselves in an inherent unsupervised setting, manual removal of the backgrounds for each image would be too costly. While not technically completely unsupervised, we used GroundedSAM [22] to segment the bulk ($\approx 98\%$) of our dataset. GroundedSAM is an open-vocabulary detection and segmentation model. It facilitates textual prompts to instruct SAM (Segment Anything, [17]) to detect and segment corresponding objects. While it took a handful of different prompts, this final prompt *"the curved metal part in the center of the image without the blue ring"* was used to segment the entire dataset. As a micro ablation, we segment images from the MPDD dataset [16] using similarly trivial prompts and on-par segmentation results[1] (Fig. 4).

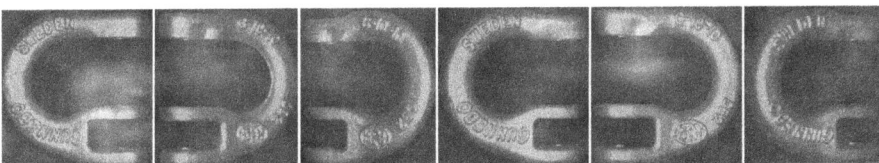

Fig. 4. Examples of spurious anomaly maps of defect samples using the masked dataset of coupling links (increased gamma and contrast).

Although the performance of training a vanilla CS-Flow on the segmented data has declined, the typical AUROC scores in the range of $[0.79, 0.81]$ would

---
[1] Among our contributions are two command-line applications that enable efficient mass-wise processing of images and their masks using a single prompt.

still suggest a somewhat skillful model. Upon inspecting the identified anomalous regions, we realize that higher scores are still assigned to the now-black background in many cases, meaning a worse version of the Husky–Snow problem is still present. Since the model cannot learn any shortcuts through spurious features of the background any longer, this result explains the lower AUROC and presents evidence for our silhouette theory. In short, it appears that the varying angles of the object seem to be disadvantageous for the chosen model.

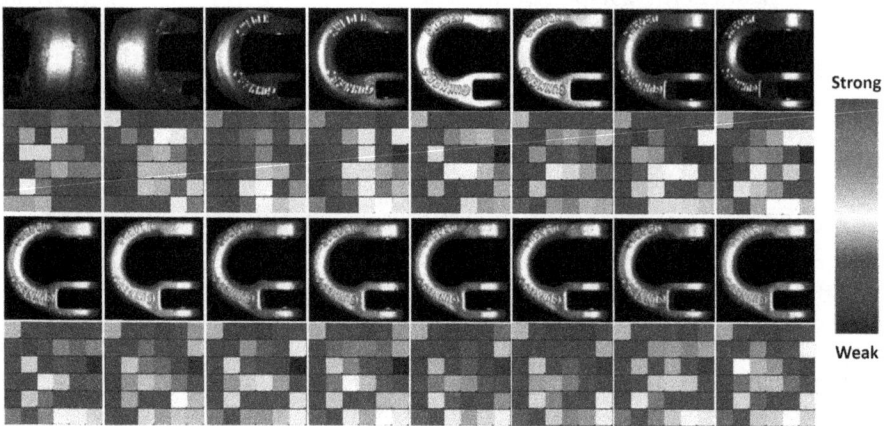

Fig. 5. A highly varying dataset causes an equivariantly varying feature map, too. Aggregated were the $6 \times 6 \times 304$ feature maps, each using max(). The lowest low is the supremum of the maximum activations across all patches and across all images (*i.e.*, max() is the global maximum).

3.5 Controlled Rotation Experiment on MVTec AD

Following our naïve approach, we hypothesized that a pronounced lack of object invariance leads to detrimental performance. However, it remains unclear whether the same holds true for image invariance—particularly relevant for equivariant models. Convolutions inherently provide some approximate local translation invariance. Pooling further amplifies this, capturing only the maximum, average, or minimum in local regions. Thus, for limited translation and scale variance, equivariant models offer partial image invariance. To quantify translation invariance, we designed a two-fold controlled experiment using a vanilla CS-Flow model with the "cable" category from the MVTec AD dataset [1]. We first trained on unmodified nominal data containing three strands: a central yellow strand at the top and blue and brown strands in the left and right corners. For testing, we added rotated versions (90°, 180°, 270°) of these nominal images. In a second test, training images were rotated using the same angles, while inference used original, as well as non-rotated images. One goal of this test was to find out to what degree CS-Flow is resilient to rotation variances. Ideally, a rotated nominal sample should not yield anomaly scores higher than typical nominal test images, indicating robust invariance. For the first experiment, the optimal threshold was ≈0.957 with AUROC ≈0.631 across all anomaly categories (e.g., bent wire, poked insulation). Rotated images had anomaly scores between ≈1.28 and ≈1.64, resulting in all of the rotated images being wrongly classified as anomalous. In contrast, the second experiment achieved a significantly higher AUROC (≈0.936) and an optimal threshold of ≈1.251. These two tests indicate that there is only very low robustness with regard to rotational invariance. Only one out of 58 non-rotated nominal samples was incorrectly classified (score ≈1.278). Thus, the second model generalized better, successfully handling rotated images. In summary, we demonstrated that rotation-based image invariances can be effectively handled when the training set explicitly includes such variance. We hypothesize that careful and limited artificially introduced image variance helps equivariant models generalize better. However, this approach may simultaneously increase model fragility through learning contradictory information—especially prominent when object invariance is introduced. Figure 5 visualizes activation magnitudes of latent features under an equivariant feature extractor (EfficientNet-B5, [29]). The first row shows rotated coupling links, revealing activations tightly localized around object regions. The second row depicts coupling links with only minimal viewpoint changes. While activation intensities vary slightly, the activation locations remain consistent as the object's position changes minimally.

3.6 Restriction to Similar Angles

Since CS-Flow is a deliberate equivariant pipeline, we alter our dataset one more time, by limiting the imagery to those shot from a very similar, front-facing angle. The idea is, again, to reduce the natural variance in the data. However, that same restriction also applies to the test data, meaning that we alter and simplify our initial problem. Therefore, the results cannot (and should not) be compared to the others. However, this method achieves an AUROC of ≈0.909. The qualitative evaluation shows that the anomaly maps often are closely located to the true region of the anomaly. However, having occasional spurious high anomaly scores assigned to the background is still a problem in this model.

4 Robust Dataset Preparation and Performance Estimation

We produce a segmented, centered, and padded version of our original dataset ("center-embedded" or "CE" short). In it, all objects are segmented and cropped to the minimum bounding box first. Then, we determine the minimum width and height that can encompass all coupling links, regardless of their spatial arrangement. We find that a resolution of 600x800 suffices. Finally, padding is added to each image such that the object remains vertically and horizontally centered. This way, the coupling links do not rotate longer around the fixture's axis, but rather around the image's center. This allows us to effectively reduce natural variation while retaining all information.

4.1 Results Using CS-Flow

We perform a last test using CS-Flow and this dataset, as previously, images were resized by it to a fixed resolution, which likely introduced more unwanted object variance, as narrow-appearing objects are perhaps stretched very wide. With an AUROC of $\approx$0.867, the model does surprisingly not perform better than our naïve tests. Spurious anomalous regions pose still a problem. It would finally appear that the too-large natural object variance makes the flow model inherently fragile as it attempts to learn contradictory information depending on object position. Recall that vanilla Normalizing Flows, even with equivariantly extracted features, lack a distinct embedding space robust enough to cope with large object-level variations like rotation and position shifts.

4.2 Results Using GLASS

Contrary to CS-Flow, GLASS is not a multi-scale model. Instead, it accepts images of a single resolution only. We identified a champion model that uses a lowered resolution of 160 × 160 that achieves an image-level AUROC of $\approx$0.941. The qualitative inspection of the results shows strong agreement between true and predicted anomaly location. Similarly, anomaly scores are practically zero for nominal parts (see Fig. 6). While sometimes the predicted anomaly scores are too high for some regions, GLASS never assigns any scores to the background, so it seems the silhouette-problem vanished. Also, judging by the qualitative results, it appears that the strong object-variance in our dataset is not problematic here, either. Interestingly though, GLASS also uses an equivariant (frozen) feature extractor, here WideResNet-50 by default. However, compared to Normalizing Flows, GLASS is a purpose-built model for AD, with two nonlinear high-capacity components, a feature adaptor (learning a suitable embedding and salient features), as well as a dense discriminator. We conclude that it is this architecture that allows the model to learn a more generalized representation of our problem.

4.3 Obtaining Unbiased Robust Performance Estimates

Once we are confident in our model and want to take it from the laboratory to the factory, we require robust estimates as to the usefulness for unsupervised industrial inspection. So far, we have only computed the AUROC. However, its usefulness lies in comparing models and/or datasets and is limited to the dataset it was determined on. In order to estimate other metrics, such as (balanced) accuracy, F1, precision and recall, etc., we have to consider the previously computed optimal threshold and use it in a decision rule on a *new* dataset. The

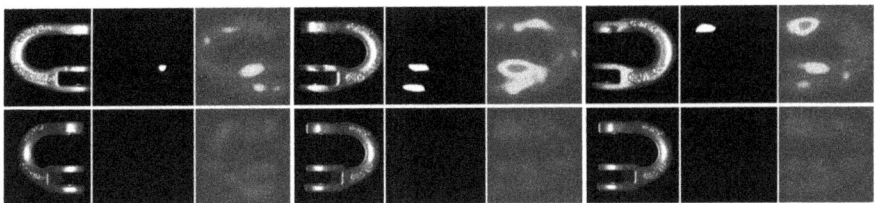

Fig. 6. Three anomalous (top row) and three nominal samples (bottom row) as predicted by GLASS. The ground truth mask for each is in the middle.

most common choice for selecting a threshold is to use Youden's index to determine the maximum value of a ROC curve. However, common alternatives are to select the threshold by, e.g., maximizing the sensitivity/specificity trade-off, maximizing a particular cost-based metric, or another criterion, such as taking into account the real-world cost of a false positive/negative (e.g., *"what is the cost of an overlooked defective part?"*).

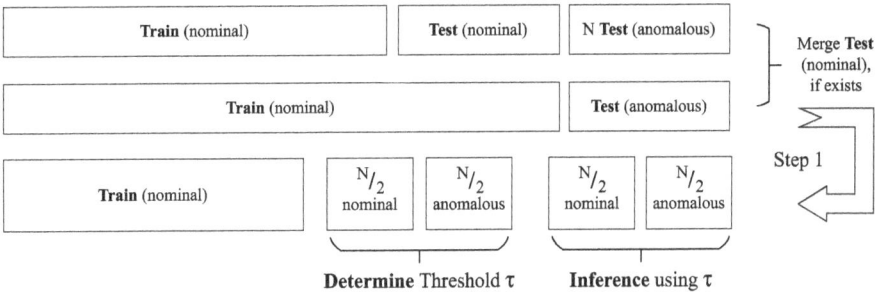

Fig. 7. Repartitioning of the training and testing data is the first step in the pipeline for obtaining robust factory-level estimates.

In the following, we describe the necessary steps that allow obtaining an unbiased estimator for the empirical risk. These steps are in accordance with existing guidelines that are recommended also in cases of limited samples sizes [31]. We assume that a three-part dataset exists to begin with: nominal training samples, as well nominal and anomalous test samples. We further assume that either the nominal test samples were drawn i.i.d. from the same distribution as the train samples, or that no nominal test set exists (second row, Fig. 7).

Step 0) (Optional) If a nominal test set exists and the i.i.d. assumption holds, merge it into the nominal train set.
Step 1) Perform a random, but deterministic three-way split Separate the anomalous test data randomly into one half each for determining the threshold

and for inferencing. Retain two partitions of the same size of nominal samples. Separate the remaining nominal samples into the training data.[2]

Step 2) Train model on remaining nominal data until convergence.

Step 3) Predict anomaly scores on *threshold* dataset and determine the optimal threshold τ for separating nominal/anomalous samples.

Step 4) Apply threshold τ to *inference* dataset and compute desired metrics. Record all results.

Step 5) Repeat K times for K-fold cross-validation (go to Step 1).

As for the number of repeats, a typical recommendation is at least 5–10. However, there exist insightful empirical guidelines for cross-validation experimentation for obtaining stable model assessments [2]. Choosing partition sizes different from $N/2$ in Step 1 will not result in an unbiased estimation. This is because ROC curve and AUROC can be overly optimistic for severely imbalanced classification problems and unsuitable when false negatives and false positives have significantly different costs [3].

5 Discussion and Future Work

Approaching the G-link problem naïvely and without prior assumptions inspired us to look beyond too-good-looking AUROCs and to iteratively identify and correct a problem that was inherently rooted in data quality and model choice. We identify an overall fragility of likelihood-based methods without representation learning (embedding) under real industrial conditions. We learn that the amount of natural variance present in a dataset strongly affects model performance and its ability to generalize and discriminate. Lastly, we highlight the importance of inspecting reported metrics and examining their applicability to factory-level operations.

We hypothesize that the synthesis of local and global anomalies is what allows GLASS to better concretize its in-distribution manifold. While the synthesis of local anomalies was done many times in previous works, the global anomaly synthesis strategy is novel. However, GLASS is specialized to imagery and, as such, the procedure using clamped gradient ascent is hard to control (hence the introduction of stochasticity). We have since begun to work on a flow-based model that exploits the fact that under a known base distribution (e.g., isotropic Gaussian), we can take controlled steps that allow us to gain insights into the geometry of the latent data manifold. This technique, in combination with controlled noise, allows us to effectively traverse the loss space linearly along all dimensions and to controllably synthesize anomalies.

Acknowledgments. Our project *"In-line visual inspection using unsupervised learning"* is a 2022 Vinnova project for Advanced Digitization, application number 2022-03018. We would like to sincerely thank our project partners and co-financers, namely

---

[2] If the image set contains multiple recordings of the same object, as is the case in our "G-link" dataset, one must ensure images of the same object are not in both train and test to prevent information leakage.

Linnaeus University and its High-Performance Computing Center, Gimic AB, SKF, and Gunnebo Industries.

Disclosure of Interests. The authors have no competing interests to declare that are relevant to the content of this article.

References

1. Bergmann, P., Batzner, K., Fauser, M., Sattlegger, D., Steger, C.: The mvtec anomaly detection dataset: a comprehensive real-world dataset for unsupervised anomaly detection. Int. J. Comput. Vis. **129**(4), 1038–1059 (2021). https://doi.org/10.1007/S11263-020-01400-4
2. Bouckaert, R.R.: Estimating replicability of classifier learning experiments. In: Machine Learning, Proceedings of the Twenty-First International Conference (ICML 2004), Banff, Alberta, Canada, 4–8 July 2004, vol. 69. ACM (2004). https://doi.org/10.1145/1015330.1015338
3. Branco, P., Torgo, L., Ribeiro, R.P.: A survey of predictive modeling on imbalanced domains. ACM Comput. Surv. **49**(2) (2016). https://doi.org/10.1145/2907070
4. Caterini, A.L., Loaiza-Ganem, G.: Entropic issues in likelihood-based OOD detection. In: Pradier, M.F., Schein, A., Hyland, S.L., Ruiz, F.J.R., Forde, J.Z. (eds.) I (Still) Can't Believe It's Not Better! Workshop at NeurIPS 2021, Virtual Workshop, 13 December 2021. Proceedings of Machine Learning Research, vol. 163, pp. 21–26. PMLR (2021). https://proceedings.mlr.press/v163/caterini22a.html
5. Chai, J., Zeng, H., Li, A., Ngai, E.W.: Deep learning in computer vision: a critical review of emerging techniques and application scenarios. Mach. Learn. Appl. **6**, 100134 (2021). https://doi.org/10.1016/j.mlwa.2021.100134
6. Chen, Q., Luo, H., Lv, C., Zhang, Z.: A unified anomaly synthesis strategy with gradient ascent for industrial anomaly detection and localization. In: Leonardis, A., Ricci, E., Roth, S., Russakovsky, O., Sattler, T., Varol, G. (eds.) Computer Vision - ECCV 2024 - 18th European Conference, Milan, Italy, 29 September–4 October 2024, Proceedings, Part LXVII. Lecture Notes in Computer Science, vol. 15125, pp. 37–54. Springer, Cham (2024). https://doi.org/10.1007/978-3-031-72855-6_3
7. Cimpoi, M., Maji, S., Kokkinos, I., Mohamed, S., Vedaldi, A.: Describing textures in the wild. In: 2014 IEEE Conference on Computer Vision and Pattern Recognition, CVPR 2014, Columbus, OH, USA, 23–28 June 2014, pp. 3606–3613. IEEE Computer Society (2014). https://doi.org/10.1109/CVPR.2014.461
8. Goodfellow, I.J., et al.: Generative adversarial nets. In: Ghahramani, Z., Welling, M., Cortes, C., Lawrence, N.D., Weinberger, K.Q. (eds.) Advances in Neural Information Processing Systems 27: Annual Conference on Neural Information Processing Systems 2014, Montreal, Quebec, Canada, 8–13 December 2014, pp. 2672–2680 (2014). https://proceedings.neurips.cc/paper/2014/hash/5ca3e9b122f61f8f06494c97b1afccf3-Abstract.html
9. Goyal, S., Raghunathan, A., Jain, M., Simhadri, H.V., Jain, P.: DROCC: deep robust one-class classification. In: Proceedings of the 37th International Conference on Machine Learning, ICML 2020, 13-18 July 2020, Virtual Event. Proceedings of Machine Learning Research, vol. 119, pp. 3711–3721. PMLR (2020). http://proceedings.mlr.press/v119/goyal20c.html
10. Gu, C., Ren, S., Duan, Q.: Unsupervised anomaly detection of industrial images based on dual generator reconstruction networks. Inf. Technol. Control. **53**(2), 331–341 (2024). https://doi.org/10.5755/J01.ITC.53.2.36018

11. Hendrycks, D., Mazeika, M., Kadavath, S., Song, D.: Using self-supervised learning can improve model robustness and uncertainty. In: Wallach, H.M., Larochelle, H., Beygelzimer, A., d'Alché-Buc, F., Fox, E.B., Garnett, R. (eds.) Advances in Neural Information Processing Systems 32: Annual Conference on Neural Information Processing Systems 2019, NeurIPS 2019, December 8-14, 2019, Vancouver, BC, Canada, pp. 15637–15648 (2019). https://proceedings.neurips.cc/paper/2019/hash/a2b15837edac15df90721968986f7f8e-Abstract.html
12. Hinton, G.E., Salakhutdinov, R.R.: Reducing the dimensionality of data with neural networks. Science **313**(5786), 504–507 (2006). https://doi.org/10.1126/science.1127647. https://www.science.org/doi/abs/10.1126/science.1127647
13. Huang, Y., Qiu, C., Yuan, K.: Surface defect saliency of magnetic tile. Vis. Comput. **36**(1), 85–96 (2020). https://doi.org/10.1007/S00371-018-1588-5
14. Hönel, S.: 3,992 Images of Blasted Forged Steel Coupling Links ("G-Links") Including Ground Truth Masks (2025). https://doi.org/10.5281/zenodo.15693611
15. Hönel, S.: Github repository: Replication package for paper: "From Lab to Factory: Pitfalls and Guidelines for Self-/Unsupervised Defect Detection on Low-Quality Industrial Images" (2025). https://doi.org/10.5281/zenodo.15693842
16. Jezek, S., Jonak, M., Burget, R., Dvorak, P., Skotak, M.: Deep learning-based defect detection of metal parts: evaluating current methods in complex conditions. In: 13th International Congress on Ultra Modern Telecommunications and Control Systems and Workshops, ICUMT 2021, Brno, Czech Republic, 25–27 October 2021, pp. 66–71. IEEE (2021). https://doi.org/10.1109/ICUMT54235.2021.9631567
17. Kirillov, A., et al.: Segment anything. In: IEEE/CVF International Conference on Computer Vision, ICCV 2023, Paris, France, 1–6 October 2023, pp. 3992–4003. IEEE (2023). https://doi.org/10.1109/ICCV51070.2023.00371
18. Papamakarios, G., Nalisnick, E.T., Rezende, D.J., Mohamed, S., Lakshminarayanan, B.: Normalizing flows for probabilistic modeling and inference. J. Mach. Learn. Res. **22**, 57:1–57:64 (2021). https://jmlr.org/papers/v22/19-1028.html
19. Park, S., Lee, K.H., Ko, B., Kim, N.: Unsupervised anomaly detection with generative adversarial networks in mammography. Sci. Rep. **13**(1), 2925 (2023). https://doi.org/10.1038/s41598-023-29521-z
20. Pless, R., Souvenir, R.: A survey of manifold learning for images. IPSJ Trans. Comput. Vis. Appl. **1**, 83–94 (2009). https://doi.org/10.2197/IPSJTCVA.1.83
21. Ren, J., et al.: Likelihood ratios for out-of-distribution detection. In: Wallach, H.M., Larochelle, H., Beygelzimer, A., d'Alché-Buc, F., Fox, E.B., Garnett, R. (eds.) Advances in Neural Information Processing Systems 32: Annual Conference on Neural Information Processing Systems 2019, NeurIPS 2019, 8–14 December 2019, Vancouver, BC, Canada, pp. 14680–14691 (2019). https://proceedings.neurips.cc/paper/2019/hash/1e79596878b2320cac26dd792a6c51c9-Abstract.html
22. Ren, T., et al.: Grounded SAM: assembling open-world models for diverse visual tasks. CoRR abs/2401.14159 (2024). https://doi.org/10.48550/ARXIV.2401.14159
23. Ribeiro, M.T., Singh, S., Guestrin, C.: "Why should I trust you?": explaining the predictions of any classifier. In: Krishnapuram, B., Shah, M., Smola, A.J., Aggarwal, C.C., Shen, D., Rastogi, R. (eds.) Proceedings of the 22nd ACM SIGKDD International Conference on Knowledge Discovery and Data Mining, San Francisco, CA, USA, 13–17 August 2016, pp. 1135–1144. ACM (2016). https://doi.org/10.1145/2939672.2939778
24. Roth, K., Pemula, L., Zepeda, J., Schölkopf, B., Brox, T., Gehler, P.V.: Towards total recall in industrial anomaly detection. In: IEEE/CVF Conference on Computer Vision and Pattern Recognition, CVPR 2022, New Orleans, LA, USA, 18–24

June 2022, pp. 14298–14308. IEEE (2022). https://doi.org/10.1109/CVPR52688.2022.01392
25. Rudolph, M., Wandt, B., Rosenhahn, B.: Same same but different: semi-supervised defect detection with normalizing flows. In: IEEE Winter Conference on Applications of Computer Vision, WACV 2021, Waikoloa, HI, USA, 3–8 January 2021, pp. 1906–1915. IEEE (2021). https://doi.org/10.1109/WACV48630.2021.00195
26. Rudolph, M., Wehrbein, T., Rosenhahn, B., Wandt, B.: Fully convolutional cross-scale-flows for image-based defect detection. In: IEEE/CVF Winter Conference on Applications of Computer Vision, WACV 2022, Waikoloa, HI, USA, 3–8 January 2022, pp. 1829–1838. IEEE (2022). https://doi.org/10.1109/WACV51458.2022.00189
27. Ruff, L., et al.: Deep one-class classification. In: Dy, J.G., Krause, A. (eds.) Proceedings of the 35th International Conference on Machine Learning, ICML 2018, Stockholmsmässan, Stockholm, Sweden, 10–15 July 2018. Proceedings of Machine Learning Research, vol. 80, pp. 4390–4399. PMLR (2018). http://proceedings.mlr.press/v80/ruff18a.html
28. Sakurada, M., Yairi, T.: Anomaly detection using autoencoders with nonlinear dimensionality reduction. In: Rahman, A., Deng, J.D., Li, J. (eds.) Proceedings of the MLSDA 2014 2nd Workshop on Machine Learning for Sensory Data Analysis, Gold Coast, Australia, QLD, Australia, 2 December 2014, p. 4. ACM (2014). https://doi.org/10.1145/2689746.2689747
29. Tan, M., Le, Q.V.: Efficientnet: rethinking model scaling for convolutional neural networks. In: Chaudhuri, K., Salakhutdinov, R. (eds.) Proceedings of the 36th International Conference on Machine Learning, ICML 2019, 9–15 June 2019, Long Beach, California, USA. Proceedings of Machine Learning Research, vol. 97, pp. 6105–6114. PMLR (2019). http://proceedings.mlr.press/v97/tan19a.html
30. Tao, X., Gong, X., Zhang, X., Yan, S., Adak, C.: Deep learning for unsupervised anomaly localization in industrial images: a survey. IEEE Trans. Instrum. Meas. **71**, 1–21 (2022). https://doi.org/10.1109/TIM.2022.3196436
31. Vabalas, A., Gowen, E., Poliakoff, E., Casson, A.J.: Machine learning algorithm validation with a limited sample size. PLOS ONE **14**(11), 1–20 (2019). https://doi.org/10.1371/journal.pone.0224365
32. Wang, S., Li, Q., Luo, H., Lv, C., Zhang, Z.: Produce once, utilize twice for anomaly detection. IEEE Trans. Circuits Syst. Video Technol. **34**(11), 11751–11767 (2024). https://doi.org/10.1109/TCSVT.2024.3420775
33. Zavrtanik, V., Kristan, M., Skocaj, D.: Dræm - a discriminatively trained reconstruction embedding for surface anomaly detection. In: 2021 IEEE/CVF International Conference on Computer Vision, ICCV 2021, Montreal, QC, Canada, 10–17 October 2021, pp. 8310–8319. IEEE (2021). https://doi.org/10.1109/ICCV48922.2021.00822

Author Index

A
Abeele, Jeriek Van den 36
Acharya, Ayan 143
Adhikari, Bijaya 476
Athanasiou, Labrini V 443
Auriau, Vincent 125

B
Baesens, Bart 195
Beeson, Alex 304
Berger, Rüdiger 3
Bernardini, Michele 338
Bizarro, Pedro 230
Bono, Jacopo 230
Borst, Vanessa 285
Botsoglou, Georgios 408
Budu, Emmanuella 321
Butt, Hans-Jürgen 3

C
Cacciatore, Alessandro 338
Chatzipanagiotidou, Irene 443
Chawla, Nitesh V. 143
Chrétien, Stéphane 391
Couper, Keith 304
Cugliari, Jairo 71

D
Da Silva, Juarez L. F. 426
Darvish, Fahimeh 3
Das, Kamalika 143
De Corte, Wouter 55
De Weerdt, Jochen 195
Dege, Tassilo 285
Désir, Jules 125
Di Cosmo, Mariachiara 338
Dimitriadis, Dimitris 408, 443
Dittus, Timo 285
Dong, Kaiwen 143
Du, Wanrou 373

E
Elsayed, Shereen 161, 178
Etminani, Farzaneh 321

F
Fehler, Luca 495
Feremans, Len 55
Fern, Xiaoli Z. 426
Ferreira, Hugo 230
Fischer, Jonas 495
Flores, Mauricio 143
Foumani, Navid Mohammadi 3
Frontoni, Emanuele 338

G
Gao, Xiang 143
Gauthier, Carl-Erik 247
Geerts, Margot 195
Giovanoudi, Eleni 356
Gupta, Priyanshi 265

H
Hahn, Kerstin 459
Hestermeyer, Lukas 161
Hönel, Sebastian 511
Husom, Erik Johannes 36

J
Jonnalagedda, Padmaja 143

K
Kansotia, Sparsh 265
Kant, Kamal 265
Kissa, Maria 143
Kothari, Kartavya 22
Kounev, Samuel 285
Kukharenko, Oleksandra 3

L

Le Cain, Aurélie 71
Le, Ngoc Son 161, 178
Lin, Fudong 373
Liu, Jinchan 373
Long, Hou-Wan 212
Lu, Tao 212
Lysitsas, Marios 408

M

Malherbe, Emmanuel 125, 247
Marathe, Kamlesh 22
Meche, Shelby 373
Metzler, Guillaume 391
Milon, Tarikul 373
Minchella, Paul 391
Montana, Giovanni 304
Možina, Martin 125

N

Nordqvist, Jonas 511

P

Pinheiro, Gabriel A. 426

Q

Qin, Xiaoqi 373
Quiles, Marcos G. 426

R

Rafailidis, Dimitrios 356
Rashed, Ahmed 161, 178
Reusens, Manon 195
Ribeiro Pereira, Ricardo 230
Ribeiro, Pedro 230
Rögnvaldsson, Thorsteinn 321

S

Sakho, Abdoulaye 247
Salehi, Mahsa 3
Scherer, Viktor 495
Schmidt-Thieme, Lars 161, 178
Schmieder, Astrid 285
Schwalie, Petra 459
Schwanecke, Ulrich 3
Scornet, Erwan 247
Segre, Alberto M. 476
Sethi, Akshay 265

Shang, Yanlei 104
Shumaly, Sajjad 3
Soares, Carlos 230
Soliman, Amira 321
Srilakshmi, Madiraju 22
Srivasatava, Nitish 265
Stricker, Markus 89
Stubbemann, Maximilian 161

T

Tang, Zhoufei 212
Treiber, Kevin 495
Tsikos, Dimitrios 443
Tsokana, Constantina N 443
Tsokana, Constantina 408
Tsoumakas, Grigorios 408, 443

U

Ulan, Maria 36

V

Valdeolivas, Alberto 459
Valiakos, George 408, 443
vanden Broucke, Seppe 195
Vasiljević, Jelica 459
Vaucher, Rémi 391
Veiga, Ines Berenguer 459
Vens, Celine 55
Venturini, Michela 55
Verlingue, Loic 391
Vu, Hieu 476

W

Weinberger, Simón 71
Wlodarczyk, Radoslaw 161

X

Xu, Wu 373

Y

Yuan, Xu 373

Z

Zhan, Zhuoyang 212
Zhang, Jianhui 212
Zhang, Lei 89
Zhang, Xiaoquan Michael 212
Zuo, Yu 104

GPSR Compliance

The European Union's (EU) General Product Safety Regulation (GPSR) is a set of rules that requires consumer products to be safe and our obligations to ensure this.

If you have any concerns about our products, you can contact us on

ProductSafety@springernature.com

In case Publisher is established outside the EU, the EU authorized representative is:

Springer Nature Customer Service Center GmbH
Europaplatz 3
69115 Heidelberg, Germany

www.ingramcontent.com/pod-product-compliance
Lightning Source LLC
Chambersburg PA
CBHW071946071025
33641CB00034BA/760